1. Investigating in a systematic way: examining. 2. Searching into or ranging over for the purpose of discovery.

Microsoft® Office Word 2010 Comprehensive

Robert T. Grauer

Michelle Hulett | Mary Anne Poatsy

Prentice Hall
Upper Saddle River London Singapore
Toronto Tokyo Sydney Hong Kong Mexico City

Library of Congress Cataloging-in-Publication Data
Grauer, Robert T.
Microsoft Office Word 2010 comprehensive / Robert T. Grauer, Michelle Hulett, Mary Anne Poatsy.
p. cm. — (Exploring series)
Includes index.
ISBN-13: 978-0-13-510440-8
ISBN-10: 0-13-510440-8
1. Microsoft Word. 2. Word processing. I. Hulett, Michelle. II. Poatsy, Mary Anne. III. Title.
Z52.5.M52G74835 2011
005.52—dc22

2010033771

Editor in Chief: Michael Payne
Acquisitions Editor: Samantha McAfee
Product Development Manager: Eileen Bien Calabro
Editorial Project Manager: Meghan Bisi
Development Editor: Laura Town
Editorial Assistant: Erin Clark
AVP/Director of Product Development: Lisa Strite
Editor-Digital Learning & Assessment: Paul Gentile
Product Development Manager-Media: Cathi Profitko
Editorial Media Project Manager: Alana Coles
Production Media Project Manager: John Cassar
Director of Marketing: Kate Valentine
Marketing Manager: Tori Olson Alves
Marketing Coordinator: Susan Osterlitz
Marketing Assistant: Darshika Vyas
Senior Managing Editor: Cynthia Zonneveld
Associate Managing Editor: Camille Trentacoste
Production Project Manager: Ruth Ferrera-Kargov
Manager of Rights & Permissions: Hessa Albader
Senior Operations Specialist: Diane Peirano
Senior Art Director: Jonathan Boylan
Cover Design: Jonathan Boylan
Cover Illustration/Photo: Courtesy of Shutterstock® Images
Composition: PreMediaGlobal
Full-Service Project Management: PreMediaGlobal
Typeface: 10.5/12.5 Minion

The drawing on page 391 is reprinted with permission of Mary Engler Guccione.

Pearson Education Ltd., London
Pearson Education Singapore, Pte. Ltd.
Pearson Education, Canada, Ltd.
Pearson Education–Japan
Pearson Education Australia PTY, Limited
Pearson Education North Asia Ltd., Hong Kong
Pearson Educación de Mexico, S.A. de C.V.
Pearson Education Malaysia, Pte. Ltd.
Pearson Education, Upper Saddle River, New Jersey

10 9 8 7 6 5 4 3 2

Prentice Hall
is an imprint of

www.pearsonhighered.com

ISBN-13: 978-0-13-510440-8
ISBN-10: 0-13-510440-8

DEDICATIONS

I would like to dedicate this book to my wonderful husband John and my sweet baby girl Dakota. They have shown an amazing amount of patience and support as I put in hours and hours of work on this project. And to my amazing friends, family, and students who offer encouragement and motivate me to be the best I can be. God bless you all.

Michelle Hulett

For my husband Ted, who unselfishly continues to take on more than his fair share to support me throughout this process; and for my children, Laura, Carolyn, and Teddy, whose encouragement and love have been inspiring.

Mary Anne Poatsy

ABOUT THE AUTHORS

Michelle Hulett, Word Author

Michelle Hulett received a B.S. degree in CIS from the University of Arkansas and an M.B.A. from Missouri State University. She has worked for various organizations as a programmer, network administrator, computer literacy coordinator, and educator. She currently serves as a Senior Instructor in the CIS department and Director of International Business Programs at Missouri State University.

When not teaching or writing, she enjoys flower gardening, traveling (Alaska and Hawaii are favorites), hiking, canoeing, and camping with her husband John, dog Dakota, and any friends or neighborhood kids who tag along.

Dr. Lynn Hogan, Office Fundamentals and File Management Author

Lynn Hogan has taught in the Computer Information Systems area at Calhoun Community College for 29 years. She is the author of *Practical Computing* and has contributed chapters for several computer applications textbooks. Primarily teaching in the areas of computer literacy and computer applications, she was named Calhoun's outstanding instructor in 2006. She received an M.B.A. from the University of North Alabama and a Ph.D. from the University of Alabama. Lynn resides in Alabama with her husband and two daughters.

Mary Anne Poatsy, Series Editor

Mary Anne is a senior faculty member at Montgomery County Community College, teaching various computer application and concepts courses in face-to-face and online environments. She holds a B.A. in psychology and education from Mount Holyoke College and an M.B.A. in finance from Northwestern University's Kellogg Graduate School of Management.

Mary Anne has more than 12 years of educational experience. She is currently adjunct faculty at Gwynedd-Mercy College and Montgomery County Community College. She has also taught at Bucks County Community College and Muhlenberg College, as well as conducted professional training. Before teaching, she was vice president at Shearson Lehman in the Municipal Bond Investment Banking Department.

Dr. Robert T. Grauer, Creator of the Exploring Series

Bob Grauer is an Associate Professor in the Department of Computer Information Systems at the University of Miami, where he is a multiple winner of the Outstanding Teaching Award in the School of Business, most recently in 2009. He has written numerous COBOL texts and is the vision behind the Exploring Office series, with more than three million books in print. His work has been translated into three foreign languages and is used in all aspects of higher education at both national and international levels. Bob Grauer has consulted for several major corporations including IBM and American Express. He received his Ph.D. in operations research in 1972 from the Polytechnic Institute of Brooklyn.

BRIEF CONTENTS

OFFICE FUNDAMENTALS AND FILE MANAGEMENT

WORD

CONTENTS

OFFICE FUNDAMENTALS AND FILE MANAGEMENT

CHAPTER ONE ➤ Office Fundamentals and File Management 1

MICROSOFT OFFICE WORD 2010

CHAPTER ONE ➤ Introduction to Word 67

CHAPTER TWO > Document Presentation 113

CHAPTER THREE > Collaboration and Research 167

CHAPTER FOUR > Document Productivity 211

CHAPTER FIVE ➤ Desktop Publishing and Graphic Design 261

CHAPTER SIX ➤ Time Saving Tools 309

CHAPTER SEVEN ➤ Document Automation 355

CHAPTER EIGHT ➤ Word and the Internet 405

ACKNOWLEDGMENTS

The Exploring team would like to acknowledge and thank all the reviewers who helped us prepare for the Exploring Office 2010 revision by providing us with their invaluable comments, suggestions, and constructive criticism:

Allen Alexander
Delaware Technical & Community College

Andrea Marchese
Maritime College, State University of New York

Andrew Blitz
Broward College, Edison State College

Angela Clark
University of South Alabama

Astrid Todd
Guilford Technical Community College

Audrey Gillant
Maritime College, State University of New York

Barbara Stover
Marion Technical College

Barbara Tollinger
Sinclair Community College

Ben Brahim Taha
Auburn University

Beverly Amer
Northern Arizona University

Beverly Fite
Amarillo College

Bonnie Homan
San Francisco State University

Brad West
Sinclair Community College

Brian Powell
West Virginia University

Carol Buser
Owens Community College

Carol Roberts
University of Maine

Cathy Poyner
Truman State University

Charles Hodgson
Delgado Community College

Cheryl Hinds
Norfolk State University

Cindy Herbert
Metropolitan Community College–Longview

Dana Hooper
University of Alabama

Dana Johnson
North Dakota State University

Daniela Marghitu
Auburn University

David Noel
University of Central Oklahoma

David Pulis
Maritime College, State University of New York

David Thornton
Jacksonville State University

Dawn Medlin
Appalachian State University

Debby Keen
University of Kentucky

Debra Chapman
University of South Alabama

Derrick Huang
Florida Atlantic University

Diana Baran
Henry Ford Community College

Diane Cassidy
The University of North Carolina at Charlotte

Diane Smith
Henry Ford Community College

Don Danner
San Francisco State University

Don Hoggan
Solano College

Elaine Crable
Xavier University

Erhan Uskup
Houston Community College–Northwest

Erika Nadas
Wilbur Wright College

Floyd Winters
Manatee Community College

Frank Lucente
Westmoreland County Community College

G. Jan Wilms
Union University

Gail Cope
Sinclair Community College

Gary DeLorenzo
California University of Pennsylvania

Gary Garrison
Belmont University

Gerald Braun
Xavier University

Gladys Swindler
Fort Hays State University

Heith Hennel
Valencia Community College

Irene Joos
La Roche College

Iwona Rusin
Baker College; Davenport University

J. Roberto Guzman
San Diego Mesa College

Jan Wilms
Union University

Janet Bringhurst
Utah State University

Jim Chaffee
The University of Iowa Tippie College of Business

Joanne Lazirko
University of Wisconsin–Milwaukee

Jodi Milliner
Kansas State University

John Hollenbeck
Blue Ridge Community College

John Seydel
Arkansas State University

Judith A. Scheeren
Westmoreland County Community College

Judith Brown
The University of Memphis

Karen Priestly
Northern Virginia Community College

Karen Ravan
Spartanburg Community College

Kathleen Brenan
Ashland University

Ken Busbee
Houston Community College

Kent Foster
Winthrop University

Kevin Anderson
Solano Community College

Kim Wright
The University of Alabama

Kristen Hockman
University of Missouri–Columbia

Kristi Smith
Allegany College of Maryland

Laura McManamon
University of Dayton

Leanne Chun
Leeward Community College

Lee McClain
Western Washington University

Linda D. Collins
Mesa Community College

Linda Johnsonius
Murray State University

Linda Lau
Longwood University

Linda Theus
Jackson State Community College

Lisa Miller
University of Central Oklahoma

Lister Horn
Pensacola Junior College

Lixin Tao
Pace University

Loraine Miller
Cayuga Community College

Lori Kielty
Central Florida Community College

Lorna Wells
Salt Lake Community College

Lucy Parakhovnik (Parker)
California State University, Northridge

Marcia Welch
Highline Community College

Margaret McManus
Northwest Florida State College

Margaret Warrick
Allan Hancock College

Marilyn Hibbert
Salt Lake Community College

Mark Choman
Luzerne County Community College

Mary Duncan
University of Missouri – St. Louis

Melissa Nemeth
Indiana University Purdue University Indianapolis

Melody Alexander
Ball State University

Michael Douglas
University of Arkansas at Little Rock

Michael Dunklebarger
Alamance Community College

Michael G. Skaff
College of the Sequoias

Michele Budnovitch
Pennsylvania College of Technology

Mike Jochen
East Stroudsburg University

Mike Scroggins
Missouri State University

Nanette Lareau
University of Arkansas Community College–Morrilton

Pam Uhlenkamp
Iowa Central Community College

Patrick Smith
Marshall Community and Technical College

Paula Ruby
Arkansas State University

Peggy Burrus
Red Rocks Community College

Peter Ross
SUNY Albany

Philip H Nielson
Salt Lake Community College

Ralph Hooper
University of Alabama

Ranette Halverson
Midwestern State University

Richard Cacace
Pensacola Junior College

Robert Dušek
Northern Virginia Community College

Robert Sindt
Johnson County Community College

Rocky Belcher
Sinclair Community College

Roger Pick
University of Missouri at Kansas City

Ronnie Creel
Troy University

Rosalie Westerberg
Clover Park Technical College

Ruth Neal
Navarro College

Sandra Thomas
Troy University

Sophie Lee
California State University, Long Beach

Steven Schwarz
Raritan Valley Community College

Sue McCrory
Missouri State University

Susan Fuschetto
Cerritos College

Susan Medlin
UNC Charlotte

Suzan Spitzberg
Oakton Community College

Sven Aelterman
Troy University

Terri Holly
Indian River State College

Thomas Rienzo
Western Michigan University

Tina Johnson
Midwestern State University

Tommy Lu
Delaware Technical and Community College

Troy S. Cash
NorthWest Arkansas Community College

Vicki Robertson
Southwest Tennessee Community College

Weifeng Chen
California University of Pennsylvania

Wes Anthony
Houston Community College

William Ayen
University of Colorado at Colorado Springs

Wilma Andrews
Virginia Commonwealth University

Yvonne Galusha
University of Iowa

We'd also like to acknowledge the reviewers of previous editions of Exploring:

Aaron Schorr
Fashion Institute of Technology

Alan Moltz
Naugatuck Valley Technical Community College

Alicia Stonesifer
La Salle University

Allen Alexander
Delaware Tech & Community College

Alok Charturvedi
Purdue University

Amy Williams
Abraham Baldwin Agriculture College

Andrea Compton
St. Charles Community College

Annette Duvall
Central New Mexico Community College

Annie Brown
Hawaii Community College

Antonio Vargas
El Paso Community College

Barbara Cierny
Harper College

Barbara Hearn
Community College of Philadelphia

Barbara Meguro
University of Hawaii at Hilo

Barbara Sherman
Buffalo State College

Barbara Stover
Marion Technical College

Bette Pitts
South Plains College

Beverly Fite
Amarillo College

Bill Daley
University of Oregon

Bill Morse
DeVry Institute of Technology

Bill Wagner
Villanova

Bob McCloud
Sacred Heart University

Bonnie Homan
San Francisco State University

Brandi N. Guidry
University of Louisiana at Lafayette

Brian Powell
West Virginia University–Morgantown Campus

Carl Farrell
Hawaii Pacific University

Carl M. Briggs
Indiana University School of Business

Carl Penzuil
Ithaca College

Carlotta Eaton
Radford University

Carole Bagley
University of St. Thomas

Carolyn DiLeo
Westchester Community College

Cassie Georgetti
Florida Technical College

Catherine Hain
Central New Mexico Community College

Charles Edwards
University of Texas of the Permian Basin

Cheryl Slavik
Computer Learning Services

Christine L. Moore
College of Charleston

Cody Copeland
Johnson County Community College

Connie Wells
Georgia State University

Dana Johnson
North Dakota State University

Dan Combellick
Scottsdale Community College

Daniela Marghitu
Auburn University

David B. Meinert
Southwest Missouri State University

David Barnes
Penn State Altoona

David Childress
Ashland Community College

David Douglas
University of Arkansas

David Langley
University of Oregon

David Law
Alfred State College

David Rinehard
Lansing Community College

David Weiner
University of San Francisco

Delores Pusins
Hillsborough Community College

Dennis Chalupa
Houston Baptist

Diane Stark
Phoenix College

Dianna Patterson
Texarkana College

Dianne Ross
University of Louisiana at Lafayette

Don Belle
Central Piedmont Community College

Douglas Cross
Clackamas Community College

Dr. Behrooz Saghafi
Chicago State University

Dr. Gladys Swindler
Fort Hays State University

Dr. Joe Teng
Barry University

Dr. Karen Nantz
Eastern Illinois University

Duane D. Lintner
Amarillo College

Elizabeth Edmiston
North Carolina Central University

Erhan Uskup
Houston Community College

Ernie Ivey
Polk Community College

Fred Hills
McClellan Community College

Freda Leonard
Delgado Community College

Gale E. Rand
College Misericordia

Gary R. Armstrong
Shippensburg University of Pennsylvania

Glenna Vanderhoof
Missouri State

Gregg Asher
Minnesota State University, Mankato

Hank Imus
San Diego Mesa College

Heidi Gentry-Kolen
Northwest Florida State College

Helen Stoloff
Hudson Valley Community College

Herach Safarian
College of the Canyons

Hong K. Sung
University of Central Oklahoma

Hyekyung Clark
Central New Mexico Community College

J Patrick Fenton
West Valley College

Jack Zeller
Kirkwood Community College

James Franck
College of St. Scholastica

James Gips
Boston College

Jana Carver
Amarillo College

Jane Cheng
Bloomfield College

Jane King
Everett Community College

Janis Cox
Tri-County Technical College

Janos T. Fustos
Metropolitan State College of Denver

Jean Kotsiovos
Kaplan University

Jeffrey A Hassett
University of Utah

Jennifer Pickle
Amarillo College

Jerry Chin
Southwest Missouri State University

Jerry Kolata
New England Institute of Technology

Jesse Day
South Plains College

Jill Chapnick
Florida International University

Jim Pepe
Bentley College

Jim Pruitt
Central Washington University

John Arehart
Longwood University

John Lee Reardon
University of Hawaii, Manoa

John Lesson
University of Central Florida

John Shepherd
Duquesne University

Joshua Mindel
San Francisco State University

Judith M. Fitspatrick
Gulf Coast Community College

Judith Rice
Santa Fe Community College

Judy Brown
The University of Memphis

Judy Dolan
Palomar College

Karen Tracey
Central Connecticut State University

Karen Wisniewski
County College of Morris

Karl Smart
Central Michigan University

Kathleen Brenan
Ashland University

Kathryn L. Hatch
University of Arizona

Kevin Pauli
University of Nebraska

Kim Montney
Kellogg Community College

Kimberly Chambers
Scottsdale Community College

Krista Lawrence
Delgado Community College

Krista Terry
Radford University

Lancie Anthony Affonso
College of Charleston

Larry S. Corman
Fort Lewis College

Laura McManamon
University of Dayton

Laura Reid
University of Western Ontario

Linda Johnsonius
Murray State University

Lisa Prince
Missouri State University

Lori Kelley
Madison Area Technical College

Lucy Parker
California State University, Northridge

Lynda Henrie
LDS Business College

Lynn Band
Middlesex Community College

Lynn Bowen
Valdosta Technical College

Malia Young
Utah State University

Margaret Thomas
Ohio University

Margie Martyn
Baldwin Wallace

Marguerite Nedreberg
Youngstown State University

Marianne Trudgeon
Fanshawe College

Marilyn Hibbert
Salt Lake Community College

Marilyn Salas
Scottsdale Community College

Marjean Lake
LDS Business College

Mark Olaveson
Brigham Young University

Martin Crossland
Southwest Missouri State University

Mary McKenry Percival
University of Miami

Meg McManus
Northwest Florida State College

Michael Hassett
Fort Hayes State University

Michael Stewardson
San Jacinto College–North

Midge Gerber
Southwestern Oklahoma State University

Mike Hearn
Community College of Philadelphia

Mike Kelly
Community College of Rhode Island

Mike Thomas
Indiana University School of Business

Mimi Duncan
University of Missouri–St. Louis

Minnie Proctor
Indian River Community College

Nancy Sardone
Seton Hall University

Pam Chapman
Waubonsee Community College

Patricia Joseph
Slippery Rock University

Patrick Hogan
Cape Fear Community College

Paul E. Daurelle
Western Piedmont Community College

Paula F. Bell
Lock Haven University of Pennsylvania

Paulette Comet
Community College of Baltimore County, Catonsville

Pratap Kotala
North Dakota State University

Ranette Halverson
Midwestern State University

Raymond Frost
Central Connecticut State University

Richard Albright
Goldey-Beacom College

Richard Blamer
John Carroll University

Richard Herschel
St. Joseph's University

Richard Hewer
Ferris State University

Robert Gordon
Hofstra University

Robert Marmelstein
East Stroudsburg University

Robert Spear
Prince George's Community College

Robert Stumbur
Northern Alberta Institute of Technology

Roberta I. Hollen
University of Central Oklahoma

Roland Moreira
South Plains College

Ron Murch
University of Calgary

Rory J. de Simone
University of Florida

Rose M. Laird
Northern Virginia Community College

Ruth Neal
Navarro College

Sally Visci
Lorain County Community College

Sandra M. Brown
Finger Lakes Community College

Sharon Mulroney
Mount Royal College

Shawna DePlonty
Sault College of Applied Arts and Technology

Stephen E. Lunce
Midwestern State University

Steve Schwarz
Raritan Valley Community College

Steven Choy
University of Calgary

Stuart P. Brian
Holy Family College

Susan Byrne
St. Clair College

Susan Fry
Boise State University

Suzan Spitzberg
Oakton Community College

Suzanne Tomlinson
Iowa State University

Thomas Setaro
Brookdale Community College

Todd McLeod
Fresno City College

Vernon Griffin
Austin Community College

Vickie Pickett
Midland College

Vipul Gupta
St. Joseph's University

Vivek Shah
Texas State University–San Marcos

Wei-Lun Chuang
Utah State University

William Dorin
Indiana University Northwest

Additionally, we'd like to thank our Instructor Resource authors:

Anci Shah
Houston Community College

Ann Rovetto
Horry-Georgetown Technical College

Arlene Eliason
Minnesota School of Business

Barbara Stover
Marion Technical College

Carol Roberts
University of Maine

David Csuha
Passaic County Community College

Emily Shephard
Central Carolina Community College

Eric Cameron
Passaic County Community College

Irene Joos
La Roche College

James Powers
University of Southern Indiana

Jayne Lowery
Jackson State Community College

Jennifer Ivey
Central Carolina Community College

Julie Boyles
Portland Community College

Kyle Stark
Macomb Community College

Linda Lau
Longwood University

Lisa Prince
Missouri State University

Lynn Bowen
Valdosta Technical College

Lynn Hogan
Calhoun Community College

Mary Lutz
Southwestern Illinois College

Meg McManus
Northwest Florida State College

NaLisa Brown
University of the Ozarks

Sally Baker
DeVry University

Sharon Behrens
Mid-State Technical College

Stephanie Jones
Texas Tech University

Steve Rubin
California State University, Monterey Bay

Susan Mahon
Collin College

Suzan Spitzberg
Oakton Community College

Tom McKenzie
James Madison University

Yvonne Leonard
Coastal Carolina Community College

Finally, we'd like to extend our thanks to the Exploring 2010 technical editors:

Chad Kirsch

Cheryl Slavik

Elizabeth Lockley

Janet Pickard

Janice Snyder

Joyce Nielsen

Julie Boyles

Lisa Bucki

Lori Damanti

Sandra Swinney

Sean Portnoy

PREFACE

The Exploring Series and You

Exploring is Pearson's Office Application series which requires students like you to think "beyond the point and click." With Office 2010, Exploring has embraced today's student learning styles to support extended learning beyond the classroom.

The goal of Exploring is, as it has always been, to go further than teaching just the steps to accomplish a task—the series provides the theoretical foundation for you to understand when and why to apply a skill. As a result, you achieve a deeper understanding of each application and can apply this critical thinking beyond Office and the classroom.

You are plugged in constantly, and Exploring has evolved to meet you half-way to work within your changing learning styles. Pearson has paid attention to the habits of students today, how you get information, how you are motivated to do well in class, and what your future goals look like. We asked you and your peers for acceptance of new tools we designed to address these points, and you responded with a resounding "YES!"

Here Is What We Learned About You

You go to college now with a different set of skills than students did five years ago. The new edition of Exploring moves you beyond the basics of the software at a faster pace, without sacrificing coverage of the fundamental skills that you need to know. This ensures that you will be engaged from page 1 to the end of the book.

You and your peers have diverse learning styles. With this in mind, we broadened our definition of "student resources" to include Compass, an online skill database; movable Visual Reference cards; relevant Set-Up Videos filmed in a familiar, commercial style; and the most powerful online homework and assessment tool around, my**it**lab. Exploring will be accessible to all students, regardless of learning style.

You read, prepare, and study differently than students used to. You use textbooks like a tool—you want to easily identify what you need to know and learn it efficiently. We have added key features that make the content accessible to you and make the text easy to use.

You are goal-oriented. You want a good grade and you want to be successful in your future career. With this in mind, we used motivating case studies and Set-Up Videos to aid in the learning now and to show the relevance of the skills to your future careers.

Moving Beyond the Point and Click and Extending Your Learning Beyond the Classroom

All of these additions will keep you more engaged, helping you to achieve a higher level of understanding and to complete this course and go on to be successful in your career. In addition to the vision and experience of the series creator, Robert T. Grauer, we have assembled a tremendously talented team of Office Applications authors who have devoted themselves to teaching you the ins and outs of Microsoft Word, Excel, Access, and PowerPoint. Led in this edition by series editor Mary Anne Poatsy, the whole team is equally dedicated to the Exploring mission of **moving you beyond the point and click, and extending your learning beyond the classroom**.

Key Features of Exploring Office 2010

- **White Pages/Yellow Pages** clearly distinguish the theory (white pages) from the skills covered in the Hands-On Exercises (yellow pages) so students always know what they are supposed to be doing.
- **Objective Mapping** enables students to skip the skills and concepts they know and quickly find those they do not know by scanning the chapter opener pages for the page numbers of the material they need.
- **Pull Quotes** entice students into the theory by highlighting the most interesting points.
- **Case Study** presents a scenario for the chapter, creating a story that ties the Hands-On Exercises together.

- **FYI Icon** indicates that an exercise step includes a skill that is common to more than one application. Students who require more information on that skill may utilize the Office Fundamentals and File Management chapter, the Visual Reference Cards, or Compass for assistance.

- **Set-Up Video** introduces the chapter's Case Study to generate student interest and attention and shows the relevance of the skills to students' future work.
- **Key Terms** are defined in the margins to ensure student comprehension.
- **End-of-Chapter Exercises** offer instructors several options for assessment. Each chapter has approximately 12–15 exercises ranging from multiple choice questions to open-ended projects.

- **Enhanced Mid-Level Exercises** include a **Creative Case**, which allows students some flexibility and creativity, not being bound by a definitive solution, as well as **Discover Steps**, which encourage students to use Help or to problem-solve to accomplish a task.

Instructor Resources

The Instructor's Resource Center, available at www.pearsonhighered.com includes the following:

- **Annotated Solution Files with Scorecards** assist with grading the Hands-On Exercises and end-of-chapter exercises.
- **Data and Solution Files**
- **Capstone Production Tests** allow instructors to assess all skills covered in a chapter with a single project.
- **Rubrics** for Mid-Level Creative Cases and Beyond the Classroom Cases in Microsoft® Word format enable instructors to customize the assignments for their classes.
- **PowerPoint® Presentations** with notes for each chapter are included for out-of-class study or review.
- **Audio PowerPoint Presentations** provide an alternate version of the PowerPoint presentations in which all the lecture notes have been prerecorded.
- **Lesson Plans** provide a detailed blueprint to achieve chapter learning objectives and outcomes.
- **Objectives List** maps chapter objectives to Hands-On Exercises and end-of-chapter exercises.
- **Multiple Choice Answer Key**
- **Complete Test Bank**, also available in TestGen format.
- **Set-Up Video Exercises** provide companion exercises for the Set-Up Video for each chapter.
- **Syllabus templates** for 8-week, 12-week, and 16-week courses.
- **Grader projects** provide live-in-the-application assessment for each chapter's Capstone Exercise and additional capstone exercises.
- **Instructor Reference Cards**, available electronically and as printed cards, for each chapter, include:
  - **Concept Summary** outlines the KEY objectives to cover in class with tips on where students get stuck as well as how to get them unstuck.
  - **Scripted Lecture** provides instructors with a lecture outline that mirrors the Hands-On Exercises.

Online Course Cartridges

Flexible, robust, and customizable content is available for all major online course platforms that include everything instructors need in one place. Please contact your Sales Representative for information on accessing course cartridges for WebCT, Blackboard, or CourseCompass.

Student Resources

Student Data CD

- Student Data Files
- Set-Up Videos introduce the chapter's Case Study to generate student interest and attention and show the relevance of the skills to students' future work.
- Compass access via computer and mobile phone

Visual Reference Cards

A two-sided reference card for each application provides students with a visual summary of information and tips specific to each application that provide answers to the most common student questions. The cards can be easily attached to and detached from the book's spiral binding to be used as a bookmark, and all cards are clearly color-coded by application.

Compass

Compass is a searchable database of Microsoft Office 2010 skills that is available for use online on a computer or on your mobile phone. Using a keyword look-up system on your computer, the database provides multimedia instructions via videos and at-a-glance frames to remind students how to perform a skill. For students on the go, you can use your mobile phone to search and access a brief description of a skill and the click-stream instructions for how to perform the skill. This is a resource for the tech savvy student, who wants help and answers right away. Students get access to Compass through my**it**lab and/or the Student CD.

Prentice Hall's Companion Web Site

www.pearsonhighered.com/exploring offers expanded IT resources and downloadable supplements. Students can find the following self-study tools for each chapter:

- Online Study Guide
- Chapter Objectives
- Glossary
- Chapter Objectives Review
- Web Resources
- Student Data Files

myitlab my**it**lab for Office 2010 is a solution designed by professors for professors that allows easy delivery of Office courses with defensible assessment and outcomes-based training. The new *Exploring Office 2010* system will seamlessly integrate online assessment, training, and projects with my**it**lab for Microsoft Office 2010!

myitlab for Office 2010 Features. . .

- **Assessment and training built to match *Exploring Office 2010*** instructional content so that my**it**lab works with *Exploring* to move students beyond the point and click.
- **Both project-based and skill-based assessment and training** allow instructors to test and train students on complete exercises or individual Office application skills.
- **Full course management functionality** includes all instructor and student resources, a complete Gradebook, and the ability to run a variety of reports including detailed student clickstream data.
- **The most open, realistic, high-fidelity simulation** of Office 2010 so students feel like they are learning Office, not just a simulation.
- **Grader, a live-in-the-application project-grading tool,** enables instructors to assign projects taken from the end-of-chapter material and additional projects included in the instructor resources. These are graded automatically, with detailed feedback provided to both instructors and students.

1 OFFICE FUNDAMENTALS AND FILE MANAGEMENT

Taking the First Step

Watch the
Set-up
Video
for this
Case Study!

CASE STUDY | Rails and Trails

You are an administrative assistant for a local historical preservation project. The project involves creating a series of trails designed for hikers, bikers, and horseback riders. The trails generally follow the route of a historic railroad line that traversed the northwestern corner of Kentucky from the early 1900s until it was discontinued in 1991. The 78 miles of trails follow the original rail route, which passed through natural hardwood forests and open meadows. Considered a major impetus of the Kentucky Historical Preservation Society, the project has received both public and private funding through legislative appropriations and private and federal grants.

As the administrative assistant, you are responsible for overseeing the production of documents, spreadsheets, newspaper articles, and presentations that will be used to increase public awareness of the Rails and Trails project. Other clerical assistants who are familiar with Microsoft Office will prepare the promotional materials, and you will proofread, make necessary corrections, adjust page layouts, save and print documents, and identify appropriate templates to simplify tasks. Your experience with Microsoft Office 2010 is limited, but you know that certain fundamental tasks that are common to Word, Excel, and PowerPoint will help you accomplish your oversight task. You are excited to get started on the project!

OBJECTIVES

AFTER YOU READ THIS CHAPTER, YOU WILL BE ABLE TO:

Files and Folders

If you stop to consider why you use a computer, you will most likely conclude that you want to produce some type of output. That output could be games, music, or the display of digital photographs. Perhaps you use a computer at work to produce reports, financial worksheets, or schedules. All of those items are considered computer ***files***. Files include electronic data such as documents, databases, slide shows, and worksheets. Even digital photographs, music, videos, and Web pages are saved as files.

Windows 7 provides tools that enable you to create folders and to save files in ways that make locating them simple.

A **file** is a document or item of information that you create with software and to which you give a name.

A **folder** is a named storage location where you can save files.

You use software to create and save files. For example, when you type a document on a computer, you first open a word processor such as Microsoft Word. Similarly, you could use a type of Web-authoring software to create a Web page. In order to access files later, you must save them to a computer storage medium such as a hard drive or flash drive. And just as you would probably organize a filing cabinet into a system of folders, you can organize storage media by ***folders*** that you name and into which you place data files. That way, you can easily retrieve the files later. Windows 7 provides tools that enable you to create folders and to save files in ways that make locating them simple. In this section, you will learn to use Windows Explorer to manage folders and files.

Using Windows Explorer

Windows Explorer is a Windows component that can be used to create and manage folders.

A **subfolder** is a folder that is housed within another folder.

Windows Explorer is a component that can be used to create and manage folders. The sole purpose of a computer folder is to provide a labeled storage location for related files so that you can easily organize and retrieve items. A folder structure can occur across several levels, so you can create folders within other folders (called ***subfolders***), arranged according to purpose. Windows 7 introduces the concept of libraries, which are folders that gather files from different locations and display the files as if they were all saved in a single folder, regardless of where they are physically stored. Using Windows Explorer, you can manage folders, work with libraries, and view favorites (areas or folders that are frequently accessed).

Understand and Customize the Interface

To open Windows Explorer, click Windows Explorer on the taskbar as shown in Figure 1.1. You can also right-click the Start button and click Open Windows Explorer. Figure 1.2 shows the Windows Explorer interface containing several areas. Some of those areas are described in Table 1.1.

FIGURE 1.1 Windows Explorer ➤

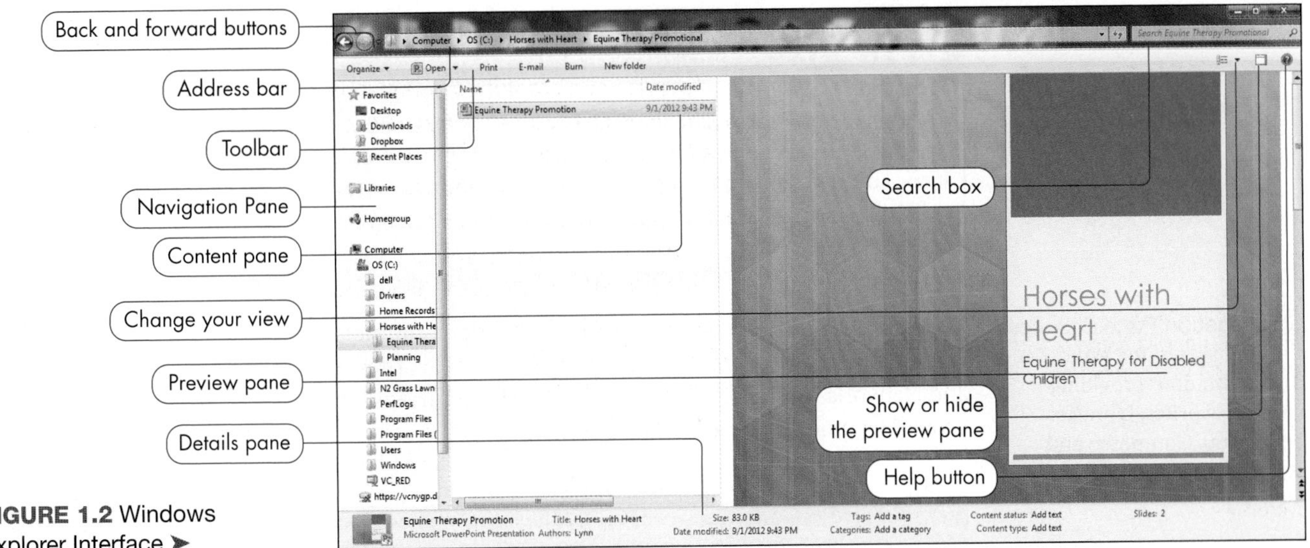

FIGURE 1.2 Windows Explorer Interface ➤

TABLE 1.1 Windows Explorer Interface	
Navigation Pane	The Navigation Pane contains five areas: Favorites, Libraries, Homegroup, Computer, and Network. Click an item in the Navigation Pane to display contents and to manage files that are housed within a selected folder.
Back and Forward Buttons	Use these buttons to visit previously opened folders or libraries.
Toolbar	The Toolbar includes buttons that are relevant to the currently selected item. If you are working with a music file, the toolbar buttons might include one for burning to a CD, whereas if you have selected a document, the toolbar would enable you to open or share the file.
Address Bar	The Address bar enables you to navigate to other folders or libraries.
Content Pane	The Content pane shows the contents of the currently selected folder or library.
Search Box	Find files and folders by typing descriptive text in the Search box. Windows immediately begins a search after you type the first character, further narrowing results as you type.
Details Pane	The Details pane shows properties that are associated with a selected file. Common properties include information such as the author name and the date the file was last modified.
Preview Pane	The Preview pane provides a snapshot of a selected file's contents. You can see file contents before actually opening the file. The Preview pane does not show the contents of a selected folder.

As you work with Windows Explorer, you might find that the view is not how you would like it. The file and folder icons might be too small for ease of identification, or you might want additional details about displayed files and folders. Modifying the view is easy. To make icons larger or to provide additional detail, click the Change your view arrow (see Figure 1.2), and select from the views provided. If you want additional detail, such as file type and size, click Details. You can also change the size of icons by selecting Small, Medium, Large, or Extra Large icons. The List view shows the file names without added detail, whereas Tiles and Content views are useful to show file thumbnails (small pictures describing file contents) and varying levels of detail regarding file locations. To show or hide Windows Explorer panes, click Organize (on the Toolbar), point to Layout, and then select the pane to hide or show. You can widen or narrow panes by dragging a border when the mouse changes to a double-headed arrow. When you click Show or hide the Preview pane, you toggle—or change between—views. If the Preview pane is not shown, clicking the button shows the pane. Conversely, if the pane is already open, clicking the button will hide it.

> **TIP** Displaying the Windows Explorer Menu Bar
>
> If you are comfortable with the menu bar that was included with previous Windows versions, you can display it in Windows 7. In the Windows Explorer window, click Organize. Point to Layout, and then click Menu bar. Following the same steps, you can remove a menu that is displayed.

Work with Groups on the Navigation Pane

The **Navigation Pane** is located on the left side of the Windows Explorer window, providing access to Favorites, Libraries, Homegroup, Computer, and Network areas.

The ***Navigation Pane*** provides ready access to computer resources, folders, files, and networked peripherals. It is divided into five areas: Favorites, Libraries, Homegroup, Computer, and Network. In Figure 1.3, the currently selected area is Libraries. Each of those components provides a unique way to organize contents.

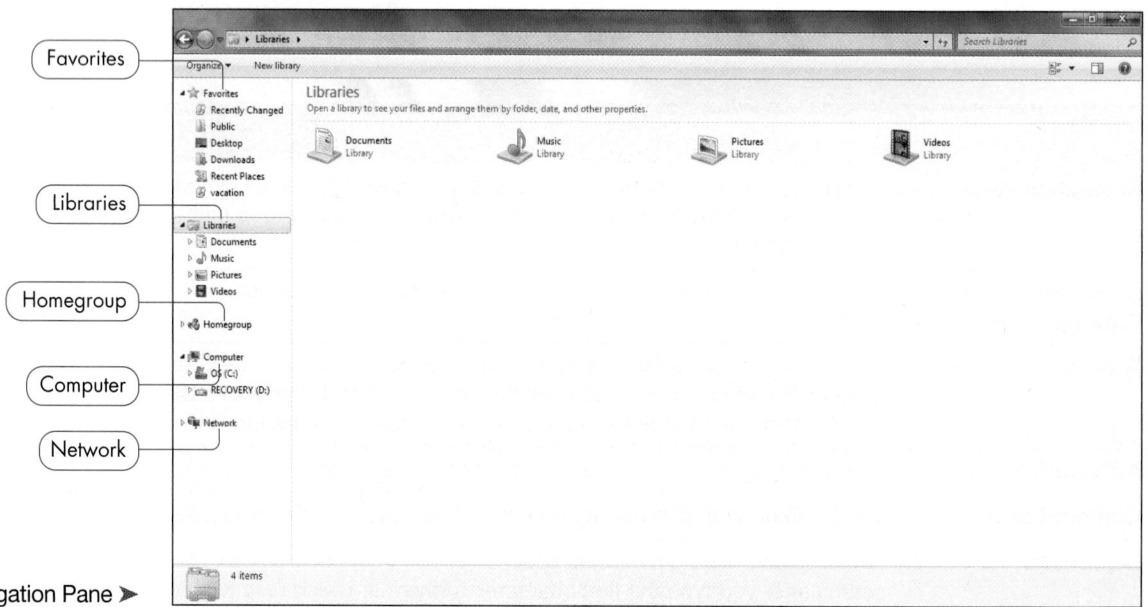

FIGURE 1.3 Navigation Pane ➤

A **library** is an organization method that collects files from different locations and displays them as one unit.

Earlier, we used the analogy of computer folders to folders in a filing cabinet. Just as you would title folders in a filing cabinet according to their contents, computer folders are also titled according to content. Folders are physically located on storage media such as a hard drive or flash drive. You can also organize folders into ***libraries***, which are collections of files from different locations that are displayed as single units. For example, the Pictures library includes files from the Pictures folder and from the Public Pictures folder, both of which are physically housed on the hard drive. Although the library content comes from two separate folders, contents are displayed as a unit.

Windows 7 includes several libraries that include default folders or devices. For example, the Documents library includes the My Documents and Public Documents folders, but you can add other folders if you wish so that they are also housed within the Documents library. To add a folder to a library, right-click the folder, and then point to Include in library. Then select a library, or select Create new library and create a new one. To remove a folder from a library, open Windows Explorer, and then click the library from which you want to remove the folder. In the Library pane shown at the right side of the Windows Explorer window, click the locations link (next to the word *Includes*). The link will indicate the number of physical locations in which the folders are housed. For example, if folders in the Pictures library are drawn from two locations, the link will read *2 locations*. Click the folder that you want to remove, click Remove, and then click OK.

The Computer area provides access to specific storage locations, such as a hard drive, CD/DVD, and removable media (including a flash drive). Files and folders housed on those storage media are accessible when you click Computer. For example, click drive C, shown under Computer in the Navigation Pane, to view its contents in the Content pane on the right. If you simply want to see the subfolders of the hard drive, click the arrow to the left of drive C to expand the view, showing all subfolders. Click the arrow again to collapse the view, removing subfolder detail. It is important to understand that clicking the arrow (as opposed to clicking the folder or area name) does not actually select an area or folder. It merely displays additional levels contained within the area. Clicking the folder or area, however, does select the item. Figure 1.4 illustrates the difference between clicking the area in the Navigation Pane and clicking the arrow to the left.

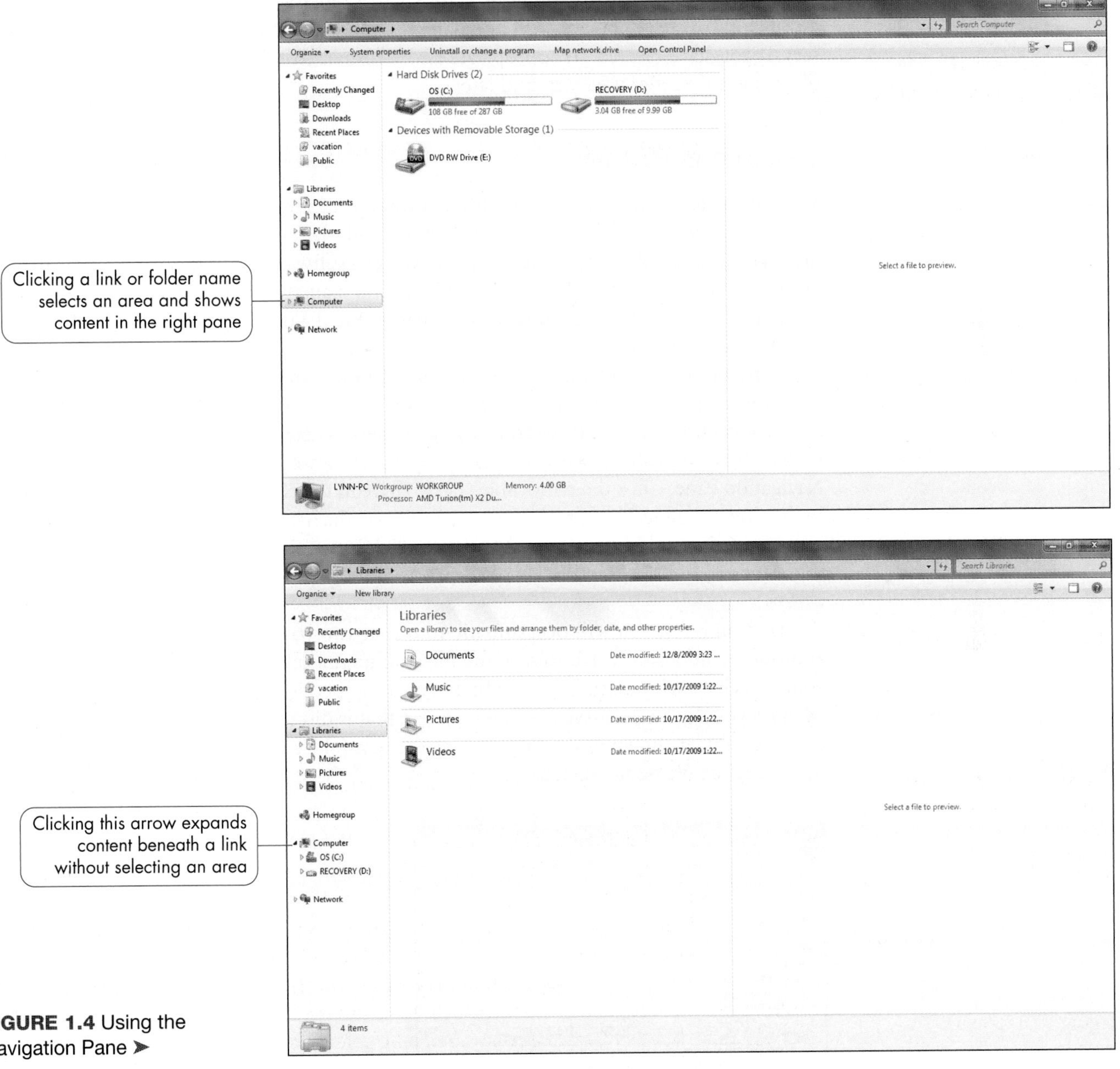

FIGURE 1.4 Using the Navigation Pane ➤

Click the drive in the Navigation Pane (or double-click the drive in the Content pane). Continue navigating through the folder structure until you find the folder that you seek. Double-click the folder (in the Content pane) or single-click the folder (in the Navigation Pane) to view its contents.

The Favorites area contains frequently accessed folders and recent searches. You can drag a folder, a saved search, a library, or a disk drive to the Favorites area. To remove a favorite, simply right-click the favorite, and then click Remove. You cannot add files or Web sites as favorites.

Homegroup is a Windows 7 feature that enables you to share resources on a home network. You can easily share music, pictures, videos, and libraries with other people in your home through a homegroup. It is password protected, so you do not have to worry about privacy.

Windows 7 makes creating a home network easy, sharing access to the Internet and peripheral devices such as printers and scanners. The Network area provides quick access to those devices, enabling you to see the contents of network computers.

Working with Folders and Files

As you work with software to create a file, such as when you type a report using Microsoft Word, your primary concern will be saving the file so that you can retrieve it later if necessary. If you have created an appropriate and well-named folder structure, you can save the file in a location that is easy to find later.

Create a Folder

You can create a folder a couple of different ways. You can use Windows Explorer to create a folder structure, providing appropriate names and placing the folders in a well-organized hierarchy. You can also create a folder from within a software application at the time that you need it. Although it would be wonderful to always plan ahead, most often you will find the need for a folder at the same time that you have created a file. The two methods of creating a folder are described below.

Suppose you are beginning a new college semester and are taking four classes. To organize your assignments, you plan to create four folders on a flash drive, one for each class. After connecting the flash drive and closing any subsequent dialog box (unless the dialog box is warning of a problem with the drive), open Windows Explorer. Click Computer in the Navigation Pane. Click the removable (flash) drive in the Navigation Pane, or double-click it in the Content pane. You can also create a folder on the hard drive in the same manner, clicking drive C instead of the removable drive. Click New folder on the Toolbar. Type the new folder name, such as English 101, and press Enter. Repeat the process for the other three classes.

Undoubtedly, you will occasionally find that you have just created a file but have no appropriate folder in which to save the file. You might have just finished the slide show for your speech class but have forgotten first to create a speech folder for your assignments. Now what do you do? As you save the file, a process that is discussed later in this chapter, you can click New folder shown in Figure 1.5. Type the new folder name, and then press Enter. After indicating the file name, click Save.

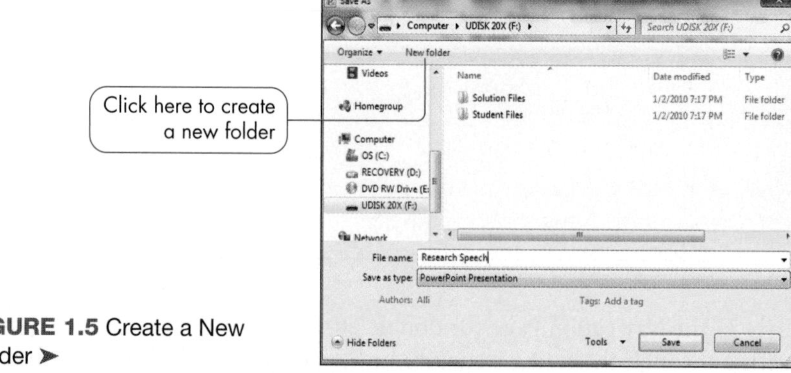

FIGURE 1.5 Create a New Folder ➤

TIP Working with the Address Bar

As you manage folders and work with files in Windows Explorer, keep a close eye on the Address bar (shown in Figure 1.2). It will always inform you of the current drive or folder, which is a very important detail. For example, if you have created a folder titled Summer Semester, and you want to create a subfolder for each class that you plan to take during the semester, you will want to be sure the Summer Semester folder is selected before creating the subfolders. If the Address bar does not show the correct folder, you should select the correct folder in the Navigation Pane before proceeding.

Open, Rename, and Delete Folders and Files

You have learned that folders can be created in Windows Explorer but that files must be created in other ways, such as within a software package. Although Windows Explorer cannot create files, you can use it to open, rename, and delete files just as you use it for folders.

Using the Navigation Pane, you can locate and select a folder containing a file that you want to open. For example, you will want to open the speech slide show so that you can practice before giving the presentation to the class. Open Windows Explorer, and navigate to the speech folder on your removable drive (flash drive). The file will display in the right pane. Double-click the file. The program that is associated with the file will open the file. For example, if you used PowerPoint to create the slide show, then PowerPoint will open the file. To open a folder and display the contents, just single-click the folder in the Navigation Pane or double-click it in the Content pane.

At times, you may find a more suitable name for a file or folder than the one that you originally gave it. Or perhaps you made a typographical mistake when you entered the name. In these situations, you should rename the file or folder. In Windows Explorer, move through the folder structure to find the folder or file. Right-click the name, and then click Rename. Type the new name, and then press Enter. You can also rename an item when you click the name twice, but much more slowly than a double-click. Type the new name, and then press Enter. Finally, you can click a file or folder once to select it, click Organize, click Rename, type the new name, and then press Enter.

TIP Renaming Several Files at Once

Suppose you are collecting digital photos that you took during a recent trip to Las Vegas. The camera gives the photo files very cryptic names, so you want to give them names that will identify them as Las Vegas photos. You can rename all the files at once. In Windows Explorer, select all of the files. To do so, click the first file, hold down Shift, and then click the last file in the list. Right-click any selected file, click Rename, and then type a new name—perhaps *Las Vegas*. Press Enter. All files will be saved with the new name and a different sequential number. Your photos will be named *Las Vegas (1)*, *Las Vegas (2)*, and so forth.

It is much easier to delete a folder or file than it is to recover it if you remove it by mistake. Therefore, be very careful when deleting items so that you are sure of your intentions before proceeding. When you delete a folder, all subfolders and all files within the folder are also removed. If you are certain you want to remove a folder or file, the process is simple. Right-click the item, click Delete, and then click Yes if asked to confirm removal to the Recycle Bin. Items are only placed in the Recycle Bin if you are deleting them from a hard drive. Files and folders deleted from a removable storage medium, such as a flash drive, are permanently deleted, with no easy method of retrieval. You can also delete an item (file or folder) when you click to select the item, click Organize, and then click Delete.

Save a File

As you create or modify a project such as a document, presentation, or worksheet, your work is placed in RAM, which is the computer's temporary memory. When you shut down the computer or inadvertently lose electrical power, the contents of RAM are erased. Even with a loss of electrical power, however, RAM on a laptop will not be erased until the battery runs down. Because you will most likely want to continue the project at another time or keep it for later reference, you need to save it to a storage medium such as a hard drive, CD, or flash drive. When you save a file, you will be working within a software package. Therefore, you must follow the procedure dictated by that software to save the file. Thankfully, most software requires that you save files in a similar fashion, so you can usually find your way through the process fairly quickly.

The first time that you save a file, you must indicate where the file should be saved, and you must assign a file name. Of course, you will want to save the file in an appropriately named folder so that you can find it easily later. Thereafter, you can quickly save the file with the same settings, or you can change one or more of those settings, perhaps saving the file to a different storage device as a backup copy. Figure 1.6 shows a typical Save As dialog box that enables you to confirm or change settings before finally saving the file.

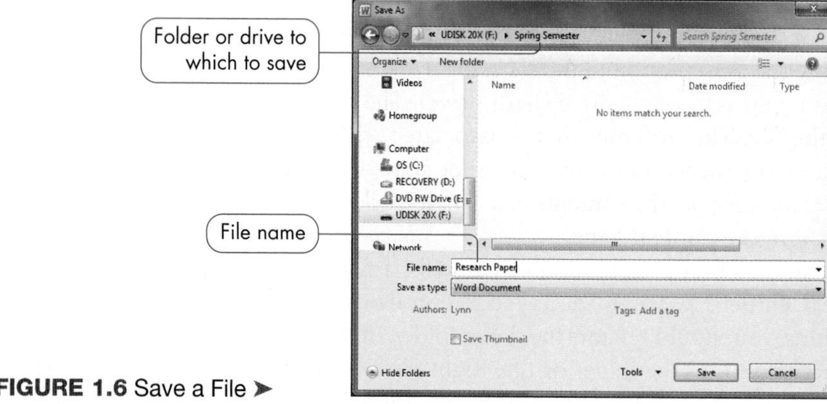

FIGURE 1.6 Save a File ➤

Selecting, Copying, and Moving Multiple Files and Folders

On occasion, you will want to select folders and files, such as when you need to rename, delete, copy, or paste them. You might want to open files and folders so that you can view the contents. Single-click a file or folder to *select* it; double-click a file or folder (in the Content pane) to *open* it. When you want to apply an operation to several files at once, such as deleting or moving them, you will want to select all of them. Knowing how to select several files and folders at one time makes the process of copying, or moving, items quick and simple.

Select Multiple Files and Folders

You can select several files and folders, regardless of whether they are adjacent to each other in the file list. Suppose that your digital pictures are contained in the Pictures folder. You might want to delete some of the pictures because you have already copied them to a CD and you want to clear up some hard drive space. To select certain pictures in the Pictures folder, open Windows Explorer, and then click the Pictures library. You will recall that the Pictures library groups and displays pictures from multiple folders. Navigate through any folder structure to locate the desired pictures in the Content pane. Assume that you want to select the first four pictures displayed. Because they are adjacent, you can select the first picture, hold down Shift, and click the fourth picture. All four pictures will be highlighted, indicating that they are selected. At that point, you can delete, copy, move, or rename the selected pictures. The next section of this chapter explains how to copy and move selections.

If the files or folders to be selected are not adjacent, simply click the first item. Hold down Ctrl while you click all other files or folders, one at a time, releasing Ctrl only when you have finished selecting all files or folders. All files or folders will be selected.

To select all items in a folder or disk, use Windows Explorer to navigate to the desired folder. Open the folder, then hold down Ctrl, and press A on the keyboard. You can also click Organize, and then Select All to select all items.

> **TIP** Using a Check Box to Select Items
>
> Windows 7 includes a file selection technique that makes it easy to make multiple selections, regardless of whether the items are adjacent. To activate the option, open Windows Explorer, and then change the view to Details. Click Organize, and then select Folder and search options. The Folder Options dialog box opens. Click the View tab, scroll down in the Advanced settings box, click Use check boxes to select items (see Figure 1.7), and then click OK. As you move the mouse pointer along the left side of files and folders, a check box appears. Click in the check box to select the file. In this manner, you can select multiple files and folders. If you want to quickly select all items in the folder, click the check box that appears in the Name column.

Click here to select items with check boxes

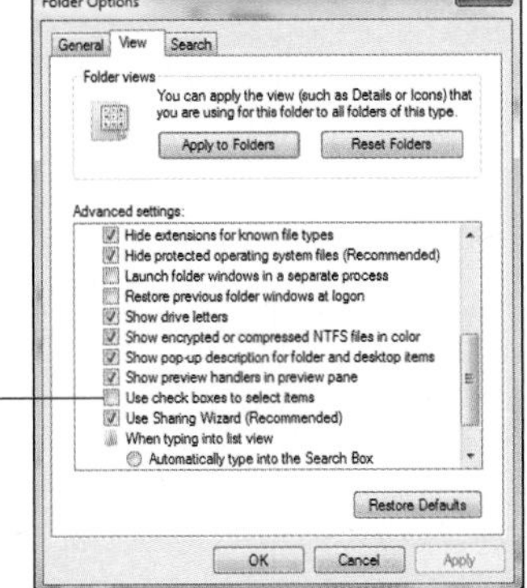

FIGURE 1.7 Use Check Boxes to Select Items ➤

Copy and Move Files and Folders

A **backup** is a copy of a file, usually on another storage medium.

When you copy or move a folder, both the folder and any files that it contains are affected. You can move or copy a folder or file to another location on the same drive or to another drive. If your purpose is to make a ***backup*** copy of an important file or folder, you will probably want to copy it to another drive.

Using a shortcut menu is one of the most foolproof ways to move or copy an item. In Windows Explorer, select the file or folder that you want to move or copy. If you want to copy or move multiple items, follow the directions in the previous section to select them all at once. Right-click the item, and select either Cut or Copy. Scroll through the Navigation Pane to locate the drive or folder to which you want to move or copy the selected item. Right-click the destination drive or folder, and then click Paste. If the moved or copied item is a folder, it should appear as a subfolder of the selected folder. If the moved or copied item is a file, it will be placed within the selected folder.

HANDS-ON EXERCISES

1 Files and Folders

You will soon begin to collect files from volunteers who are preparing promotional and record-keeping material for the Rails and Trails project. It is important that you save the files in appropriately named folders so that you can easily access them later. Therefore, you plan to create folders. You can create folders on a flash drive or a hard drive. You will select the drive on which you plan to save your student files. As you create a short document, you will save it in one of the folders. You will then make a backup copy of the folder structure, including all files, so that you do not run the risk of losing the material if the drive is damaged or misplaced.

Skills covered: Create Folders and Subfolders • Create and Save a File • Rename and Delete a Folder • Open and Copy a File

STEP 1 CREATE FOLDERS AND SUBFOLDERS

You decide to create a folder titled *Rails and Trails Project*, and then subdivide it into subfolders that will help categorize the project files. Refer to Figure 1.8 as you complete Step 1.

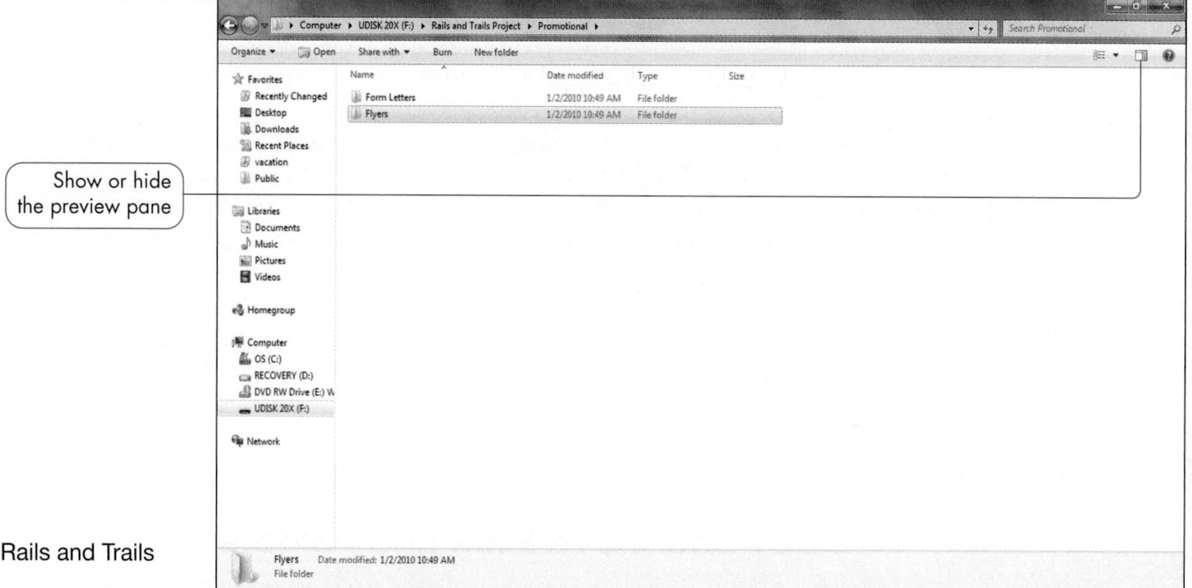

FIGURE 1.8 Rails and Trails Folders ➤

a. Insert your flash drive (if you are using a flash drive for your student files), and close any dialog box that opens (unless it is informing you of a problem with the drive). Click **Windows Explorer** on the taskbar. Click **Show the preview pane** unless the Preview pane is already displayed.

The removable drive shown in Figure 1.8 is titled UDISK 20X (F:), describing the drive manufacturer and the drive letter. Your removable drive will be designated in a different manner, perhaps also identified by manufacturer. The drive letter identifying your flash drive is likely to be different because the configuration of disk drives on your computer is unique.

TROUBLESHOOTING: If you do not have a flash drive, you can use the hard drive. In the next step, simply click drive C in the Navigation Pane instead of the removable drive.

b. Click the removable drive in the Navigation Pane (or click **drive C** if you are using the hard drive). Click **New folder** on the Toolbar, type **Rails and Trails Project**, and then press **Enter**.

You create a folder where you can organize subfolders and files for the Rails and Trails project.

> **TROUBLESHOOTING:** If the folder you create is called *New folder* instead of *Rails and Trails Project*, you probably clicked away from the folder before typing the name, so that it received the default name. To rename it, right-click the folder, click Rename, type the correct name, and then press Enter.

c. Double-click **Rails and Trails Project** in the Content pane (middle pane). The Address bar should show that it is the currently selected folder. Click **New folder**, type **Promotional**, and then press **Enter**.

   You decide to create subfolders of the Rails and Trails Project folder to contain promotional material, presentations, and office records. You create three subfolders, appropriately named.

d. Check the Address bar to make sure *Rails and Trails Project* is still the current folder. Click **New folder**, type **Presentations**, and then press **Enter**.

e. Click **New folder**, type **Office Records**, and then press **Enter**.

f. Double-click **Promotional** in the middle pane. Click **New folder**, type **Form Letters**, and then press **Enter**. Click **New folder**, type **Flyers**, and then press **Enter**.

   To subdivide the promotional material further, you create two subfolders, one to hold form letters and one to contain flyers. Your screen should appear as in Figure 1.8.

g. Close Windows Explorer.

STEP 2 CREATE AND SAVE A FILE

As the project gears up, you assign volunteers to take care of certain tasks. After creating an Excel worksheet listing those responsibilities, you will save it in the Office Records folder. Refer to Figure 1.9 as you complete Step 2.

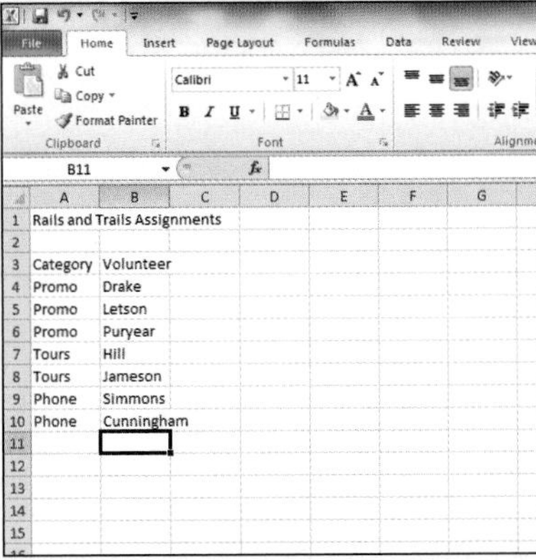

FIGURE 1.9 Volunteers Worksheet ➤

a. Click the **Start button**, and then point to **All Programs**. Scroll down the program list, if necessary, and then click **Microsoft Office**. Click **Microsoft Excel 2010**.

   You use Microsoft Excel to create the volunteers worksheet.

b. Type **Rails and Trails Assignments** in **cell A1**. Press **Enter** twice.

   Your cursor will be in cell A3.

c. Type **Category**. Press **Tab** to move the cursor one cell to the right, and then type **Volunteer**. Press **Enter**. Complete the remaining cells of the worksheet as shown in Figure 1.9.

> **TROUBLESHOOTING:** If you make a mistake, click in the cell and retype the entry.

d. Click the **File tab** (in the top-left corner of the Excel window). Click **Save**.

   The Save As dialog box displays. The Save As dialog box is where you determine the location, file name, and file type of any document. You can also create a new folder in the Save As dialog box.

e. Scroll down if necessary, and then click **Computer** in the left pane. In the Content pane, double-click the drive where you will save the file. Double-click **Rails and Trails Project** in the Content pane. Double-click **Office Records.** Click in the **File name box.** Type **f01h1volunteers_LastnameFirstname** in the **file name box**, replacing *LastnameFirstname* with your own last name and first name. Click **Save.**

   The file is now saved as *f01h1volunteers_LastnameFirstname.* You can check the title bar of the workbook to confirm the file has been saved with the correct name.

f. Click the **Close button** in the top-right corner of the Excel window to close Excel.

TROUBLESHOOTING: If you click the lower X instead of the one in the top-right corner, the current Excel worksheet will close, but Excel will remain open. In that case, click the remaining X to close Excel.

The Volunteers workbook is saved in the Office Records subfolder of the Rails and Trails Project folder.

STEP 3 RENAME AND DELETE A FOLDER

As often happens, you find that the folder structure is not exactly what you need. You will remove the Flyers folder and the Form Letters folder and will rename the Promotional folder to better describe the contents. Refer to Figure 1.10 as you complete Step 3.

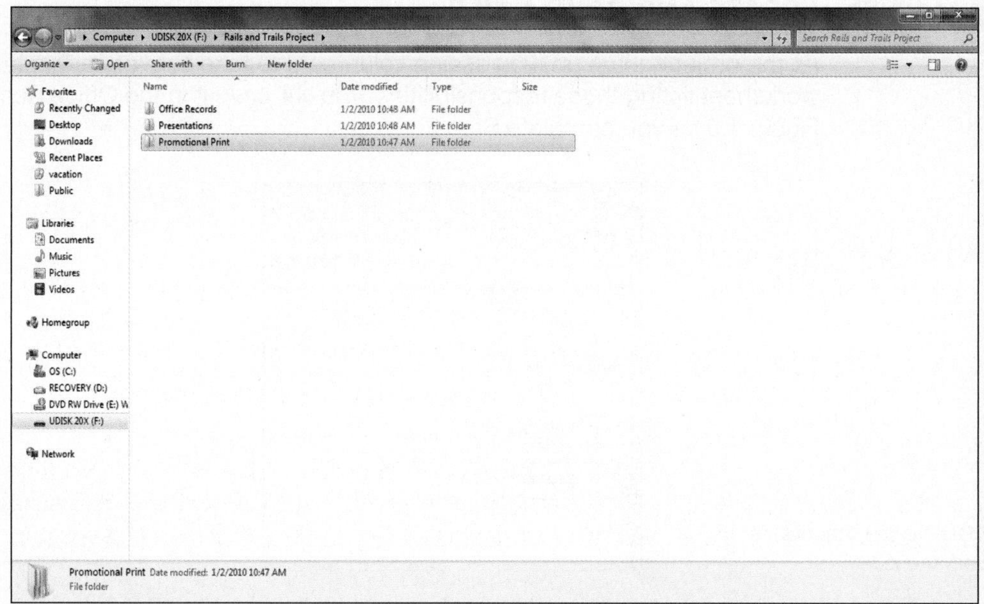

FIGURE 1.10 Rails and Trails Project Folder Structure ➤

a. Right-click the **Start button.** Click **Open Windows Explorer.** Click the disk drive where you save your files (under Computer in the Navigation Pane). Double-click **Rails and Trails Project** in the Content pane.

b. Click the **Promotional folder** to select it.

TROUBLESHOOTING: If you double-click the folder instead of using a single-click, the folder will open and you will see its title in the Address bar. To return to the correct view, click Rails and Trails Project in the Address bar.

c. Click **Organize,** click **Rename,** type **Promotional Print,** and then press **Enter.**

   Since the folder will be used to organize all of the printed promotional material, you decide to rename the folder to better reflect the contents.

d. Double-click **Promotional Print**. Click **Flyers**. Hold down **Shift**, and then click **Form Letters.** Both folders should be selected (highlighted). Right-click either folder, and then click **Delete**. If asked to confirm the deletion, click **Yes**. Click **Rails and Trails Project** in the **Address bar**. Your screen should appear as shown in Figure 1.10. Leave Windows Explorer open for the next step.

You decide that dividing the promotional material into flyers and form letters is not necessary, so you delete both folders.

STEP 4 OPEN AND COPY A FILE

You hope to recruit more volunteers to work with the Rails and Trails project. The Volunteers worksheet will be a handy way to keep up with people and assignments, and as the list grows, knowing exactly where the file is saved will be important for easy access. You will modify the Volunteers worksheet and then make a backup copy of the folder hierarchy. Refer to Figure 1.11 as you complete Step 4.

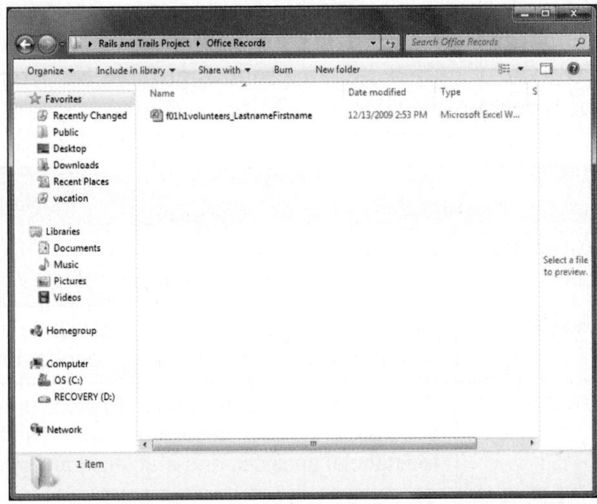

FIGURE 1.11 Rails and Trails Folder Structure ➤

a. Double-click the **Office Records folder**. Double-click *f01h1volunteers_LastnameFirstname*.

Because the file was created with Excel, that program opens, and the volunteers worksheet is displayed.

b. Click **cell A11**, and then type **Office**. Press **Tab**, type **Adams**, and then press **Enter**. Click the **File tab** in the top-left corner of the Excel window, and then click **Save**. The file is automatically saved in the same location with the same file name as before. Close Excel.

A neighbor, Samantha Adams, has volunteered to help in the office. You record that information on the worksheet and save the updated file in the Office Records folder.

c. Click the location where you save files in the Navigation Pane in Windows Explorer. Right-click **Rails and Trails Project** in the right pane. Click **Copy**.

d. Right-click **Desktop** in the Favorites group on the Navigation Pane, and then click **Paste**. Close Windows Explorer. If any other windows are open, close them also.

You make a copy of the Rails and Trails Project folder on the desktop.

e. Double-click **Rails and Trails Project** on the desktop. Double-click **Office Records**. Is the volunteers worksheet in the folder? Your screen should appear as shown in Figure 1.11. Close Windows Explorer.

f. Right-click the **Rails and Trails Project folder** on the desktop, click **Delete**, and then click **Yes** when asked to confirm the deletion.

You delete the Rails and Trails Project folder from the desktop of the computer because you may be working in a computer lab and want to leave the computer as you found it.

Microsoft Office Software

Organizations around the world rely heavily on ***Microsoft Office*** software to produce documents, spreadsheets, presentations, and databases. Microsoft Office is a productivity software suite including four primary software components, each one specializing in a particular type of output. You can use ***Word*** to produce all sorts of documents, including memos, newsletters, forms, tables, and brochures. ***Excel*** makes it easy to organize records, financial transactions, and business information in the form of worksheets. With ***PowerPoint***, you can create dynamic presentations to inform groups and persuade audiences. ***Access*** is relational database software that enables you to record and link data, query databases, and create forms and reports. You will sometimes find that you need to use two or more Office applications to produce your intended output. You might, for example, find that a Word document you are preparing for your investment club should also include a summary of stock performance. You can use Excel to prepare the summary and then incorporate the worksheet in the Word document. Similarly, you can integrate Word tables and Excel charts in a PowerPoint presentation. The choice of which software component to use really depends on what type of output you are producing. Table 1.2 describes the major tasks of the four primary programs in Microsoft Office.

Microsoft Office is a productivity software suite including four primary software components, each one specializing in a particular type of output.

Microsoft Office is a productivity software suite that includes word processing, spreadsheet, presentation, and database software components.

Word is a word processing program included in Microsoft Office.

Excel is software that specializes in organizing data in worksheet form. It is included in Microsoft Office.

PowerPoint is a Microsoft Office software component that enables you to prepare slideshow presentations for audiences.

Access is a database program included in Microsoft Office.

TABLE 1.2 Microsoft Office Software

Office 2010 Product	Application Characteristics
Word 2010	Word processing software is used with text to create, edit, and format documents such as letters, memos, reports, brochures, resumes, and flyers.
Excel 2010	Spreadsheet software is used to store quantitative data and to perform accurate and rapid calculations with results ranging from simple budgets to financial analyses and statistical analyses.
PowerPoint 2010	Presentation graphics software is used to create slide shows for presentation by a speaker, to be published as part of a Web site, or to run as a stand-alone application on a computer kiosk.
Access 2010	Relational database software is used to store data and convert it into information. Database software is used primarily for decision-making by businesses that compile data from multiple records stored in tables to produce informative reports.

As you become familiar with Microsoft Office, you will find that although each software component produces a specific type of output, all components share common features. Such commonality gives a similar feel to each software application so that learning and working with primary Microsoft Office software products is easy. In this section, you will identify features common to Microsoft Office software, including such interface components as the Ribbon, the Backstage view, and the Quick Access Toolbar. You will also learn how to get help with an application.

Identifying Common Interface Components

A **user interface** is a collection of onscreen components that facilitates communication between the software and the user.

As you work with Microsoft Office, you will find that each application shares a similar ***user interface***. The user interface is the screen display through which you communicate with the software. Word, Excel, PowerPoint, and Access share common interface elements, as shown in Figure 1.12. As you can imagine, becoming familiar with one application's interface makes it that much easier to work with other Office software.

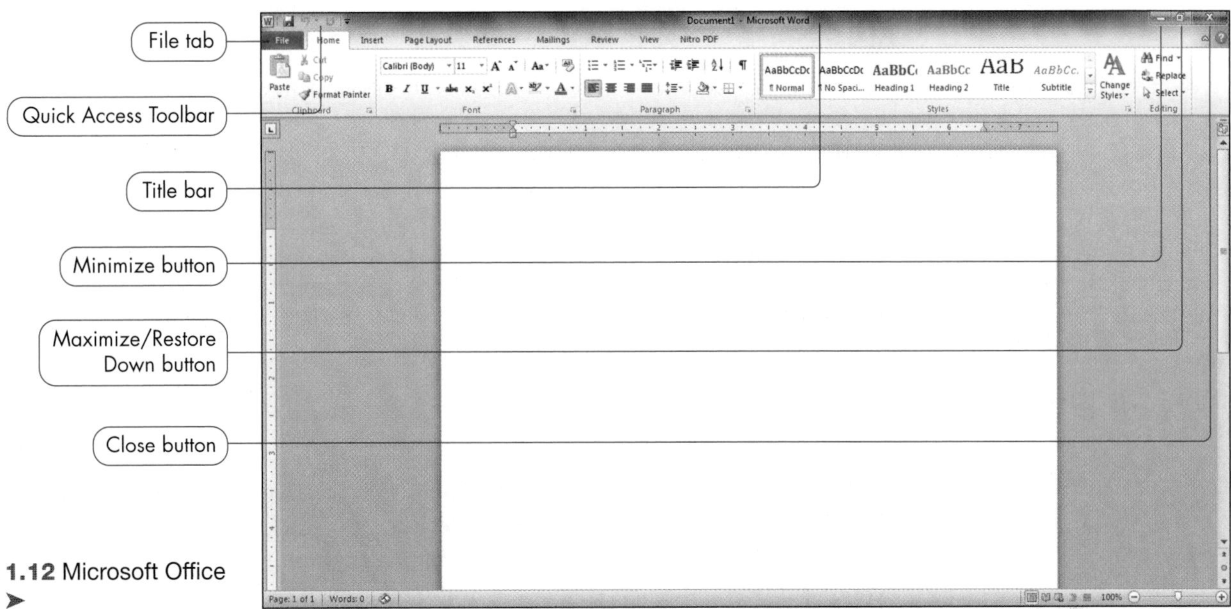

FIGURE 1.12 Microsoft Office Interface ➤

Use the Backstage View and the Quick Access Toolbar

The ***Backstage view*** is a new component of Office 2010 that provides a concise collection of commands related to an open file. Using the Backstage view, you can print, save, open, close, and share a file. In addition, you can view properties and other information related to the file. A file's properties include the author, file size, permissions, and date modified. You can access the Backstage view by clicking the File tab. The ***Quick Access Toolbar***, located at the top-left corner of the Office window, provides handy access to commonly executed tasks such as saving a file and undoing recent actions. The ***title bar*** identifies the current file name and the application in which you are working. It also includes control buttons that enable you to minimize, maximize, restore down, or close the application window. Refer to Figure 1.12 for the location of those items on the title bar.

> Using the Backstage view, you can print, save, open, close, and share a file.

The **Backstage view** displays when you click the File tab. It includes commands related to common file activities and provides information on an open file.

The **Quick Access Toolbar** provides one-click access to commonly used commands.

The **title bar** contains the current file name, Office application, and control buttons.

When you click the File tab, you will see the Backstage view, as shown in Figure 1.13. Primarily focusing on file activities such as opening, closing, saving, printing, and beginning new files, the Backstage view also includes options for customizing program settings, getting help, and exiting the program. It displays a file's properties, providing important information on file permission and sharing options. When you click the File tab, the Backstage view will occupy the entire application window, hiding the file with which you might be working. For example, suppose that as you are typing a report you need to check the document's properties. Click the File tab to display a Backstage view similar to that shown in Figure 1.13. You can return to the application—in this case, Word—in a couple of ways. Simply click the File tab again (or any other tab on the Ribbon). Alternatively, you can press Esc on the keyboard. The Ribbon is described in the next section.

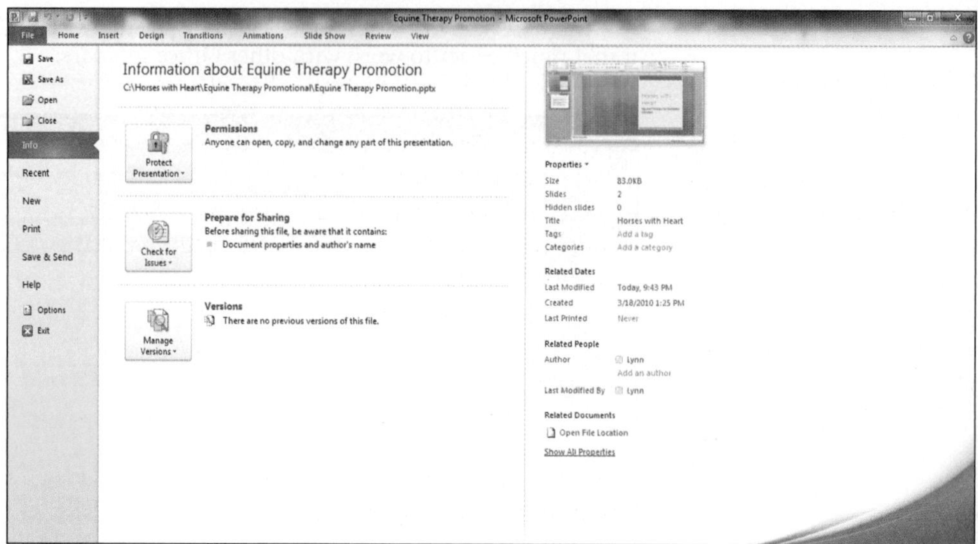

FIGURE 1.13 Backstage View ➤

The Quick Access Toolbar provides one-click access to common activities. Figure 1.14 describes the Quick Access Toolbar. By default, the Quick Access Toolbar includes buttons for saving a file and for undoing or redoing recent actions. You will probably perform an action countless times in an Office application and then realize that you made a mistake. You can recover from the mistake by clicking Undo on the Quick Access Toolbar. If you click the arrow beside Undo, you can select from a list of previous actions in order of occurrence. The Undo list is not maintained when you close a file or exit the application, so you can only erase an action that took place during the current Office session. Similar to Undo, you can also Redo (or Replace) an action that you have just undone. You can customize the Quick Access Toolbar to include buttons for frequently used commands such as printing or opening files. Because the Quick Access Toolbar is onscreen at all times, the most commonly accessed tasks are just a click away.

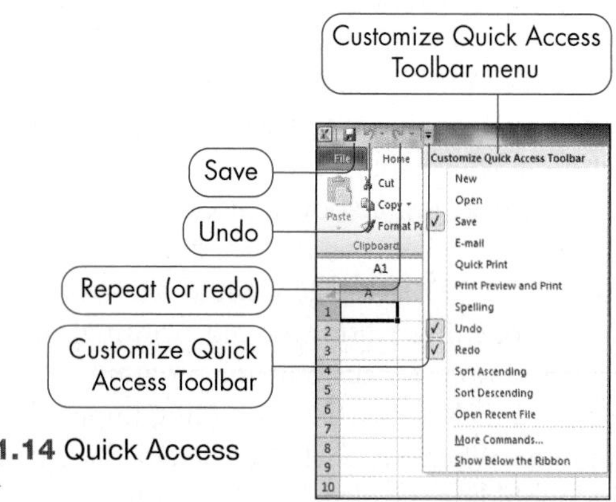

FIGURE 1.14 Quick Access Toolbar ➤

TIP Customizing the Quick Access Toolbar

To customize the Quick Access Toolbar, click Customize Quick Access Toolbar, as shown in Figure 1.14, and select from a list of commands. If a command that you want to include on the toolbar is not on the list, you can simply right-click the command on the Ribbon, and then click Add to Quick Access Toolbar. Similarly, remove a command from the Quick Access Toolbar by right-clicking the icon on the Quick Access Toolbar, and then clicking Remove from Quick Access Toolbar. If you want to display the Quick Access Toolbar beneath the Ribbon, click Customize Quick Access Toolbar (Figure 1.14), and then click Show Below the Ribbon.

Familiarize Yourself with the Ribbon

'he **Ribbon** is the long bar of abs, groups, and commands ocated just beneath the Title bar.

:ach **tab** on the Ribbon contains roups of related tasks.

The ***Ribbon*** is the command center of Office applications. It is the long bar located just beneath the Title bar, containing tabs, groups, and commands. Each ***tab*** is designed to appear much like a tab on a file folder, with the active tab highlighted. The File tab is always a darker shade than the other tabs, and a different color depending on the application. Remember that clicking the File tab opens the Backstage view. Other tabs on the Ribbon enable you to create and modify a file. The active tab in Figure 1.15 is the Home tab.

\ **group** is a subset of a tab that rganizes similar tasks together.

\ **command** is a button or area vithin a group that you click to erform tasks.

When you click a tab, the Ribbon displays several task-oriented ***groups***, with each group containing related ***commands***. Microsoft Office is designed to provide the most functionality possible with the fewest clicks. For that reason, the Home tab, displayed when you first open an Office software application, contains groups and commands that are commonly used. For example, because you will often want to change the way text is displayed, the Home tab in each Office application includes a Font group with activities related to modifying text. Similarly, other tabs contain groups of related actions, or commands, many of which are unique to the particular Office application.

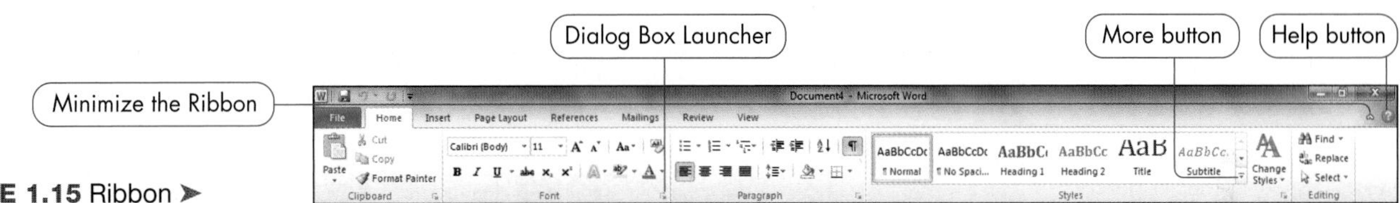

FIGURE 1.15 Ribbon ➤

Because Word, PowerPoint, Excel, and Access all share a similar Ribbon structure, you will be able to move at ease among those applications. Although the specific tabs, groups, and commands vary among the Office programs, the way in which you use the Ribbon and the descriptive nature of tab titles is the same regardless of which program you are working with. For example, if you want to insert a chart in Excel, a header in Word, or a shape in PowerPoint, you will click the Insert tab in any of those programs. The first thing that you should do as you begin to work with an Office application is to study the Ribbon. Take a look at all tabs and their contents. That way, you will have a good idea of where to find specific commands and how the Ribbon with which you are currently working differs from one that you might have used previously in another application.

> Because Word, PowerPoint, Excel, and Access all share a similar Ribbon structure, you will be able to move at ease among those applications.

TIP Hiding the Ribbon

The Ribbon occupies a good bit of space at the top of the Office interface. If you are working with a large project, you might want to maximize your workspace by temporarily hiding the Ribbon. You can hide the Ribbon in several ways. Double-click the active tab to hide the Ribbon, and then double-click any tab to redisplay it. Alternatively, you can press Ctrl+F1 to hide the Ribbon, with the same shortcut key combination redisplaying it. Finally, you can click Minimize the Ribbon (see Figure 1.15), located at the right side of the Ribbon, clicking it a second time to redisplay the Ribbon.

\ **dialog box** is a window that nables you to make selections r indicate settings beyond those rovided on the Ribbon.

\ **Dialog Box Launcher** is an con in Ribbon groups that you an click to open a related dialog ox. It is not found in all groups.

The Ribbon provides quick access to common activities such as changing number or text formats or aligning data or text. Some actions, however, are not so common but are related to commands displayed on the Ribbon. For example, you might want to change the background of a PowerPoint slide to include a picture. In that case, you will need to work with a ***dialog box*** that provides access to more precise, but less frequently used, commands. Figure 1.16 shows a dialog box. Some commands display a dialog box when they are clicked. Other Ribbon groups include a ***Dialog Box Launcher*** that, when clicked, opens a corresponding dialog box. Figure 1.15 shows a Dialog Box Launcher.

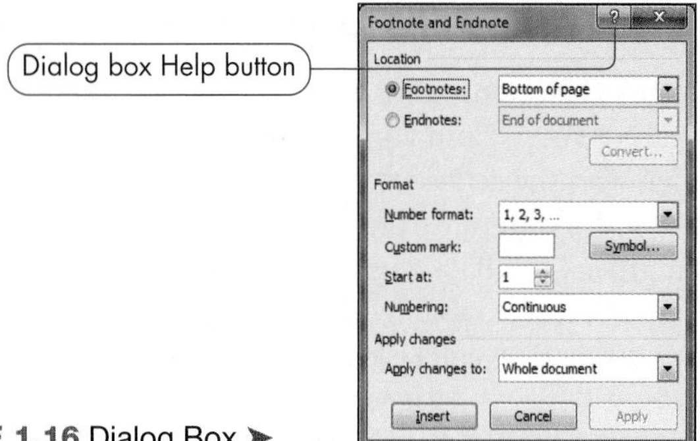

FIGURE 1.16 Dialog Box ➤

A **gallery** is a set of selections that appears when you click a More button, or in some cases when you click a command, in a Ribbon group.

The Ribbon contains many selections and commands, but some selections are too numerous to include in the Ribbon's limited space. For example, Word provides far more text styles than it can easily display at once, so additional styles are available in a ***gallery***. A gallery also provides a choice of Excel chart styles and PowerPoint transitions. Figure 1.17 gives an example of a PowerPoint Themes gallery. Most often, you can display a gallery of additional choices by clicking the More button that is found in some Ribbon selections. Figure 1.15 shows a More button.

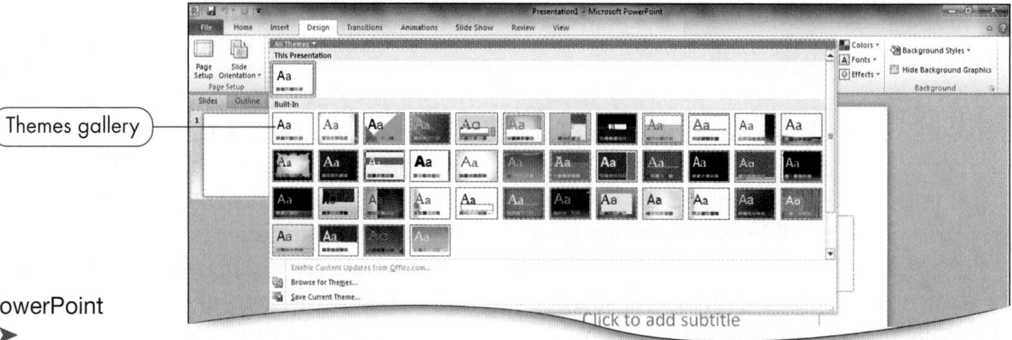

FIGURE 1.17 PowerPoint Themes Gallery ➤

Live Preview is an Office feature that provides a preview of the results of a selection when you point to an option in a list. Using Live Preview, you can experiment with settings before making a final choice.

A **contextual tab** is a Ribbon tab that displays when an object, such as a picture or clip art, is selected. A contextual tab contains groups and commands specific to the selected object.

When editing a document, worksheet, or presentation, it is helpful to see the results of formatting changes before you make final selections. You might be considering changing the font color of a selection in a document or worksheet. As you place the mouse pointer over a color selection in a Ribbon gallery or group, the selected text will temporarily display the color to which you are pointing. Similarly, you can get a preview of how color designs would appear on PowerPoint slides by pointing to specific themes in the PowerPoint Themes group and noting the effect on a displayed slide. When you click the item, such as the font color, the selection is applied. The feature enabling a preview of the results of a selection is called ***Live Preview***. It is available in various Ribbon selections among the Office applications.

Office applications make it easy for you to work with objects such as pictures, clip art, shapes, charts, and tables. When you include such objects in a project, they are considered separate components that you can manage independently. To work with an object, you must click to select it. When you select an object, the Ribbon is modified to include one or more ***contextual tabs*** containing groups of commands related to the selected object. Figure 1.18 shows a contextual tab related to a selected object in a Word document. When you click outside the selected object, the contextual tab disappears.

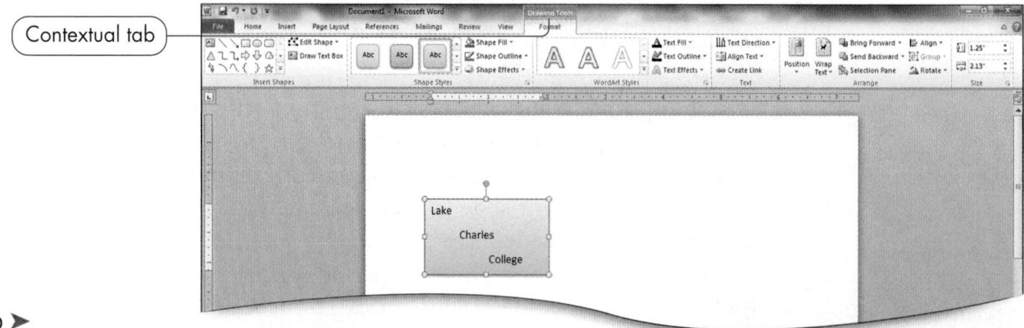

FIGURE 1.18 Contextual Tab ➤

TIP Using Keyboard Shortcuts

You might find that you prefer to use keyboard shortcuts, which are keyboard equivalents for software commands, when they are available. Keyboard shortcuts make it possible for you to keep your hands on the keyboard instead of reaching for the mouse to make Ribbon selections. Press Alt to display keyboard shortcuts, called ***Key Tips***, for items on the Ribbon and Quick Access Toolbar. You can press the letter or number corresponding to Ribbon items to invoke the action from the keyboard. Press Alt again to remove the Key Tips. You can also use universal keyboard shortcuts that have been available in past Office versions and in other Windows software, such as Ctrl+C (copy), Ctrl+X (cut), Ctrl+V (paste), and Ctrl+Z (undo). You will want to remember two very important keyboard shortcuts—Ctrl+Home and Ctrl+End. To move to the beginning of a Word document, to cell A1 in Excel, or to the first PowerPoint slide, press Ctrl+Home. To move to the end of those items, press Ctrl+End.

A **Key Tip** is the letter or number that displays over features on the Ribbon and Quick Access Toolbar. Typing the letter or number is the equivalent of clicking the corresponding item.

Use the Status Bar

The **status bar** is the horizontal bar located at the bottom of an Office application containing information relative to the open file.

The ***status bar*** is found at the bottom of the program window and contains information relative to the open file. It also includes tools for changing the view of the file and for changing the size of onscreen file contents. Contents of the status bar are unique to each specific application. When you work with Word, the status bar informs you of the number of pages and words in an open document. Excel's status bar displays summary information, such as average and sum, of selected cells. The PowerPoint status bar shows the slide number, total slides in the presentation, and the applied theme.

Regardless of the application in which you are working, the status bar includes view buttons and a Zoom slider. You can also use the View tab on the Ribbon to change the current view or zoom level of an open file. The status bar's view buttons, shown in Figure 1.19, enable you to change the ***view*** of the open file. You might, for example, view a PowerPoint slide presentation with multiple slides displayed (Slide Sorter view) or with only one slide in large size (Normal view). In Word, you could view a document in Print Layout view (showing margins, headers, and footers), Full Screen Reading view, Web Layout view, or Draft view (with the greatest amount of typing space possible). As you learn more about Office applications in the following chapters, you will become aware of the views that are specific to each application.

Changing the **view** of a file changes the way it appears onscreen.

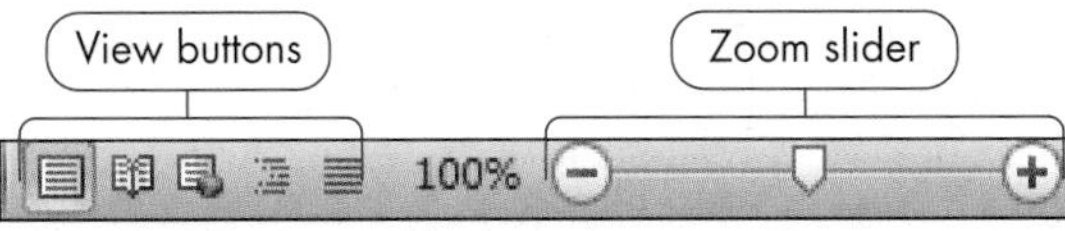

FIGURE 1.19 Word Status Bar ➤

The **Zoom slider** enables you to increase or decrease the size of file contents onscreen.

The ***Zoom slider*** always displays at the far right side of the status bar. You can drag the tab along the slider in either direction to increase or decrease the magnification of the file. Be aware, however, that changing the size of text onscreen does not increase the font size when the file is printed or saved.

Getting Office Help

One of the most frustrating things about learning new software is determining how to complete a task. Thankfully, Microsoft includes comprehensive help in Office so that you are less likely to feel such frustration. As you work with any Office application, you can access help online as well as within the current software installation. Help is also available through a short description that displays when you rest the mouse pointer on a command. Additionally, you can get help related to a currently open dialog box by clicking a question mark in the top-right corner of the dialog box or when you click the Help button in the Backstage view.

Use Office Help

To access the comprehensive library of Office Help, click the Help button, displayed as a question mark, on the far right side of the Ribbon (see Figure 1.15). You can get the same help by pressing F1 on the keyboard. The Backstage view also includes a Help feature, providing assistance with the current application as well as a direct link to online resources and technical support. Figure 1.20 shows the Help window that will display when you press F1, when you click the Help button, or when you click File, Help, Microsoft Office Help. For general information on broad topics, click a link in the window. However, if you are having difficulty with a specific task, it might be easier to simply type the request in the Search box. Suppose you are seeking help with using the Goal Seek feature in Excel. Simply type *Goal Seek* or a phrase such as *find specific result by changing variables* in the Search box, and press Enter (or click the magnifying glass on the right). Then select from displayed results for more information on the topic.

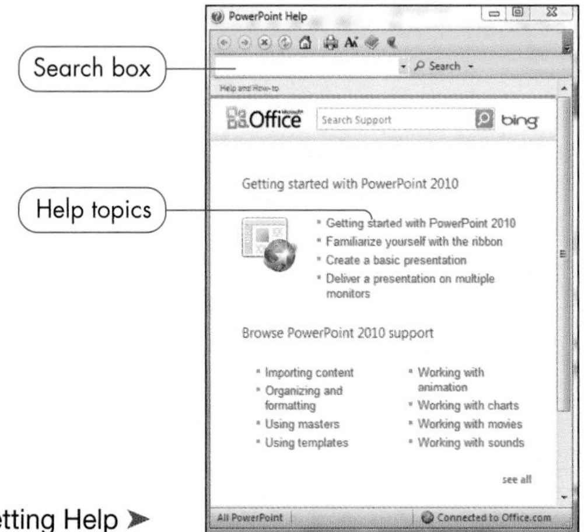

FIGURE 1.20 Getting Help ➤

Use Enhanced ScreenTips

An **Enhanced ScreenTip** provides a brief summary of a command when you place the mouse pointer over the command button.

For quick summary information on the purpose of a command button, place the mouse pointer over the button. An ***Enhanced ScreenTip*** displays, giving the purpose of the command, short descriptive text, and a keyboard shortcut if applicable. Some ScreenTips include a suggestion for pressing F1 for additional help. The Enhanced ScreenTip in Figure 1.21 provides context-sensitive assistance.

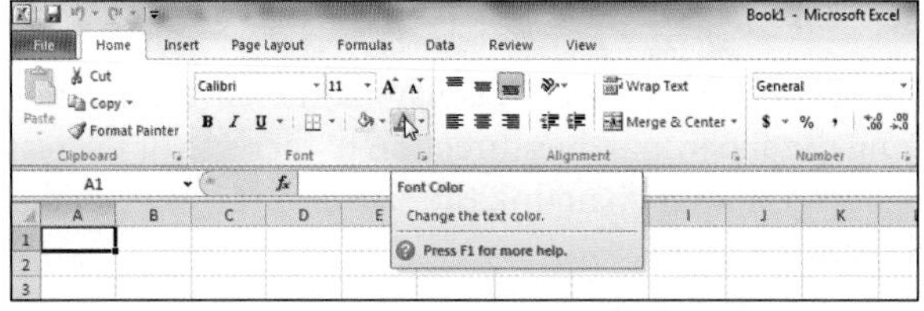

FIGURE 1.21 Enhanced ScreenTip ➤

Get Help with Dialog Boxes

Getting help while you are working with a dialog box is easy. Simply click the Help button that appears as a question mark in the top-right corner of the dialog box (see Figure 1.16). The subsequent Help window will offer suggestions relevant to your task.

2 Microsoft Office Software

As the administrative assistant for the Rails and Trails project, you need to get the staff started on a proposed fund-management worksheet. Although you do not have access to information on current donations, you want to provide a suggested format for a worksheet to keep up with donations as they come in. You will use Excel to begin design of the worksheet.

Skills covered: Open an Office Application, Get Enhanced ScreenTip Help, and Use the Zoom Slider • Get Help, Use the Backstage View • Change the View and Use Live Preview • Use the Quick Access Toolbar and Explore PowerPoint Views

STEP 1 OPEN AN OFFICE APPLICATION, GET ENHANCED SCREENTIP HELP, AND USE THE ZOOM SLIDER

Because you will use Excel to create the fund-raising worksheet, you will open the application. You will familiarize yourself with items on the Ribbon by getting Enhanced ScreenTip Help. For a better view of worksheet data, you will use the Zoom slider to magnify cell contents. Refer to Figure 1.22 as you complete Step 1.

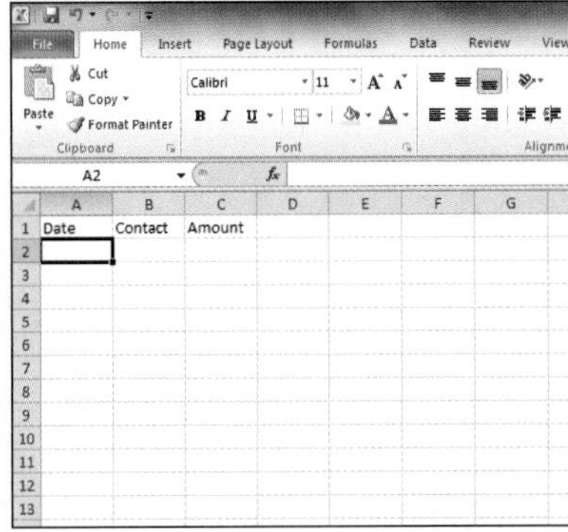

FIGURE 1.22 Fund-Raising Worksheet ➤

a. Click the **Start button** to display the Start Menu. Point to **All Programs**. Scroll down the list, if necessary, and click **Microsoft Office**. Click **Microsoft Excel 2010**.

   You have opened Microsoft Excel because it is the program in which the fund-raising worksheet will be created.

b. Type **Date**. As you type, the text appears in the current worksheet cell, **cell A1**. Press **Tab**, and then type **Contact**. Press **Tab**, and then type **Amount**. Press **Enter**. Your worksheet should look like the one in Figure 1.22.

   The worksheet that you create is only a beginning. Your staff will later suggest additional columns of data that can better summarize the hoped-for donations.

c. Hover the mouse pointer over any command on the Ribbon and note the Enhanced ScreenTip that displays, informing you of the purpose of the command. Explore other commands and identify their purpose.

d. Click the **Page Layout tab**, click **Orientation** in the Page Setup group, and then click **Landscape**.

   The Page Layout tab is also found in Word, enabling you to change margins, orientation, and other page settings. Although you will not see much difference in the Excel screen display after you change the orientation to landscape, the worksheet will be oriented so that it is wider than it is tall when printed.

e. Drag the tab on the **Zoom slider**, located at the far right side of the status bar, to the right to temporarily magnify the text. Click the **View tab**, and then click **100%** in the Zoom group to return the text to its original size. Keep the workbook open for the next step in this exercise.

When you change the zoom, you do not change the text size that will be printed or saved. The change merely magnifies or decreases the view while you work with the file.

STEP 2 GET HELP, USE THE BACKSTAGE VIEW

Because you are not an Excel expert, you occasionally rely on the Help feature to provide information on tasks. You need assistance with saving a worksheet, previewing it before printing, and printing the worksheet. From what you learn, you will find that the Backstage view enables you to accomplish all of those tasks. Refer to Figure 1.23 as you complete Step 2.

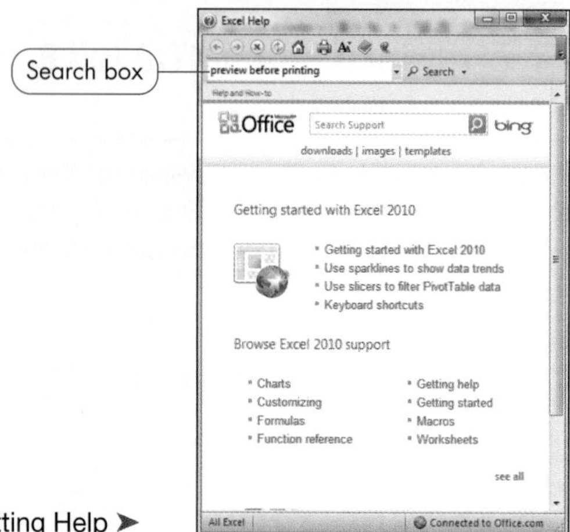

FIGURE 1.23 Getting Help ➤

a. Click the **Help button**, which is the question mark in the top-right corner of the Ribbon.

The Help dialog box displays.

b. Click in the white text box to the left of the word *Search* in the Help dialog box, as shown in Figure 1.23. Type **preview before printing** and click **Search**. In the Help window, click **Preview worksheet pages before printing**. Read about how to preview a worksheet before printing. From what you read, can you identify a keyboard shortcut for previewing worksheets? Click the **Close button**.

Before you print the worksheet, you would like to see how it will look when printed. You can use Help to find information on previewing before printing.

TROUBLESHOOTING: You must be connected to the Internet to get context-sensitive help.

c. Click the **File tab**, and then click **Print**.

Having used Office Help to learn how to preview before printing, you follow the directions to view the document as it will look when printed. The preview of the worksheet displays on the right. To print the worksheet, you would click Print. However, you can first select any print options, such as the number of copies, from the Backstage view.

d. Click the **Help button**. Excel Help presents several links related to the worksheet. Explore any that look interesting. Return to previous Help windows by clicking **Back** at the top-left side of the Help window. Close the Help dialog box.

e. Click the **Home tab**. Point to **Bold** in the Font group.

You will find that, along with Excel, Word and PowerPoint also include formatting features in the Font group, such as Bold and Italic. When the Enhanced ScreenTip appears, identify the shortcut key combination that could be used to bold a selected text item. It is indicated as Ctrl plus a letter. What is the shortcut?

f. Click the **Close button** in the red box in the top-right corner of the Excel window to close both the workbook and the Excel program. When asked whether you want to save changes, click **Don't Save**.

You decide not to print or save the worksheet right now. Instead, you will get assistance with its design and try it again later.

> **TROUBLESHOOTING:** If you clicked the Close button on the second row from the top, you closed the workbook but not Excel. Click the remaining Close button to close the program.

STEP 3 CHANGE THE VIEW AND USE LIVE PREVIEW

It is important that the documents you prepare or approve are error-free and as attractive as possible. Before printing, you will change the view to get a better idea of how the document will look when printed. In addition, you will use Live Preview to experiment with font settings before actually applying them. Refer to Figure 1.24 as you complete Step 3.

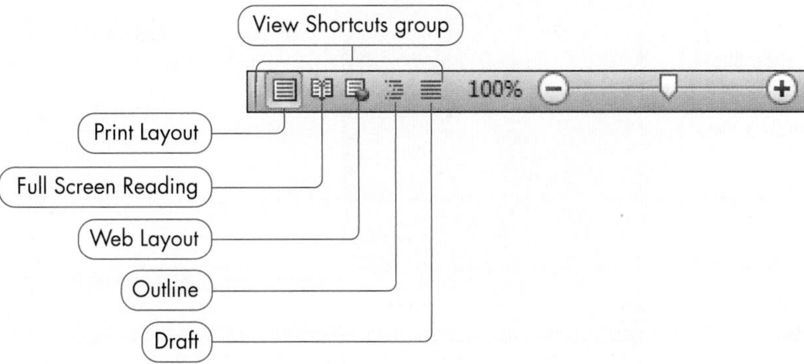

FIGURE 1.24 Word Views ➤

a. Click the **Start button**, and then point to **All Programs**. Scroll down, if necessary, and click **Microsoft Office**. Click **Microsoft Word 2010**.

You have opened a blank Word document. You plan to familiarize yourself with the program for later reference.

b. Type your full name, and then press **Enter**. Drag to select your name (or position the mouse pointer immediately to the left of your name so that the pointer looks like a white arrow, and then click). Your name should be shaded, indicating that it is selected.

You have selected your name because you want to experiment with using Word to change the way text looks.

c. Click the **Font Size arrow** in the Font group on the Home tab. If you need help locating Font Size, check for an Enhanced ScreenTip. Place the mouse pointer over any number in the subsequent list, but do not click. As you move to another number, notice the size of your name change. The feature you are using is called Live Preview. Click any number in the list to change the text size of your name.

d. Click **Draft** in the View Shortcuts group on the status bar to change the view (see Figure 1.24).

When creating a document, you might find it helpful to change the view. Word's Print Layout view is useful when you want to see both the document text and such features as margins and page breaks. Draft view provides a full screen of typing space without displaying margins or other print features, such as headers or footers. PowerPoint, Excel, and Access also provide view options, although they are unique to the application. The most common view options are accessible from View Shortcuts on the status bar of each application.

e. Click the **Close button** in the top-right corner of the Word window to close both the current document and the Word program. When asked whether you want to save the file, click **Don't Save**.

STEP 4 USE THE QUICK ACCESS TOOLBAR AND EXPLORE POWERPOINT VIEWS

During the course of the Rails and Trails project, you will be asked to review documents, presentations, and worksheets. It is important that you explore each application to familiarize yourself with operations and commonalities. Specifically, you know that the Quick Access Toolbar is common to all applications and that you can place commonly used commands there to streamline processes. Also, learning to change views will enable you to see the project in different ways for various purposes. Refer to Figure 1.25 as you complete Step 4.

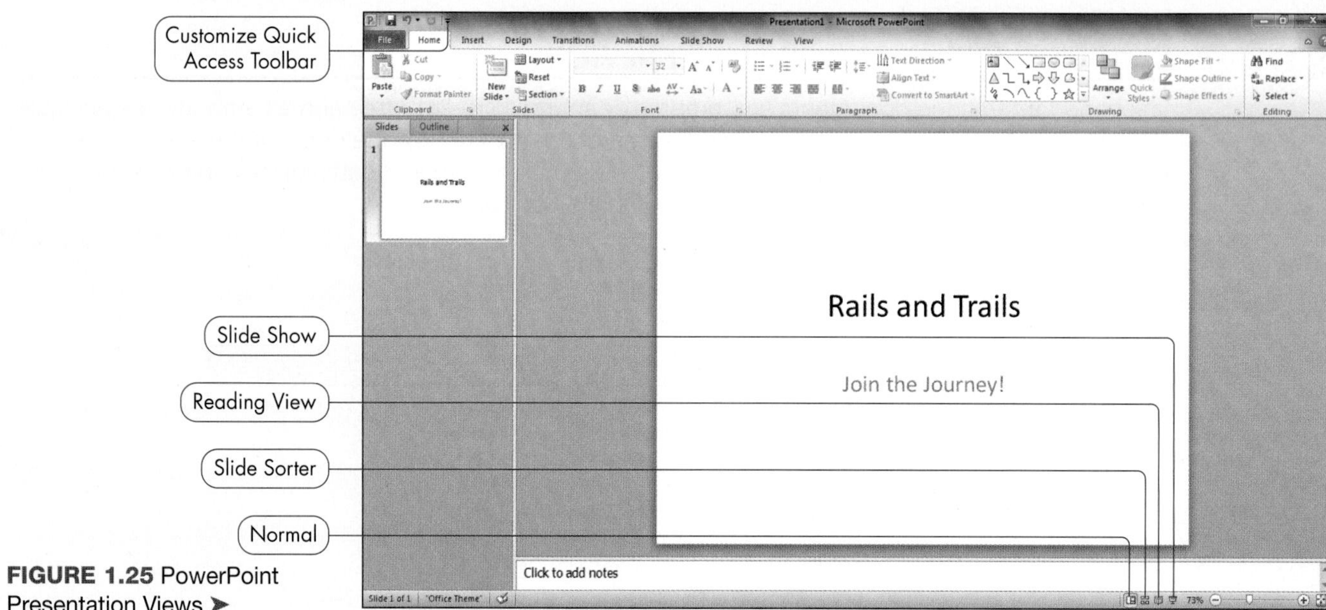

FIGURE 1.25 PowerPoint Presentation Views ➤

a. Click the **Start button**, and then point to **All Programs**. Scroll down, if necessary, and click **Microsoft Office**. Click **Microsoft PowerPoint 2010.**

   You have opened PowerPoint. You see a blank presentation.

b. Click **Click to add title**, and then type **Rails and Trails**. Click in the bottom, subtitle box, and then type **Join the Journey!** Click the bottom-right corner of the slide to deselect the subtitle. Your PowerPoint presentation should look like that shown in Figure 1.25.

c. Click **Undo** on the Quick Access Toolbar.

   The subtitle on the current slide is removed because it is the most recent action.

d. Click **Slide Sorter** in the View Shortcuts group on the status bar.

   The Slide Sorter view shows thumbnails of all slides in a presentation. Because this presentation has only one slide, you see a small version of one slide.

e. Move the mouse pointer to any button on the Quick Access Toolbar and hold it steady. See the tip giving the button name and the shortcut key combination, if any. Move to another button and see the description.

   The Quick Access Toolbar has at least three buttons, Save, Undo, and Redo (or Repeat). In addition, a small arrow is included at the far-right side. If you hold the mouse pointer steady on the arrow, you will see the ScreenTip Customize Quick Access Toolbar.

f. Click **Customize Quick Access Toolbar**. From the menu, click **New**. The New button enables you to quickly create a new presentation (also called a document).

g. Click **Customize Quick Access Toolbar**, and then click **New**. The button is removed from the Quick Access Toolbar.

   You can customize the Quick Access Toolbar by adding and removing items.

h. Click **Normal** in the View Shortcuts group on the status bar.

The presentation returns to the original view in which the slide displays in full size.

i. Click **Slide Show** in the View Shortcuts group on the status bar.

The presentation is shown in Slide Show view, which is the way it will be presented to audiences.

j. Press **Esc** to end the presentation.

k. Close the presentation without saving it. Exit PowerPoint.

Backstage View Tasks

When you work with Microsoft Office files, you will often want to open previously saved files, create new ones, print items, and save and close files. You will also find it necessary to indicate options, or preferences, of settings. For example, you might want a spelling check to occur automatically, or you might prefer to initiate a spelling check only occasionally. Getting Help is also a common selection that you want to find easily. Because those tasks are applicable to each software application within the Office 2010 suite, they are accomplished through a common area in the Office interface—the Backstage view. Open the Backstage view by clicking the File tab. Figure 1.26 shows the area that displays when you click the File tab. The Backstage view also enables you to exit the application and to identify file information, such as the author or date created. In this section, you will explore the Backstage view, learning to create, open, close, and print files.

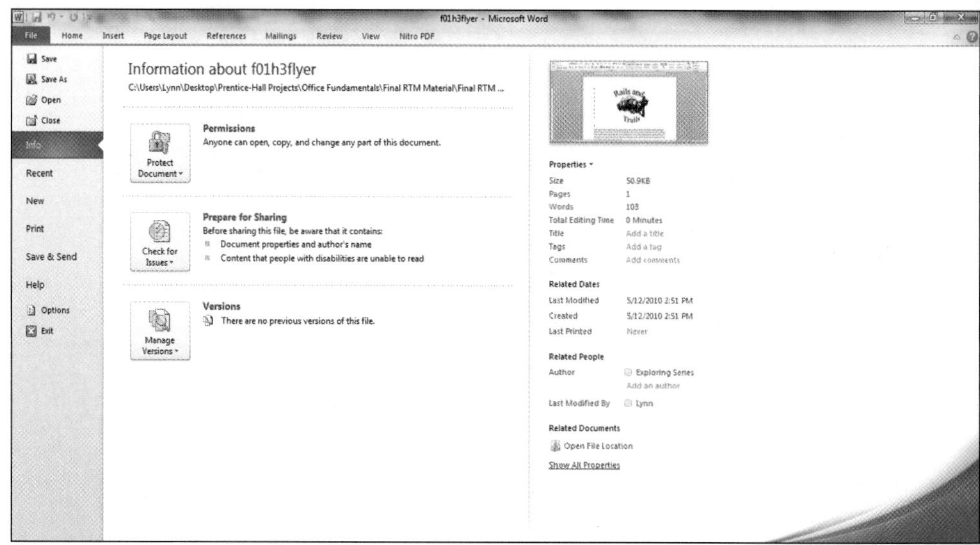

FIGURE 1.26 Backstage View ➤

Opening a File

When working with an Office application, you can begin by opening an existing file that has already been saved to a storage medium, or you can begin work on a new file. Both actions are available when you click the File tab. When you first open Word, Excel, or PowerPoint, you will be presented with a new blank work area that you can begin using immediately. When you first open Access, you will need to save the file before you can begin working with it. You can also open a project that you previously saved to a disk.

Create a New File

After opening an Office application, such as Word, Excel, or PowerPoint, you will be presented with a blank document area. The word *document* is sometimes used generically to refer to any Office file, including a Word document, an Excel worksheet, or a PowerPoint presentation. Perhaps you are already working with a document in an Office application but want to create a new file. Simply click the File tab, and then click New. Double-click Blank document (or Blank presentation or Blank workbook, depending on the specific application). You can also single-click Blank document, and then click Create.

Open a File Using the Open Dialog Box

If you choose to open a previously saved file, as you will need to do when you work with the data files for this book, you will work with the Open dialog box as shown in Figure 1.27. That dialog box appears after you select Open from the File tab. Using the Navigation Pane, you will make your way to the file to be opened. Double-click the file or click the file name once, and then click Open. Most likely, the file will be located within a folder that is appropriately named to make it easy to find related files. Obviously, if you are not well aware of the file's location and file name, the process of opening a file could become quite cumbersome. However, if you have created a well-designed system of folders, as you learned to do in the *Files and Folders* section of this chapter, you will know exactly where to find the file.

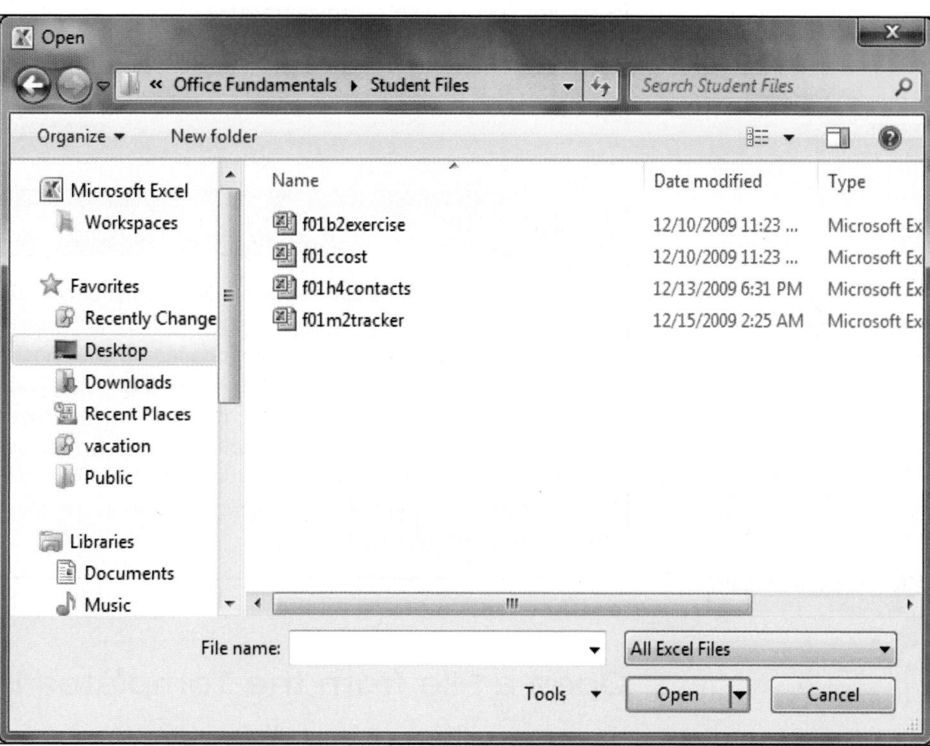

FIGURE 1.27 Open Dialog Box ➤

Open a File Using the Recent Documents List

You will often work with a file, save it, and then continue the project at a later time. Office simplifies the task of reopening the file by providing a Recent Documents list with links to your most recently opened files. See Figure 1.28 for an example of a Recent Documents list. To access the list, click the File tab, and then click Recent. Select from any files listed in the right pane. The list constantly changes to reflect only the most recently opened files, so if it has been quite some time since you worked with a particular file, you might have to work with the Open dialog box instead of the Recent Documents list.

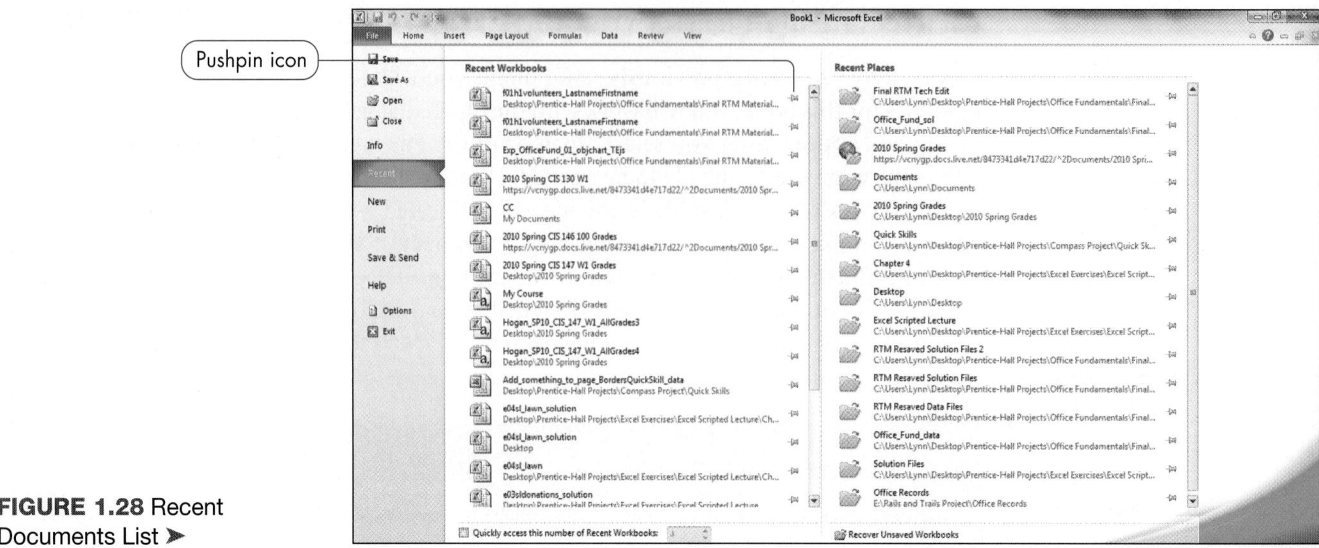

FIGURE 1.28 Recent Documents List ➤

TIP Keeping Files on the Recent Documents List

The Recent Documents list displays a limited list of only the most recently opened files. You might, however, want to keep a particular file in the list regardless of how recently it was opened. In Figure 1.28, note the pushpin icon that appears to the right of each file. Click the icon to cause the file to remain in the list. At that point, you will always have access to the file by clicking the File tab and selecting the file from the Recent Documents list. The pushpin of the "permanent" file will change direction so that it appears to be inserted, indicating that it is a pinned item. If later you want to remove the file from the list, simply click the inserted pushpin, changing its direction and allowing the file to be bumped off the list when other, more recently opened, files take its place.

Open a File from the Templates List

A **template** is a predesigned file that you can modify to suit your needs.

You do not need to create a new file if you can access a predesigned file that meets your need or one that you can modify fairly quickly to complete your project. Office provides such files called ***templates***, making them available when you click the File tab and then New. Refer t Figure 1.29 for an example of a Templates list. The top area is comprised of template group available within the current Office installation on your computer The lower category includes template groups that are availabl from Office.com. When you click to select a group, you are some times presented with additional choices to narrow your selectio to a particular file. For example, you might want to prepare home budget. After opening Excel, click the File tab, and the click New. From the template categories, you could click Budget from the Office.com Templates area, click Monthly Famil Budget, and then click Download to display the associated worksheet (or simply double click Monthly Family Budget). If a Help window displays along with the worksheet template click to close it, or explore Help to learn more about the template. If you know only a little bi about Excel, you could then make a few changes so that the worksheet would accurately rep resent your family's financial situation. The budget would be prepared much more quickl than if you began the project with a blank workbook, designing it yourself.

You do not need to create a new file if you can access a predesigned file that meets your needs or one that you can modify fairly quickly to complete your project. Office provides such files, called templates.

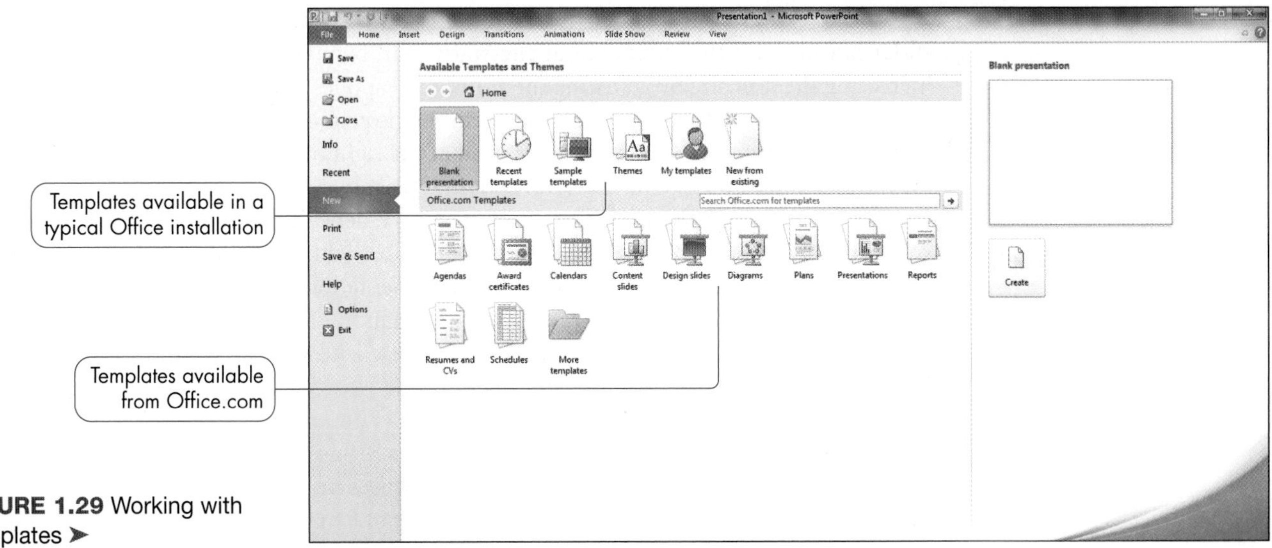

FIGURE 1.29 Working with Templates ➤

Printing a File

There will be occasions when you will want to print an Office project. Before printing, you should preview the file to get an idea of how it will look when printed. That way, if there are obvious problems with the page setup, you can correct them before wasting paper on something that is not correct. When you are ready to print, you can select from various print options, including the number of copies and the specific pages to print. If you know that the page setup is correct and that there are no unique print settings to select, you can simply print the project without adjusting any print settings.

It is a good idea to take a look at how your document will appear before you print it. The Print Preview feature of Office enables you to do just that.

It is a good idea to take a look at how your document will appear before you print it. The Print Preview feature of Office enables you to do just that. In Print Preview, you will see all items, including any headers, footers, graphics, and special formatting. To view a project before printing, click the File tab, and then click Print. The subsequent Backstage view shows the file preview on the right, with print settings located in the center of the Backstage screen. Figure 1.30 shows a typical Backstage print view.

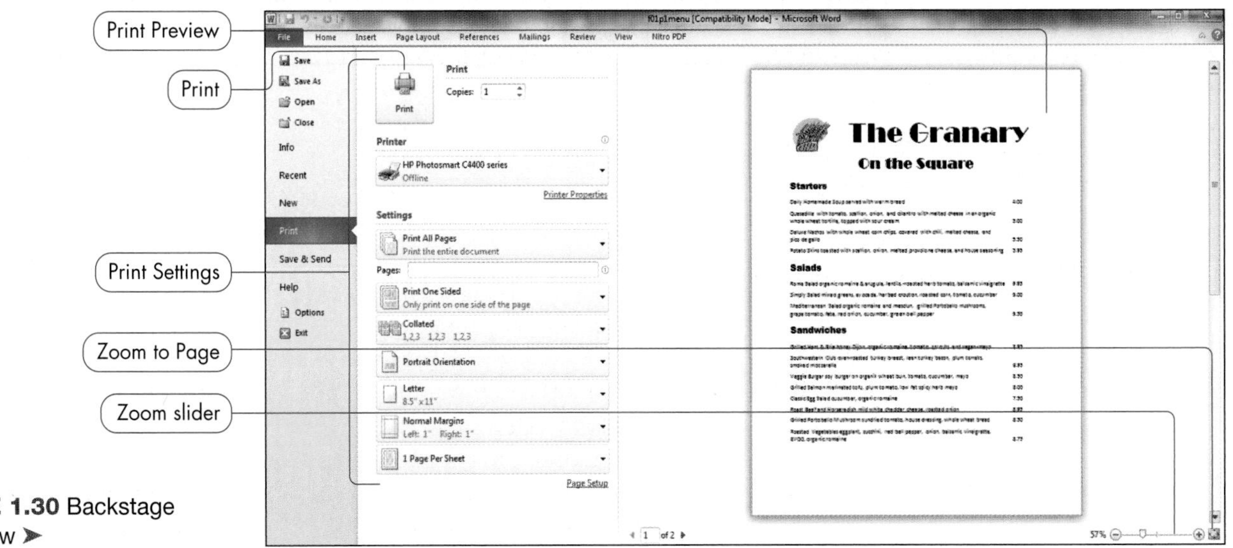

FIGURE 1.30 Backstage Print View ➤

To increase the size of the file preview, drag the Zoom slider to the right. The Zoom slider is found on the right side of the status bar, beneath the preview. Remember that increasing the font size by adjusting the zoom only applies to the current display. It does not actually increase the font size when the document is printed or saved. To return the preview to its original size, click Zoom to Page found at the right of the Zoom slider. See Figure 1.30 for the location of the Zoom slider and Zoom to Page.

Other options on the Backstage Print view vary, depending on the application in which you are working. Regardless of the Office application, you will be able to access Print Setup options from the Backstage view, including page orientation (landscape or portrait), margins and page size. You will find a more detailed explanation of those settings in the *Page Layout Tab Tasks* section later in this chapter. To print a file, click Print (shown in Figure 1.30).

The Backstage Print view shown in Figure 1.30 is very similar across all Office applications. However, you will find slight variations specific to each application. For example PowerPoint's Backstage Print view includes options for printing slides and handouts in various configurations and colors, whereas Excel's focuses on worksheet selections and Word's includes document options. Regardless of software, the manner of working with Backstage's print options remains consistent.

Closing a File and Application

Although you can have several documents open at one time, limiting the number of open files is a good idea. Office applications have no problem keeping up with multiple open files but you can easily become overwhelmed with them. When you are done with an open project, you will need to close it along with the application itself.

You can easily close any files that you no longer need. With the desired file on the screen click the File tab, and then click the Close button. Respond to any prompt that might appear suggesting that you save the file. The application remains open, but the selected file is closed. To close the application, click the File tab, and then click Exit.

TIP Closing a File and an Application

When you close an application, all open files within the application are also closed. You will be prompted to save any files before they are closed. A quick way to close an application is to click the X in the top-right corner of the application window.

HANDS-ON EXERCISES

3 Backstage View Tasks

Projects related to the Rails and Trails project have begun to come in for your review and approval. You have received an informational flyer to be distributed to civic and professional groups around the city. It contains a new logo along with descriptive text. Another task on your agenda is to keep the project moving according to schedule. You will identify a calendar template to print and distribute. You will explore printing options, and you will save the flyer and the calendar to a disk as directed by your instructor.

Skills covered: Open and Save a File • Preview and Print a File • Open a File from the Recent Documents List and Open a Template

STEP 1 OPEN AND SAVE A FILE

You have asked your staff to develop a logo that can be used to promote the Rails and Trails project. You will open a Word document that includes a proposed logo and you will save the document to a disk drive. Refer to Figure 1.31 as you complete Step 1.

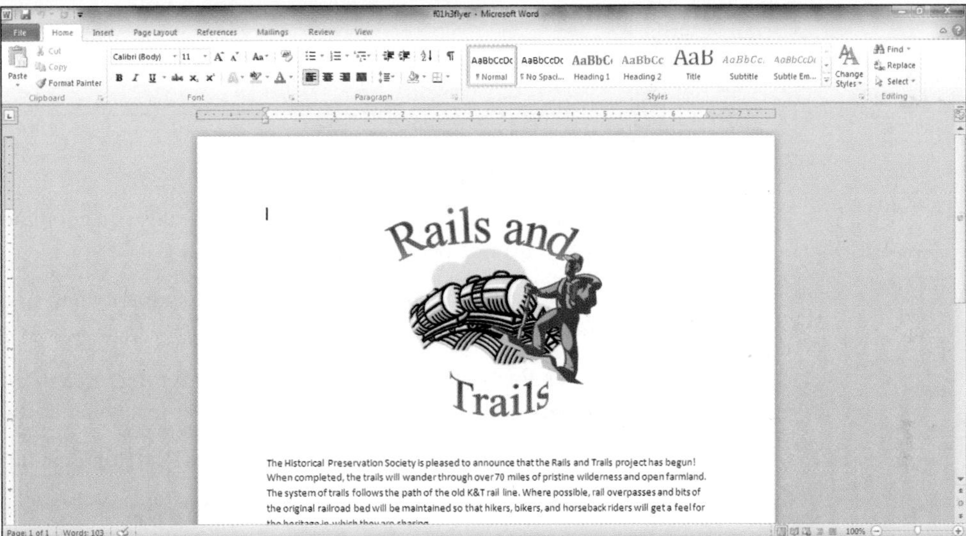

FIGURE 1.31 Promotional Flyer (Word Document) ➤

a. Click the **Start button** to display the Start Menu, and then click **All Programs**. Scroll down the list, if necessary, and then click **Microsoft Office**. Click **Microsoft Word 2010**.

   You have opened Microsoft Word because it is the program in which the promotional flyer is saved.

b. Click the **File tab**, and then click **Open**. Navigate to the location of your student files. Because you are working with Microsoft Word, the only files listed are those that were created with Microsoft Word. Double-click *f01h3flyer* to open the file shown in Figure 1.31. Familiarize yourself with the document.

   The logo and the flyer are submitted for your approval. A paragraph underneath the logo will serve as the launching point for an information blitz and the beginning of the fund-raising drive.

c. Click the **File tab**, and then click **Save As**.

   You choose the Save As command because you know that it enables you to indicate the location to which the file should be saved, as well as the file name.

d. Click the drive where you save your files, and then double-click **Rails and Trails Project**. Double-click **Office Records**, click in the **File name box**, type **f01h3flyer_LastnameFirstname**, and then click **Save**. Keep the file open for the next step in this exercise.

STEP 2 PREVIEW AND PRINT A FILE

You approve of the logo, so you will print the document for future reference. You will first preview the document as it will appear when printed. Then you will print the document. Refer to Figure 1.32 as you complete Step 2.

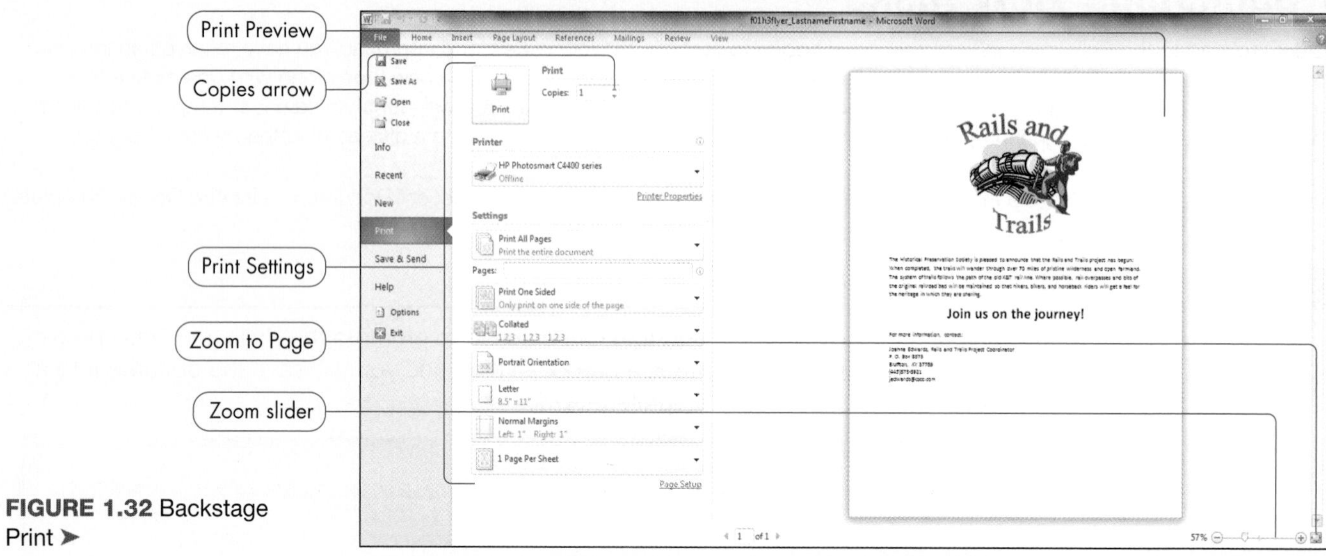

FIGURE 1.32 Backstage Print ➤

a. Click the **File tab**, and then click **Print.**

   Figure 1.32 shows the flyer preview. It is always a good idea to check the way a file will look when printed before actually printing it.

b. Drag the **Zoom slider** to increase the document view. Click **Zoom to Page** to return to the original size.

c. Click **Portrait Orientation** in the Print settings area in the center of the screen. Click **Landscape Orientation** to show the flyer in a wider and shorter view.

d. Click **Landscape Orientation,** and click **Portrait Orientation** to return to the original view.

   You decide that the flyer is more attractive in portrait orientation, so you return to that setting.

e. Click the **Copies arrow** repeatedly to increase the copies to **5**.

   You will need to print five copies of the flyer to distribute to the office assistants for their review.

f. Press **Esc** to leave the Backstage view.

   You choose not to print the flyer at this time.

g. Click the **File tab,** and then click the **Close button**. When asked, click **Don't Save** so that changes to the file are not saved. Leave Word open for the next step in this exercise.

STEP 3 OPEN A FILE FROM THE RECENT DOCUMENTS LIST AND OPEN A TEMPLATE

A large part of your responsibility is proofreading Rails and Trails material. You will correct a typo in a phone number in the promotional flyer. You must also keep the staff on task, so you will identify a calendar template on which to list tasks and deadlines. Refer to Figure 1.33 as you complete Step 3.

Recently opened flyer

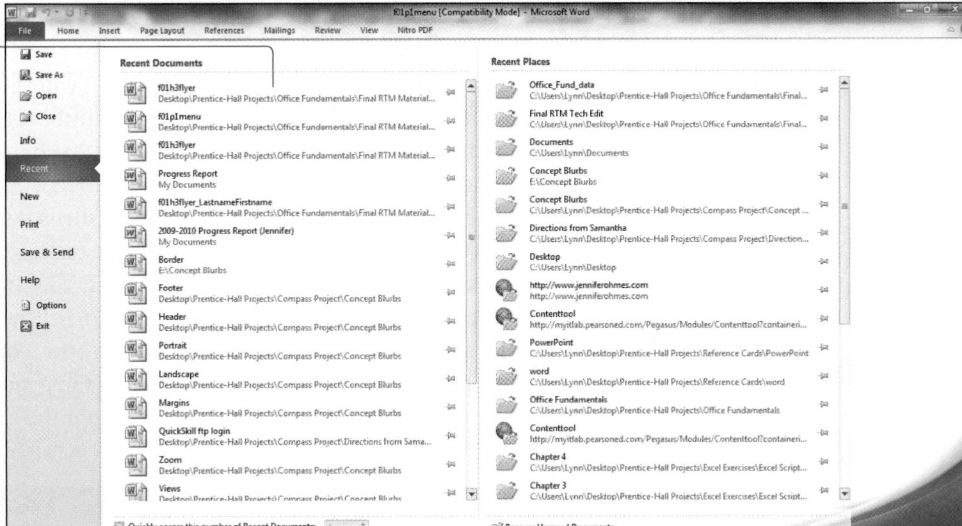

FIGURE 1.33 Recent Documents List ➤

a. Click the **File tab**, click **Recent** if necessary, and then click *f01h3flyer_LastnameFirstname* in the **Recent Documents list**.

Figure 1.33 shows the Recent Documents list. After clicking the document, the promotional flyer opens.

b. Scroll down, and then click after the number 1 in the telephone number in the contact information. Press **Backspace** on the keyboard, and then type **2**.

You find that the phone number is incorrect, so you make a correction.

c. Click **Save** on the Quick Access Toolbar, click the **File tab**, and then click the **Close button**.

When you click Save on the Quick Access Toolbar, the document is saved in the same location with the same file name as was indicated in the previous save.

d. Click the **File tab**, and then click **New**. From the list of template categories available from Office.com, click **Calendars**, and then click the current year's calendar link.

Office.com provides a wide range of calendar choices. You will select one that is appealing and that will help you keep projects on track.

e. Click a calendar of your choice from the gallery, and then click **Download**. Close any Help window that may open.

The calendar that you selected opens in Word.

> **TROUBLESHOOTING:** It is possible to select a template that is not certified by Microsoft. In that case, you might have to confirm your acceptance of settings before you click Download.

f. Click **Save** on the Quick Access Toolbar. If necessary, navigate to **Office Records** (a subfolder of Rails and Trails Project) on the drive where you save your student files. Save the document as **f01h3calendar_LastnameFirstname**. Click **OK**, if necessary. Close the document, and then exit Word.

Because this is the first time to save the calendar file, the Save button on the Quick Access Toolbar opens a dialog box in which you must indicate the location of the file and the file name.

Home Tab Tasks

You will find that you will repeat some tasks often, whether in Word, Excel, or PowerPoint. You will frequently want to change the format of numbers or words, selecting a different font or changing font size or color. You might also need to change the alignment of text or worksheet cells. Undoubtedly, you will find a reason to copy or cut items and paste them elsewhere in the document, presentation, or worksheet. And you might want to modify file contents by finding and replacing text. All of those tasks, and more, are found on the Home tab of the Ribbon in Word, Excel, and PowerPoint. The Access interface is unique, sharing little with other Office applications, so this section will not address Access. In this section, you will explore the Home tab, learning to format text, copy and paste items, and find and replace words or phrases. Figure 1.34 shows Home tab groups and tasks in the various applications. Note the differences and similarities between the groups.

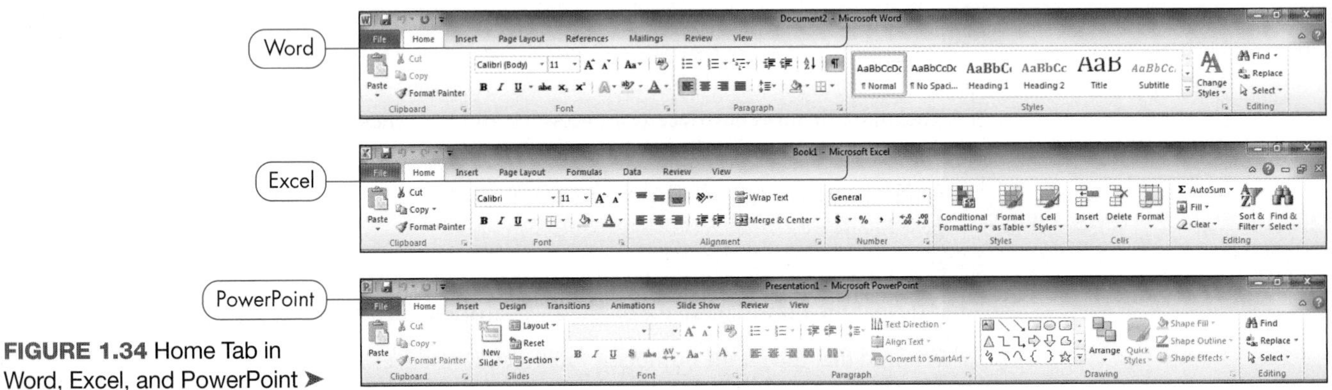

FIGURE 1.34 Home Tab in Word, Excel, and PowerPoint ➤

Selecting and Editing Text

After creating a document, worksheet, or presentation, you will probably want to make some changes. You might prefer to center a title, or maybe you think that certain worksheet totals should be formatted as currency. You can change the font so that typed characters are larger or in a different style. You might even want to underline text to add emphasis. In all Office applications, the Home tab provides tools for selecting and editing text. You can also use the Mini toolbar for quick changes to selected text.

Select Text to Edit

Before making any changes to existing text or numbers, you must first select the characters. A general rule that you should commit to memory is "Select, then do." A foolproof way to select text or numbers is to place the mouse pointer before the first character of the text you want to select, and then drag to highlight the intended selection. Before you drag, be sure that the mouse pointer takes on the shape of the letter *I*, called the I-bar. Although other methods for selecting exist, if you remember only one way, it should be the click-and-drag method. If your attempted selection falls short of highlighting the intended area, or perhaps highlights too much, simply click outside the selection and try again.

Before making any changes to existing text or numbers, you must first select the characters. A general rule that you should commit to memory is "Select, then do."

Sometimes it can be difficult to precisely select a small amount of text, such as a single character or a single word. Other times, the task can be overwhelming, such as when selecting an entire 550-page document. Shortcut methods for making selections in Word and PowerPoint are shown in Table 1.3. When working with Excel, you will more often need to select multiple cells. Simply drag the intended selection, usually when the mouse pointer appears as a large white plus sign. The shortcuts shown in Table 1.3 are primarily applicable to Word and PowerPoint.

TABLE 1.3 Shortcut Selection in Word and PowerPoint	
Item Selected	**Action**
One Word	Double-click the word.
One Line of Text	Place the mouse pointer at the left of the line, in the margin area. When the mouse changes to a right-pointing arrow, click to select the line.
One Sentence	Press and hold Ctrl while you click in the sentence to select.
One Paragraph	Triple-click in the paragraph.
One Character to the Left of the Insertion Point	Press and hold Shift while you press ←.
One Character to the Right of the Insertion Point	Press and hold Shift while you press →.
Entire Document	Press and hold Ctrl while you press the letter A on the keyboard.

After having selected a string of characters, such as a number, word, sentence, or document, you can do more than simply format the selection. Suppose you have selected a word. If you begin to type another word, the newly typed word will immediately replace the selected word. With an item selected, you can press Delete to remove the selection. You will learn later in this chapter that you can also find, replace, copy, move, and paste selected text.

Use the Mini Toolbar

The **Mini toolbar** is an Office feature that provides access to common formatting commands. It is displayed when text is selected.

You have learned that you can always use commands on the Ribbon to change selected text within a document, cell, or presentation. All it takes is locating the desired command on the Home tab and clicking to select it. Although using Home tab commands is simple enough, an item called the ***Mini toolbar*** provides an even shorter way to accomplish some of the same formatting changes. When you select any amount of text within a worksheet, document, or presentation, you can move the mouse pointer only slightly within the selection to display the Mini toolbar, as shown in Figure 1.35. The Mini toolbar provides access to the most common formatting selections, such as boldfacing, italicizing, or changing font type or color. Unlike the Quick Access Toolbar, the Mini toolbar is not customizable, which means that you cannot add or remove options from the toolbar. The Mini toolbar will only appear when text is selected. The closer the mouse pointer is to the Mini toolbar, the darker the toolbar. As you move the mouse pointer away from the Mini toolbar, it becomes almost transparent. Make any selections from the Mini toolbar by clicking the corresponding button.

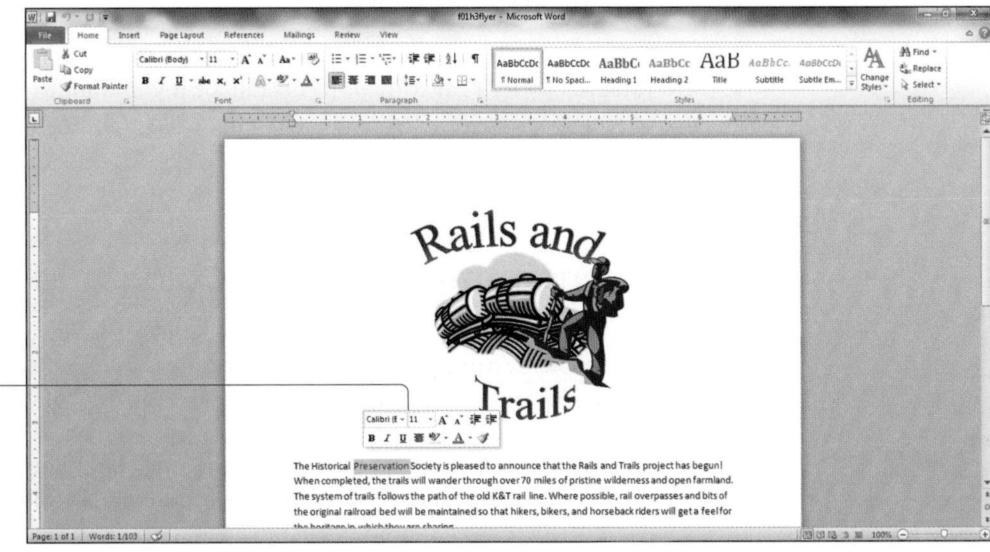

FIGURE 1.35 Mini Toolbar ➤

To temporarily remove the Mini toolbar from view, press Esc. If you want to permanently disable the Mini toolbar so that it does not appear in any open file when text is selected, click the File tab and click Options. As shown in Figure 1.36, click General, if necessary. Deselect the Show Mini Toolbar on selection setting by clicking the check box to the left of the setting and clicking OK.

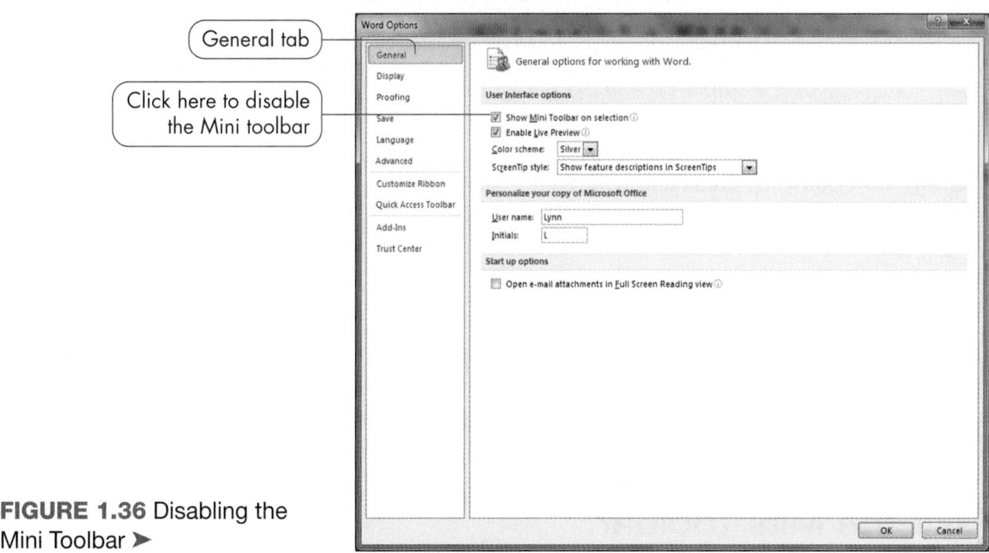

FIGURE 1.36 Disabling the Mini Toolbar ➤

Apply Font Attributes

A **font** is a character design that includes size, spacing, and shape.

To **toggle** is to switch from one setting to another. Several Home tab tasks, such as Bold and Italic, are actually toggle commands.

A ***font*** is a character design. More simply stated, it is the way characters appear onscreen, including qualities such as size, spacing, and shape. Each Office application has a default font, which is the font that will be in effect unless you change it. Other font attributes include boldfacing, italicizing, and font color, all of which can be applied to selected text. Some formatting changes, such as Bold and Italic, are called ***toggle*** commands. They act somewhat like light switches that you can turn on and off. For example, after having selected a word that you want to boldface, click Bold in the Font group of the Home tab to turn the setting "on." If at a later time you want to remove boldface from the word, select it again, and then click Bold. This time, the button turns "off" the bold formatting.

Change the Font

All applications within the Office suite provide a set of fonts from which you can choose. If you prefer a font other than the default, or if you want to apply a different font to a section of your project, you can easily make the change by selecting a font from within the Font group on the Home tab. You can also change the font by selecting from the Mini toolbar, although that only works if you have first selected text.

Change the Font Size, Color, and Attributes

At times, you want to make the font size larger or smaller, change the font color, underline selected text, or apply other font attributes. Because such changes are commonplace, Office places those formatting commands in many convenient places within each Office application.

You can find the most common formatting commands in the Font group on the Home tab. As shown in Figure 1.34, Word, Excel, and PowerPoint all share very similar Font groups that provide access to tasks related to changing the character font. Remember that you can place the mouse pointer over any command icon to view a summary of the icon's purpose, so although the icons might at first appear cryptic, you can use the mouse pointer to quickly determine the purpose and applicability to your desired text change. You can also find a subset of those commands plus a few additional choices on the Mini toolbar, which becomes available when you make a text selection.

If the font change that you plan to make is not included as a choice on either the Home tab or the Mini toolbar, you can probably find what you are looking for in the Font dialog box. Click the Dialog Box Launcher in the bottom-right corner of the Font group. Figure 1.37 shows a sample Font dialog box. Since the Font dialog box provides many formatting choices in one window, you can make several changes at once. Depending on the application, the contents of the Font dialog box vary slightly, but the purpose is consistent—providing access to choices related to modifying characters.

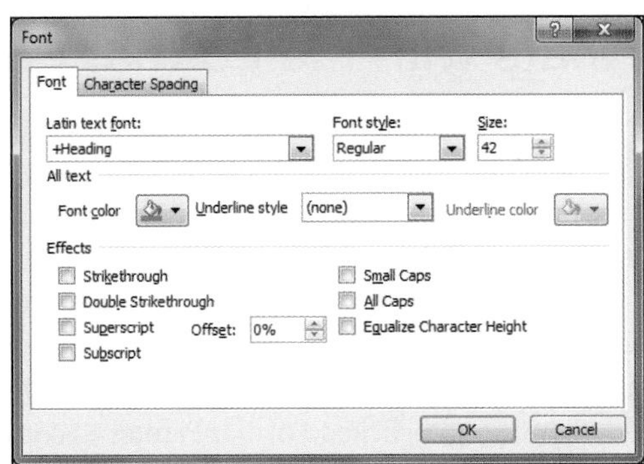

FIGURE 1.37 Font Dialog Box ➤

Using the Clipboard Group Tasks

The **Clipboard** is an Office feature that temporarily holds selections that have been cut or copied. It also enables you to paste those selections in other locations within the current or another Office application.

When you **cut** a selection, you remove it from the original location and place it in the Office Clipboard.

When you **copy** a selection, you duplicate it from the original location and place the copy in the Office Clipboard.

On occasion, you will want to move or copy a selection from one area to another. Suppose that you have included text on a PowerPoint slide that you believe would be more appropriate on a previous slide. Or perhaps an Excel formula should be copied from one cell to another because both cells should be totaled in the same manner. You can easily move the slide text and copy the Excel formula by using options found in the Clipboard group on the Home tab. The ***Clipboard*** is an area of memory reserved to temporarily hold selections that have been ***cut*** or ***copied***. Although the Clipboard can hold up to 24 items at one time, the usual procedure is to ***paste*** the cut or copied selection to its final destination fairly quickly. When the computer is shut down or loses power, the contents of the Clipboard are erased, so it is important to finalize the paste procedure during the current session.

The Clipboard group enables you not only to copy and cut items, but also to copy formatting. Perhaps you have applied a font style to a major heading of a report and you realize that the same formatting should be applied to other headings. Especially if the heading includes multiple formatting features, you will save a great deal of time by copying the entire package of formatting to the other headings. In so doing, you will ensure the consistency of formatting for all headings because they will appear exactly alike. Using the Clipboard group's ***Format Painter***, you can quickly and easily copy all formatting from one area to another in Word, PowerPoint, and Excel.

> The Clipboard group enables you not only to copy and cut text, but also to copy formatting.

When you **paste** a selection, you place a cut or copied item in another location.

The **Format Painter** is a Clipboard group command that copies the formatting of text from one location to another.

A **shortcut menu** provides choices related to the selection or area at which you right-click.

TIP Using a Shortcut Menu

In Office, you can usually accomplish the same task in several ways. Although the Ribbon provides ample access to formatting and Clipboard commands (such as Format Painter, cut, copy, and paste), you might find it convenient to access the same commands on a ***shortcut menu***. Right-click a selected item or text to open a shortcut menu such as the one shown in Figure 1.38. A shortcut menu is also sometimes called a *context menu* because the contents of the menu vary depending on the location at which you right-clicked.

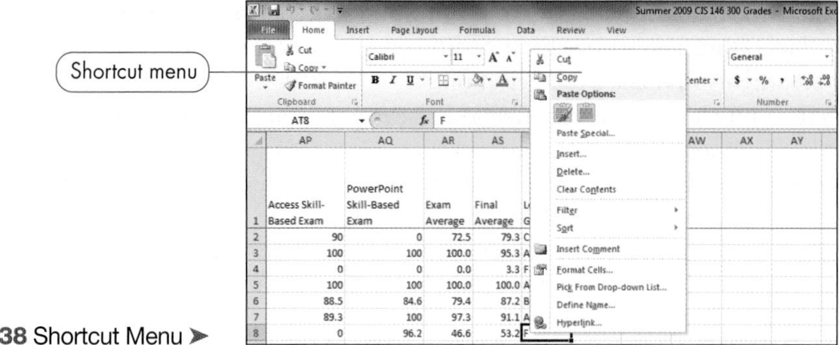

FIGURE 1.38 Shortcut Menu ➤

Copy Formats with the Format Painter

As described earlier, the Format Painter makes it easy to copy formatting features from one selection to another. You will find the Format Painter command conveniently located in the Clipboard group of the Home tab. Figure 1.39 shows Clipboard group tasks. To copy a format, you must first select the text containing the desired format. If you want to copy the format to only one other selection, *single-click* Format Painter. If, however, you plan to copy the same format to multiple areas, *double-click* Format Painter. As you move the mouse pointer, you will find that it has the appearance of a paintbrush with an attached I-bar. Select the area to which the copied format should be applied. If you single-clicked Format Painter to copy the format to one other selection, Format Painter turns off once the formatting has been applied. If you double-clicked Format Painter to copy the format to multiple locations, continue selecting text in various locations to apply the format. Then, to turn off Format Painter, click Format Painter again, or press Esc.

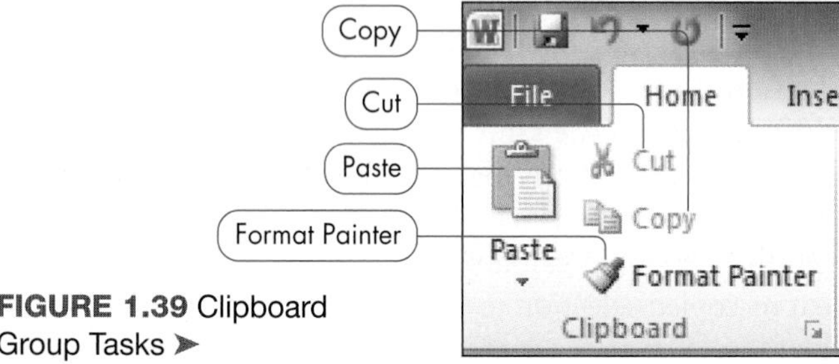

FIGURE 1.39 Clipboard Group Tasks ➤

Move and Copy Text

Undoubtedly, there will be times when you want to revise a project by moving or copying items such as Word text, PowerPoint slides, or Excel cell contents, either within the current application or among others. For example, a section of a Word document might be appropriate as PowerPoint slide content. To keep from retyping the Word text in the PowerPoint slide, you can copy the text and paste it in a blank PowerPoint slide. At other times, it might be necessary to move a paragraph within a Word document or to copy selected cells from one Excel worksheet to another. The Clipboard group contains a Cut command with which you can select text to move. You can also use the Copy command to duplicate items and the Paste command to place moved or copied items in a final location. See those command icons in Figure 1.39.

TIP Using Ribbon Commands with Arrows

Some commands, such as Paste in the Clipboard group, contain two parts: the main command and an arrow. The arrow may be below or to the right of the command, depending on the command, window size, or screen resolution. Instructions in the Exploring series use the command name to instruct you to click the main command to perform the default action (e.g., Click Paste). Instructions include the word *arrow* when you need to select an additional option (e.g., Click the Paste arrow).

The first step in moving or copying text is to select the text. After that, click the appropriate icon in the Clipboard group either to cut or copy the selection. Remember that cut or copied text is actually placed in the Clipboard, remaining there even after you paste it to another location. It is important to note that you can paste the same item multiple times because it will remain in the Clipboard until you power down your computer or until the Clipboard exceeds 24 items. To paste the selection, click the location where you want the text to be placed. The location can be in the current file or in another open file within any Office application. Then click Paste in the Clipboard group. In addition to using the Clipboard group icons, you can also cut, copy, and paste in any of the ways listed in Table 1.4.

TABLE 1.4 Cut, Copy, and Paste Options

Result	Actions
Cut	• Click Cut in Clipboard group. • Right-click selection, and then click Cut. • Press Ctrl+X
Copy	• Click Copy in Clipboard group. • Right-click selection, and then click Copy. • Press Ctrl+C.
Paste	• Click in destination location, and then click Paste in Clipboard group. • Right-click in destination location, and then click Paste. • Click in destination location, and then press Ctrl+V. • Click the Clipboard Dialog Box Launcher to open the Clipboard task pane. Click in destination location. With the Clipboard task pane open, click the arrow beside the intended selection, and then click Paste.

Use the Office Clipboard

When you cut or copy selections, they are placed in the Office Clipboard. Especially if you cut or copy multiple items, you might need to view the contents of the Clipboard so that you can select the correct item to paste. Regardless of which Office application you are using, you can view the Clipboard by clicking the Clipboard Dialog Box Launcher as shown in Figure 1.40.

FIGURE 1.40 Clipboard Task Pane ➤

Unless you specify otherwise when beginning a paste operation, the most recently added Clipboard item is pasted. You can, however, select an item from the Clipboard task pane to paste. Similarly, you can delete items from the Clipboard by making a selection in the Clipboard task pane. You can remove all items from the Clipboard by clicking Clear All. The Options button in the Clipboard task pane enables you to control when and where the Clipboard is displayed. Close the Clipboard task pane by clicking the Close button in the top-right corner of the task pane or by clicking the arrow in the title bar of the Clipboard task pane and selecting Close.

Using the Editing Group Tasks

The process of finding and replacing text is easily accomplished through options in the Editing group of the Home tab. You will at times find it necessary to locate each occurrence of a text item so that you can replace it with another or so that you can delete, move, or copy it. If you have consistently misspelled a person's name throughout a document, you can find the misspelling and replace it with the correct spelling in a matter of a few seconds, no matter how many times the misspelling occurs in the document. The Editing group also enables you to select all contents of a project document, all text with similar formatting, or specific objects, such as pictures, clip art, or charts. The Editing group is found at the far-right side of the Home tab in all Office applications except Access.

The Excel Editing group is unique in that it also includes provisions for sorting, filtering, and clearing cell contents; filling cells; and summarizing numeric data. Because those commands are relevant only to Excel, this chapter will not address them specifically. Figure 1.41 shows the Editing group of Excel, Word, and PowerPoint. Note the differences.

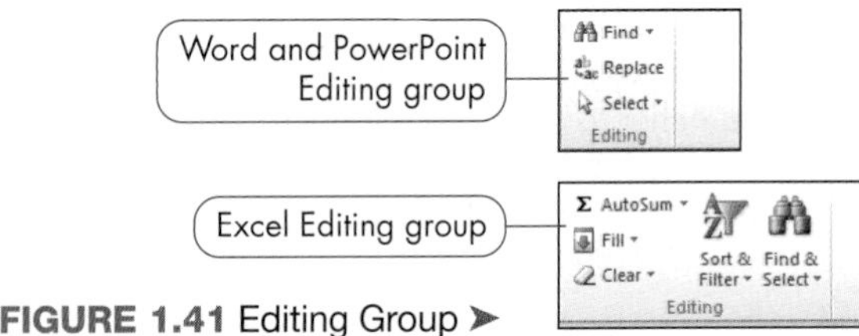

FIGURE 1.41 Editing Group ➤

Find and Replace Text

Find locates a word or phrase that you indicate in a document.

Replace finds text and replaces it with a word or phrase that you indicate.

Especially if you are working with a lengthy project, manually seeking a specific word or phrase can be time-consuming. Office enables you not only to ***find*** each occurrence of a series of characters, but also to ***replace*** what it finds with another series.

To begin the process of finding a specific item, click Replace in the Editing group on the Home tab of Word or PowerPoint. To begin a find and replace procedure in Excel, you must click Find & Select, and then click Replace. The subsequent dialog box enables you to indicate a word or phrase to find and replace. See Figure 1.42 for the Find and Replace dialog box in each Office application.

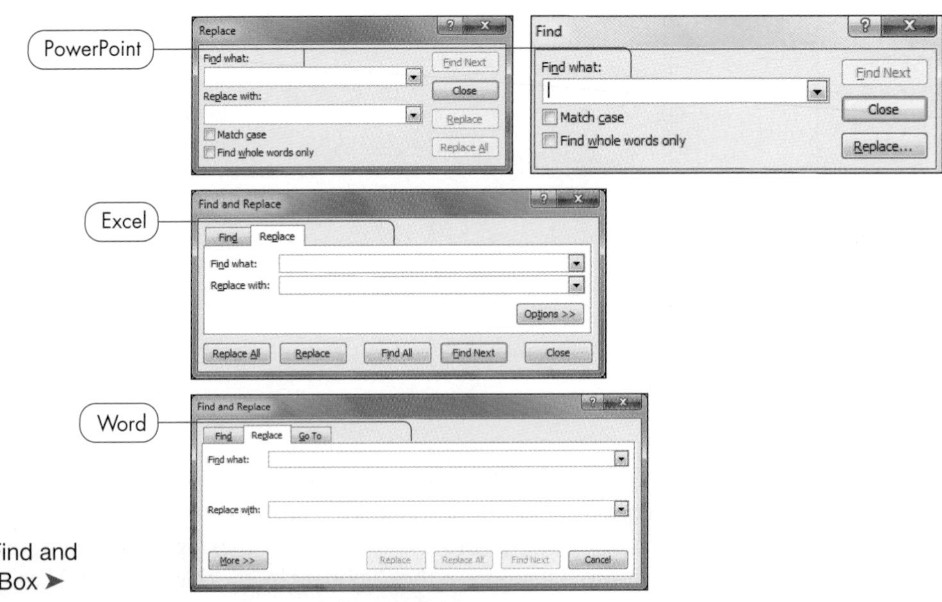

FIGURE 1.42 Find and Replace Dialog Box ➤

Using a Shortcut to Finding Items

Ctrl+F is a shortcut to finding items in a Word, Excel, or PowerPoint file. When you press Ctrl+F, the Find and Replace dialog box shown in Figure 1.42 displays in Excel and PowerPoint. Pressing Ctrl+F in Word displays a feature—the Navigation task pane—at the left side of a Word document. When you type a search term in the Search Document area, Word finds and highlights all occurrences of the search term. The Navigation task pane also makes it easy to move to sections of a document based on levels of headings. The Navigation task pane is only found in Word 2010.

To find and replace selected text, type the text to locate in the *Find what* box and the replacement text in the *Replace with* box. You can narrow the search to require matching case or find whole words only. If you want to replace all occurrences of the text, click Replace All. If you want to replace only some occurrences, click Find Next repeatedly until you reach the occurrence that you want to replace. At that point, click Replace. Click the Close button (or Cancel).

Go to a Location in a File

An Excel worksheet can include more than 1,000,000 rows of data. A Word document's length is unlimited. Moving to a specific point in large files created in either of those applications can be a challenge. That task is simplified by the Go To option, found in the Editing group as an option of the Find command (or under Find & Select in Excel). Click Go To and enter the page number (or other item, such as section, comment, bookmark, or footnote) or the specific Excel cell. Click Go To (in Word) or OK in Excel.

HANDS-ON EXERCISES

4 Home Tab Tasks

You have created a list of potential contributors to the Rails and Trails project. You have used Excel to record that list in worksheet format. Now you will review the worksheet and format its appearance to make it more attractive. You will also modify the promotional flyer that you reviewed in the last Hands-On Exercise. In working with those projects, you will put into practice the formatting, copying, moving, and editing information from the preceding section.

Skills covered: Move, Copy, and Paste Text • Select Text, Apply Font Attributes, and Use the Mini Toolbar • Use Format Painter and Work with a Shortcut Menu • Use the Font Dialog Box and Find and Replace Text

STEP 1 MOVE, COPY, AND PASTE TEXT

Each contributor to the Rails and Trails project is assigned a contact person from the project. You manage the worksheet that keeps track of those assignments, but the assignments sometimes change. You will copy and paste some worksheet selections to keep from having to retype data. You will also reposition a clip art image to improve the worksheet's appearance. Refer to Figure 1.43 as you complete Step 1.

Minimize button

Potential Partners

Name	Phone	Rails and Trails Contact
Alexander, June	(335)232-0912	Nester, Alli
Allen, Willis	(335)233-1139	Ullman, Linda
Bello, Daniel	(410)988-9991	Lynn, Rayford
Chapman, Bill	(335)232-1133	Ullman, Linda
Childers, Claire	(410)988-1832	Vinzant, Jackie
Compton, Scott	(410)909-2321	Ullman, Linda
Dietz, Diego	(410)282-3417	Lynn, Rayford
Dillon, J.H.	(335)381-1300	Sammons, Roger
Foster, Harris	(410)988-3901	Sammons, Roger
Freeman, Jennifer	(335)233-1111	Lynn, Rayford
Gewin, David	(254)389-9114	Vinzant, Jackie
Hairell, Hilda	(335)232-2288	Blackburn, Miriam
Holmes, Betty	(410)844-9745	Lynn, Rayford
Horton, Garland	(335)233-7653	Sammons, Roger
Johns, Amanda	(254)667-2955	Blackburn, Miriam
Joiner, Tracy	(335)888-1283	Sammons, Roger
Lambert, Russeau	(254)766-3318	Ullman, Linda
Layton, Dot	(410)877-3298	Vinzant, Jackie
McClain, Randy	(254)838-2983	Ullman, Linda

FIGURE 1.43 Contributor List (Excel) ➤

a. Click the **Start button** to display the Start menu, point to **All Programs**, scroll down the list if necessary, and then click **Microsoft Office**. Click **Microsoft Excel 2010**.

   The potential contributors list is saved as an Excel worksheet. You will first open Excel.

b. Open the student data file *f01h4contacts*. Save the file as **f01h4contacts_LastnameFirstname** in the Office Records folder on the drive where you save your files.

   The potential contributors list shown in Figure 1.43 is displayed.

c. Click **cell C7** to select the cell that contains *Alli Nester*, and then click **Copy** in the Clipboard group on the Home tab. Click **cell C15** to select the cell that contains *Roger Sammons*, click **Paste** in the Clipboard group, and then press **Esc** to remove the selection from *Alli Nester*.

   Alli Nester has been assigned as the Rails and Trails contact for Harris Foster, replacing Roger Sammons. You make that replacement on the worksheet by copying and pasting Alli Nester's name in the appropriate worksheet cell.

d. Click the picture of the train. A box displays around the image, indicating that it is selected. Click **Cut** in the Clipboard group, click **cell A2**, click **Paste**, and then click anywhere outside the train picture to deselect it.

> **TROUBLESHOOTING:** A Paste Options icon might appear in the worksheet after you have moved the train picture. It offers additional options related to the paste procedure. You do not need to change any options, so ignore the button.

You decide that the picture of the train will look better if it is placed on the left side of the worksheet instead of the right. You move the picture by cutting and pasting the object.

e. Click **Save** on the Quick Access Toolbar. Click the **Minimize button** to minimize the worksheet without closing it.

STEP 2 SELECT TEXT, APPLY FONT ATTRIBUTES, AND USE THE MINI TOOLBAR

As the opening of Rails and Trails draws near, you are active in preparing promotional materials. You are currently working on an informational flyer that is almost set to go. You will make a few improvements before approving the flyer for release. Refer to Figure 1.44 as you complete Step 2.

Rails and

Trails

The Historical Preservation Society is pleased to announce that the Rails and Trails project has begun! When completed, the trails will wander through over 70 miles of pristine wilderness and open farmland. The system of trails follows the path of the old K&T rail line. Where possible, rail overpasses and bits of the original railroad bed will be maintained so that hikers, bikers, and horseback riders will get a feel for the heritage in which they are sharing.

Construction of the trail will be funded in several ways. Thanks to the persistent efforts of local interest groups and individuals, we have secured 13.5 million dollars through local, state, and federal departments and grants. The journey has only begun, however. At its completion, the trail is estimated to cost $15 million. In an effort to fully fund the project, we need private contributions. Will you help us create an everlasting tribute to our community's history? Please consider donating any amount that is within your means, as every donation counts.

For further information, please contact Rhea Mancuso (335)555-9813.

Join us on the journey!

FIGURE 1.44 Promotional Flyer (Word) ➤

a. Click the **Start button** to display the Start menu. Click **All Programs**, scroll down if necessary, and then click **Microsoft Office**. Click **Microsoft Word 2010**. Open *f01h4flyer* and save the document as **f01h4flyer_LastnameFirstname** in the Promotional Print folder (a subfolder of Rails and Trails project) on the drive where you save your files.

You plan to modify the promotional flyer slightly to include additional information about the Rails and Trails project.

> **TROUBLESHOOTING:** If you make any major mistakes in this exercise, you can close the file without saving it, open *f01h4flyer* again, and start this exercise over.

b. Click after the period after the word *sharing* at the end of the first paragraph. Press **Enter**, and then type the text below. As you type, do not press Enter at the end of each line. Word will automatically wrap the lines of text.

Construction of the trail will be funded in several ways. Thanks to the persistent efforts of local interest groups and individuals, we have secured $13.5 million through local, state, and federal departments and grants. The journey has only begun, however. At its completion, the

trail is estimated to cost $15 million. In an effort to fully fund the project, we need private contributions. Will you help us create an everlasting tribute to our community's history? Please consider donating any amount that is within your means, as every donation counts. For further information, please contact Rhea Mancuso at (335)555-9813.

> **TROUBLESHOOTING:** If you make any mistakes while typing, press Backspace and correct them.

c. Scroll down and select all of the text at the end of the document, beginning with **For more information, contact:**. Press **Delete**.

   When you press Delete, selected text (or characters to the right of the cursor) are removed. Deleted text is not placed in the Clipboard.

d. Select the words *Join us on the journey!* Click **Italic** in the Font group, and then click anywhere outside the selection to see the result.

e. Select both paragraphs but not the final italicized line. While still within the selection, move the mouse pointer slightly to display the Mini toolbar, click the **font arrow** on the Mini toolbar, and then select **Arial**.

> **TROUBLESHOOTING:** If you do not see the Mini toolbar, you might have moved too far away from the selection. In that case, click outside the selection, and then drag to select it once more. Without leaving the selection, move the mouse pointer slightly to display the Mini toolbar.

   You have changed the font of the two paragraphs.

f. Click after the period following the word *counts* before the last sentence in the second paragraph. Press **Enter**, and then press **Delete** to remove the extra space before the first letter, if necessary. Move the mouse pointer to the margin area at the immediate left of the new line. The mouse pointer should appear as a white arrow. Click once to select the line, click **Underline** in the Font group, and then click anywhere outside the selected area. Your document should appear as shown in Figure 1.44.

   You have underlined the contact information to draw attention to the text.

g. Save the document and keep it open for the next step in this exercise.

STEP 3 USE FORMAT PAINTER AND WORK WITH A SHORTCUT MENU

You are on a short timeline for finalizing the promotional flyer, so you will use a few shortcuts to avoid retyping and reformatting more than is necessary. You know that you can easily copy formatting from one area to another using Format Painter. Shortcut menus can also help make changes quickly. Refer to Figure 1.45 as you complete Step 3.

The Historical Preservation Society is pleased to announce that the **Rails and Trails** project has begun! When completed, the trails will wander through over 70 miles of pristine wilderness and open farmland. The system of trails follows the path of the old K&T rail line. Where possible, rail overpasses and bits of the original railroad bed will be maintained so that hikers, bikers, and horseback riders will get a feel for the heritage in which they are sharing.

Construction of the trail will be funded in several ways. Thanks to the persistent efforts of local interest groups and individuals, we have secured $13.5 million through local, state, and federal departments and grants. The journey has only begun, however. At its completion, the trail is estimated to cost $15 million. In an effort to fully fund the project, we need private contributions. Will you help us create an everlasting tribute to our community's history? Please consider donating any amount that is within your means, as every donation counts.

For further information, please contact Rhea Mancuso at (335)232-9813.

Join us on the journey!

FIGURE 1.45 Promotional Flyer (Word) ➤

a. Select the words **Rails and Trails** in the first paragraph, and then click **Bold** in the Font group.

b. Click **Format Painter** in the Clipboard group, and then select the second to last line of the document, containing the contact information. Click anywhere outside the selection to deselect the line.

   The format of the area that you first selected (Rails and Trails) is applied to the line containing the contact information.

c. Select the text *Join us on the journey!* Right-click in the selected area, click **Font** on the shortcut menu, click **22** in the **Size box** to reduce the font size slightly, and then click **OK**. Click outside the selected area.

   Figure 1.45 shows the final document as it should now appear.

d. Save the document and close Word.

   The flyer will be saved with the same file name and in the same location as it was when you last saved the document in Step 2. As you close Word, the open document will also be closed.

STEP 4 USE THE FONT DIALOG BOX AND FIND AND REPLACE TEXT

The contributors worksheet is almost complete. However, you first want to make a few more formatting changes to improve the worksheet's appearance. You will also quickly change an incorrect area code by using Excel's Find and Replace feature. Refer to Figures 1.46 and 1.47 as you complete Step 4.

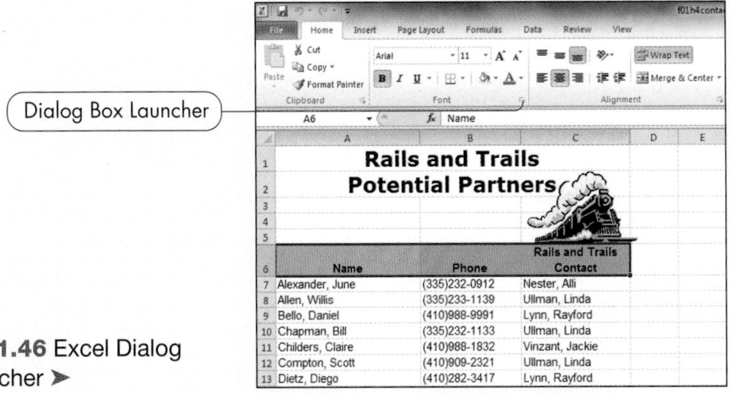

FIGURE 1.46 Excel Dialog Box Launcher ➤

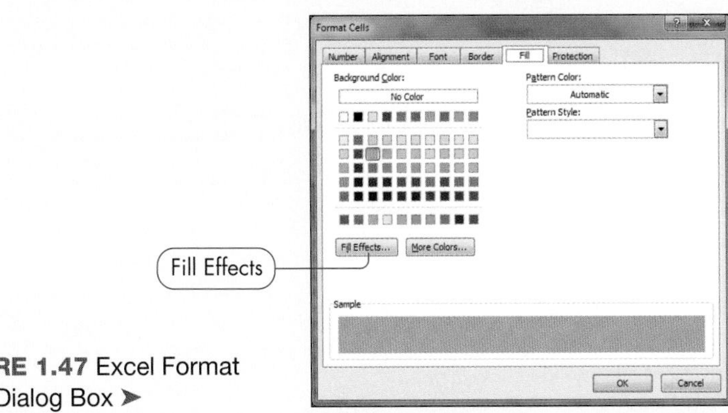

FIGURE 1.47 Excel Format Cells Dialog Box ➤

a. Click the **Excel icon** on the taskbar to redisplay the contributors worksheet that you minimized in Step 1.

   The Excel potential contributors list displays.

b. Drag to select **cells A6 through C6**.

TROUBLESHOOTING: Make sure the mouse pointer looks like a large white plus sign before dragging. It is normal for the first cell in the selected area to be a different shade. If you click and drag when the mouse pointer does not resemble a white plus sign, text may have been moved or duplicated. In that case, click Undo on the Quick Access Toolbar.

c. Click the **Dialog Box Launcher** in the Font group as shown in Figure 1.46. Click the **Fill tab**, and then click **Fill Effects** as shown in Figure 1.47. Click any style in the Variants group, click **OK**, and then click **OK** once more to close the Format Cells dialog box. Click outside the selected area to see the final result.

   The headings of the worksheet are shaded more attractively.

d. Click **Find & Select** in the Editing group, click **Replace**, and then type **410** in the **Find what box**. Type **411** in the **Replace with box**, click **Replace All**, and then click **OK** when notified that Excel has made 10 replacements. Click **Close.**

   You discover that you consistently typed an incorrect area code. You use Find and Replace to make a correction quickly.

e. Save the *f01h4contacts_LastnameFirstname* workbook. Close the workbook and exit Excel.

   The workbook will be saved with the same file name and in the same location as it was when you last saved the document in Step 1. As you exit Excel, the open workbook will also be closed.

Insert Tab Tasks

As its title implies, the Insert tab enables you to insert, or add, items into a file. Much of the Insert tab is specific to the particular application, with little commonality to other Office applications. Word's Insert tab includes text-related commands, whereas Excel's is more focused on inserting such items as charts and tables. PowerPoint's Insert tab includes multimedia items and links. Despite their obvious differences in focus, all Office applications share a common group on the Insert tab—the Illustrations group. In addition, all Office applications enable you to insert headers, footers, text boxes, and symbols. Those options are also found on the Insert tab in various groups, depending on the particular application. In this section, you will work with common activities on the Insert tab, including inserting pictures and clip art.

Despite their obvious differences in focus, all Office applications share a common group on the Insert tab—the Illustrations group.

Inserting Objects

With few exceptions, all Office applications share common options in the Illustrations group of the Insert tab. PowerPoint places some of those common features in the Images group. You can insert pictures, clip art, shapes, screenshots, and SmartArt. Those items are considered objects, retaining their separate nature when they are inserted in files. That means that you can select them and manage them independently of the underlying document, worksheet, or presentation.

After an object has been inserted, you can click the object to select it or click anywhere outside the object to deselect it. When an object is selected, a border of small dots, or "handles," surrounds it, appearing at each corner and in the middle of each side. Figure 1.48 shows a selected object, surrounded by handles. Unless an object is selected, you cannot change or modify it. When an object is selected, the Ribbon expands to include one or more contextual tabs. Items on the contextual tabs relate to the selected object, enabling you to modify and manage it.

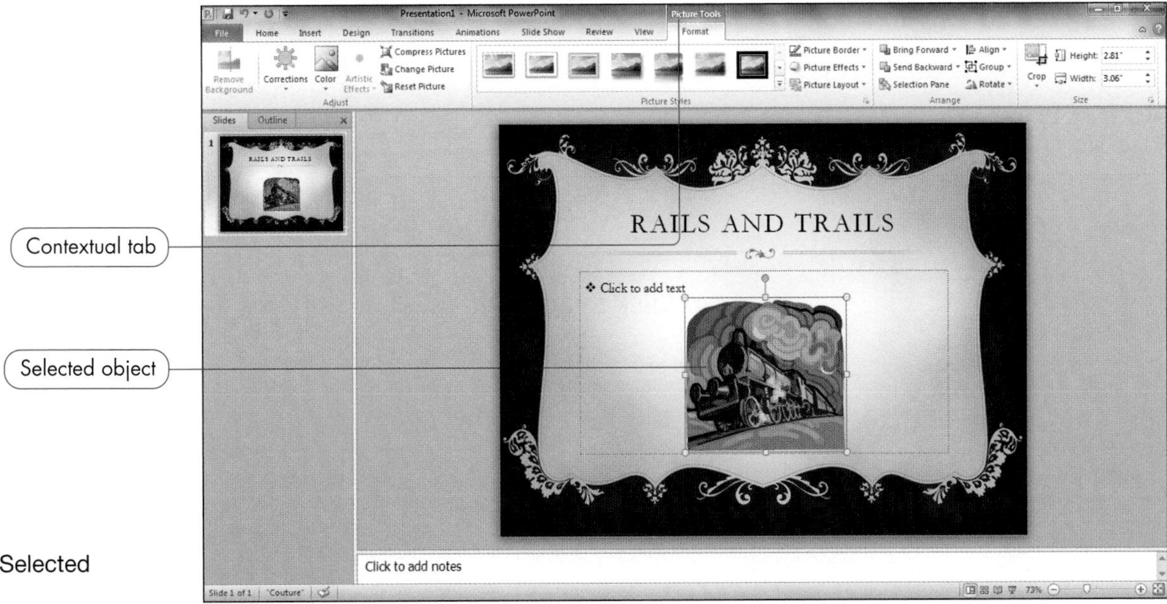

FIGURE 1.48 Selected Object ➤

Resizing and Moving a Selected Object

You can resize and move a selected object. Place the mouse pointer on any handle, and then drag (when the mouse pointer looks like a two-headed arrow) to resize the object. Be careful! If you drag a side handle, the object is likely to be skewed, possibly resulting in a poor image. Instead, drag a corner handle to proportionally resize the image. To move an object, drag the object when the mouse pointer looks like a four-headed arrow.

Insert Pictures

A **picture** is a graphic file that is retrieved from storage media and placed in an Office project.

Documents, worksheets, and presentations can include much more than just words and numbers. You can easily add energy and description to the project by including pictures and other graphic elements. Although a ***picture*** is usually just that—a digital photo—it is actually defined as a graphic element retrieved from storage media such as a hard drive or a CD. A picture could actually be a clip art item that you saved from the Internet onto your hard drive.

The process of inserting a picture is simple. First, click in the project where you want the picture to be placed. Make sure you know where the picture that you plan to use is stored. Click the Insert tab. Then, in the Illustrations group (or Images group in PowerPoint), click Picture. The Insert Picture dialog box shown in Figure 1.49 displays. Select a picture and click Insert (or simply double-click the picture). In addition, on some slide layouts, PowerPoint displays an Insert Picture from File button (Figure 1.50) that you can click to select and position a picture on the slide.

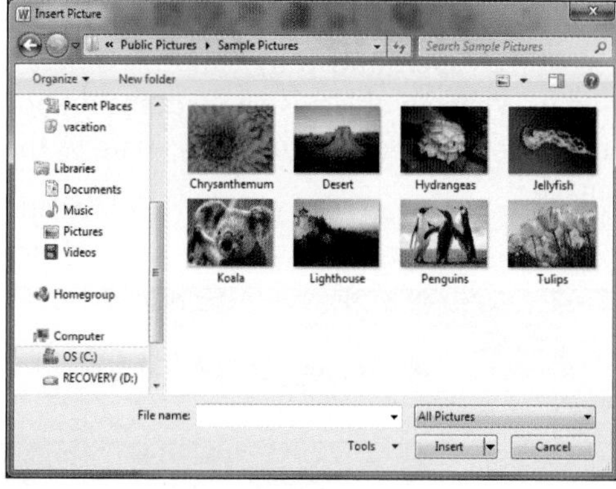

FIGURE 1.49 Insert Picture Dialog Box ➤

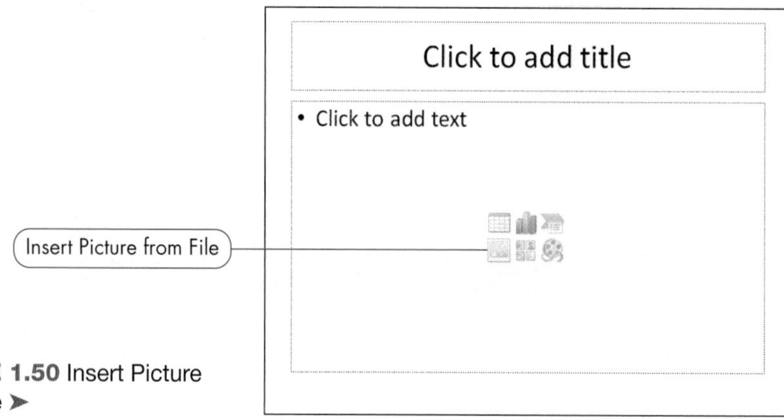

FIGURE 1.50 Insert Picture from File ➤

Insert Clip Art

Clip art is an electronic illustration that can be inserted into an Office project.

A large library of ***clip art*** is included with each Office installation. Office.com, an online resource providing additional clip art and Office support, is also available from within each Office application. To explore available clip art, click the Insert tab within an Office program, and then click Clip Art in the Illustrations group (or the Images group in PowerPoint). Figure 1.51 shows the Clip Art task pane that displays. Suppose that you are looking for some clip art to support a fund-raising project. Having opened the Clip Art task pane, you could click in the *Search for* box and type a search term, such as *money*. To limit the results to a particular media type, click the arrow beside the *Results should be* box, and make a selection. Click Go to initiate the search.

FIGURE 1.51 Clip Art Task Pane ➤

You can resize and move clip art just as you have learned to similarly manage pictures. All Office applications enable you to insert clip art from the Illustrations group. However, PowerPoint uses a unique approach to working with graphics, including the ability to insert clip art by selecting from a special-purpose area on a slide.

Review Tab Tasks

As a final touch, you should always check a project for spelling, grammatical, and word-usage errors. If the project is a collaborative effort, you and your colleagues might add comments and suggest changes. You can even use a thesaurus to find synonyms for words that are not quite right for your purpose. The Review tab in each Office application provides all these options and more. In this section, you will learn to review a file, checking for spelling and grammatical errors. You will also learn to use a thesaurus to identify synonyms.

Reviewing a File

As you create or edit a file, you will want to make sure no spelling or grammatical errors exist. You will also be concerned with wording, being sure to select words and phrases that best represent the purpose of the document, worksheet, or presentation. On occasion, you might even find yourself at a loss for an appropriate word. Not to worry. Word, Excel, and PowerPoint all provide standard tools for proofreading, including a spelling and grammar checker and a thesaurus.

Check Spelling and Grammar

In general, all Office applications check your spelling and grammar as you type. If a word is unrecognized, it is flagged as misspelled or grammatically incorrect. Misspellings are identified with a red wavy underline, grammatical problems are underlined in green, and word usage errors (such as using *bear* instead of *bare*) have a blue underline. If the word or phrase is truly in error—that is, it is not a person's name or an unusual term that is not in the application's dictionary—you can correct it manually or you can let the software correct it for you. If you right-click a word or phrase that is identified as a mistake, you will see a shortcut menu similar to that shown in Figure 1.52. If the application's dictionary can make a suggestion as to the correct spelling, you can click to accept the suggestion and make the change. If a grammatical rule is violated, you will have an opportunity to select a correction. However, if the text is actually correct, you can click Ignore (to bypass that single occurrence) or Ignore All (to bypass all occurrences of the flagged error in the current document). Click Add to Dictionary if you want the word to be considered correct whenever it appears in all documents. Similar selections on a shortcut menu enable you to ignore grammatical mistakes if they are not errors.

In general, all Office applications check your spelling and grammar as you type.

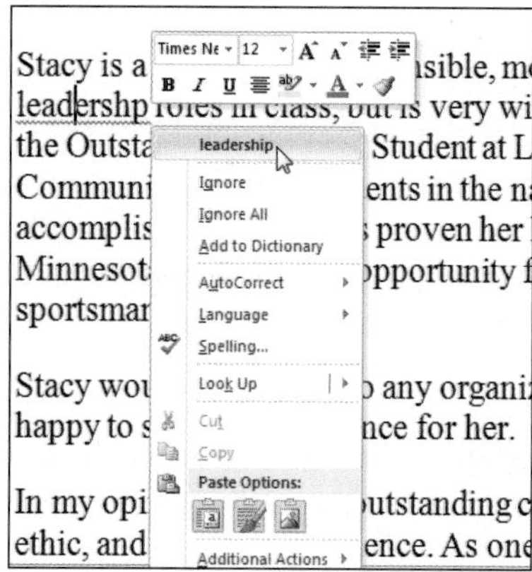

FIGURE 1.52 Correcting Misspelling ➤

You might prefer the convenience of addressing possible misspellings and grammatical errors without having to examine each underlined word or phrase. To do so, click Spelling & Grammar in the Proofing group of the Review tab. Beginning at the top of the document, each identified error is highlighted in a dialog box similar to Figure 1.53. You can then choose how to address the problem by making a selection in the dialog box.

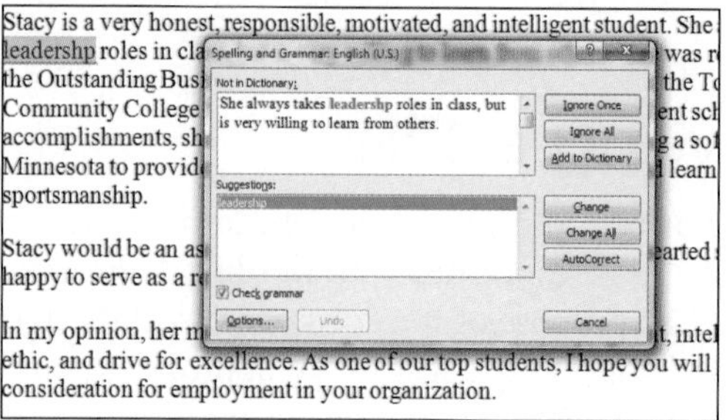

FIGURE 1.53 Checking for Spelling and Grammatical Errors ➤

A **default** setting is one that is in place unless you specify otherwise.

> **TIP** Understanding Software Options
>
> Many Office settings are considered ***default*** options. Thus, unless you specify otherwise, the default options are in effect. One such default option is the automatic spelling and grammar checker. If you prefer to enable and disable certain options or change default settings in an Office application, you can click the File tab and click Options. From that point, you can work through a series of categories, selecting or deselecting options at will. For example, if you want to change how the application corrects and formats text, you can select or deselect settings in the Proofing group.

Use the Thesaurus

As you write, there will be times when you are at a loss for an appropriate word. Perhaps you feel that you are overusing a word and want to find a suitable substitute. The Thesaurus is the Office tool to use in such a situation. Located in the Proofing group of the Review tab, Thesaurus enables you to search for synonyms, or words with similar meanings. Select a word, then click Thesaurus, in the Proofing group on the Review tab. A task pane displays on the right side of the screen, and synonyms are listed similar to those shown in Figure 1.54. You can also use the Thesaurus before typing a word to find substitutes. Simply click Thesaurus and type the word for which you are seeking a synonym in the Search for box. Press Enter or click the green arrow to the right of the Search box for some suggestions. Finally, you can also identify synonyms when you right-click a word and point to Synonyms (if any are available). Click any word to place it in the document.

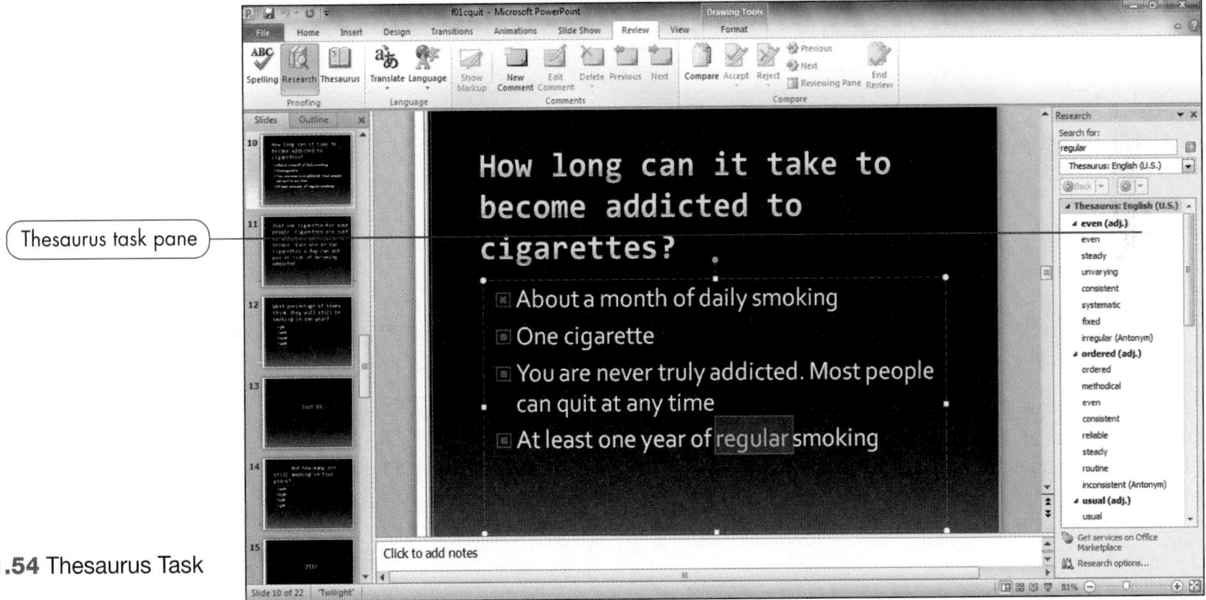

FIGURE 1.54 Thesaurus Task Pane ➤

Page Layout Tab Tasks

When you prepare a document or worksheet, you are concerned with the way the project appears onscreen and possibly in print. Unlike Word and Excel, a PowerPoint presentation is usually designed as a slide show, so it is not nearly as critical to concern yourself with page layout settings. The Page Layout tab in Word and Excel provides access to a full range of options such as margin settings and page orientation. In this section, you will identify page layout settings that are common to Office applications. These settings include margins and page orientation.

The Page Layout tab in Word and Excel provides access to a full range of options such as margin settings and page orientation.

Changing Page Settings

Because a document is most often designed to be printed, you will want to make sure it looks its best in printed form. That means that you will need to know how to adjust margins and how to change the page orientation. Perhaps the document or spreadsheet should be centered on the page vertically or the text should be aligned in columns. By adjusting page settings, you can do all these things and more. You will find the most common page settings, such as margins and page orientation, in the Page Setup group of the Page Layout tab. For less common settings, such as determining whether headers should print on odd or even pages, you can use the Page Setup dialog box.

Change Margins

A **margin** is the blank space around the sides, top, and bottom of a document or worksheet.

A ***margin*** is the area of blank space that appears to the left, right, top, and bottom of a document or worksheet. Margins are only evident if you are in Print Layout or Page Layout view or if you are in the Backstage view, previewing a document to print. To change or set margins, click the Page Layout tab. As shown in Figure 1.55, the Page Setup group enables you to change such items as margins and orientation. To change margins, click Margins. If the margins that you intend to use are included in any of the preset margin options, click a selection. Otherwise, click Custom Margins to display the Page Setup dialog box in which you can create custom margin settings. Click OK to accept the settings, and close the dialog box. You can also change margins when you click Print on the File tab.

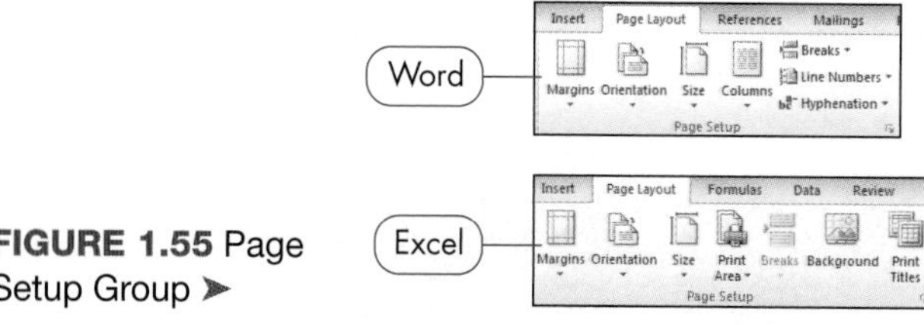

FIGURE 1.55 Page Setup Group ➤

Change Page Orientation

A page or worksheet displayed in **portrait** orientation is taller than it is wide.

A page or worksheet displayed in **landscape** orientation is wider than it is tall.

Documents and worksheets can be displayed in ***portrait*** orientation or in ***landscape***. A page displayed or printed in portrait orientation is taller than it is wide. A page in landscape orientation is wider than it is tall. Word documents are usually more attractive displayed in portrait orientation, whereas Excel worksheets are often more suitable in landscape. To select page orientation, click Orientation in the Page Setup group on the Page Layout tab. See Figure 1.55 for the location of the Orientation command. Orientation is also an option in the Print area of the Backstage view.

Use the Page Setup Dialog Box

The Page Setup group contains the most commonly used page options in the particular Office application. Some are unique to Excel, and others are more applicable to Word. Other less common settings are only available in the Page Setup dialog box, displayed when you click the Page Setup Dialog Box Launcher. The subsequent dialog box includes options for customizing margins, selecting page orientation, centering vertically, printing gridlines, and creating headers and footers, although some of those options are only available when working with Word, and others are unique to Excel. Figure 1.56 gives a glimpse of both the Excel and Word Page Setup dialog boxes.

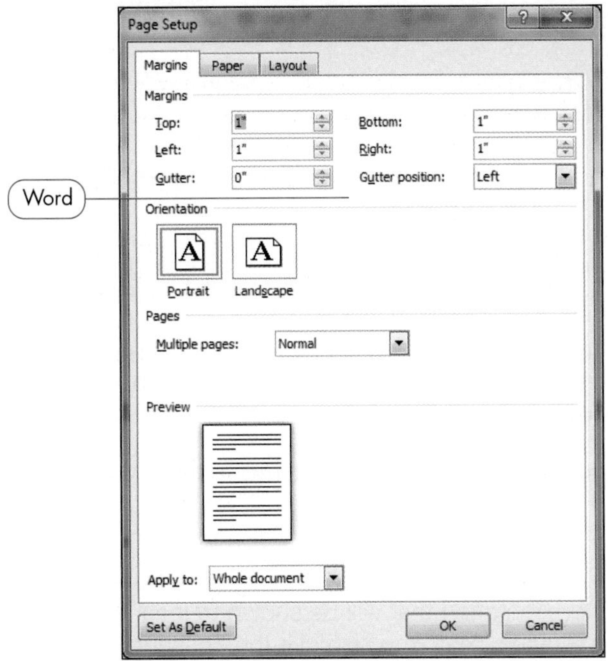

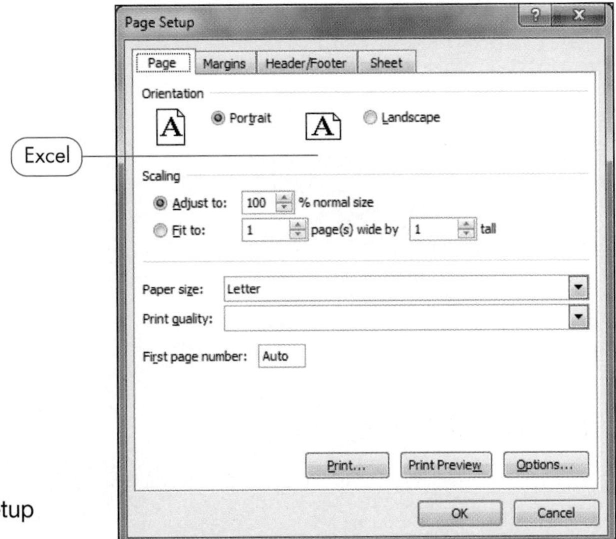

FIGURE 1.56 Page Setup Dialog Boxes ➤

HANDS-ON EXERCISES

5 Tasks on the Insert Tab, Page Layout Tab, and Review Tab

The Rails and Trails project is nearing kickoff. You are helping plan a ceremony to commemorate the occasion. To encourage interest and participation, you will edit a PowerPoint presentation that is to be shown to civic groups, the local retiree association, and to city and county leaders. You know that pictures and clip art add energy to a presentation when used appropriately, so you will check for those elements, adding whatever is necessary. A major concern is making sure the presentation is error free and that it is available in print so that meeting participants can review it later. As a reminder, you also plan to have available a handout giving the time and date of the dedication ceremony. You will use the Insert tab to work with illustrations and the Review tab to check for errors, and you will use Word to generate an attractive handout as a reminder of the date.

Skills covered: Check Spelling and Use the Thesaurus • Insert Clip Art and Pictures • Select Margins and Page Orientation

STEP 1 CHECK SPELLING AND USE THE THESAURUS

As you check the PowerPoint presentation that will be shown to local groups, you make sure no misspellings or grammatical mistakes exist. You also use the Thesaurus to find a suitable substitution for a word you feel should be replaced. Refer to Figure 1.57 as you complete Step 1.

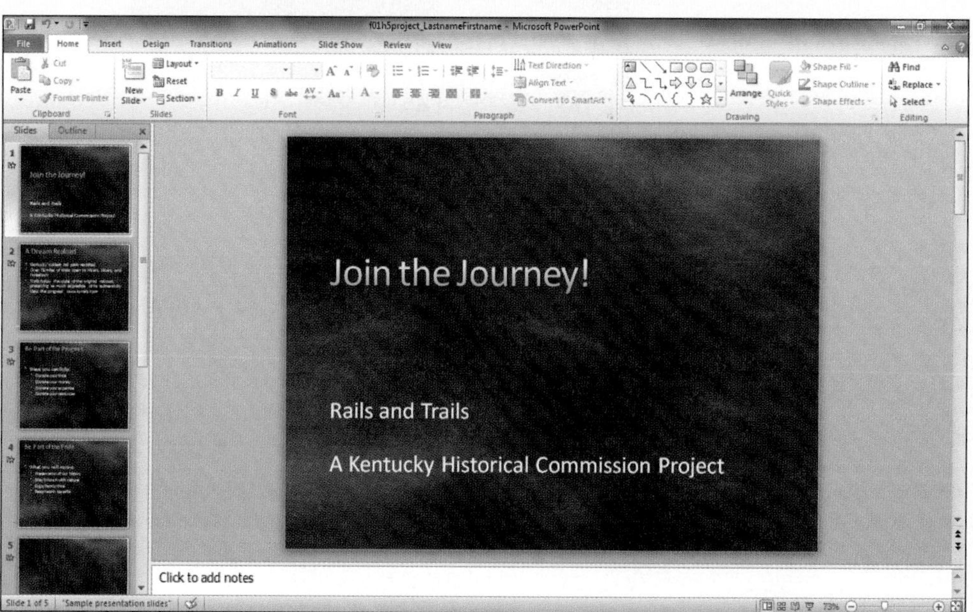

FIGURE 1.57 Project Presentation ➤

a. Click the **Start button** to display the Start menu, and then point to **All Programs**. Click **Microsoft Office**, and then click **Microsoft PowerPoint 2010**. Open *f01h5project* and save it as **f01h5project_LastnameFirstname** in the Presentations folder (a subfolder of Rails and Trails Projects) on the drive where you save your files. The presentation displays as shown in Figure 1.57.

   The PowerPoint presentation opens, with Slide 1 shown in Normal view.

b. Click **Slide Show** and the **Slide Show tab**, and then click **From Beginning** in the Start Slide Show group to view the presentation. Click to advance from one slide to another. After the last slide, click to return to Normal view.

c. Click the **Review tab**, and then click **Spelling** in the Proofing group. The first misspelling is not actually misspelled. It is the name of a city. Click **Ignore** to leave it as is. The next flagged misspelling is truly misspelled. With the correct spelling selected, click **Change** to correct the mistake. Correct any other words that are misspelled. Click **OK** when the spell check is complete.

d. Click **Slide 2** in the Slides pane on the left. Double-click the word *route*, click **Thesaurus** in the Proofing group, point to **path** in the Research pane, click the arrow to the right of the word path, and then click **Insert**. Press the **Spacebar**.

   The word *route* is replaced with the word *path*.

e. Click the **Close button** in the top-right corner of the Research pane.

f. Save the presentation and keep it open for the next step.

STEP 2 INSERT CLIP ART AND PICTURES

Although the presentation provides the necessary information and encourages viewers to become active participants in the project, you believe that pictures and clip art might make it a little more exciting. Where appropriate, you will include clip art and a picture. Refer to Figures 1.58 and 1.59 as you complete Step 2.

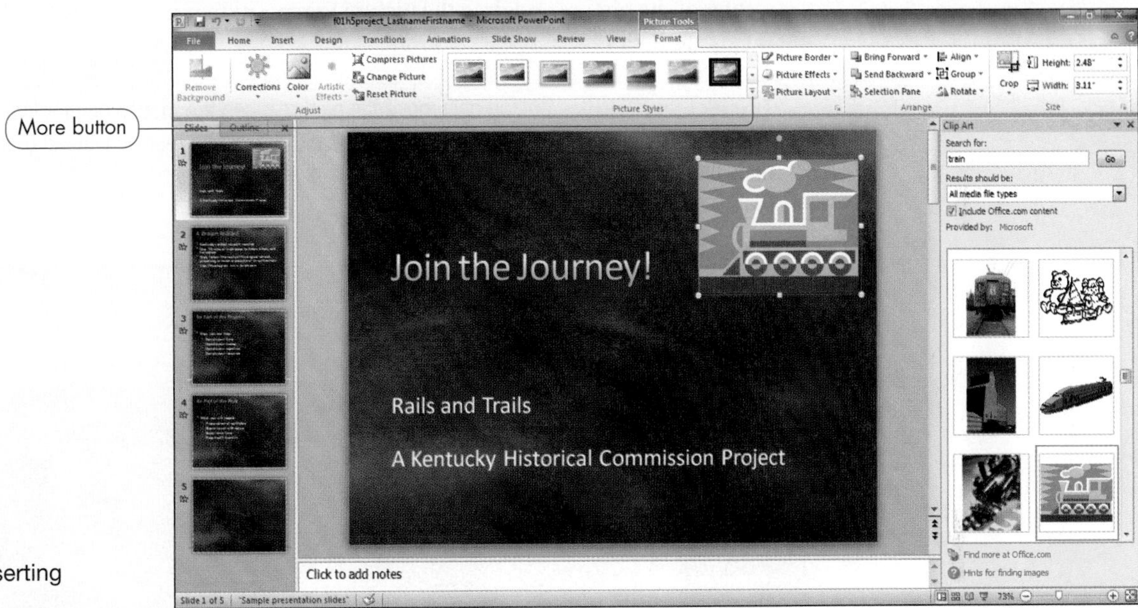

FIGURE 1.58 Inserting Clip Art ➤

a. Display Slide 1, click the **Insert tab**, and then click **Clip Art**.

   The Clip Art task pane opens on the right side of the screen.

b. Type **train** in the **Search for box** in the Clip Art task pane. Click the check box beside *Include Office.com content* (unless it is already checked), click the arrow beside *Results should be*, and then click the check box beside *All media types* (unless it is already checked). Narrow results to illustrations by clicking the check box beside *Illustrations*, and then click **Go**.

   You will identify clip art to be displayed on Slide 1.

c. Click to select any clip art image of a train.

> **TROUBLESHOOTING:** Be sure to click the clip art image, not the arrow to the right. If you click the arrow, you will then need to click Insert to place the clip art image on the slide.

> **TROUBLESHOOTING:** It is very easy to make the mistake of inserting duplicate clip art images on a slide, perhaps because you clicked the image more than once in the Clip Art task pane. If that should happen, you can remove any unwanted clip art by clicking to select it on the slide and pressing Delete.

The clip art image probably will not be placed as you would like, but you will move and resize it in the next substep. Also, the clip art is selected, as indicated by the box and handles surrounding it.

d. Click a corner handle (small circle) on the border of the clip art. Make sure the mouse pointer appears as a double-headed arrow. Drag to resize the image so that it appears similar to that shown in Figure 1.58. Click in the center of the clip art. The mouse pointer should appear as a four-headed arrow. Drag the clip art to the top-right corner of the slide. Make sure the clip art is still selected (it should be surrounded by a box and handles). If it is not selected, click to select it.

e. Click the **More button** of the Picture Styles group (see Figure 1.58) to reveal a gallery of styles. Position the mouse pointer over any style to see a preview of the style applied to the clip art. Click to apply a style of your choice. Close the Clip Art task pane.

f. On Slide 5, type **The Journey Begins** in the **Title box**. Click **Insert Picture from File** in the Content Placeholder (see Figure 1.50), navigate to the student data files, and then double-click *f01h5rails*.

   A picture is placed on the final slide.

g. Click to select the picture, if necessary. Drag a corner handle to resize the picture. Click the center of the picture and drag the picture to reposition it in the center of the slide as shown in Figure 1.59.

TROUBLESHOOTING: You can only move the picture when the mouse pointer looks like a four-headed arrow. If instead, you drag a handle, the picture will be resized instead of moved. Click Undo on the Quick Access Toolbar and try it again.

Picture Effects

FIGURE 1.59 Inserting a Picture ➤

h. Click **Picture Effects** in the Picture Styles group on the Format tab, point to **Soft Edges**, and then click **5 Point**.

i. Click the **Slide Show tab**, and then click **From Beginning** in the Start Slide Show group. Click to advance from one slide to another. After the last slide, click to return to Normal view.

j. Save the presentation and exit PowerPoint.

STEP 3 SELECT MARGINS AND PAGE ORIENTATION

You are ready to finalize the flyer, but before printing it you want to see how it will look. You wonder if it would be better in landscape or portrait orientation, so you will try both. After adjusting the margins, you are ready to save the flyer for later printing and distribution. Refer to Figure 1.60 as you complete Step 3.

Join the Journey!
Rails and Trails Dedication Ceremony
May 25, 2011
9:00 a.m.
110 Overton Drive

FIGURE 1.60 Word Handout ➤

a. Click the **Start button** to display the Start menu, and then point to **All Programs**. Click **Microsoft Office**, and then click **Microsoft Word 2010**. Open *f01h5handout* and save it as **f01h5handout_LastnameFirstname** in the Promotional Print folder on the drive where you save your files. The handout that you developed to help publicize the dedication ceremony displays as shown in Figure 1.60.

b. Click the **Page Layout tab**, click **Orientation** in the Page Setup group, and then click **Landscape** to view the flyer in landscape orientation.

   You want to see how the handout will look in landscape orientation.

c. Click the **File tab**, click **Print**, and then click **Next Page** (right-directed arrow at the bottom center of the preview page).

   The second page of the handout shows only the address. You can see that the two-page layout is not an attractive option.

d. Click the **Home tab**. Click **Undo** on the Quick Access Toolbar. Click the **File tab**, and then click **Print**.

   The document fits on one page. Portrait orientation is a much better choice for the handout.

e. Click the **Page Layout tab**, click **Margins**, and then select **Custom Margins**. Click the **spin arrow** beside the Left margin box to increase the margin to **1.5**. Similarly, change the right margin to **1.5**. Click **OK**.

f. Save the document and exit Word.

CHAPTER OBJECTIVES REVIEW

After reading this chapter, you have accomplished the following objectives:

1. **Use Windows Explorer.** You can use Windows Explorer to manage files and folders and to view contents of storage media. In addition to viewing the contents of physical folders, you can also manage libraries, which are collections of related data from various physical locations. Windows Explorer provides information on networked resources and shared disk drives, as well. Using the Favorites area of Windows Explorer, you can locate areas of frequent access.
2. **Work with folders and files.** Using Windows Explorer, you can create folders and rename, delete, move, and copy files and folders. You can also open files through Windows Explorer.
3. **Select, copy, and move multiple files and folders.** Backing up, or copying, files and folders is necessary to ensure that you do not lose important data and documents. You can quickly move or copy multiple items by selecting them all at one time.
4. **Identify common interface components.** You can communicate with Office software through the Microsoft Office user interface. Common interface components, found in all Microsoft Office applications, include the Ribbon, Quick Access Toolbar, title bar, status bar, and the Backstage view. The Ribbon is organized by commands within groups within tabs on the Ribbon. The Quick Access Toolbar provides one-click access to such activities as Save, Undo, and Repeat (Redo). The Backstage view is an Office feature that enables such common activities as opening, closing, saving, and printing files. It also provides information on an open file. The status bar contains information relative to the open file. The title bar identifies the open file's name and contains control buttons (minimize, maximize/restore down, and close).
5. **Get Office Help.** You can get help while you are using Microsoft Office by clicking the Help button, which appears as a question mark in the top-right corner of the Ribbon. You can also click the File tab to open the Backstage view, and then click the Help button. Assistance is available from within a dialog box by clicking the Help button in the top-right corner of the dialog box. When you rest the mouse pointer over any command on the Ribbon, you will see an Enhanced ScreenTip that provides a brief summary of the command.
6. **Open a file.** After a file has been saved, you can open it by clicking the File tab and selecting Open. If you recently worked with a file, you can reopen it from the Recent Documents list, which is displayed when you click Recent on the Backstage view. Finally, you can open a file from a template. Templates are predesigned files supplied by Microsoft from within the current Office installation or from Office.com.
7. **Print a file.** Often, you will want to print a file (a document, worksheet, or presentation). The Backstage view makes it easy to preview the file, change print settings, and print the file.
8. **Close a file and application.** When you close a file, it is removed from memory. If you plan to work with the file later, you will need to save the file before closing it. The Office application will prompt you to save the file before closing if you have made any changes since the last time the file was saved. When you close an application, all open files within the application are also closed.
9. **Select and edit text.** The Home tab includes options to change the appearance of text. You can change the size, color, and type of font, as well as other font attributes. The font is the typeface, or the way characters appear and are sized. Before changing existing text, you must select what you want to change. Although shortcuts to text selection exist, you can always select text by dragging to highlight it. Any formatting changes that you identify apply only to selected text or to text typed after the changes are invoked.
10. **Use the Clipboard group tasks.** The Clipboard is a holding area for selections that you have cut or copied. Although you can view the Clipboard by clicking the Dialog Box Launcher in the Clipboard group, doing so is not necessary before pasting a cut or copied item to a receiving location. Another option in the Clipboard group is Format Painter, which enables you to copy formatting from one area to another within a file.
11. **Use the Editing group tasks.** You can easily find selected words or phrases and replace them, if necessary, with substitutions. There may be occasions when you simply want to find an occurrence of selected text without replacing it, whereas at other times you want to make replacements immediately. The Find option enables you to locate text, whereas Replace enables you to find all occurrences of an item quickly and replace it with another.
12. **Insert objects.** Pictures, clip art, shapes, screenshots, headers and footers, and text boxes are objects that you can insert in Office projects. After you have inserted an object, you can click to select it and manage it independently of the underlying worksheet, document, or presentation. When you select an object, a contextual tab appears on the Ribbon to provide formatting options specific to the selected object.
13. **Review a file.** You can check spelling, grammar, and word usage using any Office application. In fact, applications are usually set to check for such errors as you type, underlining possible misspellings in red, grammatical mistakes in green, and incorrect word usage in blue. Errors are not always correctly identified, as the Office application might indicate a misspelling when it is simply a word that is not in its dictionary. You can also check spelling and grammar by selecting Spelling & Grammar in the Proofing group on the Review tab.
14. **Change page settings.** You can change margins and page orientation through commands in the Page Setup group of the Page Layout tab. The Page Setup dialog box, accessible when you click the Dialog Box Launcher in the Page Setup group, provides even more choices of page settings.

KEY TERMS

Access ***p.14***
Backstage view ***p.15***
Backup ***p.9***
Clip art ***p.49***
Clipboard ***p.37***
Command ***p.17***
Contextual tab ***p.18***
Copy ***p.37***
Cut ***p.37***
Default ***p.51***
Dialog box ***p.17***
Dialog Box Launcher ***p.17***
Enhanced ScreenTip ***p.20***
Excel ***p.14***
File ***p.2***
Find ***p.40***
Folder ***p.2***
Font ***p.36***
Format Painter ***p.37***
Gallery ***p.18***
Group ***p.17***
Key Tip ***p.19***
Landscape ***p.52***
Library ***p.4***
Live Preview ***p.18***
Margin ***p.52***
Microsoft Office ***p.14***
Mini toolbar ***p.35***
Navigation Pane ***p.4***
Paste ***p.37***
Picture ***p.48***
Portrait ***p.52***
PowerPoint ***p.14***
Quick Access Toolbar ***p.15***
Replace ***p.40***
Ribbon ***p.17***
Shortcut menu ***p.37***
Status bar ***p.19***
Subfolder ***p.2***
Tab ***p.17***
Template ***p.28***
Title bar ***p.15***
Toggle ***p.36***
User interface ***p.14***
View ***p.19***
Windows Explorer ***p.2***
Word ***p.14***
Zoom slider ***p.19***

MULTIPLE CHOICE

1. The Recent Documents list:
   (a) Shows documents that have been previously printed.
   (b) Shows documents that have been previously opened.
   (c) Shows documents that have been previously saved in an earlier software version.
   (d) Shows documents that have been previously deleted.

2. Which of the following Windows Explorer features collects related data from folders and gives them a single name?
   (a) Network
   (b) Favorites
   (c) Libraries
   (d) Computer

3. When you want to copy the format of a selection, but not the content:
   (a) Double-click Copy in the Clipboard group.
   (b) Right-click the selection, and then click Copy.
   (c) Click Copy Format in the Clipboard group.
   (d) Click Format Painter in the Clipboard group.

4. Which of the following is not an object that can be inserted in an Office document?
   (a) Picture
   (b) Clip art
   (c) Paragraph box
   (d) Text box

5. What does a red wavy underline in a document, spreadsheet, or presentation mean?
   (a) A word is misspelled or not recognized by the Office dictionary.
   (b) A grammatical mistake exists.
   (c) An apparent word-usage mistake exists.
   (d) A word has been replaced with a synonym.

6. When you close a file:
   (a) You are prompted to save the file (unless you have made no changes since last saving it).
   (b) The application (Word, Excel, or PowerPoint) is also closed.
   (c) You must first save the file.
   (d) You must change the file name.

7. Live Preview:
   (a) Opens a predesigned document or spreadsheet that is relevant to your task.
   (b) Provides a preview of the results of a choice you are considering before you make a final selection.
   (c) Provides a preview of an upcoming Office version.
   (d) Enlarges the font onscreen.

8. You can get help when working with an Office application in which one of the following areas?
   (a) Help tab
   (b) Status bar
   (c) The Backstage view
   (d) Quick Access Toolbar

9. The Find and Replace feature enables you to do which of the following?
   (a) Find all instances of misspelling and automatically correct (or replace) them.
   (b) Find any grammatical errors and automatically correct (or replace) them.
   (c) Find any specified font settings and replace them with another selection.
   (d) Find any character string and replace it with another.

10. A document or worksheet printed in portrait orientation is:
    (a) Taller than it is wide.
    (b) Wider than it is tall.
    (c) A document with 2″ left and right margins.
    (d) A document with 2″ top and bottom margins.

PRACTICE EXERCISES

1 Editing a Menu

You have gone into partnership with a friend to open a health food restaurant in a golf and tennis community. With the renewed emphasis on healthy living and the large number of high-income renters and condominium owners in the community, the specialty restaurant should do well. In preparation for the opening, your partner has begun a menu that you will review and edit. This exercise follows the same set of skills as used in Hands-On Exercises 1, 2, 3, 4, and 5 in the chapter. Refer to Figure 1.61 as you complete this exercise.

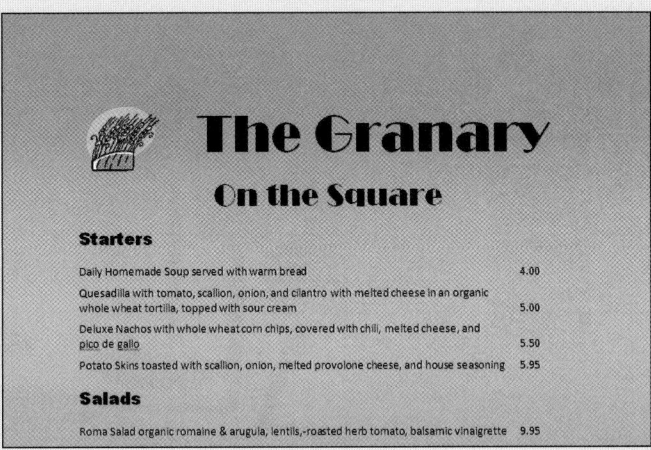

FIGURE 1.61 Restaurant Menu ➤

a. Click **Windows Explorer** on the taskbar, and then select the location where you save your files. Click **New folder**, type **The Granary**, and then press **Enter**. Close Windows Explorer.

b. Start Word. Open *f01p1menu* and save it as **f01p1menu_LastnameFirstname** in the The Granary folder.

c. Click the **Review tab**, and then click **Spelling & Grammar** in the Proofing group. The words *pico*, *gallo*, and *mesclun* are not misspelled, so you should ignore them when they are flagged. Other identified misspellings should be changed.

d. Click after the word *bread* in the first item under *Starters*. Press the **Spacebar**, and then type **or cornbread**.

e. Double-click **Desserts** on page 2 to select the word, and then type **Sweets**.

f. Drag to select the **Sandwiches section**, beginning with the word *Sandwiches* and ending after *8.75*. Click the **Home tab**, click **Cut** in the Clipboard group, click to place the insertion point before the word *Salads*, and then click **Paste** in the Clipboard group. The *Sandwiches* section should be placed before the *Salads* section.

g. Click **Undo** twice on the Quick Access Toolbar to return the *Sandwiches* section to its original location.

h. Change the price of Daily Homemade Soup to **4.95**.

i. Press **Ctrl+End** to place the insertion point at the end of the document, and then type your name.

j. Click the **Page Layout tab**, click **Orientation**, and then click **Landscape**. Click the **File tab**, and then click **Print** to see a preview of the document. Click the **Home tab**. Because the new look does not improve the menu's appearance, click **Undo** to return to the original orientation.

k. Press **Ctrl+Home** to move to the top of the document. Compare your results to Figure 1.61.

l. Drag the **Zoom slider** on the status bar slightly to the right to magnify text. Click the **View tab**, and then click **100%** in the Zoom group to return to the original size.

m. Save and close the file, and submit based on your instructor's directions.

2 Web Design Business

You have always been interested in Web design and have worked in the field for several years. You now have an opportunity to devote yourself full-time to your career as the CEO of a company dedicated to designing and supporting Web sites. One of the first steps in getting the business off the ground is developing a business plan so that you can request financial support. You will use PowerPoint to present your business plan. This exercise follows the same set of skills as used in Hands-On Exercises 2, 3, and 4 in the chapter. Refer to Figure 1.62 as you complete this exercise.

FIGURE 1.62 Business Plan Presentation ➤

a. Start PowerPoint. Open *f01p2business* and save it as **f01p2business_ LastnameFirstname.**

b. Click the **Slides tab** in the Slides pane (on the left), if necessary. Slide 1 should be displayed. If not, click the first slide in the left pane.

c. Position the mouse pointer to the immediate left of the word *Company*. Drag to select the words *Company Name*, and then type **Inspire Web Design**.

d. Click the **Insert tab**, and then click **Clip Art** in the Images group.
   - Click in the **Search for box** in the Clip Art task pane, remove any text that might be in the box, and then type **World Wide Web**. Make sure *Include Office.com content* is checked, and then click **Go**.
   - Select any image (or the one shown in Figure 1.62). Resize and position the clip art as shown. *Hint: To reposition clip art, drag when the mouse pointer is a four-headed arrow.*
   - Click the **Format tab**, click the **More button** in the Picture Styles group, and then click the **Reflected Rounded Rectangle picture style** (fifth from the left on the top row).
   - Click outside the clip art and compare your slide to Figure 1.62. Close the Clip Art task pane.

e. On Slide 2, click after the period on the bulleted point ending with *them*, and then press **Enter**. Type **Support services will include continued oversight, modification, and redesign of client Web sites.**

f. Press **Enter**, and then type **Web hosting services will ensure uninterrupted 24/7 Web presence for clients.**

g. On Slide 3, complete the following steps:
   - Position the mouse pointer over the first bullet so that the pointer appears as a four-headed arrow, and then click the bullet. All of the text in the bullet item is selected. As you type text, it will replace the selected text.
   - Type ***your name*** **(CEO)** [replacing *your name* with your first and last names], **Margaret Atkins (Financial Manager), Daniel Finch (Web Design), Susan Cummings (Web Support and Web Hosting).**

h. Click the second bullet, and then type **Team members collectively possess over 28 years' experience in Web design and business management. All have achieved success in business careers and are redirecting their efforts to support Inspire Web Design as full-time employees.**
i. Click to select the third bullet, and then press **Delete**, removing the bullet and text.
j. On Slide 1, click **Slide Show** on the status bar. After viewing a slide, click the mouse button to proceed to the next slide. Continue to click until the slide show ends.
k. Click **Slide Sorter** on the status bar. You and your partners have decided to rename the company. The new name is **Inspired Web Design**.
    - Click the **Home tab**, and then click **Replace** in the Editing group. Be careful to click the button, not the arrow to the right.
    - Type **Inspire** in the **Find what box**. Type **Inspired** in the **Replace with box**.
    - Click **Replace All**. Three replacements should be made. Click **OK**, and then click **Close** in the Replace dialog box.
l. Save and close the file, and submit based on your instructor's directions.

3 Planning Ahead

You and a friend are starting a lawn care service and have a few clients already. Billing will be a large part of your record keeping, so you are planning ahead by developing a series of folders to maintain those records. This exercise follows the same set of skills as used in Hands-On Exercises 1 and 4 in the chapter. Refer to Figure 1.63 as you complete this exercise.

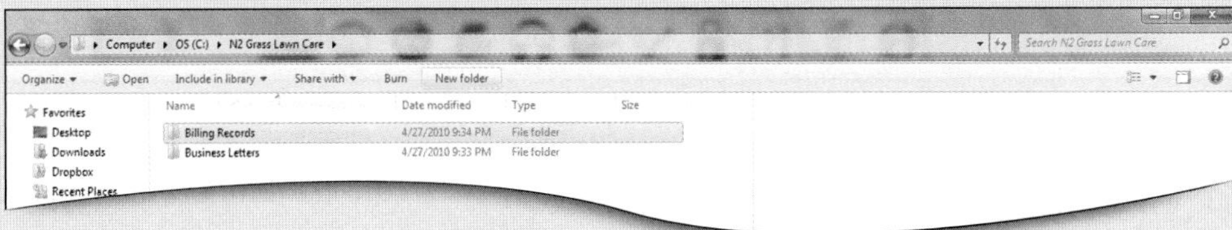

FIGURE 1.63 N2 Grass Folder Structure ➤

a. Click **Windows Explorer** on the taskbar, and then select the location where you save your files. Click **New folder**, type **N2 Grass Lawn Care**, and then press **Enter**.
b. Double-click **N2 Grass Lawn Care** in the Content pane.
    - Click **New folder**, type **Business Letters**, and then press **Enter**.
    - Click **New folder**, type **Billing Records**, and then press **Enter**. Compare your results to Figure 1.63. Close Windows Explorer.
c. Start Word. Open *f01p3lawn*. Use Find and Replace to replace the text *Your Name* with your name.
d. Click the **File tab**, and then click **Save As**.
    - Click **Computer** in the left pane.
    - Click the drive (in the Navigation Pane) where you save your student files. Double-click **N2 Grass Lawn Care**, and then double-click **Business Letters**.
    - Save the file as **f01p3lawn_LastnameFirstname**. Click **OK**, if necessary. Close the document and exit Word.
e. Open Windows Explorer.
    - Click **Computer** in the Navigation Pane.
    - In the Content pane, double-click the drive where you earlier placed the N2 Grass Lawn Care folder. Double-click **N2 Grass Lawn Care**.
    - Right-click **Billing Records**, click **Rename**, type **Accounting Records,** and then press **Enter**.
f. Click the **Start button**, click **All Programs**, click **Accessories**, and then click **Snipping Tool**. You will use the Snipping Tool to capture the screen display for submission to your instructor.
    - Click the **New arrow**, and then click **Full-screen Snip**.
    - Click **File**, and then click **Save As**.
g. Save the file as **f01p3snip_LastnameFirstname**. Close the file and submit based on your instructor's directions.

MID-LEVEL EXERCISES

1 Reference Letter

You are an instructor at a local community college. A student has asked you to provide her with a letter of reference for a job application. You have used Word to prepare the letter, but now you need to make a few changes before it is finalized.

a. Open Windows Explorer. Create a new folder on the drive where you save your student files, naming it **Letters of Reference**. Close Windows Explorer.
b. Start Word. Open *f01m1letter* and save it in the Letters of Reference folder as **f01m1letter_LastnameFirstname**.
c. Type your name, address, and the current date in the address area, replacing the generic text. The letter is to go to **Ms. Samantha Blake, CEO, Ridgeline Industries, 410 Wellington Parkway, Huntsville AL 35611**. The salutation should read **Dear Ms. Blake:**.
d. Bold the student's first and last names in the first sentence.
e. Find each occurrence of the word *Stacy* and replace it with **Stacey**.
f. Find and insert a synonym for the word *intelligent* in the second paragraph.
g. Move the last paragraph (beginning with *In my opinion*) to position it before the third paragraph (beginning with *Stacey*).
h. Press **Ctrl+Home** to move the insertion point to the beginning of the document. Check spelling, selecting a correction for each misspelled word and ignoring spelling or grammatical mistakes that are not actually incorrect.
i. Type your name and title in the area beneath the word *Sincerely.*
j. Preview the document as it will appear when printed.
k. Save and close the file, and submit based on your instructor's directions.

2 Medical Monitoring

You are enrolled in a Health Informatics program of study in which you learn to manage databases related to health fields. For a class project, your instructor requires that you monitor your blood pressure, recording your findings in an Excel worksheet. You have recorded the week's data and will now make a few changes before printing the worksheet for submission.

a. Start Excel. Open *f01m2tracker* and save it as **f01m2tracker_LastnameFirstname**.
b. Preview the worksheet as it will appear when printed.
c. Change the orientation of the worksheet to **Landscape**. Preview the worksheet again. Click the **Home tab**.
d. Click in the cell beside *Name*, and then type your first and last names. Press **Enter**.
e. Change the font of the text in **cell C1** to **Verdana** and the font size to **20**.
f. Copy the function in **cell E22** to **cells F22 and G22**. *Hint: After selecting cell E22 and clicking Copy, drag cells F22 and G22. Before you drag, be sure the mouse pointer has the appearance of a large white plus sign. Then click Paste to copy the formula to those two cells.* Press **Esc** to remove the selection from around **cell E22**.

g. Get Help on showing decimal places. You want to increase the decimal places for the values in **cells E22, F22, and G22**, so that each value shows two places to the right of the decimal. Use Excel Help to learn how to do that. You might use *Increase Decimals* as a Search term. When you find the answer, select the three cells and increase the decimal places to **2**.
h. Click **cell A1**, and insert a clip art image of your choice related to blood pressure. Be sure the images include content from Office.com. If necessary, resize and position the clip art attractively. *Hint: To resize clip art, drag a corner handle (small circle). To reposition, drag the clip art when the mouse pointer is a four-headed arrow.*
i. Open the Backstage view, and adjust print settings to print two copies. You will not actually print two copies unless directed by your instructor.
j. Save and close the file, and submit based on your instructor's directions.

CAPSTONE EXERCISE

You are a member of the Student Government Association (SGA) at your college. As a community project, the SGA is sponsoring a "Stop Smoking" drive designed to provide information on the health risks posed by smoking cigarettes and to offer solutions to those who want to quit. The SGA has partnered with the local branch of the American Cancer Society as well as the outreach program of the local hospital to sponsor free educational awareness seminars. As the SGA Secretary, you will help prepare a PowerPoint presentation that will be displayed on plasma screens around campus and used in student seminars. You will use Microsoft Office to help with those tasks.

Manage Files and Folders

You will open, review, and save an Excel worksheet providing data on the personal monetary cost of smoking cigarettes over a period of years.

a. Create a folder called **SGA Drive** on the drive where you save your files.

b. Start Excel. Open *f01ccost* from the student data files and save it in the SGA Drive folder as **f01ccost_LastnameFirstname**.

c. Click **cell A10**, and then type your first and last names. Press **Enter**.

Modify Font

To highlight some key figures on the worksheet, you will format those cells with additional font attributes.

a. Draw attention to the high cost of smoking for 10, 20, and 30 years by changing the font color in **cells G3 through I4** to **Red**.

b. Italicize the Annual Cost cells (**F3 and F4**).

c. Click **Undo** on the Quick Access Toolbar to remove the italics. Click **Redo** to return the text to italics.

Insert Clip Art

You will add a clip art image to the worksheet and then resize it and position it.

a. Click **cell G7**, and then insert clip art appropriate for the topic of smoking.

b. Resize the clip art and reposition it near cell B7, if necessary.

c. Click outside the clipart to deselect it. Close the Clip Art task pane.

Preview Print, Change Page Layout, and Print

To get an idea of how the worksheet will look when printed, you will preview the worksheet. Then you will change the orientation and margins before printing it.

a. Preview the document as it will appear when printed.

b. Change the page orientation to **Landscape**. Click the **Page Layout tab**, and then change the margins to **Narrow**.

c. Preview the document as it will appear when printed.

d. Adjust the print settings to print two copies. You will not actually print two copies unless directed by your instructor.

e. Save the workbook and exit Excel.

Find and Replace

You have developed a PowerPoint presentation that you will use to present to student groups and for display on plasma screens across campus. The presentation is designed to increase awareness of the health problems associated with smoking. The PowerPoint presentation has come back from the reviewers with only one comment: A reviewer suggested that you spell out Centers for Disease Control and Prevention, instead of abbreviating it. You do not remember exactly which slide or slides the abbreviation might have been on, so you use Find and Replace to make the change quickly.

a. Start PowerPoint. Open *f01c1quit* and save it in the SGA Drive folder as **f01c1quit_LastnameFirstname**.

b. Replace all occurrences of *CDC* with **Centers for Disease Control and Prevention**.

Cut and Paste and Insert a Text Box

The Mark Twain quote on Slide 1 might be more effective on the last slide in the presentation, so you will cut and paste it there in a text box.

a. On Slide 1, select the entire Mark Twain quote, including the author name, and then cut it.

b. On Slide 22, paste the quote, reposition it more attractively, and then format it in a larger font size.

Check Spelling and Change View

Before you call the presentation complete, you will spell check it and view it as a slide show.

a. Check spelling. The word *hairlike* is not misspelled, so it should not be corrected.

b. View the slide show, and then take the smoking quiz. Click after the last slide to return to the presentation.

c. Save and close the presentation. Exit PowerPoint. Submit both files included in this project as directed by your instructor.

Employment Résumé

GENERAL CASE 

You have recently graduated from a university and are actively seeking employment. You know how important it is to have a comprehensive résumé to include with job applications, so you will use Word to prepare one. Instead of beginning a new document, you will modify a résumé template that is installed with Word. You can locate an appropriate résumé template by clicking the File tab and then clicking New. Select a résumé template from the Office.com area. Save the résumé as **f01b1resume_LastnameFirstname** in an appropriately named folder where you save your student files. Modify the résumé in any way you like, but make sure to complete the following activities:

- Include your name on the résumé. All other information, including address, education, employment history, and job objective, can be fictional.
- Format some text differently. The choice of text is up to you, but you should change font size and type and apply appropriate character attributes to improve the document's appearance.
- Find and replace all occurrences of the word *education* with **academic preparation**.
- Check the document for spelling errors, correcting or ignoring any that you find.
- Change the margins to **1.5″** right and left. Preview the document as it will appear when printed. Save and close the document. Keep Word open.
- Open a new blank document. Create a cover letter that will accompany the résumé. You can use a template for the cover letter if you find an appropriate one. The letter should serve as your introduction, highlighting anything that you think makes you an ideal employee.
- Save the cover letter as **f01b1cover_LastnameFirstname** and exit Word. Submit the file as directed by your instructor.

Fitness Planner

RESEARCH CASE 

Microsoft Excel is an excellent organizational tool. You will use it to maintain a fitness planner. Start Excel. Open *f01b2exercise*, and then save it as **f01b2exercise_LastnameFirstname**. The fitness planner is basically a template, which means that all exercise categories are listed, but without actual data. To personalize the planner to improve its appearance, complete the following activities:

- Change the orientation to **Landscape**. Preview the worksheet as it will appear when printed.
- Move the contents of **cell A2** (*Exercise Planner*) to **cell A1**.
- Click **cell A8**, and then use **Format Painter** to copy the format of that selection to **cells A5 and A6.** Increase the font size of **cell A1** to **26.**
- Use Excel Help to learn how to insert a header. Then insert a header on the worksheet with your first and last names.
- Insert a fitness-related clip art item in **cell A21**, positioning and sizing it so that it is attractive. Click outside the clip art to deselect it.
- Begin the fitness planner, entering at least one activity in each category (warm-up, aerobics, strength, and cool-down). Use **Find and Select** to replace all occurrences of *Exercises* with **Activities.** Save and close the file, and submit as directed by your instructor.

Household Records

You recently received a newsletter from the insurance company with which you have homeowners insurance. An article in the newsletter suggested that you maintain detailed records of your household appliances and other items of value that are in your home. In case of burglary or disaster, an insurance claim is expedited if you are able to itemize what was lost along with identifying information such as serial numbers. You will use Excel to prepare such a list. You will then make a copy of the record on another storage device for safekeeping outside your home (in case your home is destroyed by a fire or weather-related catastrophe).

- Connect a flash drive to your computer, and then close any dialog box that may appear (unless it is informing you of a problem with the drive). Use Windows Explorer to create a folder on the hard drive titled **Home Records.**
- Start Excel. Design a worksheet listing at least five fictional appliances and electronic equipment along with the serial number of each. Design the worksheet in any way you like. Save the workbook as **f01b3household_LastnameFirstname** in the Home Records folder of the hard drive. Close the workbook and exit Excel.
- Use Windows Explorer to copy the Home Records folder from the hard drive to your flash drive. Click the **flash drive** in the Navigation Pane of Windows Explorer. Double-click the **Home Records folder** in the Content pane.
- Click the **Start button**, click **All Programs**, click **Accessories**, and then click **Snipping Tool**. Click the **New arrow**, and then click **Full-screen Snip**. Click **File**, and then click **Save As**. Save the screen display as **f01b3disaster_LastnameFirstname.**
- Close all open windows and submit the files as directed by your instructor.

WORD

1 INTRODUCTION TO WORD

Organizing a Document

Watch the
Set-up Video
for this Case Study!

CASE STUDY | First River Outfitter

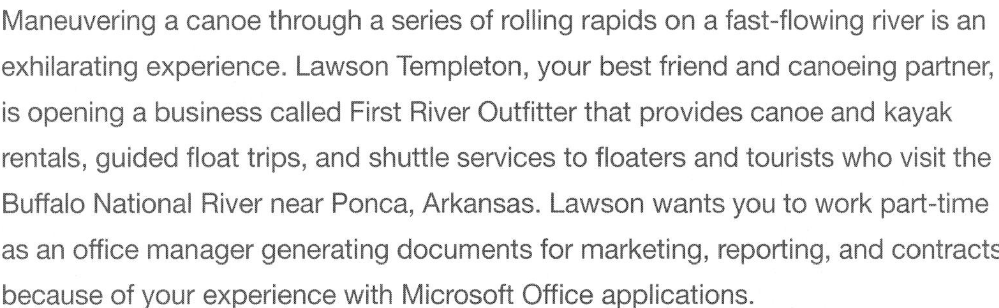

Maneuvering a canoe through a series of rolling rapids on a fast-flowing river is an exhilarating experience. Lawson Templeton, your best friend and canoeing partner, is opening a business called First River Outfitter that provides canoe and kayak rentals, guided float trips, and shuttle services to floaters and tourists who visit the Buffalo National River near Ponca, Arkansas. Lawson wants you to work part-time as an office manager generating documents for marketing, reporting, and contracts because of your experience with Microsoft Office applications.

Preparation for the new business includes acquiring real estate and equipment, but it also demands the development of marketing materials that generate new business. Your first project is to transform the rough draft of a document about river distances, safety precautions, and rental fees into a professional-looking article. This article will not only be posted on the First River Outfitter's Web site, but also printed and mailed to customers after they book a trip or reserve a rental. Your training in Microsoft Office Word 2010 enables you to modify the document easily and efficiently. After you complete the modifications, you both can go float the river!

OBJECTIVES

AFTER YOU READ THIS CHAPTER, YOU WILL BE ABLE TO:

1. Understand how word processors work ***p.69***
2. Customize Word ***p.74***
3. Use features that improve readability ***p.81***
4. Check spelling and grammar ***p.85***
5. Display a document in different views ***p.86***
6. Prepare a document for distribution ***p.94***
7. Modify document properties ***p.99***

Introduction to Word Processing

Word processing software is the most commonly used type of software. You can create letters, reports, research papers, newsletters, brochures, and other documents with Word. You can even create and send e-mail, produce Web pages, and update blogs with Word.

Word processing software, often called a word processor, is the most commonly used type of software. People around the world—students, office assistants, managers, and professionals in all areas—use word processing programs such as Word for a variety of tasks. You can create letters, reports, research papers, newsletters, brochures, and other documents with Word. You can even create and send e-mail, produce Web pages, and update blogs with Word. Figure 1.1 shows examples of documents created in Word.

Word processing software enables you to produce documents such as letters, reports, and research papers.

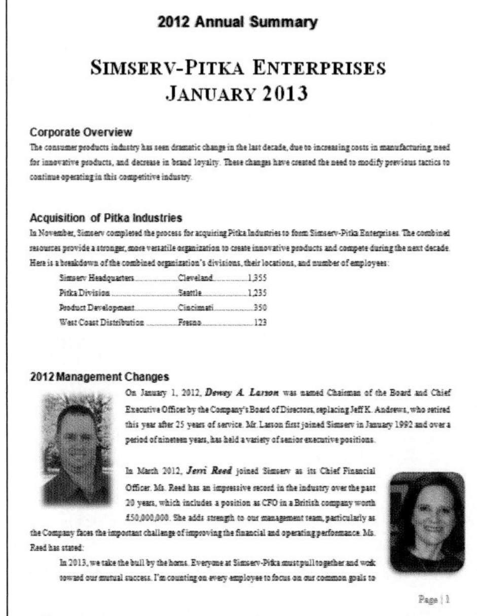

2012 Annual Summary

SIMSERV-PITKA ENTERPRISES
JANUARY 2013

Corporate Overview

The consumer products industry has seen dramatic change in the last decade, due to increasing costs in manufacturing, need for innovative products, and decrease in brand loyalty. These changes have created the need to modify previous tactics to continue operating in this competitive industry.

Acquisition of Pitka Industries

In November, Simserv completed the process for acquiring Pitka Industries to form Simserv-Pitka Enterprises. The combined resources provide a stronger, more versatile organization to create innovative products and compete during the next decade. Here is a breakdown of the combined organization's divisions, their locations, and number of employees:

Simserv Headquarters.......Cleveland.......1,355
Pitka Division.......Seattle.......1,235
Product Development.......Cincinnati.......350
West Coast Distribution.......Fresno.......123

2012 Management Changes

On January 1, 2012, ***Dewey A. Larson*** was named Chairman of the Board and Chief Executive Officer by the Company's Board of Directors, replacing Jeff K. Andrews, who retired this year after 25 years of service. Mr. Larson first joined Simserv in January 1992 and over a period of nineteen years, has held a variety of senior executive positions.

In March 2012, ***Jerri Reed*** joined Simserv as its Chief Financial Officer. Ms. Reed has an impressive record in the industry over the past 20 years, which includes a position as CFO in a British company worth £50,000,000. She adds strength to our management team, particularly as the Company faces the important challenge of improving the financial and operating performance. Ms. Reed has stated:

In 2013, we take the bull by the horns. Everyone at Simserv-Pitka must pull together and work toward our mutual success. I'm counting on every employee to focus on our common goals to

Page | 1

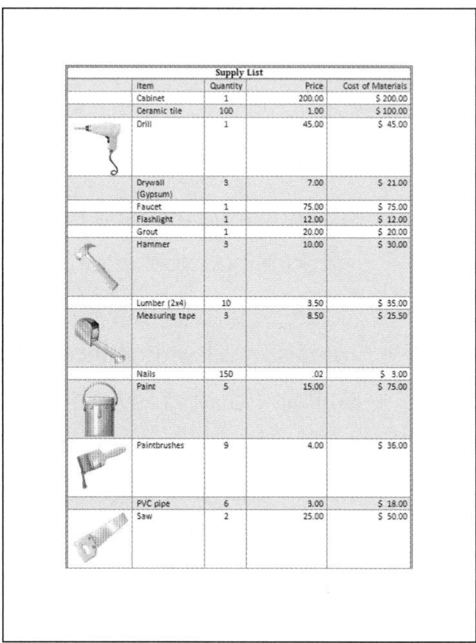

Supply List				
	Item	Quantity	Price	Cost of Materials
	Cabinet	1	200.00	$ 200.00
	Ceramic tile	100	1.00	$ 100.00
	Drill	1	45.00	$ 45.00
	Drywall (Gypsum)	3	7.00	$ 21.00
	Faucet	1	75.00	$ 75.00
	Flashlight	1	12.00	$ 12.00
	Grout	1	20.00	$ 20.00
	Hammer	3	10.00	$ 30.00
	Lumber (2x4)	10	3.50	$ 35.00
	Measuring tape	3	8.50	$ 25.50
	Nails	150	.02	$ 3.00
	Paint	5	15.00	$ 75.00
	Paintbrushes	9	4.00	$ 36.00
	PVC pipe	6	3.00	$ 18.00
	Saw	2	25.00	$ 50.00

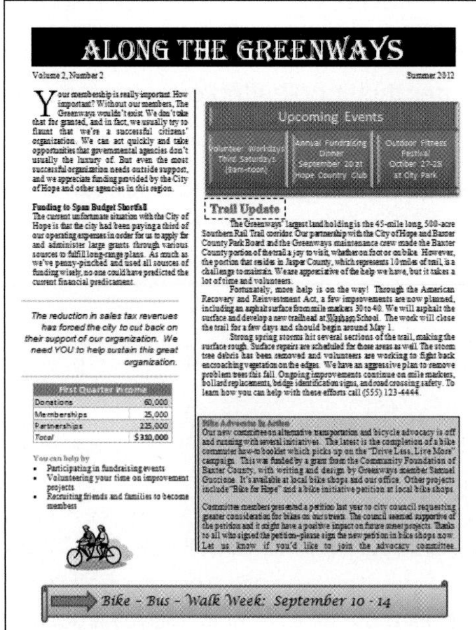

ALONG THE GREENWAYS

Volume 2, Number 2 — Summer 2012

Your membership is really important. How important? Without our members, The Greenways wouldn't exist. We don't take that for granted, and in fact, we usually try to flaunt that we're a successful citizens' organization. We can act quickly and take opportunities that governmental agencies don't usually the luxury of. But even the most successful organization needs outside support, and we appreciate funding provided by the City of Hope and other agencies in this region.

Funding to Span Budget Shortfall

The current unfortunate situation with the City of Hope is that the city had been paying a third of our operating expenses in order for us to apply for and administer large grants through various sources to fulfill long-range plans. As much as we've penny-pinched and used all sources of funding wisely, no one could have predicted the current financial predicament.

The reduction in sales tax revenues has forced the city to cut back on their support of our organization. We need YOU to help sustain this great organization.

First Quarter Income	
Donations	60,000
Memberships	25,000
Partnerships	225,000
Total	$310,000

You can help by

- Participating in fundraising events
- Volunteering your time on improvement projects
- Recruiting friends and families to become members

Upcoming Events

Volunteer Workdays Third Saturdays (8am-noon)
Annual Fundraising Dinner September 20 at Hope Country Club
Outdoor Fitness Festival October 27-28 at City Park

Trail Update

The Greenways' largest land holding is the 45-mile long, 500-acre Southern Rail Trail corridor. Our partnership with the City of Hope and Baxter County Park Board and the Greenways maintenance crew made the Baxter County portion of the trail a joy to visit, whether on foot or on bike. However, the portion that resides in Jasper County, which represents 10 miles of trail, is a challenge to maintain. We are appreciative of the help we have, but it takes a lot of time and volunteers.

Fortunately, more help is on the way! Through the American Recovery and Reinvestment Act, a few improvements are now planned, including an asphalt surface from mile markers 30 to 40. We will asphalt the surface and develop a new trailhead at [illegible] School. The work will close the trail for a few days and should begin around May 1.

Strong spring storms hit several sections of the trail, making the surface rough. Surface repairs are scheduled for those areas as well. The storm tree debris has been removed and volunteers are working to fight back encroaching vegetation on the edges. We have an aggressive plan to remove problem trees this fall. Ongoing improvements continue on mile markers, bollard replacements, bridge identification signs, and road crossing safety. To learn how you can help with these efforts call (555) 123-4444.

Bike Advocates In Action

Our new committee on alternative transportation and bicycle advocacy is off and running with several initiatives. The latest is the completion of a bike commuter how-to booklet which picks up on the "Drive Less, Live More" campaign. This was funded by a grant from the Community Foundation of Baxter County, with writing and design by Greenways member Samuel Guccione. It's available at local bike shops and our office. Other projects include "Bike for Hope" and a bike initiative petition at local bike shops.

Committee members presented a petition last year to city council requesting greater consideration for bikes on our streets. The council seemed supportive of the petition and it might have a positive impact on future street projects. Thanks to all who signed the petition–please sign the new petition in bike shops now. Let us know if you'd like to join the advocacy committee.

Bike - Bus - Walk Week: September 10 - 14

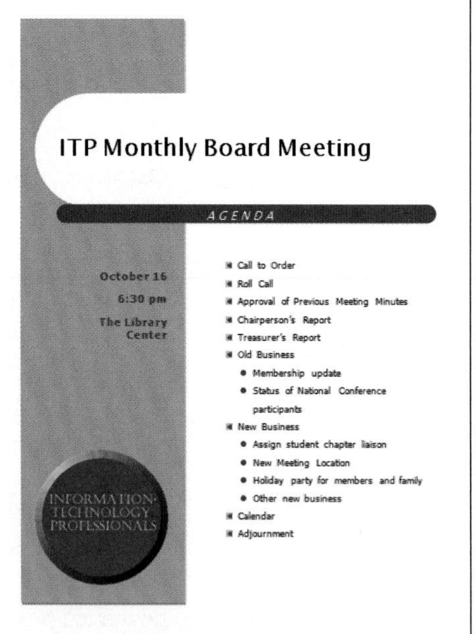

ITP Monthly Board Meeting

AGENDA

October 16
6:30 pm
The Library Center

- Call to Order
- Roll Call
- Approval of Previous Meeting Minutes
- Chairperson's Report
- Treasurer's Report
- Old Business
  - Membership update
  - Status of National Conference participants
- New Business
  - Assign student chapter liaison
  - New Meeting Location
  - Holiday party for members and family
  - Other new business
- Calendar
- Adjournment

INFORMATION TECHNOLOGY PROFESSIONALS

FIGURE 1.1 Versatility of Microsoft Office Word 2010 ➤

Word provides several features that enable you to enhance documents with only a few clicks of the mouse. You can change colors, add interesting styles of text, insert graphics, use a table to present data, track changes made to a document, view comments made about document content, combine several documents into one, and quickly create reference pages such as a table of contents, an index, or a bibliography.

This chapter provides a broad-based introduction to word processing and Word in general. All word processors adhere to certain basic concepts that must be understood to use the program effectively.

In this section, you will learn about the Word interface and word wrap. You will also learn how to move around quickly in a document and how to turn features on and off quickly by toggling. Finally, you will learn about breaks in a document, how to add page numbers, how to insert cover pages quickly, and how to customize Word.

Understanding How Word Processors Work

The Exploring series authors used Word to write this book. You will use Word to complete the exercises in this chapter. When you start Word, your screen might look different than the screen shown in Figure 1.2. This is because the commands are customizable, and elements that display will be affected. However, you should recognize the basic elements emphasized in Figure 1.2.

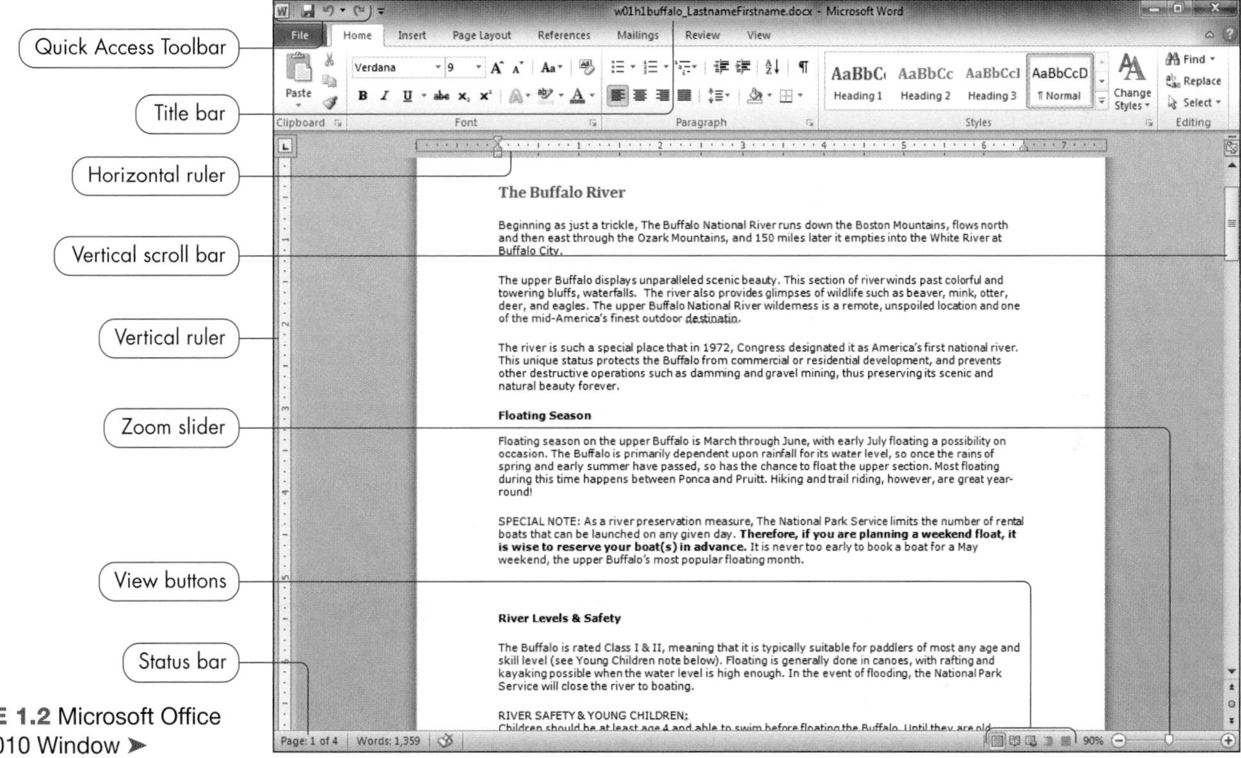

FIGURE 1.2 Microsoft Office Word 2010 Window ➤

When Word opens, several basic features are available. These features include the Ribbon, the Quick Access Toolbar, vertical and horizontal scroll bars, and the status bar, which you learned about in the Office Fundamentals chapter. The status bar at the bottom of the window displays information about the open Word document such as the page number where the insertion point is currently positioned, the total number of pages in the document, and the total number of words in the document.

Learn About Word Wrap

Whether you are new to using a word processor or have been using one for a period of time, you will notice that certain functions seem to happen automatically. As you type, you probably do not think about how much text can fit on one line or where the sentences roll from

Word wrap moves words to the next line if they do not fit on the current line.

A **hard return** is created when you press Enter to move the insertion point to a new line.

A **soft return** is created by the word processor as it wraps text to a new line.

one line to the other. Fortunately, Word takes care of that for you. This feature is called ***word wrap*** and enables you to type continuously without pressing Enter at the end of a line within a paragraph. The only time you press Enter is when you want the insertion point to move to the next line.

Word wrap is closely associated with another concept: the hard and soft return. A ***hard return*** is created when you press Enter at the end of a line or paragraph. A ***soft return*** is created by the word processor as it wraps text from one line to the next. The locations of the soft returns change automatically as text is inserted or deleted. Only the user, who must intentionally insert or delete each hard return, can change the location of such returns.

The paragraphs at the top of Figure 1.3 show two hard returns, one at the end of each paragraph. Figure 1.3 also includes four soft returns in the first paragraph (one at the end of every line except the last) and three soft returns in the second paragraph. Now, assume the margins in the document are made smaller (that is, the line is made longer), as shown in the bottom paragraphs of Figure 1.3. The number of soft returns decreases as more text fits on a line and fewer lines are needed. The revised document still contains the two original hard returns—one at the end of each paragraph.

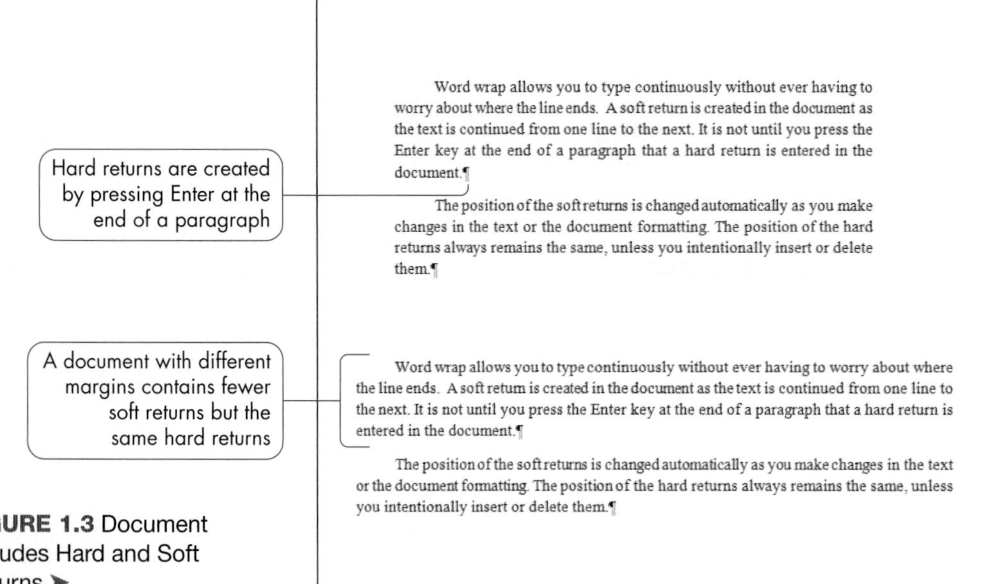

FIGURE 1.3 Document Includes Hard and Soft Returns ➤

Use Keyboard Shortcuts to Move Around a Document

The horizontal and vertical scrollbars and the scroll arrows are frequently used to view different pages in a document. However, clicking the scrollbars or arrows does not move the insertion point; it merely lets you see different parts of the document and leaves the insertion point where it was last positioned. To move the insertion point in a document you use the mouse or the keyboard. Table 1.1 shows useful keyboard shortcuts for navigating a document and relocating the insertion point.

TABLE 1.1 Keyboard Navigation Controls

Keys	Moves the Insertion Point	Keys	Moves the Insertion Point
←	One character to the left	**Ctrl+Home**	To the beginning of the document
→	One character to the right	**Ctrl+End**	To the end of the document
↑	Up one line	**Ctrl+←**	One word to the left
↓	Down one line	**Ctrl+→**	One word to the right
Home	To the beginning of the line	**Ctrl+↑**	Up one paragraph
End	To the end of the line	**Ctrl+↓**	Down one paragraph
Page Up	Up to the previous page	**Ctrl+Page Up**	To the top of the previous page
Page Down	Down to the next page	**Ctrl+Page Down**	To the top of the next page

Discover Toggle Switches

To **toggle** is to switch from one setting to another.

A ***toggle***, when pressed or clicked, causes the computer to switch from one setting to another. Caps Lock is an example of a toggle button. Each time you press it, newly typed text will change from uppercase to lowercase, or vice versa. In the Office Fundamentals chapter you read about other toggle buttons. Sometimes you can invoke a toggle by pressing keys on the keyboard, such as Caps Lock. You invoke many toggle features, such as the Bold, Italic, and Underline commands, by clicking a combination of keys or a ribbon command to turn the feature on and off.

The **Show/Hide feature** reveals where formatting marks, such as spaces, tabs, and returns, are used in the document.

A toggle that enables you to reveal formatting applied to a document is the ***Show/Hide feature***. Click Show/Hide (¶) in the Paragraph group on the Home tab to reveal where formatting marks, such as spaces, tabs, and hard returns, are in the document. Figure 1.4 displays formatting marks when the Show/Hide (¶) feature is on.

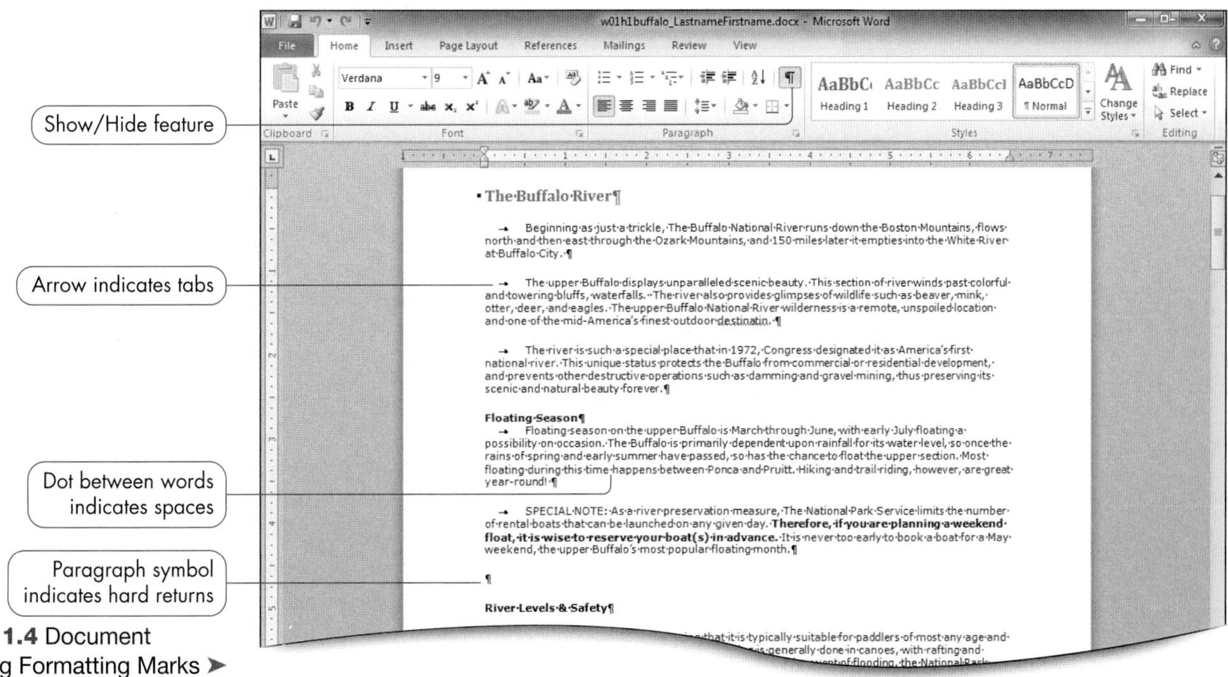

FIGURE 1.4 Document Displaying Formatting Marks ➤

Insert Page Breaks

A **soft page break** is inserted when text fills an entire page, then continues onto the next page.

When you type more text than can fit on a page, Word continues the text on another page using soft and hard page breaks. The ***soft page break*** is a hidden marker that automatically continues text on the top of a new page when text no longer fits on the current page. These breaks adjust automatically when you add and delete text. For the most part, you rely on soft page breaks to prepare multiple-page documents. However, at times you need to start a new page before Word inserts a soft page break.

A **hard page break** forces the next part of a document to begin on a new page.

When this occurs, you can insert a ***hard page break***, a hidden marker, to force text to begin on a new page. You can insert a hard page break into a document using the Breaks command in the Page Setup group on the Page Layout tab or using Page Break in the Pages group on the Insert tab. To view the page break markers in Print Layout view you must click Show/Hide (¶) on the Home tab to toggle on the formatting marks, as shown in Figure 1.5. You can view the page break markers without Show/Hide toggled on when you switch to Draft view.

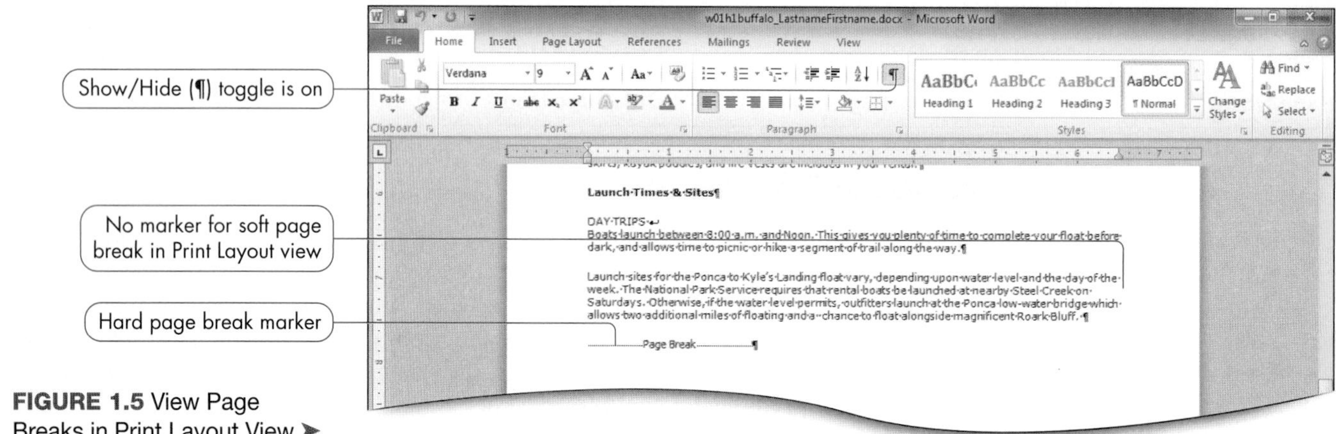

FIGURE 1.5 View Page Breaks in Print Layout View ➤

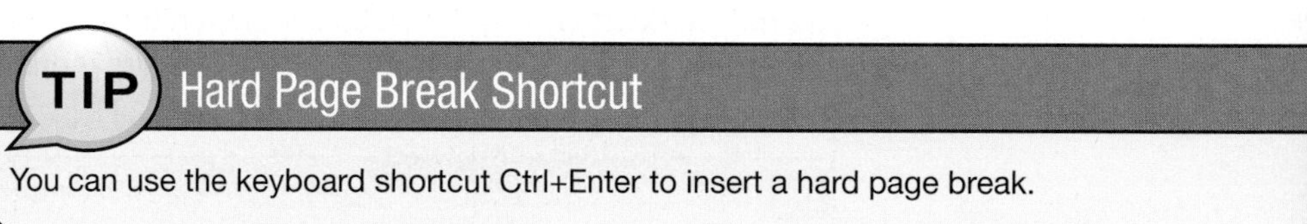

TIP Hard Page Break Shortcut

You can use the keyboard shortcut Ctrl+Enter to insert a hard page break.

Add Page Numbers

Page numbers are essential in long documents. They serve as convenient reference points for the writer and reader. If you do not include page numbers in a long document, you will have difficulty trying to find text on a particular page or trying to tell someone where to locate a particular passage in the document. Have you ever tried to reassemble a long document without page numbers that was out of order? It can be very frustrating, and it makes a good case for inserting page numbers in your documents.

The Page Number command in the Header & Footer group on the Insert tab is the easiest way to place page numbers in a document. When you use this feature, Word not only inserts page numbers, but also automatically adjusts the page numbers when you add or delete pages. Page numbers can appear at the top or bottom of a page in the header or footer areas, and can be left, center, or right aligned. Word 2010 provides several options for formatting page numbers. Your decision on where to place page numbers might stem from personal preference, the writing specifications for your paper, or other information you must include with the page number. Figure 1.6 displays a few gallery options for placing a page number at the bottom of a page.

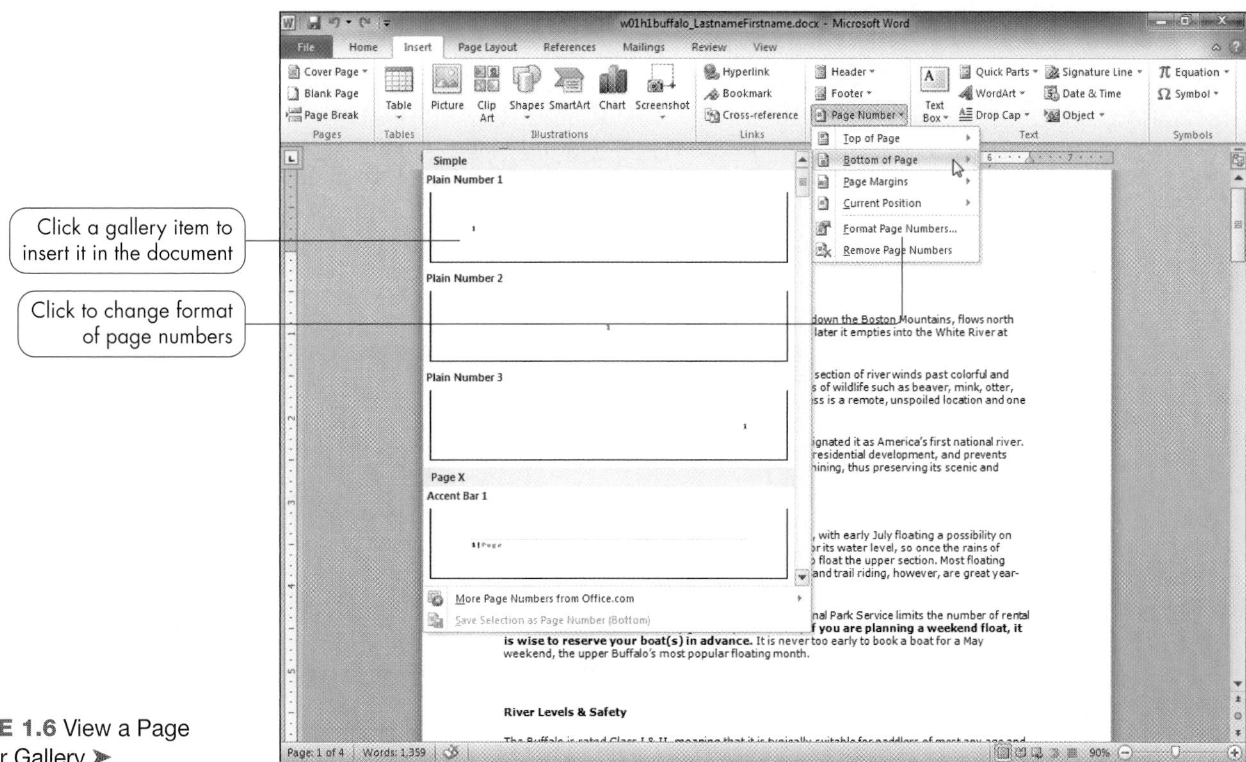

FIGURE 1.6 View a Page Number Gallery ➤

Word enables you to customize the format of page numbers. For example, at the beginning of a document you can use Roman numerals instead of Arabic numerals for preface pages. You also can adjust the page numbering so that it starts numbering on a page other than the first. This is useful when you have a report with a cover page; you typically do not consider the cover as page one and therefore begin numbering the page that follows it. You use the Format Page Number feature to display the Page Number Format dialog box (see Figure 1.7). If you are not satisfied with the page numbering in a document, use the Remove Page Numbers command to remove them.

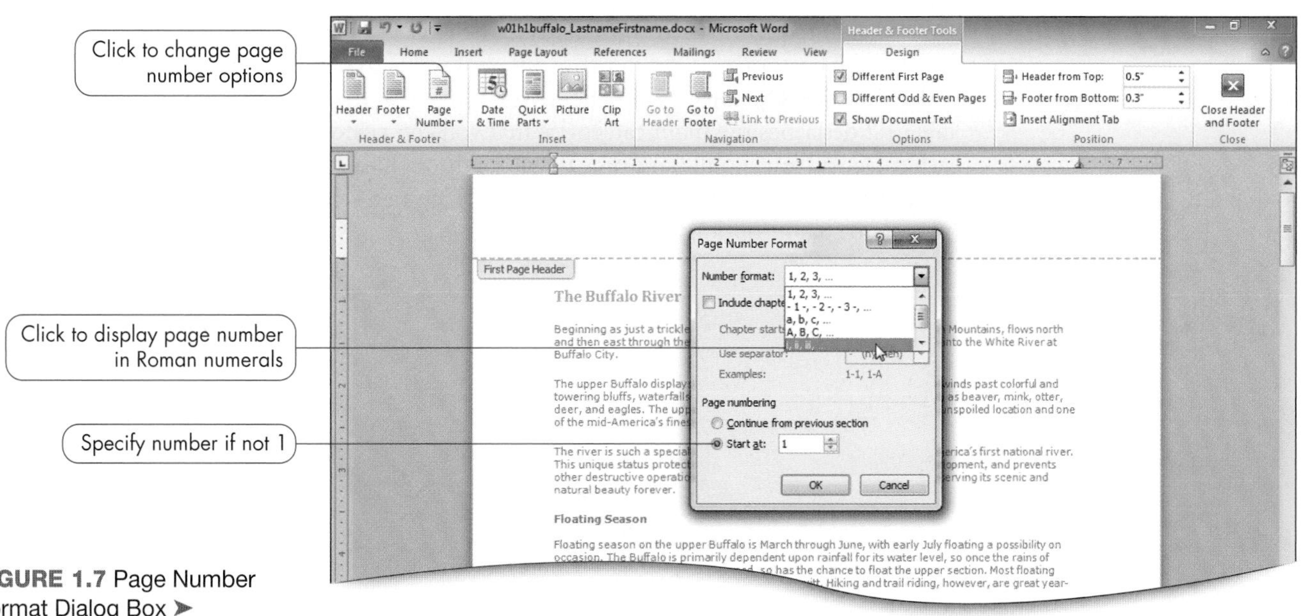

FIGURE 1.7 Page Number Format Dialog Box ➤

Insert a Cover Page

You can use commands such as page break and keystrokes such as Ctrl+Enter to insert a blank page to use as a cover page for a document. Word 2010 also offers a feature to quickly insert a preformatted cover page into your document. The Cover Page feature in the Pages group on the Insert tab includes a gallery with several designs, as shown in Figure 1.8. Each design includes fields such as Document Title, Company Name, Date, and Author, which you can personalize or remove. After you personalize this feature, your document will include an attractive cover page.

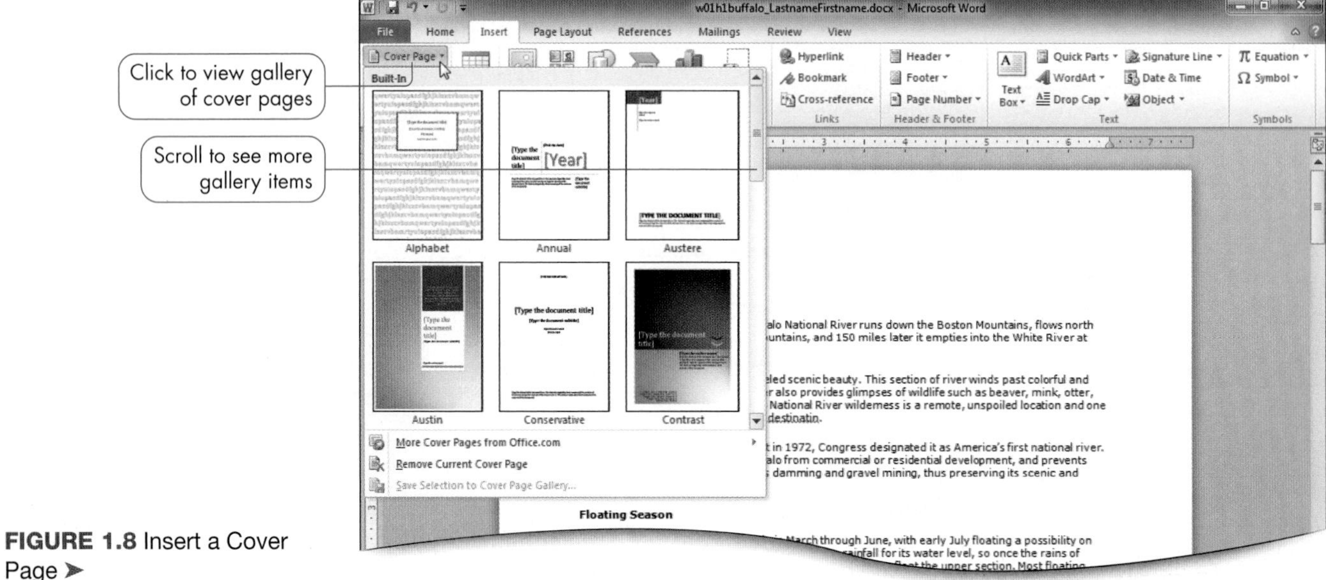

FIGURE 1.8 Insert a Cover Page ➤

Customizing Word

As installed, Word is immediately useful. However, you might find options that you would prefer to customize, add, or remove from the document window. For example, you can add commands to the Quick Access Toolbar (QAT) that do not currently display on any tab. You can also add frequently used commands to the QAT.

You can customize Word in many different ways. To begin the process, click the File tab, and then click Options. From there, you can view the options that are customizable. Table 1.2 describes the main categories that you can customize and some of the features in each category. You should take time to glance through each category as you continue to read this chapter. Keep in mind that if you are working in a school lab, you might not have permission to change options permanently.

TABLE 1.2 Word Options

Menu Category	Description	Sample of Options to Change
General	Change options that customize the window area and identify the user.	Show Mini toolbar; show Enhanced ScreenTips; change color scheme; change user name and initials.
Display	Change how documents are displayed on the screen and in print.	Show white space between pages in Print Layout view; always show formatting marks such as spaces on the screen; print document properties.
Proofing	Modify how Word corrects and formats your text.	Ignore words in uppercase (don't flag as incorrect in your text); use spelling checker; use contextual spelling and mark grammatical errors.
Save	Customize how documents are saved.	Default locations and format to save files; AutoRecover file location; Web server location.
Language	Set preference for one or more languages to use, which also invokes supporting resources such as dictionaries and grammar checking.	Editing language, language priority order.
Advanced	Specify editing options; cut, copy, and paste options; show document content options; display options; print options; and save options.	Enable text to be dragged and dropped; enable click and type; default paragraph style; show paste option buttons; show smart tags; number of recent documents to show in file menu; print pages in reverse order; always create backup copy; embed smart tags; update automatic links at open; compatibility options.
Customize Ribbon	Customize the existing Ribbon or create a new tab.	Add or remove tasks from the default tabs; create a new tab; reset all tabs to default tasks.
Quick Access Toolbar	Customize the Quick Access Toolbar and other keyboard shortcuts.	Add or remove buttons from the QAT; determine location of QAT; customize keyboard shortcuts.
Add-Ins	View the add-ins previously installed, customize settings for add-ins, and install more add-ins.	View settings for active and inactive application add-ins; manage smart tags, templates, and disabled items.
Trust Center	View online documentation about security and privacy and change settings to protect documents from possible infections.	Enable and disable macros; change ActiveX settings; set privacy options; select trusted publishers and locations.

As you can see, you are able to customize dozens of settings in Word. Table 1.2 offers only a small sample of what can be customized. You may not need to make any changes at all! But as you become more familiar with features in Word, you may want to use options to customize the application to fit your specific needs.

HANDS-ON EXERCISES

1 Introduction to Word Processing

As the new office manager for First River Outfitter, you must preview the document Lawson drafted for use as a marketing brochure. You will proofread the current document and make modifications to improve readability and the way the document looks in print.

Skills covered: Use Keyboard Shortcuts to Navigate a Document and Insert a Page Break • Insert a Page Number • Add a Cover Page and Revise Page Numbers • Change Word Options

STEP 1 USE KEYBOARD SHORTCUTS TO NAVIGATE A DOCUMENT AND INSERT A PAGE BREAK

When you open the file that contains information about the Buffalo River, you look to see if paragraph breaks are in odd places, making the content difficult to read. When you find them, you insert page breaks to improve readability. Refer to Figure 1.9 as you complete Step 1.

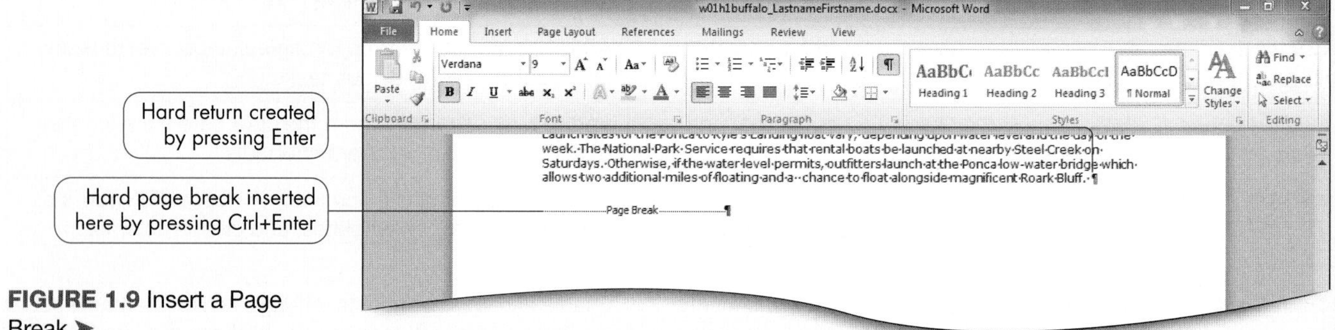

FIGURE 1.9 Insert a Page Break ➤

FYI

a. Start Word. Open *w01h1buffalo* and save it as **w01h1buffalo_LastnameFirstname.**

> **TROUBLESHOOTING:** If you make any major mistakes in this exercise, you can close the file, open *w01h1buffalo* again, and then start this exercise over.

When you save files, use your last and first names. For example, as the Word author, I would name my document w01h1buffalo_HulettMichelle.

> **TIP** Save and Save Again
>
> You should practice saving your files often. If you open a document and you do not want to change its name or where it is stored, the easiest way to save it is to click Save on the Quick Access Toolbar. You can also click the File tab and then click Save, or you can press the keyboard command Ctrl+S to save quickly and often.

b. Press **Page Down** five times, stopping on each page to view the document contents. Press **Ctrl+Home** to return to the top of the document.

c. Scroll down until you can view the last line of the second page.

d. Click **Show/Hide** (¶) in the Paragraph group on the Home tab.

This toggle enables you to see exactly where the paragraphs and other text break on each line and across pages.

e. Click to the left of the *Glass, Trash, & Other Regulations* paragraph title.

This paragraph begins at the bottom of page 2 and continues to the top of page 3. It would be best if the heading and each paragraph below the heading displays together on one page, so inserting a hard return will move them all together.

f. Press **Ctrl+Enter** to insert a hard page break.

The hard page break is marked as a Page Break. Now the paragraph heading displays on the same page as the paragraph, as shown in Figure 1.9.

g. Click **Save** in the Quick Access Toolbar.

STEP 2 INSERT A PAGE NUMBER

The next step you take to improve readability of this document is the addition of page numbers. If someone prints the document and the pages become scattered, he or she should be able to use page numbers to reassemble it in the proper order. Refer to Figure 1.10 as you complete Step 2.

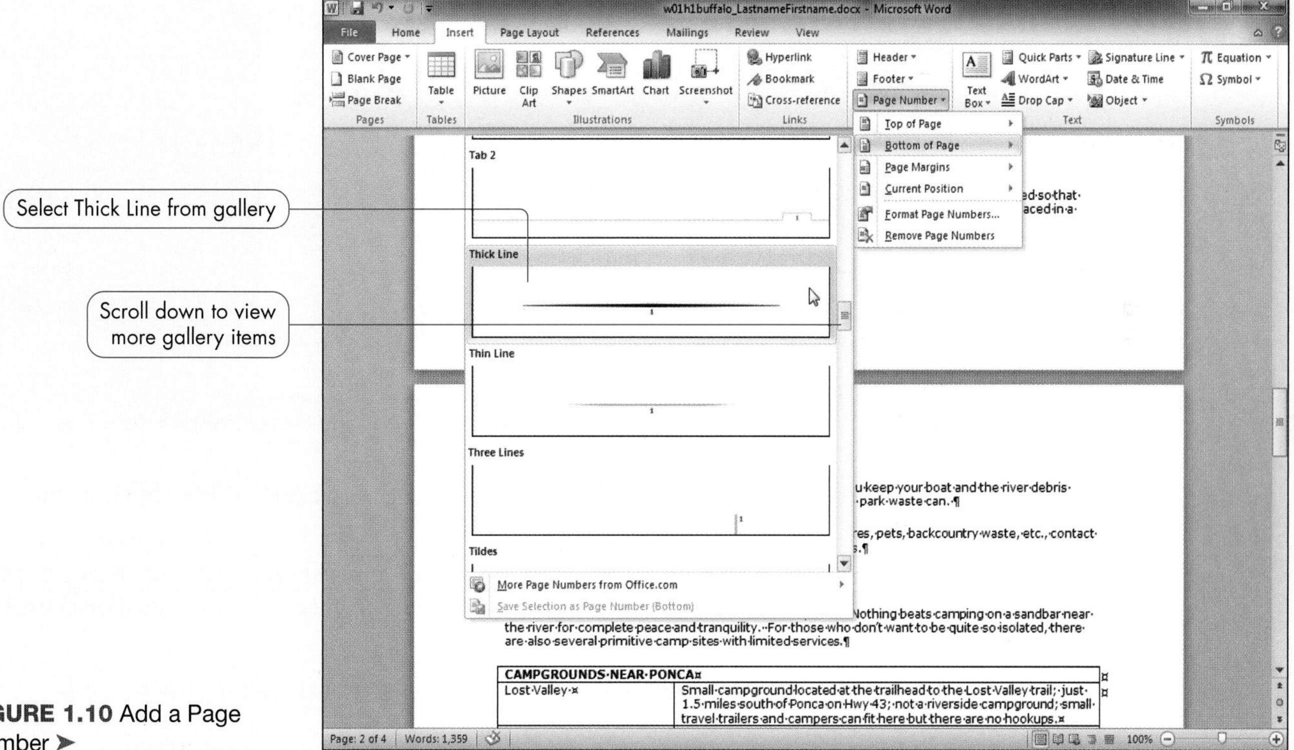

FIGURE 1.10 Add a Page Number ➤

a. Click the **Insert tab**. Click **Page Number** in the Header & Footer group, and then point to **Bottom of Page**. Scroll down the gallery, and then click **Thick Line**, as shown in Figure 1.10.

A dark line and the page number display on the bottom of each page. The Header & Footer Tools tab displays in the Ribbon area.

b. Click the **Footer from Bottom arrow** in the Position group until **0.3** displays.

You make this modification to enable the footer to rest closer to the bottom of the page and reduce the white space that displays. Reducing this number is one way to utilize the paper more efficiently and display more text on a page. In the case of very long documents, this can reduce the number of sheets of paper used for printing.

c. Click **Close Header and Footer**. Click the **Home tab**, and then click **Show/Hide** (¶) in the paragraph group to turn off formatting marks.

d. Press **Ctrl+S** to save the document.

STEP 3 ADD A COVER PAGE AND REVISE PAGE NUMBERS

Because you are working with a document that will be used for advertising purposes, you want to add an attractive cover page. You will use a Word feature to insert a cover page very quickly and easily. You will then make adjustments to the page numbering to reflect the addition of the cover page. Refer to Figure 1.11 as you complete Step 3.

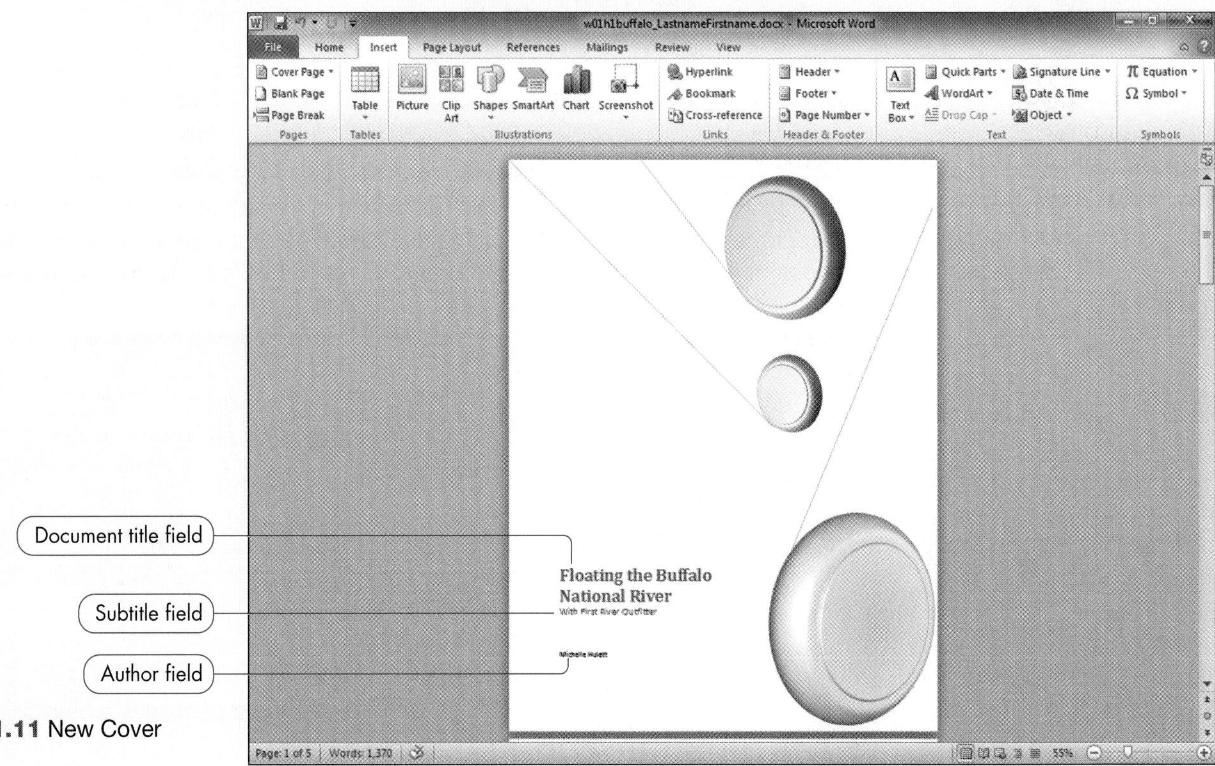

FIGURE 1.11 New Cover Page ➤

a. Click the **Insert tab**, click **Cover Page** in the Pages group, and then click **Mod** from the gallery.

Now that the cover page displays, the rest of the document begins at the top of page 2. The insertion point does not have to be at the beginning of a document to insert a cover page; it inserts automatically as the first page.

b. Type **Floating the Buffalo National River** to replace the text *Type the document title.*

TROUBLESHOOTING: If you begin to type and the existing text remains, just click inside the title area to position your cursor there, and then begin to type. You can also scroll to select the existing text, and then replace it when you type.

c. Press **Tab** to select the **Subtitle field**, and then replace the text *Type the document subtitle* with **with First River Outfitter**. Replace the capital *W* with a lower case *w* on the word *with*, if necessary.

When you fill in the document subtitle, Word automatically capitalizes the first letter of the first word. In this case, it is inappropriate to capitalize the word *with*, so you must revise the subtitle to remove the capitalization.

d. Right-click the **Abstract field** below the subtitle, and then select **Cut.** Press **Tab** two times to select the **Author field**, and then type your name. Right-click the **Date field**, and then select **Cut.** Compare your cover page to Figure 1.11.

e. Look at the status bar at the bottom of the page to determine the page where the insertion point is located. If necessary, scroll to page 2, and then double-click the white space at the top of the second page to place your insertion point in the header.

   Notice that the Different First Page option is selected in the Options group on the Header & Footer Tools Design tab. The cover page you created does not require a header or footer, and this setting prevents them from displaying on the first page. This setting is checked automatically when you insert a cover page.

f. Click **Close Header and Footer.**

   When you scroll to view the bottom of the second page, the number 1 displays.

g. Save the document.

STEP 4 CHANGE WORD OPTIONS

You remember that the Word Options dialog box has a few settings that you want to change or confirm. First, you want to make sure your name is applied to this installation of Word. Your next concern is that backups occur in a timely manner so that you will lose minimal information in the event of a system crash; therefore, you decide to reduce the time between backups. You often preview your document to see how it looks for printing, so you add the Print Preview command to the Quick Access Toolbar. Refer to Figure 1.12 as you complete Step 4.

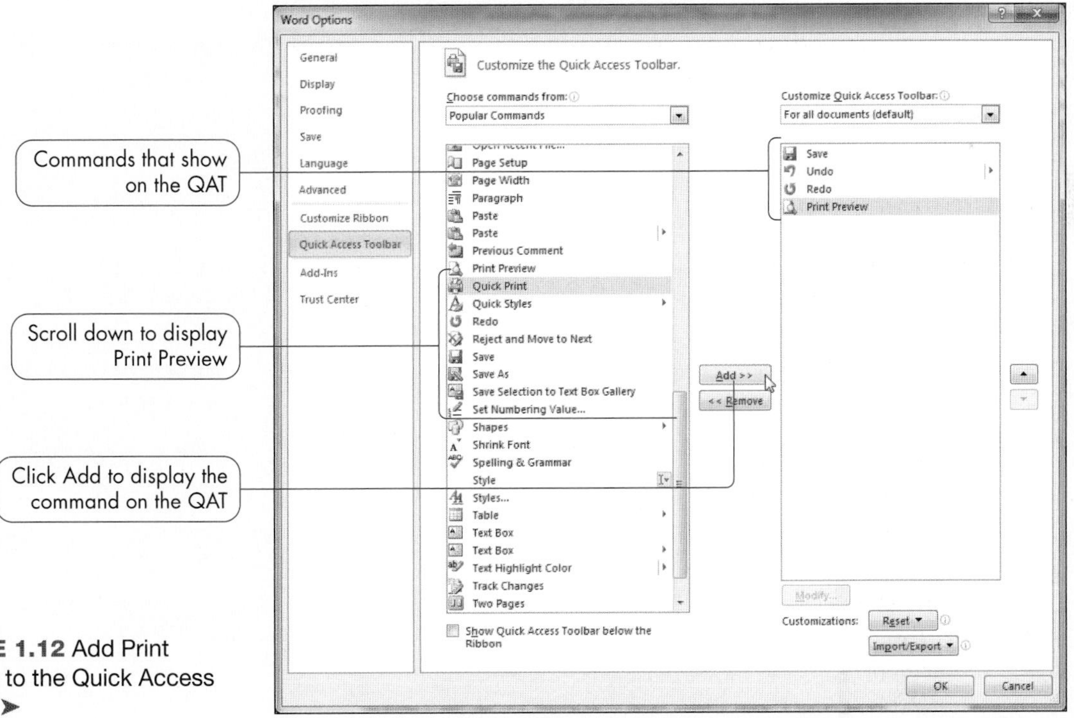

FIGURE 1.12 Add Print Preview to the Quick Access Toolbar ➤

a. Click the **File tab**, and then click **Options** near the bottom of the menu.

b. Type your name in the **User name box** that displays in the General category of options.

   When you change this setting, your name is attached to a file as the author of that document. Other features presented later also use this setting.

c. Click **Save** on the left side of the Word Options dialog box. Reduce the time that currently displays next to *Save AutoRecover information every 10 minutes* to **3**.

   You do a lot of work within the time span of a few minutes, so you may prefer to have the backups happen every three minutes instead of every ten minutes.

d. Click **Quick Access Toolbar** on the left side of the Word Options dialog box.

e. Scroll down the list of commands on the left side until *Print Preview and Print* displays. Click **Print Preview and Print**, and then click **Add** to copy the Print Preview and Print command, as shown in Figure 1.12.

f. Click **OK** to close the Word Options dialog box.

   The Print Preview and Print command now displays on the Quick Access Toolbar at the top of the page on the title bar.

TROUBLESHOOTING: If you work in a lab environment, you might not have permission to modify the Word settings. Accept any error messages you might see when saving the Word options, and then proceed to the next step.

g. Save the document and keep it onscreen if you plan to continue with the next Hands-On Exercise. If not, close the document, and then exit Word.

Document Organization

Throughout your college and professional career, you will create a variety of documents. As you compose and edit you want to set the documents up so that some parts display differently than others when you view or print them. Word has settings that enable you to segment a document just for this purpose.

In this section, you will learn how to make changes to a Word document, such as inserting section breaks, adding headers and footers, and displaying watermarks. You will also learn about features that help you monitor spelling and grammar, and you will learn about different view modes.

Using Features That Improve Readability

When you create a document you consider the content you will insert, but you also should consider how you want the document to look when you print or display it. Many of the settings you use for this purpose are on the Page Layout tab. For example, when you create a short business letter, you want to increase the margins to a width such as 1.5″ on all sides, so the letter contents are balanced on the printed page. If you print a formal or research paper, you want to use a 1.5″ left margin and a 1″ right margin to provide extra room on the left for binding.

When you create a document, you consider the content you will insert, but you also should consider how you want the document to look when you print or display it.

Another setting to consider for a document is orientation. Most documents, such as letters and research papers, use portrait orientation. However, a brochure, large graphic, chart, or table might display better on a page with landscape orientation.

If you need to print a document on special paper, such as legal size (8½″ x 14″) paper or an envelope, you should select the paper size before you create the document text. The Size command in the Page Setup group on the Page Layout tab contains several different document sizes that you can use. If you have special paper requirements, you can select More Paper Sizes to enter your own custom size. If you do not select the special size before you print, you will waste paper and find yourself with a very strange-looking printout.

Insert Headers and Footers

A **header** is information that displays at the top of each document page.

A **footer** is information that displays at the bottom of each document page.

Headers and footers give a professional appearance to a document. A ***header*** consists of one or more lines at the top of each page. A ***footer*** displays at the bottom of each page. The advantage of using a header or footer is to specify the content only once, after which it appears automatically on all pages. Although you can type the text yourself at the top or bottom of every page, it is time-consuming, and the possibility of making a mistake is great. You also can insert a field, such as a page number or file name, and Word will automatically insert the correct information. A document may display headers but not footers, footers but not headers, both headers and footers, or neither. A page number is a simple header or footer and can be created by clicking Page Number, selecting the location where it will display, and selecting the style you prefer. Footers might also contain the date the document was created or the file name. Headers might contain the name of an organization, the author, or the title of the document. Take a moment to notice the type of information you see in the headers and footers of the books or magazines you are reading.

Headers and footers are added from the Insert tab and are formatted like any other paragraph. They can be center, left, or right aligned. You can format headers and footers in any typeface or point size and can include special fields to insert automatically information such as author, date, or time a document is saved. The content of the headers and footers is adjusted for changes in page breaks caused by modifications to the body of the document. This happens most often for page numbers because the addition or deletion of information in a document can alter the page numbering.

Word 2010 offers many built-in formatting options that enable you to add a professional look quickly. It also enables you to control how headers and footers display throughout a document. These options display on the Header & Footer Tools Design tab (see Figure 1.13). For instance, you can specify a different header or footer for the first page; this is advisable when you have a cover page and do not want the header (or footer) to display on that page. You can also have different headers and footers for odd and even pages. This feature is useful when you plan to print a document that will be bound as a book. Notice the different information this book prints on the footer of odd versus even pages and how the page numbers display in the corners of each page. If you want to change the header (or footer) midway through a document, you need to insert a section break at the point where the new header (or footer) is to begin. These breaks are discussed in the next section.

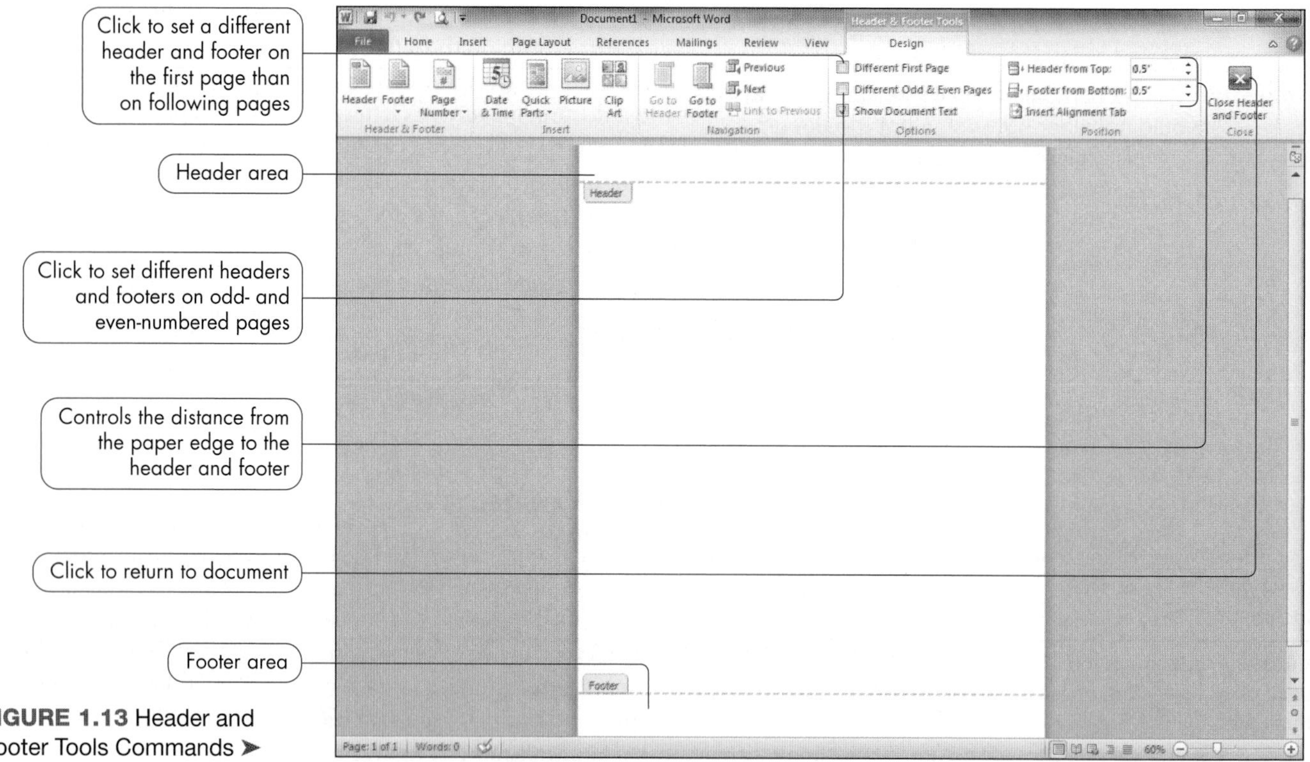

FIGURE 1.13 Header and Footer Tools Commands ➤

Create Sections

Formatting in Word occurs on three levels: character, paragraph, and section. Formatting at the section level controls headers and footers, page numbering, page size and orientation, margins, and columns. Most documents you work with, unless intentionally changed, probably consist of a single section, and thus any formatting is applied to the entire document. You can, however, divide a document into sections and format each section independently.

A **section break** is a marker that divides a document into sections, thereby enabling different formatting in each section.

You determine where one section ends and another begins by clicking Breaks in the Page Setup group on the Page Layout tab. A ***section break*** is a marker that divides a document into sections. It enables you to control where text is placed and how it will be formatted on the printed page; that is, you can specify that text in the new section displays on the same page or on a new page. Formatting at the section level gives you the ability to create more sophisticated documents. Word stores the formatting characteristics of each section within the section break at the end of a section. Thus, deleting a section break also deletes the section formatting, causing the text above the break to assume the formatting characteristics of the next section.

Word has four types of section breaks, as shown in Table 1.3.

TABLE 1.3 Section Breaks

Type	Description	Example
Next Page	When inserted, text that follows must begin at the top of the next page.	Use to force a chapter to start at the top of a page.
Continuous	When inserted, text that follows can continue on the same page.	Use to format text in the middle of the page into columns.
Even Page	When inserted, text that follows must begin at the top of the next even-numbered page.	Use to force a chapter to begin at the top of an even-numbered page.
Odd Page	When inserted, text that follows must begin at the top of the next odd-numbered page.	Use to force a chapter to begin at the top of an odd-numbered page.

When you use section breaks, you can do the following:

- Change the margins within a multipage letter, where the section containing only the first page (the letterhead) requires a larger top margin than the other pages in the letter.
- Change the orientation in one section from portrait to landscape to accommodate a wide table or graphic in the middle or end of the document.
- Change the page numbering in one section to use Roman numerals for a table of contents and Arabic numerals thereafter on pages in remaining sections.
- Change the number of columns in a newsletter, which may contain a section with a single column at the top of a page for the masthead and another section with two or three columns in the body of the newsletter.

Figure 1.14 displays the last page of the Buffalo River document. The document has been divided into two sections, and the insertion point is currently on the last page of the document, which is also the first page of the second section. Note the difference in page number on the footer and in the status bar.

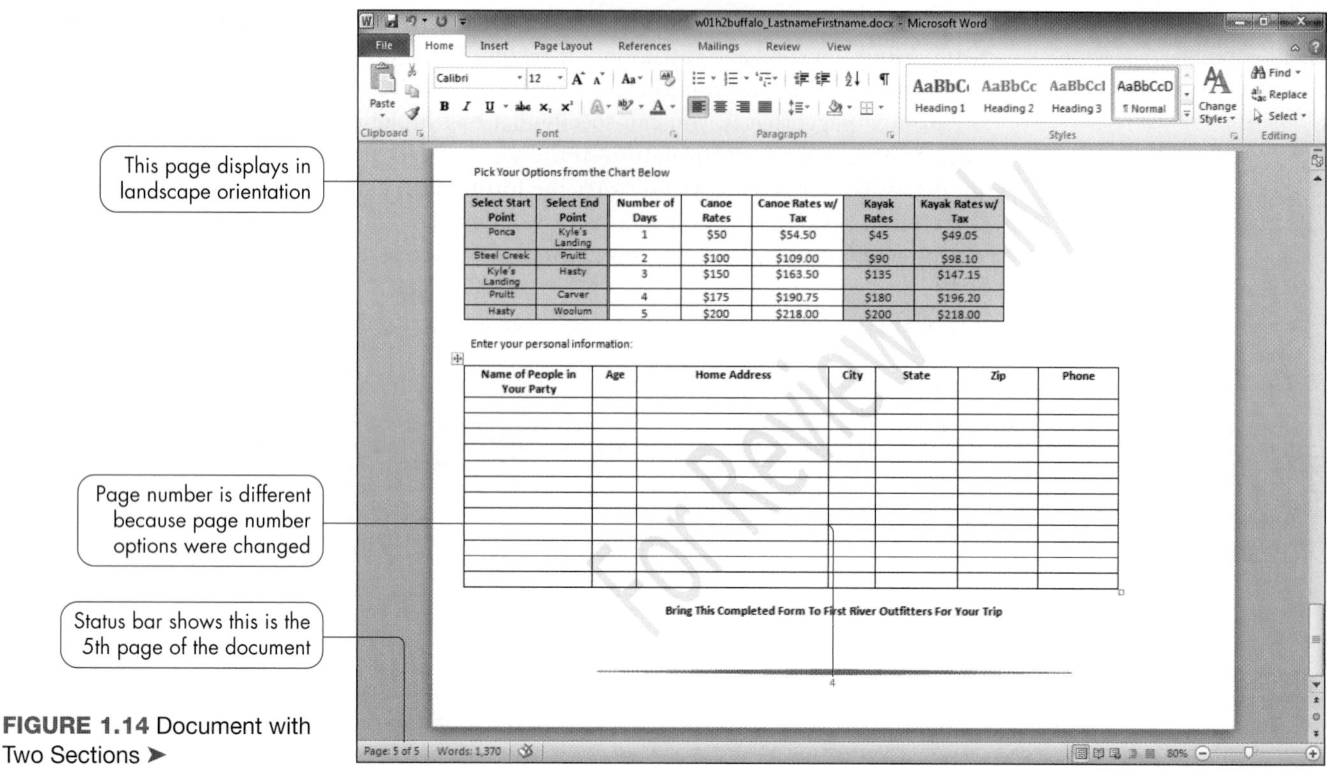

Select Start Point	Select End Point	Number of Days	Canoe Rates	Canoe Rates w/ Tax	Kayak Rates	Kayak Rates w/ Tax
Ponca	Kyle's Landing	1	$50	$54.50	$45	$49.05
Steel Creek	Pruitt	2	$100	$109.00	$90	$98.10
Kyle's Landing	Hasty	3	$150	$163.50	$135	$147.15
Pruitt	Carver	4	$175	$190.75	$180	$196.20
Hasty	Woolum	5	$200	$218.00	$200	$218.00

Name of People in Your Party	Age	Home Address	City	State	Zip	Phone

FIGURE 1.14 Document with Two Sections ➤

When a document has multiple sections, the Link to Previous feature in the Header & Footer Tools tab is important to consider. If you want page numbering to continue sequentially so the numbering is not interrupted from section to section, activate the Link to Previous toggle. It displays with an orange color when active. If you want to restart page numbering when a section changes, turn off the Link to Previous toggle. Additionally, you can move from the header or footer of one section to another section by clicking Next or Previous in the Navigation group on the Design tab, as shown in Figure 1.15.

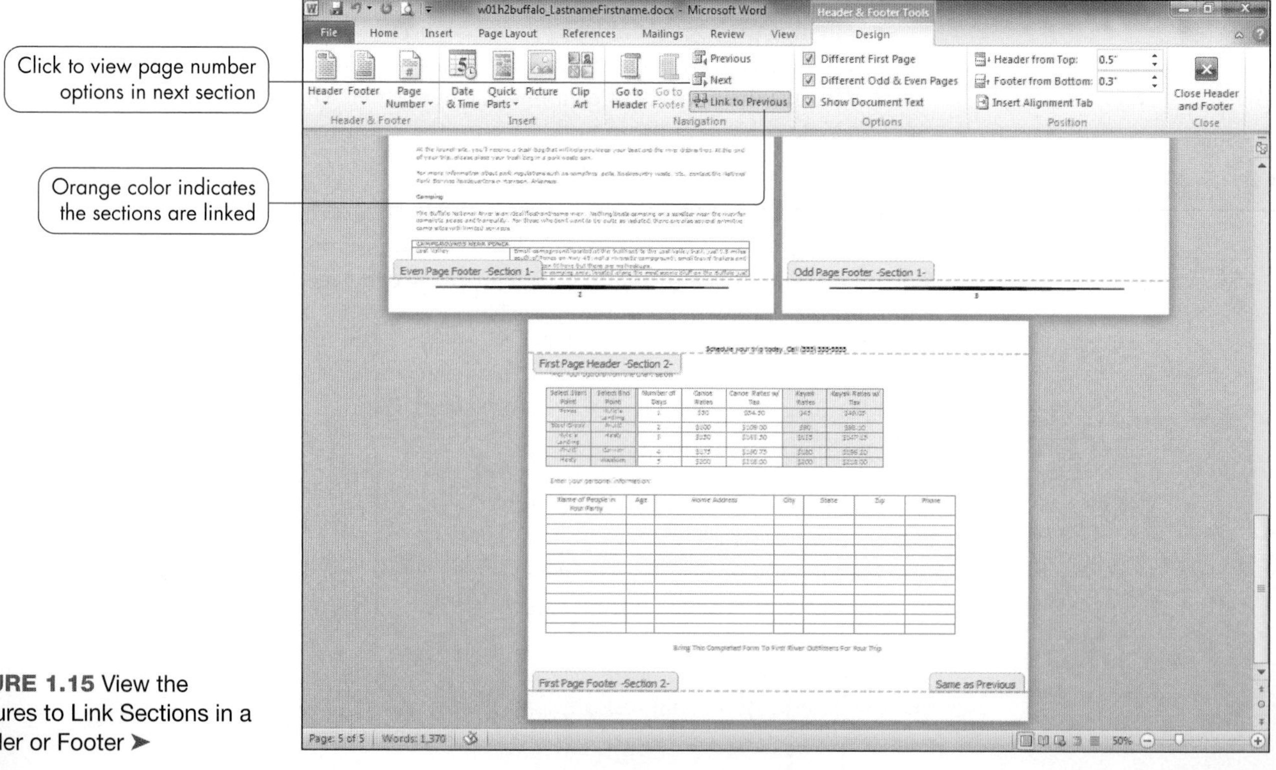

FIGURE 1.15 View the Features to Link Sections in a Header or Footer ➤

TIP Viewing Section Breaks

The best way to view the location of a section break in a document is to change to Draft view. The best way to determine which section each page is in is to double-click on the header or footer of a page. If a document has multiple sections, the section number is indicated with the header and footer.

Insert a Watermark

A **watermark** is text or a graphic that displays behind text.

A ***watermark*** is text or a graphic that displays behind text. Watermarks are often used to display a very light, washed-out logo for a company. They are also frequently used to indicate the status of a document, such as *FOR REVIEW ONLY*, as shown in Figure 1.16. Watermarks do not display on a document that is saved as a Web page, nor will they display in Web Layout view.

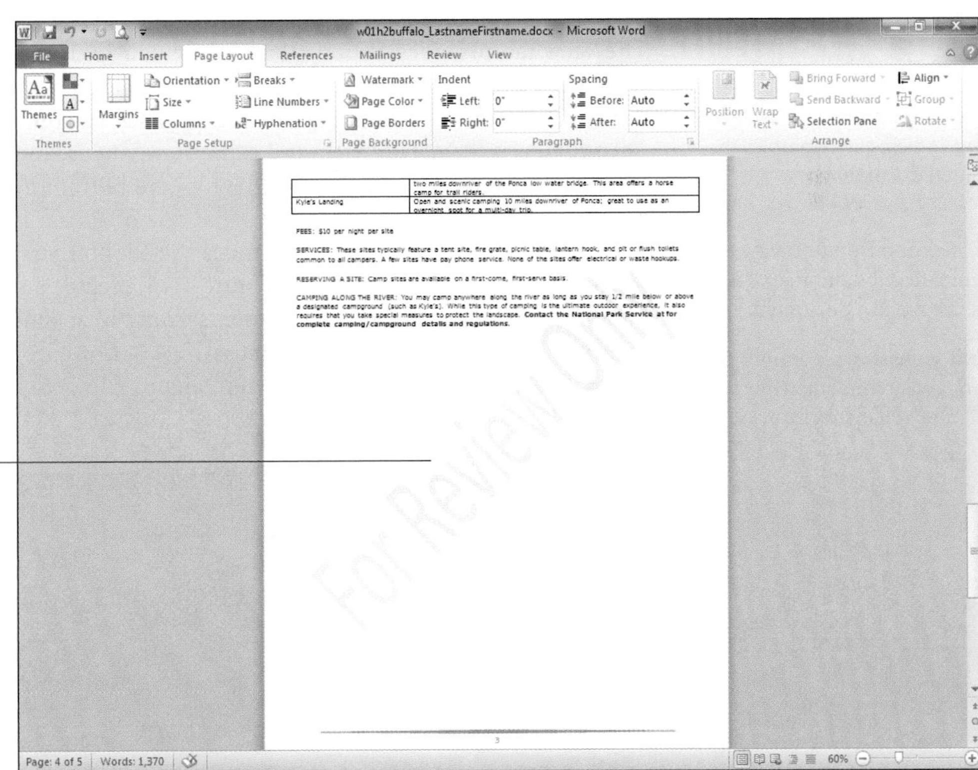

For Review Only displays as a watermark behind text on the page

FIGURE 1.16 Document That Includes a Watermark ➤

Checking Spelling and Grammar

It is important to create a document that is free of typographical and grammatical errors. With the automated spelling and grammar checker tools in Word, it is relatively easy to do so. However, you should always proofread a document because the spelling and grammar checker will not always find every possible error.

In addition to spelling and grammar checking, Word provides many features that correct a variety of grammatical mistakes. Word has a contextual spelling feature that attempts to locate a word that is spelled correctly but used incorrectly. For example, many people confuse the usage of words such as *their* and *there*, *two* and *too*, and *which* and *witch*. The visual indication that a contextual spelling error exists is a blue wavy line under the word, as shown in Figure 1.17.

When you invoke the spelling and grammar checking feature, contextual spelling mistakes will also display, and you can change them during this process.

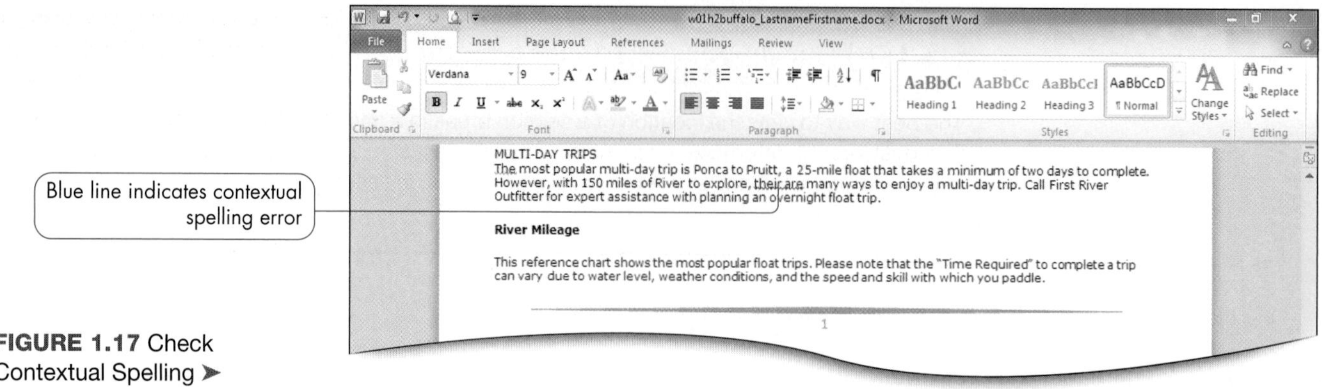

FIGURE 1.17 Check Contextual Spelling ➤

Displaying a Document in Different Views

Print Layout view is the default view and closely resembles the printed document.

Full Screen Reading view eliminates tabs and makes it easier to read a document.

Draft view shows a simplified work area, removing white space and other elements from view.

The View tab provides options that enable you to display a document in many different ways. Each view can display your document at a different magnification, which in turn determines the amount of scrolling necessary to see remote parts of a document. The ***Print Layout view*** is the default view and is the view you use most frequently. It closely resembles the printed document and displays the top and bottom margins, headers and footers, page numbers, graphics, and other features that do not appear in other views.

The ***Full Screen Reading view*** hides the Ribbon, making it easier to read your document. The ***Draft view***, shown in Figure 1.18, creates a simple area in which to work; it removes white space and certain elements from the document, such as headers, footers, and graphics, but leaves the Ribbon. Because view options are used frequently, buttons for each are located on the status bar, as shown in Figure 1.18.

FIGURE 1.18 Display a Document in Draft View ➤

When you click Zoom in the Zoom group on the View tab, the Zoom dialog box displays with several options (see Figure 1.19). You can use the Zoom controls to display the document onscreen at different magnifications—for example, 75%, 100%, or 200%. This command does not affect the size of the text on the printed page. It is helpful to be able to zoom in to view details or to zoom out and see the effects of your work on a full page.

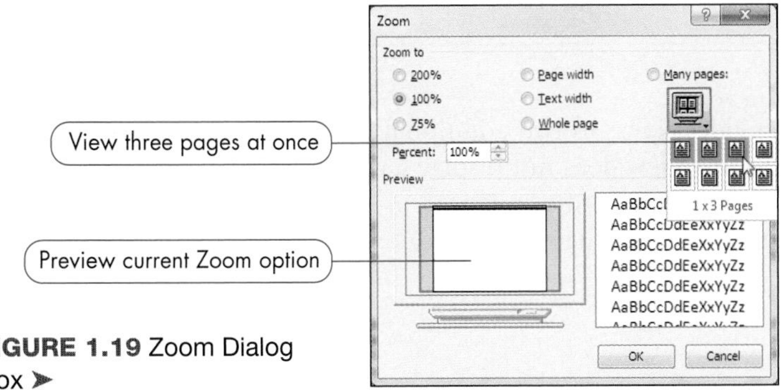

FIGURE 1.19 Zoom Dialog Box ➤

Word will automatically determine the magnification if you select one of the Zoom options—Page width, Text width, Whole page, or Many pages (Whole page and Many pages are available only in the Print Layout view). Figure 1.20, for example, displays the Buffalo River document in Print Layout view. The 27% magnification is determined automatically after you specify the number of pages, in this case 2 × 2. If you use a wide screen, the magnification size might differ slightly.

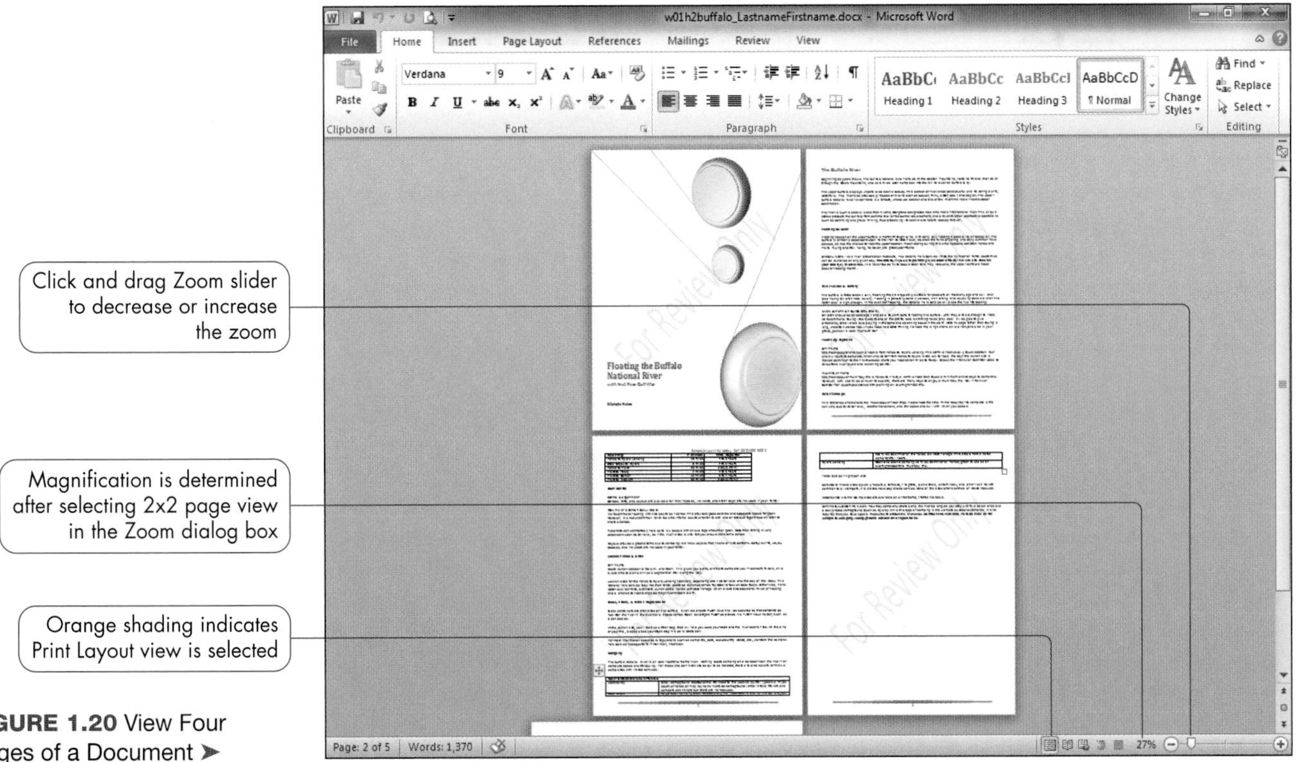

FIGURE 1.20 View Four Pages of a Document ➤

TIP Use the Status Bar to Change View Options

The status bar repeats commands from the View tab in a handy location for quick access. You can switch to Print Layout, Full Screen Reading, Web Layout, Outline, or Draft view from the buttons on the status bar. You also can use the Zoom slider to change the zoom of the current document or click the Zoom command to display the Zoom dialog box, which contains more viewing options.

The **Outline view** displays a structural view of the document that can be collapsed or expanded.

The **Web Layout view** is used when creating a Web page.

The View tab also provides access to two additional views—the Outline view and the Web Layout view. The ***Outline view*** does not display a conventional outline, but rather a structural view of a document that can be collapsed or expanded as necessary. The ***Web Layout view*** is used when you are creating a Web page.

2 Document Organization

You have made some introductory edits to the document that will be used in marketing the First River Outfitter, but you plan to make more changes that will improve organization and readability. These improvements require a section break at the end that will enable you to format the last page differently from the others. You also remember to check spelling and grammar.

Skills covered: Change Page Margins and Insert a Page Break • Insert Headers in Sections • Add a Watermark • Check Spelling and Grammar

STEP 1 CHANGE PAGE MARGINS AND INSERT A PAGE BREAK

One step in conserving the amount of paper used in marketing materials is to reduce the margins on the pages that will print. In this step you change margins and insert a page break to create a new section at the end of the document. Then you change orientation on the last page to make it easier to view a lengthy table. Refer to Figure 1.21 as you complete Step 1.

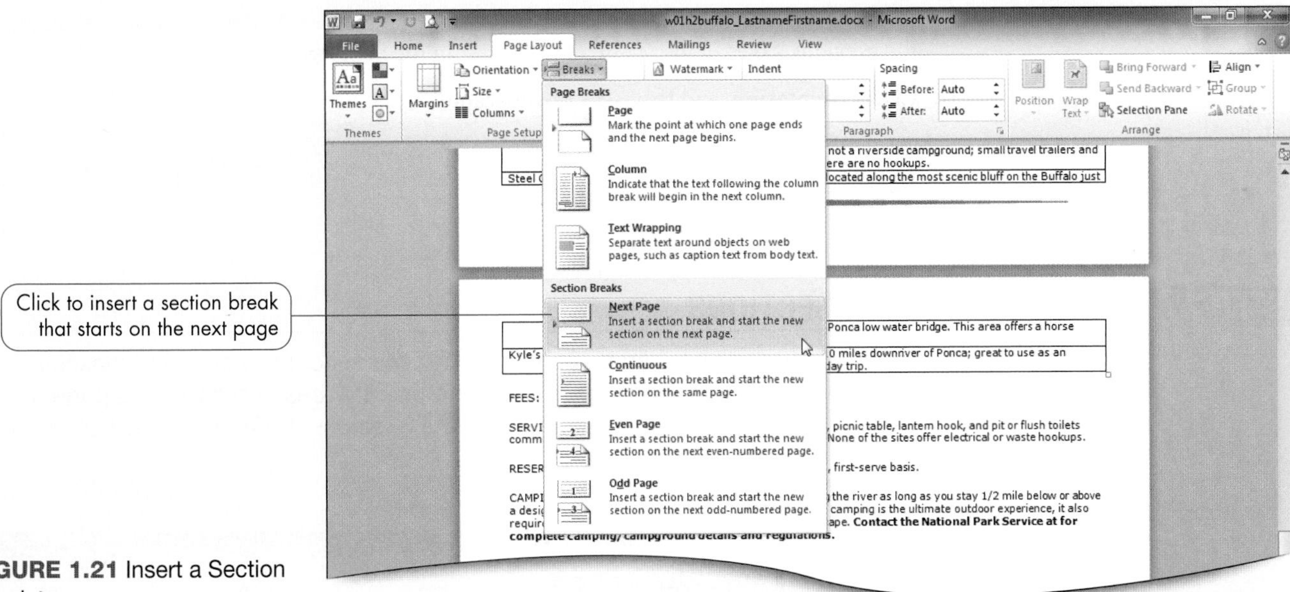

FIGURE 1.21 Insert a Section Break ➤

a. Open *w01h1buffalo_LastnameFirstname* if you closed it at the end of Hands-On Exercise 1. Save the document with the new name **w01h2buffalo_LastnameFirstname**, changing *h1* to *h2*.

b. Click the **Page Layout tab**, and then click **Margins** in the Page Setup group. Click **Custom Margins.**

   The Page Setup dialog box displays.

c. Click the **Margins tab**, if necessary. Type **.5** in the **Top margin box.** Press **Tab** to move the insertion point to the Bottom margin box. Type **.5** and press **Tab** to move to the Left margin box.

   0.5″ is the equivalent of 1/2 of one inch.

d. Click the **Left margin arrow** to set the left margin at **0.6**, and then repeat the procedure to set the right margin to **0.6**.

The top and bottom margins are now set at 0.5″, and the left and right margins are set at 0.6″.

e. Check that these settings apply to the **Whole document**, located in the lower portion of the dialog box. Click **OK** to close the dialog box.

You can see the change in layout as a result of changing the margins. The content now displays with less white space around the text. And the page break at the beginning of the *Glass, Trash, & Other Regulations* section that you inserted earlier is no longer needed.

f. Scroll down and position the insertion point on the left side of the *Glass, Trash, & Other Regulations* title. Press **Backspace**.

> **TROUBLESHOOTING:** If the page break does not disappear immediately, you might have to press Backspace a second time.

g. Scroll down and place the insertion point on the left side of the heading *Plan Your Trip Now!* Click **Breaks** in the Page Setup group, and then click **Next Page** under *Section Breaks*, as shown in Figure 1.21.

The table for personal information that displays on the last page is very wide and does not show the entire table in the portrait orientation. By inserting this section break you can now make modifications, such as turning this page to landscape orientation, without changing the previous pages. Those changes will occur in the next steps.

h. Click **Orientation**, and then select **Landscape**.

The table of personal information now displays completely.

i. Press **Ctrl+S** to save the document.

STEP 2 INSERT HEADERS IN SECTIONS

The document you are preparing will be read by potential customers. To make sure you maximize all areas of the document to market the company, you decide to use the area at the top of a page to add a small amount of information, such as phone numbers for the business. Refer to Figure 1.22 as you complete Step 2.

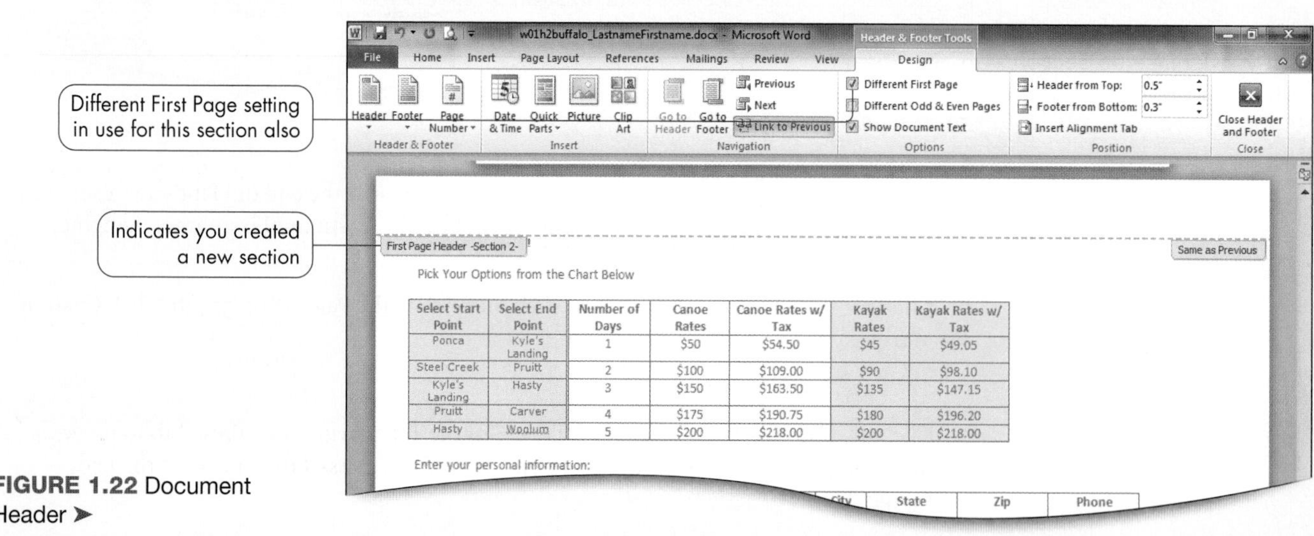

FIGURE 1.22 Document Header ➤

a. Click the **Insert tab**, click **Header** in the Header & Footer group, and then click **Edit Header.**

The Insertion point displays in the header of the last page, and the Header & Footer Tools Design tab displays in the Ribbon. Notice also that the Header tab for this page indicates this is Section 2, as seen in Figure 1.22.

b. Scroll up and click in a header or footer in Section 1. Click **Different Odd & Even Pages** in the Options group to turn on this feature.

c. Scroll and click to position the insertion point in a header identified as *Even Page Header -Section 1-*, if necessary.

Any information you insert in this header will only show up on even-numbered pages. It looks more professional to omit headers from the first page of text and add them on following pages. This enables you to place information on only even-numbered pages throughout the document. The setting can be used in addition to the Different First Page feature, which is already being used to prevent any header or footer from displaying on the cover page.

d. Press **Tab** two times to move the insertion point to the right side of the header. Type **Schedule your trip today. Call (555) 555-5555.**

The text and phone number display in the header. Scroll down and notice the header displays on this page only.

e. Scroll down and position the insertion point in the header for Section 2. Click **Link to Previous** in the Navigation group to turn that setting off.

The creation of the new section automatically invokes the Link to Previous command. When turned on, it enables the same header or footer to display on the first page in each section. To prevent this contact information from displaying on the cover page you disable that setting in Section 2.

f. Press **Tab** two times, and then type **Schedule your trip today. Call (555) 555-5555.**

Because you insert a separate section for the last page, the headers and footers in the previous section do not automatically display there. To continue the trend of placing the contact information at the top of every even-numbered page, you must insert it again in the new section.

g. Scroll up to the previous page, select the entire odd page footer from Section 1, and then click **Ctrl+C.**

Another consequence of invoking the Different Odd & Even Pages setting is that the footers for the even pages in Section 1 were removed. The next steps copy the footer from the odd pages and insert it into the even pages.

h. Scroll up to the *Even Page Footer -Section 1-*, and then place the insertion point in the footer. Press **Ctrl+V** to insert the page number and heavy line.

TROUBLESHOOTING: If you insert an extra line return and the cursor displays on the line below the page number at the end of the paste operation, press Backspace to remove the extra line return so it does not needlessly extend the space for the footer.

i. Scroll through the document and notice the sequential page numbering only on the middle pages, not the cover sheet or last page. Click **Close Header and Footer.**

j. Save the document.

STEP 3 ADD A WATERMARK

You plan to send a copy of your current work to Lawson for review. You want to make sure this document is marked so anyone who views it will know it is not complete or ready to distribute to customers. You insert a watermark that will display faintly on each page. Later, when the document is complete, you will remove the watermark. Refer to Figure 1.23 as you complete Step 3.

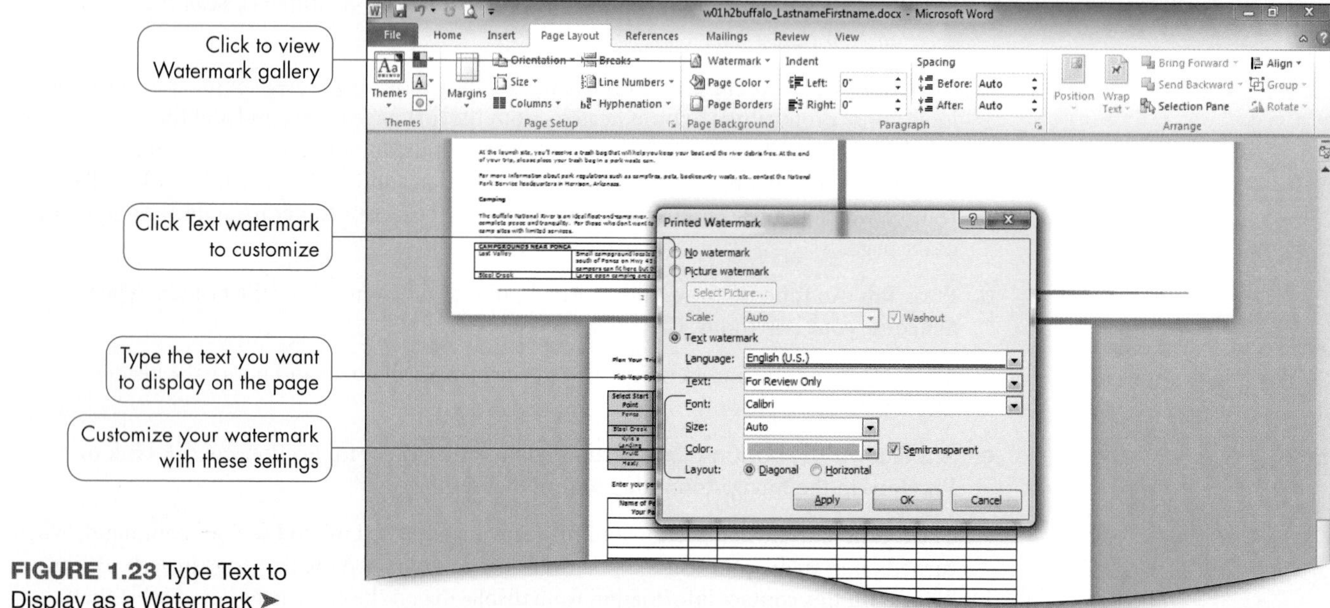

FIGURE 1.23 Type Text to Display as a Watermark ➤

a. Click the **Page Layout tab**. Click **Watermark** in the Page Background group, and then click **Custom Watermark**.

   The Watermark dialog box displays with several options available. You decide to enter your own words to communicate the message that displays as a watermark on this page.

b. Click **Text watermark**.

c. Select the text *ASAP* that displays beside *Text*, and then type **For Review Only** to replace *ASAP*, as shown in Figure 1.23. Click **OK**. Scroll to page 4, which displays *3* as the page number in the footer, to get a better view of the watermark.

   The watermark is in place and displays on each page in each section. It is easier to see it on page 4 because this page has less text.

TIP Frequently Used Watermarks

When you click Watermark in the Page Background group, several of the most commonly used watermark statements display, such as *DRAFT* or *CONFIDENTIAL*. You can also select the option to view more Watermarks from Office.com.

d. Click **Print Preview** in the Quick Access Toolbar, and notice the watermark in the preview of the document.

e. Click the **File tab** to close Print Preview. Press **Ctrl+S** to save the document.

STEP 4 CHECK SPELLING AND GRAMMAR

You are always careful to check spelling and grammar before distributing a document for others to read. After several edits, you decide it is time to run the spelling and grammar check feature in Word and make changes to remove any mistakes. Refer to Figure 1.24 as you complete Step 4.

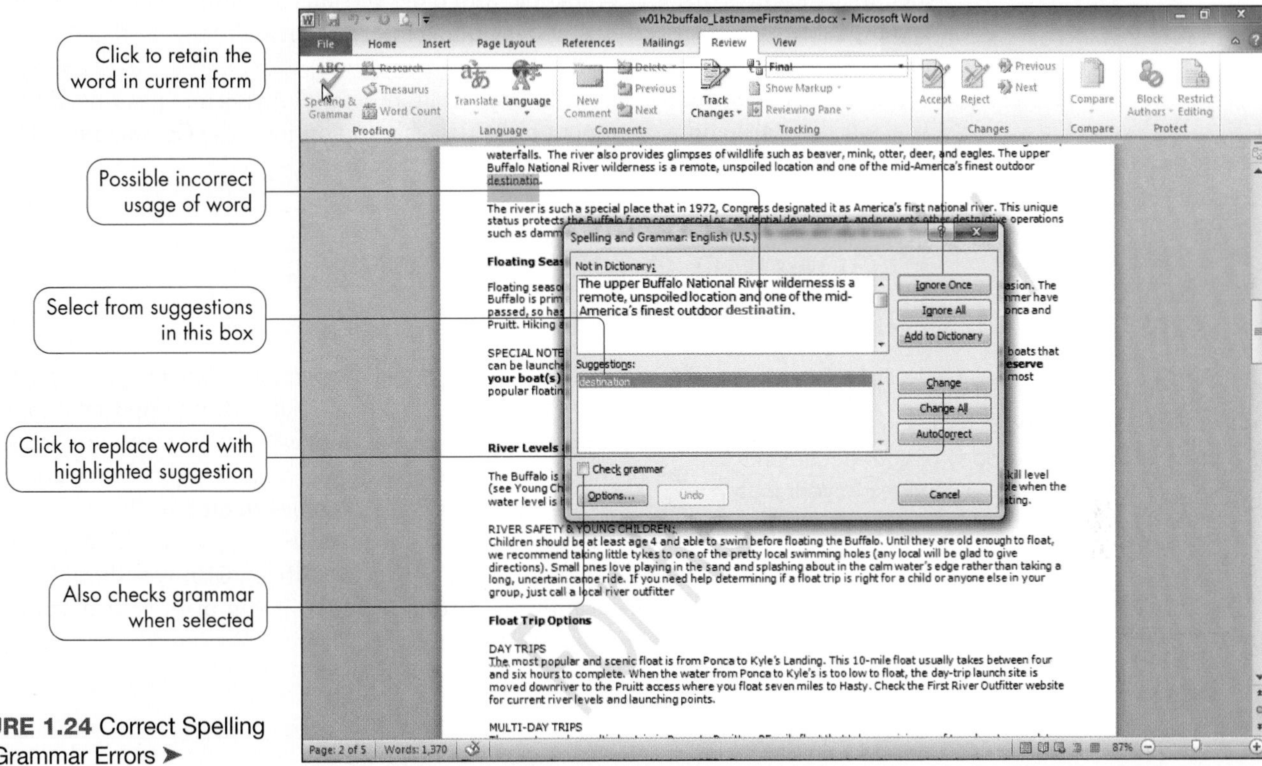

FIGURE 1.24 Correct Spelling and Grammar Errors ➤

a. Place the cursor at the top of page 2, on the left side of the text *The Buffalo River.* Click the **Review tab**, and then click **Spelling & Grammar** in the Proofing group.

FYI

The Spelling and Grammar dialog box displays with the first error indicated in red text, as shown in Figure 1.24.

b. Remove the check from the *Check grammar* option. If necessary, click **Yes** in the dialog box that asks if you want to continue checking the document.

Many of the headings in the document will be flagged for incorrect grammar, so this will let you bypass all of them and check the spelling only.

TROUBLESHOOTING: If additional text is flagged, such as *you've*, click Ignore All. This indicates that Word is checking grammar and style. To do a simple spelling and grammar check, click the File tab, click Options, click Proofing, click the Writing Style arrow, choose Grammar Only, and then click OK.

c. Click **Change All** to replace all misspellings of the word *destinatin* with the correct *destination*, and then view the next error.

d. Click **Change** to replace the contextual spelling error *their are* with *there are* near the bottom of the first page.

e. Click **Ignore once** to the remaining spelling errors in the document. These words are spelled correctly, but are not included in the spelling checker dictionary, and therefore, are flagged as spelling errors. Click **OK** in the box that informs you the spelling and grammar check is complete.

f. Save the document and keep it onscreen if you plan to continue with the next Hands-On Exercise. If not, close the document and exit Word.

Finalize a Document

After you organize your document and make all the formatting changes you desire, you need to save the document in its final form and prepare it for use by others. You can take advantage of features in Word that enable you to manipulate the file in a variety of ways, such as identifying features that are compatible with older versions of Word, saving in a format that is compatible with older versions, and including information about the file that does not display in the document.

In this section, you will revisit the important process of saving and printing documents. You will also learn about document properties, backup options, the Compatibility Checker, and the Document Inspector.

Preparing a Document for Distribution

It is not a question of *if* it will happen but *when*. You should use resources that Word provides to create a copy of your documents and back up the changes to your files at every opportunity.

It is not a question of *if* it will happen but *when*. Files are lost, systems crash, and viruses infect a system. That said, the importance of saving work frequently cannot be overemphasized. For this reason, you should use resources that Word provides to create a copy of your documents and back up the changes to your files frequently. By default, documents will save as Word 2010 files. If you plan to share a document with someone who is not using Office 2010, you should consider using the tools provided for locating compatibility issues. If you print your document, be sure to use preview features so you can avoid wasting paper.

Save a Document in Compatible Format

Because some people may have a different version of Word, you should know how to save a document in a format that they can use. People cannot open a Word 2010 document in the 97-2003 versions of Word unless they install the Compatibility Pack that contains a converter. If you are sure they have not installed the Compatibility Pack, you should save the document in Word 97-2003 format.

After reading the Office Fundamentals chapter, you know the Save and Save As commands are used to copy your documents to disk and should be used frequently to avoid loss of work and data. To save a document so that someone with a 97-2003 version of Office can open it, do the following:

1. Click the File tab.
2. Click Save As.
3. Select the Save as type arrow, and then select Word 97-2003 (see Figure 1.25).
4. Enter a name for your file in the Save As dialog box. The saved file will have the .doc extension instead of the Word 2010 extension, .docx.

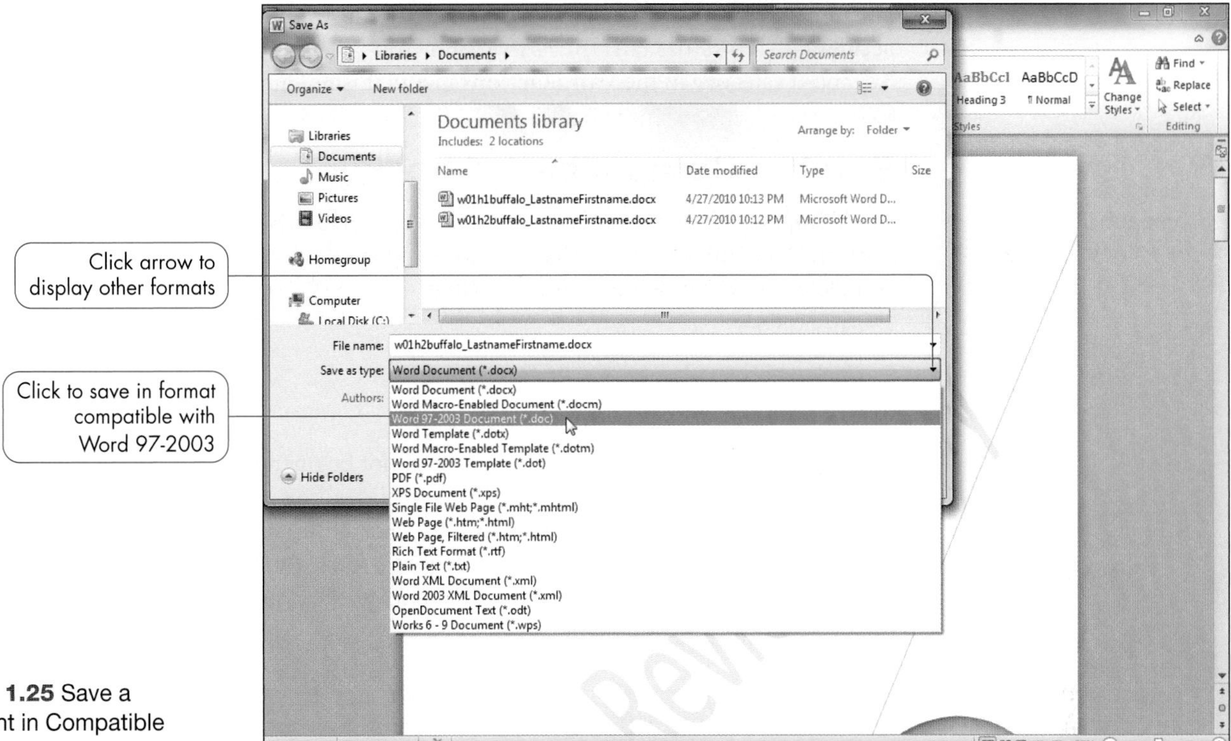

FIGURE 1.25 Save a Document in Compatible Format ➤

If you open a Word document created in an earlier version, such as Word 2003, the title bar will include *(Compatibility Mode)* at the top. You can still work with the document and even save it back in the same format for Word 97-2003 users. However, some features introduced in Word 2007 and used in Word 2010, such as SmartArt and graphic enhancement options used in the cover page, are not viewable or available for use in compatibility mode.

To remove the file from compatibility mode, click the File tab, and then click Convert. It will convert the file and remove the *(Compatibility Mode)* designator, but the .doc extension will still display. The next time you click Save, the extension will change to .docx, indicating that the file is converted into a Word 2010 file; you will then be able to use all of the Word 2010 features.

Understand Backup Options

AutoRecover enables Word to recover a previous version of a document.

Word enables you to back up files in different ways. One option is to use a feature called ***AutoRecover***. If Word crashes when AutoRecover is enabled, the program will be able to recover a previous version of your document when you restart the program. The only work you will lose is anything you did between the time of the last AutoRecover operation and the time of the crash, unless you happen to save the document in the meantime. The default *Save AutoRecover information every 10 minutes* ensures that you will never lose more than 10 minutes of work. AutoRecover is enabled from the Save category in the Word Options menu.

You can also set Word to create a backup copy with every save. Assume that you have created the simple document with the phrase *The fox jumped over the fence*, and have saved it under the name *Fox*. Assume further that you edit the document to read *The quick brown fox jumped over the fence*, and that you save it a second time. The second Save command changes the name of the original document from *Fox* to *Backup of Fox*, then saves the current contents of memory as *Fox*. In other words, the disk now contains two versions of the document: the current version *Fox* and the most recent previous version *Backup of Fox*.

The cycle goes on indefinitely, with *Fox* always containing the current version and *Backup of Fox* the most recent previous version. So, if you revise and save the document a third time, the original (first) version of the document disappears entirely because only two versions are kept. The contents of *Fox* and *Backup of Fox* are different, but the existence of the latter enables you to retrieve the previous version if you inadvertently edit beyond repair or accidentally erase the current *Fox* version. You set this valuable backup option from the Advanced category in the Word Options menu; it is not automatically enabled.

Run the Compatibility Checker

The **Compatibility Checker** looks for features that are not supported by previous versions of Word.

The ***Compatibility Checker*** is a feature in Word 2010 that enables you to determine if your document includes features that are not supported by Word 97-2003 versions. After you complete your document, do the following:

1. Click the File tab.
2. Click Check for Issues.
3. Click Check Compatibility.

If the document contains anything that could not be opened in a different version of Word, the Microsoft Word Compatibility Checker dialog box lists it. From this dialog box you also can indicate that you want to always check compatibility when saving this file (see Figure 1.26). If you are saving the document in a format to be used by someone with an earlier version, you will want to make corrections to the items listed in the dialog box before saving again and sending the file.

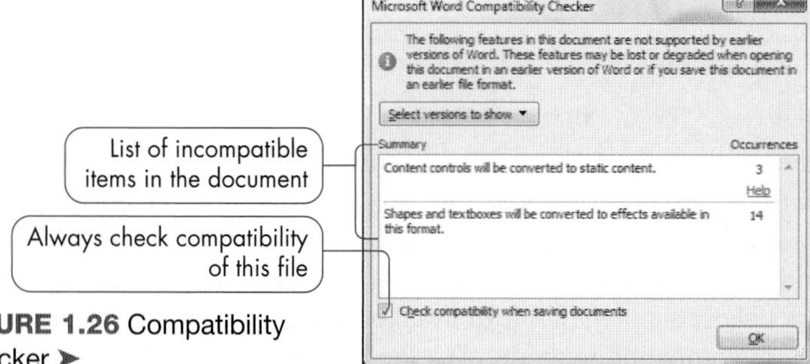

FIGURE 1.26 Compatibility Checker ➤

Run the Document Inspector

The **Document Inspector** checks for and removes different kinds of hidden and personal information from a document.

Before you send or give a document to another person, you should run the ***Document Inspector*** to reveal any hidden or personal data in the file. For privacy or security reasons, you might want to remove certain items contained in the document such as author name, comments made by one or more persons who have access to the document, or document server locations. Some inspectors are specific to individual Office applications, such as Excel and PowerPoint. Word provides inspectors that you can invoke to reveal different types of information, including the following:

- Comments, Revisions, Versions, and Annotations
- Document Properties and Personal Information
- Custom XML Data
- Headers, Footers, and Watermarks
- Invisible Content
- Hidden Text

The inspectors can also locate information in documents created in older versions of Word. Because some information that the Document Inspector might remove cannot be recovered with the Undo command, you should save a copy of your original document, using a different name, just before you run any of the inspectors. After you save the copy, do the following:

1. Click the File tab.
2. Click Check for Issues.
3. Click Inspect Document.

The Document Inspector dialog box displays first, enabling you to select the types of content you want it to check (see Figure 1.27). When the check is complete, Word lists the results and enables you to choose whether to remove the content from the document. If you forget to save a backup copy of the document, you can use the Save As command to save a copy of the document with a new name after you run the inspector.

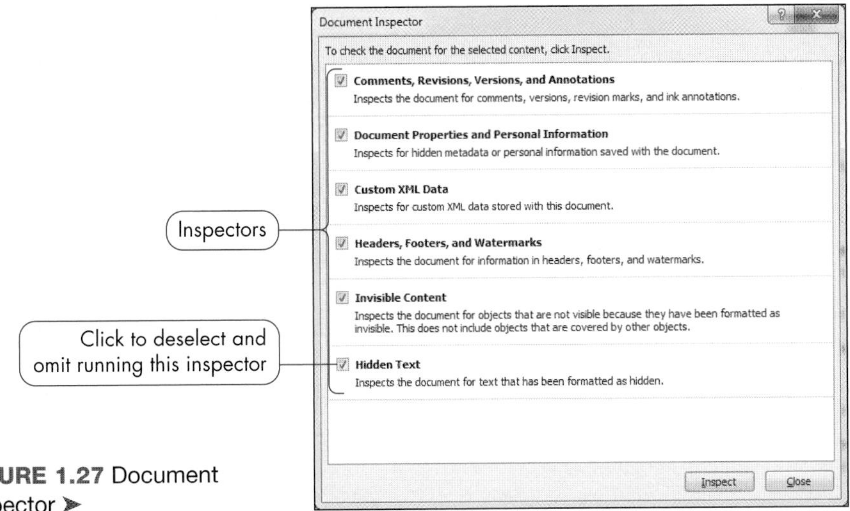

FIGURE 1.27 Document Inspector ➤

Select Printing Options

People often print an entire document when they want to view only a few pages. All computer users should be mindful of the environment, and limiting printer use is a perfect place to start. Millions of sheets of paper have been wasted because someone did not take a moment to preview his or her work and then had to reprint due to a minor error that is easily noticed in a preview window.

Click the File tab, and click Print to view the Backstage view settings and options for printing. Fortunately, the print preview displays automatically, so you know how your document will print in its current form. You see one page at a time, but you can use the Previous Page and Next Page arrows to navigate to other pages. You can also use the zoom slider or Zoom to Page setting at the bottom of the Preview pane to magnify the page or preview several pages at once.

After evaluating the preview carefully, you can select from many print options in the Backstage view, as shown in Figure 1.28. At the top of the screen you can scroll to select the number of copies. To select a different printer, if you have access to more than one, click the Printer arrow. Word has other print settings; Table 1.4 lists a sampling of options available for each setting. Settings might vary from one computer to another because of the difference in printers.

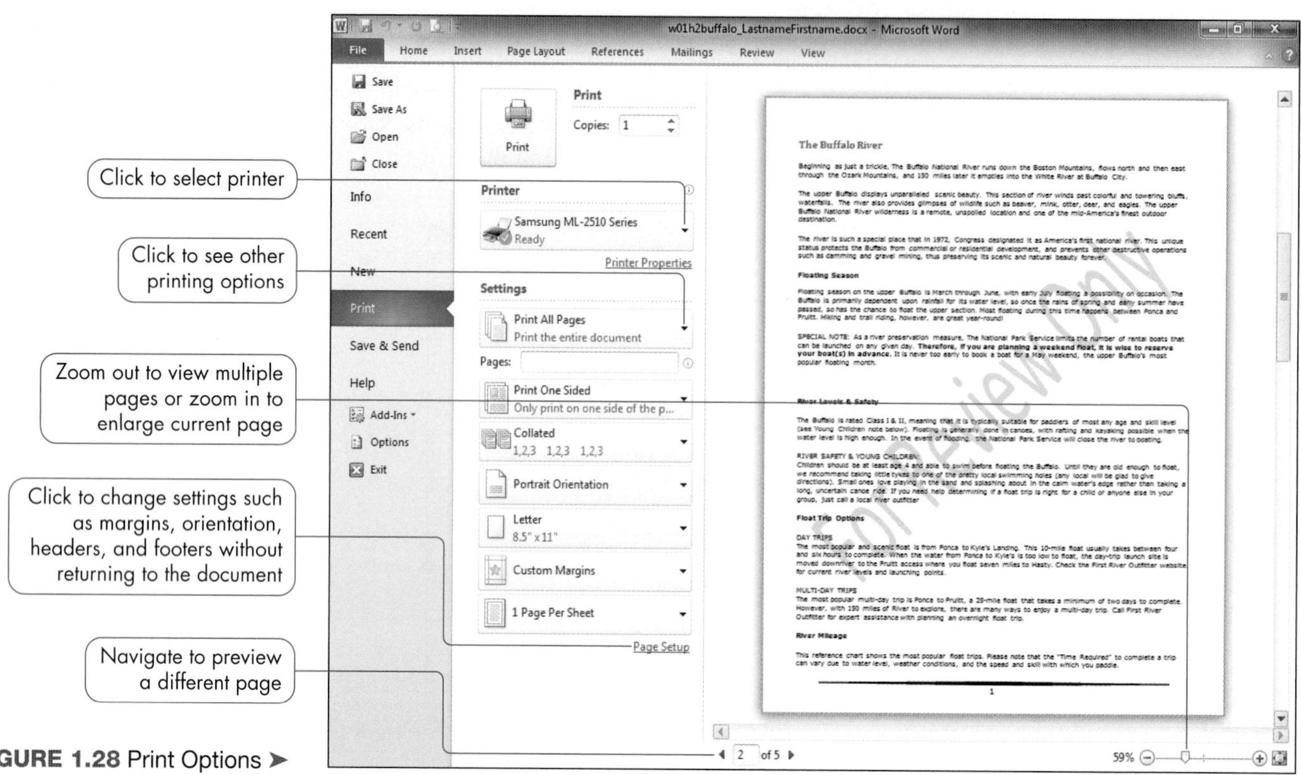

FIGURE 1.28 Print Options ➤

TABLE 1.4 Print Settings

Setting	Options
Print All Pages	Print Selection Print Current Page Print Custom Range Document Properties Only Print Odd Pages Only Print Even Pages
Print One Sided	Print Both Sides (only listed if your printer is capable of duplex printing) Manually Print on Both Sides
Collated	Collated (1,2,3; 1,2,3; 1,2,3) Uncollated (1,1,1; 2,2,2; 3,3,3)
Portrait Orientation	Portrait Orientation Landscape Orientation
Letter	Legal (8.5″ × 14″) A4 (8.27″ × 11.69″) More Paper Sizes
Normal Margins	Normal Narrow Custom Margins
1 Page Per Sheet	2 Pages Per Sheet 4 Pages Per Sheet 16 Pages Per Sheet Scale to Paper Size

Modifying Document Properties

Sometimes, you want to record detailed information about a document but do not want to display the information directly in the document window. You use the Document Panel to store descriptive information such as a title, subject, author, keywords, and summary.

Sometimes, you want to record detailed information about a document but do not want to display the information directly in the document window. For example, you might want to record some notes to yourself about a document, such as the document's author, purpose, or intended audience. You use the ***Document Panel*** to store descriptive information such as a title, subject, author, keywords, and summary.

The **Document Panel** enables you to enter descriptive information about a document.

When you click the File tab and display the Backstage view, you see a thumbnail version of the current page. Below that thumbnail you see information about the document such as the size, number of pages, word count, title, date modified, and author. You can modify some document information in this view, but you can also display the full Document Panel to view and edit other properties. To display the Document Panel, as shown in Figure 1.29, do the following:

1. Click the File tab.
2. Click the Properties arrow.
3. Click Show Document Panel.

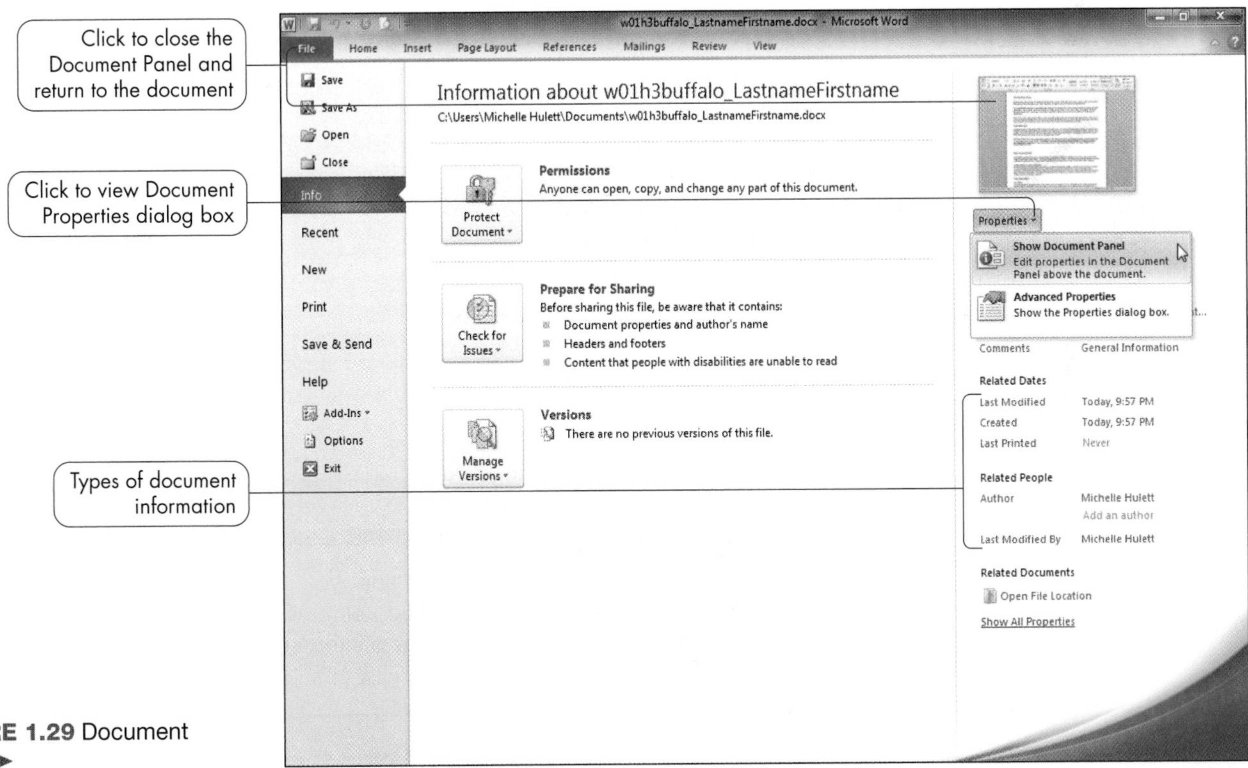

FIGURE 1.29 Document Panel ➤

When you save the document, Word saves this information with the document. You can update the descriptive information at any time by opening the Document Panel for the respective document.

TIP Exiting the Backstage View

You can return to a document from the Backstage view in three ways:

- Click the File tab.
- Click the document thumbnail.
- Click ESC on the keyboard.

Customize Document Properties

In addition to creating, modifying, and viewing a document summary, you may want to customize the document properties in the Document Panel. For example, you might want to add a *Date completed* property and specify an exact date for reference. This date would reflect the completion date, not the date the file was last saved—in case someone opens a file and saves it without making changes. You also might create a field to track company information such as warehouse location or product numbers.

When you click Document Properties and then click Advanced Properties, the Properties dialog box displays. Most commonly used properties display in the General tab. The Custom tab of the Properties dialog box enables you to add custom property categories and assign values to them. The Statistics tab provides useful information about the document, such as the creation date, the total editing time, and the word count.

Print Document Properties

You can print document properties to store hard copies for easy reference. To do this,

1. Click the File tab.
2. Click Print.
3. Click Print All Pages.
4. Click Document Properties.
5. Click Print.

Search for a Document Using Document Properties

After you insert information into the Document Panel, you can use it as search criteria when using the Windows search tool. The information entered as document title, comments, author, or any other field will be searched in the same manner as text that displays in the document.

3 Finalize a Document

As office manager for First River Outfitter, you are responsible for the security, management, and backup of all documents the business uses. Your formatting changes to the marketing document make it look more professional; now you must perform last-minute checks before sending it to Lawson for a final check. You also change document properties so it will be easy to locate and identify from your system storage device.

Skills covered: Modify Document Properties • Run the Document Inspector and a Compatibility Check • Save in a Compatible Format • Use Print Preview Features

STEP 1 MODIFY DOCUMENT PROPERTIES

You want to add data to your document so you can identify information such as the author, title, purpose, and date that it was completed—not just the last revision date, which is assigned by the computer. Since you don't want this information to show up in your document, you include it in the Document Properties. Refer to Figure 1.30 as you complete Step 1.

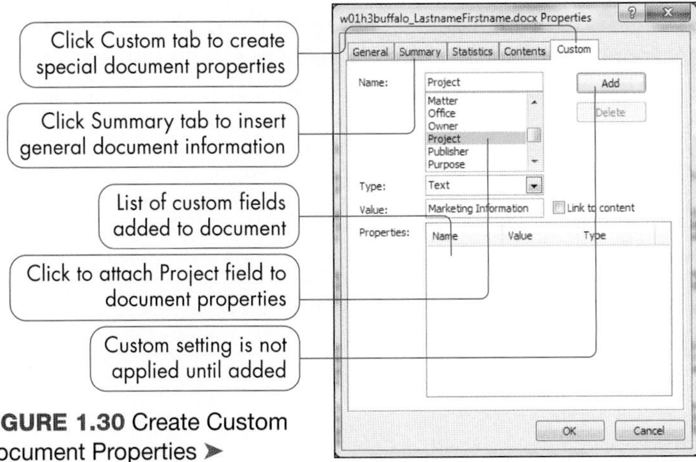

FIGURE 1.30 Create Custom Document Properties ➤

a. Open *w01h2buffalo_LastnameFirstname* if you closed it at the end of Hands-On Exercise 2. Save the document with the new name **w01h3buffalo_LastnameFirstname**, changing *h2* to *h3*.

b. Click the **File tab**, click **Properties**, and then click **Show Document Panel**.

   The Document Panel displays above your document. The document title and author name you entered on the cover page display in their respective boxes here. The subtitle you entered on the cover page displays in the Subject box.

> **TROUBLESHOOTING:** If the Document Panel disappears, repeat step b above to display it again.

c. Click one time in the **Comments box**, and then type **General Information**.

d. Click the **Document Properties arrow** in the top-left of the Document Properties panel, and then select **Advanced Properties** to display the w01h3buffalo_LastnameFirstname.docx Properties dialog box.

e. Create a custom property by completing the following steps:
   - Click the **Custom tab**, and then select **Project** in the **Name list**.
   - Type **Marketing Information** in the **Value box**, as shown in Figure 1.30, and then click **Add**.
   - Click **OK** to close the dialog box.

   You want to catalog the documents you create for First River Outfitter, and one way to do that is to assign a project scope using the custom properties that are stored with each document. Because you set up a custom field in the Document Properties, you can later perform searches and find all documents in that Project category.

f. Click **Close the Document Information Panel** in the top-right corner of Document Properties. Save the document.

TIP Document Properties and Windows Explorer

When you hover your mouse over a document in Windows Explorer, information stored as Document Properties will display.

STEP 2 RUN THE DOCUMENT INSPECTOR AND A COMPATIBILITY CHECK

You cannot remember if Lawson is using Office 2010 or an earlier version of Word. You decide to take precautions and run the Document Inspector and Compatibility check prior to saving the file in a compatible version. Refer to Figure 1.31 as you complete Step 2.

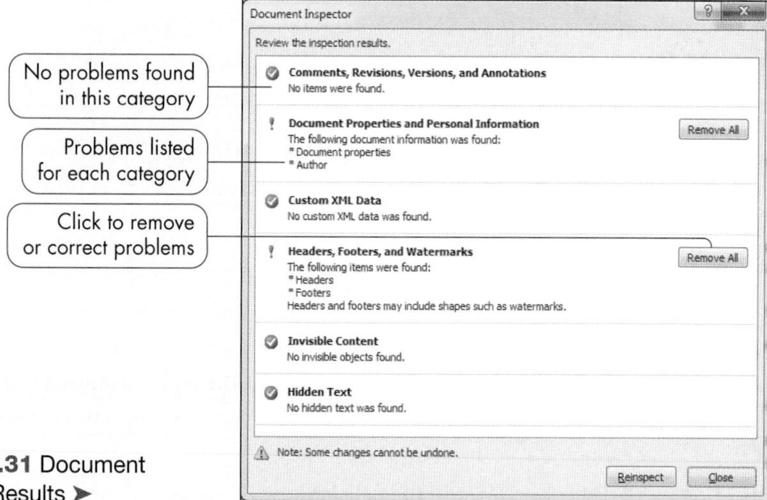

FIGURE 1.31 Document Inspector Results ➤

a. Click the **File tab**, click **Check for Issues** in the center part of the window, and then select **Check Compatibility**.

   Any noncompatible items in the document will display in the Microsoft Office Word Compatibility Checker dialog box. For this document, 17 occurrences of a feature are not compatible with earlier versions of Word.

b. Click **OK** after you view the incompatible listings.

c. Click the **File tab**, and then click **Save As**. Save the document as **w01h3buffalo2_LastnameFirstname**, adding the number *2* at the end of *buffalo*.

   Before you run the Document Inspector, you save the document with a different name in order to have a backup. You should always create a backup of the document because the Document Inspector might make changes that you cannot undo.

d. Click the **File tab**, click **Check for Issues**, and then select **Inspect Document**.

TROUBLESHOOTING: An informational window might display with instructions to save the document before you run the Document Inspector. You should always create a backup of the document because the Document Inspector might make changes that you cannot undo.

e. Click to select any inspector check box that is not already checked. Click **Inspect**.

   The Document Inspector results display and enable you to use Remove All buttons to eliminate the items found in each category.

f. Click the **Close button**; do not remove any items at this time.

g. Save the document as **w01h3buffalo_LastnameFirstname**, deleting the *2* at the end of *buffalo* and reverting back to the previous name. Click **OK** to replace the existing file with the same name.

STEP 3 SAVE IN A COMPATIBLE FORMAT

You know Lawson is anxious to review a copy of this document. You have learned that Lawson is running Word 2000 in his office, so you decide to convert the file so he will be able to open and view it easily. After you save it in compatible mode, you convert it again so Lawson can view your work using the current version. Refer to Figure 1.32 as you complete Step 3.

FIGURE 1.32 File Saved in Word 97-2003 Format ➤

a. Click the **File tab**, click **Save As**, click the **Save as type arrow**, and then select **Word 97-2003 Document**.

b. Confirm the Save as type box displays *Word 97-2003 Document (*.doc)*, and then click **Save**.

   The Microsoft Word Compatibility Checker dialog box displays to confirm the compatibility issues you have already seen.

c. Click **Continue** to accept the alteration.

   The title bar displays *(Compatibility Mode)* following the file name *w01h3buffalo_LastnameFirstname.doc*. If you set the option to display file extensions on your computer, the document extension .doc displays in the title bar, as shown in Figure 1.32.

d. Click the **File tab**, and then click **Convert**.

   The Compatibility Mode designation is removed from the title bar. If a dialog box displays stating the document will be converted to the newest file format, click OK. You can check the option that prevents the dialog box from displaying each time this situation occurs.

e. Click **Save** on the Quick Access Toolbar. Click **Save** in the Save As dialog box, and then click **OK** if the authorization to replace the current file displays.

   The document extension has been restored to .docx.

STEP 4 USE PRINT PREVIEW FEATURES

Since you believe you have made the final changes to the document for now, you preview it onscreen. When you preview it this way, you are not wasting paper on unnecessary printouts. Refer to Figure 1.33 as you complete Step 4.

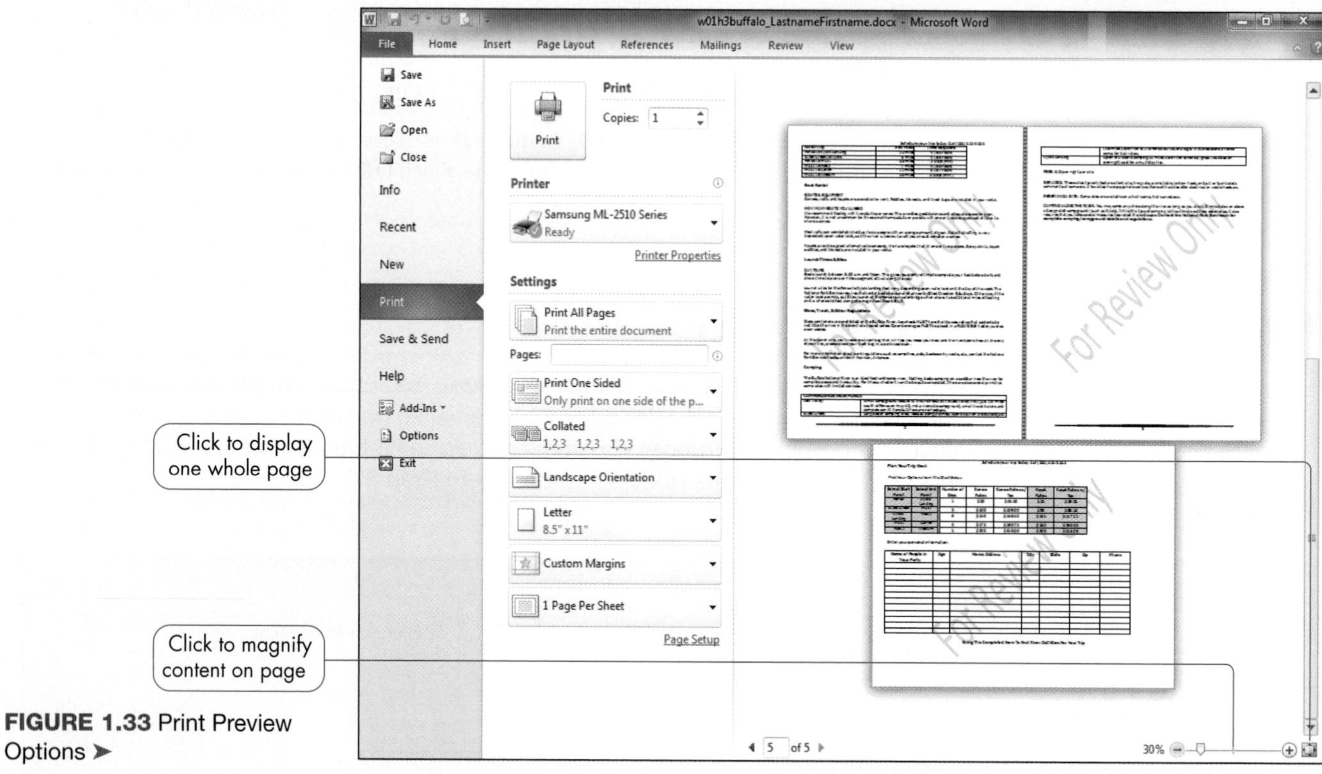

FIGURE 1.33 Print Preview Options ➤

a. Click **Ctrl+Home**, if necessary, to move to the beginning of the document. Click the **File tab**, and then click **Print**.

   The Print Preview window displays the first page.

b. Click **Zoom out** on the Zoom slider until the first four pages display.

   The display can vary depending on your settings, but you should see four pages of the document.

c. Click the **Next Page** navigation arrow four times until the last page of the document displays.

   You can see how the last page is formatted differently due to the section break inserted previously.

d. Click the **File tab** again to return to the application.

e. Close *w01h3buffalo_LastnameFirstname* and submit based on your instructor's directions.

CHAPTER OBJECTIVES REVIEW

After reading this chapter, you have accomplished the following objectives:

1. **Understand how word processors work.** Word provides a multitude of features that enable you to enhance documents easily while typing or with only a few clicks of the mouse. As you type, the word wrap feature automatically positions text for you using soft returns; however, you can insert a hard return to force text to the next page or to increase spacing between paragraphs. Keyboard shortcuts are useful for navigating a document, and toggle switches are often used to alternate between two states while you work. Page numbers are easy to add, and they serve as a convenient reference point to assist in reading through a document. Word also offers a feature to quickly insert a preformatted cover page in your document. The Cover Page feature includes a gallery with several designs.
2. **Customize Word.** Word is useful immediately. However, many options can be customized. The Word Options dialog box contains ten categories of options that you can change, including General, Proofing, and Add-Ins.
3. **Use features that improve readability.** When you create a document, you should consider how it will look when you print or display it. Margins determine the amount of white space from the text to the edge of the page, and you can set pages to display in portrait or landscape orientation. Headers and footers give a professional appearance to a document and are the best location to store page numbers. A section break is a marker that divides a document into sections, thereby enabling different formatting in each section. By using section breaks, you can change the margins within a multipage letter, where the first page (the letterhead) requires a larger top margin than the other pages in the letter. You can also change the page numbering within a document.
4. **Check spelling and grammar.** In conjunction with the spelling and grammar check feature, the contextual spelling feature attempts to locate a word that is spelled correctly but used incorrectly. For example, it looks for the correct usage of the words *there* and *their*. A contextual spelling error is underlined with a blue wavy line.
5. **Display a document in different views.** The View tab provides options that enable you to display a document in many different ways. Views include Print Layout, Full Screen Reading, Web Layout, Outline, and Draft. To change the view quickly, click a button on the status bar in the lower-right corner of the window. The Zoom dialog box includes options to change to whole page or multipage view.
6. **Prepare a document for distribution.** To prevent loss of data you should save and back up your work frequently. You should also be familiar with commands that enable you to save your documents in a format compatible with older versions of Word. Several backup options can be set, including an AutoRecover setting you can customize. You can also require Word to create a backup copy in conjunction with every save operation. Word 2010 includes a compatibility checker to look for features that are not supported by previous versions of Word, and it also offers a Document Inspector that checks for and removes different kinds of hidden or personal information from a document. The Backstage view print area contains many useful options including options to print only the current page, a specific range of pages, or a specific number of copies.
7. **Modify document properties.** You can create a document summary that provides descriptive information about a document, such as a title, subject, author, keywords, and comments. When you create a document summary, Word saves the document summary with the saved document. You also can print document properties.

KEY TERMS

AutoRecover ***p.95***
Compatibility Checker ***p.96***
Document Inspector ***p.96***
Document Panel ***p.99***
Draft view ***p.86***
Footer ***p.81***
Full Screen Reading view ***p.86***
Hard page break ***p.72***
Hard return ***p.70***
Header ***p.81***
Outline view ***p.88***
Print Layout view ***p.86***
Section break ***p.83***
Show/Hide feature ***p.71***
Soft page break ***p.71***
Soft return ***p.70***
Toggle ***p.71***
Watermark ***p.85***
Web Layout view ***p.88***
Word processing software ***p.68***
Word wrap ***p.70***

MULTIPLE CHOICE

1. How do you display the Backstage view Print options?
   (a) Click Print on the Quick Access Toolbar.
   (b) Click the File tab, and then click Print.
   (c) Click the Print Preview command.
   (d) Click the Home tab.

2. Which view removes white space, headers, and footers from the screen?
   (a) Full Screen Reading
   (b) Print Layout
   (c) Draft
   (d) Print Preview

3. You are the only person in your office to upgrade to Word 2010. Before you share documents with coworkers you should do which of the following?
   (a) Print out a backup copy.
   (b) Run the Compatibility Checker.
   (c) Burn all documents to CD.
   (d) Have no concerns that coworkers can open your documents.

4. A document has been entered into Word using the default margins. What can you say about the number of hard and soft returns if the margins are increased by 0.5″ on each side?
   (a) The number of hard returns is the same, but the number and/or position of the soft returns increases.
   (b) The number of hard returns is the same, but the number and/or position of the soft returns decreases.
   (c) The number and position of both hard and soft returns is unchanged.
   (d) The number and position of both hard and soft returns decreases.

5. Which of the following is detected by the contextual spelling checker?
   (a) Duplicate words
   (b) Use of the word *their* when you should use *there*
   (c) Irregular capitalization
   (d) Improper use of commas

6. If your cursor is near the bottom of a page and you want to display the next paragraph you type at the top of a new page, you should use which of the following?
   (a) Enter
   (b) Ctrl+Page Down
   (c) Ctrl+Enter
   (d) Page Layout, Breaks, Line Numbers

7. You need to insert a large table in the middle of a report that contains page numbers in the footer. The table is too wide to fit on a standard page. Which of the following is the best option to use in this case?
   (a) Put the table in a separate document, and do not worry about page numbering.
   (b) Insert a section break, and change the format of the page containing the table to landscape orientation.
   (c) Change the whole document to use landscape orientation.
   (d) Change margins to 0″ on the right and left.

8. What feature adds organization to your documents?
   (a) Print Preview
   (b) Orientation
   (c) Page Numbers
   (d) Find and Replace

9. If you cannot determine why a block of text starts at the top of the next page, which toggle switch should you invoke to view the formatting marks in use?
   (a) Word wrap
   (b) Show/Hide
   (c) Bold font
   (d) Caps Lock

10. What visual clue tells you that a document is not in Word 2010 format?
    (a) The status bar includes the text *(Compatibility Mode)*.
    (b) The file extension is .docx.
    (c) The title bar is a different color.
    (d) The title bar includes *(Compatibility Mode)* after the file name.

1 Executive Assistant Training Tools

To prepare for a position as an executive assistant, you decide to learn more about the keyboard shortcuts that are available in Word. Keyboard shortcuts are especially useful if you are a good typist because your hands can remain on the keyboard, as opposed to continually moving to and from the mouse. Although people usually learn the shortcuts as they work in Word, it is helpful to view a list to determine which shortcuts you might be inclined to use on a more regular basis. It is nice to know the same shortcuts apply to multiple applications, such as Microsoft Office Excel, PowerPoint, and Access. This exercise follows the same set of skills as used in Hands-On Exercises 1, 2, and 3 in the chapter. Refer to Figure 1.34 as you complete this exercise.

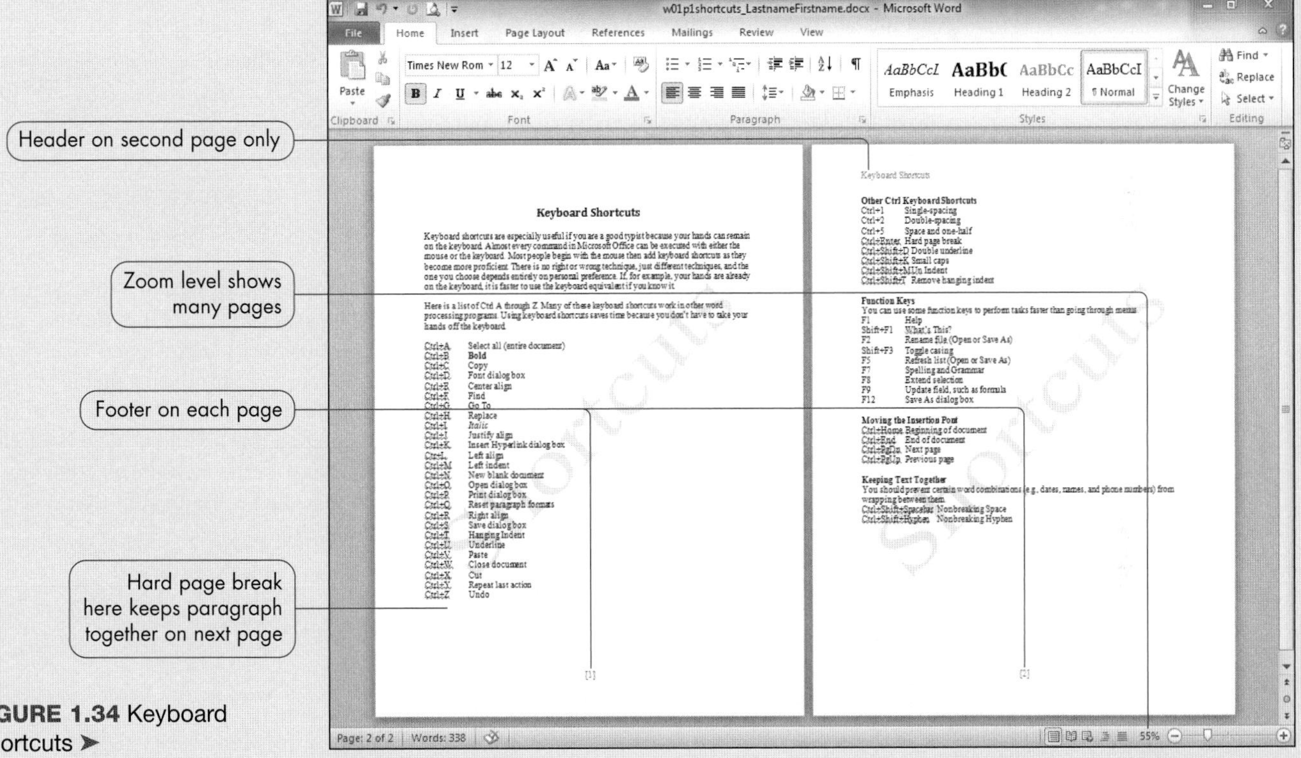

FIGURE 1.34 Keyboard Shortcuts ➤

a. Open the *w01p1shortcuts* document. Click the **File tab**, click **Convert**, and then click **OK** in the dialog box that might display. Save the document as **w01p1shortcuts_LastnameFirstname**, paying special attention that it is saved in Word format (*.docx).

b. Place your cursor at the end of the first paragraph. Press **Enter** two times, and then type **Here is a list of Ctrl A through Z. Many of these keyboard shortcuts work in other word processing programs. Using keyboard shortcuts saves time because you don't have to take your hands off the keyboard.**

c. Click the **Page Layout tab**, click **Margins** in the Page Setup group, and then select **Normal.** Click **Orientation**, and then select **Portrait.**

d. Click the **Home tab**, and then click **Show/Hide** (¶) in the Paragraph group, if necessary, to display formatting marks.

e. Move the insertion point to the left side of the hard return mark at the end of the line containing *Ctrl+B*. Press **Ctrl+B**, and then type the word **Bold**. Using keyboard shortcuts prior to typing applies the format to all typed text that follows. Alternately, you can type and then select the text prior to applying the format. The format used on text is stored in the hard return mark that follows the text.

f. Move the insertion point to the left side of the hard return mark at the end of the line containing *Ctrl+I*. Press **Ctrl+I**, and then type the word **Italic**.

g. Scroll to the bottom of the first page, and then place the insertion point on the left side of the title *Other Ctrl Keyboard Shortcuts.* Press **Ctrl+Enter** to insert a hard page break and keep the group together on one page.
h. Click the **Insert tab**, click **Page Number** in the Header & Footer group, point to **Bottom of Page**, and then click **Brackets 1** from the gallery.
i. Click **Header** in the Header & Footer group, and then select **Edit Header**. Click **Different First Page** in the Options group to insert a check mark. Place the insertion point in the header area of the second page, if necessary, and then type **Keyboard Shortcuts.**
j. Move the insertion point to the first page footer. Click **Page Number** in the Header & Footer group, point to **Bottom of Page**, and then click **Brackets 1** from the gallery. Click **Close Header and Footer**. After selecting the option for Different First Page in the previous step, the headers and footers on the first page were removed. This enables you to insert information on the first page, which won't display in the header or footer of the remaining pages.
k. Click the **Page Layout tab**, click **Watermark**, and then click **Custom Watermark**. Click **Text watermark**, select the text *ASAP*, and then type **Shortcuts**. Click **OK**.
l. Click **Zoom level** in the status bar, click the **Many pages icon**, and then drag to select **1 × 2 Pages**. Click **OK** to close the Zoom dialog box. Click **Show/Hide** (¶) in the Paragraph group on the Home tab to toggle off the formatting marks. Compare your document to Figure 1.34.
m. Click the **File tab**, click **Print**, click the **1 Page per sheet arrow**, and then click **2 Pages Per Sheet**. If instructed, click **Print** to print the document.
n. Save and close the file, and submit based on your instructor's directions.

2 Aztec Computers

As the owner of Aztec Computers, you are frequently asked to provide information about computer viruses and backup procedures. You are quick to tell anyone who asks about data loss that it is not a question of if it will happen, but when—hard drives die, removable disks are lost, and viruses may infect systems. You advise customers and friends alike that they can prepare for the inevitable by creating an adequate backup before the problem occurs. Because people appreciate a document to refer to about this information, you have started one that contains information that should be taken seriously. After a few finishing touches, you will feel comfortable about passing it out to people who have questions about this topic. This exercise follows the same set of skills as used in Hands-On Exercises 1, 2, and 3 in the chapter. Refer to Figure 1.35 as you complete this exercise.

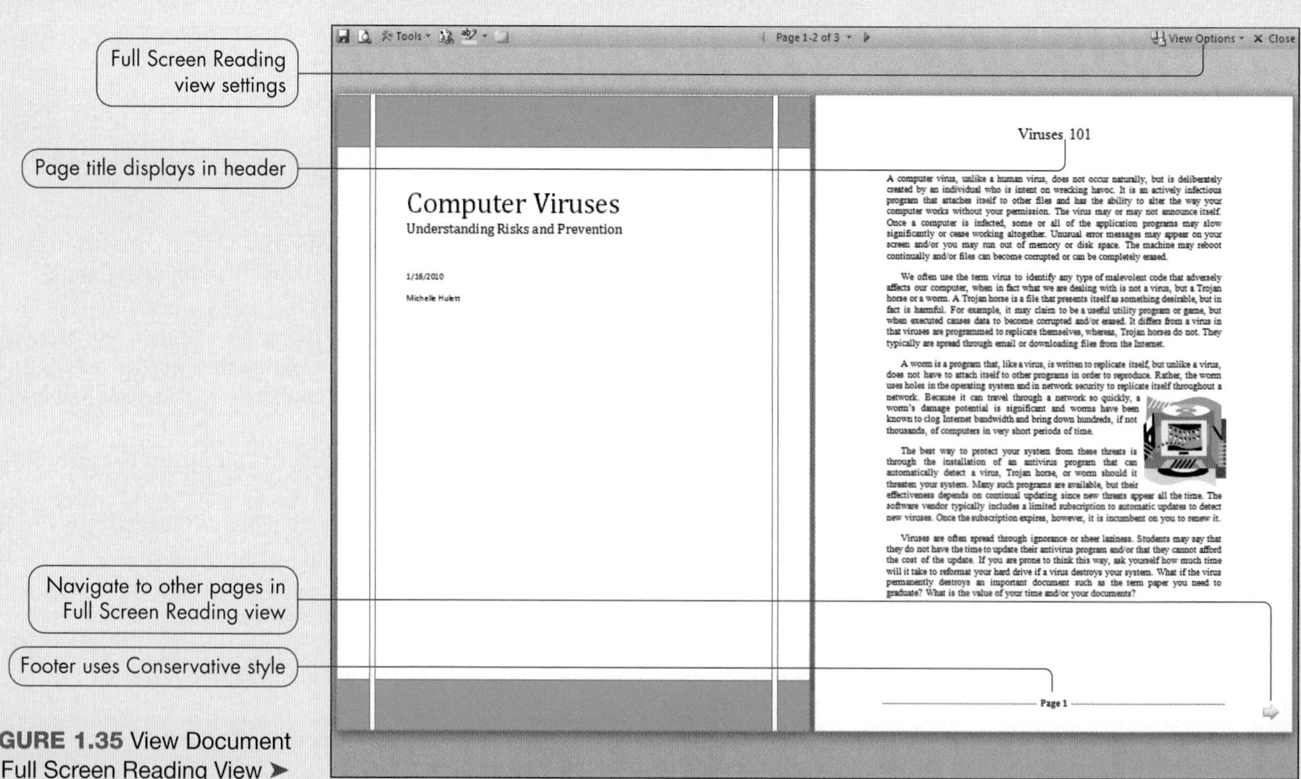

FIGURE 1.35 View Document in Full Screen Reading View ➤

a. Open the *w01p2virus document* and save it as **w01p2virus_LastnameFirstname**.
b. Create a cover page by completing the following steps:
    - Click the **Insert tab**, click **Cover Page** in the Pages group, and then click **Pinstripes.**
    - Click **Type the document subtitle**, and then type the text **Understanding Risks and Prevention.**
    - Click **Pick the Date**, click the arrow, and then select **Today**.
    - Right-click **Type the company name**, and then select **Cut**.
    - Click **Type the author name**, and then type your name.
c. Scroll to the bottom of the first page of the report, and then place the insertion point on the left side of the title *The Essence of Backup*. Click the **Page Layout tab**, click **Breaks**, and then click **Next Page**.
d. Set up headers and footers by completing the following steps:
    - Click the **Insert tab**, click **Footer**, and then click **Conservative**. A page number footer is added to *First Page Footer -Section 2-*.
    - Select the page number footer in *First Page Footer -Section 2-*, and then press **Ctrl+C** to copy the page number footer to the clipboard.
    - Click **Previous** in the Navigation group to place the insertion point in the Section 1 footer, and then press **Ctrl+V** to paste the page number and graphic into this footer. Since this document has two sections, you must duplicate the steps when you want to display the same footer (or header) in both.
    - Place the insertion point in *First Page Header -Section 2-*. Click **Page Number** in the Header & Footer group, click **Format Page Numbers**, and then click **Continue from Previous Section**. Click **OK.**
    - Click **Previous** in the Navigation group to place the insertion point in *Header -Section 1-*. Type **Viruses 101** and press **Ctrl+E** to center it. Use the Mini toolbar to increase the font to **20 pt**.
    - Place the insertion point in *First Page Header -Section 2-*. Click **Link to Previous** in the Navigation group to turn the setting off and enable you to create a unique header for this section instead of displaying the header from the previous section.
    - Type **The Essence of Backup**, press **Ctrl+E** to center it, and then use the Mini toolbar to increase the font to **20 pt**.
    - Click **Close Header and Footer**.
e. Delete the lines that contain the text *Viruses 101* and *The Essence of Backup* from the two pages of the report because these titles now display in the header.
f. Click the **Review tab**, and click **Spelling & Grammar**. Click **Change** to correct the contextual spelling error reported on backup, and then click **OK** when complete.
g. Complete the following steps to display the document in different views:
    - Click **Draft** in the status bar, and then scroll to view the location of the section break.
    - Click **Full Screen Reading** on the status bar.
    - Click **View Options** in the top-right corner, and then click **Show Two Pages**, if necessary.
    - Click **View Options** again, and then click **Show Printed Page**.
    - Click the arrows in the bottom corners to view each page, and then return to the first page. Compare your document to Figure 1.35.
    - Click the **Close button** to return to Print Layout view.
h. Click the **File tab**, click **Properties**, and then select **Show Document Panel**. Click in the **Comments box**, and then type **General information for understanding computer viruses**. Click **Close the Document Information Panel**.
i. Save the document. Click the **File tab**, click **Check for Issues**, and then click **Check Compatibility**. Click **OK** to close the Microsoft Word Compatibility Checker dialog box after you review the results.
j. Click the **File tab**, click **Check for Issues**, select **Inspect Document**, and then click **Inspect**. Click **Close** after you review the results.
k. Save and close the file, and submit based on your instructor's directions.

MID-LEVEL EXERCISES

1 Heart Disease Prevention

Millions of people suffer from heart disease and other cardiac-related illnesses. Of those people, several million will suffer a heart attack this year. Your mother volunteers for the American Heart Association and has brought you a document that explains what causes a heart attack, the signs of an attack, and what you can do to reduce your risk of having one. The information in the document is very valuable, but she needs you to put the finishing touches on this document before she circulates it in the community.

a. Open the *w01m1heart document* and save it as **w01m1heart_LastnameFirstname**.
b. Convert *w01m1heart_LastnameFirstname* so it does not save in Compatibility Mode.
c. Create a cover page for the report. Use Stacks in the cover page gallery. Add text where necessary to display the report title **Heart Attacks:** and the subtitle **What You Should Know**. Insert your name as author, replacing *Exploring Series.*
d. Change the document margins to **0.75″** on all sides.
e. Create a section break between the cover page and the first page of the report.

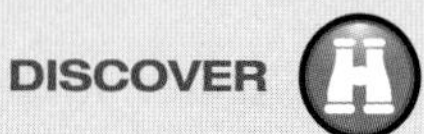

f. Create a footer in Section 2 by typing the text **Page**, leave a space, and then insert a page number field. The page number should only display at the bottom of the pages in Section 2. The first page of Section 2, not the cover page, should display page number 1.
g. Create a header that displays the report title and subtitle. It should not display on the cover or first page of the report. Confirm that the headers and footers in the second section are not linked to the first section.
h. Insert hard page breaks where necessary to prevent a paragraph or list from breaking across pages. View the document in Full Screen Reading view to confirm it is formatted as instructed and ready for printing.
i. Check spelling in the document. Change the document properties to include a custom field for Date completed.
j. Check Word Options and verify that AutoRecover backups occur every five minutes or less.
k. Print the document properties if approved by your instructor.
l. Save and close the file, and submit based on your instructor's directions.

2 Career Considerations

Your Introduction to College Life teacher has requested you consider the career path you might like to follow and write a paper about it. In this paper, you decide to discuss the field of Optometry, and you even describe your experience shadowing a doctor of Optometry one day last summer. The first draft is written, but you make a few more revisions before submitting the paper to your instructor for a preliminary check on your progress.

a. Open *w01m2career* and save it as **w01m2career_LastnameFirstname**.
b. Set margins to **1″** on the top, bottom, left, and right.
c. Turn on **Show/Hide** (¶), if necessary, to view formatting marks in the document. Correct the absence of a tab that is needed to indent the first paragraph.
d. Display the document in Draft view. Use keyboard shortcuts to move to the end of the document, and then remove unnecessary page returns and breaks below the last paragraph. Return to Print Layout view when complete.
e. Insert page numbers, at the bottom of the pages, using the **Bold Numbers 3 style**. Create a header that starts on page 2 and displays the title of the paper on the left and your name on the right.
f. Insert a watermark that displays **Draft** when you print the document.
g. Use the Spelling & Grammar tool to check the document.
h. Insert Page Breaks where necessary to display the document in a manner that prevents paragraphs from breaking across a page.
i. Run the Compatibility Checker and Document Inspector, and then save the document in Word 97-2003 format.
j. Save and close the file, and submit based on your instructor's directions.

CAPSTONE EXERCISE

Ethical conflicts occur all the time and result when one person or group benefits at the expense of another. Your Philosophy 101 instructor assigned a class project whereby students must consider the question of ethics and society. The result of your research includes a collection of questions every person should ask him- or herself. Your paper is nearly complete but needs a few modifications before you submit it.

Spelling, Margins, and Watermarks

You notice Word displays spelling and grammar errors with the colored lines, so you must correct those as soon as possible. Additionally, you want to adjust the margins and then insert a watermark that displays when you print so that you will remember that this is not the final version.

a. Open the file *w01c1ethics* and save it as **w01c1ethics_LastnameFirstname**.

b. Display the Word Options dialog box, and then engage the Contextual Spelling feature if it is not already in use.

c. Run the Spelling & Grammar tool to correct all misspelled words and contextual errors.

d. Change the margins to use a setting of **0.75″** on all sides.

e. Insert a watermark that displays **Version 1** when printed.

Cover Page, Headers, and Footers

You want to add a cover page that will attractively introduce your paper. Then you will set up page numbering, but it must not display on the cover page. Because you are going to customize headers and footers very precisely, you must use several of the custom settings available for Headers and Footers.

a. Insert a Cover Page that uses the Puzzle style. Select **Today** in the two Date fields. Type the title of the paper in the appropriate field, and then add your name as author, but remove all other fields from the cover page.

b. Insert a page number at the bottom of the first page of the report (the page that follows the cover page) using **Accent Bar 2 style**. There should be no header on this page.

c. Display the page number in the header of the remaining page of the report using the **Accent Bar 2 style**. (Hint: Use the Different Odd & Even Pages Header & Footer option.) In the footer of this page, display the report title on the left and your name on the right.

Set Properties and Finalize Document

After improving the readability of the document, you remember that you have not yet saved it. Your professor still uses an older version of Word, so you save the document in a compatible format that will display easily. You also remove the watermark just before saving the final copy.

a. Save the document.

b. Run the Compatibility Checker and Document Inspector, but do not take any suggested actions at this time.

c. Add **Ethics**, **Responsibility**, and **Morals** to the Keywords: field in the document properties.

d. Remove the watermark.

e. Save the document again, in Word 97-2003 format, as **w01c1ethics_LastnameFirstname**.

f. Use the Print Preview and Print feature to view the document before printing. If allowed by your instructor, print one copy of the document using the 2 Pages per sheet setting.

BEYOND THE CLASSROOM

More Career Choices

GENERAL CASE 

Have you taken time to think about the career you wish to pursue when you complete your education? In Mid-Level Exercise 2, you modified a documentary written by a student with interest in optometry. Now it is your turn to develop a similar paper about a different career field. After you write your own documentary using Word, use the skills from this chapter to format it with a professional look, and then name the document **w01b1job_LastnameFirstname**. Save and close the file, and submit based on your instructor's directions.

Animal Concerns

RESEARCH CASE 

As the population of family pets continues to grow, it is imperative that we learn how to be responsible pet owners. Very few people take the time to perform thorough research on the fundamental care of and responsibility for animal populations. Open the *w01b2animal* document, and then save it as **w01b2animal_LastnameFirstname**. Search the Internet for information that will contribute to this report on animal care and concerns. Compare information from at least three sources. Give consideration to information that is copyrighted; any information you quote should be cited in the document. As you enter the information and sources into the document, you will be reminded of concepts learned in this chapter, such as word wrap and soft returns. Use your knowledge of other formatting techniques, such as hard returns, page numbers, and margin settings, to create an attractive document. Create a cover page for the document, perform a spelling check, and then view the print preview before submitting this assignment to your instructor. Create headers and/or footers to improve readability. Save and close the file, and submit based on your instructor's directions.

TMG Newsletter

Open *w01b3tmgnews*, and then save it as **w01b3tmgnews_LastnameFirstname**.The document was started by an office assistant, but he quickly gave up on it after he moved paragraphs around until it became unreadable. The document contains significant errors, which cause the newsletter to display in a very disjointed way. Use your knowledge of Page Layout options and other Word features to revise this newsletter in time for the monthly mailing. Save and close the file, and submit based on your instructor's directions.

WORD

2 DOCUMENT PRESENTATION

Editing and Formatting

CASE STUDY | Simserv-Pitka Enterprises

Watch the
Set-up Video
for this Case Study!

Simserv Enterprises, a consumer products manufacturing company, has recently acquired a competitor in an effort to become a stronger company poised to meet the demands of the market. Each year, Simserv generates a corporate annual summary and distributes it to all employees and stockholders. You are the executive assistant to the president of Simserv, and your responsibilities include preparing and distributing the corporate annual summary. This year, the report emphasizes the importance of acquiring Pitka Industries to form Simserv-Pitka Enterprises.

The annual report always provides a synopsis of recent changes to upper management, and this year, it will introduce a new Chairman of the Board and Chief Executive Officer, as well as a new Chief Financial Officer. Information about these newly appointed executives and other financial data has been gathered, but the report needs to be formatted to display the information clearly and professionally before it can be distributed to employees and stockholders.

OBJECTIVES AFTER READING THIS CHAPTER, YOU WILL BE ABLE TO:

1. Apply font attributes through the Font dialog box ***p.114***
2. Control word wrap ***p.118***
3. Set off paragraphs with tabs, borders, lists, and columns ***p.122***
4. Apply paragraph formats ***p.128***
5. Understand styles ***p.137***
6. Create and modify styles ***p.137***
7. Format a graphical object ***p.147***
8. Insert symbols into a document ***p.151***

Text Formatting Features

Typography is the appearance of printed matter.

The arrangement and appearance of printed matter is called ***typography***. You may also define it as the process of selecting typefaces, type styles, and type sizes. The importance of these decisions is obvious, for the ultimate success of any document depends greatly on its appearance. Typeface should reinforce the message without calling attention to itself and should be consistent with the information you want to convey. For example, a paper prepared for a professional purpose, such as a résumé, should have a standard typeface instead of one that looks funny or cute. Additionally, you want to minimize the variety of typefaces in a document to maintain a professional look.

The ultimate success of any document depends greatly on its appearance. Typeface should reinforce the message without calling attention to itself and should be consistent with the information you want to convey.

A **typeface** or **font** is a complete set of characters.

A **serif typeface** contains a thin line at the top and bottom of characters.

A **sans serif typeface** does not contain thin lines on characters.

A ***typeface*** or ***font*** is a complete set of characters—upper- and lowercase letters, numbers, punctuation marks, and special symbols. A definitive characteristic of any typeface is the presence or absence of thin lines that end the main strokes of each letter. A ***serif typeface*** contains a thin line or extension at the top and bottom of the primary strokes on characters. A ***sans serif typeface*** (*sans* from the French meaning *without*) does not contain the thin lines on characters. Times New Roman is an example of a serif typeface. Arial is a sans serif typeface.

Serifs help the eye to connect one letter with the next and generally are used with large amounts of text. The paragraphs in this book, for example, are set in a serif typeface. A sans serif typeface is more effective with smaller amounts of text such as titles, headlines, corporate logos, and Web pages. For example, the blue heading Text Formatting Features and the quote by the first paragraph on this page are set in a sans serif font.

A **monospaced typeface** uses the same amount of horizontal space for every character.

A **proportional typeface** allocates horizontal space to each character.

Type style is the characteristic applied to a font, such as bold.

A second characteristic of a typeface is whether it is monospaced or proportional. A ***monospaced typeface*** (such as `Courier New`) uses the same amount of horizontal space for every character regardless of its width. A ***proportional typeface*** (such as Times New Roman or Arial) allocates space according to the width of the character. For example, the lowercase *m* is wider than the lowercase *i*. Monospaced fonts are used in tables and financial projections where text must be precisely lined up, one character underneath the other. Proportional typefaces create a more professional appearance and are appropriate for most documents, such as research papers, status reports, and letters. You can set any typeface in different ***type styles*** such as regular, **bold**, *italic*, or ***bold italic***.

In this section, you will apply font attributes through the Font dialog box, change case, and highlight text so that it stands out. You will also control word wrap by inserting nonbreaking hyphens and nonbreaking spaces between words.

Applying Font Attributes Through the Font Dialog Box

In the Office Fundamentals chapter, you learn how to use the Font group on the Home tab to apply font attributes. In addition to applying commands from the Font group, you can display the Font dialog box when you click the Font Dialog Box Launcher. Making selections in the Font dialog box before entering text sets the format of the text as you type (see Figure 2.1).

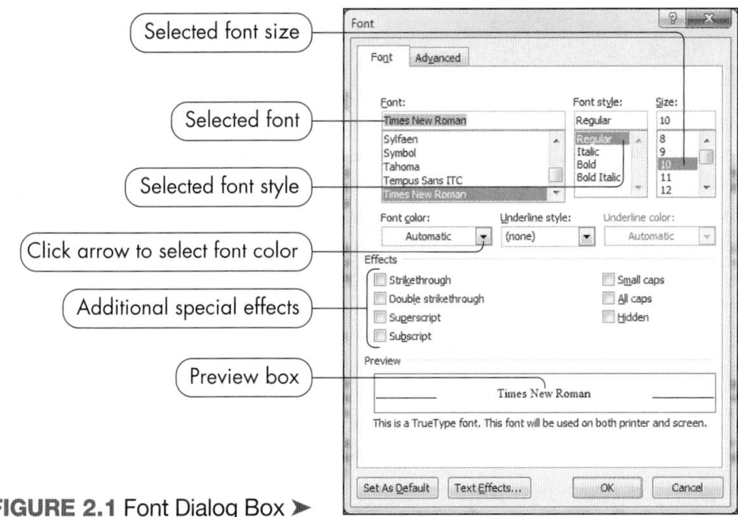

FIGURE 2.1 Font Dialog Box ➤

Select Font Options

In addition to changing the font, font style, and size, you can apply other font attributes to text. Although the Font group on the Home tab contains special effects commands such as strikethrough, subscript, and superscript, the Effects section in the Font tab in the Font dialog box contains other options for applying color and effects, such as small caps and double strikethrough. From this dialog box you can change the underline options and indicate if spaces are to be underlined or just words. You can even change the color of the text and the color of the underline.

New to Office 2010 is the Text Effects feature in the Font group. When you click Text Effects you can choose from a variety of colors and styles to immediately apply to text. The feature enables you to customize the effects by selecting colors, line widths, and amount of transparency. In addition to the Home tab, you can access Text Effects from the Font dialog box. When you use that path, another dialog box opens, showing custom options for each effect. Table 2.1 gives a general description of these special effects.

TABLE 2.1 Font Effects

Effect	Description and Options	Sample of Options to Change	Sample of Effect
Text Fill	Select a color to apply to the font.	No fill Solid fill Gradient fill	Sample
Text Outline	Select a color and line type to outline the font.	No line Solid line Gradient line	Sample
Outline Style	Select line width, type (solid, dashed), and cap on the font.	Width Dash type Arrow settings	Sample
Shadow	Select amount of shadow to apply to the font.	Color Transparency Angle	Sample
Reflection	Select a reflection style to apply to the font.	Presets Size Blur	Sample
Glow and Soft Edges	Select a glow or soft edge that displays around the font.	Color Size Presets	Sample
3-D Format	Select features that present the font in 3-D form.	Bevel Depth Surface	Sample

TIP Hidden Text

Hidden text does not appear onscreen.

Hidden text is document text that does not appear onscreen, unless you click Show/Hide (¶) in the Paragraph group on the Home tab. You can use this special effect format to hide confidential information before printing documents for other people. For example, an employer can hide employees' Social Security numbers before printing a company roster. Note, however, that if you e-mail a document that contains hidden text, the recipient will be able to view it.

Set Character Spacing

Character spacing is the horizontal space between characters.

Character spacing refers to the amount of horizontal space between characters. Although most character spacing is acceptable, some character combinations appear too far apart or too close together in large-sized text when printed. If so, you might want to adjust for this spacing discrepancy. The Advanced tab in the Font dialog box contains options in which you manually control the spacing between characters. The Advanced tab shown in Figure 2.2 displays four options for adjusting character spacing: Scale, Spacing, Position, and Kerning.

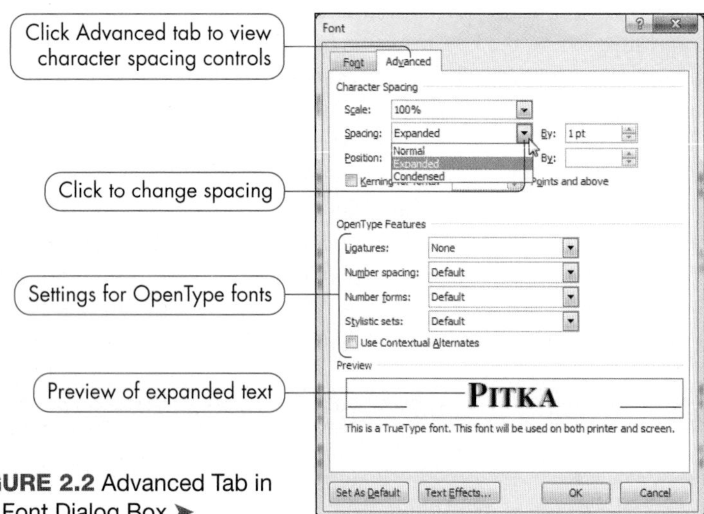

FIGURE 2.2 Advanced Tab in the Font Dialog Box ➤

Scale or **scaling** is the adjustment of height or width by a percentage of the image's original size.

Scale or ***scaling*** adjusts height and width by a percentage of the original size. For text, adjustments to scale will increase or decrease the text horizontally as a percentage of its size; it does not change the vertical height of text. You may use the scale feature on justified text, which does not produce the best-looking results—adjust the scale by a low percentage (90%–95%) to improve text flow without a noticeable difference to the reader. You may select the Expanded option to stretch a word or sentence so it fills more space; for example, use it on a title you want to span across the top of a page. The Condensed option is useful to squeeze text closer together, such as when you want to prevent one word from wrapping to another line.

Position raises or lowers text from the baseline.

Kerning enables more even spacing between characters.

Position raises or lowers text from the baseline without creating superscript or subscript size. Use this feature when you want text to stand out from other text on the same line, or use it to create a fun title by raising and/or lowering every few letters. ***Kerning*** automatically adjusts spacing between characters to achieve a more evenly spaced appearance. Kerning primarily enables letters to fit closer together, especially when a capital letter can use space unoccupied by a lowercase letter beside it. For example, you can kern the letters *Va* so the top of the *V* extends into the empty space above the *a* instead of leaving an awkward gap between them.

OpenType is a form of font designed for use on all platforms.

Word 2010 introduces support for OpenType fonts. ***OpenType*** is an advanced form of font that is designed for all platforms, including Windows and Macintosh. OpenType font technology has advantages over the commonly used TrueType Font because it can hold more characters in a set and is more compact, enabling smaller file sizes. If you install OpenType fonts on your PC, you can use the OpenType font settings in the Advanced tab of the Font dialog box.

Change Text Case (Capitalization)

Use **Change Case** to change capitalization of text.

To change the capitalization of text in a document quickly, use ***Change Case*** in the Font group on the Home tab. When you click Change Case, the following list of options display:

- **Sentence case** (capitalizes only the first word of the sentence or phrase).
- **lowercase** (changes the text to all lowercase).
- **UPPERCASE** (changes the text to all capital letters).
- **Capitalize Each Word** (capitalizes the first letter of each word; effective for formatting titles, but remember to lowercase first letters of short prepositions, such as *of*).
- **tOGGLE cASE** (changes lowercase to uppercase and uppercase to lowercase).

This feature is useful when generating a list and you want to use the same case formatting for each item. If you do not select text first, the casing format will take effect on the text where the insertion point is located. You can toggle among uppercase, lowercase, and sentence case formats by pressing Shift+F3.

Apply Text Highlighting

Use the **Highlighter** to mark text that you want to locate easily.

People often use a highlighting marker to highlight important parts of textbooks, magazine articles, and other documents. In Word, you use the ***Highlighter*** to mark text that you want to stand out or locate easily. Highlighted text draws the reader's attention to important information within the documents you create, as illustrated in Figure 2.3. The Text Highlight Color command is located in the Font group on the Home tab and on the Mini toolbar. You can click Text Highlight Color before or after selecting text. When you click Text Highlight Color before selecting text, the mouse pointer resembles a pen that you can click and drag across text to highlight it. The feature stays on so you can highlight additional text. When you finish highlighting text, click Text Highlight Color again, or press Esc to turn it off. If you select text first, click Text Highlight Color to apply the color. To remove highlights, select the highlighted text, click the Text Highlight Color arrow, and choose No Color.

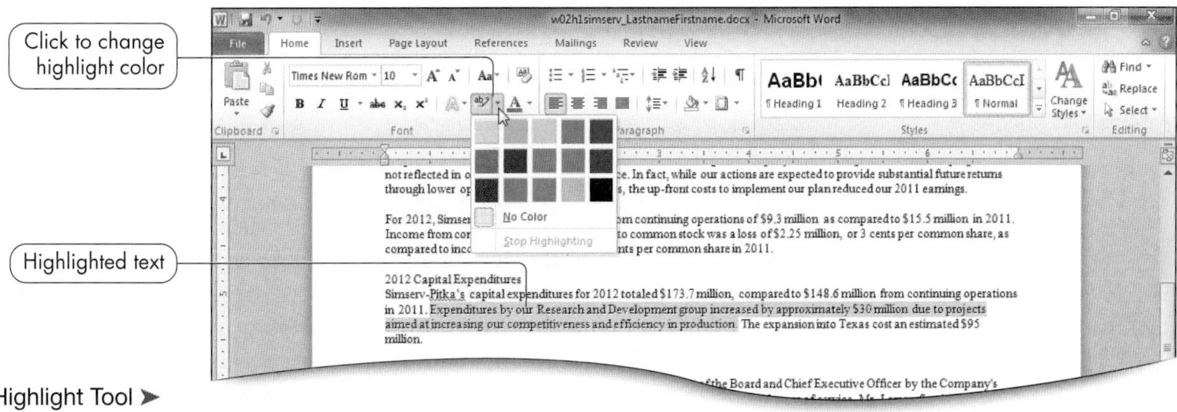

FIGURE 2.3 Highlight Tool ➤

If you use a color printer, you see the highlight colors on your printout. If you use a monochrome printer, the highlight appears in shades of gray. Use Print Preview prior to printing to be sure that you can easily read the text with the gray highlight. If not, select a lighter highlight color, and preview your document again. You can create a unique highlighting effect by choosing a dark highlight color, such as Dark Blue, and applying a light font color, such as White.

Controlling Word Wrap

In Word, text wraps to the next line when the current line of text is full. Most of the time, the way words wrap is acceptable. Occasionally, however, text may wrap in an undesirable location. To improve the readability of text, you need to proofread word-wrapping locations and insert special characters. Two general areas of concern are hyphenated words and spacing within proper nouns.

Insert Nonbreaking Hyphens

A **nonbreaking hyphen** prevents a word from becoming separated at the hyphen.

If a hyphenated word falls at the end of a line, the first word and the hyphen may appear on the first line, and the second word may wrap to the next line. However, certain hyphenated text, such as phone numbers, should stay together to improve the readability of the text. To keep hyphenated words together, replace the regular hyphen with a nonbreaking hyphen. A ***nonbreaking hyphen*** keeps text on both sides of the hyphen together, thus preventing the hyphenated word from becoming separated at the hyphen, as shown in Figure 2.4. To insert a nonbreaking hyphen, press Ctrl+Shift+Hyphen. When you click Show/Hide in the Paragraph group on the Home tab to display formatting symbols, a regular hyphen looks like a hyphen, and a nonbreaking hyphen appears as a wider hyphen. However, the nonbreaking hyphen looks like a regular hyphen when printed.

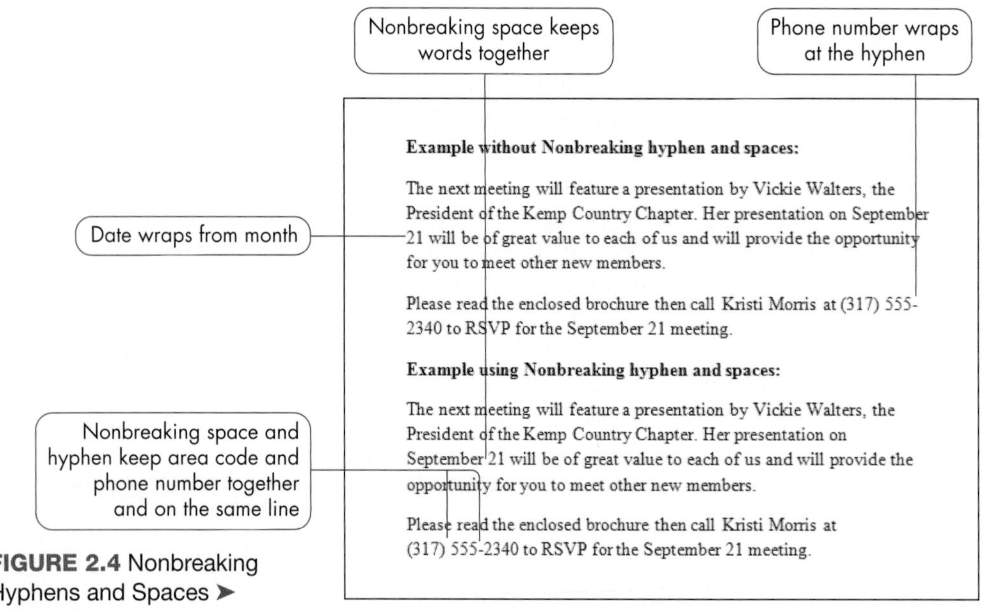

FIGURE 2.4 Nonbreaking Hyphens and Spaces ➤

Insert Nonbreaking Spaces

A **nonbreaking space** keeps two or more words together on a line.

Because text will wrap to the next line if a word does not fit at the end of the current line, occasionally word wrapping between certain types of words is undesirable; that is, some words should be kept together for improved readability and understanding. For example, in Figure 2.4 the date September 21 should stay together instead of separating on two lines. Other items that should stay together include names, such as Ms. Stevenson, and page references, such as page 15. To prevent words from separating due to the word wrap feature, you can insert a ***nonbreaking space***—a special character that keeps two or more words together. To insert a nonbreaking space, press Ctrl+Shift+Spacebar between the two words that you want to keep together. If a space already exists, the result of pressing the Spacebar, you should delete it before you insert the nonbreaking space.

HANDS-ON EXERCISES

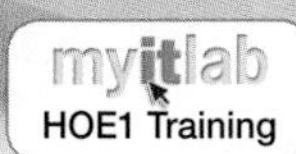

1 Text Formatting Features

As the executive assistant to the president at Simserv-Pitka Enterprises, you are responsible for preparing and distributing the Annual Summary. A report of this importance should be easy to read, attractive, and professional. You have the basic information to include in the report, and your first step is to change the formatting of some text so that it displays nicely in print, to include highlighting where appropriate, and to look for places where you might need to insert nonbreaking hyphens or spaces.

Skills covered: Change Text Appearance • Insert Nonbreaking Spaces and Nonbreaking Hyphens • Highlight Text

STEP 1 CHANGE TEXT APPEARANCE

As you begin to prepare the report for the Board and stockholders, you know the first thing that requires your attention is changing the font of the whole document so that it is easier to read. Additionally, you will change the font properties of the heading and subheading so they stand out from the rest of the text. Refer to Figure 2.5 as you complete Step 1.

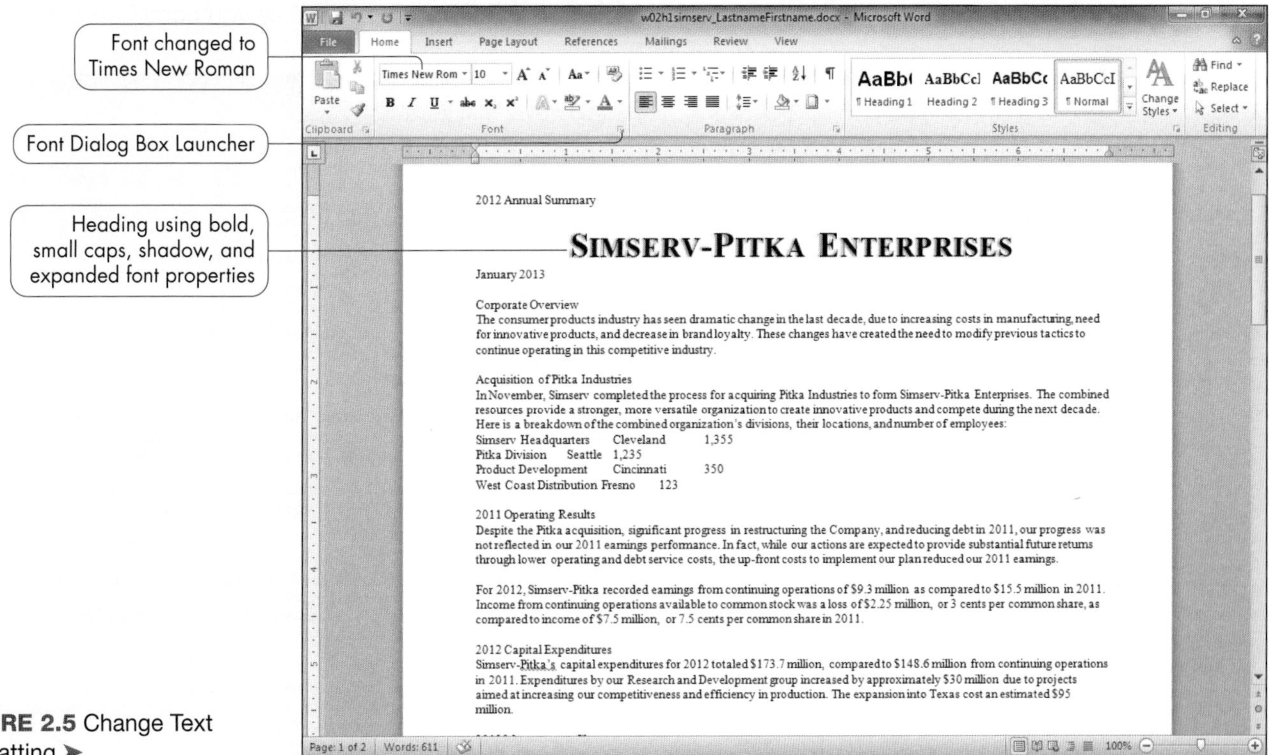

FIGURE 2.5 Change Text Formatting ➤

a. Open *w02h1simserv* and save it as **w02h1simserv_LastnameFirstname.**

TROUBLESHOOTING: If you make any major mistakes in this exercise, you can close the file, open *w02h1simserv* again, and then start this exercise over.

b. Click **Ctrl+A** to select all of the text in the document. Click the **Font arrow** in the Font group on the Home tab, and then select **Times New Roman.**

You use a serif font on the whole document because it is easier to read in print.

c. Select the second line of the document, *Simserv-Pitka Enterprises.* Click **Center** on the Mini toolbar.

d. Click the **Font Dialog Box Launcher** in the Font group.

The Font dialog box displays with the Font tab options.

e. Click the **Font tab**, if necessary, and then click **Bold** in the Font style box. Select **26** in the Size box. Click to select the **Small caps Effect**.

f. Click **Text Effects**. Click **Shadow**, click **Presets**, and then click **Offset Left** (third row, third column). Click the **Close button** to return to the Font dialog box.

g. Click the **Advanced tab**, and then click the **Spacing arrow**. Select **Expanded**, and then notice how the text changes in the preview box. Click **OK.**

Word expands the spacing between letters in the subtitle as shown in Figure 2.5. You will apply this formatting to the third line in a later exercise.

h. Save the document.

STEP 2 INSERT NONBREAKING SPACES AND NONBREAKING HYPHENS

Since the company's new name, Simserv-Pitka, is hyphenated, you want to keep the name together and not split it if it appears at the end of a text line. Therefore, you will replace existing hyphens in Simserv-Pitka, as well as in other areas of the document, with nonbreaking hyphens. You will also replace existing spaces with nonbreaking spaces to make sure the information displays properly when the report is completed and ready for printing. Refer to Figure 2.6 as you complete Step 2.

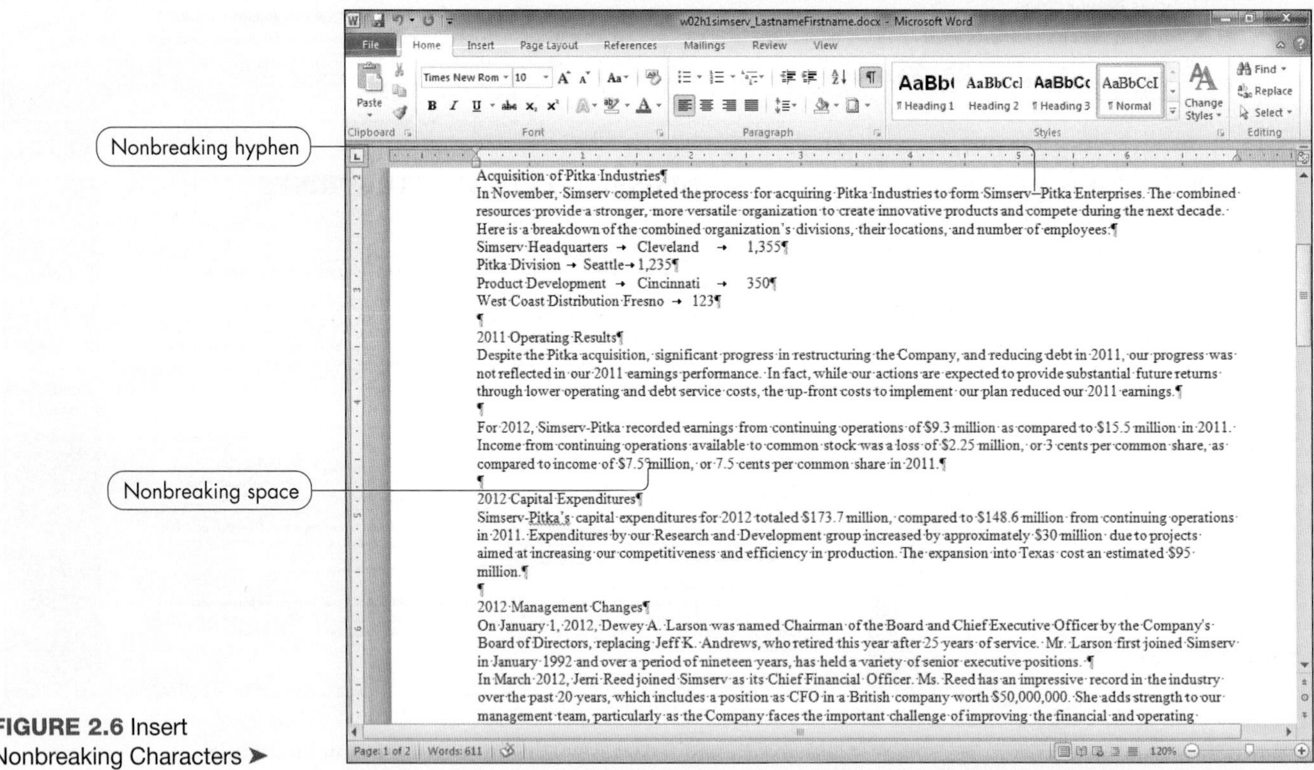

FIGURE 2.6 Insert Nonbreaking Characters ➤

a. Select the hyphen between the text *Simserv-Pitka* in the first sentence of the *Acquisition of Pitka Industries* paragraph. Press **Delete**, and then press **Ctrl+Shift+Hyphen** to insert a nonbreaking hyphen.

TROUBLESHOOTING: If text continues word wrapping between two words after you insert a nonbreaking space or nonbreaking hyphen, click Show/Hide (¶) in the Paragraph group on the Home tab to display symbols, and then identify and delete regular spaces or hyphens that still exist between words.

b. Place the insertion point between *$7.5* and *million* in the last sentence of the second paragraph under the *2011 Operating Results* heading.

   Before inserting a nonbreaking space, you must position the insertion point between the two words you want to keep together.

c. Delete the existing space, and then press **Ctrl+Shift+Spacebar** to insert a nonbreaking space.

d. Click **Show/Hide** (¶) in the Paragraph group, and then notice the different format for the nonbreaking hyphen and space, as seen in Figure 2.6.

   If text is enlarged, the nonbreaking space keeps *$7.5 million* together, preventing word wrapping between the two words.

e. Click **Show/Hide** (¶) again to remove the formatting marks. Save the document.

TIP Another Way to Insert Nonbreaking Spaces and Hyphens

An alternative to using keyboard shortcuts to insert nonbreaking spaces and hyphens is to use the Symbols gallery on the Insert tab. From the Insert tab, click the Symbol arrow and click More Symbols to display the Symbol dialog box. Click the Special Characters tab, select the Nonbreaking Hyphen or the Nonbreaking Space character option, and click Insert to insert a nonbreaking hyphen or a nonbreaking space, respectively. Close the Symbol dialog box after inserting the nonbreaking hyphen or nonbreaking space.

STEP 3 HIGHLIGHT TEXT

Some information in a document is so important that you want to be sure to draw attention to it. The Highlighting tool is useful for this purpose and you use it in the next step to make sure the reader knows about the great investment in Research and Development at Simserv-Pitka Enterprises. Refer to Figure 2.7 as you complete Step 3.

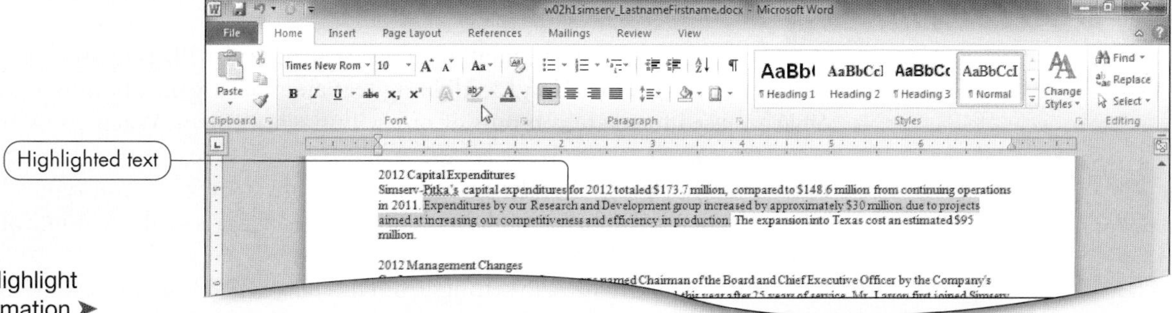

FIGURE 2.7 Highlight Important Information ➤

a. Select the second sentence in the *2012 Capital Expenditures* paragraph that starts with *Expenditures by our Research and Development group.*

b. Click **Text Highlight Color** in the Font group.

   Word highlighted the selected sentence in the default highlight color, yellow, as seen in Figure 2.7.

TROUBLESHOOTING: If Word applies a color other than yellow to the selected text, that means another highlight color was selected after starting Word. If this happens, select the text again, click the Text Highlight Color arrow, and select Yellow.

c. Save the document and keep it onscreen if you plan to continue with the next Hands-On Exercise. If not, close the document and exit Word.

Paragraph Formatting Features

A change in typography is only one way to alter the appearance of a document. You also can change the alignment, indentation, tab stops, or line spacing for any paragraph(s) within the document. You can control the pagination and prevent the occurrence of awkward page breaks by specifying that an entire paragraph must appear on the same page, or that a heading should appear on the same page as the next paragraph. You can include borders or shading for added emphasis around selected paragraphs.

A change in typography is only one way to alter the appearance of a document. You also can change the alignment, indentation, tab stops, or line spacing for any paragraph(s) within the document.

Word implements all of these paragraph formats for all selected paragraphs. If no paragraphs are selected, Word applies the formats to the current paragraph (the paragraph containing the insertion point), regardless of the position of the insertion point within the paragraph when you apply the paragraph formats.

In this section, you will set tabs, apply borders, create lists, and format text into columns to help offset text for better readability. You will also change text alignment, indent paragraphs, set line and paragraph spacing, and control pagination breaks.

Setting Off Paragraphs with Tabs, Borders, Lists, and Columns

Many people agree that their eyes tire and minds wander when they read page after page of plain black text on white paper. To break up long blocks of text or draw attention to an area of a page, you can format text with tabs, borders, lists, or columns. These formatting features enable you to modify positioning, frame a section, itemize for easy reading, order steps in a sequence, or create pillars of text for visual appeal and easy reading. For example, look through the pages of this book and notice the use of bulleted lists, tables for reference points, and borders around TIP boxes to draw your attention and enhance the pages.

Set Tabs

A **tab** is a marker for aligning text in a document.

One way to enhance the presentation of text on a page visually is to use tabs. ***Tabs*** are markers that specify the position for aligning text and add organization to a document. They often are used to create columns of text within a document. When you start a new document, the default tab stops are set every one-half inch across the page and are left aligned. Every time you press Tab, the insertion point moves over .5″. You typically press Tab to indent the first line of paragraphs in double-spaced reports or the first line of paragraphs in a modified block style letter.

You can access many Tab settings from the Tabs dialog box. To view the Tabs dialog box, click the Paragraph Dialog Box Launcher in the Paragraph group on the Home tab, then click Tabs from the Indents and Spacing tab. You can also display the Tabs dialog box by double-clicking a tab setting on the ruler. Table 2.2 describes the different types of tabs.

A **left tab** marks the position to align text on the left.

A **center tab** marks where text centers as you type.

A **right tab** marks the position to align text on the right.

A **decimal tab** marks where numbers align on a decimal point as you type.

A **bar tab** marks the location of a vertical line between columns.

TABLE 2.2 Tab Markers

Tab Icon on Ruler	Type of Tab	Function
L	***left tab***	Sets the start position on the left so as you type, text moves to the right of the tab setting.
⊥	***center tab***	Sets the middle point of the text you type; whatever you type will be centered on that tab setting.
┘	***right tab***	Sets the start position on the right so as you type, text moves to the left of that tab setting and aligns on the right.
⊥.	***decimal tab***	Aligns numbers on a decimal point. Regardless of how long the number, each number lines up with the decimal in the same position.
|	***bar tab***	This tab does not position text or decimals, but inserts a vertical bar at the tab setting. This bar is useful as a separator for text printed on the same line.

An alternative to using the Tabs dialog box is to set tabs directly on the ruler. Click the Tabs selector on the left side of the ruler (refer to Figure 2.8) until it displays the tab alignment you want. Then click the ruler in the location where you want to set the type of tab you selected. To delete a tab, click the tab marker on the ruler, and then drag it down and off the ruler.

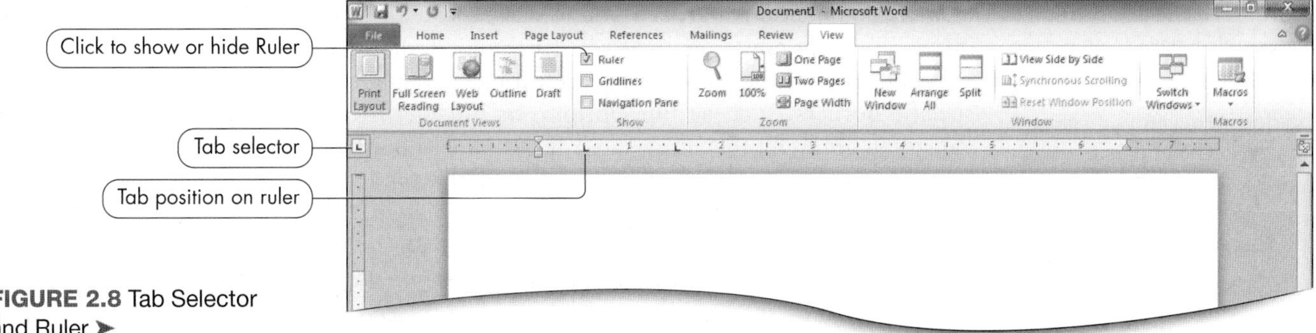

FIGURE 2.8 Tab Selector and Ruler ➤

TIP Deleting Tabs

When you set a new tab by clicking on the ruler, Word deletes all tab settings to the left of the tab you set. If you need to delete a single tab setting, for example the tab at 1.5″, click the 1.5″ tab marker on the ruler and drag it off of the ruler. When you release the mouse, you delete only that tab setting. If a marker does not display on the ruler for a tab, use the Tabs dialog box to adjust tab settings.

A **leader character** is dots or hyphens that connect two items of information.

In the Tabs dialog box, you also can specify a ***leader character***, typically dots or hyphens, which display on the left side of the tab and serve to draw or lead the reader's eye across the page to connect two items of information. For example, in Figure 2.9, it is easier to read the location and number of employees for each division because tab leader characters connect each piece of information. When dot characters connect items, they are often called *dot leaders* or just *leaders*. Notice also in the Tab dialog box in Figure 2.9, the default tab settings have been cleared and new tab settings are in place at .5″ and 2.5″; additionally, a right tab is set at 4″.

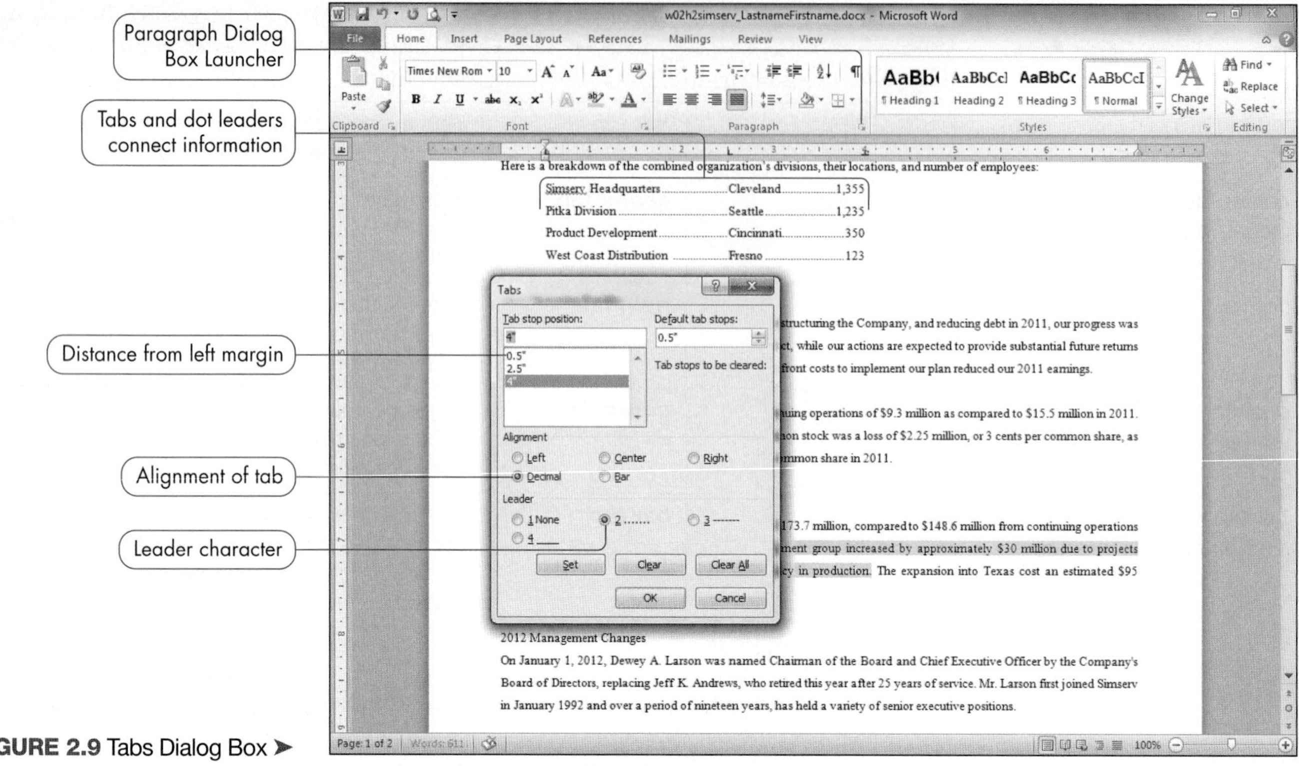

FIGURE 2.9 Tabs Dialog Box ➤

Apply Borders and Shading

A **border** is a line that surrounds a paragraph, a page, a table, or an image.

Shading is background color that appears behind text.

You can draw attention to a document or an area of a document by using the Borders and Shading command. A ***border*** is a line that surrounds a paragraph, a page, a table, or an image, similar to how a picture frame surrounds a photograph or piece of art. ***Shading*** is a background color that appears behind text in a paragraph, a page, or a table. You can apply specific borders, such as top, bottom, or outside, from the Border command in the Paragraph group on the Home tab. For customized borders, click the Borders arrow in the Paragraph group on the Home tab to open the Borders and Shading dialog box (see Figure 2.10). Borders or shading is applied to selected text within a paragraph, to the entire paragraph if no text is selected, or to the entire page if the Page Border tab is selected. Even though other features can highlight text with color, you can use the Borders and Shading commands to add boxes and/or shading around text, as well as place horizontal or vertical lines around different quantities of text. A good example of this practice is used in the Exploring series: The TIP boxes are surrounded by a border with dark shading and use a white font color for the headings to attract your attention.

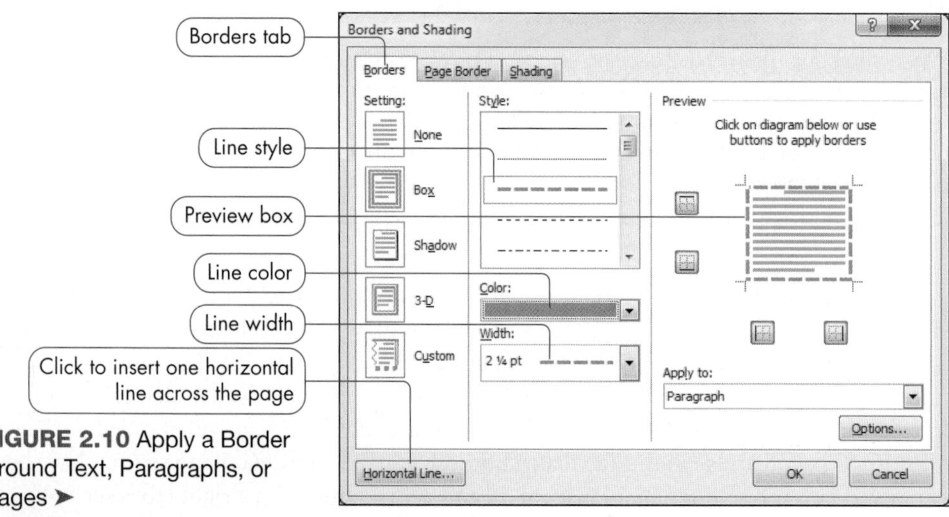

FIGURE 2.10 Apply a Border Around Text, Paragraphs, or Pages ➤

You can choose from several different line styles in any color, but remember you must use a color printer to display the line colors on the printed page. Colored lines appear in gray on a monochrome printer. Using the Box setting, you can place a uniform border around a paragraph, or you can choose a shadow effect with thicker lines at the right and bottom. You also can apply lines to selected sides of a paragraph by selecting a line style, and then clicking the desired sides as appropriate.

The horizontal line button at the bottom of the Borders and Shading dialog box provides access to a variety of attractive horizontal line designs. This is useful for displaying a horizontal line across a page to separate two elements. It also makes a nice border in a header or footer.

The Page Border tab enables you to place a decorative border around one or more selected pages. As with a paragraph border, you can place the border around the entire page, or you can select one or more sides. The page border also provides an additional option to use preselected clip art as a border instead of ordinary lines. Note that it is appropriate to use page borders on documents such as fliers, newsletters, and invitations, but not on formal documents such as research papers and professional reports.

Use page borders on ... fliers, newsletters, and invitations, but not on formal documents such as research papers and professional reports.

Shading is applied independently of the border and is accessed from the Borders and Shading dialog box or from Shading in the Paragraph group on the Home tab. Clear (no shading) is the default. Solid (100%) shading fills in a box around the text, and in some instances, the text is turned white so you can read it. Shading of 10% or 20% generally is most effective to add emphasis to the selected paragraph (see Figure 2.11). The Borders and Shading command is implemented on the paragraph level and affects the entire paragraph unless text has been selected within the paragraph.

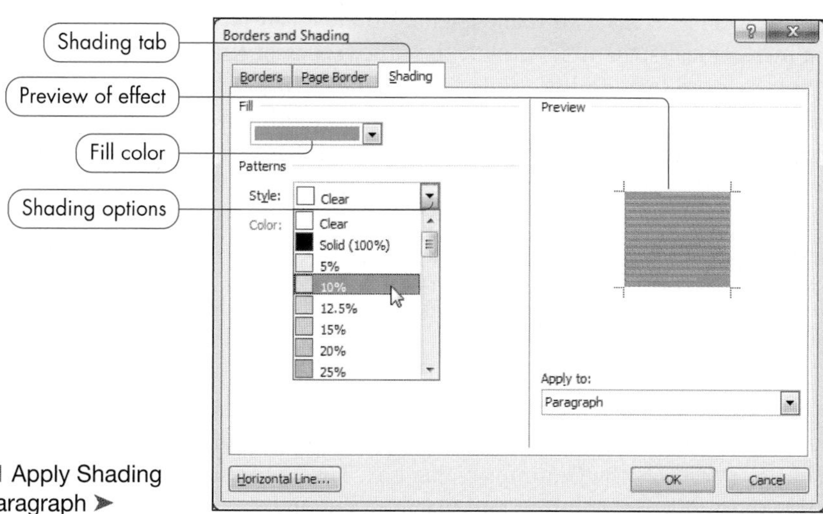

FIGURE 2.11 Apply Shading to Text or a Paragraph ➤

Create Bulleted and Numbered Lists

A **bulleted list** itemizes and separates paragraph text to increase readability.

A **numbered list** sequences and prioritizes items.

A **multilevel list** extends a numbered list to several levels.

A list helps you organize information by highlighting important topics. A ***bulleted list*** itemizes and separates paragraphs to increase readability. A ***numbered list*** sequences and prioritizes the items and is automatically updated to accommodate additions or deletions. A ***multilevel list*** extends a numbered list to several levels, and it too is updated automatically when topics are added or deleted. You create each of these lists from the Paragraph group on the Home tab.

To apply bullet formatting to a list, click the Bullets arrow and choose one of several predefined symbols in the Bullet library (see Figure 2.12). Position your mouse over one of the bullet styles in the Bullet Library and a preview of that bullet style will display in your document. To use that style, simply click the bullet. If you want to use a different bullet symbol, click the Define New Bullet option below the Bullet Library to choose a different symbol or picture for the bullet.

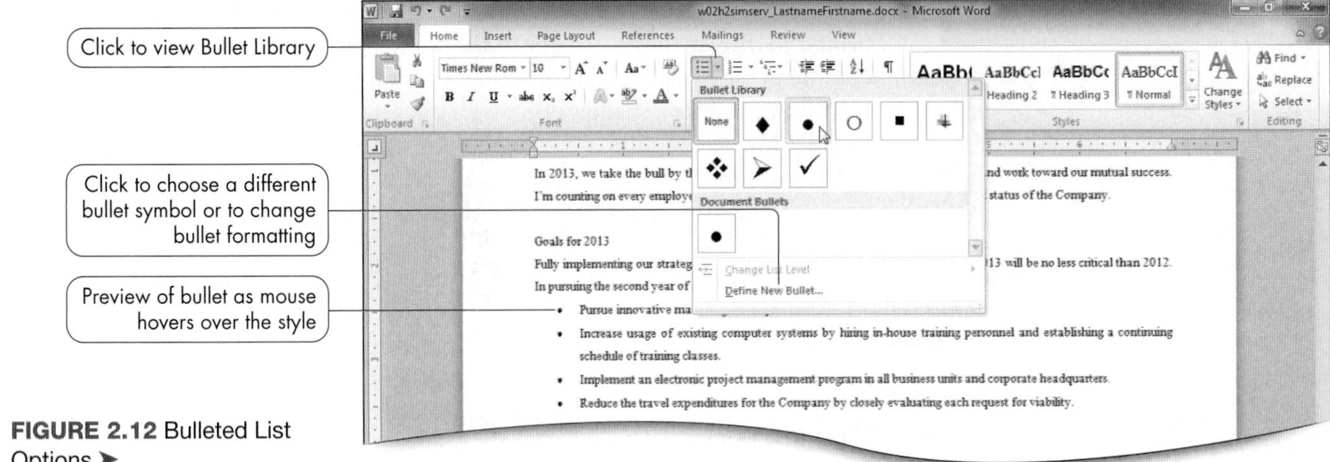

FIGURE 2.12 Bulleted List Options ➤

After you select text, you can click the Numbering arrow in the Paragraph group to apply Arabic or Roman numerals, or upper- or lowercase letters, for a numbered list. When you position the mouse pointer over a style in the Numbering Library, you see a preview of that numbering style in your document. As with a bulleted list, you can define a new style by selecting the Define New Number Format option below the Numbering Library. Note, too, the options to restart or continue numbering found by selecting the Set Numbering Value option. These become important if a list appears in multiple places within a document. In other words, each occurrence of a list can start numbering anew, or it can continue from where the previous list left off.

The Multilevel List command enables you to create an outline to organize your thoughts in a hierarchical structure. As with the other types of lists, you can choose one of several default styles and/or modify a style through the Define New Multilevel List option below the List Library. You also can specify whether each outline within a document is to restart its numbering, or whether it is to continue numbering from the previous outline.

Format Text into Columns

A **column** formats a section of a document into side-by-side vertical blocks.

Columns format a section of a document into side-by-side vertical blocks in which the text flows down the first column and then continues at the top of the next column. The length of a line of columnar text is shorter, enabling people to read through each document faster. To format text into columns, click the Page Layout tab and click Columns in the Page Setup group. From the Columns gallery, you can specify the number of columns or select More Columns to display the Columns dialog box. The Columns dialog box provides options for setting the number of columns and spacing between columns. Microsoft Word calculates the width of each column according to the left and right document margins on the page and the specified (default) space between columns.

The dialog box in Figure 2.13 implements a design of two equal columns. The width of each column is computed based on current left and right document margins and the spacing between columns. The width of each column is determined by subtracting the sum of the margins and the space between the columns from the page width of 8.5″. The result of the subtraction results in column widths of 3.25″.

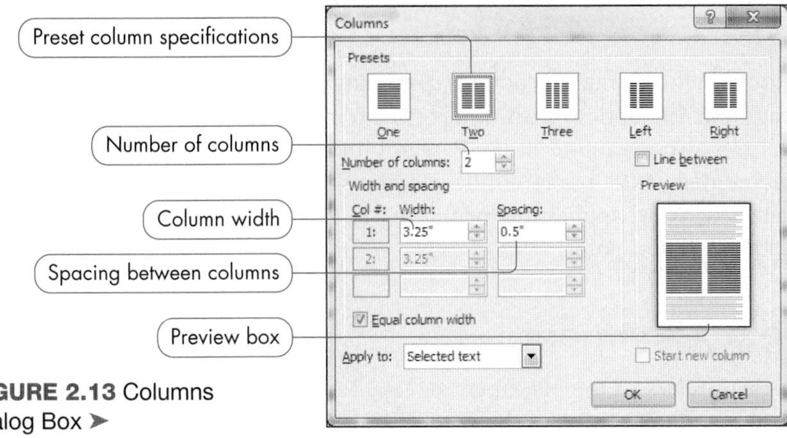

FIGURE 2.13 Columns Dialog Box ➤

One subtlety associated with column formatting is the use of sections, which control elements such as the orientation of a page (landscape or portrait), margins, page numbers, and the number of columns. Most of the documents you work with consist of a single section, so section formatting is not an issue. It becomes important only when you want to vary formatting in different parts, or sections, of the document. For example, you could use section formatting to create a document that has one column on its title page and two columns on the remaining pages. Creating this type of formatting requires you to divide the document into two sections by inserting a section break. You then format each section independently and specify the number of columns in each section.

Display Nonprinting Formatting Marks

As you type text, Word inserts nonprinting marks or symbols. While these symbols do not display on printouts, they do affect the appearance. For example, Word inserts a code every time you press Spacebar, Tab, and Enter. When you press Enter, it leaves a paragraph mark, no matter whether it is at the end of a single word, a single line, or a complete group of sentences. Word interprets the Paragraph mark as the completion of a paragraph, and so the paragraph mark (¶) at the end of a paragraph does more than just indicate the presence of a hard return. It also stores all of the formatting in effect for the paragraph. To preserve the formatting when you move or copy a paragraph, you must include the paragraph mark in the selected text. Click Show/Hide (¶) in the Paragraph group on the Home tab to display the paragraph mark and make sure it has been selected. Table 2.3 lists several common formatting marks. Both the hyphen and nonbreaking hyphen look like a regular hyphen when printed.

Word interprets the Paragraph mark as the completion of a paragraph.... It also stores all of the formatting in effect for the paragraph.

TABLE 2.3 Nonprinting Symbols

Symbol	Description	Create by
•	Regular space	Pressing Spacebar
°	Nonbreaking space	Pressing Ctrl+Shift+Spacebar
-	Regular hyphen	Pressing Hyphen
–	Nonbreaking hyphen	Pressing Ctrl+Shift+Hyphen
→	Tab	Pressing Tab
¶	End of paragraph	Pressing Enter
... **(shows under text)**	Hidden text	Selecting Hidden check box in Font dialog box
↵	Line break	Pressing Shift+Enter

Applying Paragraph Formats

The Paragraph group on the Home tab contains commands to set and control several format options for a paragraph. The options include alignment, indentation, line spacing, and pagination. These features also are found in the Paragraph dialog box. All of these formatting features are implemented at the paragraph level and affect all selected paragraphs. If no paragraphs are selected, Word applies the formatting to the current paragraph—the paragraph containing the insertion point.

Change Text Alignment

Horizontal alignment refers to the placement of text between the left and right margins.

Horizontal alignment refers to the placement of text between the left and right margins. Text is aligned in four different ways, as shown in Figure 2.14. Alignment options are justified (flush left/flush right), left aligned (flush left with a ragged right margin), right aligned (flush right with a ragged left margin), or centered within the margins (ragged left and right). The default alignment is left aligned.

We, the people of the United States, in order to form a more perfect Union, establish justice, insure domestic tranquility, provide for the common defense, promote the general welfare, and secure the blessings of liberty to ourselves and our posterity, do ordain and establish this Constitution for the United States of America.

Justified (flush left/flush right)

We, the people of the United States, in order to form a more perfect Union, establish justice, insure domestic tranquility, provide for the common defense, promote the general welfare, and secure the blessings of liberty to ourselves and our posterity, do ordain and establish this Constitution for the United States of America.

Left Aligned (flush left/ragged right)

We, the people of the United States, in order to form a more perfect Union, establish justice, insure domestic tranquility, provide for the common defense, promote the general welfare, and secure the blessings of liberty to ourselves and our posterity, do ordain and establish this Constitution for the United States of America.

Right Aligned (ragged left/flush right)

We, the people of the United States, in order to form a more perfect Union, establish justice, insure domestic tranquility, provide for the common defense, promote the general welfare, and secure the blessings of liberty to ourselves and our posterity, do ordain and establish this Constitution for the United States of America.

Centered (ragged left/ragged right)

FIGURE 2.14 Horizontal Alignment ➤

Left-aligned text is perhaps the easiest to read. The first letters of each line align with each other, helping the eye to find the beginning of each line. The lines themselves are of irregular length. Uniform spacing exists between words, and the ragged margin on the right adds white space to the text, giving it a lighter and more informal look.

Justified text, sometimes called fully justified, produces lines of equal length, with the spacing between words adjusted to align at the margins. Look closely and you will see many books, magazines, and newspapers fully justify text to add formality and "neatness" to the text. Some find this style more difficult to read because of the uneven (sometimes excessive) word spacing and/or the greater number of hyphenated words needed to justify the lines. However, it also can enable you to pack more information onto a page when space is constrained.

Text that is centered or right aligned is usually restricted to limited amounts of text where the effect is more important than the ease of reading. Centered text, for example, appears frequently on wedding invitations, poems, or formal announcements. In research papers, first-level titles often are centered as well. Right-aligned text is used with figure captions, in short headlines, and in document headers and footers.

The Paragraph group on the Home tab contains the four alignment options: Align Text Left, Center, Align Text Right, and Justify. To apply the alignment, select text, then click the alignment option on the Home tab. You can also set alignment from the Paragraph dialog box; the Indents and Spacing tab contains an Alignment arrow in the General section from which you can choose one of the four options.

 Alignment Keyboard Shortcuts

You can quickly apply alignment by using keyboard shortcuts. After you select the text, click Ctrl+L to align left, click Ctrl+E to align center, click Ctrl+R to align right, or click Ctrl+J to justify.

Indent Paragraphs

You can indent individual paragraphs so they appear to have different margins from the rest of a document. Indentation is established at the paragraph level; thus, it is possible to apply different indentation properties to different paragraphs. You can indent one paragraph from the left margin only, another from the right margin only, and a third from both the left and right margins. For example, the sixth edition of the *Publication Manual of the American Psychological Association,* which establishes the APA editorial style of writing, specifies that quotations consisting of 40 or more words should be contained in a separate paragraph that is indented .5″ from the left margin. Additionally, you can indent the first line of any paragraph differently from the rest of the paragraph. Finally, a paragraph may have no indentation at all, so that it aligns on the left and right margins.

Three settings determine the indentation of a paragraph: the left indent, the right indent, and a special indent (see Figure 2.15). The left and right indents are set to 0 by default, as is the special indent, and produce a paragraph with no indentation at all. Positive values for the left and right indents offset the paragraph from both margins.

A **first line indent** marks the location to indent only the first line in a paragraph.

A **hanging indent** marks how far to indent each line of a paragraph except the first.

The two types of special indentation are first line and hanging. The ***first line indent*** affects only the first line in the paragraph, and you apply it by pressing the Tab key at the beginning of the paragraph or by setting a specific measurement in the Paragraph dialog box. Remaining lines in the paragraph align at the left margin. A ***hanging indent*** aligns the first line of a paragraph at the left margin and indents the remaining lines. Hanging indents are often used with bulleted or numbered lists and to format citations on a bibliography page.

When you view the ruler, characters display to identify any special indents that are in use. A grey triangle pointing down identifies the indention for a First Line Indent, a grey arrow pointing up identifies the indention for a Hanging Indent, and a grey square identifies the Left Indent. You can slide the characters along the ruler to modify the location of the indents.

 Decrease Indent and Increase Indent

You can click Decrease Indent in the Paragraph group on the Home tab to decrease (bring text to the left) indented text by .5″. Click Increase Indent to move text to the right for an additional 1/2″.

Set Line and Paragraph Spacing

Line spacing is the space between the lines in a paragraph.

Line spacing determines the space between the lines in a paragraph and between paragraphs. Word provides complete flexibility and enables you to select any multiple of line spacing (single, double, line and a half, and so on). You also can specify line spacing in terms of points (1″ vertical contains 72 pt). Click Line and Paragraph Spacing in the Paragraph group on the Home tab to establish line spacing for the current paragraph. You can also set line spacing in the *Spacing* section on the Indents and Spacing tab in the Paragraph dialog box.

Paragraph spacing is the amount of space before or after a paragraph.

Paragraph spacing is the amount of space before or after a paragraph, as indicated by the paragraph mark when you press Enter between paragraphs. Unlike line spacing that controls *all* spacing within and between paragraphs, paragraph spacing controls only the spacing between paragraphs.

Sometimes you need to single-space text within a paragraph but want to have a blank line between paragraphs. Instead of pressing Enter twice between paragraphs, you can set the paragraph spacing to control the amount of space before or after the paragraph. You can set paragraph spacing in the *Spacing* section on the Indents and Spacing tab in the Paragraph dialog box. Setting a 12-pt After spacing creates the appearance of a double-space after the paragraph even though the user presses Enter only once between paragraphs.

The Paragraph dialog box is illustrated in Figure 2.15. The Indents and Spacing tab specifies a hanging indent, 1.5 line spacing, and justified alignment. The Preview area within the Paragraph dialog box enables you to see how the paragraph will appear within the document.

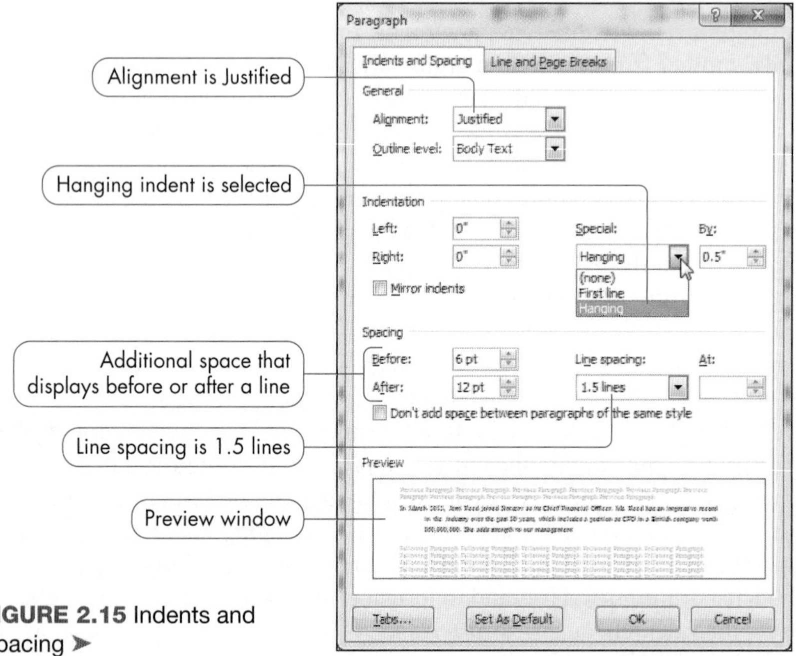

FIGURE 2.15 Indents and Spacing ➤

> **TIP** Indents and Paragraph Spacing
>
> To avoid opening the Paragraph dialog box, you can quickly change Indent or Paragraph Spacing from the Paragraph group on the Page Layout tab.

Control Widows and Orphans

A **widow** is the last line of a paragraph appearing by itself at the top of a page.

An **orphan** is the first line of a paragraph appearing by itself at the bottom of a page.

Some lines become isolated from the remainder of a paragraph and seem out of place at the beginning or end of a multipage document. A ***widow*** refers to the last line of a paragraph appearing by itself at the top of a page. An ***orphan*** is the first line of a paragraph appearing by itself at the bottom of a page. You can prevent these from occurring by checking the Widow/Orphan control in the *Pagination* section of the Line and Page Breaks tab of the Paragraph dialog box.

To prevent a page break from occurring within a paragraph and ensure that the entire paragraph appears on the same page use the *Keep lines together* option in the *Pagination* section of the Line and Page Breaks tab of the Paragraph dialog box. The paragraph is moved to the top of the next page if it does not fit on the bottom of the current page. Use the *Keep with next* option in the *Pagination* section to prevent a soft page break between the two paragraphs. This option is typically used to keep a heading (a one-line paragraph) with its associated text in the next paragraph. Figure 2.16 displays the Paragraph dialog box settings to control soft page breaks that detract from the appearance of a document.

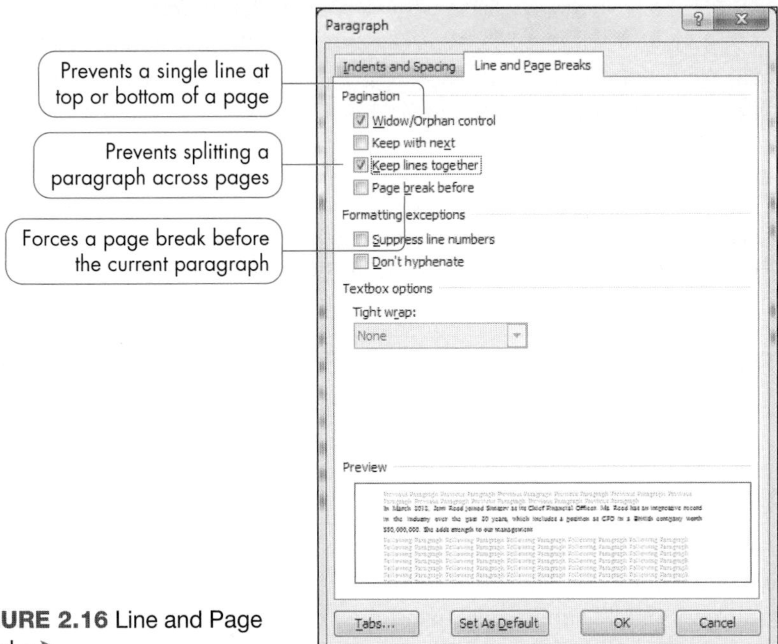

FIGURE 2.16 Line and Page Breaks ➤

TIP The Section Versus the Paragraph

Line spacing, alignment, tabs, and indents are implemented at the paragraph level. Change any of these parameters anywhere within the current (or selected) paragraph(s) and you change *only* those paragraph(s). Margins, page numbering, orientation, and columns are implemented at the section level. Change these parameters anywhere within a section and you change the characteristics of every page within that section.

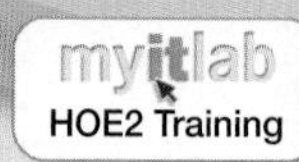

2 Paragraph Formatting Features

The next step in preparing the Annual Summary for distribution is to apply paragraph formatting to several areas of the document that will make it easier to read. You also want to apply special formatting, such as indentions and borders, to certain paragraphs for emphasis and to draw the readers' eye to that information.

Skills covered: Specify Line Spacing and Justification • Set Tabs and Indent a Paragraph • Apply Borders and Shading • Create a Bulleted and Numbered List • Create Columns

STEP 1 SPECIFY LINE SPACING AND JUSTIFICATION

The Annual Summary is an important document for your company, so you want to be sure it is easy to read and looks professional when printed. To help in that endeavor, you increase the line spacing and adjust justification of this document quickly and easily using the paragraph formatting features in Word. Refer to Figure 2.17 as you complete Step 1.

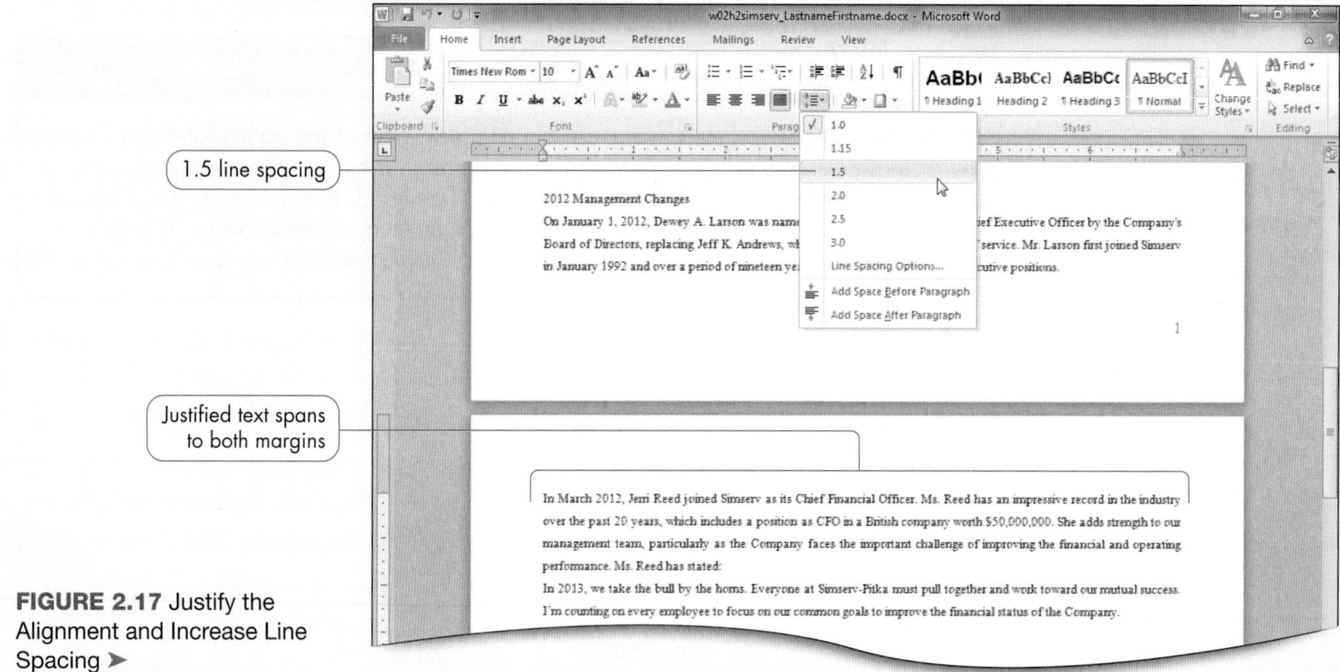

FIGURE 2.17 Justify the Alignment and Increase Line Spacing ➤

a. Open the *w02h1simserv_LastnameFirstname* document if you closed it at the end of Hands-On Exercise 1, and save it as **w02h2simserv_LastnameFirstname**, changing *h1* to *h2*.

b. Drag to select all of the text in the document, starting with the first sentence, *The consumer products industry has seen dramatic change …*, and then click **Justify** in the Paragraph group.

c. Click **Line and Paragraph Spacing** in the Paragraph group, and then select **1.5**, as seen in Figure 2.17.

These settings align the text on the right and left margins and add spacing before and after lines of text, making it easier to read.

d. Save the document.

STEP 2 SET TABS AND INDENT A PARAGRAPH

You want to display the information about divisions that were acquired so that it is easy to read across the page and not jumbled together as you see it now. You decide to insert two tabs to line up the division and cities. A third tab is needed for the number of employees, and since you are aligning a number, you wisely insert a decimal tab. You also decide to indent a quotation by the new CFO so it does not blend in with the rest of the paragraph. Refer to Figure 2.18 as you complete Step 2.

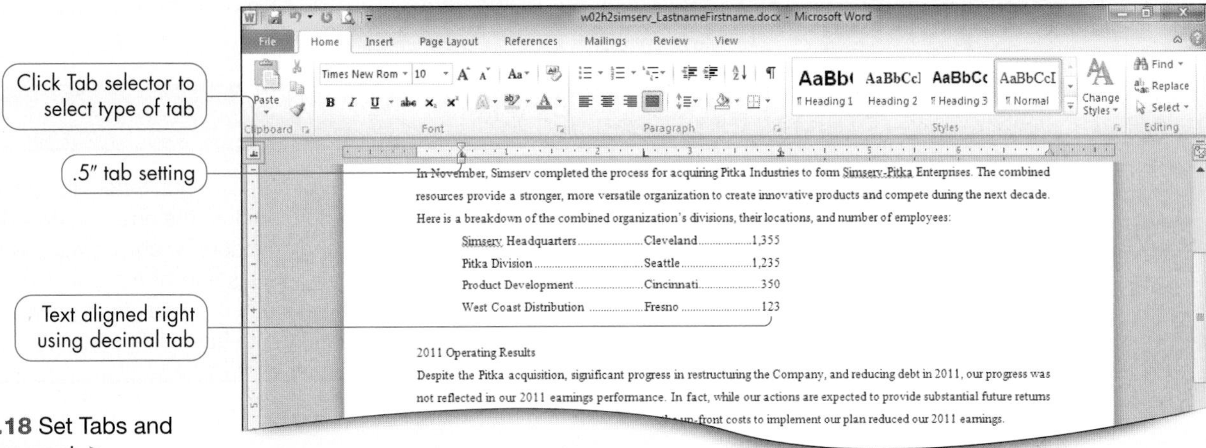

FIGURE 2.18 Set Tabs and Indent a Paragraph ➤

a. Select the last four lines of the *Acquisition of Pitka Industries* paragraph.

   These lines describe facility locations and number of employees at each.

b. Click the **Paragraph Dialog Box Launcher** in the Paragraph group. Click **Tabs** in the bottom left to display the Tabs dialog box.

c. Type **.5** in the **Tab stop position box**, confirm *Left* is selected in the Alignment area, and then click **Set**.

d. Type **2.5** in the **Tab stop position box**, confirm it is a Left-aligned tab, click **2...** in the Leader area, and then click **Set** again. Click **OK** to close the Tabs dialog box.

   You set two tab stops for the Division and locations.

e. Click the **View tab**, and then click **Ruler**, if necessary, to view the Ruler at the top of the window. Select the last four lines again, if necessary, and then click the **Tab selector** at the left end of the ruler until the Decimal tab displays.

TROUBLESHOOTING: If you miss the Decimal tab selector, keep clicking. All tab selections will cycle through the selector area and then repeat as you click.

f. Click the **4"** mark on the ruler to apply the Decimal tab.

   When you set the decimal tab, the numbers line up along the right edge. It is always best to display numbers aligning on the right.

g. Right-click the selected text, click **Paragraph**, and then click **Tabs**. Click the **4" tab**, click **2...** in the Leader area, and then click **OK**.

   When you add the dot leaders, it is easier to follow the information across the page for each location.

h. Click the **Home tab**, and then click **Increase Indent** in the Paragraph group to indent the list to the first tab stop.

i. Place your cursor on the left side of *Fresno* on the last line, and press **Tab** to align the data at the new tab stops, as shown in Figure 2.18.

j. Select the quote by Jerri Reed at the end of the second paragraph following the *2012 Management Changes* heading. The quote starts *In 2013, we take the bull by the horns.*

k. Click the **Page Layout tab**. Click the **Indent Left arrow** until *0.5″* displays.

l. Click the **Indent Right arrow** until *0.5″* displays.

The paragraph is equally indented from the right and left margins and now displays with additional white space on the right and left sides.

m. Save the document.

TIP Indents and the Ruler

You can use the ruler to change the special, left, and/or right indents. Select the paragraph (or paragraphs) in which you want to change indents, and then drag the appropriate indent markers to the new location(s) on the ruler. If you get a hanging indent when you wanted to change the left indent, it means you dragged the bottom triangle instead of the box. Click Undo on the Quick Access Toolbar and try again. You can always use the Paragraph group settings or Paragraph Dialog Box rather than the ruler if you continue to have difficulty.

STEP 3 APPLY BORDERS AND SHADING

To make sure your company's financial position is recognized, you decide to place a border around that paragraph and shade it with color to make it really stand out. You know that this is another way to draw the reader's attention to important data—by highlighting with color and borders. Refer to Figure 2.19 as you complete Step 3.

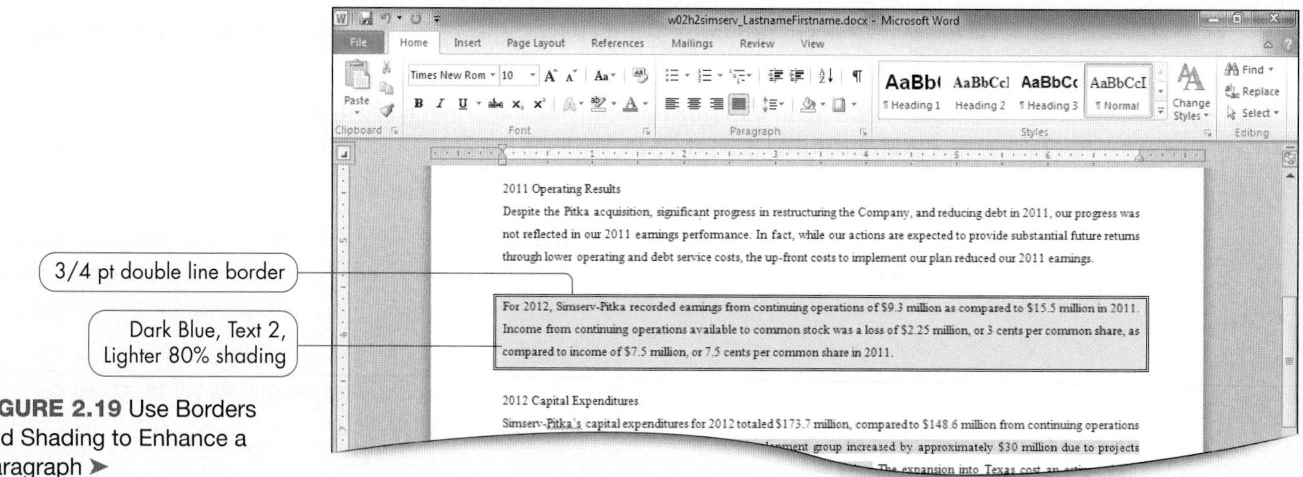

FIGURE 2.19 Use Borders and Shading to Enhance a Paragraph ➤

a. Select the second paragraph following the *2011 Operating Results* heading, which starts *For 2012, Simserv-Pitka recorded earnings.*

b. Click the **Home tab**, click the **Borders arrow**, and then click **Borders and Shading** to display the Borders and Shading dialog box.

c. Click the **Borders tab**, if necessary, and then select the **double line style** in the **Style list**. Click the **Width arrow**, select **3/4 pt**, and then click **Box** in the *Setting* section.

A preview of these settings will display on the right side of the window in the Preview area.

d. Click the **Shading tab**, click the **Fill arrow**, and then select **Dark Blue, Text 2, Lighter 80%** from the palette (second row, fourth column). Click **OK** to accept the settings for both Borders and Shading.

The paragraph is surrounded by a 3/4-pt double-line border, and light blue shading appears behind the text.

e. Click outside the paragraph to deselect it, and then compare your work to Figure 2.19.

f. Save the document.

STEP 4 CREATE A BULLETED AND NUMBERED LIST

The Annual Summary includes paragraphs that describe the goals for 2012. To display the key goals so each one is easily distinguishable, you decide to format them into a bulleted list. The goals described in the final paragraph should be formatted similarly, but since they are described as steps, which assume an order, you format them using a numbered list instead of simple bullets. Refer to Figure 2.20 as you complete Step 4.

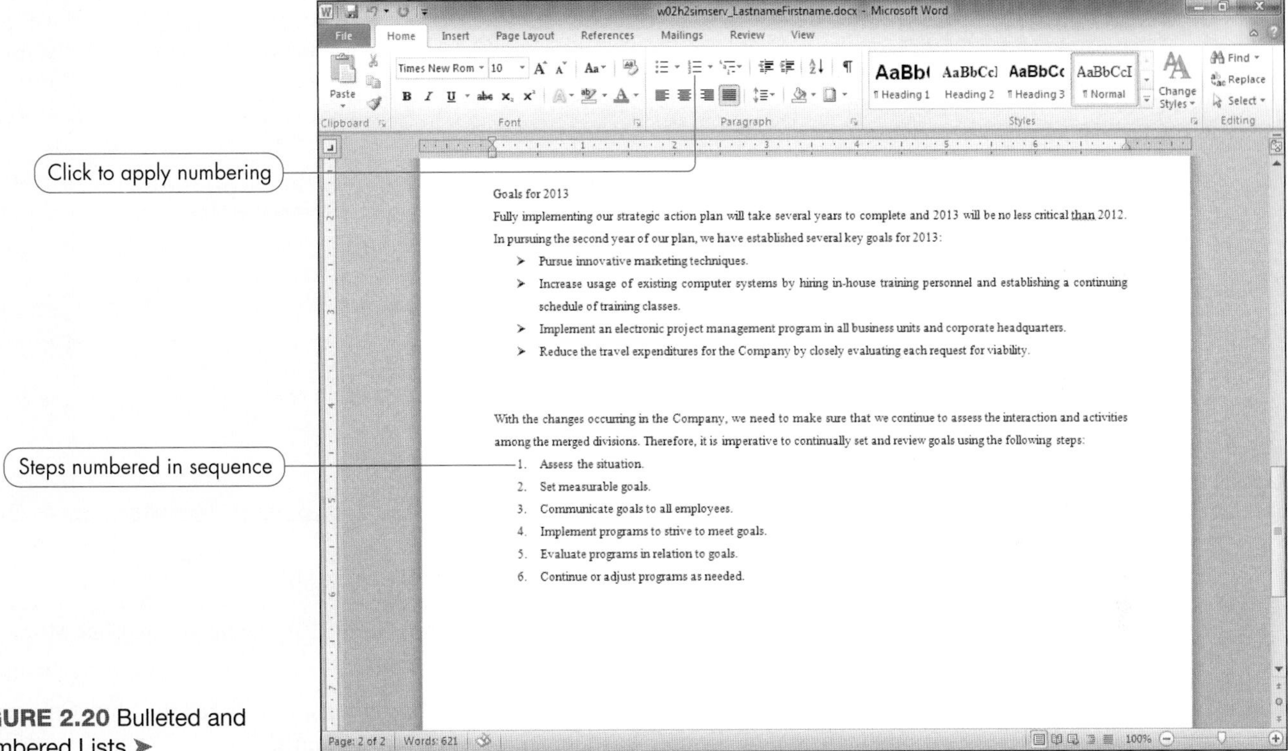

FIGURE 2.20 Bulleted and Numbered Lists ➤

a. Select the five lines of text in the first paragraph that follows the *Goals for 2013* heading, starting with *Pursue innovative marketing techniques.*

b. Click the **Home tab**, if necessary, and then click the **Bullets arrow** to display the Bullet Library.

   Here you select from a variety of bullet styles. The most recently used bullets display at the top.

c. Click a bullet that is in the shape of an arrow or arrowhead. If that style does not display, click the bullet of your choice.

d. Select the last six lines of text in the last paragraph that follows the *Goals for 2013* heading.

e. Click **Numbering** in the paragraph group.

   The steps are numbered in sequence from 1 to 6 as shown in Figure 2.20. Because it is important to perform these steps in this order, you use a numbered list instead of bullets.

f. Save the document.

STEP 5 CREATE COLUMNS

The goals you formatted with bullets in the last step look fine, but you realize the bullets are somewhat short and would look good if displayed in columns on the page. Columns would also add an element of variety to the way the information displays on the page. Refer to Figure 2.21 as you complete Step 5.

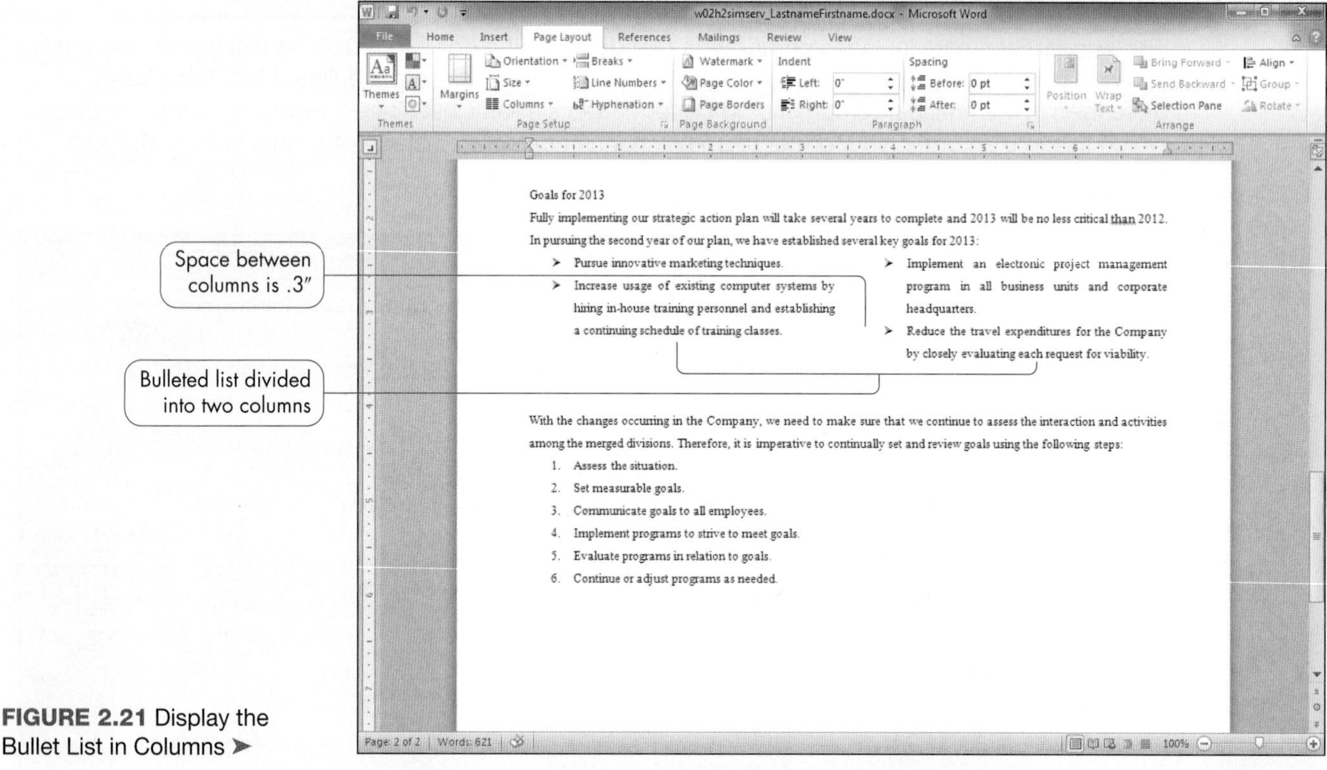

FIGURE 2.21 Display the Bullet List in Columns ➤

a. Select the four bulleted items in the *Goals for 2013* paragraph.

b. Click the **Page Layout tab**, and then click **Columns** in the Page Setup group. Click **More Columns** to display the Columns dialog box.

   Because you will change several settings related to columns, you clicked the More Columns option instead of clicking the gallery option to create columns.

c. Click **Two** in the *Presets* section of the dialog box. The default spacing between columns is 0.5″, which leads to a column width of 3.25″. Change the Spacing to **.3**″, which automatically changes the column Width to *3.35″*.

d. Click **OK** to close the Columns dialog box, and compare your document to Figure 2.21.

   The bulleted list is now formatted in two columns and makes efficient use of space on the page.

e. Click the **View tab**, and then click **Ruler** to turn off the ruler.

f. Save the document and keep it onscreen if you plan to continue with the next Hands-On Exercise. If not, close the document and exit Word.

Styles

As you complete reports, assignments, and projects for other classes or in your job, you probably apply the same text, paragraph, table, and list formatting for similar documents. Instead of formatting each document individually, you can create your own custom style to save time in setting particular formats for titles, headings, and paragraphs. Styles and other features in Word then can be used to automatically generate reference pages such as a table of contents and indexes. In this section, you will create and modify styles.

Understanding Styles

> Styles automate the formatting process and provide a consistent appearance to a document... Change the style and you automatically change all text defined by that style.

One characteristic of a professional document is the uniform formatting that is applied to similar elements throughout the document. Different elements have different formatting. For headings you can use one font, color, style, and size, and then use a completely different format design on text below those headings. The headings may be left aligned, whereas the text is fully justified. You can format lists and footnotes in entirely different styles.

A **style** is a set of formatting options you apply to characters or paragraphs.

One way to achieve uniformity throughout the document is to use the Format Painter to copy the formatting from one occurrence of each element to the next. If you change your mind after copying the formatting throughout a document, you have to repeat the entire process all over again. A much easier way to achieve uniformity is to store all the formatting information together, which is what we refer to as a ***style***. Styles automate the formatting process and provide a consistent appearance to a document. It is possible to store any type of character or paragraph formatting within a style, and once a style is defined, you can apply it to any element within a document to produce identical formatting. Change the style and you automatically change all text defined by that style.

Creating and Modifying Styles

A **character style** stores character formatting and affects only selected text.

A **paragraph style** stores formats used on text in an entire paragraph.

Styles are created on the character or paragraph level. A ***character style*** stores character formatting (font, size, and style) and affects only the selected text. A ***paragraph style*** stores paragraph formatting such as alignment, line spacing, indents, tabs, text flow, and borders and shading, as well as the font, size, and style of the text in the paragraph. A paragraph style affects the current paragraph or, if selected, multiple paragraphs. You cannot apply a paragraph style to only part of a paragraph. You create and apply styles from the Styles group on the Home tab, as shown in Figure 2.22.

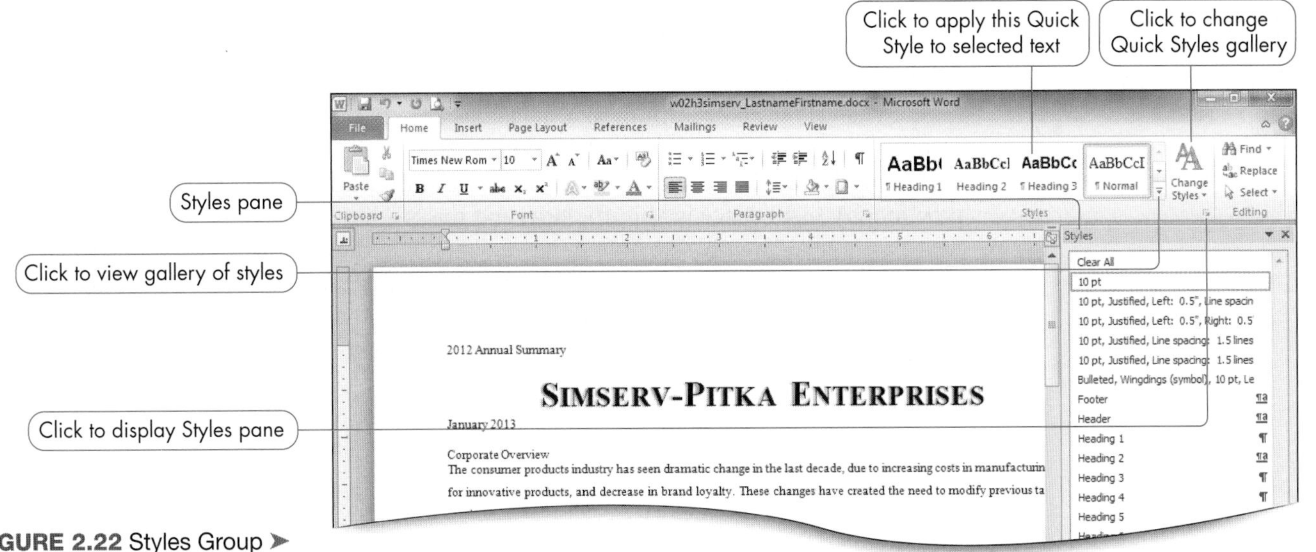

FIGURE 2.22 Styles Group ➤

The Normal template contains more than 100 styles. Unless you specify a style, Word uses the Normal style. The Normal style contains these settings: 11-pt Calibri, 1.15 line spacing, 10-pt spacing after, left horizontal alignment, and Widow/Orphan control. To apply a different style to an existing paragraph, place the insertion point anywhere within the paragraph, click the Styles Dialog Box Launcher on the Home tab to display the Styles pane, and then click the name of the style you want to use. You can create your own styles to use in a document, modify or delete an existing style, and even add your new style to the Normal template for use in other documents. The Clear All style removes all formatting from selected text.

In Figure 2.23, the task pane displays all of the styles available for use in the Simserv-Pitka Enterprises Annual Summary. The Normal style contains the default paragraph settings (left aligned, 1.15 line spacing, 10-pt spacing after, and 11-pt Calibri font) and is assigned automatically to every paragraph unless a different style is specified. It is the Heading 1 and Heading 3 styles, however, that are of interest to us, as these styles have been applied throughout the document to titles and paragraph headings. To view the style names with their styles applied, click the Show Preview check box near the bottom of the Styles pane.

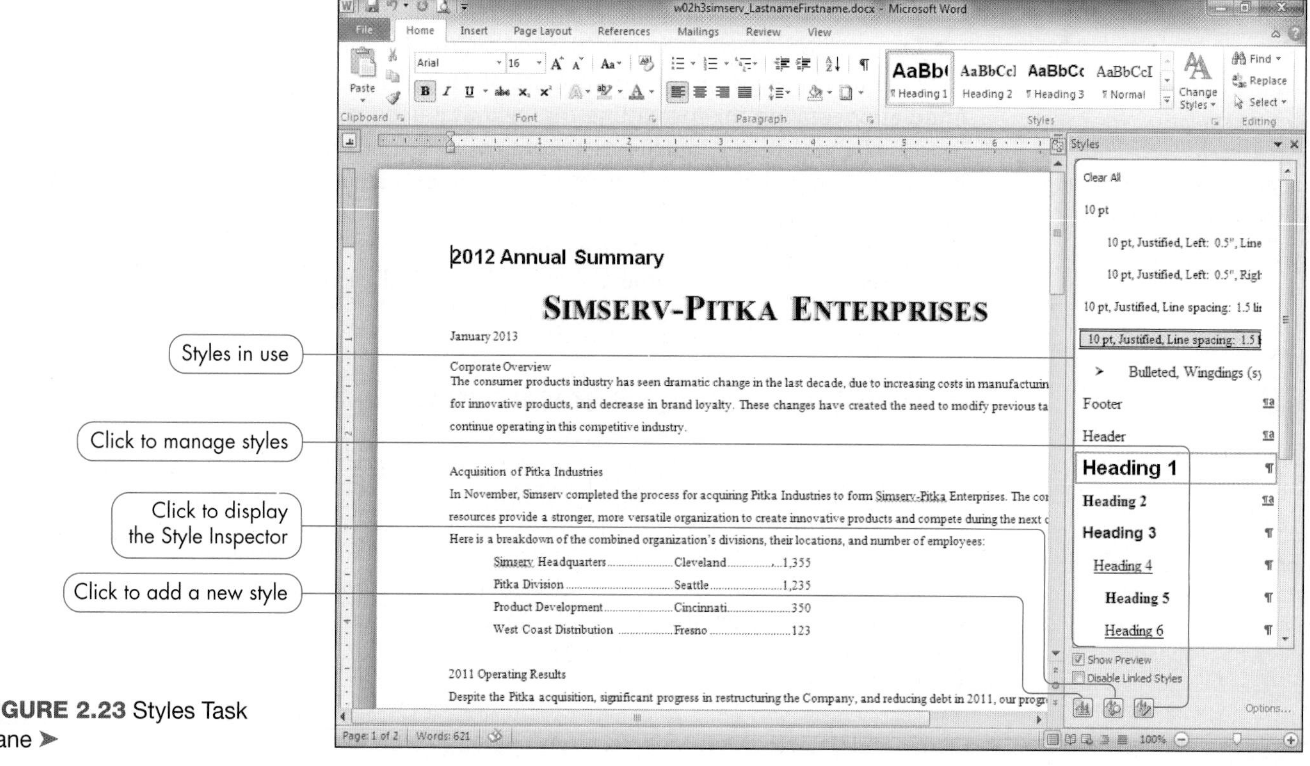

FIGURE 2.23 Styles Task Pane ➤

To change the specifications of a style, hover the mouse over the style name to view the arrow, click the arrow, and then select Modify. The specifications for the Heading 1 style are shown in Figure 2.24. The current settings within the Heading 1 style use 18-pt Arial bold type font. A 14-pt space is after the text, and the heading appears on the same page as the next paragraph. The preview frame in the dialog box shows how paragraphs formatted in this style display. Click Format in the Modify Style dialog box to select and open other dialog boxes where you modify settings used in the style. In addition, as indicated earlier, any changes to the style are reflected automatically in any text or element defined by that style.

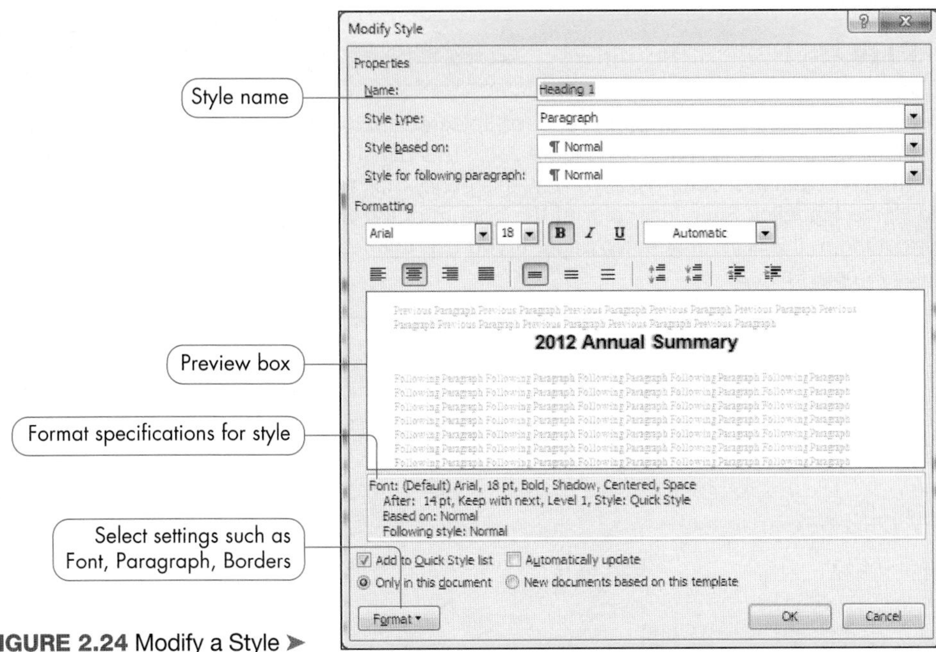

FIGURE 2.24 Modify a Style ➤

Use the Styles Pane Options

The Styles pane can display in several locations. Initially it might display as a floating window, but you can drag the title bar to move it. Drag to the far left or right side, and it will dock on that side of the window. When you display the Styles pane in your document, it might contain only the styles used in the document, as in Figure 2.23, or it might list every style in the Word document template. If the Styles pane only displays styles used in the document, you are unable to view or apply other styles.

You can change the styles that display in the Styles pane by using the Styles Pane Options dialog box, which displays when you click Options in the bottom-right corner of the Styles pane. In the *Select styles to show* box, you select from several options including Recommended, In use, In current document, and All styles, as shown in Figure 2.25. Select *In use* to view only styles used in this document; select *All styles* to view all styles created for the document template as well as any custom styles you create. Other options are available in this dialog box, including how to sort the styles when displayed, and whether to show Paragraph or Font or both types of styles.

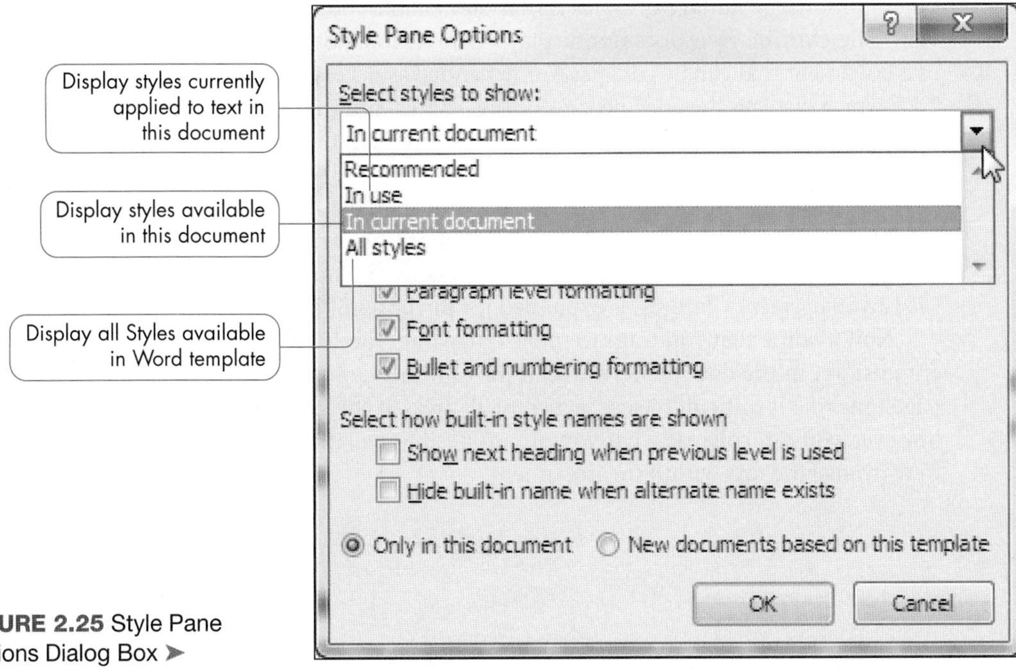

FIGURE 2.25 Style Pane Options Dialog Box ➤

TIP Reveal Formatting

To display complete format properties for selected text in the document, use the Reveal Formatting task pane as shown in Figure 2.26. This panel is often helpful for troubleshooting a format problem in a document. To view this pane, click the Styles Dialog Box Launcher on the Home tab, click Style Inspector at the bottom of the Styles pane, and then click Reveal Formatting in the Style Inspector pane. If you use this feature often, you can add it to the Quick Access Toolbar.

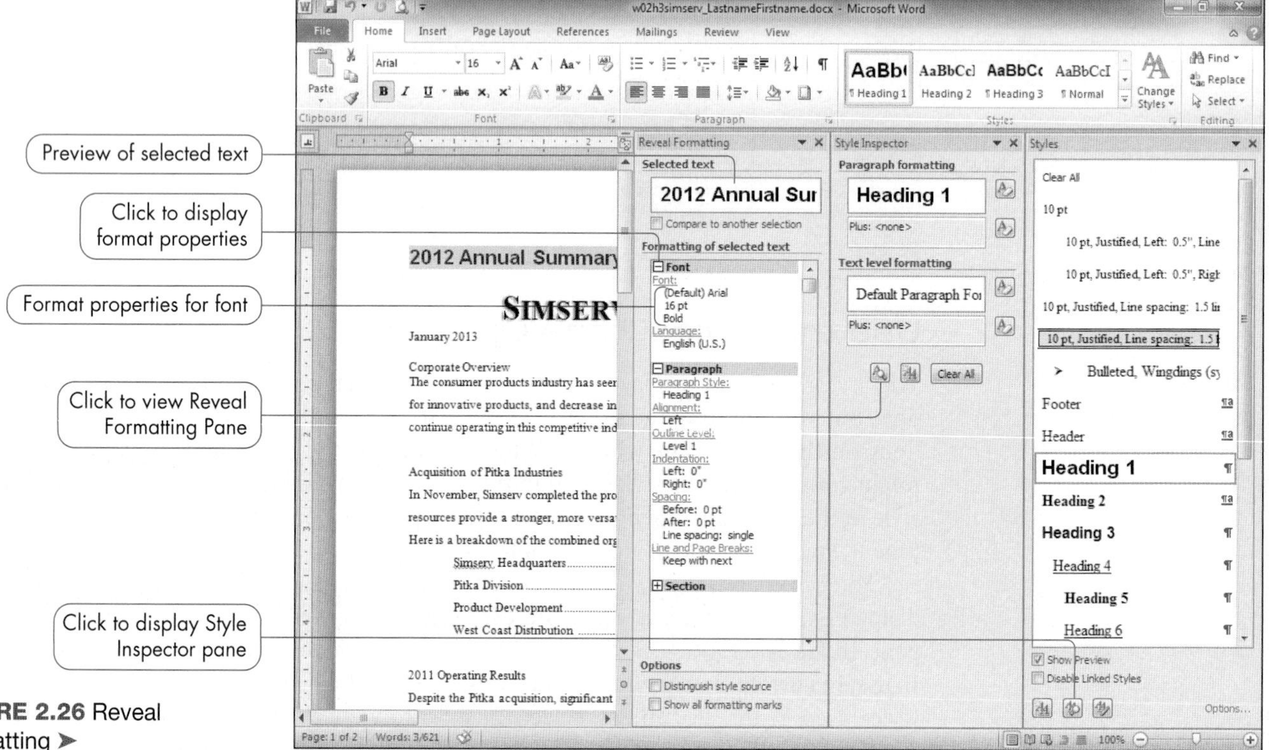

FIGURE 2.26 Reveal Formatting ➤

Use the Outline View

Outline view is a structural view that displays varying amounts of detail.

One additional advantage of styles is that they enable you to view a document in the Outline view. The ***Outline view*** does not display a conventional outline, but rather a structural view of a document that can be collapsed or expanded as necessary. Consider, for example, Figure 2.27, which displays the Outline view of the Annual Summary for Simserv-Pitka Enterprises. To display a document in Outline view, click Outline in the status bar. You can also click the View tab, and then click Outline.

The advantage of Outline view is that you can collapse or expand portions of a document to provide varying amounts of detail. Almost the entire document in Figure 2.27 is collapsed, displaying the headings while suppressing the body text. The text for one section (*2012 Management Changes*) is expanded for purposes of illustration.

Now assume that you want to move one paragraph from its present position to a different position in the document. Without the Outline view, the text might stretch over several pages, making it difficult to see the text of all areas at the same time. Using the Outline view, however, you can collapse what you do not need to see, then simply click and drag headings to rearrange the text within the document.

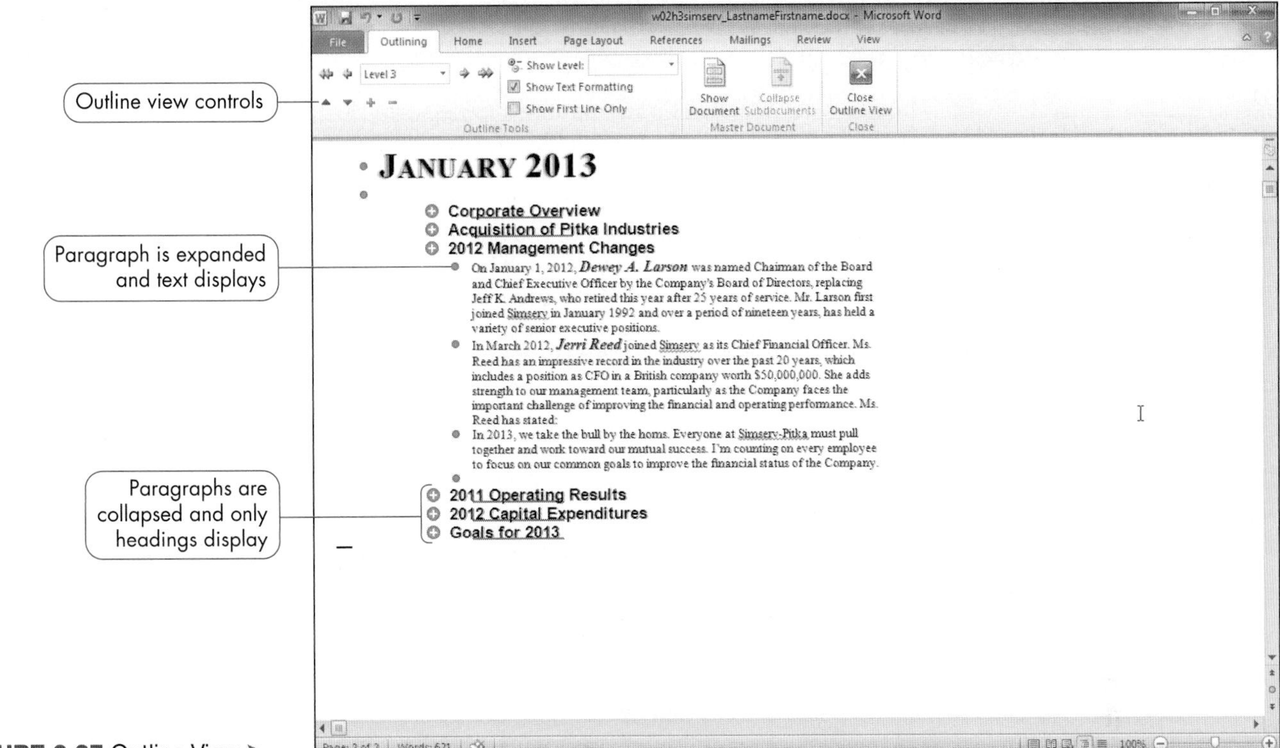

FIGURE 2.27 Outline View ➤

TIP The Outline Versus the Outline View

A conventional outline is created as a multilevel list using the Multilevel List command in the Paragraph group on the Home tab. Text for the outline is entered in the Print Layout view, *not* the Outline view. The latter provides a condensed view of a document that is used in conjunction with styles.

HANDS-ON EXERCISES

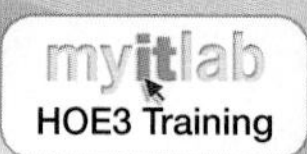

3 Styles

After you enhance several paragraphs of the document with formatting, you decide to format the paragraph headings with styles, and you create a custom style of your own. By using styles on the paragraph headings, you are certain that formatting is consistent and you have the option of making a change to all the headings in one step, if necessary.

Skills covered: Apply Style Properties • Modify the Heading 1 Style • Create a Paragraph and Character Style • Select the Outline View

STEP 1 APPLY STYLE PROPERTIES

For convenience, and because they are designed in a style you like, you decide to use the Heading 1 style on the document title and Heading 3 style on the paragraph headings. Fortunately, your work goes quickly when you use the Format Painter to copy the style from one heading to all the rest. Refer to Figure 2.28 as you complete Step 1.

Click to view more style formats

Heading 1 style applied to document title

Heading 3 style applied to paragraph headings

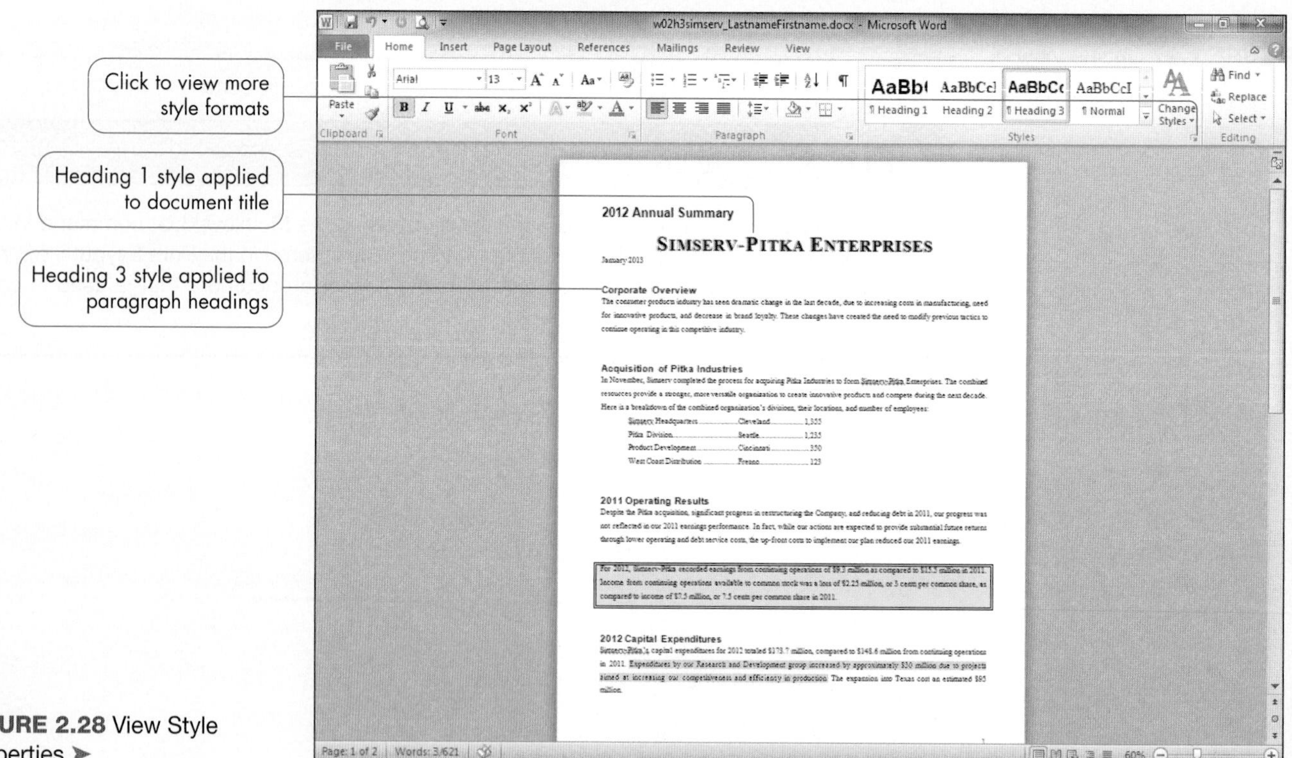

FIGURE 2.28 View Style Properties ➤

a. Open *w02h2simserv_LastnameFirstname* if you closed it at the end of Hands-On Exercise 2, and save it as **w02h3simserv_LastnameFirstname**, changing *h2* to *h3*.

b. Press **Ctrl+Home** to move to the beginning of the document.

c. Select the first line of the document, *2012 Annual Summary*, click the **Home tab**, if necessary, and then click **Heading 1** from the Quick Style gallery in the Styles group.

   When you hover your mouse over the different styles in the gallery, the Live Preview feature displays the style on your selected text but will not apply it until you click the style.

d. Select the paragraph heading *Corporate Overview*. Click the **More buttom** on the right side of the Quick Style gallery to display more styles, and then click the **Heading 3 style**.

e. Double-click the **Format Painter** in the Clipboard group, and then select the five remaining paragraph headings in the document to apply the **Heading 3 style**. Press **Esc** to turn off the Format Painter.

All paragraph headings in this document are formatted as shown in Figure 2.28.

f. Save the document.

STEP 2 MODIFY THE HEADING 1 STYLE

After you look at the document title, you decide it should be centered on the page and formatted to match the subtitle. Because you anticipate using that style frequently, you decide to modify the style to add center alignment and to include the font attributes used on the subtitle. Refer to Figure 2.29 as you complete Step 2.

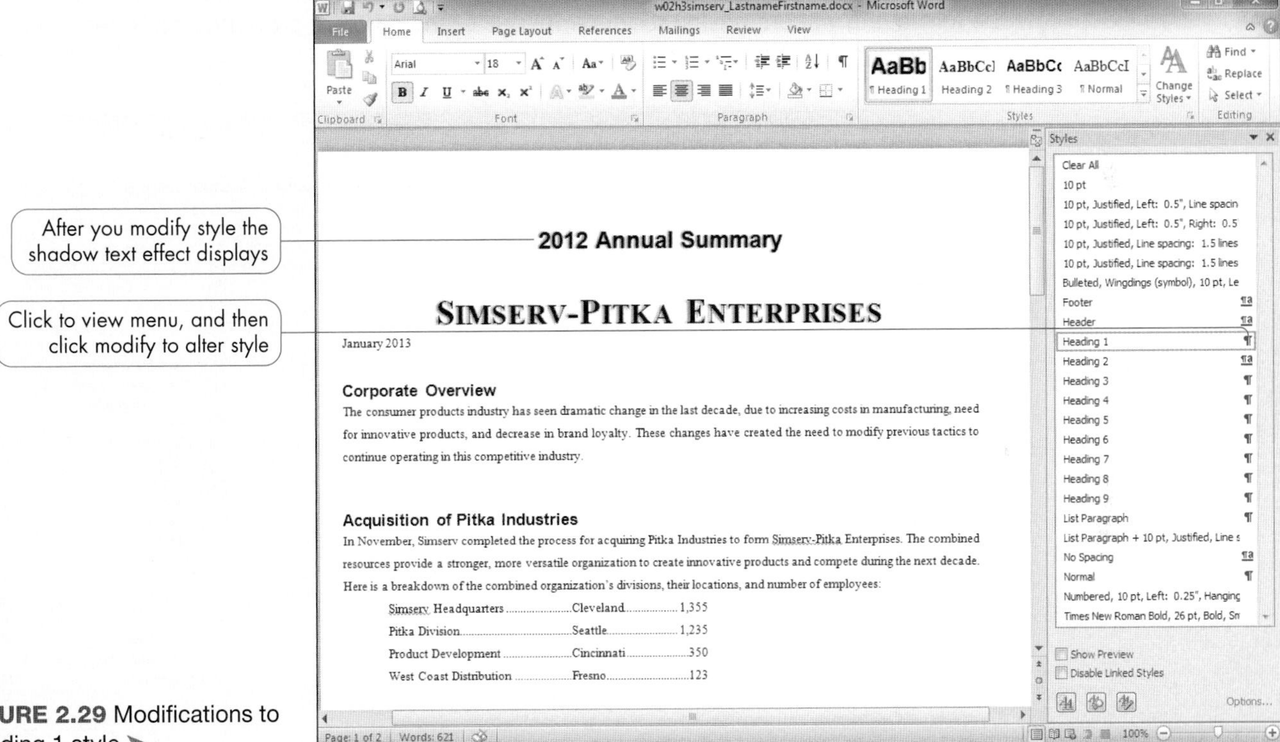

FIGURE 2.29 Modifications to Heading 1 style ➤

a. Click the **Styles Dialog Box Launcher** in the Styles group. Double-click the title bar of the Styles pane to dock it, if necessary, so it does not float on the screen.

b. Click **Ctrl+Home** to move to the beginning of the document. Notice the Heading 1 style is selected in the Styles pane. Hover your mouse over the style description in the Styles pane to display the arrow, click the arrow, and then select **Modify** to display the Modify Style dialog box.

> **TROUBLESHOOTING:** If you click the style name instead of the arrow, you will apply the style to the selected text instead of modifying it. Click Undo on the Quick Access Toolbar to cancel the command. Click the arrow next to the style name to display the associated menu, and select the Modify command to display the Modify Style dialog box.

c. Click **Center** in the *Formatting* section to change the alignment of this title. Click **Format** in the bottom-left corner of the window, and then click **Font** to display the Font dialog box. If necessary, click the **Font tab**. Change Font size to **18**, and then click **OK** to close the Font dialog box and return to the Modify Style dialog box.

d. Click **Format**, and then select **Text Effects**. Click **Shadow**, click **Presets,** and then click **Offset Left** (second row, third column). Click the **Close button**.

e. Click **Format**, and then select **Paragraph**. If necessary, click the **Indents and Spacing tab**. In the *Spacing* section, type **14** in the **After box.**

   Since 14 is not one of the predefined options you see when scrolling in the Spacing After box, you must type it in.

f. Click **OK** to close the Paragraph dialog box, and then click **OK** to close the Modify Style dialog box. Compare your results to Figure 2.29.

g. Save the document.

STEP 3 CREATE A PARAGRAPH AND CHARACTER STYLE

You decide the format used on the subtitle should also be saved as a style so you can apply it to other text. You also decide to create a character style that you use on specific text to make it stand out from other text in the paragraph. Creating the paragraph and character styles enables you to duplicate the formatting without having to remember all of the different attributes you used previously. Refer to Figure 2.30 as you complete Step 3.

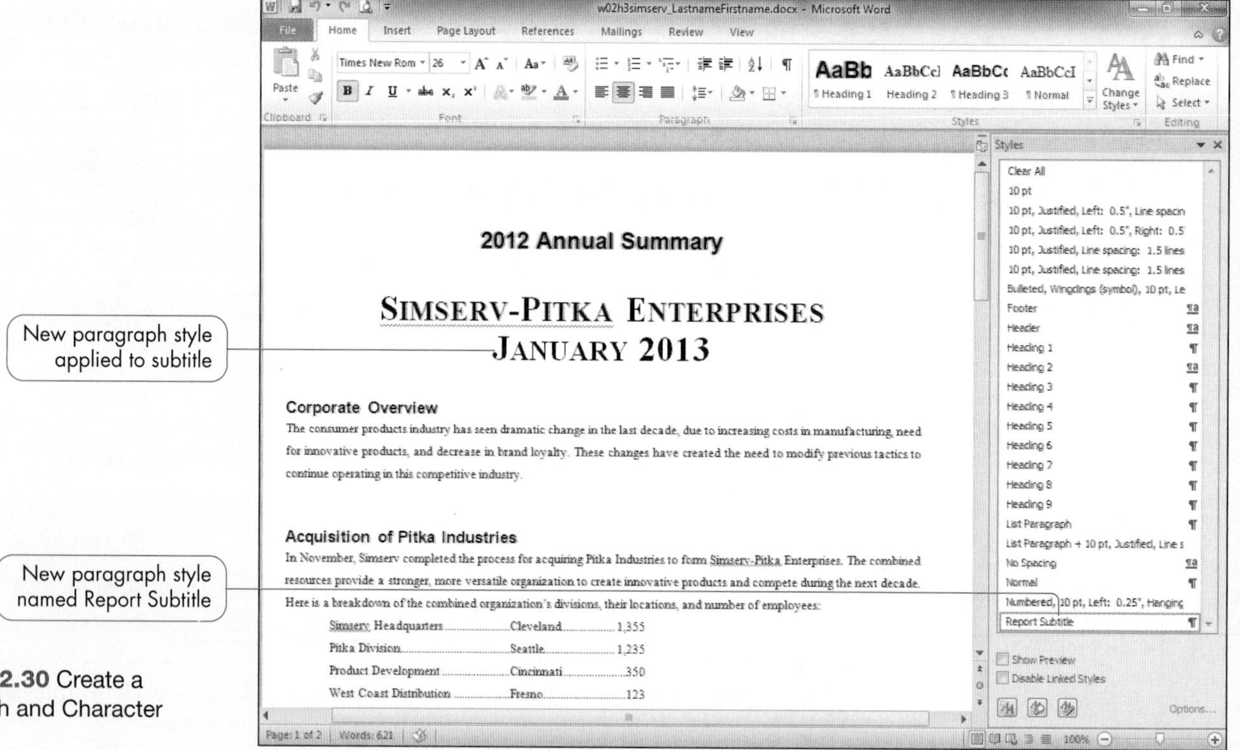

FIGURE 2.30 Create a Paragraph and Character Style ➤

a. Move the insertion point to the left side of the subtitle *Simserv-Pitka Enterprises* that displays just below the main title. Point to the description for this subtitle on the Styles Pane (you may only be able to see the first or last few format effects listed), hover your mouse over the description to display the arrow, click the arrow, and then select **Modify Style** to display the Modify Style dialog box.

   The Styles task pane displays the specifications for this style. You have created a new style by changing the font options earlier, but the style is not yet named.

b. Click in the **Name box** in the Properties area, and then type **Report Subtitle** as the name of the new style. Click **OK**.

c. Select the third line of the document, *January 2013*, and then click **Report Subtitle** in the Styles pane to apply the new style to this line of text.

The two lines of text that make up the subtitle of the document share the same formatting, as shown in Figure 2.30. However, the shadow special effect does not save. You will modify the style to add it back and it will then display on all text that uses the Report Subtitle style.

d. Hover your mouse over the *Report Subtitle* style until the arrow displays, and then click **Modify**. Click **Format**, and then click **Text Effects**. Click **Shadow**, click **Presets**, and then click **Offset Left** (third row, third column). Click the **Close button**. Click **OK** to close the dialog box.

   Notice the shadow effect displays on both lines of text that use the Report Subtitle style. Once you apply a style, any modifications to that style will automatically show on all text that uses the style; you do not have to change text individually.

e. Select the name *Dewey A. Larson* that appears within the *2012 Management Changes* paragraph. Click **Bold** and **Italic** in the Font group. Click **Grow Font** in the Font group two times to increase the size to **12**.

f. Click **New Style** on the bottom of the Styles pane, and then type **Emphasize** as the name of the style.

g. Click the **Style type arrow**, and then select **Character**. Click **OK** to close the dialog box.

   The style named *Emphasize* is listed in the Style pane and can be used throughout your document. You create and use this character style because you only want to use it on certain words, not entire paragraphs.

h. Select the name *Jerri Reed*, also in the *2012 Management Changes* paragraph. Click **Emphasize** in the Quick Style gallery to apply the newly created Emphasize character style to the selected text.

   You can also select this character style from the Styles pane.

i. Close the Styles task pane and save the document.

STEP 4 SELECT THE OUTLINE VIEW

You want to view the structure of the document quickly by looking only at titles and paragraph headings, so you invoke the Outline view in Word. By viewing the outline, you determine you should move one paragraph up, and you quickly make it so by using the Outline tools on the ribbon. Refer to Figure 2.31 as you complete Step 4.

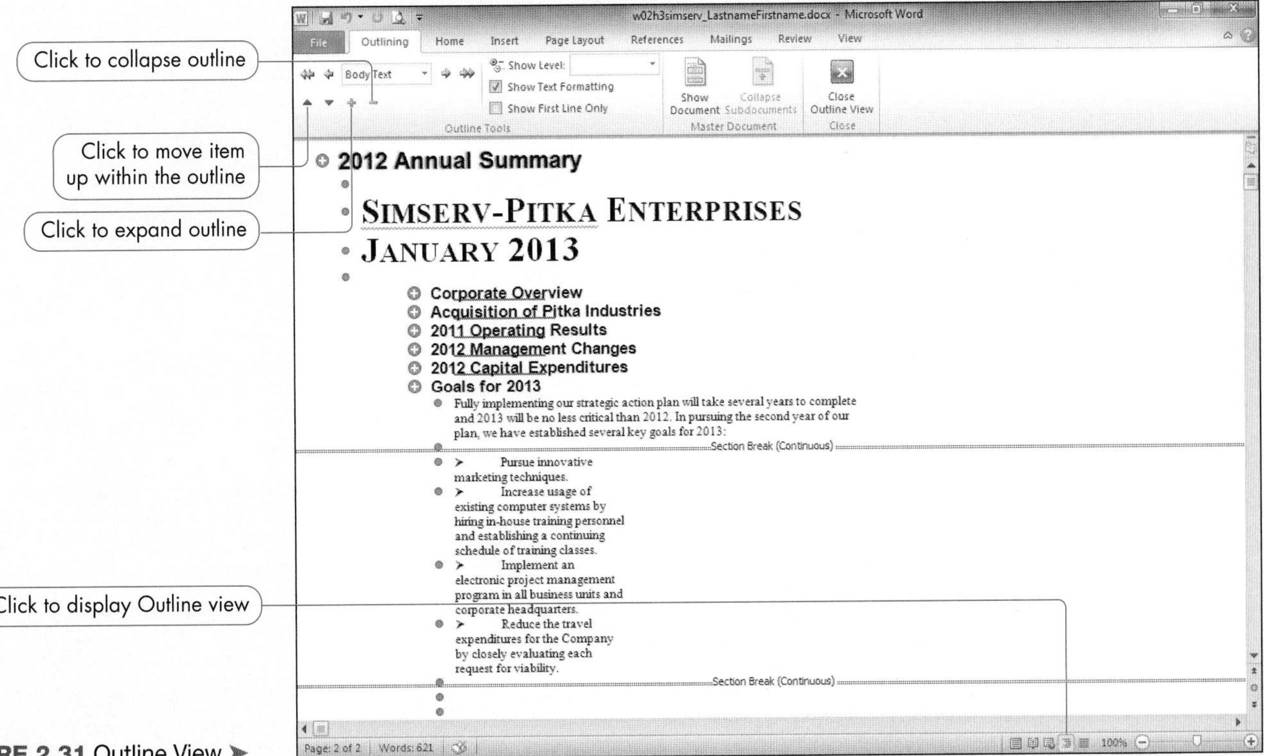

FIGURE 2.31 Outline View ➤

a. Click the **View tab**, then click **Outline** to display the document in Outline view.

b. Place the insertion point to the left of the first paragraph heading, *Corporate Overview*, and then select the rest of the document. Click the **Outlining tab**, if necessary, and then click **Collapse** in the Outline Tools group.

   The entire document collapses so that only the headings display.

c. Click in the heading titled *Goals for 2013*, and then click **Expand** in the Outline Tools group to expand the subordinate paragraphs under this heading.

d. Select the paragraph heading *2012 Management Changes*, and then click **Move Up** in the Outline Tools group one time.

   You moved the paragraph above the paragraph that precedes it in the outline. It now displays just below the *2011 Operating Results* paragraph, as shown in Figure 2.31. Note that you also can drag and drop a selected paragraph.

e. Click **Print Layout** in the status bar so you can view the entire document.

f. Save the document and keep it onscreen if you plan to continue with the next Hands-On Exercise. If not, close the document and exit Word.

Graphical Objects

One of the most exciting features of Word is its graphic capabilities. You can use clip art, images, drawings, scanned photographs, and symbols to visually enhance brochures, newsletters, announcements, and reports. After inserting a graphical object, you can adjust size, choose placement, and perform other formatting options.

One of the most exciting features of Word is its graphic capabilities. You can use clip art, images, drawings, and scanned photographs to visually enhance brochures, newsletters, announcements, and reports.

In this section, you will format the image by changing the height and width, applying a text-wrapping style, applying a quick style, and adjusting graphic properties. Finally, you will insert symbols in a document.

Formatting a Graphical Object

In addition to the collection of clip art and pictures that you can access from Word, you also can insert your own pictures into a document. If you have a scanner or digital camera attached to your computer, you can scan or download a picture for use in Word. After you insert the picture, many commands are available that you can use to format the picture or any other graphical element you use in the document. Remember that graphical elements should enhance a document, not overpower it.

Adjust the Height and Width of an Image

When you insert an image in a document, it comes in a predefined size. For example, the graphic image in Figure 2.32 was very large and took up much space on the page before it was resized. Most times, you need to adjust an image's size so it fits within the document and does not greatly increase the document file size.

Word provides different tools you can use to adjust the height or width of an image, depending on how exact you want the measurements. The Picture Tools Format tab contains Height and Width commands that enable you to specify exact measurements. You can use ***sizing handles***, the small circles and squares that appear around a selected object, to size an object by clicking and dragging any one of the handles. When you use the circular sizing handles in the corner of a graphic to adjust the height (or width), Word also adjusts the width (or height) simultaneously. If needed, hold down Shift while dragging the corner-sizing handle to maintain the correct proportion of the image. If you use square sizing handles on the right, left, top, or bottom, you adjust that measurement without regard to any other sides.

Sizing handles are the small circles and squares that appear around a selected object and enable you to adjust the height and width of an object.

For more precise measurements use the scale or scaling feature. Similar to the effects on text mentioned earlier in the chapter, you can adjust the height or width of an image by a percentage of its original size. The scale adjustment is located in the Size dialog box, which you display by clicking the Size Dialog Box Launcher on the Format tab.

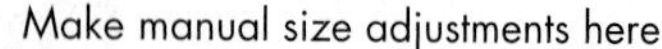

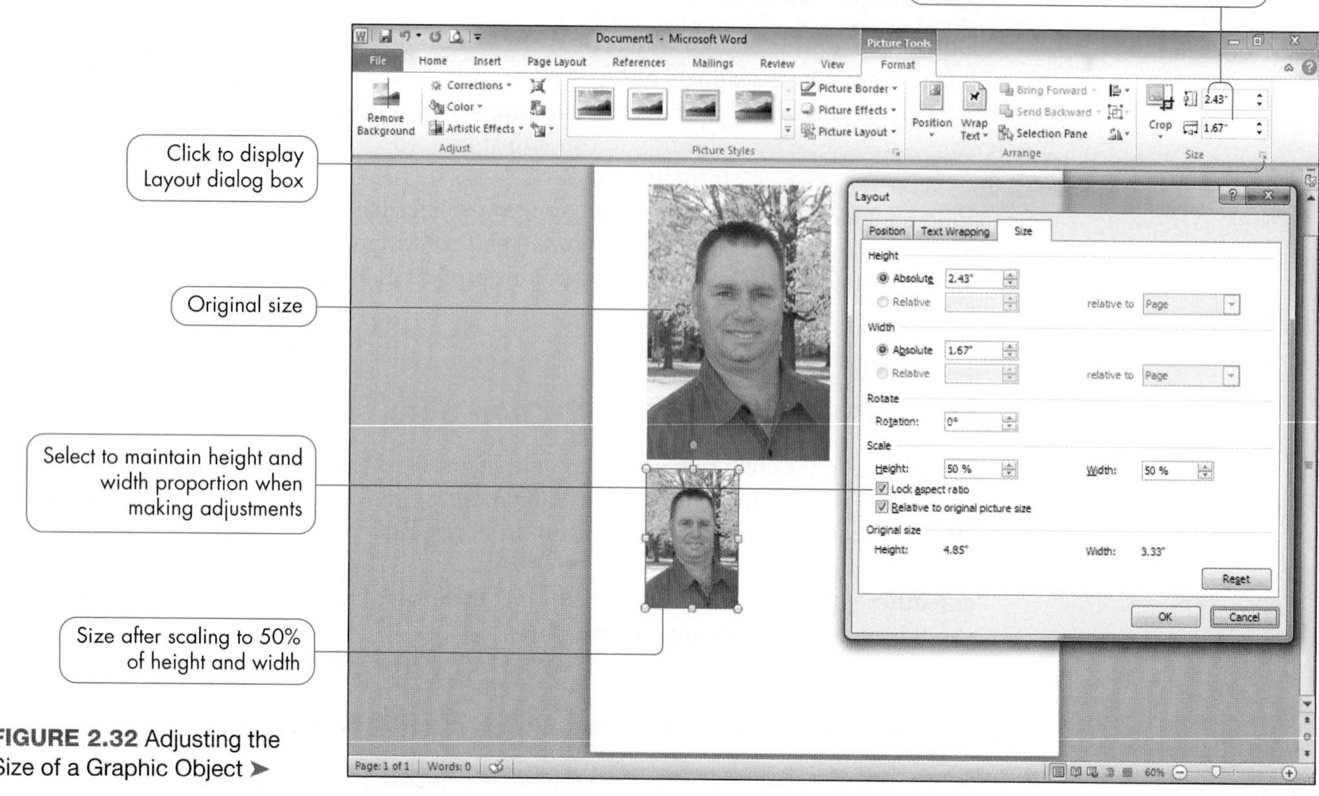

FIGURE 2.32 Adjusting the Size of a Graphic Object ➤

Adjust Text Wrapping

Text wrapping style refers to the way text wraps around an image.

When you first insert an image, Word treats it as a character in the line of text, which leaves a lot of empty space on the left or right side of the image. You may want it to align differently, perhaps enabling text to display very tightly around the object or even placing it behind the text. ***Text wrapping style*** refers to the way text wraps around an image. Table 2.4 describes the different options, which may also display as Wrap Text options.

TABLE 2.4 Text Wrapping Styles

Wrap Text Style	Description
In Line with Text	Graphic displays on the line where inserted so that as you add or delete text, causing the line of text to move, the image moves with it.
Square	Enables text to wrap around the graphic frame that surrounds the image.
Tight	Enables text to wrap tightly around the outer edges of the image itself instead of the frame.
Through	Select this option to wrap text around the perimeter and inside any open portions of the object.
Top and Bottom	Text wraps to the top and bottom of the image frame, but no text appears on the sides.
Behind Text	Enables the image to display behind the text in such a way that the image appears to float directly behind the text and does not move if text is inserted or deleted.
In Front of Text	Enables the image to display on top of the text in such a way that the image appears to float directly on top of the text and does not move if text is inserted or deleted.

Apply Picture Quick Styles

The **Picture Styles** gallery contains preformatted options that can be applied to a graphical object.

Word includes a ***Picture Styles*** gallery that contains many preformatted picture formats. The gallery of styles you can apply to a picture or clip art is extensive, and you can modify the style after you apply it. The quick styles provide a valuable resource if you want to improve the appearance of a graphic but are not familiar with graphic design and format tools. For example, after you insert a graphic, with one click you can choose a style from the Quick Styles gallery that adds a border and displays a reflection of the picture. You might want to select a style that changes the shape of your graphic to an octagon, or select a style that applies a 3-D effect to the image. To apply a quick style, select the graphical object, then choose a quick style from the Picture Styles group on the Picture Tools Format tab. Other style formatting options, such as Soft Edges or 3-D Rotation, are listed in Picture Effects on the Picture Styles group as shown in Figure 2.33.

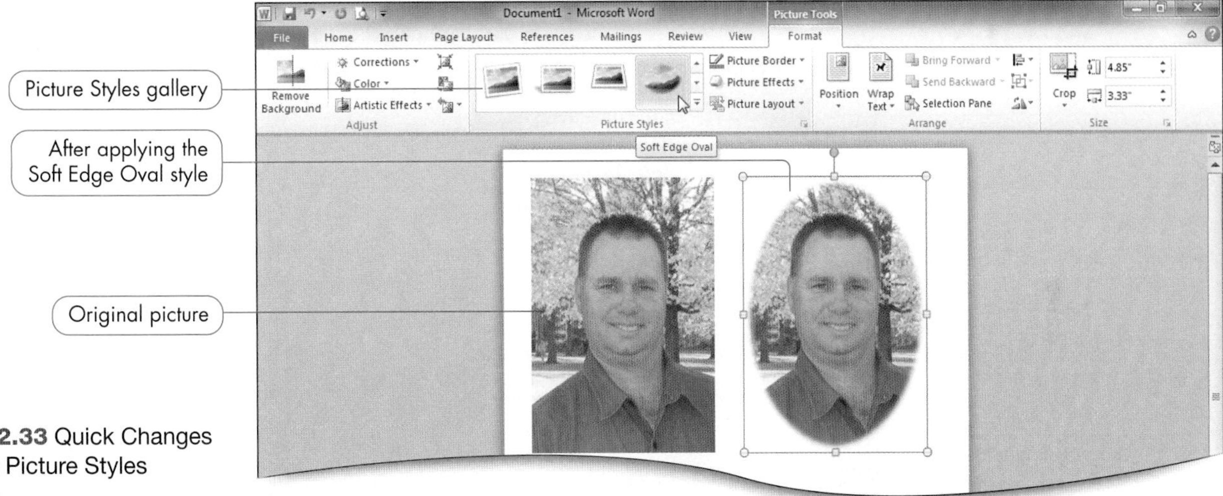

FIGURE 2.33 Quick Changes Using the Picture Styles Gallery ➤

Adjust Graphic Properties

Cropping (or to **crop**) is the process of trimming the edges of an image or other graphical object.

After you insert a graphic or an image, you might find that you need to edit it before using a picture style. One of the most common changes is to ***crop*** (also called ***cropping***), which is the process of trimming edges or other portions of an image or other graphical object that you do not wish to display. Cropping enables you to call attention to a specific area of a graphical element while omitting any unnecessary detail, as shown in Figure 2.34. When you add images to enhance a document, you may find clip art that has more objects than you desire, or you may find an image that has damaged edges that you do not wish to appear in your document. You can solve the problems with these graphics by cropping. The cropping tool is located in the Size group on the Format tab.

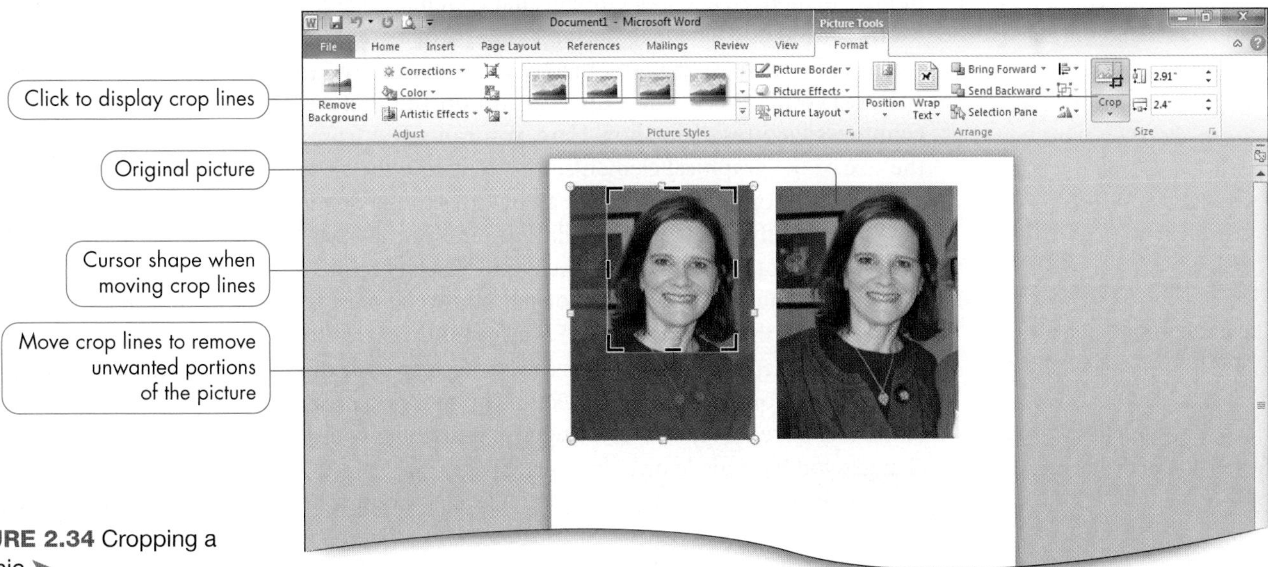

FIGURE 2.34 Cropping a graphic ➤

Even though cropping enables you to adjust the amount of a picture that displays, it does not actually delete the portions that are cropped out. Nor does cropping reduce the size of the graphic and the Word document in which it displays. Therefore, if you want to reduce the size of an image so it does not greatly increase the size of the file, you should not use only the crop tool.

Contrast is the difference between light and dark areas of an image.

Brightness is the ratio between lightness and darkness of an image.

Other common adjustments to a graphical object include contrast and/or brightness. Adjusting the ***contrast*** increases or decreases the difference in dark and light areas of the image. Adjusting the ***brightness*** lightens or darkens the overall image. These adjustments often are made on a picture taken with a digital camera in poor lighting or if a clip art image is too bright or dull to match other objects in your document. Adjusting contrast or brightness can improve the visibility of subjects in a picture. You may want to increase contrast for a dramatic effect or lower contrast to soften an image. The Brightness and Contrast adjustment is combined in the Adjust group on the Format tab, as shown in Figure 2.35.

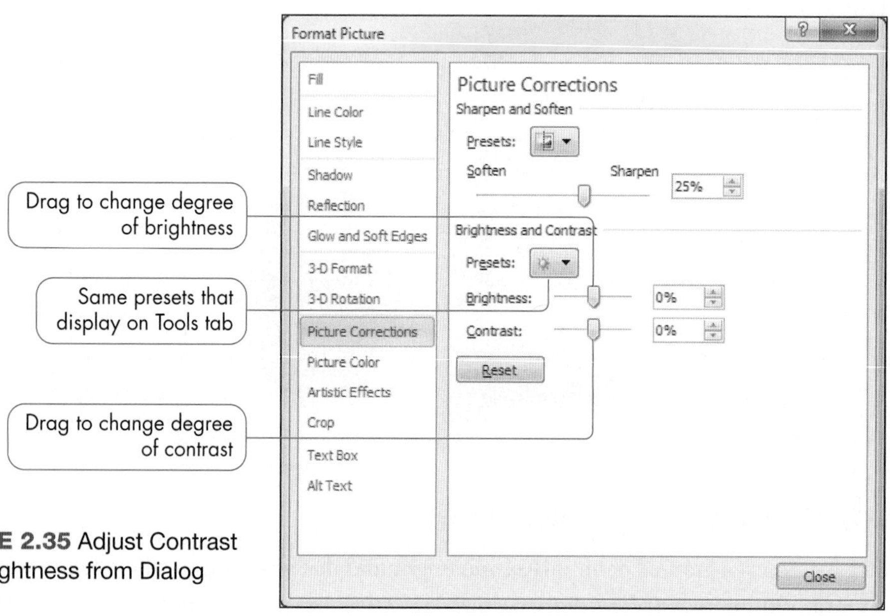

FIGURE 2.35 Adjust Contrast and Brightness from Dialog Box ➤

Compress reduces the file size of an object.

Even though graphical objects add a great deal of visual enhancement to a document, they also can increase the file size of the document. If you add several graphics to a document, you should view the file size before you copy or save it to a portable storage device, and then confirm the device has enough empty space to hold the large file. Additional consideration should be given to files you send as e-mail attachments. Many people have space limitations in their mailboxes, and a document that contains several graphics can fill their space or take a long time to download. To decrease the size of a graphic, you can use the ***Compress*** feature, which reduces the size of an object. After you select a graphical object, click the Compress Pictures command in the Adjust group on the Picture Tools Format tab to display the Compress Pictures dialog box. Here, you can select from options that enable you to reduce the size of the graphical elements, thus reducing the size of the file when you save. You can also select the option to compress all pictures in the document.

The **background** of a picture is the portion of a picture to be removed.

The **foreground** of a picture is the portion of the picture to be kept.

New to Office 2010 is the ability to remove the background or other portions of a picture you do not want to keep. When you select a picture and click the Remove Background tool in the Adjust group on the Format tab, Word creates automatic marquee selection area in the picture that determines the ***background***, or area to be removed, and the ***foreground***, or area to be kept. Word identifies the background selection with magenta coloring. You can then adjust Word's automatic selection by marking areas you want to keep, marking areas you want to remove, and deleting any markings you do not want. You can discard any changes you have made or keep your changes.

The Picture Tools Format tab offers many graphic editing features, some of which are described in Table 2.5.

TABLE 2.5 Graphic Editing Features

Feature	Button	Description
Height	1.5"	Height of an object in inches.
Width	1.37"	Width of an object in inches.
Crop		Remove unwanted portions of the object from top, bottom, left, or right to adjust size.
Align		Adjust edges of object to line up on right or left margin or center between margins.
Group		Process of selecting multiple objects so you can move and format them together.
Rotate		Ability to change the position of an object by rotating it around its own center.
Wrap Text		Refers to the way text wraps around an object.
Position		Specify location on page where object will reside.
Picture Border		The outline surrounding an object; it can be formatted using color, shapes, or width, or can be set as invisible.
Picture Effects		Enhance an object by adding effects such as shadow, bevel, or reflection.
Compress Pictures		Reduce the file size of an object.
Corrections		Increase or decrease brightness of an object. Increase or decrease difference between black and white colors of an object (contrast).
Color		Apply color alterations for effect, such as grayscale, sepia, or match document content colors.
Artistic Effects		Apply effects that make a picture appear as a painting or sketch.
Remove Background		Remove unwanted background in a picture. Enables customization to define unwanted areas.

Inserting Symbols into a Document

The Symbol command enables you to enter typographic symbols and/or foreign language characters into a document in place of ordinary typing—for example, ® rather than (R), © rather than (c), and ½ and ¼, rather than 1/2 and 1/4. These special characters give a document a very professional look.

You may have already discovered that some of this formatting can be done automatically through the AutoCorrect feature that is built into Word. If, for example, you type (c) it will automatically convert to the copyright symbol. You can use the Symbol command to insert other symbols, such as accented letters like the é in résumé or those in a foreign language such as *¿Cómo está usted?*

The installation of Microsoft Office adds a variety of fonts onto your computer, each of which contains various symbols that can be inserted into a document. Selecting "normal text," however, as was done in Figure 2.36, provides access to the accented characters as well as other common symbols. Other fonts—especially the Wingdings, Webdings, and Symbol fonts—contain special symbols, including the Windows logo. The Wingdings, Webdings, and Symbol fonts are among the best-kept secrets in Microsoft Office. Each font contains a variety of symbols that are actually pictures. You can insert any of these symbols into a document as text, or custom bullets, or you can even select the character and enlarge the point size, change the color, then copy the modified character to create a truly original document.

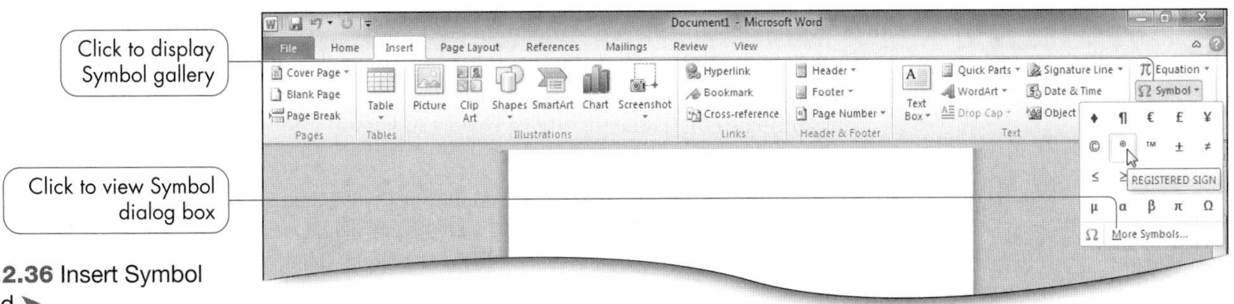

FIGURE 2.36 Insert Symbol Command ➤

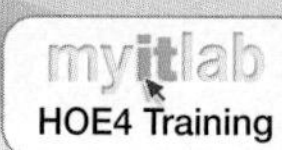

4 Graphical Objects

To finalize the Annual Summary for Simserv-Pitka Industries, you decide to include pictures of the two new executives. As is the case with most pictures inserted into a document, they need to be resized and formatted so they will display next to the paragraphs where you insert them. You also insert a euro symbol into the document, and finish by inserting a page number in the footer.

Skills covered: Insert Picture Objects • Change Picture Formatting • Insert a Symbol

STEP 1 INSERT PICTURE OBJECTS

The new executives hired to lead Simserv-Pitka are important assets to the company, so you want to honor them by placing their pictures in the Annual Summary. You display the picture of each person beside the paragraph that describes his or her position and credentials. Refer to Figure 2.37 as you complete Step 1.

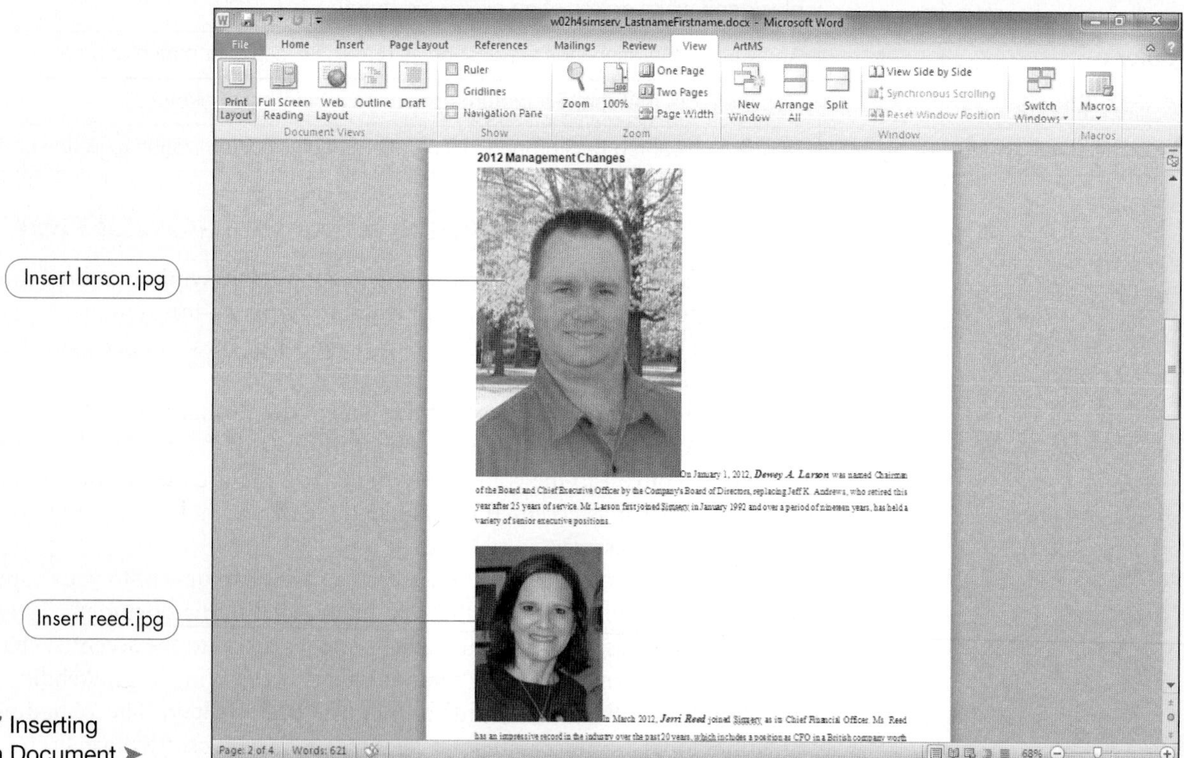

FIGURE 2.37 Inserting Pictures into a Document ➤

a. Open *w02h3simserv_LastnameFirstname* if you closed it at the end of Hands-On Exercise 3, and save it as **w02h4simserv_LastnameFirstname**, changing *h3* to *h4*.

b. Click to the left of the *2012 Management Changes* paragraph heading. Press **Ctrl+Enter** to insert a page break. Click the **Insert tab**, and then click **Picture** in the Illustrations group. Navigate to the location where files for this book are stored, and then double-click **larson.jpg** to insert the picture of Dewey A. Larson into your document.

TROUBLESHOOTING: If the graphic files for these photos do not display, click the File type arrow, and then select All Files (*.*) so all file types display rather than just Word documents. Also, be certain you are clicking Insert Picture, not File, Open, to insert the graphic files.

c. Click to the left of the text *In March 2012* in the *2012 Management Changes* section. Press **Enter** to insert a blank line. Click the **Insert tab**, if necessary, and then click **Picture**. This time, double-click **reed.jpg** to insert the picture of Jerri Reed into your document. Compare your results to Figure 2.37.

d. Save the document.

STEP 2 CHANGE PICTURE FORMATTING

After you insert the pictures, you must adjust them, by changing size or cropping, so they are not disproportionate in size to the rest of the text in the document. You also want to adjust the wrapping style of each picture so you have the control you need to position them with the paragraphs they support. You correct colors as needed, and finally, for effect, you decide to add a border around the pictures. Refer to Figure 2.38 as you complete Step 2.

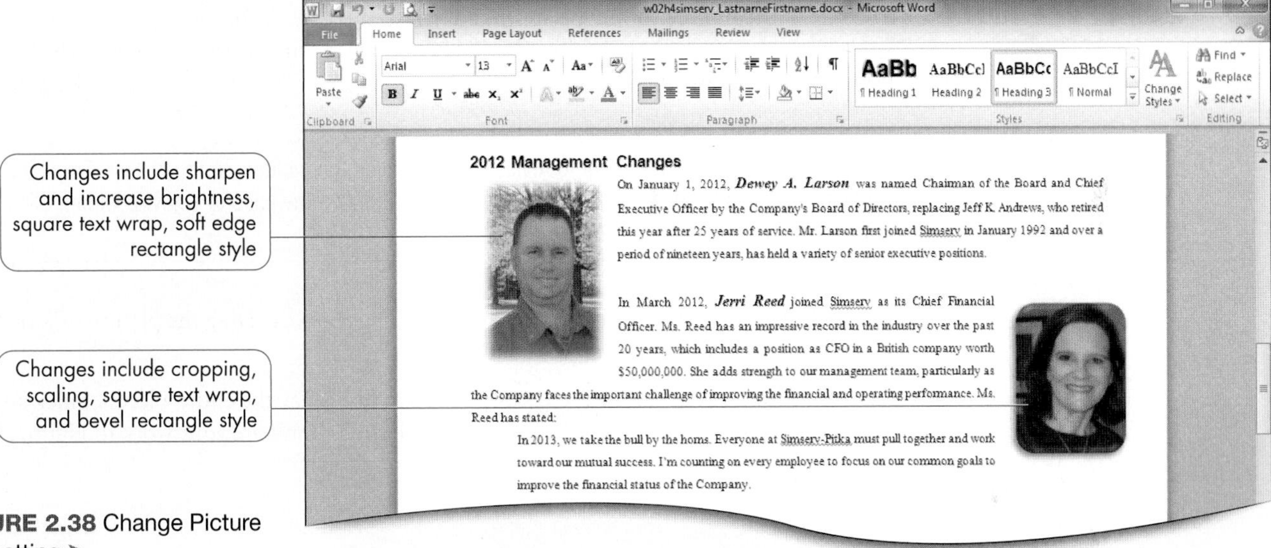

FIGURE 2.38 Change Picture Formatting ➤

a. Select the picture of Dewey A. Larson. Click the **Height arrow** in the Size group on the Picture Tools Format tab until the height is reduced to *2.0″*.

   The width will change in proportion to the height, which should display approximately 1.38″.

b. Click **Corrections** in the Adjust group, and then click **Picture Corrections Options**. In the *Brightness and Contrast* section, decrease **Brightness** to *–5%*, and increase **Contrast** to *5%*. Click the **Close button**.

c. Click **WrapText** in the Arrange group, and then select **Square**.

   The paragraph text displays around the right side of the picture.

d. Click the **More button** in the Picture Styles group to display the entire Picture quick style gallery. Click **Soft Edge Rectangle** (second row, first column).

e. Use your mouse to drag the picture down slightly so the paragraph heading displays on the left margin and the picture displays on the left of the paragraph text only.

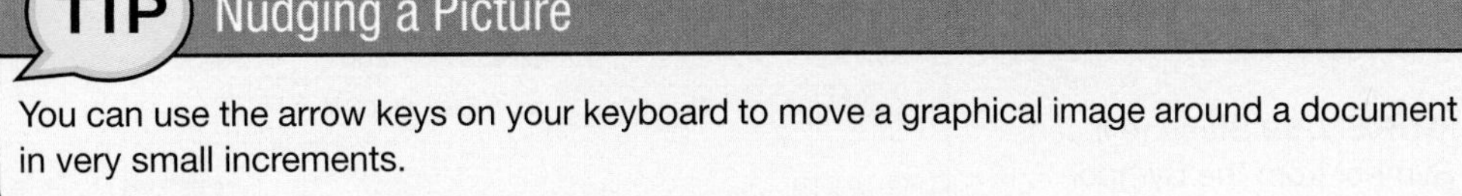

TIP Nudging a Picture

You can use the arrow keys on your keyboard to move a graphical image around a document in very small increments.

f. Click **Compress Pictures** in the Adjust group. Click **Apply only to this picture** to deselect the option, and then click **OK**.

Most digital picture files are quite large and can increase the size of the document substantially when you insert them. The Compression feature is vital to use in that situation. This picture of Dewey A. Larson is not extremely large, but you decide to compress the picture and make sure the size of the document stays small. By deselecting the option in this step, all graphics in the document will compress as well.

g. Select the picture of Jerri Reed. Click the **Size Dialog Box Launcher**. In the *Scale* section, click **Lock aspect ratio**, if necessary. Click the **height arrow** until *70%* displays. Click **OK**.

Because you locked the aspect ratio, which preserves proportions as the picture is resized, the Width percentage changed automatically when you reduced the height.

h. Click **Crop**, and then drag the crop lines inward from right, left, and bottom until she displays from the shoulders up. When complete, press **Crop** again to remove the crop lines.

The size of the picture should be approximately 1.6″ by 1.25″. You crop out the bill of a cap worn by a person who was standing beside her and also remove excess space on the left and bottom of the picture.

TROUBLESHOOTING: If you want to revise the crop, click the picture, and then click Crop. The crop lines and original picture size display, and you can move the lines to a new position. Click Crop again to remove all crop lines.

i. Click **Wrap Text** in the Arrange group, and then click **Square**. Drag the picture of Jerri Reed to the right side of the paragraph that introduces her.

j. Click the **More button** in the Picture Styles group to display the entire Picture quick style gallery. Click **Bevel Rectangle** (fifth row, first column). Compare your work to Figure 2.38.

k. Save the document.

STEP 3 INSERT A SYMBOL

The financial manager at Simserv-Pitka reminds you that it is appropriate to use the correct currency symbols when referring to monetary assets in a document such as this, especially when the currency is not U.S. dollars. To conform to that rule, you change the symbol used to reference the value of a European company to the euro instead of using the dollar symbol. To complete the document, you insert a page number in the footer of the document. Even though it is short, page numbering helps the reader follow the order of the document. Refer to Figure 2.39 as you complete Step 3.

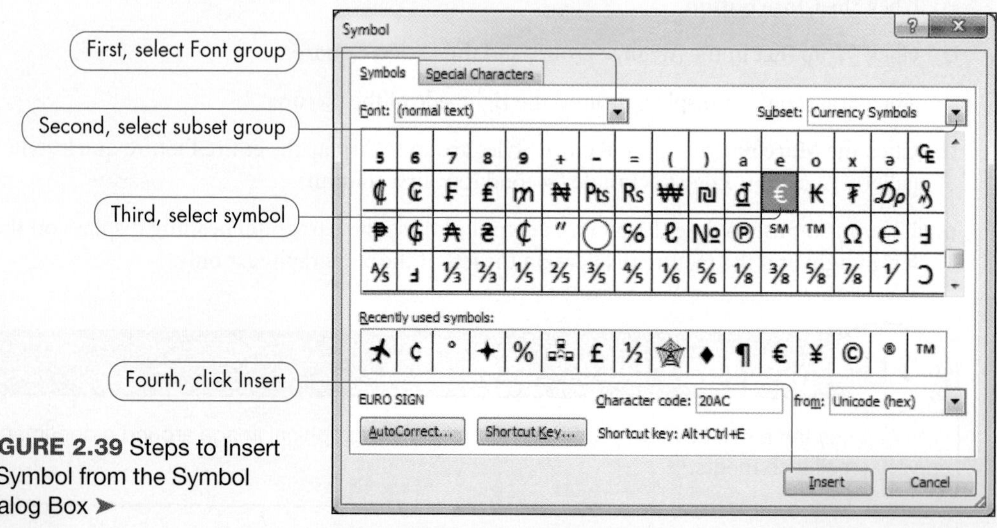

FIGURE 2.39 Steps to Insert a Symbol from the Symbol Dialog Box ➤

a. Select **$** in the second sentence in the paragraph that describes the new CFO, Jerri Reed. Press **Delete** to remove the dollar sign.

b. Click the **Insert tab**, and then click **Symbol** in the Symbols group. Click **More Symbols** to view the Symbol dialog box, as seen in Figure 2.39.

c. Change the Font group to **(normal text)**, if necessary, and then change the Subset to **Currency Symbols**. Click the **Euro sign (€)**, click **Insert**, and then click the **Close button**.

   When you click Insert, the symbol appears in your document at the location of your cursor. While the Symbol dialog box is open, you can return to your document, move your cursor, then return to the symbol dialog box and insert other symbols before you close.

d. Click **Page Number** in the Header and Footer group, hover the mouse over *Bottom of Page*, and then scroll down and select **Accent Bar 4**. Click **Close Header and Footer**.

e. Save and close *w02h4simserve_LastnameFirstname*, and submit based on your instructor's directions.

CHAPTER OBJECTIVES REVIEW

After reading this chapter, you have accomplished the following objectives:

1. **Apply font attributes through the Font dialog box.** Formatting occurs at the character, paragraph, or section level. The Font dialog box enables you to change the spacing of the characters and you can change attributes including font size, font color, underline color, and effects. Use the character spacing options to control horizontal spacing between letters and also adjust the scale, position, and kerning of characters. You can quickly modify the capitalization and text highlight color from the Home tab.
2. **Control word wrap.** Occasionally, text wraps in an undesirable location in your document, or you just want to keep words together for better readability. To keep hyphenated words together on one line, use a nonbreaking hyphen to replace the regular hyphen. You also can keep words together on one line by inserting a nonbreaking space instead of using the spacebar.
3. **Set off paragraphs with tabs, borders, lists, and columns.** You can change appearance and add interest to documents by using paragraph formatting options. Tabs enable you to set markers in the document to use for aligning text. Borders and shading enable you to use boxes and/or shading to highlight an area of your document. A bulleted or numbered list helps to organize information by emphasizing or ordering important topics. Columns add interest by formatting text into side-by-side vertical blocks of text.
4. **Apply paragraph formats.** The Paragraph dialog box contains many formatting options, such as alignment. Another option to adjust the distance from margins is indention. Line spacing determines the space between lines in a document, such as single or double, and can be customized. You also can specify an amount of space to insert before or after a paragraph, which is more efficient than pressing Enter. Widow/Orphan control prevents a single line from displaying at the top or bottom of a page, separate from the rest of a paragraph.
5. **Understand styles.** A style is a set of formatting instructions that has been saved under a distinct name. Styles are created at the character or paragraph level and provide a consistent appearance to similar elements throughout a document. Styles provide the foundation to use other tools such as outlines and the table of contents.
6. **Create and modify styles.** You can modify any existing style to change the formatting of all text defined by that style. You can even create a new style for use in the current or any other document.
7. **Format a graphical object.** Graphics are often added to enhance a document. After you insert one, a variety of tools can make it fit and display where you want—such as changing height and width, scaling, or cropping unwanted portions. You can position the graphic more exactly by wrapping text, and you can use the Picture Styles gallery to add borders or reflections. You can refine imperfections or add creative touches to pictures using features to sharpen, change brightness, and adjust contrast. You can compress a graphic to reduce its size as well as the size of the document.
8. **Insert symbols into a document.** Insert Symbol makes it easy to place typographic characters in a document. The symbols can be taken from any font and can be displayed in any point size.

KEY TERMS

Background ***p. 150***
Bar tab ***p. 123***
Border ***p. 124***
Brightness ***p. 150***
Bulleted list ***p. 125***
Center tab ***p. 123***
Change Case ***p. 117***
Character spacing ***p. 116***
Character style ***p. 137***
Column ***p. 126***
Compress ***p. 150***
Contrast ***p. 150***
Cropping or crop ***p. 149***
Decimal tab ***p. 123***
First line indent ***p. 129***
Font ***p. 114***
Foreground ***p. 150***
Hanging indent ***p. 129***
Hidden text ***p. 116***
Highlighter ***p. 117***
Horizontal alignment ***p. 128***
Kerning ***p. 116***
Leader character ***p. 123***
Left tab ***p. 123***
Line spacing ***p. 129***
Monospaced typeface ***p. 114***
Multilevel list ***p. 125***
Nonbreaking hyphen ***p. 118***
Nonbreaking space ***p. 118***
Numbered list ***p. 125***
OpenType ***p. 116***
Orphan ***p. 130***
Outline view ***p. 140***
Paragraph spacing ***p. 129***
Paragraph style ***p. 137***
Picture Styles ***p. 149***
Position ***p. 116***
Proportional typeface ***p. 114***
Right tab ***p. 123***
Sans serif typeface ***p. 114***
Scale or scaling ***p. 116***
Serif typeface ***p. 114***
Shading ***p. 124***
Sizing handles ***p. 147***
Style ***p. 137***
Tab ***p. 122***
Text wrapping style ***p. 148***
Type style ***p. 114***
Typeface ***p. 114***
Typography ***p. 114***
Widow ***p. 130***

MULTIPLE CHOICE

1. Which of the following is not true about typeface?
   (a) A serif typeface helps the eye connect one letter with the next.
   (b) A monospaced typeface allocates space according to the width of the character.
   (c) A san serif typeface is more effective with titles and headlines.
   (d) A typeface is a complete set of characters.

2. What is the easiest way to change the alignment of five paragraphs scattered throughout a document, each of which is formatted with the same style?
   (a) Select the paragraphs individually, then click the appropriate alignment button.
   (b) Use CTRL to select all of the paragraphs, then click the appropriate alignment button on the Home tab.
   (c) Change the format of the existing style, which changes the paragraphs.
   (d) Retype the paragraphs according to the new specifications.

3. If you want to be sure the date June 21, 2012, does not word wrap what should you do?
   (a) Use a nonbreaking hyphen in place of the comma.
   (b) Use expanded spacing on the whole number.
   (c) Use nonbreaking spaces between the month, date, and year.
   (d) Press Ctrl+Enter before you type the date.

4. Which wrap style enables text to wrap around the graphic frame that surrounds the image?
   (a) Square
   (b) Tight
   (c) Behind Text
   (d) Right and Left

5. A(n) _________ occurs when the first line of a paragraph is isolated at the bottom of a page and the rest of the paragraph continues on the next page.
   (a) widow
   (b) section break
   (c) footer
   (d) orphan

6. Which of the following is a false statement about the Outline view?
   (a) It can be collapsed to display only headings.
   (b) It can be expanded to show the entire document.
   (c) It requires the application of styles.
   (d) It is used to create a multilevel list.

7. What happens if you modify the Body Text style in a Word document?
   (a) Only the paragraph where the insertion point is located is changed.
   (b) All paragraphs in the document will be changed.
   (c) Only those paragraphs formatted with the Body Text style will be changed.
   (d) It is not possible to change a Word default style such as Body Text.

8. If you want to display text in side-by-side sections, what feature should you use to format the text?
   (a) Styles
   (b) Borders
   (c) Multilevel lists
   (d) Columns

9. Which of the following is a true statement regarding indents?
   (a) Indents are measured from the edge of the page.
   (b) The left, right, and first line indents must be set to the same value.
   (c) The insertion point can be anywhere in the paragraph when indents are set.
   (d) Indents must be set within the Paragraph dialog box.

10. The spacing in an existing multipage document is changed from single spacing to double spacing throughout the document. What can you say about the number of hard and soft page breaks before and after the formatting change?
    (a) The number of soft page breaks is the same, but the number and/or position of the hard page breaks are different.
    (b) The number of hard page breaks is the same, but the number and/or position of the soft page breaks are different.
    (c) The number and position of both hard and soft page breaks are the same.
    (d) The number and position of both hard and soft page breaks are different.

1 Engler, Guccione, & Partners

You are the Marketing Director for the Architect firm Engler, Guccione, & Partners. Lately, the firm has less work due to a reduction in construction spending. In order to bring in new business, you design a marketing plan to pursue new customers by advertising your ability to consult in legal cases. The plan is typed and in a raw form, so you use formatting features to enhance the document and impress the partners with your own skills. This exercise follows the same set of skills as used in Hands-On Exercises 1, 2, 3, and 4 in the chapter. Refer to Figure 2.40 as you complete this exercise.

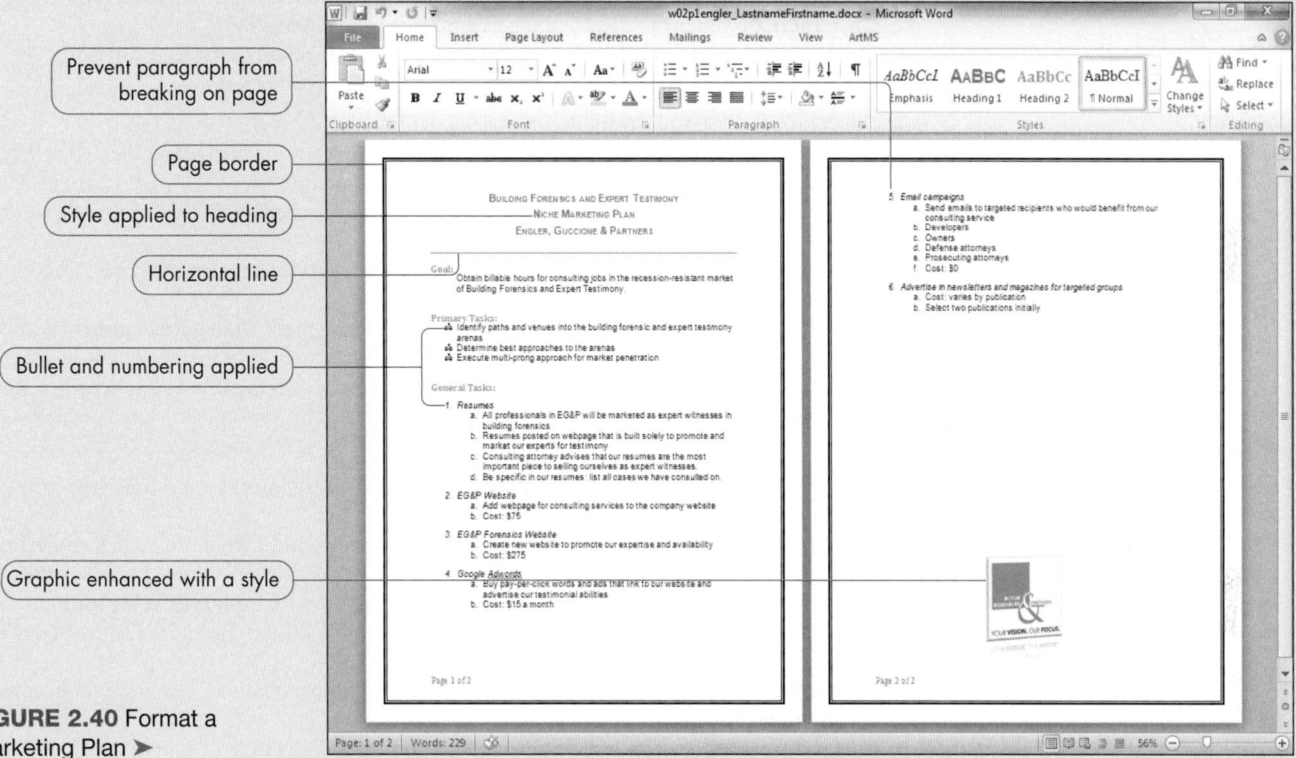

FIGURE 2.40 Format a Marketing Plan ➤

a. Open *w02p1engler* and save the document as **w02p1engler_LastnameFirstname**.

b. Add a page border around the text by completing the following steps:
   - Click the **Home tab**, and then click the **Borders arrow** in the Paragraph group.
   - Select **Borders and Shading** to open the dialog box.
   - Click the **Page Border tab**, and then click **Box** in the *Setting* section.
   - Scroll down and select the **ninth** style—a double line border with a thick line outside and a thin line inside.
   - Click **OK** to close the Borders and Shading dialog box.

c. Click **Ctrl+A** to select the whole document. Click the **Font arrow** in the Font group on the Home tab, and then select **Arial**.

d. Select the first three lines, which make up the document title, and complete the following steps:
   - Click **Heading 1** in the Quick Styles gallery.
   - Right-click the **Heading 1 entry** in the Quick styles pane, and then select **Modify**.
   - Change the alignment to **Center**.
   - Change the font to **Arial**.
   - Click **Format, Font,** and then click **Small caps.** Click **OK** to close the Font dialog box.
   - Click **Format, Paragraph,** and then click the **Indents and Spacing tab**, if necessary.
   - Reduce the **Spacing Before** to **0 pt**.
   - Increase **Spacing After** to **6 pt**.

- Click **OK** to close the Paragraph dialog box.
- Click **OK** to close the Modify Style dialog box.

e. Place the insertion point on the blank line that follows the third line of the title. Click the **Borders and Shading arrow**, and then click **Horizontal Line**.

f. Select the three lines under the *Primary Tasks:* paragraph heading, and then click the **Bullets arrow** in the Paragraph group. Click **Define New Bullet**, click **Symbol** to open the Symbol dialog box, and then select **Webdings** from the **Font list**. Select the symbol that resembles a computer network (character code 194) located in the third row, third column, and then click **OK**. Click **OK** to create the bullet list, and then close the Define New Bullet dialog box.

g. Create a numbered list for the General Tasks by completing the following steps:
   - Right-click the italicized word *Resumes* directly under *General Tasks*, point to *Styles* in the menu, and then click **Select Text with Similar Formatting** to select all italicized headings.
   - Click the **Numbering arrow**, and then select the format that displays lowercase alphabet numbering (*a., b., c.*).
   - Select the four sub-points for *Resumes*, and then click **Numbering** in the paragraph group. Click **Increase Indent** to display them as a multilevel list item.
   - Double-click the **Format Painter** in the Clipboard group. Select each set of sub-points in the remainder of the numbered list. Press **Esc** to turn off the format painter.

h. Make the bullet lists easier to read by completing the following steps:
   - Right-click the first General Task, *Resumes.* Point to *Styles* in the menu, and then click **Select Text with Similar Formatting** to select all italicized headings.
   - Click the **Paragraph Dialog Box Launcher**, and then click the **Spacing Before arrow** until *12 pt* displays.
   - Click **Don't add space between paragraphs of the same style** to remove the check mark from the check box. Click **OK.**
   - Select item number five, *Email campaigns.* Click the **Paragraph Dialog Box Launcher**, and then click the **Line and Page Breaks tab.** Click **Keep with next**, and then click **OK.**
   - Select the six sub-points for item five. Click the **Paragraph Dialog Box Launcher**, click **Keep with next**, click **Keep lines together**, and then click **OK.** This prevents the break, which enables one paragraph to split between two pages.

i. Press **Ctrl+End** to move the cursor to the end of the document. To insert a graphical image complete the following steps:
   - Click the **Insert tab**, click **Picture**, browse to the data files, and then double-click **englerlogo**.
   - Click the **Size Dialog Box Launcher**, and then reduce the Scale Height to **25%**. Click **OK**.
   - Click **Position**, and then click **Position in Bottom Center with Square Text Wrapping.**
   - Click the **More button** in the Picture Quick Styles group to display the entire Picture Styles gallery.
   - Click **Reflected Perspective Right** (fifth row, third column) to apply a border and reflective effects around the graphic.
   - Click **Compress Pictures** in the Adjust group, and then click **OK.**

j. Click the **Insert tab**, click **Page Number**, point to *Bottom of Page*, and select **Bold Numbers 1**. Click **Close Header and Footer.**

k. Press **Ctrl+Home**. Click the **Styles Dialog Box Launcher**. Click **Options**, and then click the **Select styles to show arrow**. Click **All styles**, and then click **OK**. Right-click the **Emphasis style** in the Styles gallery, and then select **Select All 3 Instance(s)**. Scroll down the Styles pane, and then select **Heading 2** to change all headings to a new style. Close the Style pane.

l. Place the insertion point on the left side of the paragraph under the *Goal:* heading. Press **Tab**. Press **Ctrl+T** to indent the whole paragraph the same distance as the tab setting.

m. Compare your work to Figure 2.40. Save and close the file, and submit based on your instructor's directions.

2 Queen City Medical Equipment

You are the training coordinator for Queen City Medical Equipment, and your responsibilities include tracking all employees' continuing education efforts. The company urges employees to pursue educational opportunities that add experience and knowledge to their positions, including taking any certification exams that enhance their credentials. The human resources director wants you to provide him with a list of employees who have met minimum qualifications to take an upcoming certification exam. In its present state the memo prints on two pages; you will format the memo using columns in order to save paper and display the entire list on one page. This exercise follows the same set of skills as used in Hands-On Exercises 1 and 2 in the chapter. Refer to Figure 2.41 as you complete this exercise.

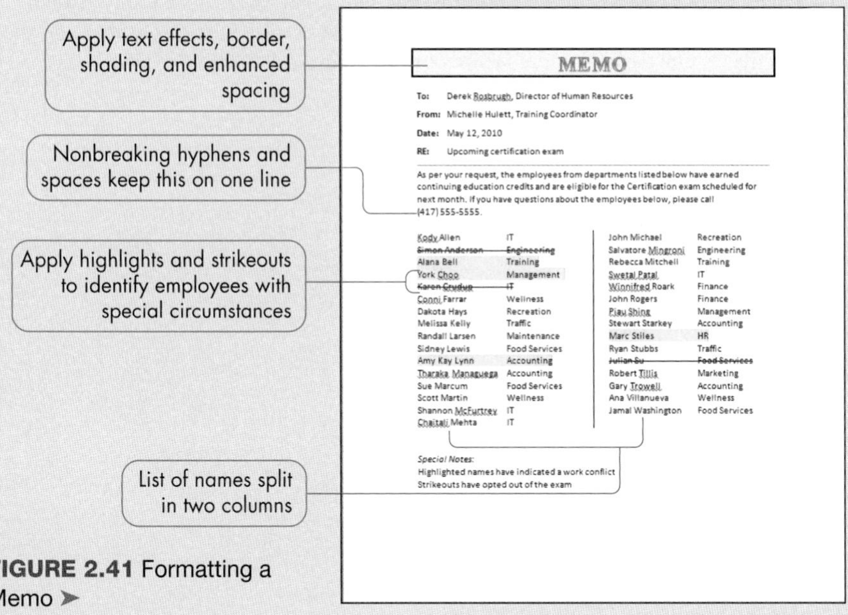

FIGURE 2.41 Formatting a Memo ➤

a. Open *w02p2memo* and save it as **w02p2memo_LastnameFirstname.**

b. Select the word *Memo,* and then complete the following steps:
   - Click **Center** in the Paragraph group, click **Change Case** in the Font group, and then select **UPPERCASE**. Click the **Font arrow**, and then select **Times New Roman**.
   - Click the **Font Size arrow**, and then select **24**. Click **Text Effects**, and then click **Gradient Fill - Gray, Outline - Gray** (third row, third column). Click the **Font Dialog Box Launcher**, click the **Advanced tab**, click the **Spacing arrow**, select **Expanded**, click **By**, and then type the number **2**. Click **OK** to close the Font dialog box.
   - Click the **Borders arrow** in the Paragraph group, and then click **Borders and Shading**. Click the **Box setting**, click the **Width arrow**, and then click **2 1/4**.
   - Click the **Shading tab**, click the **Fill arrow**, and then select **White, Background 1, Darker 5%** (second row, first column). Click **OK** to close the dialog box.

c. Select the highlighted text **Your Name Here**, and then replace it with your name. Select the highlighted text **Insert current date**, and then type today's date. Select the job title *director*, which follows Derek Rosbrugh's name, hold down **Ctrl**, select **human resources**, click **Change Case** in the Font group, and then select **Capitalize Each Word**.

d. Select the space between the area code *(417)* and phone number *(555)*, and then press **Shift+Ctrl+Spacebar** to insert a nonbreaking space. Select the hyphen in the middle of the phone number, between *555* and *5555*, and then press **Shift+Ctrl+Hyphen** to insert a nonbreaking hyphen. Now the entire phone number should display together on one line.

e. Select the line that contains *Alana Bell* to select her name and department. On the Mini toolbar, click the **Text Highlight Color arrow**, and then click the **Yellow square**. You do this to show which employees have a work conflict and will be unable to sit for the upcoming certification exam. To identify other people who fall into that category, double-click the **Format Painter**, and then click the names *York Choo, Amy Kay Lynn,* and *Marc Stiles.* Each name is now highlighted in yellow. Press **Esc** to turn off the format painter.

f. Select *Simon Anderson*, hold down **Ctrl**, and then select *Karen Crudup* and *Julian Su.* Release Ctrl, and then click **Strikethrough** in the Font group. These employees are opting out of the exam for personal reasons, and we need to identify them as well.

g. Insert tabs to separate the names and departments by completing the following steps:
   - Click **Show/Hide** (¶) in the Paragraph group to display the tab characters.
   - Select the list of people, click the **Paragraph Dialog Box launcher**, and then click **Tabs**.
   - Type **1.5** in the **Tab stop position**, and then click **Set**.
   - Click **OK** to close the dialog box. The departments now align in a column on the right side of the employee names. Click **Show/Hide** (¶) again to turn off the formatting marks.

h. Display the list of employees in two columns, so you can print the memo on one sheet of paper instead of two, by completing these steps:
   - Select all the names.
   - Click the **Page Layout tab**, click **Columns**, and then select **More Columns**.
   - Click **Two** in the *Presets* section in the Columns dialog box, and then check **Line between**.
   - Click **OK** to close the Columns dialog box. The names now display in two columns, and the entire memo fits on one page. Compare your work to Figure 2.41.

i. Save and close the file, and submit based on your instructor's directions.

MID-LEVEL EXERCISES

1 Technology Training Conference

You created a status report to inform committee members about an upcoming conference of which you are in charge. You want the report to look attractive and professional, so you decide to create and apply your own styles rather than use those already available in Word. You create a paragraph style named Side Heading to format the headings, and then you create a character style named Session to format the names of the conference sessions and apply these formats to document text. You then copy these two styles to the Normal template.

a. Open *w02m1conference* and save it as **w02m1conference_LastnameFirstname**.
b. Create a new paragraph style named **Side Heading** using the following properties: Style based on is **Normal**, style for following paragraph is **Normal**. Font properties are **Arial**, **14 pt**, **Bold**; and font color is **Red, Accent 2, Darker 50%.**
c. Set the following paragraph formats for this style: **12 pt Before** paragraph spacing, **6 pt After** paragraph spacing.
d. Apply the **Side Heading style** to the two-line report title, and then **Center** both lines. Apply the **Side Heading style** to the three headings *The Committee*, *Training Sessions*, and *Training Goal*.
e. Create a new character style named **Session** using the following specifications: **Bold** and **Red, Accent 2, Darker 50%** font color. Apply the **Session style** to the following words in the highlighted area: *Word*, *Web Page Development*, *Multimedia*, and *Presentation Graphics*.
f. Use the highlighted text to create a bulleted list. Remove the highlighting, and then indent the bullet list **.8″** from the right side.
g. Modify the Side Heading style to use the **Small caps font effect** and expand spacing by **1.5 pt**.
h. Save *w02m1conference_LastnameFirstname*.

DISCOVER

i. Open the Manage Styles dialog box, and then export the **Side Heading** and **Session styles** from *w02m1conference_ LastnameFirstname.docx* to *Normal.dotm*.
j. Open a new document. Display the Styles pane, if necessary, and then verify that the Session and Side Heading styles display. After confirming they are imported, delete the two styles from the *Normal.dotm* list. If working in a computer lab, this resets the Normal template for the next user. Close the blank document without saving it.
k. Insert a nonbreaking hyphen and a nonbreaking space in the phone number that displays at the end of the report.
l. Save and close *w02m1conference_LastnameFirstname*, and submit based on your instructor's directions.

2 Association for Administrative Professionals

CREATIVE CASE

You are president of the Association for Administrative Professionals and you recently composed a letter to welcome new members. Now, you want to make the letter look more professional by applying paragraph formatting, such as alignment, paragraph spacing, and a paragraph border and shading. In addition, you want to create a customized bulleted list that describes plans for the organization and insert the organization's logo.

a. Open the document *w02m2welcome* and save it as **w02m2welcome_LastnameFirstname**.
b. Change the capitalization of the recipient Emily Gibson and her address so that each word is capitalized and the state abbreviation displays in uppercase. Change Ken's name to your name in the signature block.
c. Apply **Justified alignment** to each paragraph in the document. Delete the asterisk (*), and then create a customized bulleted list, selecting a picture bullet of your choice. Type the following items in the bulleted list:

Asking administrative professionals to be guest speakers at meetings.
Participating in the regional and national conferences.
Shadowing an administrative professional for a day.
Finding internships for members of the organization.

d. Select text from the salutation *Dear Emily*: through the last paragraph that ends with *next meeting*. Set **12 pt spacing After paragraph**.
e. Use the **Small Cap font effect** on *Association for Administrative Professionals* in the first paragraph.
f. Replace the word *cent* in the title of the presentation with the cent symbol found in the (normal text) Latin-1 Supplement subset.
g. Select the italicized lines of text that give date, time, and location of the meeting. Remove the italics, and then complete the following:
  - Increase left and right indents to **1.5″**, and set **0 pt spacing After paragraph**.
  - Apply a double-line border using the color **Red, Accent 2, Darker 50%**, **3/4 pt border width**, and **Red, Accent 2, Lighter 40% shading** color.
h. Click the line containing the text *Room 255*, and set **12 pt spacing After** paragraph.
i. Select the entire document, and then change the font to **12-pt Bookman Old Style**. If necessary, delete the extra tab formatting mark to the left of *Community College* to prevent it from word wrapping.
j. Use nonbreaking hyphens and nonbreaking spaces to display the telephone number on one line.
k. Insert the graphic **logo.jpg** and display it in the top-right corner of the document. Resize the graphic so it does not display larger than 1.6″ x 2.0″. Apply the **Reflected Round Rectangle style** to the logo. Increase the brightness settings by **15%**. Apply **Color settings** or **Artistic Effects** to your preference.
l. Save and close the file, and submit based on your instructor's directions.

CAPSTONE EXERCISE

In this project, you work with a document prepared for managers involved in the hiring process. This report analyzes the validity of the interview process and suggests that selection does not depend only on quality information, but on the quality of the interpretation of information. The document requires formatting to enhance readability and important information; you will use skills from this chapter to format multiple levels of headings and figures. To make it easy for readers to locate topics in your document, create and use various supplemental document components such as a table of contents and index.

Applying Styles

This document is ready for enhancements, and the styles feature is a good tool that enables you to add them quickly and easily.

a. Open *w02c1interview* and save it as **w02c1interview_LastnameFirstname.**

b. Create a paragraph style named **Title_Page_1** with these formats: **22-pt font size, Shadow font effect Offset Diagonal Top Right, character spacing expanded by 2 pt, horizontally centered,** using Font color **Dark Blue, Text 2, Darker 50%.** Apply this style to the first line of the document, *Understanding the Personal Interview.*

c. Create a paragraph style named **Title_Page_2** based on the first style you created, with these additional formats: **20-pt font size, custom color 66, 4, 66.** Apply this style to the subtitle, *A Study for Managers Involved in the Hiring Process.*

d. Replace the * in the middle of the first page with your name. Change the capitalization for your name to uppercase.

e. Select the remainder of the text in the document that follows your name, starting with *Understanding the Personal Interview.* **Justify** the alignment of all paragraphs and change line spacing to **1.15.** Place your cursor on the left side of the title *Understanding the Personal Interview,* and then insert a page break so the document starts at the top of the page.

f. Apply the **Heading 1 style** to the main headings throughout the document and the **Heading 2 style** to the paragraph headings, such as *Introduction* and *Pre-interview Impressions.*

g. Modify the Heading 2 style to use **Dark Red font color.**

Formatting the Paragraphs

Next, you will apply paragraph formatting to the document. These format options will further increase the readability and attractiveness of your document.

a. Apply a bulleted list format for the five-item list in the *Introduction.* Use the symbol of a four-sided star from the Wingdings group (symbol 170) for the bullet.

b. Select the second paragraph in the *Introduction* section that begins with *Personal interviewing continues,* and then apply these formats: **0.6″ left and right indent, 6 pt spacing after the paragraph, boxed 1½ pt border using the color Blue, Accent 1, Darker 25%,** and the shading color **Blue, Accent 1, Lighter 80%.**

c. Apply the first numbered-list format (1., 2., 3.) for the three phases in the *Pre-Interview Impressions* section.

d. Select the second and third paragraphs in *The Unfavorable Information Effect* section, and then display them in two columns with a line between the columns.

Inserting Graphics and Page Numbers

To put the finishing touches on your document, you will add graphics that enhance the explanations given in some paragraphs. Captions are already in place for the graphics, but final formatting must occur to display them properly. Additionally, you will create a footer to display page numbers in this long document.

a. Insert the picture file **perceptions.jpg** at the beginning of the line that contains the caption *Figure 1: Perception in the Interview* and that displays at the bottom of page 2. Center the graphic horizontally, change text wrapping, and then insert any line breaks necessary so the graphic displays on a line by itself just above the caption. Use scaling to reduce the size to 75% of the original size. Apply the **Rounded Diagonal Corner, White picture style.**

b. Insert the picture file **phases.jpg** at the beginning of the line that contains the caption *Figure 2: Diboye's Interview phases.* Change text wrapping, and then insert any line breaks necessary so the graphic displays on a line by itself just above the caption. Apply **Offset Center shadow effect** to the graphic.

c. Display a page number in the footer of each page using the **Accent Bar 4 format.** Prevent the footer from displaying on the title page, and then start numbering on the page that follows the title page.

d. Review the entire document, and if necessary, use **Keep Lines Together controls** to prevent headings and paragraphs from being separated across pages. Invoke the **Widow/Orphan control** also.

e. Insert nonbreaking spaces and nonbreaking hyphens where appropriate.

f. Display the document in Outline view. Collapse all paragraphs so only the headings display.

g. Save and close the file, and submit based on your instructor's directions.

BEYOND THE CLASSROOM

Review the Skills

GENERAL CASE

You learned many skills and features of Word 2010 in this chapter. Take a few minutes to refresh yourself on these and other features by creating an outline of this chapter. Use the Multilevel list feature to type out each heading and subheading, and write a short paragraph to summarize the skills. Adjust tabs as necessary so the second and third level headings are indented at least .5″ beyond the first. Use styles for each type of heading so they appear different (as they do in the chapter). Save your work as **w02b1outline_LastnameFirstname** and submit based on your instructor's directions.

The Invitation

RESEARCH CASE

Search the Internet for an upcoming local event at your school or in your community and produce the perfect invitation. You can invite people to a charity ball, a fun run, or to a fraternity party. Your color printer and abundance of fancy fonts, as well as your ability to insert page borders, enable you to do anything a professional printer can do. Save your work as **w02b2invitation_LastnameFirstname** and submit based on your instructor's directions.

A Fundraising Letter

DISASTER RECOVERY

Each year, you update a letter to several community partners soliciting support for an auction. The auction raises funds for your organization, and your letter should impress your supporters. Open *w02b3auction* and notice how unprofessional and unorganized the document looks so far. You must make changes immediately to improve the appearance. Consider replacing much of the formatting that is in place now and instead using columns for auction items, bullets to draw attention to the list of forms, page borders, and pictures or Clip Art—and that is just for starters! Save your work as **w02b3auction_LastnameFirstname** and submit based on your instructor's directions.

WORD

3 COLLABORATION AND RESEARCH

Communicating Easily and Producing Professional Papers

CASE STUDY | Marketing Plan for Take Note Paperie

Watch the
Set-up
Video
for this
Case Study!

Your marketing professor assigned you to work with Rachel Starkey and your team project is to create a marketing plan for a new small business. You and Rachel have chosen a custom printing service named Take Note Paperie as the company for which you will develop a plan.

The research is complete, and the document is typed. Rachel last updated the document and has sent it to you to view and modify as you see fit. You check the comments Rachel made and perform modifications based on her notes. You also notice it is lacking vital features of a research paper that all professors require, such as the table of contents, bibliography, and table of figures, so you plan to add those. However, you also want to provide Rachel the opportunity to view your changes to the document and to provide feedback before you submit it for grading, so you leave a note for her as well. You hope this is the last round of changes before you turn it in and earn an A!

OBJECTIVES AFTER YOU READ THIS CHAPTER, YOU WILL BE ABLE TO:

1. Insert comments in a document ***p.168***
2. Track changes in a document ***p.171***
3. Acknowledge a source ***p.179***
4. Create and modify footnotes and endnotes ***p.182***
5. Insert a table of contents and index ***p.187***
6. Add other reference tables ***p.191***
7. Create cross-references ***p.193***

Document Revisions

This chapter introduces several Word features that you can use for research papers while in school. These same skills will also be useful as you work with others on collaborative projects. One of the first things you need to do when working on a collaborative project is workgroup editing, where suggested revisions from one or more individuals can be stored electronically within a document. This feature enables the original author to review each suggestion individually before it is incorporated into the final version of the document, and further, enables multiple people to work on the same document in collaboration with one another. Another feature that is useful in workgroup settings enables you to insert comments in a document for other editors to view and respond to.

In this section, you will insert comments to provide feedback or to pose questions to the document author. Then you will track editing changes you make so that others can see your suggested edits.

Inserting Comments in a Document

In today's organizational environment, teams of people with diverse backgrounds, skills, and knowledge prepare documentation.... When you work with a team, you can use collaboration tools in Word such as the Comments feature.

In today's organizational environment, teams of people with diverse backgrounds, skills, and knowledge prepare documentation. Team members work together while planning, developing, writing, and editing important documents. If you have not participated in a team project yet, most likely you will. When you work with a team, you can use collaboration tools in Word such as the Comments feature. A ***comment*** is a note or annotation that appears in the document to ask a question or provide a suggestion about the content of a document. Frequently, the comment appears in a balloon on the side of the document.

A **comment** is a note or annotation about the content of a document.

Before you use the comments and other collaboration features, you should click File, click Options, and then view the General section of the Word Options dialog box to confirm that your name and initials display as the user. Word uses this information to identify the person who uses collaboration tools, such as Comments. If you are in a lab environment, you might not have permission to modify settings or change the User name; however, you should be able to change these settings on a home computer.

Add a Comment

You add comments to a document to remind a reviewer, or yourself, of action that needs to be taken. To insert a comment, select a word or phrase where you want it to appear, display the Review tab, click New Comment in the Comments group to open the markup balloon (see Figure 3.1), and then type the text of the comment. If you do not select anything prior to clicking New Comment, Word assigns the comment to the word or object closest to the insertion point. When you click outside the comment area, the comment is recorded in the document. Most comments display in ***markup balloons***, which are colored circles in the margin with a line drawn to the object of the comment. After you complete the comment, the text and markup balloon are highlighted in the color assigned to the reviewer.

A **markup balloon** is a colored circle that contains comments and displays in the margin.

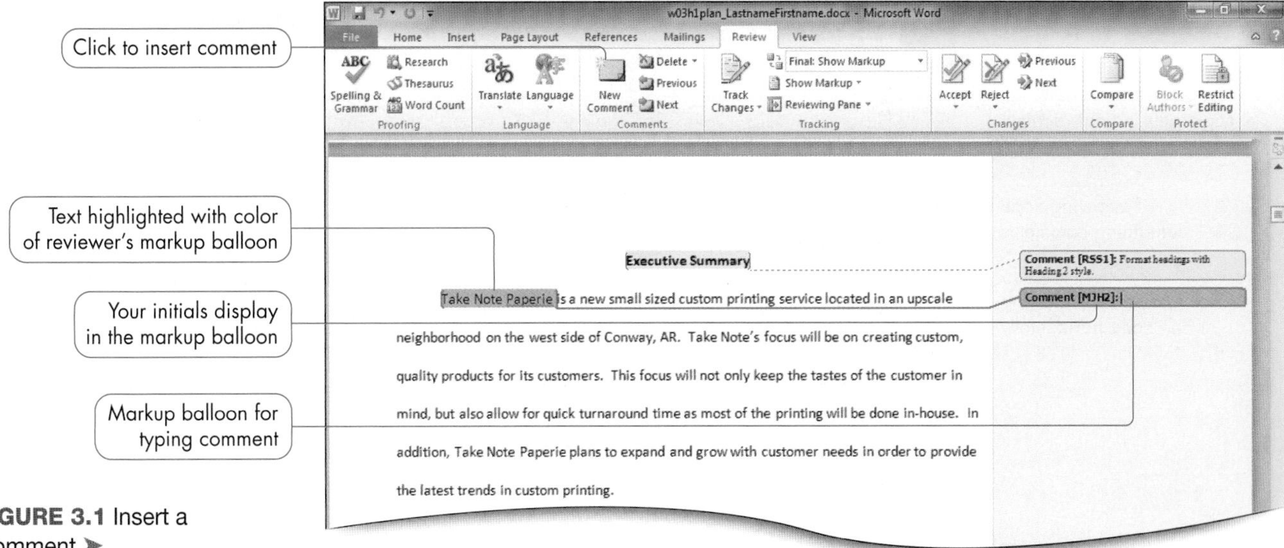

FIGURE 3.1 Insert a Comment ➤

TIP Response Comments

You can build a dialog through comments. If you select or put the insertion point in a comment markup balloon, and then click New Comment, a new markup balloon displays adjoining the first balloon, and *R1* will follow the reviewer's initials that display inside. The *R* stands for response, so the reader knows it is a response to the original comment.

View, Modify, and Delete Comments

The **Reviewing Pane** displays comments and changes made to a document.

Comments appear in markup balloons in Print Layout, Full Screen Reading, and Web Layout views. In Draft view, comments appear as tags embedded in the document; when you hover the cursor over the tag, it displays the comment. In any view, you can display the ***Reviewing Pane***, which displays all comments and editorial changes made to the main document. To display the Reviewing Pane vertically on the left side of the document, as shown in Figure 3.2, click Reviewing Pane on the Review tab. To hide the Reviewing Pane click Reviewing Pane again—it is a toggle. You can display the Reviewing Pane horizontally at the bottom when you click the Reviewing Pane arrow. The Reviewing Pane is useful when the comments are too long to display completely in a markup balloon.

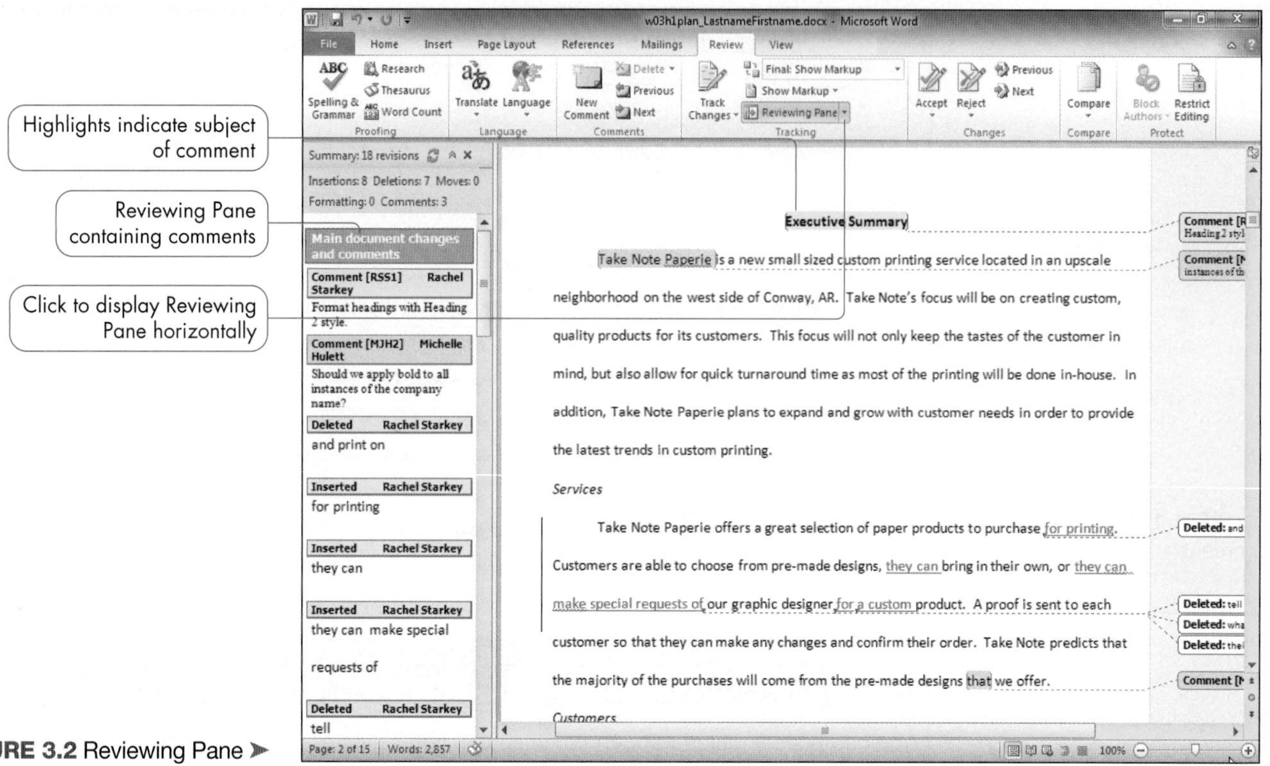

FIGURE 3.2 Reviewing Pane ➤

Show Markup enables you to view document revisions by reviewers.

If you do not see comments initially, click Show Markup on the Review tab and confirm that Comments is toggled on. The ***Show Markup*** feature enables you to view document revisions by reviewers. It also enables you to choose which type of revisions you want to view such as Comments, Ink annotations (made on a tablet PC), insertions and deletions, or formatting changes. Each can be toggled on or off, and you can view several at the same time, as shown in Figure 3.3. Show Markup also color-codes each revision or comment by using a different color for each reviewer. If you want to view only changes by a particular reviewer, click Show Markup, click Reviewers, and deselect all reviewers except the one you prefer.

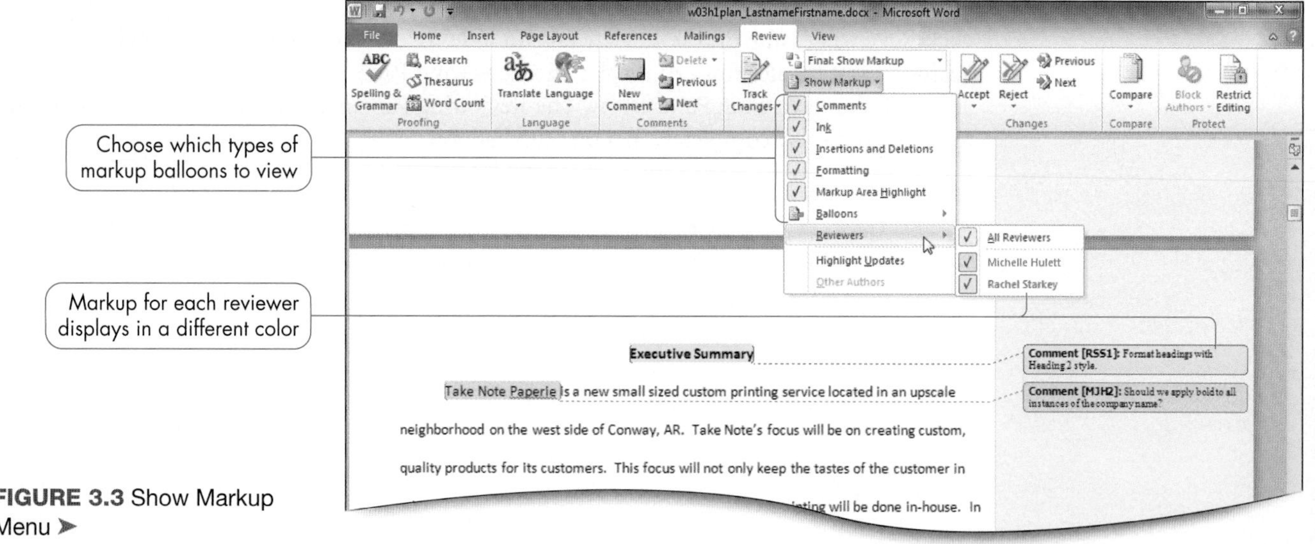

FIGURE 3.3 Show Markup Menu ➤

You can modify comments easily. When you click inside a markup balloon, the insertion point will relocate in the balloon, and you can use word processing formatting features, such as bold, italic, underline, and color, in the comment. If a document contains many comments, or the document is lengthy, you can click Previous and Next in the Comments group on the Review tab to navigate from comment to comment. This is a quick way to move between comments without scrolling through the entire document, and it places the insertion point in the comment automatically. You can edit comments when viewing them in the Reviewing Pane also.

After reading or acting on comments, you can delete them from the document or the Reviewing Pane by clicking Delete in the Comments group on the Review tab. When you click the Delete arrow, your options include deleting the current comment, all comments shown, or deleting all comments in the document at one time. You also can right-click a comment markup balloon and select Delete Comment from the shortcut menu. If you print a document that has comments, the comments also print. To omit the comments from the printout, click File, click Print, click the first Settings arrow (which shows Print All Pages by default), and then click Show Markup to remove the checkmark.

Tracking Changes in a Document

Use **Track Changes** to insert revision marks and markup balloons for additions, deletions, and formatting changes.

Whether you work individually or with a group, you can monitor any revisions you make to a document. The ***Track Changes*** feature monitors all additions, deletions, and formatting changes you make. It is useful in situations where a document must be reviewed by several people—each of whom can offer suggestions or changes—and then returned to one person who will finalize the document.

A **revision mark** indicates where text is added, deleted, or formatted while the Track Changes feature is active.

A **changed line** is a vertical bar in the margin to pinpoint the area where changes are made.

When Track Changes is not active, any change you make to a document is untraceable and no one will know what you change unless he or she compares your revised document with the previous version. When Track Changes is active, it applies ***revision marks***, which indicate where a person added, deleted, or formatted text. Like Comments, the revision marks will be colored differently for each reviewer. Revision marks can vary depending on your preference in viewing them, but include strikeout lines for deleted text, underlines for inserted text, markup balloons, and changed lines. ***Changed lines*** are vertical bars that display in the right or left margins to specify the line that contains revision marks. You can position the mouse pointer over revision marks or markup balloons to see who made the change and on what date and time, as shown in Figure 3.4.

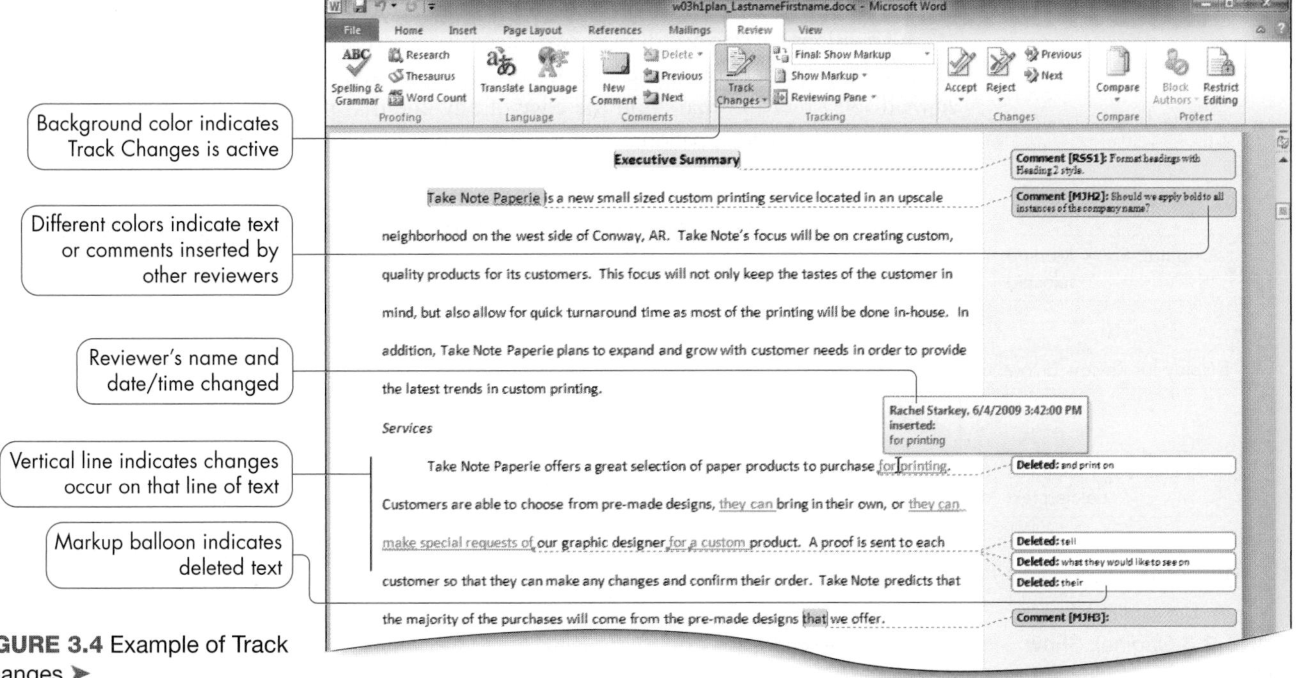

FIGURE 3.4 Example of Track Changes ➤

Word also includes markup tools, which enable you to accept or reject changes indicated by revision marks. The Changes group on the Review tab includes Accept, to accept a suggested change, and Reject, to remove a suggested change. When you accept or reject a change, the revision marks, markup balloon, and changed lines disappear. The Changes group also includes Previous and Next. When you click Previous, the insertion point moves to the beginning of any comment or change that occurs just prior to the current position. Similarly, clicking Next will move the insertion point to the beginning of the next comment or change.

If the review process takes place using paper copies of a document, it is difficult to visualize all the suggested changes at one time, and then the last person must manually change the original document. While writing the Exploring series, the authors, editors, and reviewers each inserted comments and tracked changes to the manuscript for each chapter using Word. Each person's comments or changes displayed in different colored balloons, and because all edits were performed in the same document, the Series Editor could accept and reject changes before sending the manuscript to the production department.

TIP Accepting or Rejecting All Changes

To accept all changes in a document at once, click the Accept arrow on the Review tab and select Accept All Changes in Document. To delete all changes in a document at once, click the Reject arrow on the Review tab and select Reject All Changes in Document.

Select Markup Views

Original: Show Markup view shows a line through deleted text and puts inserted text in a markup balloon.

Final: Show Markup view shows inserted text in the body and puts deleted text in a markup balloon.

The suggested revisions from the various reviewers display in one of two ways, as the Original Showing Markup or as the Final Showing Markup. The ***Original: Show Markup*** view shows the deleted text within the body of the document (with a line through the deleted text) and displays the inserted text in a balloon to the right of the actual document, as shown in Figure 3.5. The ***Final: Show Markup*** view is the opposite; that is, it displays the inserted text in the body of the document and shows the deleted text in a balloon. The difference is subtle and depends on personal preference with respect to displaying the insertions and deletions in a document. You can change the way markups display by clicking Show Markup, Balloons, and selecting from three choices: Show Revisions in Balloons, Show All Revisions Inline, or Show Only Comments and Formatting in Balloons.

All revisions fall into one of these two categories: insertions or deletions. Even if you substitute one word for another, you are deleting the original word and then inserting its replacement. Both views display revision marks on the edge of any line that has been changed. Comments are optional and enclosed in balloons in the side margin of a document.

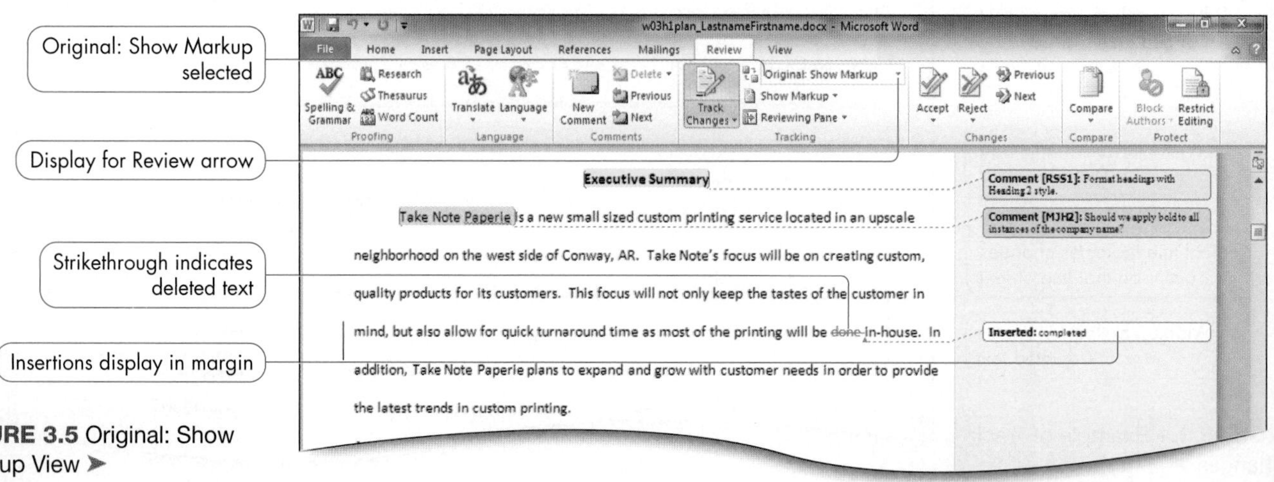

FIGURE 3.5 Original: Show Markup View ➤

To select one of the markup views you click the Display for Review arrow in the Tracking group on the Review tab (see Figure 3.5). When you click the Display for Review arrow, two additional view options are listed—Final and Original. Final shows how the document looks if you accept and incorporate all tracked changes. Original shows the document prior to using the Track Changes feature.

Customize Track Changes Options

The Track Changes feature has many options for viewing and displaying changes, which you can customize. When you click Change Tracking Options from the Track Changes arrow, the Track Changes Options dialog box displays with many features you can change. For example, you can choose the type of underline to display under inserted text (single line or double line). You can choose the type of strikethrough line to display on deleted text (strikethrough or double strikethrough). You can choose the location where the balloons display (right or left margins), and you can even choose the size of the balloons.

The beginning of this chapter mentioned that you should check the Word Options, making changes if necessary, so your name and initials are associated with any tracked changes you make in the document. You also can access those settings from the Review tab when you click the Track Changes arrow and select Change User Name, as shown in Figure 3.6. This step takes you to the General category of the Word Options dialog box, where you have the opportunity to enter your name and initials in the *Personalize your copy of Microsoft Office* section.

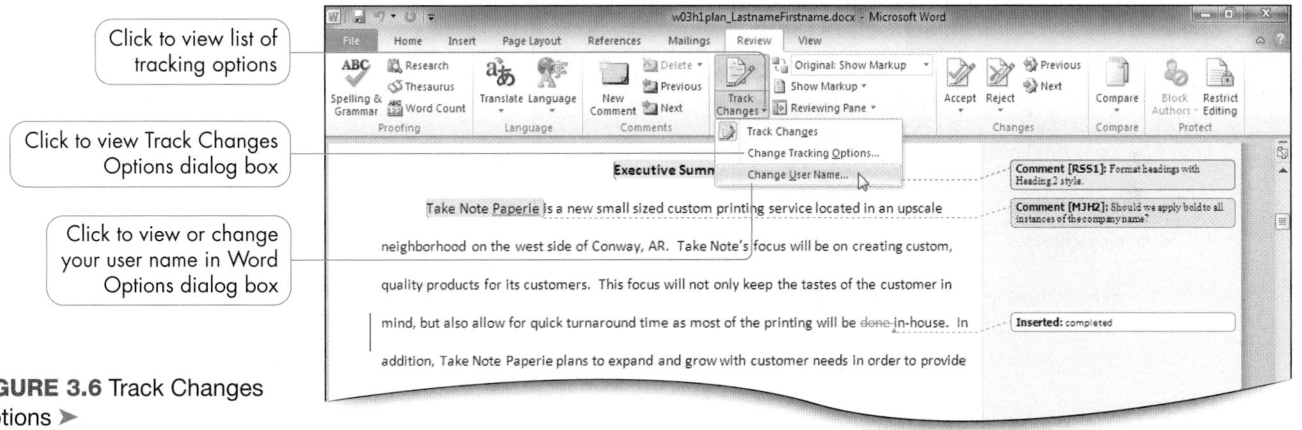

FIGURE 3.6 Track Changes Options ➤

HANDS-ON EXERCISES

1 Document Revisions

You open the document that Rachel Starkey prepared and find the comments she left for you. You also see her recent edits because she tracked her changes. Your task is to address any questions or requests in the comment balloons and also accept or reject the changes she made when revising the document.

Skills covered: Set User Name and Customize the Track Changes Options • Track Document Changes • View, Add, and Delete Comments • Accept and Reject Changes

STEP 1 SET USER NAME AND CUSTOMIZE THE TRACK CHANGES OPTIONS

You want to make sure the Word Options are customized so your name displays when comments are added or changes are tracked in a document. Then you decide to modify some of the track changes options to use settings that are distinguishable from those other editors might use. Refer to Figure 3.7 as you complete Step 1.

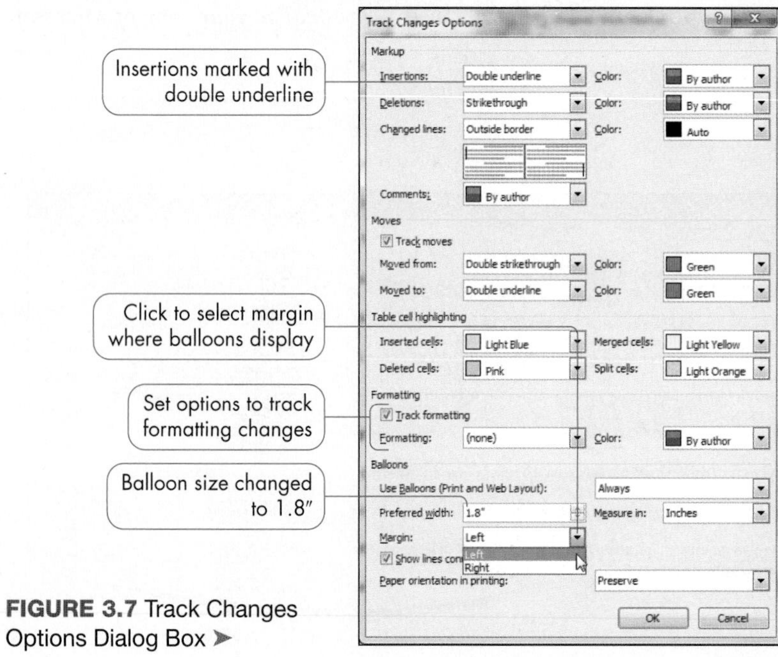

FIGURE 3.7 Track Changes Options Dialog Box ➤

a. Open *w03h1plan* and save it as **w03h1plan_LastnameFirstname**.

> **TROUBLESHOOTING:** If you make any major mistakes in this exercise, you can close the file, open *w03h1plan* again, and then start this exercise over.

b. Delete the text *YourName* in the subtitle and insert your first and last names. Click the **Review tab**, and then click **Track Changes** in the Tracking group.

> **TROUBLESHOOTING:** Track Changes in the Tracking group, like some other commands in Word, contain two parts: the main command icon and an arrow. Click the main command icon when instructed to click Track Changes and turn on the feature. Click the arrow when instructed to click the Track Changes arrow for additional command options.

The command displays with an orange background color, indicating the feature is turned on. When you click Track Changes, you toggle the feature on or off.

c. Click the **Track Changes arrow**, and then click **Change User Name**. In the *Personalize your copy of Microsoft Office* section, type your name in the **User name box**, and then type your initials in the **Initials box**, if necessary. Click **OK** to close the Word Options dialog box.

   You want to be sure your name and initials are correct before you add any comments or initiate any changes in the document. After you update the user information, your initials display with all comments or changes you make.

> **TROUBLESHOOTING:** Personalizing your copy of Microsoft Office might not be possible in a lab environment. If you cannot make the change, just continue with the exercise.

d. Click the **Track Changes arrow**, and then click **Change Tracking Options** to open the dialog box. In the *Markup* section, click the **Insertions arrow**, and then click **Double underline**. In the *Formatting* section, click the **Track formatting check box**, if necessary, to turn on this feature.

   Your revisions to the Track Changes options enable you to view any additions to the document quickly because they will be identified in balloons and your insertions will display with a double underline. Markups on formatting may not display automatically, but you confirm that option is on so you will see marks next to formatting changes that you make.

e. Click the **Use Balloons (Print and Web Layout) arrow** in the *Balloons* section, and then click **Always**, if necessary. Click the **Preferred width arrow** until **1.8"** displays. Click the **Margin arrow**, and then select **Left**, as shown in Figure 3.7. Click **OK** to close the Track Changes Options dialog box.

   You altered the location of all comment and editing balloons to display on the left side of your document instead of on the right, which is the default. You also decreased the width of the markup balloons so they will take up less space in the margins.

f. Save the document.

STEP 2 TRACK DOCUMENT CHANGES

Now that the settings are set to your preference, you make a few changes so you can see how your editing is tracked separately from Rachel's. You first change the views so you can see the tracked changes made by both of you while you work, and then you later change the view so you see how the document looks as a final version. Refer to Figure 3.8 as you complete Step 2.

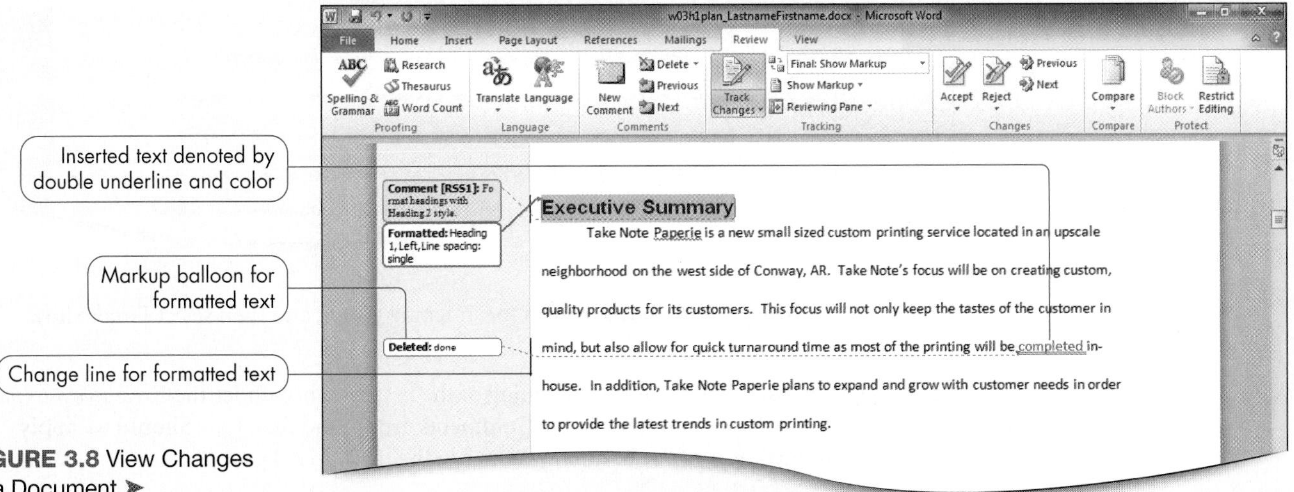

FIGURE 3.8 View Changes in a Document ➤

a. Click the **Display for Review arrow** in the Tracking group on the Review tab, and then select **Final: Show Markup**, if necessary. Scroll down the document until you see the heading *Executive Summary* on the second page of the document.

   One comment displays in a balloon and several changes are marked in color. Because of the changes you made in Step 1, any future changes you make in the document also display in balloons in the margin of the document.

b. Replace the word *done* with **completed** in the third sentence of the first paragraph that follows the *Executive Summary* heading.

   The text you inserted is colored and has a double underline beneath it.

TROUBLESHOOTING: If a balloon does not display, indicating the word replacement, make sure Track Changes is on. When on, Track Changes is highlighted in an orange color on the Review tab. If necessary, click Undo, click Track Changes again to turn it on, and then repeat Step 2b.

c. Select the **Executive Summary heading**, click the **Home tab**, and then apply the **Heading 1 style** from the Styles gallery.

   The heading is now left justified, and a changed line appears on the left side. A markup balloon describes the formatting change, as seen in Figure 3.8.

d. Click the **Review tab**, click the **Display for Review arrow** in the Tracking group, and then select **Final**.

   The formatting change indicators do not display, and the *Executive Summary* heading displays in the new style.

e. Save the document.

STEP 3 VIEW, ADD, AND DELETE COMMENTS

As you work through the document, you think of a question you would like to ask Rachel before the plan is finalized, so you insert a comment of your own. You also remove one of her comments about an issue that is resolved. Refer to Figure 3.9 as you complete Step 3.

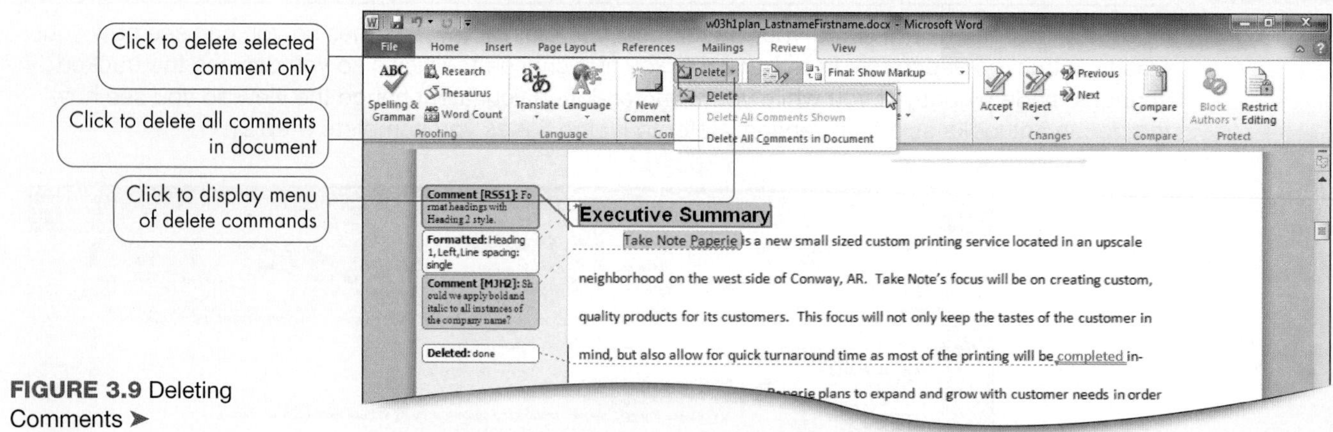

FIGURE 3.9 Deleting Comments ➤

a. Click the **Display for Review arrow** in the Tracking group, and then select **Final: Show Markup**.

b. Select **Take Note Paperie** at the beginning of the first sentence under the *Executive Summary* heading. Click **New Comment** in the Comments group, and then type **Should we apply bold to all instances of the company name?** in the markup balloon.

   If you do not select anything prior to clicking New Comment, Word selects the word or object nearest the insertion point for the comment reference.

c. Click inside the markup balloon you created. Place your cursor to the left of the word *to*, edit the comment by typing **and italic**, and then press **Spacebar**. Click outside of the balloon to deselect it.

Your comment now displays *Should we apply bold and italic to all instances of the company name?*

d. Position the mouse pointer over the comment balloon attached to the *Executive Summary* heading.

When you position the mouse pointer over a markup balloon, Word displays a ScreenTip that tells you who created the comment and when.

e. Click Rachel Starkey's comment one time to select it, and then click **Delete** in the Comments group.

You removed the selected comment and the markup balloon. If you click the arrow on the right side of Delete in the Comments group, you can select from several options, including Delete all Comments in Document (see Figure 3.9). You can also right-click a comment and select Delete Comment.

f. Save the document.

STEP 4 ACCEPT AND REJECT CHANGES

Now you are ready to consider the changes that Rachel made and tracked. Some are good and will improve the readability of the paper; some will not. You remember how quick and easy it is to accept and reject changes by using features on the Review tab and that makes you smile. Refer to Figure 3.10 as you complete Step 4.

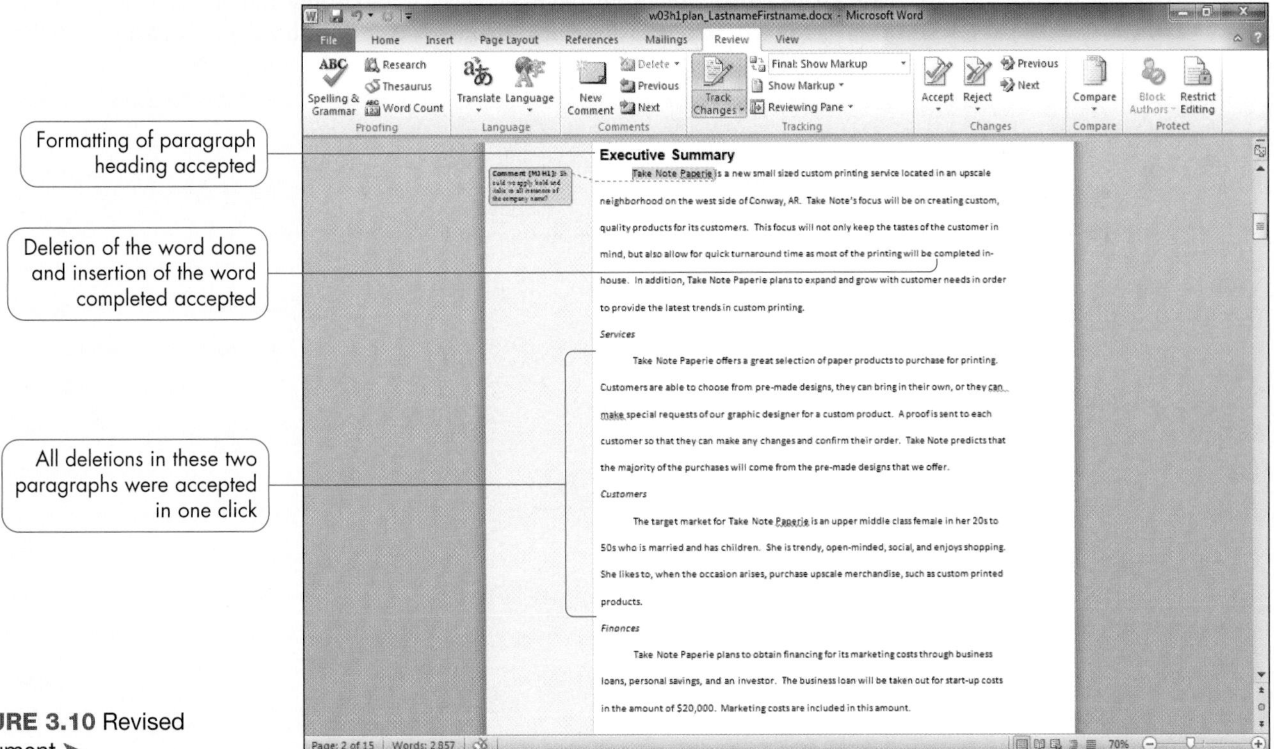

FIGURE 3.10 Revised Document ➤

a. Press **Ctrl+Home** to place the insertion point at the beginning of the document.

b. Click **Next** in the Changes group to highlight the first change, and then position the mouse pointer over the tracked change.

The formatting change to the *Executive Summary* heading is highlighted. When you position the mouse pointer on the revision, a ScreenTip appears that tells you who made the change and the date and time the change was made.

TROUBLESHOOTING: If you click Next in the Comments group instead of Next in the Changes group, click Previous in the Comments group to return the cursor to the beginning of the document, and then click Next in the Changes group.

c. Click **Accept** in the Changes group.

The formatting change is accepted. When the suggested change is accepted, the markup balloons and other Track Changes markups disappear. Additionally, the markup balloon for the next change or comment is highlighted. As with other commands, you can click Accept to accept this change only, or you can click the Accept arrow to view options for accepting changes.

d. Click **Next** in the Changes group to pass the comment and view the next markup balloon. Click **Accept** two times to accept the replacement of *done* to *completed.*

The first time you accept the change it applies to the deletion of the word *done.* The second time you accept the change it applies to the insertion of *completed.*

e. Select the entire second and third paragraphs in the *Executive Summary* section. Click **Accept** to retain all revisions in the paragraphs. Click **Reject** to remove the empty comment that displays in this paragraph.

All the changes in those paragraphs are accepted, the blank comment is removed, and the next change, a deletion of a complete section of the report, is highlighted. Figure 3.10 shows the first page after accepting changes.

f. Click **Reject** in the Changes group to retain the *Goals* heading and following paragraphs.

g. Save *w03h1plan_LastnameFirstname* and keep it onscreen if you plan to continue with the next Hands-On Exercise. Close the file and exit Word if you will not continue with the next exercise at this time.

Research Paper Basics

Well-prepared documents often include notes that provide supplemental information or citations for sources quoted in the document. Some documents also contain other valuable supplemental components, such as a list of figures or legal references. Word includes many features that can help you create these supplemental references, as well as many others described in the following paragraphs.

In this section, you will use Word to create citations used for reference pages, create a bibliography page that displays works cited in the document, and select from a list of writing styles that are commonly used to dictate the format of reference pages. You will also create and modify footnote and endnote citations, which display at the bottom of a page or the end of the document.

Acknowledging a Source

Plagiarism is the act of using and documenting the works of another as one's own.

It is common practice to use a variety of sources to supplement your own thoughts when writing a paper, report, legal brief, or many other types of document. Failure to acknowledge the source of information you use in a document is a form of plagiarism. *Webster's New Collegiate Dictionary* defines ***plagiarism*** as the act of using and documenting the ideas or writings of another as one's own. It may also apply to spoken words, multimedia works, or graphics. Plagiarism has serious moral and ethical implications and is taken seriously in the academic community; it is often classified as academic dishonesty.

Failure to acknowledge the source of information you use in a document is a form of plagiarism.... Word includes a robust feature for tracking sources and producing the supplemental resources to display them.

To assist in your efforts to avoid plagiarism, which is frequently a thoughtless oversight rather than a malicious act, Word includes a robust feature for tracking sources and producing the supplemental resources to display them.

Create a Source

A **citation** is a note recognizing a source of information or a quoted passage.

Word provides the citation feature to track, compile, and display your research sources for inclusion in several types of supplemental references. To use this feature you use the Insert Citation command in the Citations & Bibliography group on the References tab to add data about each source, as shown in Figure 3.11. A ***citation*** is a note recognizing the source of information or a quoted passage. The Create Source dialog box includes fields to catalog information, such as author, date, publication name, page number, or Web site address, from the following types of sources:

- Book
- Book Section
- Journal Article
- Article in a Periodical
- Conference Proceedings
- Report
- Web site
- Document from Web site
- Electronic Source
- Art
- Sound Recording
- Performance
- Film
- Interview
- Patent
- Case
- Miscellaneous

After you create the citation sources, you can insert them into a document using the Insert Citation command. When you click the command, a list of your sources displays; click a source from the list, and the proper citation format is inserted in your document.

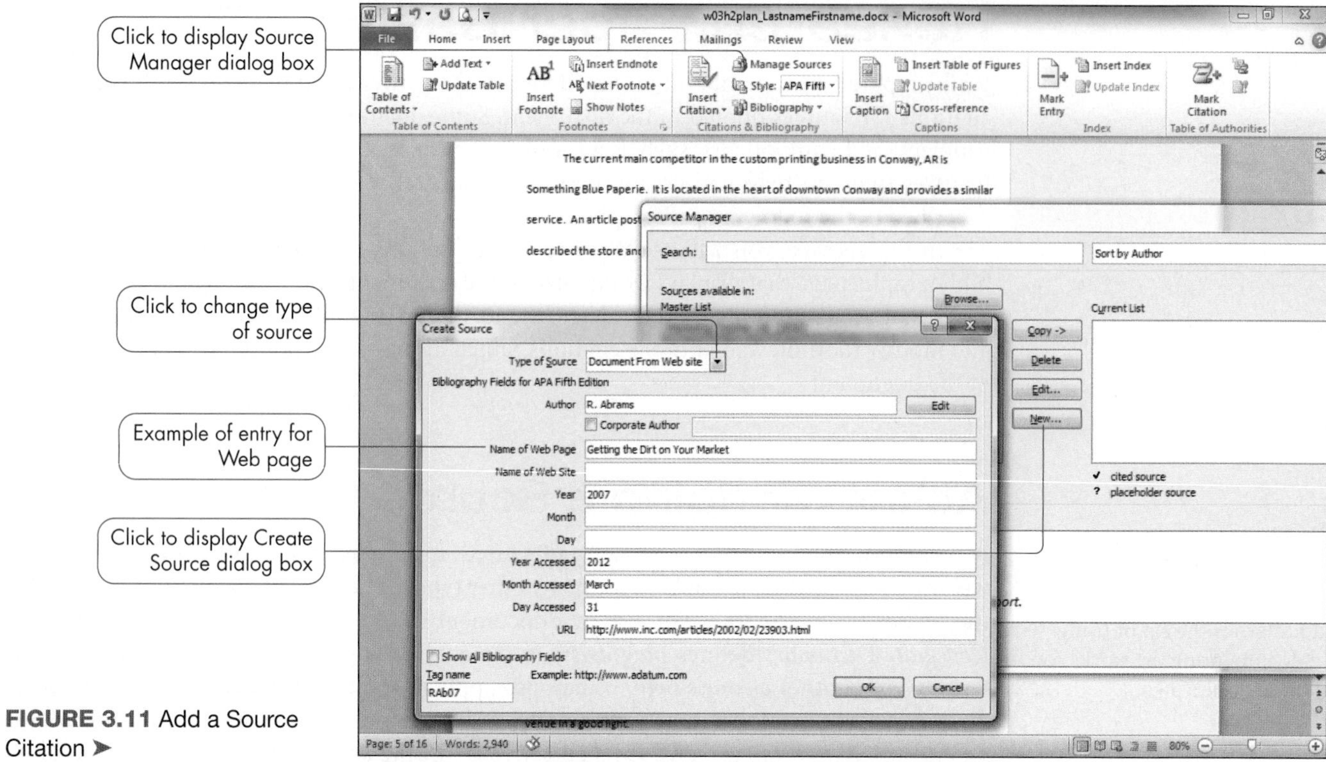

FIGURE 3.11 Add a Source Citation ➤

Share and Search for a Source

The **Master List** is a database of all citation sources created in Word.

The **Current List** includes all citation sources you use in the current document.

After you add sources, they are saved in a Master List. The ***Master List*** is a database of all citation sources created in Word on a particular computer. The source also is stored in the ***Current List***, which contains all sources you use in the current document. Sources saved in the Master List can be used in any Word document. This feature is helpful to those who use the same sources on multiple occasions. Master Lists are stored in XML format, so you can share the Master List file with coworkers or other authors, eliminating the need to retype the information and ensuring accuracy. The Master List file is stored in \AppData\Roaming\Microsoft\Bibliography, which is a subfolder of the user account folder stored under C:\Users. For example, a path to the Master File might be C:\Users\MichelleHulett\AppData\Roaming\Microsoft\Bibliography\Sources.xml.

The Source Manager dialog box (see Figure 3.12) displays the Master List you created, and you also can browse to find other XML files that contain source information. After you open a Master List, you can copy sources to your Current List. You can also copy, delete, or edit sources in either the Master or Current List from the Source Manager.

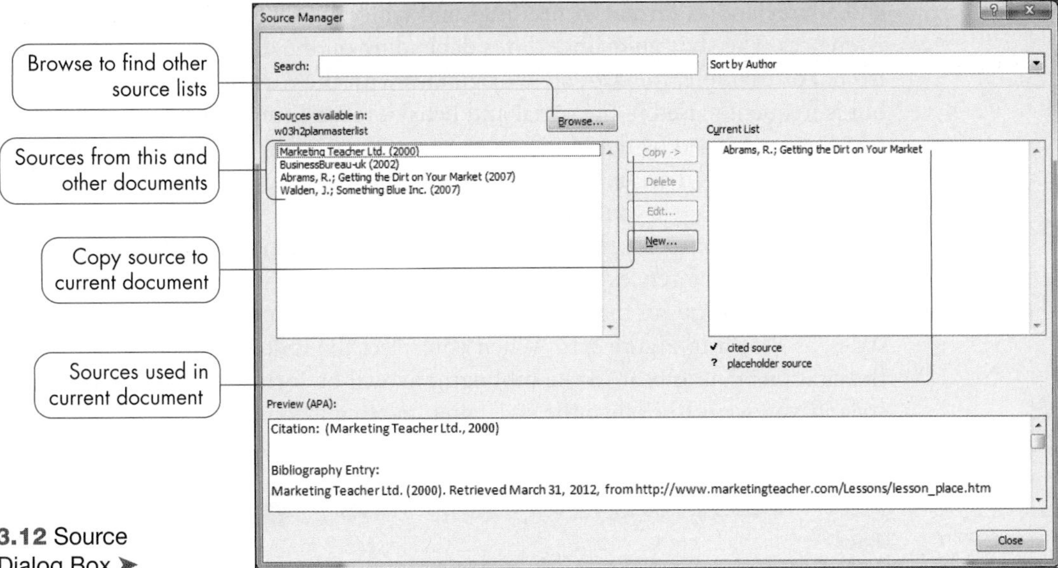

FIGURE 3.12 Source Manager Dialog Box ➤

Creating a Bibliography

A **bibliography** is a list of works cited or consulted by an author in a document.

A ***bibliography*** is a list of works cited or consulted by an author and should be included with the document when published. Some reference manuals use the terms Works Cited or References instead of Bibliography. A bibliography is just one form of reference that gives credit to the sources you consulted or quoted in the preparation of your paper. The addition of a bibliography to your completed work demonstrates respect for the material consulted. In addition to the bibliography, you should cite your source within a document, near any quotations or excerpts, to avoid plagiarizing. It also gives the reader an opportunity to validate your references for accuracy.

Word includes a bibliography feature that makes the addition of this reference page very easy. After you add the sources using the Insert Citation feature, you click Bibliography in the Citations & Bibliography group on the References tab, and then click Insert Bibliography. Any sources used in the current document will display in the appropriate format as a bibliography, as shown in Figure 3.13.

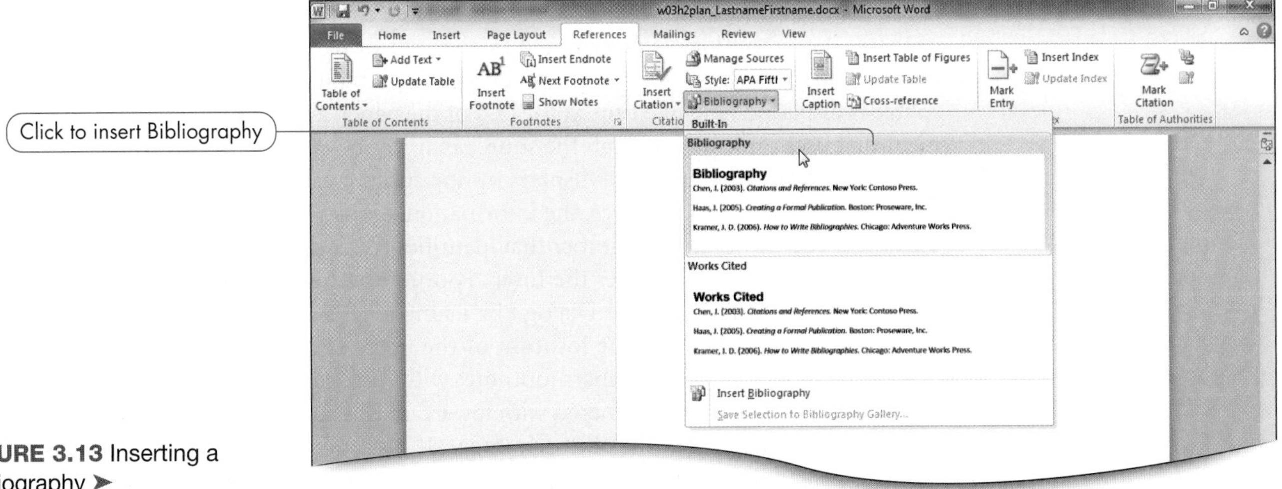

FIGURE 3.13 Inserting a Bibliography ➤

Selecting the Writing Style

When research papers are prepared the author often must conform to a particular writing style. The writing style, also called an editorial style, consists of rules and guidelines set forth by a publisher of a research journal to ensure consistency in presentation of research documents. Some of the presentation consistencies that a style enforces are use of punctuation and abbreviations, format of headings and tables, presentation of statistics, and citation of references. The style guidelines differ depending on the discipline the research topic comes from. For example, the APA style originates with the American Psychological Association, but is frequently used in the social and behavioral sciences. Another common style is MLA, which is sanctioned by the Modern Language Association and is often used in the humanities and business disciplines. The topic of your paper and the audience you write to will determine which style you should use while writing.

Word incorporates several writing style guidelines, making it easier for you to generate supplemental references in the required format. The Style list in the Citations & Bibliography group on the References tab includes the most commonly used international styles, as shown in Figure 3.14. When you select the style before creating the bibliography, the citations that appear in the bibliography will be formatted exactly as required by that style. If you want to change the style after creating it, simply position the cursor anywhere within the bibliography, and then select a different style from the list.

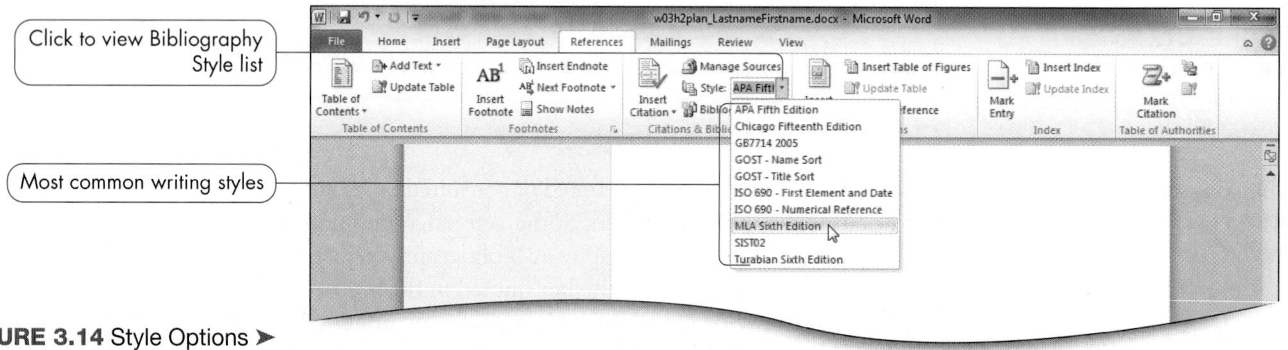

FIGURE 3.14 Style Options ➤

Creating and Modifying Footnotes and Endnotes

A **footnote** is a citation that appears at the bottom of a page.

An **endnote** is a citation that appears at the end of a document.

A ***footnote*** is a citation that appears at the bottom of a page, and an ***endnote*** is a citation that appears at the end of a document. You use footnotes or endnotes to credit the sources you quote or cite in your document. You also can use footnotes or endnotes to provide supplemental information about a topic that is too distracting to include in the body of the document. Footnotes, endnotes, and bibliographies often contain the same information. Your use of these citation options is determined by the style of paper (MLA, for example) or by the person who oversees your research. When you use a bibliography, the information about a source is displayed only one time at the end of the paper, and the exact location in the document that uses information from the source may not be obvious. When you use a footnote, the information about a source displays on the specific page where a quote or information appears. When you use endnotes, the information about a source displays only at the end of the document; however, the number that identifies the endnote displays on each page.

The References tab includes the Insert Footnote and Insert Endnote commands. If you click the Footnote and Endnote Dialog Box Launcher, the Footnote and Endnote dialog box opens, and you can modify the location of the notes and the format of the numbers. By default, Word sequentially numbers footnotes with Arabic numerals (1, 2, and 3) as shown in Figure 3.15. Endnotes are numbered with lowercase Roman numerals (i, ii, and iii) based on the location of the note within the document. If you add or delete notes, Word renumbers the remaining notes automatically.

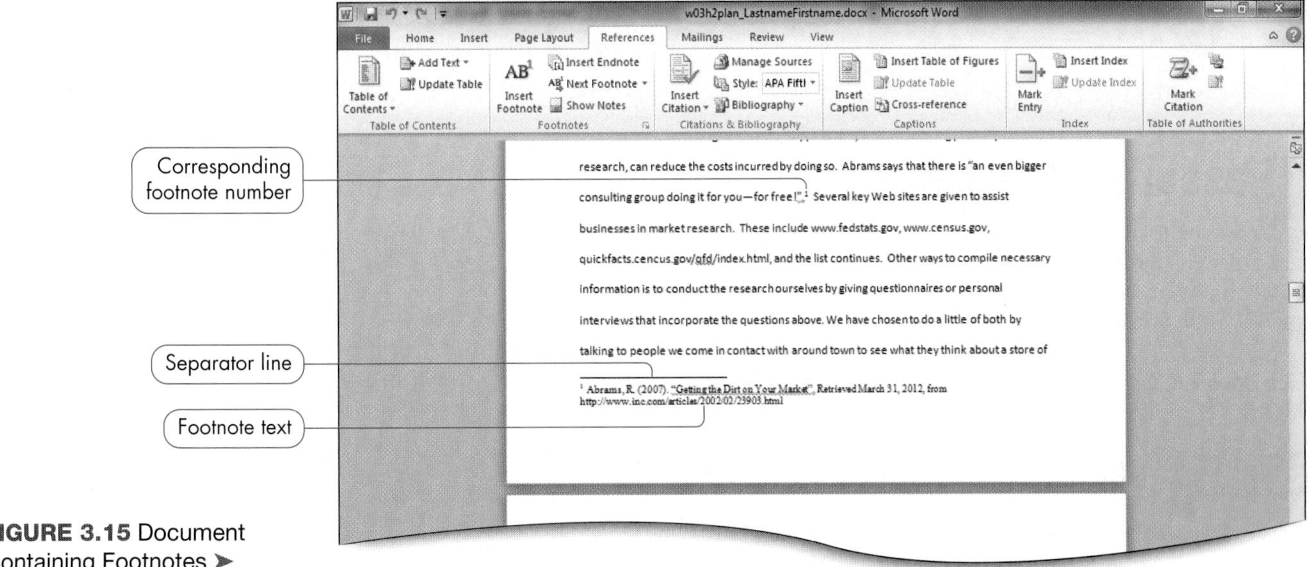

FIGURE 3.15 Document Containing Footnotes ➤

You can easily make modifications to footnotes and endnotes. In Print Layout view, scroll to the bottom of the page (or for endnotes, to the end of the document or section), click inside the note, and then edit it. In Draft view, double-click the footnote or endnote reference mark to display the Footnotes or Endnotes pane, and then you can edit the note.

TIP Relocating a Footnote or Endnote

If you created a note in the wrong location, select the note reference mark within the text, cut it from its current location, and then paste it in the correct location within the document text. You also can use the drag-and-drop method to move a selected note reference mark to a different location.

HANDS-ON EXERCISES

2 Research Paper Basics

The Marketing Plan that you and Rachel Starkey have written makes good use of external sources of information. You want to make sure all sources are properly credited and display in footnotes where appropriate in the document. You also plan to include a bibliography at the end of the paper, so you can display citations there as well, and you must remember to format it to use the required writing style, such as APA.

Skills covered: Create and Search for a Source • Select a Writing Style and Insert a Bibliography • Create and Modify Footnotes

STEP 1 CREATE AND SEARCH FOR A SOURCE

You used several sources in the document, so you decide to use the Citations and Bibliography feature in Word to prepare the citations. You insert the first citation, and then you import the other citations from a document that Rachel sent you, thus eliminating duplication of efforts. Refer to Figure 3.16 as you complete Step 1.

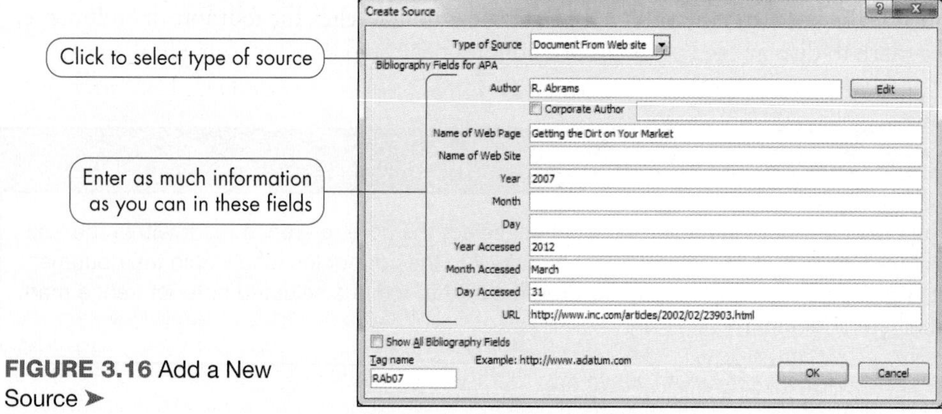

FIGURE 3.16 Add a New Source ➤

a. Open the *w03h1plan_LastnameFirstname* document if you closed it after the last Hands-On Exercise, and save it as **w03h2plan_LastnameFirstname**, changing *h1* to *h2*.

b. Click the **Display for Review arrow** in the Tracking group on the Review tab, and then select **Final**.

   You are still tracking changes in the document, but the information that displays can distract your attention, so you change the view to display it as if all your changes are accepted.

c. Click the **References tab**, click **Manage Sources** in the Citations & Bibliography group, and then click **New** in the middle of the dialog box.

   The Source Manager dialog box displays, as shown in Figure 3.16. Because you want to create a citation source without inserting the citation directly into the document, you use the Source Manager instead of clicking Insert Citation, Add New Source. After you click New in the Source Manager, the Create Source dialog box displays.

d. Click the **Type of Source arrow**, and then select **Document From Web site**. Type the source information as noted in the following table and as seen in Figure 3.16. After you enter each entry, click **OK** to add the source to your document and return to the Source Manager dialog box.

Author	R. Abrams
Name of Web Page	Getting the Dirt on Your Market
Year	2007
Year Accessed	2012
Month Accessed	March
Day Accessed	31
URL	http://www.inc.com/articles/2002/02/23903.html

To cite a source properly, you need as much information as you can provide, but you do not have to fill out all of the boxes in the Create Source dialog box. In some sources, such as the one above, the URL is more descriptive than the Web site name, and therefore more informative to anyone who wants to check your source.

e. Click **Browse** in the Source Manager dialog box to display the Open Source List dialog box. Click the drive and folder in the Folders list on the left side of the Open Source List dialog box where the student data files that accompany this book are located. Select *w03ho2planmasterlist*, and then click **OK**.

   You return to the Source Manager dialog box, and three sources that Rachel Starkey had created in a separate document display in the *Sources available in* box along with the source you just created.

f. Click the first source entry, if necessary, to select it. Then press and hold **Ctrl** and select the other two new entries. Click **Copy** to insert the sources into the current document.

   The three sources you copied and the one source you created display in the Current List box as well as in the Master List.

g. Click **Close** to return to the document. Save the document.

STEP 2 SELECT A WRITING STYLE AND INSERT A BIBLIOGRAPHY

Now that sources are cited and stored in the document, you can quickly insert the bibliography at the end. You also select the writing style, which affects the way each source displays in the bibliography listing. Luckily, you can select the style before or after inserting the bibliography and Word changes it accordingly. Refer to Figure 3.17 as you complete Step 2.

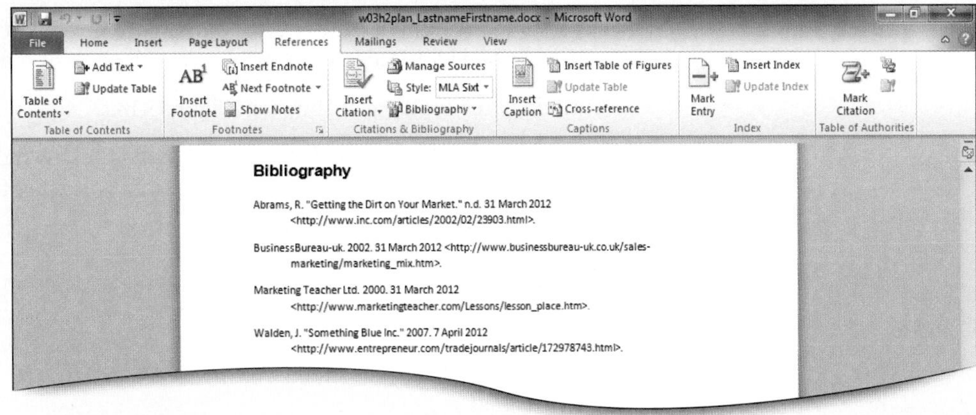

FIGURE 3.17 Bibliography in MLA Style ➤

a. Click the **Style arrow** in the Citations and Bibliography group, and then select **MLA Sixth Edition**.

b. Press **Ctrl+End** to position the insertion point at the end of the document, press **Ctrl+Enter** to add a blank page, and then type **Bibliography** at the top of the new page. Click the **Home tab**, and then apply the **Heading 1 style** from the Styles gallery. Press **End**, and then press **Enter** two times.

c. Click the **References tab**, click **Bibliography** in Citations & Bibliography, and then click **Insert Bibliography**.

The sources cited in the document display in the MLA format for bibliographies, as shown in Figure 3.17.

d. Click the **Style arrow** again, and then select **APA Fifth Edition**.

The format of the bibliography changes to reflect the standards of the APA style.

e. Save the document.

STEP 3 CREATE AND MODIFY FOOTNOTES

Rachel inserted some footnotes, but you realize she forgot one, so you add it. You also notice one footnote needs revising so that it accurately reflects the source information. Refer to Figure 3.18 as you complete Step 3.

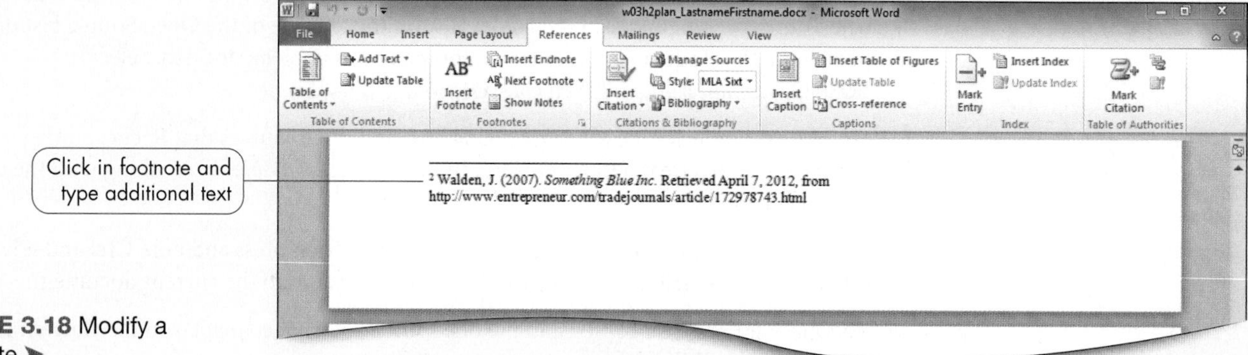

FIGURE 3.18 Modify a Footnote ➤

a. Scroll to the middle of page 4. Click one time at the end of the sentence that ends with *doing it for you—for free!* to relocate the insertion point. Click **Insert Footnote** in the Footnotes group.

The insertion point displays at the bottom of the page, below a horizontal line. This is where your footnote displays in the document.

b. Type **Abrams, R. (2007). "Getting the Dirt on Your Market". Retrieved March 31, 2012, from http://www.inc.com/articles/2002/02/23903.html**. Format the footnote as displayed with periods and commas, but do not bold the citation.

c. Scroll to the bottom of page 6. Click one time at the end of the footnote, a reference to an article written by J. Walden in 2007. Replace the date of retrieval with the date **April 7, 2012**.

You edited the footnote as shown in Figure 3.18.

d. Save *w03h2plan_LastnameFirstname* and keep it onscreen if you plan to continue with the next Hands-On Exercise. Close the file and exit Word if you will not continue with the next exercise at this time.

Research Paper Enhancements

The previous section mentioned several types of reference features that should be used when a document refers to outside information or sources. Some reference features are used less frequently, yet are valuable for creating professional quality documents. These supplements include a list of captions used on figures, a list of figures presented in a document, references to other locations in a document, and a list of legal sources referenced. You also can attach information that refers to the contents and origin of a document.

In this section, you will generate a table of contents at the beginning of a document. You will then learn how to designate text to include in an index and then generate the index at the end of a document. You will add captions to visual elements and create a list of the visuals used in a document, and you will create a list of references from a legal document. Finally, you will create a cross-reference, or note that refers the reader to another location in the document.

Inserting a Table of Contents and Index

Well-prepared long documents include special features to help readers locate information easily. For example, people often refer to the table of contents or the index in a long document—such as a book, reference manual, or company policy—to locate particular topics within that document. You can use Word to help you create these supplemental document components with minimal effort.

Well-prepared long documents include special features to help readers locate information easily.... You can use Word to help you create these supplemental document components with minimal effort.

Create a Table of Contents

A **table of contents** lists headings and the page numbers where they appear in a document.

A ***table of contents*** lists headings in the order they appear in a document and the page numbers where the entries begin. Word can create the table of contents automatically, if you apply a style to each heading in the document. You can use built-in styles, Heading 1 through Heading 9, or identify your own custom styles to use when generating the table of contents. Word also will update the table to accommodate the addition or deletion of headings or changes in page numbers brought about through changes in the document.

The table of contents feature is located on the References tab. After you apply a heading style to selected text in the document, you click the References tab and click Table of Contents to insert a predefined table of the styled text and page numbers. If you want more control over the way the table of contents displays in your document, you can click the Insert Table of Contents command to select from other styles such as Classic and Formal, as well as determine how many levels to display in the table; the latter correspond to the heading styles used within the document using the custom feature. You can determine whether to right-align the page numbers, and you also can choose to include a leader character to draw the reader's eyes across the page from a heading to a page number. Table 3.1 shows the variety of styles you can choose for your table of contents.

TABLE 3.1 Table of Contents Styles

Fancy Format

Table of Contents

Formal Format

Table of Contents

Modern Format

Table of Contents

Simple Format

Table of Contents

Create an Index

An **index** is a listing of topics and the page numbers where the topics are discussed.

An index puts the finishing touch on a long document. The ***index*** provides an alphabetical listing of topics covered in a document, along with the page numbers where the topic is discussed. Typically, the index appears at the end of a book or document. Word will create an index automatically, provided that the entries for the index have been previously marked. This requires you to go through a document, select the terms to be included in the index, and mark them accordingly. You can select a single occurrence of an entry and select an option to mark all occurrences of that entry for the index. You also can refer the reader to a different location in the document when you create an index entry, such as "see also Internet."

To mark an Index entry you follow these steps:

1. Select the word or phrase in your document that you want to display in the Index.
2. Click the References tab, and then click Mark Entry in the Index group. You can also use the shortcut Alt+Shift+X.
3. If necessary, revise the Main Entry text that displays in the Mark Index Entry dialog box. For example, if you mark a word that is not capitalized in the document, you want to revise the Main Entry so it is capitalized in the Index. The text that displays in the Main Entry box will display in the Index.
4. Click Mark for this selected word or phrase or click Mark All to include all occurrences of this word or phrase in the Index.
5. In a long document, it is helpful to use the Find feature to locate the next word or phrase to mark.
6. When all words or phrases are marked, close the Mark Entry dialog box.

After you specify the entries, create the index by choosing Insert Index in the Index group on the References tab. You can choose a variety of styles for the index, just as you can for the table of contents, as shown in Table 3.2. Word arranges the index entries in alphabetical order and enters the appropriate page references. You also can create additional index entries or move text within a document, then update the index with the click of a mouse.

TABLE 3.2 Index Styles

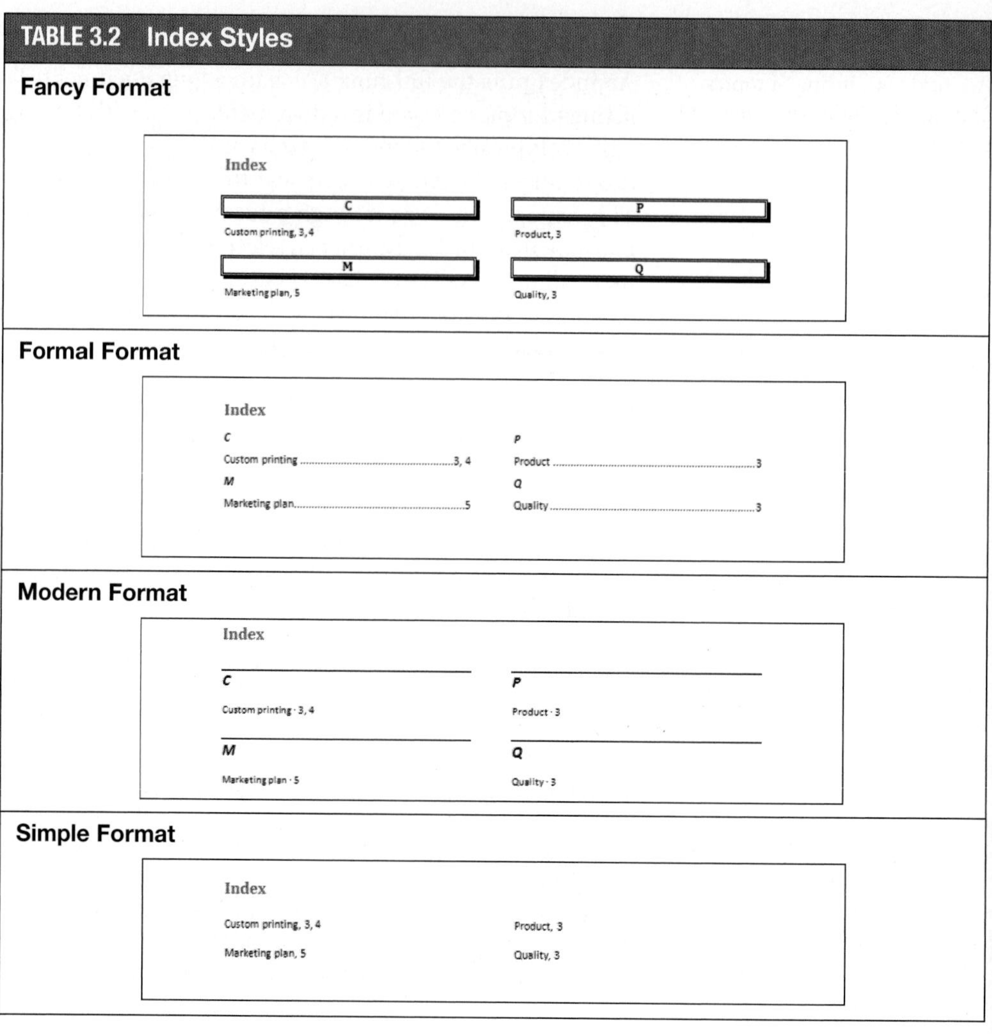

To modify an Index entry, you must display the index fields by clicking Show/Hide (¶) in the Paragraph group on the Home tab. Locate the entry that you wish to modify and edit the text inside the quotation marks. Do not change the entry in the finished Index, or the next time you update the index, your changes will be lost. To delete an entry, select the entire entry field, including the braces {}, and then press Delete. After you modify or delete a marked entry, click Update Index in the Index group on the References tab to display the changes in the table.

When you have a lengthy list of words to mark for index entries, you can use a separate Word document as a source to help you automatically mark all occurrences of each word. When you select the AutoMark command from the Index dialog box it prompts you to open the Word document that contains a list of terms you want to mark for an index. It then marks the entries automatically. The advantage is that it is fast. The disadvantage is that every occurrence of an entry is marked and displays in the index so that a commonly used term may have too many page references. You can, however, delete superfluous entries by manually deleting the field codes. Click Show/Hide (¶) in the Paragraph group of the Home tab if you do not see the entries in the document.

Adding Other Reference Tables

You will likely use the Table of Contents and Index features most often in your research and other long documents. However, you can include additional reference tables to highlight other important information in your document. Some documents might contain so many tables or pictures that listing each one in a format similar to a table of contents can be helpful. Legal documents also often include a listing of the documents they use as a reference. Word includes features to enable you to include reference tables correctly for these situations.

Assign Figure Captions

A **caption** is a descriptive title for an equation, a figure, or a table.

Documents and books often contain several images, charts, or tables. For example, this textbook contains several screenshots in each chapter. To help readers refer to the correct image or table, you can add a caption. A ***caption*** is a descriptive title for an image, a figure, or a table. To add a caption click Insert Caption in the Captions group on the References tab. By default, Word assigns a number to the equation, figure, or table at the beginning of the caption. When you click Insert Caption, the Caption dialog box appears, as shown in Figure 3.19, and you can edit the default caption by adding descriptive text.

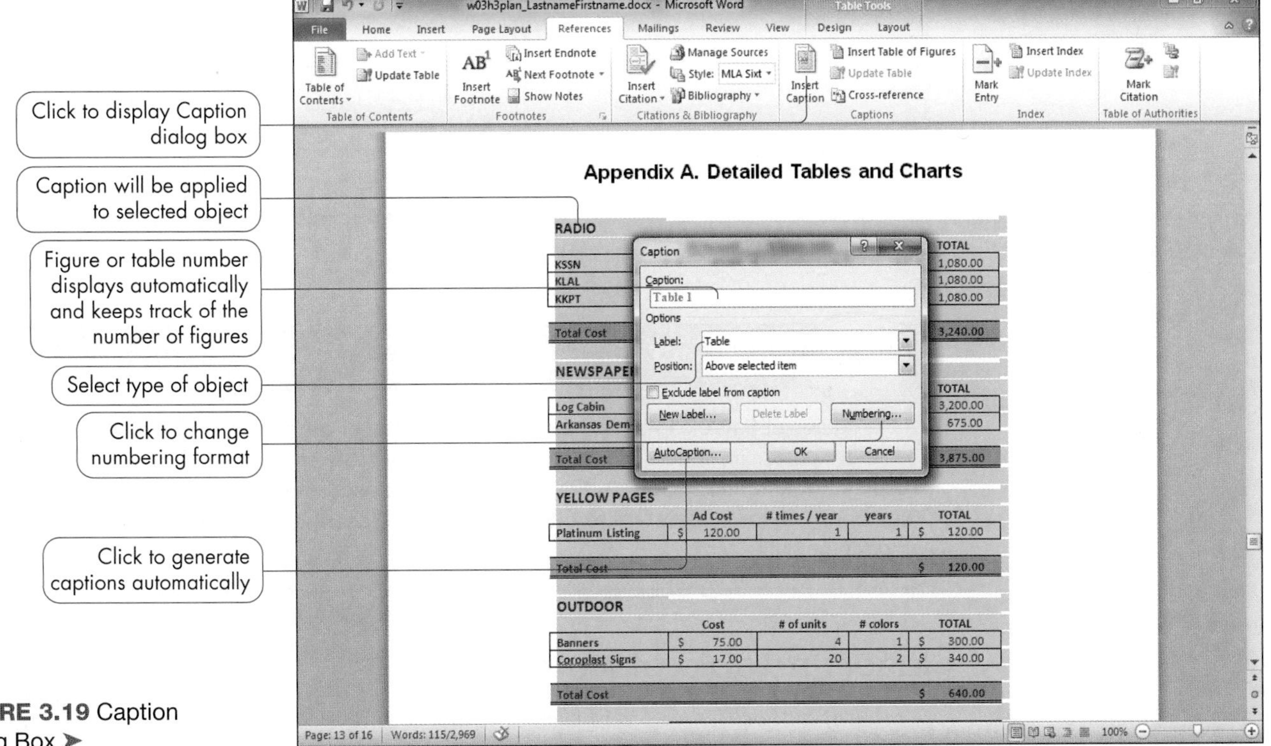

FIGURE 3.19 Caption Dialog Box ➤

To automatically generate captions, click AutoCaption in the Caption dialog box. In the *Add caption when inserting* list, in the AutoCaption dialog box, click the check box next to the element type for which you want to create AutoCaptions. Specify the default caption text in the *Use label* box, and specify the location of the caption by clicking the Position arrow. If your document will contain several captions, this feature helps to ensure each caption is named and numbered sequentially.

Insert a Table of Figures

A **table of figures** is a list of the captions in a document.

If your document includes pictures, charts and graphs, slides, or other illustrations along with a caption, you can include a ***table of figures***, or list of the captions, as a reference. To build a table of figures, Word searches a document for captions, sorts the captions by number, and displays the table of figures in the document. A table of figures is placed after the table of contents for a document. The Insert Table of Figures command is in the Captions group on the References tab. The Table of Figures dialog box, shown in Figure 3.20, enables you to select page number, format, and caption label options.

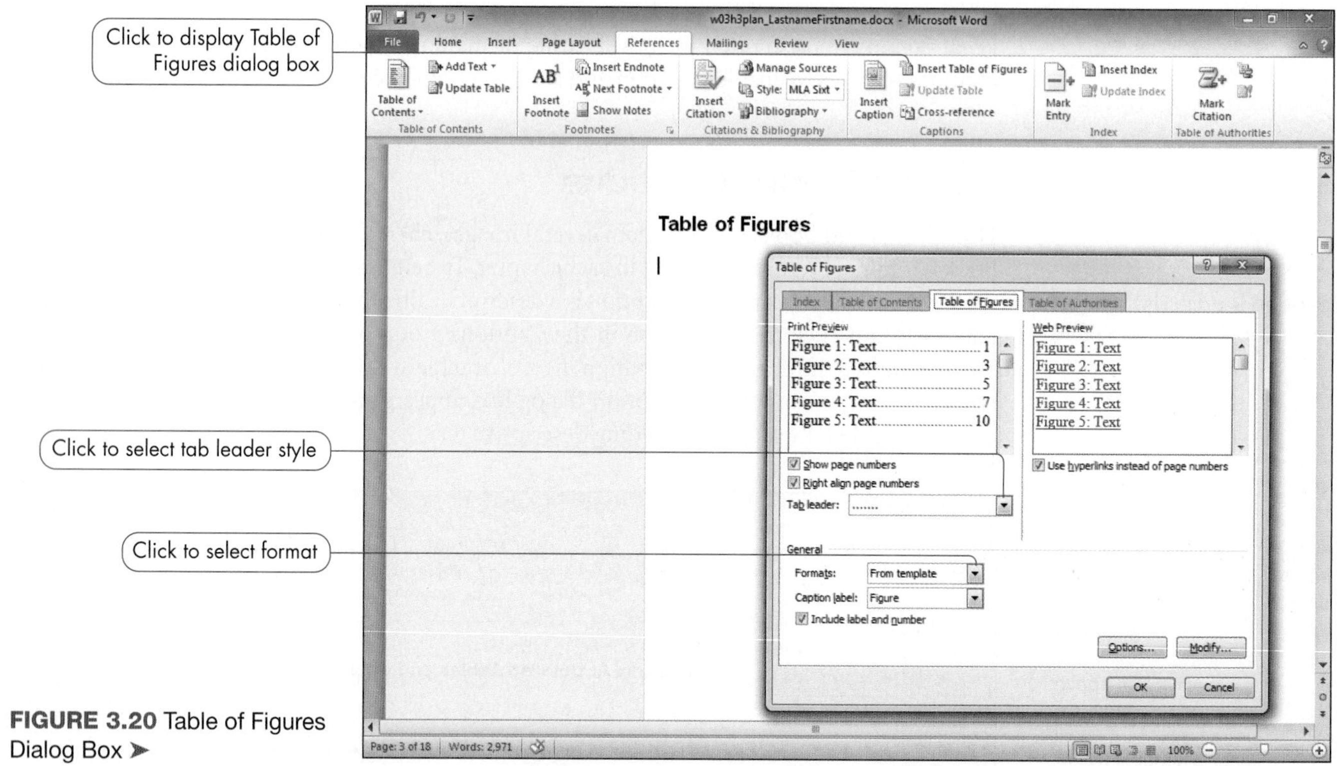

FIGURE 3.20 Table of Figures Dialog Box ➤

> **TIP** Update a Table of Figures
>
> If the figures or figure captions in a document change or are removed, you should update the table of figures. To update the table, right-click any table entry to select the entire table and display a menu. Click Update Field, and then choose between the options Update Page Numbers only or Update entire table. If significant changes have been made, you should update the entire table.

Insert a Table of Authorities

A **table of authorities** is used in legal documents to reference cases and other documents referred to in a legal brief.

A ***table of authorities*** is used in legal documents to reference cases, rules, treaties, and other documents referred to in a legal brief. You typically compile the table of authorities on a separate page at the beginning of a legal document. Word's Table of Authorities feature enables you to track, compile, and display citations, or references to specific legal cases and other legal documents, to be included in the table of authorities. Before you generate the table of authorities, you must indicate which citations you want to include using the Mark Citation command in the Table of Authorities group on the References tab. To mark citations, select text, and then click Mark Citation. The Mark Citation dialog box displays, as shown in Figure 3.21, and you can choose to mark this one case or mark all references to this case in the document. After you mark the citations in your document, click Insert Table of Authorities in the Table of Authorities group to generate the table at the location of your insertion point.

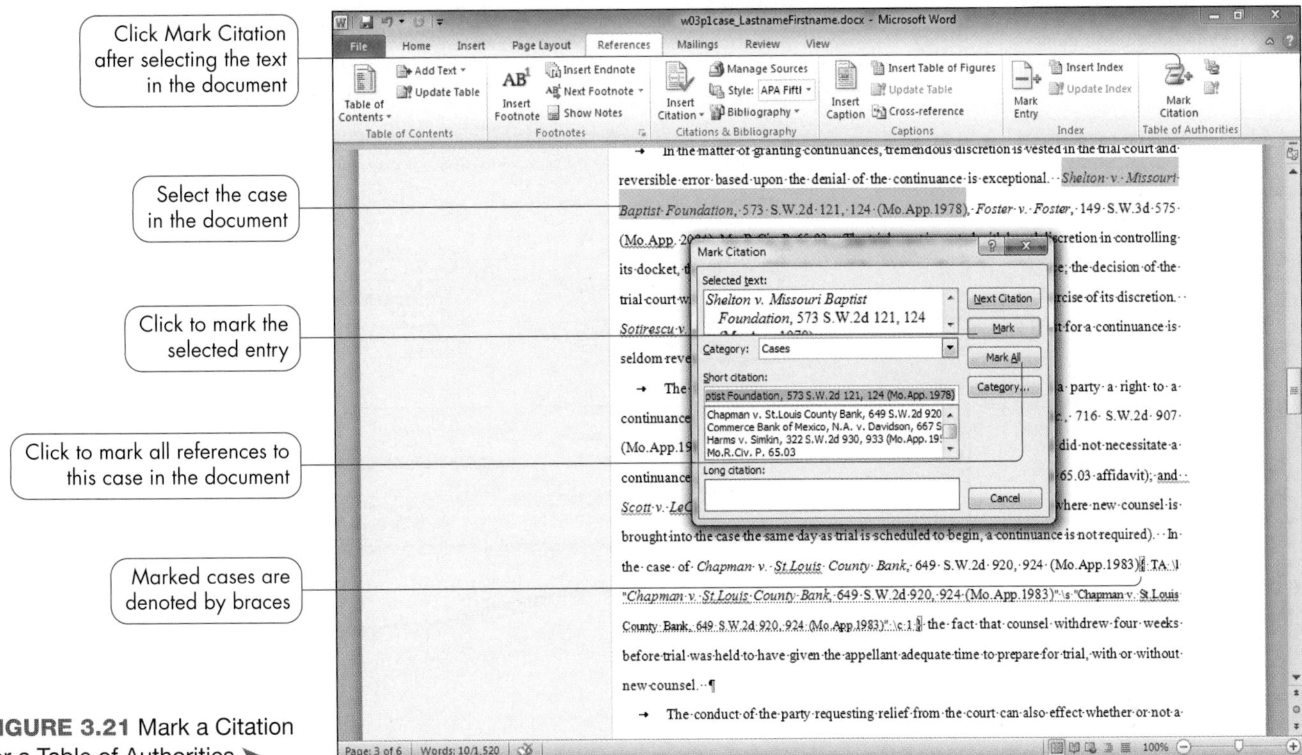

FIGURE 3.21 Mark a Citation for a Table of Authorities ➤

To modify an entry in the table of authorities, you must display the table of authorities fields by clicking Show/Hide (¶) in the Paragraph group on the Home tab. Locate the entry that you wish to modify and edit the text inside the quotation marks. Do not change the entry in the finished table of authorities, or the next time you update the table of authorities, your changes will be lost.

To delete a table of authorities entry, select the entire entry field, including the braces {}, and press Delete. After you modify or delete a marked entry, click Update Table in the Table of Authorities group on the References tab to display the changes in the table.

Creating Cross-References

A **cross-reference** is a note that refers the reader to another location for more information about a topic.

A ***cross-reference*** is a note that refers the reader to another location for more information about a topic. You can create automated cross-references to headings, bookmarks, footnotes, endnotes, captions, and tables. A typical cross-reference looks like this: *See page 4 for more information about local recreation facilities.* When using the automated cross-reference feature, Word tracks the location of the reference and inserts the correct page number in the place you designate in the document. For files you make available via e-mail or on an intranet, this creates an electronic cross-reference that enables the reader to hyperlink to that location.

To create a cross-reference, position the insertion point in the location where the reference occurs. On the References tab click Cross-reference in the Captions group. When the Cross-reference dialog box displays, as shown in Figure 3.22, you choose the type of reference (such as Heading, Bookmark, Figure, or Footnote) and then the reference element to display (such as page number or paragraph text). You can specify whether it displays as a hyperlink in the document, causing a ScreenTip to appear when the mouse pointer is over the cross-reference and moving you to that location when clicked, or as a static entry that simply displays a page number.

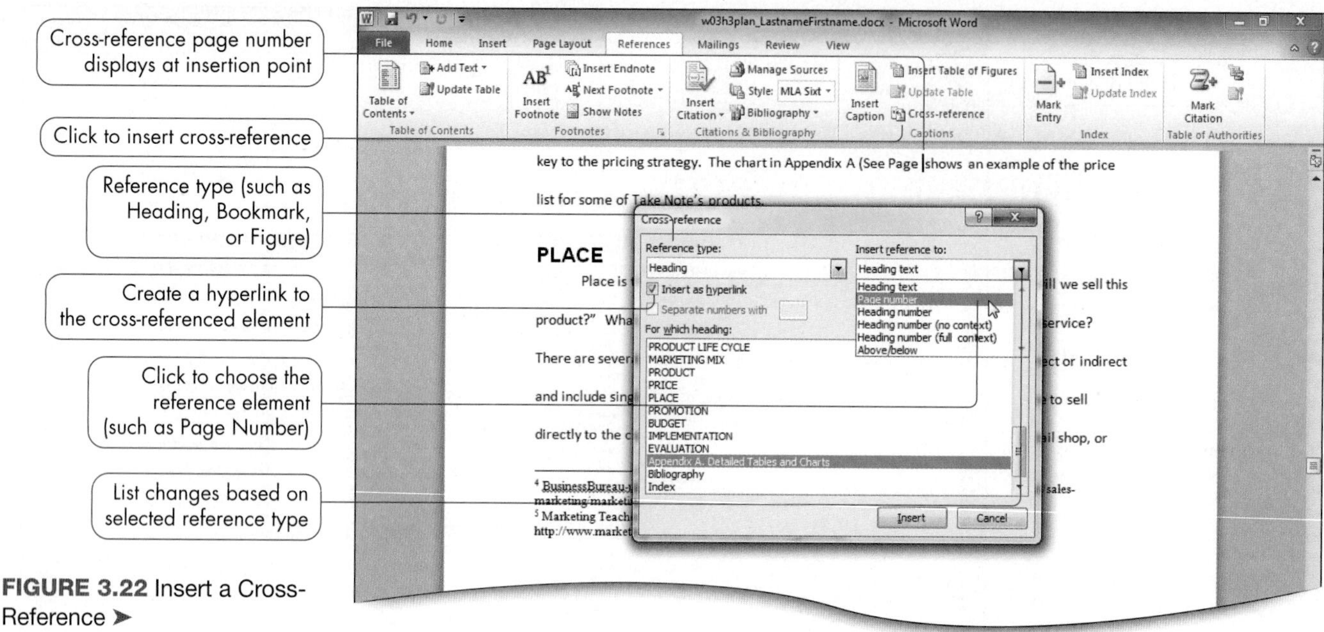

FIGURE 3.22 Insert a Cross-Reference ➤

HANDS-ON EXERCISES

3 Research Paper Enhancements

This version of the marketing plan is nearly done. Only a few more enhancements will make it complete, so you decide to add a table of contents to the beginning of the document. Because of the number of graphic elements, you also decide to include a table of figures. An index will help the reader find information in this lengthy document, and you insert a cross-reference as well.

Skills covered: Apply Styles and Insert a Table of Contents • Define an Index Entry • Create the Index and Add Page Numbers • Add Captions and Create a Table of Figures • Create a Cross-Reference • Update the Table of Contents and View the Completed Document

STEP 1 APPLY STYLES AND INSERT A TABLE OF CONTENTS

Adding a table of contents (ToC) will enhance the professionalism of the marketing plan you and Rachel have developed for your class. You know that a table of contents is easy to insert if you apply styles to text first, so you take care of that and then insert the ToC. Refer to Figure 3.23 as you complete Step 1.

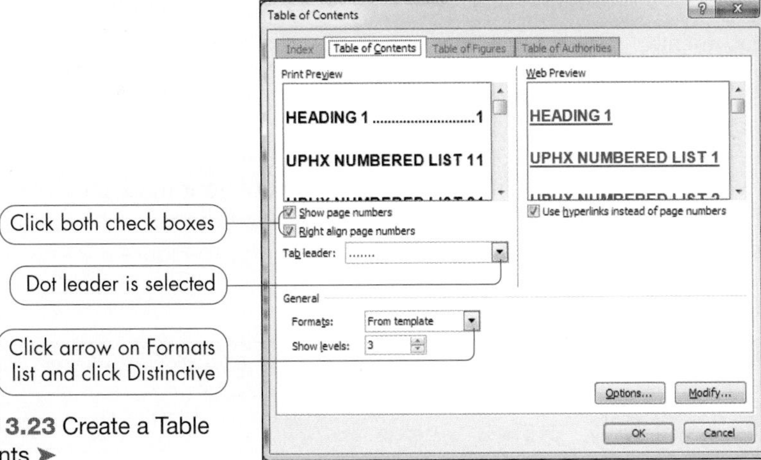

FIGURE 3.23 Create a Table of Contents ➤

a. Open the *w03h2plan_LastnameFirstname* document if you closed it after the last Hands-On Exercise. Save the document as **w03h3plan_LastnameFirstname**, changing *h2* to *h3*.

b. Click to the left of the *Executive Summary* title on the second page. Type **Table of Contents** and press **Enter** two times. Press **Ctrl+Enter** to insert a page break.

   The ToC displays on a page between the title page and the body of the document using the Heading 1 style you applied in the previous exercise.

> **TROUBLESHOOTING:** If the Heading 1 style does not display, apply Heading 1 from the Quick Style gallery on the Home Tab to the *Table of Contents* heading.

c. Select the entire **Table of Contents heading**. Click the **Home tab**, and then apply the **Strong style**. **Center** the heading.

   If you continue to use the Heading 1 style, the *Table of Contents* heading will display in the ToC itself.

d. Apply the **Heading 1 style** to the paragraph heading *Organizational Overview* on the fourth page. Continue to apply the **Heading 1 style** to the paragraph headings on the next three pages using the Format Painter.

e. Scroll up and place the insertion point on the line following the *Table of Contents* title.

f. Click the **References tab**, and then click **Table of Contents** in the Table of Contents group. Select **Insert Table of Contents.**

   The Table of Contents dialog box displays (see Figure 3.23). You will see several preformatted styles provided when you click Table of Contents, but you are not using them because you want to customize the table. To customize you will select features in the Table of Contents dialog box, which you do in the next steps.

g. Click the **Show page numbers check box** and the **Right align page numbers check box,** if necessary.

h. Click the **Formats arrow** in the *General* section, and then select **Distinctive.** Click the **Tab leader arrow** in the *Print Preview* section, and then choose a dot leader. Click **OK.**

   Word takes a moment to create the table of contents and then displays all paragraph headings and their associated page numbers in the location of your insertion point.

TROUBLESHOOTING: If your Table of Contents includes text from the paragraphs instead of just paragraph headings, check the style applied to the text. Remove the Heading 1 or 2 styles, if they are in use, and apply a different one to avoid inclusion in the ToC. Press F9 to update your table to reflect the change.

i. Save the document.

STEP 2 DEFINE AN INDEX ENTRY

Rachel has marked several words already that will display in the index of your marketing plan. You decide to add the word *customer*, so you take steps to mark all occurrences of it; you use the Find feature to speed up the process of locating it in the document. Refer to Figure 3.24 as you complete Step 2.

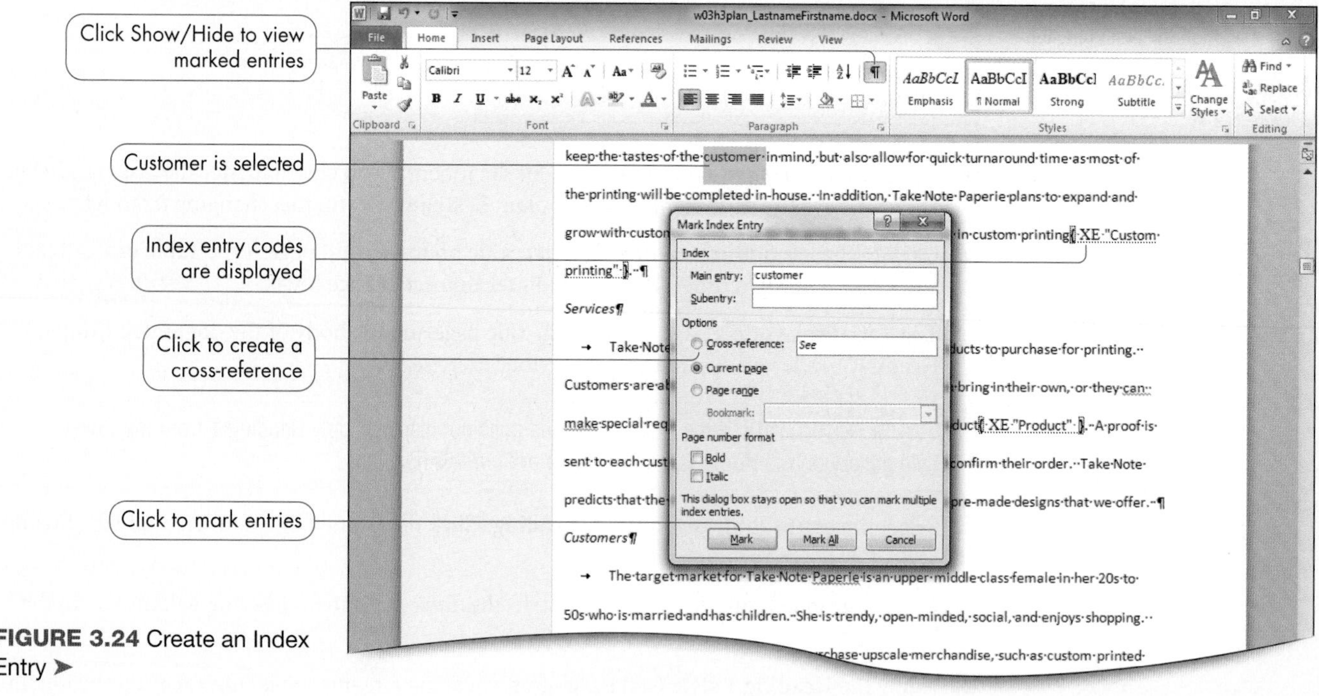

FIGURE 3.24 Create an Index Entry ➤

a. Press **Ctrl+Home** to move to the beginning of the document. Click **Ctrl+F** to display the Navigation Pane, and type **Customer** in the **text box**. Click the second entry in the results list.

You click the second occurrence because it is in singular form. The first occurrence is in plural form, but that is not what you want to mark for the index.

b. Click the **Home tab**, if necessary, and then click **Show/Hide** (¶) in the Paragraph group so you can see the nonprinting characters in the document.

The index entries already created by Rachel appear in curly brackets and begin with the letters *XE*.

c. Confirm that the entry for *customer* you just found is selected within the document. Click the **References tab**, and then click **Mark Entry** to display the Mark Index Entry dialog box, as shown in Figure 3.24.

d. Replace the lowercase *c* in the **Main Entry box** with a capital **C** so the word *Customer* displays capitalized.

The word that displays in the dialog box, and later as a hidden mark in the document text, will display in the index, so you want it to be capitalized. Capitalizing it in the index entry does not affect the way it displays in the document.

e. Click **Mark** to create the index entry.

After you create the index entry, you see the field code *{XE "Customer"}* to indicate that the index entry is created. The Mark Index Entry dialog box stays open so that you can create additional entries by selecting additional text.

f. Type **customer** in the **text box** in the Navigation Pane, if necessary, and then click the fourth entry, which is the next occurrence of the word *customer* in the document. Close the Navigation Pane.

g. Click anywhere on the Mark Index Entry dialog box, change capitalization to display *Customer* in the **Main Entry box**, and then click **Mark All** to create the index entry on all instances of the word in the remainder of the document.

You know this word occurs many times in the document and each should be referenced in the Index; this is the most efficient way to mark all occurrences simultaneously.

h. Click **Close** to close the Mark Index Entry dialog box. Click the **Home tab**, and then click **Show/Hide** (¶) to hide the formatting marks.

i. Save the document.

STEP 3 CREATE THE INDEX AND ADD PAGE NUMBERS

You have just marked all the words you want to include in the Index, so it is time to add it. You remember to insert the index on a blank page at the end of the document, after the bibliography, You also decide it is time to add page numbers, which are appropriate to display in a multi-page document. Refer to Figure 3.25 as you complete Step 3.

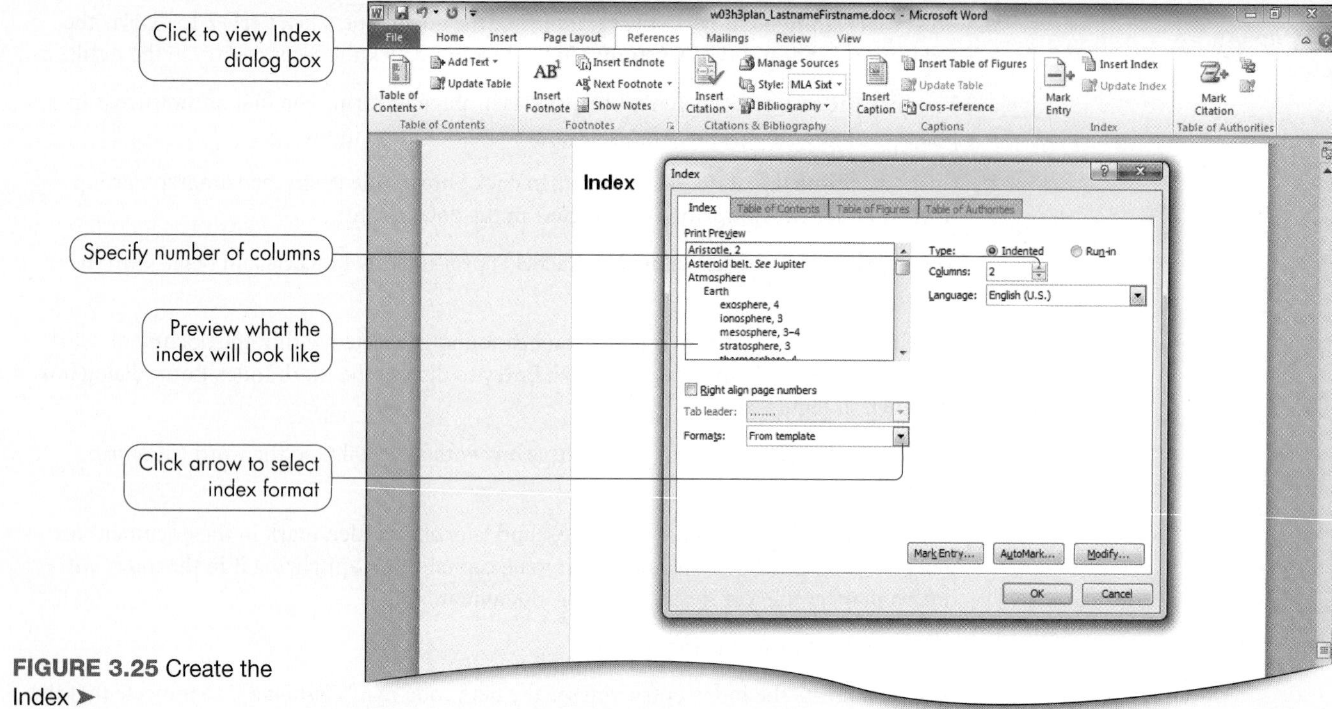

FIGURE 3.25 Create the Index ➤

a. Press **Ctrl+End** to move to the end of the document, and then press **Ctrl+Enter** to add a new blank page.

   This is where you will insert the index.

b. Type **Index** and press **Enter** one time. Select **Index**, and then click **Heading 1** in the Styles gallery. Position your cursor on the line that follows the *Index* heading.

c. Click the **References tab**, and then click **Insert Index** in the Index group.

   The Index dialog box displays as shown in Figure 3.25.

d. Click the **Formats arrow**, and then select **Classic**. If necessary, click the **Columns arrow** until 2 displays. Click **OK** to create the index.

TROUBLESHOOTING: Click Undo on the Quick Access Toolbar if the index does not display at the end of the document, reposition the cursor, and then repeat Steps 3c and 3d.

TIP Check the Index Entries

Every entry in the index should begin with an uppercase letter. If this is not the case, it is because the original entry within the body of the document was marked improperly. Click Show/Hide (¶) in the Paragraph group on the Home tab to display the indexed entries within the document, which appear within brackets, e.g., {XE "Customer"}. Change each entry to begin with an uppercase letter as needed.

e. Click the **Insert tab**, click **Page Number** in the Header & Footer group, point to **Bottom of Page**, and then click **Plain Number 3**. Click **Close Header and Footer**.

f. Save the document.

STEP 4 ADD CAPTIONS AND CREATE A TABLE OF FIGURES

Because the marketing plan contains multiple tables and a graphic, you take steps to insert a table of figures. Similar to other reference items you insert, before you create this table you must do some preliminary work by adding captions to the tables and graphic first, which are then used in the table. Refer to Figure 3.26 as you complete Step 4.

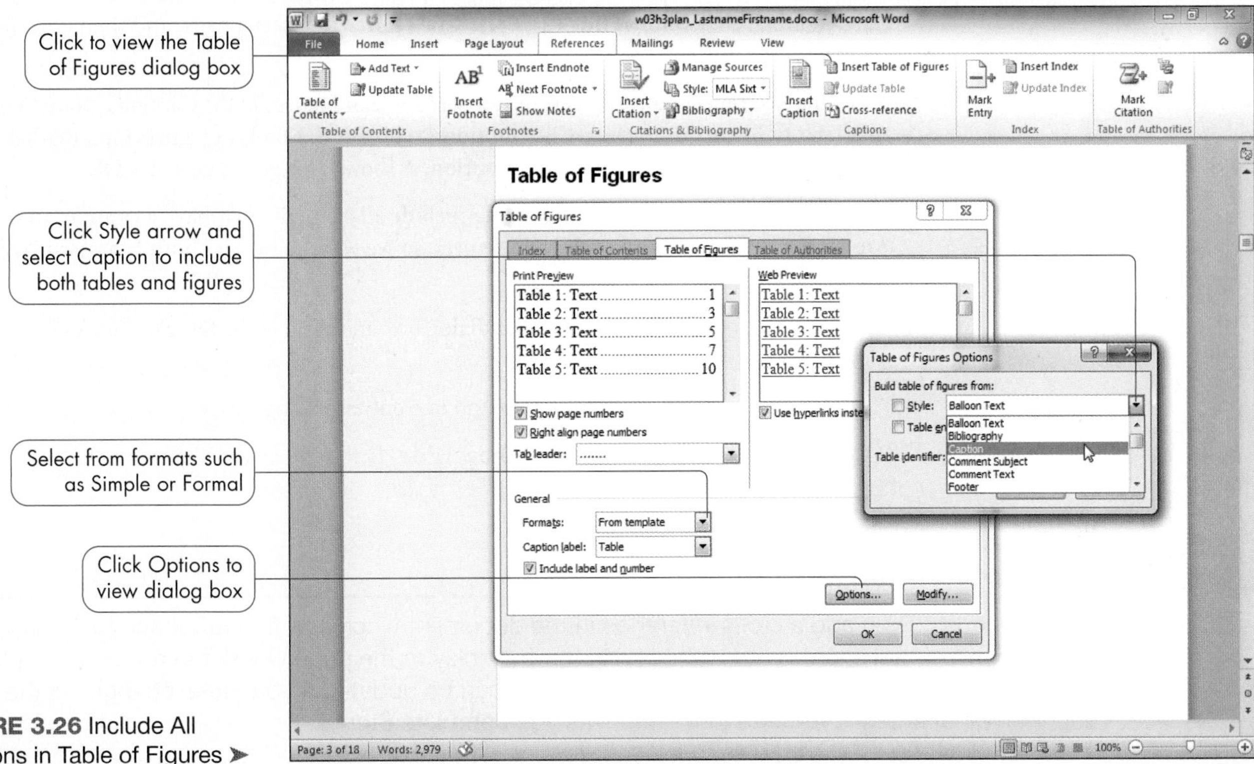

FIGURE 3.26 Include All Captions in Table of Figures ➤

FYI

a. Go to page 14 where Appendix A begins. Hold your mouse over the top-left corner of the table until the cursor turns into a crosshair with arrows on each end. Click once to select the entire table. Click the **References tab**, and then click **Insert Caption** in the Captions group.

> **TROUBLESHOOTING:** Your page numbers may vary slightly. If so, find the page where *Appendix A* displays.

The Caption dialog box displays, and the insertion point is positioned at the end of the caption text that displays automatically.

b. Press the **Colon key** (:), and then press **Spacebar** two times. Type **Initial Advertising Plan Budget** in the **Caption box**. Click the **Position arrow**, and then select **Above selected item**, if necessary. Click **OK**.

The caption *Table 1: Initial Advertising Plan Budget* displays above the chart. By default, captions for tables are placed above the table, and captions for images are placed below the image. However, you can relocate them by making a change in the Caption dialog box.

c. Scroll to the top of the next page, and then select the organization chart. Click **Insert Caption** in the Captions group to open the Caption dialog box.

d. Click the **Label arrow**, and then select **Figure**. Click to place the cursor after *Figure 1* in the **Caption box**, press the **Colon key** (:), press **Spacebar** two times, and then type **Marketing Organization**. Click the **Position arrow**, and then click **Above selected item**. Click **OK** to close the dialog box.

The caption for this figure now displays *Figure 1: Marketing Organization.*

e. Scroll to the top of the next page, and then select the chart. Click **Insert Caption**, press the **Colon key** (:), press **Spacebar** one time, and then type **Take Note Paperie—Price List** in the **Caption box**. Click the **Label arrow**, and then select **Table**. Click the **Position arrow**, and then select **Above selected item**, if necessary. Click **OK** to close the dialog box.

   You have now created three captions in this paper—two for tables and one for a figure.

f. Move your insertion point to the bottom of page 2, which contains the ToC. Click the **Home tab**, and then click **Show/Hide** (¶). Press **Ctrl+Enter** to insert a page, and then type **Table of Figures**. Press **Enter** two times.

g. Click the **References tab**, and then click **Insert Table of Figures** in the Captions group to display the Table of Figures dialog box. Click **Options** to display the Table of Figures Options dialog box. Click the **Style arrow**, and then select **Caption**, as shown in Figure 3.26. Click **OK**.

   This option forces the table of figures to include all elements that have a caption. In our case, we apply captions to both tables and figures, so we want to be sure both types display in the table.

h. Click **OK** to close the Table of Figures dialog box and display the table of figures in your document.

   The table shows two entries for tables and one entry for a figure.

i. Click the **Home tab**, and then click **Show/Hide** (¶) to remove the formatting marks.

j. Save the document.

STEP 5 CREATE A CROSS-REFERENCE

Rachel suggests you add a cross-reference in the document where the first reference to Appendix A occurs, which will enable your instructor to jump quickly to the page where the appendix starts. By using the cross-reference tool, the page number can be updated if you make changes in the document that affect it. Refer to Figure 3.27 as you complete Step 5.

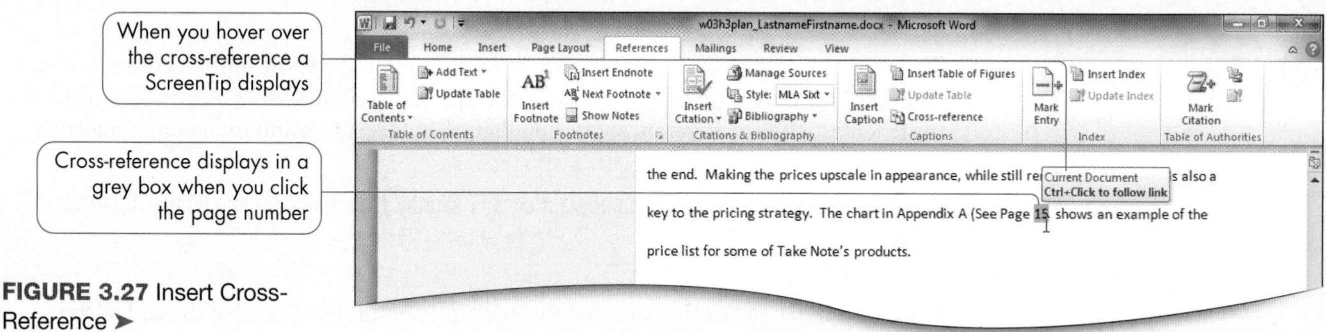

FIGURE 3.27 Insert Cross-Reference ➤

a. Scroll to page 11, and then place the insertion point on the right side of the text *Appendix A* in the last sentence of the *Price* section.

b. Press **Spacebar**, and then type **(See page** . Click the **References tab**, if necessary, and then click **Cross-reference** in the Captions group. Click the **Reference type arrow**, and then select **Heading**. Click **Appendix A. Detailed Tables and Charts** in the **For which heading list**. Click the **Insert reference to arrow**, select **Page number**, and then click **Insert**. Click **Close** to close the Cross-reference dialog box.

   The cross-reference displays the number *15*, which is the page where the chart displays.

c. Type) to close the parenthesis around the cross-reference. Click one time on the number *15* in the cross-reference, and then notice it is shaded with a dark grey box. Hold your mouse over the cross-reference page number, and then view the ScreenTip, as shown in Figure 3.27.

   The ScreenTip instructs you to press *Ctrl+Click to follow link* while you click the number *15*; if you do, Word will move the insertion point to the location of the chart on page 15.

d. Save the document.

STEP 6 UPDATE THE TABLE OF CONTENTS AND VIEW THE COMPLETED DOCUMENT

Before you finish you want to make sure the additions of the table of figures, bibliography, and index display in your table of contents, so you take steps to update it and all page numbers. Then you view the marketing plan as a final copy without markup. Then you save it so Rachel can look at it before you submit it to your professor. Refer to Figure 3.28 as you complete Step 6.

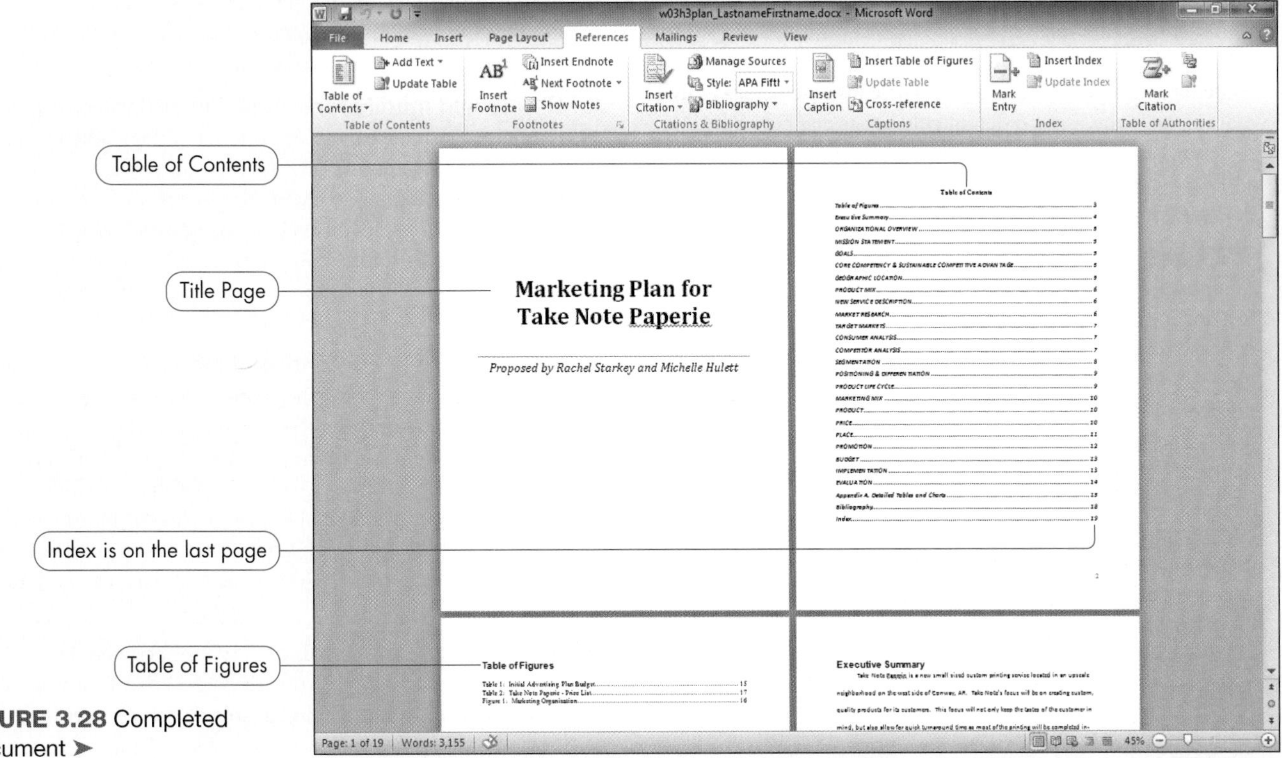

FIGURE 3.28 Completed Document ➤

a. Scroll to view the page that contains the *Table of Contents*. Right-click anywhere in the ToC, click **Update Field**, click **Update Entire Table**, and then click **OK**.

   The entries for *Table of Figures*, *Bibliography*, and *Index* display, and page numbers adjust throughout the ToC to reflect these additions.

> **TROUBLESHOOTING:** If one or more of these tables do not display in the ToC, reapply the Heading 1 style to them, and update the ToC again. Also, remove any extra page breaks that might occur when you refresh the table—you do not want blank pages in between reference pages.

b. Click **Zoom level** on the status bar. Click the **Many pages icon** and drag to display **2 × 2 Pages**. Click **OK**.

   You view several pages of the document, as seen in Figure 3.28.

c. Save and close the *w03h3plan_LastnameFirstname* file, and submit based on your instructor's directions.

CHAPTER OBJECTIVES REVIEW

After reading this chapter, you have accomplished the following objectives:

1. **Insert comments in a document.** When you work as part of a team, you can use the Comment feature to collaborate. Comments enable you to ask a question or provide a suggestion to another person within a document, without modifying the content of the document. Comments are inserted using colored markup balloons, and a different color is assigned to each reviewer. Comments appear in the Print Layout, Web Layout, and Full Screen Reading views. You can display comments in the margins of a document or in a reading pane.
2. **Track changes in a document.** You use this feature to monitor all additions, deletions, and formatting changes made to a document. When active, the Track Changes feature applies revision marks to indicate where a change occurs. When you move your mouse over a revision mark, it will display the name of the person who made the change as well as the date and time of the change. You can use markup tools to accept or reject changes that have been tracked. These tools are especially helpful when several people make changes to the same document. If comments and tracked changes do not display initially, you can turn on the Show Markup feature to view them. You also can view the document as a final copy if all tracked changes are accepted or as the original before any changes were made and tracked. You can modify the Track Changes options to change settings such as fonts, colors, location, and size of markup balloons.
3. **Acknowledge a source.** It is common practice to use a variety of sources to supplement your own thoughts when authoring a paper, report, legal brief, or many other types of document. Failure to acknowledge the source of information you use in a document is a form of plagiarism. Word provides the citation feature to track, compile, and display your research sources for inclusion in several types of supplemental references such as a bibliography. A bibliography is a list of works cited or consulted by an author and should be included with the document when published. Any sources added with the citation feature and used in the current document will display in the appropriate format as a bibliography. When research papers are prepared, the author often must conform to a particular writing style. The Style list on the References tab includes the most commonly used international styles. When you select the style the citations that appear in the bibliography will be formatted exactly as required by that style.
4. **Create and modify footnotes and endnotes.** A footnote is a citation that appears at the bottom of a page, and an endnote is a citation that appears at the end of a document. You use footnotes or endnotes to credit the sources you quote or cite in your document. If you click the Footnotes Dialog Box Launcher, the Footnotes and Endnotes dialog box opens, and you can modify the location of the notes and the format of the numbers.
5. **Insert a table of contents and index.** A table of contents lists headings in the order they appear in a document with their respective page numbers. Word can create it automatically, provided the built-in heading styles were applied previously to the items for inclusion. Word also will create an index automatically, provided that the entries for the index have been marked previously. This result, in turn, requires you to go through a document, select the appropriate text, and mark the entries accordingly.
6. **Add other reference tables.** If your document includes pictures, charts, or graphs you can create captions for them. Using captions, you can create a table of figures, or list of the captions, for a point of reference. A table of figures is commonly placed after the table of contents for a document. A table of authorities is used in legal documents to reference cases, rules, treaties, and other documents referred to in a legal brief. Word's Table of Authorities feature enables you to mark, track, compile, and display citations, or references to specific legal cases and other legal documents, to be included in the table of authorities.
7. **Create cross-references.** A cross-reference is a note that refers the reader to another location in the document for more information about a topic. You can create cross-references to headings, bookmarks, footnotes, endnotes, captions, and tables.

KEY TERMS

Bibliography ***p.181***
Caption ***p.191***
Changed line ***p.171***
Citation ***p.179***
Comment ***p.168***
Cross-reference ***p.193***
Current List ***p.180***
Endnote ***p.182***
Final: Show Markup ***p.172***
Footnote ***p.182***
Index ***p.189***
Markup balloon ***p.168***
Master List ***p.180***
Original: Show Markup ***p.172***
Plagiarism ***p.179***
Reviewing Pane ***p.169***
Revision mark ***p.171***
Show Markup ***p.170***
Table of authorities ***p.192***
Table of contents ***p.187***
Table of figures ***p.191***
Track Changes ***p.171***

MULTIPLE CHOICE

1. Which of the following statements about comments is true?
   (a) You cannot edit a comment that was created by another person.
   (b) Comment balloons appear on the right side in Print Layout view by default.
   (c) You cannot ever print comments with the rest of the document.
   (d) You can use the Show Markup feature on the Review tab to filter markup balloons so comments display both inline and also in balloons.

2. What option enables you to preview how a document will look if you accept all tracked changes?
   (a) Final: Show Markup
   (b) Final
   (c) Original: Show Markup
   (d) Original

3. How do you view and edit footnote text?
   (a) Position the mouse pointer over the footnote reference mark and click inside the ScreenTip that appears.
   (b) Open the Footnote and Endnote dialog box.
   (c) Double-click the footnote reference mark and type in the footnote.
   (d) Click Citation on the References tab.

4. Which option is not true about plagiarism?
   (a) It is the act of using another person's work and claiming it as your own.
   (b) It is considered academic dishonesty in academic communities.
   (c) It only applies to written works; ideas, spoken words, or graphics are not included.
   (d) It has serious moral and ethical implications.

5. What document item directs a reader to another location in a document by mentioning its location?
   (a) Cross-reference
   (b) Bookmark
   (c) Endnote
   (d) Thumbnail

6. A table of figures is generated from what type of entries?
   (a) Index
   (b) Bookmarks
   (c) Comments
   (d) Captions

7. What does a table of authorities display?
   (a) A list of pictures, tables, and figures in a document
   (b) A list of cases, rules, treaties, and other documents cited in a legal document
   (c) A list of key words and phrases in the document
   (d) A sequential list of section headings and their page numbers

8. Select the sequence of events to include a bibliography in your document.
   (a) Select writing style, insert bibliography, and then insert citations.
   (b) Type footnotes into document, insert bibliography, and then select writing style.
   (c) Select writing style, mark legal references, and then insert bibliography.
   (d) Insert a citation, select writing style, and then insert bibliography.

9. After you create and insert a table of contents into a document:
   (a) Any subsequent page changes arising from the insertion or deletion of text to existing paragraphs must be entered manually.
   (b) Any additions to the entries in the table arising due to the insertion of new paragraphs defined by a heading style must be entered manually.
   (c) An index cannot be added to the document.
   (d) You can right-click, then select Update Field to update the table of contents.

10. You are participating in a group project in which each member makes changes to the same document. Which feature in Word should you suggest the members use so each can see the edits made by fellow group members?
    (a) Mark index entries.
    (b) Track changes.
    (c) Mark citations.
    (d) Create cross-references.

1 Odom Law Firm

You work as a clerk in the Odom Law Firm and are responsible for preparing documentation used in all phases of the judicial process. A senior partner in the firm asks you to work on a document by inserting a table of authorities based on the cases cited in the document. As you work you notice it also needs another footnote and a caption on a graphic. So that the partner can double-check your work, you track the changes you make to the document. This exercise follows the same set of skills as used in Hands-On Exercises 1, 2, and 3 in the chapter. Refer to Figure 3.29 as you complete this exercise.

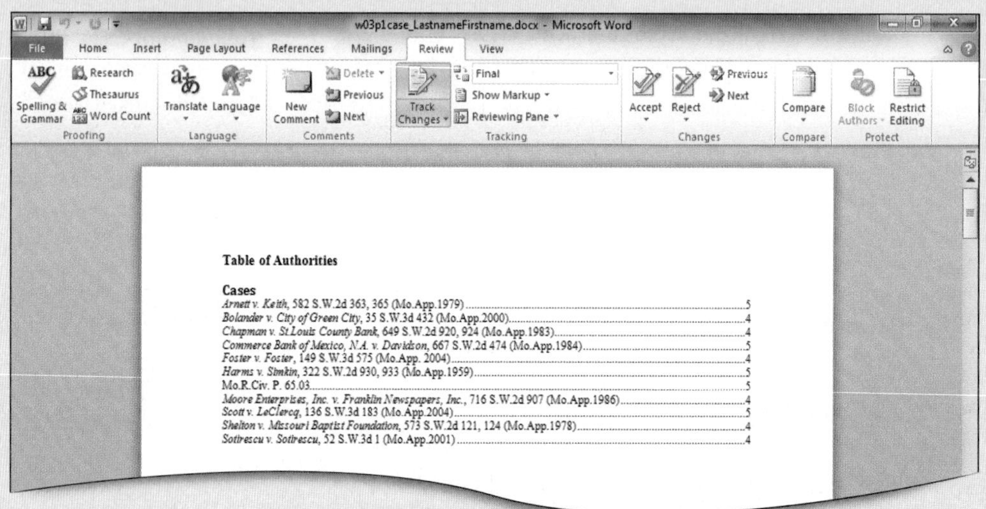

FIGURE 3.29 Table of Authorities ➤

a. Open *w03p1case* and save it as **w03p1case_LastnameFirstname**.
b. Press **Ctrl+Home** to move the insertion point to the beginning of the document.
c. Click the **Review tab**, click the **Track Changes arrow** in the Tracking group, and click **Change User Name**. Verify that your name displays as the *User Name* on this PC, and that your initials display in the Initials box; if necessary, type your name and initials in the appropriate text box, and then click **OK** to close the Word Options dialog box.
d. Click **Track Changes** in the Tracking group so the feature displays in orange and your edits are marked as you work.
e. Click **New Comment** in the Comments group, and then type **Second edit by *your name* on *date*.**
f. Click **Next** in the Comments group two times to select the balloon containing the comment about a change you need to make to the footer. Read the comment.
g. Place the insertion point at the end of the footer on the bottom of the first page. Replace the year *2008* with **2012**.
h. Click **Previous** in the Comments group to select the comment balloon you previously read. Move the insertion point to the end of the comment inside the balloon, and then type the sentence **Completed by *your name*** after the existing text. Remember to use your name.
i. Scroll to the bottom of page 2. Position your cursor at the end of the last sentence in the first paragraph under the heading *Attorney Blanchard's withdrawal.* When your cursor is on the right side of the period after the words *anything on the case,* click the **References tab**, and then click **Insert Footnote** in the Footnotes group. Type **See Exhibit 9, attached** in the **footnote area** where your cursor is blinking at the bottom of the page.
j. Press **Ctrl+End** to move to the end of the document. Select the picture of the bicycle, and then click **Insert Caption** in the Captions group. If necessary, click the **Label arrow**, and then select **Figure** so that *Figure 1* displays as the caption. Place the insertion point at the end of the caption, press **colon** (:), press **Spacebar** one time, and then type **Assembled Bicycle**. Click **OK** to close the Caption dialog box.
k. Go to page 3 in the document. Locate the *Shelton v. Missouri Baptist Foundation* case, and then select the case information from *Shelton* through and including the date *(1978)*. Select the closing

parenthesis but not the comma after it. Click **Mark Citation** in the Table of Authorities group. Click **Mark All**, and then click **Close**.

l. Scan the remainder of that page, and then mark all citations for the following cases: *Foster, Sotirescu, Moore Enterprises, Scott, Chapman, Bolander*, and *Arnett*. After you mark the final citation on that page, click **Cancel** to close the dialog box. Click the **Home tab**, and then click **Show/Hide** (¶) in the Paragraph group to turn off display of formatting marks.

m. Press **Ctrl+Home** to position the insertion point at the beginning of the document, and then press **Ctrl+Enter** to add a blank page. Press **Ctrl+Home** to place the insertion point at the top of the new page, type **Table of Authorities**, and then press **Enter** one time. Click the **References tab**, and then click **Insert Table of Authorities** in the Table of Authorities group. Click **OK.**

n. Right-click the comment by William Kincaid on page 2 that says *Please add the Table of Authorities to this document*, and then click **Delete Comment**.

o. Press **Ctrl+F**, and then type **bike** in the **text box**. Place the insertion point after the first occurrence of the word *bike* that displays in the first sentence of the *Background* paragraph. Press **Spacebar** one time, and then type (**See picture on page** . Be sure to add a blank space after you type the word *page*. Click the **References Tab**, and then click **Cross-reference** in the Captions group.

p. Click the **Reference type arrow**, and then select **Figure**. Click **Figure 1 Assembled Bicycle** in the **For which caption list**, click the **Insert reference to arrow**, select **Page Number**, and then click **Insert** to complete the cross-reference. Click **Close** to close the Cross-reference dialog box. Type) to complete the parentheses that hold the cross-reference.

q. Click the **Review tab**, click the **Display for Review arrow**, and then click **Final** to display the document without markup. Press **Ctrl+Home** to view the table of authorities, and then compare to Figure 3.29.

r. Save and close the file, and submit based on your instructor's directions.

2 The Great Depression

Dr. Jared Dockery, your history professor, has assigned a short research paper project. You decide to write about the Great Depression, which started in 1929. In addition to writing an interesting overview of the financial struggles in the United States during that time, you intend to impress Dr. Dockery with your technical skills—submitting a paper that includes proper citations, reference tables, and even an index. This exercise follows the same set of skills as used in Hands-On Exercises 1, 2, and 3 in the chapter. Refer to Figure 3.30 as you complete this exercise.

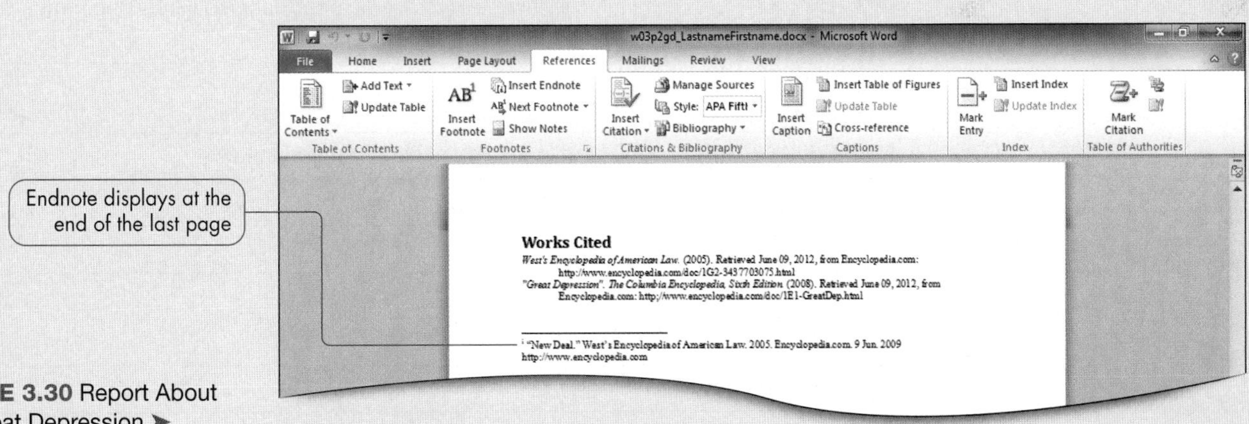

FIGURE 3.30 Report About the Great Depression ➤

a. Open *w03p2gd* and save it as **w03p2gd_LastnameFirstname.**

b. Click the **Insert tab**, and then click **Cover Page** in the Pages group. Choose the **Alphabet style**, and then type **1929-1933** as the document subtitle. Click the date, click the date arrow, and then choose **Today**. Replace the current author, *Exploring Series*, with your name.

c. Press **Ctrl+Home** to move the insertion point to the beginning of the document. Click the **Review Tab**, and then click **Next** in the Changes group. Click **Reject** to prevent the insertion of the lines that are now included in the title page. Click the **Accept arrow**, and then click **Accept All Changes in Document.**

d. Place the insertion point on the left side of the heading *Introduction* at the top of this page. Press **Ctrl+Enter** to create a hard page break. At the top of page 3, select the **Introduction heading,** click the **Home tab**, and then apply the **Heading 1 style** from the Styles gallery. Apply the **Heading 1 style** to the remaining boldfaced paragraph headings in the document using the Format Painter.

e. Scroll to the top of page 2, which is the blank page you created in the last step, and place the insertion point on the first line. Click the **References tab**, click **Table of Contents**, and then click **Automatic Table 2.**

f. Scroll down to the third page, and then select the picture. Click **Insert Caption** in the Captions group. Press **Spacebar** two times, and then type **Families in Dismay**. Click the **Position arrow**, and then click **Below selected item**. Click **OK** to close the Caption dialog box.

g. Use the instructions from step f to apply the following captions to the remaining pictures in the document:
   - **Struggling Main Street**
   - **Recovery in Sight**

h. Place the insertion point at the end of the Table of Contents. Press **Ctrl+Enter** to insert a page break. Scroll to the top of the blank page you just created, if necessary, and then place the insertion point on the first line. Type **Table of Figures** and press **Enter** two times. Click **Insert Table of Figures** in the Captions group, and then click **OK**. Select the **Table of Figures heading**, click the **Home tab**, and then click **Heading 1** from the Styles gallery.

i. Click the **References tab**, and then click **Manage Sources** in the Citations & Bibliography group. Click **New**, and then select **Document from Web site**, if necessary, from the Type of Source menu. Use the following table to enter information for the two sources used in this paper. After both sources are created, click **Close** to close the Source Manager dialog box.

Field in Create Source Dialog box	Source #1
Name of Web Page	"Great Depression." The Columbia Encyclopedia, Sixth Edition
Name of Web Site	Encyclopedia.com
Year	2008
Year Accessed	2012
Month Accessed	June
Day Accessed	09
URL	http://www.encyclopedia.com/doc/1E1-GreatDep.html

Field in Create Source Dialog box	Source #2
Name of Web Page	West's Encyclopedia of American Law
Name of Web Site	Encyclopedia.com
Year	2005
Year Accessed	2012
Month Accessed	June
Day Accessed	09
URL	http://www.encyclopedia.com/doc/1G2-3437703075.html

j. Press **Ctrl+End** to move the insertion point to the end of the document, and then press **Ctrl+Enter** to insert a hard page break. Click the **Style arrow** in the Citations & Bibliography group, and then click **APA Fifth Edition**, if necessary. Click **Bibliography**, and then click **Works Cited.**

k. Place your cursor at the end of the first sentence (after the period) in the first paragraph under *The New Deal* paragraph heading. Click **Insert Endnote** in the Footnotes group. Type the following: **"New Deal." West's Encyclopedia of American Law. 2005. Encyclopedia.com. 9 June 2009 http://www.encyclopedia.com.** Compare your work to Figure 3.30.

l. Scroll to the page that contains the Table of Contents. Click one time anywhere in the table of contents, and then press **F9**. Click **Update Entire Table**, and then click **OK**.

m. Save and close the file, and submit based on your instructor's directions.

MID-LEVEL EXERCISES

1 WWW Web Services Agency

You work as a Web designer at WWW Web Services Agency and have been asked to provide some basic information to be used in a senior citizens workshop. You want to provide the basic elements of good Web design and format the document professionally. Use the basic information you have already, in a Word document, and revise it to include elements appropriate for a research-oriented paper.

a. Open *w03m1web* and save it as **w03m1web_LastnameFirstname.**
b. Insert your name at the bottom of the cover page.
c. Place the insertion point at the end of the *Proximity and Balance* paragraph on the second page of the document. Insert the following text into an endnote: **Max Rebaza, Effective Web Sites, Chicago: Windy City Publishing, Inc. (2004): 44.**

d. Change all endnotes into footnotes.
e. Insert a table of contents after the cover page. Use a style of your choice.
f. In preparation for adding a bibliography to your document, create a citation source using the source from step c. (Hint: It is a book section.) Use the **Source Manager** to create the source and prevent the citation from displaying in the document. Also create citation sources for the two additional sources identified in the document footnotes.
g. Insert a bibliography at the end of the document using the Chicago style. Use the default format and settings for the bibliography. Apply **Heading 2 style** to the *Bibliography* heading.
h. Add captions to each graphic that displays in the paper. Use the default caption for each; you do not have to create a description. Display the caption below the graphic. Add a caption to the table on page 6 and display the caption below the table.
i. Create a table of figures at the beginning of the document on a separate page after the table of contents. The table should provide a list of figures only. Give the page an appropriate heading and format the heading using the **Heading 2 style**.
j. Insert a cross-reference at the end of the *Font Size and Attributes* paragraph on the seventh page. Type **See also** and insert a cross-reference that uses the **Heading reference type** and the *Contrast and Focus* heading. End the sentence with a period.
k. Update the entire table of contents and the table of figures. Remove any unnecessary blank pages in the document.
l. Save and close the file, and submit based on your instructor's directions.

2 Tips for Healthy Living

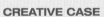

As a student in the Physician Assistant program at a local university, you create a document containing tips for healthier living. The facts have been entered into a Word document but are thus far unformatted. You will modify it to incorporate styles, and then you will create a comprehensive document by including a table of contents and index.

a. Open *w03m2healthy* and save it as **w03m2healthy_LastnameFirstname.**
b. Scroll through the document and view the changes that are currently marked in the document, and then accept each change. Turn on **Track Changes** so your changes will also be flagged. Change the Track Changes Options to display all formatting changes in color only.
c. Apply the **Heading 1** and **Body Text styles** throughout the document. It has been completed on the first and last paragraphs already.
d. Create a title page for the document consisting of the title, **Tips for Healthy Living**, and the subtitle, **Prepared by your name.** Replace *your name* with your name.
e. Create a footer for the document consisting of the title, **Tips for Healthy Living**, and a page number—use the page number style of your choice. The footer should not appear on the title page; that is, page 1 is actually the second page of the document.
f. Create a page specifically for the table of contents, and then give the page a title and generate a table of contents using the Healthy Living tip headings. Use a dashed leader to connect the headings to the page numbers in the table.

g. Mark the following text for inclusion in the index: *diet, exercise, metabolism, vegetables, fat.* At the end of your document, create the index and take necessary steps so the index heading displays in the table of contents.
h. Change the Display for Review setting to show the document as a final copy.

i. Print only a **List of markup**, if allowed by your instructor.
j. Save and close the file, and submit based on your instructor's directions.

3 Table of Authorities

As the junior partner in a growing law firm, you must proofread and update all legal briefs before they are submitted to the courts. You are in the final stage of completing a medical malpractice case, but the brief cannot be filed without a table of authorities.

a. Open *w03m3legal* and save it as **w03m3legal_LastnameFirstname**.
b. Mark all references to legal cases throughout the document.
c. Insert a table of authorities at the beginning of the document. Insert an appropriate heading at the top of the page, and format it using **Heading 1 style**.
d. Insert a comment at the beginning of the document, and then type **Ready to include in court records**.
e. Save and close the file, and submit based on your instructor's directions.

CAPSTONE EXERCISE

You are a member of the Horticulture Society and have been asked to assist in the development of information packets about a variety of flowers and plants. A report about tulips has been started, and you are responsible for completing the document so that it is ready for the fall meeting. You know of many features in Word that you can use to finish and present an easy-to-follow report.

Track Revisions

The document you receive has a few comments and shows the last few changes by the author. You will accept or reject the changes, and then make a few of your own. You will turn on track changes to differentiate between your changes and the author's.

a. Open *w03c1tulip* and save it as **w03c1tulip_Lastname Firstname**.

b. Scroll through the document and review the comment. Return to the third page and reject the insertion of a sentence about squirrels.

c. Accept all other tracked changes in the document. Keep all comments.

d. Change all headings that use Heading 3 style so they use **Heading 1 style**, as per the comment left by the author

e. Click inside the author's comment, and then insert a new comment. In the new comment, type a message indicating you have made the style replacement. This new comment will display *R1* after your name in the balloon to indicate it is a response to the previous comment.

Credit Sources

You are now ready to add the citations for resources that the author used when assembling this report. The author sent some source citations as an external file, and she typed some of the source information at the end of the document. She did not format it appropriately for use as a citation, nor did she insert citations in the appropriate places in the document as a footnote or endnote.

a. Use the **Source Manager tool** to open the file *tulips.xml*, and then copy the citations into the current list for this document.

b. Scroll to the end of the document to view a list of sources. Use the **Source Manager tool** to create new citations for each source. After you create the citations, delete the *Sources* paragraph heading and each source below it.

c. Modify the source from the Gardenersnet Web site to indicate the information was retrieved on June 7, 2012. Modify the source only in your current list.

d. Create a bibliography using MLA style on a separate page at the end of the document.

e. Insert an endnote on page 3, at the end of the third paragraph in the *Planting* section, which ends with *made by the planter*. Type the following for the endnote: **Swezey, Lauren Bonar, A Westerner's Guide to Tulips (Sunset, October 1999).** Change the number format for endnotes to **1, 2, 3** in the Footnotes dialog box launcher.

Figure References

The graphics in the document are quite informative, and you want to add descriptive captions to them and to list them on a reference page.

a. Select the tulip picture on the left side of the first row, and then assign the following caption below the photo: **Figure 1. Angelique**.

b. Assign captions to the remaining tulip photos on that page using information in the comments fields. Delete the comments after you create the captions.

c. Assign the caption **Planting Depth Guide** to the graphic titled *Planting Guide at a Glance*.

d. Create a blank page following the cover page, and then insert a table of figures, using the **Distinctive format**. Type **Table of Figures** at the top, and then format with the **Heading 1 style**.

Finish with Table of Contents and Index

To put the finishing touches on your document, you add a table of contents and an index. The document is short, but you decide to include both because they demonstrate a higher level of professionalism in your work.

a. Automatically generate a table of contents and display it on a page between the cover page and the table of figures.

b. Mark the following words as index entries: *Holland*, *perennials*, *deadheading*, *soil*, *store*. Create an index cross-reference entry using the word *storage* in the index to indicate where the word *store* is used in the document.

c. Add an index to the end of the document. Use the **Classic index format**. Format the Index title using the **Heading 1 style**.

d. Find the sentence *See the depth chart in Figure 6*, which displays in the third paragraph in the *Planting* section. Before the period and following the number 6, add the following text: **on page** . Then insert a cross reference to Figure 6. If correct, it informs the reader that the graphic is found on page 5.

e. Display a page number in the footer of the document using **Accent Bar 4 format**. Start numbering on the page that contains the Table of Contents. Also, in the left side of the footer, display the text **Compiled by *your name***, but use your first and last name.

f. Update all tables to reflect any changes made throughout this project.

g. Save and close the file, and submit based on your instructor's directions.

BEYOND THE CLASSROOM

Group Collaboration

GENERAL CASE 

This case requires collaboration between members of a group. Create groups of two or three people; the first person will open *w03b1_collaborate* and save it as **w03b1collaborate_LastnameFirstname**. The first person will turn on track changes and make at least two corrections, add comments to the document, and type his or her name in the footer. The first person will then save and send the document to the next group member, who also will turn on track changes, make additional corrections and suggestions, and add his or her name to the footer. It is acceptable to correct the previous member's corrections, but do not accept or reject changes at this time. Each member can also customize the track changes options. After each member adds corrections and comments to the document, and adds his or her name to the footer, the last person should save the document, and then print one copy of the document that shows markup and a second copy that shows final without markup. Save and close the file, and submit based on your instructor's directions.

Learn to Use Writing Styles

RESEARCH CASE 

Do you know someone who has been the victim of identity theft? It occurs every day. But what exactly is involved in this growing crime? Use your research skills to locate information about identity theft. You should find at least one source from the Internet, at least one source from a book, and at least one source from a journal. Use your school's library or online library resources to help locate the information sources. After you find your sources, write a two-page report, double-spaced, describing identity theft. Include information about the crime, statistics, government policies, laws that have been passed because of this crime, and the crime's effects on victims. Cite the sources in your paper, use footnotes where appropriate, and develop a bibliography for your paper based on the APA writing style. Save the report as **w03b2idtheft_LastnameFirstname**. Save and close the file, and submit based on your instructor's directions.

Repairing Tables

DISASTER RECOVERY 

You work in the city's Planning and Zoning department as an analyst. You begin to prepare the *Guide to Planned Developments* document for posting on the city's intranet. The administrative clerk who typed the document attempted to insert a table of contents and a table of figures, but he was not successful in displaying either table accurately. Open his file, *w03b3table*, and save your revised document as **w03b3table_LastnameFirstname**. He also attempted to insert cross-references, but they do not work correctly either. Before this document can be posted, you must repair both tables at the beginning of the document and the erroneous cross-references. The cross-references are highlighted in the document so you can locate them easily; the highlights should be removed when you have corrected the references. When you have corrected the problems, save and close the file, and submit based on your instructor's directions.

WORD

4 DOCUMENT PRODUCTIVITY

Working with Tables and Mail Merge

Watch the
Set-up
Video
for this
Case Study!

CASE STUDY | Community Disaster Relief Center

Wacey Rivale is the Director of Fundraising at the local Community Disaster Relief Center (CDRC). She spends many hours giving speeches to local companies, organizations, and civic groups so they will be familiar with the efforts and activities of the Relief Center. Because the CDRC is a nonprofit organization, Wacey and other CDRC staffers must demonstrate the need, the benefits, and the success of the service they provide.

Wacey always sends a letter of appreciation to the people who donate and support the CDRC, but her latest marketing efforts have increased the response of the community. Typically, she sends one or two per week, but now she is in a position where she needs to send several dozen letters. She asks you, her co-worker, to start a list of donors, their addresses, and their contribution amounts so no donor is overlooked when it comes time to send the letters. You decide to document donor information in a table in Word. Then it will be part of a mail merge to create thank-you letters quickly and efficiently.

OBJECTIVES

AFTER YOU READ THIS CHAPTER, YOU WILL BE ABLE TO:

1. Insert a table ***p.212***
2. Format a table ***p.214***
3. Sort and apply formulas to table data ***p.223***
4. Convert text to a table ***p.225***
5. Select a main document ***p.232***
6. Select or create recipients ***p.233***
7. Insert merge fields ***p.237***
8. Merge a main document and a data source ***p.238***

Tables

A **table** is a series of columns and rows that organize data.

A **cell** is the intersection of a column and row in a table.

A ***table*** is a series of columns and rows that organizes data effectively. The columns and rows in a table intersect to form ***cells***. The table feature is one of the most powerful in Word and is an easy way to organize a series of data in a columnar list format. For example, you can create tables to organize data such as employee lists with phone numbers and e-mail addresses. The donor registry in Figure 4.1, for example, is actually an 8 × 13 table (8 columns and 13 rows). The completed table looks impressive, but it is very easy to create once you understand how a table works. In addition to the organizational benefits, tables make an excellent alignment tool. Although you can align text with tabs, you have more format control when you create a table. (See the Practice Exercises at the end of the chapter for other examples.)

> The table feature is one of the most powerful in Word and is an easy way to organize a series of data.... In addition to the organizational benefits, tables make an excellent alignment tool.

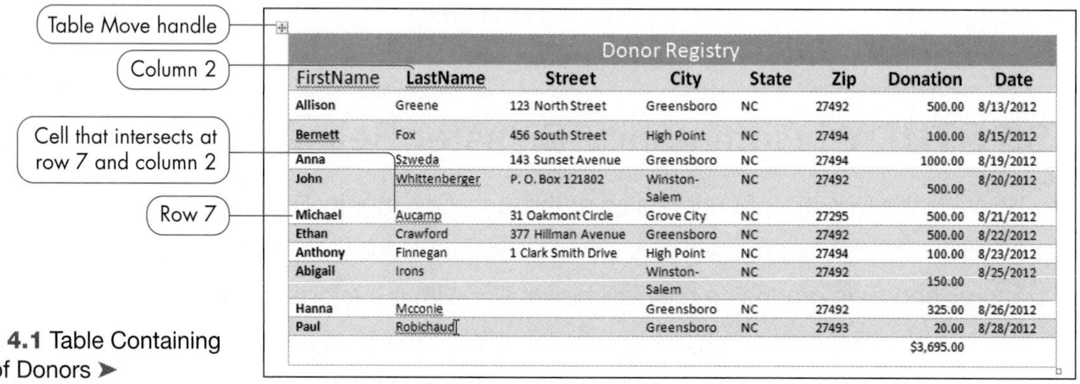

Donor Registry							
FirstName	LastName	Street	City	State	Zip	Donation	Date
Allison	Greene	123 North Street	Greensboro	NC	27492	500.00	8/13/2012
Bernett	Fox	456 South Street	High Point	NC	27494	100.00	8/15/2012
Anna	Szweda	143 Sunset Avenue	Greensboro	NC	27494	1000.00	8/19/2012
John	Whittenberger	P. O. Box 121802	Winston-Salem	NC	27492	500.00	8/20/2012
Michael	Aucamp	31 Oakmont Circle	Grove City	NC	27295	500.00	8/21/2012
Ethan	Crawford	377 Hillman Avenue	Greensboro	NC	27492	500.00	8/22/2012
Anthony	Finnegan	1 Clark Smith Drive	High Point	NC	27494	100.00	8/23/2012
Abigail	Irons		Winston-Salem	NC	27492	150.00	8/25/2012
Hanna	Mcconie		Greensboro	NC	27492	325.00	8/26/2012
Paul	Robichaud		Greensboro	NC	27493	20.00	8/28/2012
						$3,695.00	

FIGURE 4.1 Table Containing Names of Donors ➤

After you create a basic table, you want to enhance the appearance to create interest for the reader and improve readability. Word includes many tools to assist with these efforts, and you will use several of them to complete the table used for the Donor Registry. In this section, you will insert a table in a document. After inserting the table, you can insert or delete columns and rows if you need to change the structure. Furthermore, you will learn how to merge and split cells within the table and how to change the row height and column width to accommodate data in the table. You also will learn how to format a table using borders, shading, and the styles provided by Word. Finally, you will modify table alignment and position.

Inserting a Table

You create a table from the Insert tab. Click Table in the Tables group on the Insert tab to see a gallery of cells on which you drag to select the number of columns and rows you require in the table, or you can choose the Insert Table command below the gallery to display the Insert Table dialog box and enter the table composition you prefer. When you select the table dimension from the gallery or from the Insert Table dialog box, Word creates a table structure with the number of columns and rows you specify. After you create a table, you can enter text, numbers, or graphics in individual cells. The text wraps as it is entered within a cell, so that you can add or delete text without affecting the entries in other cells.

You format the contents of an individual cell the same way you format an ordinary paragraph; that is, you change the font, apply boldface or italic, change the text alignment, or apply any other formatting commands. You can select multiple cells, rows, or columns and apply formatting to the selection all at once, or you can format a cell independently of every other cell.

After you insert a table in your document, use commands in the Table Tools Design and Layout tabs to modify and enhance it. Place the insertion point anywhere in the table, and then click either the Design or Layout tab to view the commands. In either tab just point to a command and a ScreenTip describes its function. When you hover the mouse over any cell of a table the ***Table Move handle*** displays (see Figure 4.1). You can click this handle once to select the whole table at one time, which is useful when working with design and layout features.

Click the **Table Move handle** to select a whole table at one time.

TIP Using Tabs to Move Within Tables

The Tab key on your keyboard functions differently in a table than in a regular document. Press Tab to move to the next cell in the current row, or to the first cell in the next row if you are at the end of a row. Press Tab when you are in the last cell of a table to add a new blank row to the bottom of the table. Press Shift+Tab to move to the previous cell in the current row (or to the last cell in the previous row). You must press Ctrl+Tab to insert a regular tab character within a cell.

Insert and Delete Rows and Columns

You can change the structure of a table after it has been created. If you need more rows or columns to accommodate additional data in your table, it is easy to add or insert them using the Rows & Columns group on the Table Tools Layout tab. The Insert and Delete commands enable you to add new or delete existing rows or columns. When you add a column, you can specify if you want to insert it to the right or left of the current column. Likewise, you can specify where to place a new row—either above or below the currently selected row.

You can delete complete rows and columns using the commands mentioned previously, or you can delete only the data in those rows and columns using the Delete key on your keyboard. Keep in mind that when you insert or delete a complete row or a column, the remaining rows and columns will adjust to the positioning. For example, if you delete the third row of a 5×5 table, the data in the fourth and fifth rows move up and become the third and fourth rows. If you delete only the data in the third row, the cells would be blank and the fourth and fifth rows would not change at all.

Inserting Multiple Rows (or Columns) Simultaneously

If you need to insert more than one row (or column) at a time, simply select multiple rows (or columns), right-click, and select the Insert command, and the same number of blank rows (or columns) you selected will display. For example, if you select three rows before you click the Insert row command, three blank rows will appear.

Merge and Split Cells

You can use the Merge Cells command in the Merge group on the Table Tools Layout tab to join individual cells together (merge) to form a larger cell, as was done in the first row of Figure 4.1. People often merge cells to enter a main title at the top of a table. Conversely, you can use the Split Cells command in the Merge group to split a single cell into multiple cells if you require more cells to hold data.

Change Row Height and Column Width

When you create a table, Word builds evenly spaced columns. Frequently you need to change the row height or column width to fit your data. ***Row height*** is the vertical distance from the top to the bottom of a row. ***Column width*** is the horizontal space or width of a column. You might increase the column width to display a wide string of text, such as first and last name,

Row height is the vertical space from the top to the bottom of a row.

Column width is the horizontal space or length of a column.

to prevent it from wrapping in the cell. You might increase row height to better fit a header that has been enlarged for emphasis.

The Table command is easy to master, and as you might have guessed, you will benefit from reviewing the available commands listed in the Design and Layout tabs. Features in the Layout tab are described in Table 4.1. You will use many of these commands as you create a table in the Hands-On Exercises.

TABLE 4.1 Table Tools Layout Tab

Group	Commands	Enables You to
Table	Select, View Gridlines, Properties (Table)	• Select particular parts of a table (cell, column, row, or entire table). • Show or hide the gridlines around the table. • Display the Table Properties dialog box to format the table.
Rows & Columns	Delete, Insert Above, Insert Below, Insert Left, Insert Right (Rows & Columns)	• Delete cells, columns, rows, or the entire table. • Insert rows and columns. • Display the Insert Cells dialog box.
Merge	Merge Cells, Split Cells, Split Table (Merge)	• Merge (join) selected cells together. • Split cells into separate cells. • Split the table into two tables.
Cell Size	6.65", 0.25", AutoFit (Cell Size)	• Adjust the row height and column width. • Adjust the column width automatically based on the data in the column. • Display the Table Properties dialog box.
Alignment	Text Direction, Cell Margins (Alignment)	• Specify the combined horizontal and vertical alignment of text within a cell. • Change the text direction. • Set margins within a cell.
Data	Sort, Repeat Header Rows, Convert to Text, Formula (Data)	• Sort data within a table. • Repeat header rows when tables span multiple pages. • Convert tabulated text to table format. • Insert a formula in a table.

Formatting a Table

Shading affects the background color within a cell.

Border refers to the line style around each cell.

You can use basic formatting options to enhance the appearance of your table. The Borders and Shading commands, for example, offer a wide variety of choices for formatting the table structure. ***Shading*** affects the background color within a cell or group of cells. Table shading is similar to the Highlight feature that places a color behind the contents in a cell. You often apply shading to the header row of a table to make it stand out from the data. ***Border*** refers to the line style around each cell in the table. The default is a single line, but you can choose from many styles to outline a table such as a double, triple, or a wavy line. You can even choose invisible borders if you want only data to display in your document without the outline of a table. Borders and Shading commands are located on both the Home tab and the Table Tools Design tab, but you will probably find it more convenient to access the command from the Table Tools Design tab while you work with tables. The Design tab features are described in Table 4.2.

TIP Right-Click for Table Formatting Options

As an alternative to using the Layout tab, you can find many table options in the context-sensitive menu that displays when you right-click the mouse. The insertion point can be anywhere in the table, and after you right-click you see several table options including Insert, Delete Cells, and Split Cells. You also can change format and alignment of table cells using the Borders and Shading, Cell Alignment, and Text Direction commands in this menu. The Table Properties option is available in the menu if you need to access features such as table alignment and cell spacing.

TABLE 4.2 Table Tools Design Tab		
Group	**Commands**	**Enables You to**
Table Style Options	Header Row, First Column, Total Row, Last Column, Banded Rows, Banded Columns (Table Style Options)	• Turn Header Row on or off. • Turn Total Row on or off. • Display banded rows; formats even- and odd-numbered rows differently. • Display special formatting for first column. • Display special formatting for last column. • Display banded columns; formats even- and odd-numbered columns differently.
Table Styles	Shading, Borders (Table Styles)	• Select predefined style from gallery. • Apply color behind the selected cell(s) or table. • Customize borders of selected cell(s) or table.
Draw Borders	½ pt, Pen Color, Draw Table, Eraser (Draw Borders)	• Alter style of line used around border of cell or table. • Alter size of line used for borders. • Change Pen Color feature; use with Draw Table feature. • Manually draw borders of cell(s) or table. • Erase borders of cell(s) or table. • Display the Borders and Shading dialog box.

Apply Table Styles

A **table style** contains borders, shading, and other attributes to enhance a table.

Word provides many predefined ***table styles*** that contain borders, shading, font sizes, and other attributes that enhance the readability of a table. The Table Styles feature is helpful in situations where you want to apply a professional-looking format to a table; when you are coordinating the design of a table with other features in Word, Excel, or PowerPoint; or when you do not have time to apply custom borders and shading. The styles are available in the Table Styles group on the Design tab. To use a predefined table style, click anywhere in your table, and then click a style from the Table Styles gallery. A few styles from the gallery display, but you can select from many others by clicking the More button on the right side of the gallery, as shown in Figure 4.2. The Live Preview of a style displays on your table when you hover your mouse over it in the gallery. To apply a style, click it one time.

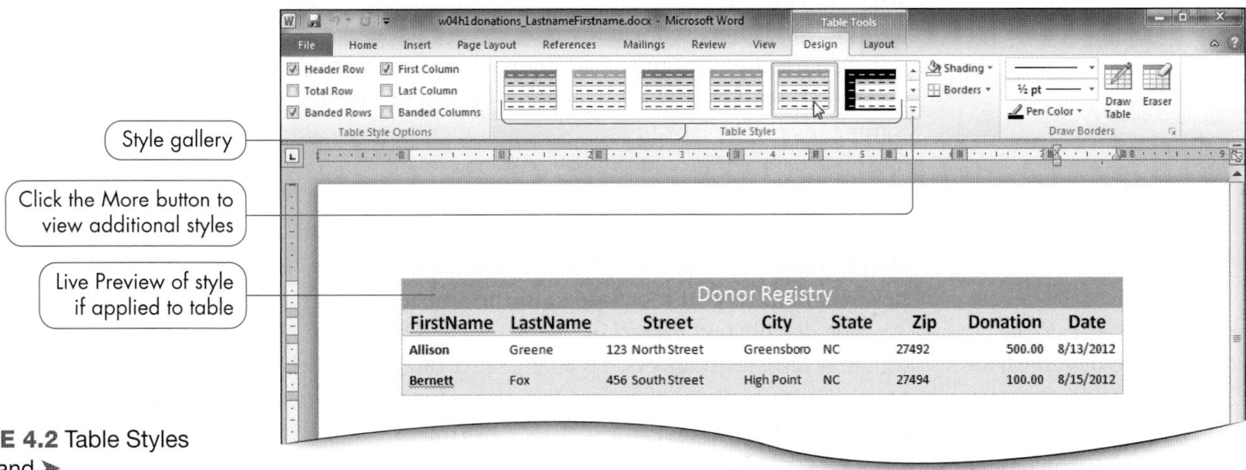

FIGURE 4.2 Table Styles Command ➤

You can modify a predefined style if you wish to make changes to features such as color or alignment. You also can create your own table style and save it for use in the current document, or add it to a document template for use in other Word documents. Click the More button in the Table Styles group to access the Modify Table Style and New Table Style commands.

Select the Table Position and Alignment

Table alignment is the position of a table between the left and right margins.

Table alignment refers to the position of a table between the left and right document margins. When you insert a table, Word aligns it at the left margin by default. However, you can click Properties in the Table group on the Layout tab to display the Table Properties dialog box, as seen in Figure 4.3. The *Alignment* section of the dialog box offers four choices for table alignment—Left, Center, Right, or a custom setting in which you specify an amount that the table is indented from the left margin. For example, you might want to use the custom setting to indent the table exactly two inches from the left margin so it aligns with other indented text.

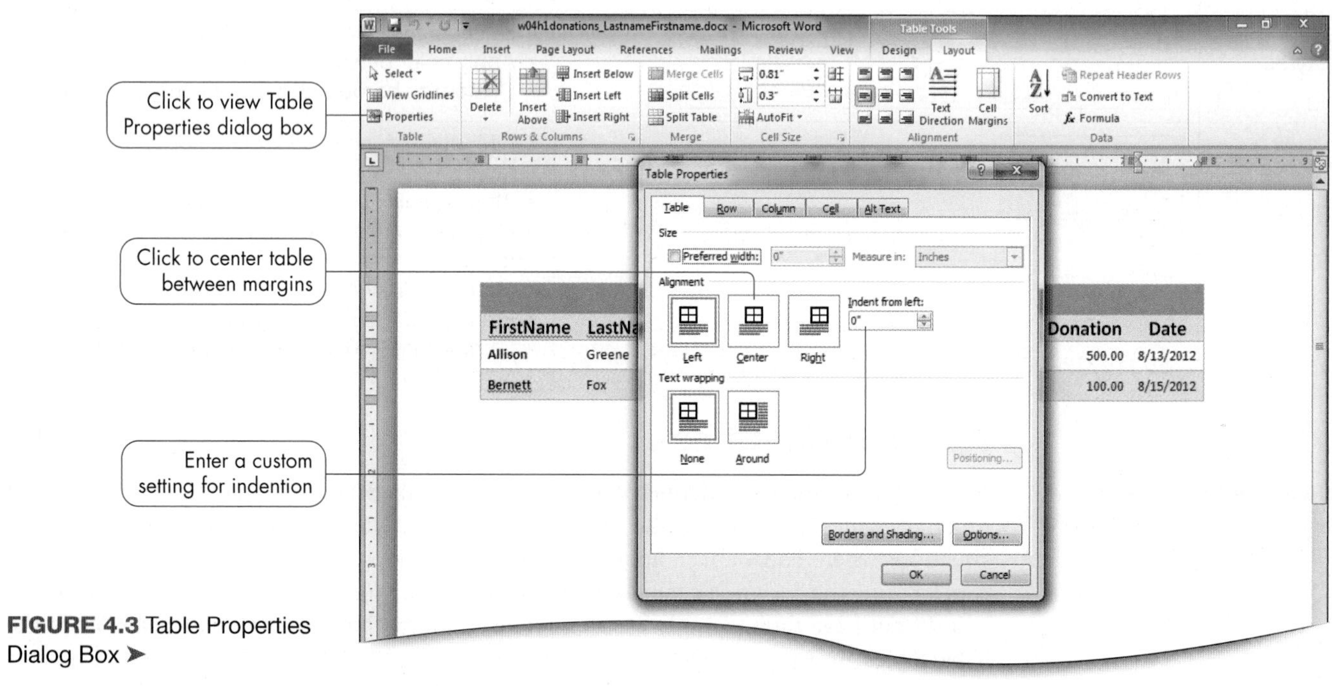

FIGURE 4.3 Table Properties Dialog Box ➤

You can also choose from two text wrapping options in the Table Properties dialog box. The option to wrap text Around will enable you to display text on the side of the table. This is useful if you have a small table so you will not waste a great deal of space on the page by displaying the table and text close together. The option for None prevents text from displaying beside the table, and will force text to display above or below it. If your table is small, this will enable a large amount of white space to display beside it.

You also can change alignment of the data in a table separately from the table itself using commands on the Layout tab. The Alignment group contains many options to quickly format table data. Table data can be formatted to align in many different horizontal and vertical combinations. We often apply horizontal settings, such as Center, to our data, but using vertical settings also increases readability. For example, when you want your data to be centered both horizontally and vertically within a cell so it is easy to read and does not appear to be elevated on the top or too close to the bottom, click Align Center in the Alignment group.

Text direction refers to the degree of rotation in which text displays.

The default ***text direction*** places text in a horizontal position. However, you can rotate text so it displays sideways. To change text direction, click Text Direction in the Alignment group. Each time you click Text Direction, the text rotates. This is a useful tool for aligning text that is in the header row of a narrow column.

A **cell margin** is the amount of space between data and the cell border in a table.

The ***Cell Margins*** command in the Alignment group on the Layout tab enables you to adjust the amount of white space inside a cell as well as spacing between cells. Use this setting to improve readability of cell contents by adjusting white space around your data or between cells if they contain large amounts of text or data. If you increase cell margins, it prevents data from looking squeezed together.

1 Tables

Since you will be tracking information about the donors and donations that Wacey Rivale receives for the Community Disaster Relief Center (CDRC), you quickly determine that a table is the logical choice for a professional and easy-to-read document. It also gives you flexibility in adding more information because you expect the donations to keep pouring in.

Skills covered: Create a Table • Insert Data, Rows, and Columns • Change Row Height and Column Width • Merge Cells to Create a Title Row • Apply a Table Style and Align Data

STEP 1 CREATE A TABLE

After a discussion with Wacey, you now know the donor information that should be documented. You determine the size of the table you will use is based on the fact that it must display the donor's name, address, date, and amount of donation. Refer to Figure 4.4 as you complete Step 1.

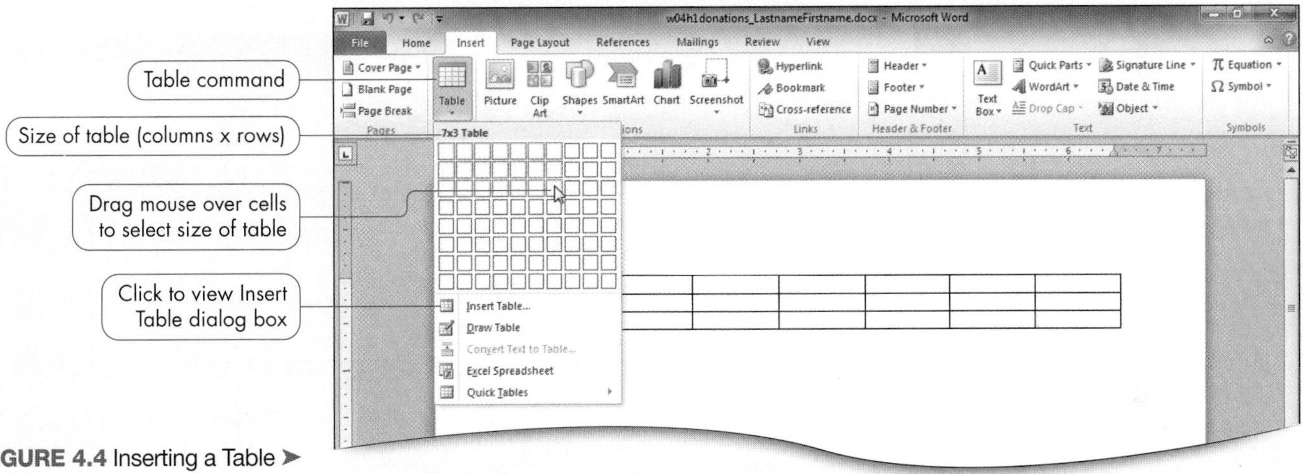

FIGURE 4.4 Inserting a Table ➤

a. Open a new blank document and save it as **w04h1donations_LastnameFirstname**.

b. Press **Enter** twice in the blank document, and then click the **Insert tab**.

   You will find it easier to work with a table if it does not begin on the very first line of the document. The Insert tab contains the Table command.

c. Click **Table** in the Tables group, and then drag your mouse over the cells until you select seven columns and three rows; you will see the table size, 7 × 3, displayed above the cells, as shown in Figure 4.4. Click the bottom-right cell (where the seventh column and the third row intersect) to insert the table into your document.

   Word creates an empty table that contains seven columns and three rows. The default columns have identical widths, and the table spans from the left to the right margin.

d. Practice selecting various elements from the table, something that you will have to do in subsequent steps:

   - Select a single cell by pointing inside the left grid line. The pointer changes to a black slanted arrow when you are in the proper position, and then you can click to select the cell.

- Select a row by clicking in the left margin of the first cell in that row (the pointer changes to a right slanting white arrow).
- Select a column by pointing just above the top of the column (the pointer changes to a small black downward pointing arrow) and click.
- Select adjacent cells by clicking a cell and dragging the mouse over the adjacent cells.
- Select the entire table by dragging the mouse over the table or by clicking the Table Move handle that appears at the top-left corner of the table.

e. Save the document.

STEP 2 INSERT DATA, ROWS, AND COLUMNS

With the table in place, you can now begin entering the headings for each column, and then you can add the donor information later. When you realize you need one more column, you relax because Word makes it easy to add one just where you need it. Refer to Figure 4.5 as you complete Step 2.

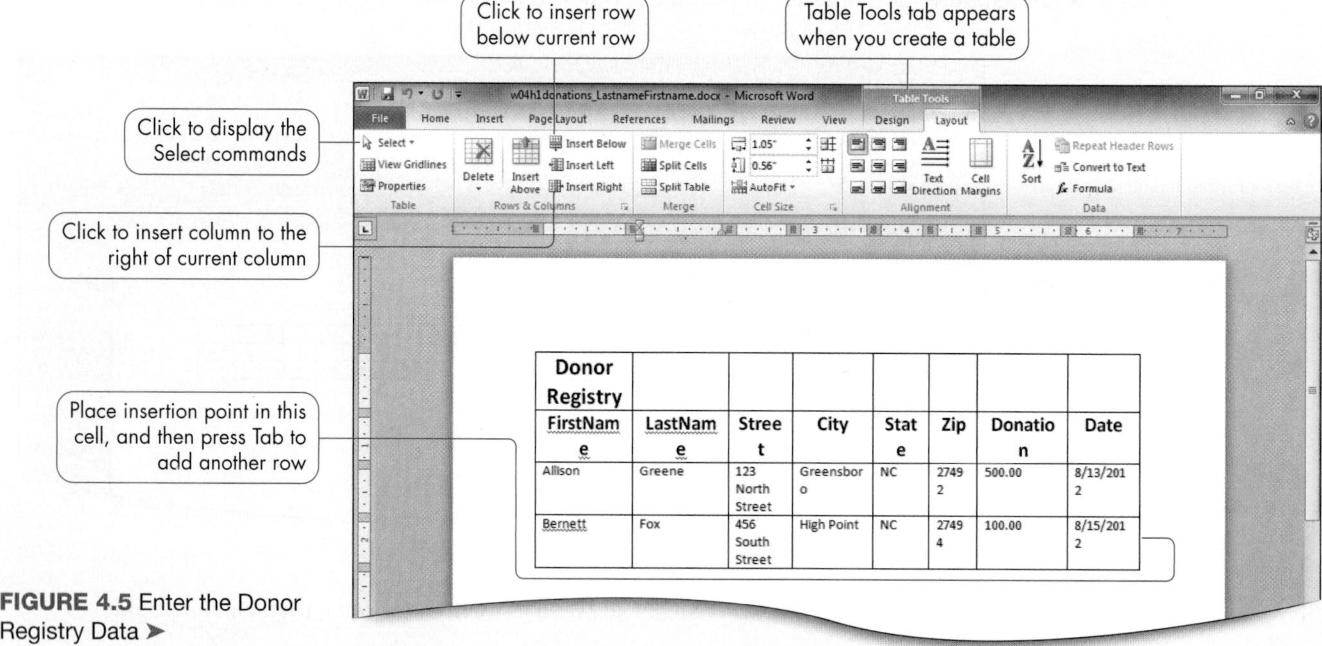

FIGURE 4.5 Enter the Donor Registry Data ➤

a. Enter data into the table by completing the following steps:

- Click in the first cell of the first row, and then type **Donor Registry**.
- Press ↓ to move to the first cell in the second row, and then type **FirstName** (this displays directly below *Donor Registry*).

  You do not insert spaces in the First Name column heading because this format is used in documents we later use to associate with this information.
- Press **Tab** (or →) to move to the next cell, and then type **LastName**.
- Press **Tab** to move to the next cell, and then type **Street**.
- Enter the following labels in the next four cells: **City**, **State**, **Zip**, and **Donation**.

  You realize you need one more column for the date of the donation.

b. Add another column by completing the following steps:

- Click anywhere in the last column of your table, and then click the **Layout tab**, if necessary. Click **Insert Right** in the Rows & Columns group to add a new column to your table.
- Click in the second row of the new column, and then type **Date**.

  You added a new column on the right side of the table. Notice that the column widths decrease to make room for the new column you just added.

TROUBLESHOOTING: If the column you insert is not in the correct location within the table, click Undo on the Quick Access Toolbar, confirm your insertion point is in the last column, and then click the appropriate Insert command.

FYI

c. Select the text *Donor Registry* in the first row. On the Mini toolbar, click the **Font Size arrow**, select **18**, click **Bold**, and then click **Center** to center the heading within the cell.

The table title stands out with the larger font size, bold, and center horizontal alignment.

d. Click in the left margin to select the entire second row. On the Mini toolbar, click the **Font Size arrow**, select **16**, and then click **Bold** and **Center**.

Now the labels in the second row stand out as well. They are not quite as large as the first row because they should not overpower the title.

e. Insert the donor information into your new table using data in the table below. When you get to the last column and find you need another row to hold the next row of data, press **Tab** to add a row to the end of your table, and then enter the next item and amounts. Compare your results to Figure 4.5.

FirstName	LastName	Street	City	State	Zip	Donation	Date
Allison	Greene	123 North Street	Greensboro	NC	27492	500.00	8/13/2012
Bernett	Fox	456 South Street	High Point	NC	27494	100.00	8/15/2012

f. Save the document.

Other Ways to Select a Table

You can click Select in the Table group on the Layout tab to display commands for selecting a cell, a column, a row, or the entire table. Figure 4.5 shows the location of the Select command.

STEP 3 CHANGE ROW HEIGHT AND COLUMN WIDTH

Now that you have donor information in the table, you decide to adjust the way it displays so it is easier to read. Adjusting the orientation of the page enables you to increase column widths so text does not need to wrap as much. This is especially useful for addresses, which are easier to read if they do not wrap. Refer to Figure 4.6 as you complete Step 3.

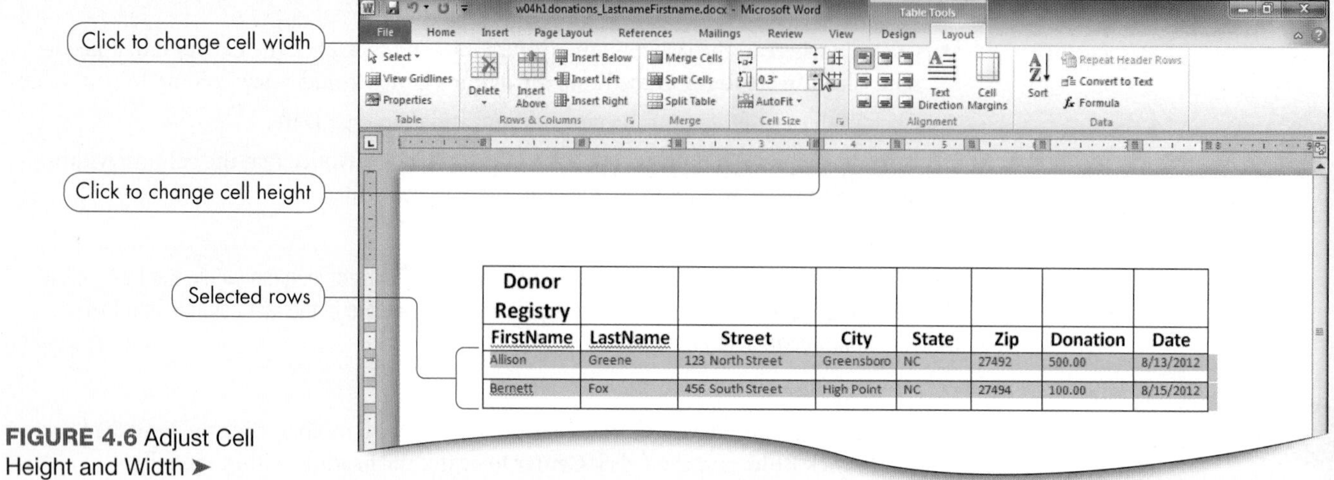

FIGURE 4.6 Adjust Cell Height and Width ➤

a. Click the **Page Layout tab**, click **Orientation**, and then click **Landscape**.

You have more room to display the donor information without wrapping the text if your page orientation is in landscape mode.

b. Hold your mouse above the top cell in the third column of data until the small black arrow appears, and then click to select the column that displays the street address.

c. Click the **Layout tab**, and then click the **Width arrow** in the Cell Size group until **1.5″** displays.

You changed the width of the column so that the whole address displays without wrapping. Other column widths did not change, even though the table stretches to the right of the page.

d. Change the height of the row by completing the following steps:

- Place the insertion point anywhere in the cell that contains the text *Allison*, and then click **Select** in the Table group.
- Click **Select Row**, and then hold down **Shift** and press ↓ on your keyboard to select the remaining row in the table.
- Click the **Height arrow** in the Cell Size group until **.3″** displays, as shown in Figure 4.6.

You changed the height of the last two rows in the table to 0.3″ tall, which makes the data easier to read.

e. Save the document.

> **TIP Adjusting Column Width and Row Height**
>
> If you are not certain of the exact measurements needed for row height or column width, you can use the mouse to increase or decrease the size. Position the mouse pointer on the grid-line that separates the rows (or columns) until the pointer changes to a two-headed arrow. The two-headed arrow indicates you can adjust the height (or width) by dragging the gridline up or down (right or left) to resize the cell.

STEP 4 MERGE CELLS TO CREATE A TITLE ROW

Any table that displays important information should have a title to explain the contents, and it should be easy to read and look professional. You recognize this table fits that description, so you merge the cells in the first row and center the text. Refer to Figure 4.7 as you complete Step 4.

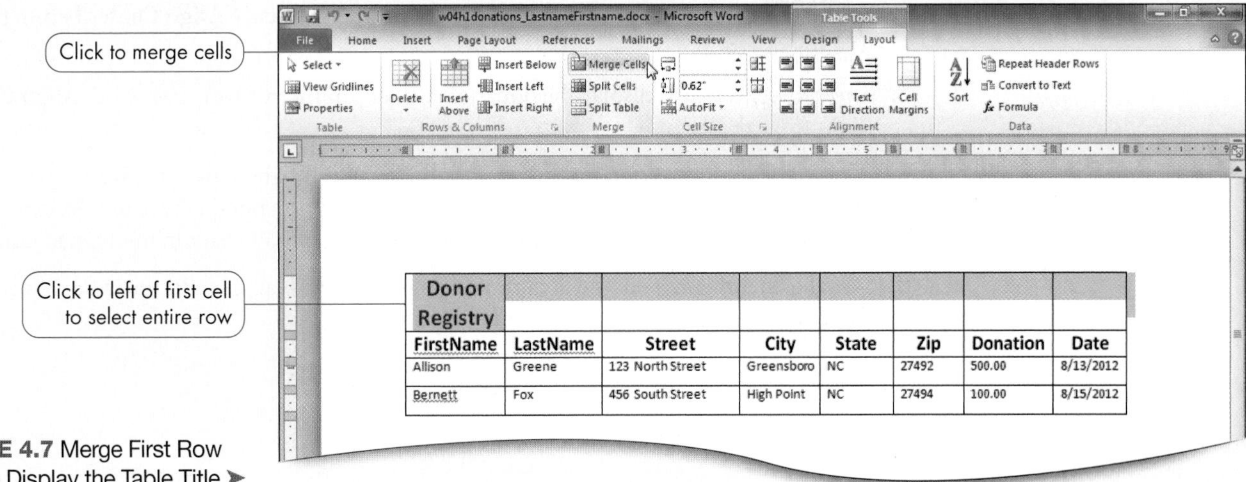

FIGURE 4.7 Merge First Row Cells to Display the Table Title ➤

a. Click outside the table to the left of the first cell in the first row to select the entire first row.

b. Click **Merge Cells** in the Merge group, as shown in Figure 4.7.

   You merged the selected cells. The first row now contains a single cell.

c. Right-click the row to display the Mini toolbar, and then click **Center**.

d. Save the document.

STEP 5 APPLY A TABLE STYLE AND ALIGN DATA

The table is sufficient for holding information, but you want to format it using Table Styles in Word so that the information is easy to read when it displays. Using alternating colors across the rows prevents the data from being blurred together or mixed up when you read it. It is also a good practice to apply proper alignment to the columns that contain monetary values. Refer to Figure 4.8 as you complete Step 5.

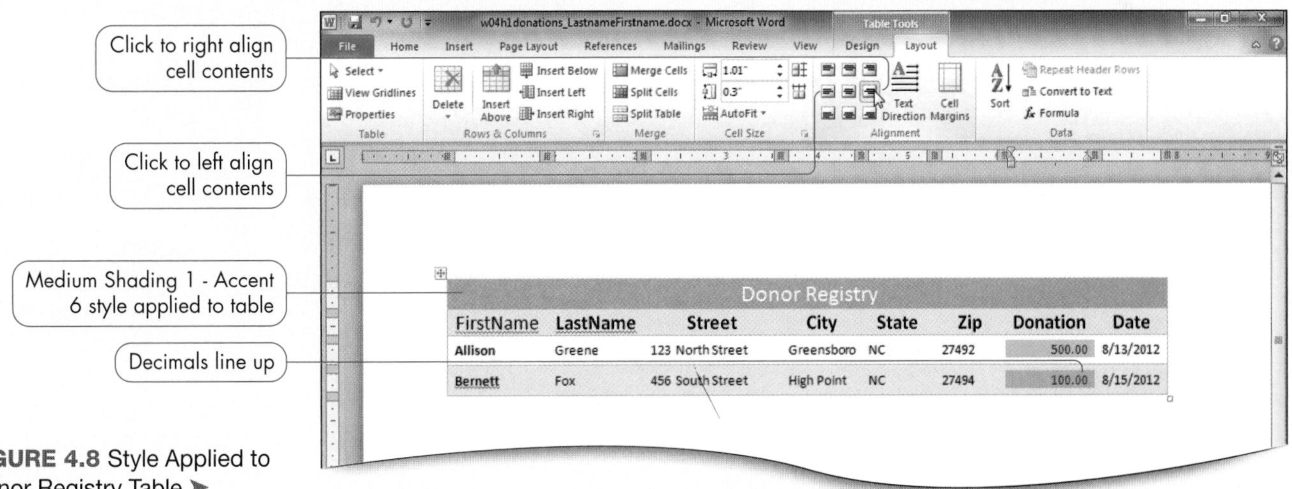

FIGURE 4.8 Style Applied to Donor Registry Table ➤

a. Apply a style to your table by completing the following steps:
   - Click the **Design tab**, and then click the **More button** in the Table Styles group.
   - Hover your mouse over several styles and notice how the table changes to preview that style.
   - Click **Medium Shading 1 - Accent 6** (last column, fourth row) to apply it to your table.

     Previous formatting such as alignment and cell shading, if it exists, may be replaced by the formatting attributes for a style when applied to a table.

b. Select rows three and four. Click the **Layout tab**, and then click **Align Center Left** in the Alignment group.

c. Select the cells which display the donation amount in the last two rows. Click **Align Center Right** from the Alignment group.

   Because this column contains monetary values, you right align them to give the effect of decimal alignment, as shown in Figure 4.8. Technically, the numbers are not decimal aligned, so if you display an additional digit in a value, it will result in misaligned numbers.

d. Save the document. Keep the document onscreen if you plan to continue with Hands-On Exercise 2. If not, close the document and exit Word.

Advanced Table Features

You now have a good understanding of table features and realize there are many uses for them in your Word documents. But did you know you can use tables to perform simple tasks that are typically performed in a spreadsheet? Word includes features that enable the user to sort and perform simple mathematical calculations to data in a table. You can also convert plain text into a table.

> Word includes features that enable the user to sort and perform simple mathematical calculations to data in a table.

In this section, you will learn how to sort data within a table and insert formulas to perform calculations. Finally, you convert text to a table format.

Sorting and Applying Formulas to Table Data

Sorting is the process of arranging data in a specific order.

Because tables provide an easy way to arrange numbers within a document, it is important to know how to use table calculations. This feature gives a Word document the power of a simple spreadsheet. Additional organization of table data is possible by ***sorting***, or rearranging, data based on certain criteria. Figure 4.9 displays the donor list you created previously, but this table illustrates two additional capabilities of the table feature—sorting and calculating.

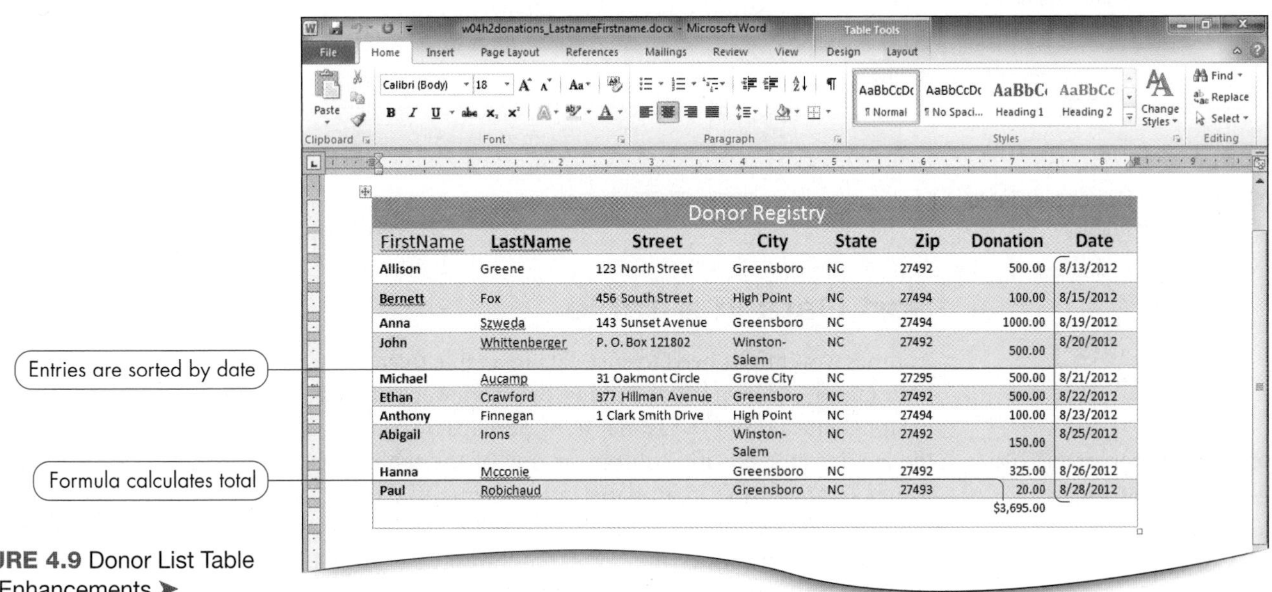

Donor Registry							
FirstName	LastName	Street	City	State	Zip	Donation	Date
Allison	Greene	123 North Street	Greensboro	NC	27492	500.00	8/13/2012
Bernett	Fox	456 South Street	High Point	NC	27494	100.00	8/15/2012
Anna	Szweda	143 Sunset Avenue	Greensboro	NC	27494	1000.00	8/19/2012
John	Whittenberger	P. O. Box 121802	Winston-Salem	NC	27492	500.00	8/20/2012
Michael	Aucamp	31 Oakmont Circle	Grove City	NC	27295	500.00	8/21/2012
Ethan	Crawford	377 Hillman Avenue	Greensboro	NC	27492	500.00	8/22/2012
Anthony	Finnegan	1 Clark Smith Drive	High Point	NC	27494	100.00	8/23/2012
Abigail	Irons		Winston-Salem	NC	27492	150.00	8/25/2012
Hanna	Mcconie		Greensboro	NC	27492	325.00	8/26/2012
Paul	Robichaud		Greensboro	NC	27493	20.00	8/28/2012
						$3,695.00	

FIGURE 4.9 Donor List Table with Enhancements ➤

Calculate Using Table Formulas

You know that the intersection of a row and column forms a cell, and the rows and columns are identified by numbers and letters, respectively. Word uses the column letter and row number of that intersection to identify the cell and to give it an address. Thus, the rows in the Donor Registry table are numbered top to bottom from 1 to 13 while the columns are labeled left to right from A to H. The row and column labels do not appear in the table, but are used in the formula for reference. The last entry in the Donation column in the table in Figure 4.9 is actually a formula entered into the table to perform a calculation. The entry is similar to that in a spreadsheet because it is adding the values in all the cells above it.

Syntax refers to the rules for constructing an equation.

The formula is not entered (typed) into the cell explicitly, but is created using the Formula command in the Data group on the Layout tab. You often do not need to know the formula ***syntax***, or rules for constructing the formula, because Word provides a dialog box that supplies basic formulas such as sum and average. But sometimes you construct a unique formula from your table entries. Once you use the table formula feature to create a formula, you will find it easy to understand because it uses field codes to identify the data and formats you use in the formula. You could, of course, use a calculator and type in the total in the cell. However, it is better to use the Formula command to calculate totals than to type the result because if you add data or change data already in the table, you can use formula tools to recalculate the total for you.

Figure 4.10 is a slight variation of Figure 4.9 in which the field codes have been toggled on to display formulas, as opposed to the calculated values. The cells are shaded to emphasize that these cells contain formulas (also called *fields*), as opposed to numerical values. The field codes are toggled on and off by selecting the formula and pressing Shift+F9 or by right-clicking the entry and selecting the Toggle Field Codes command.

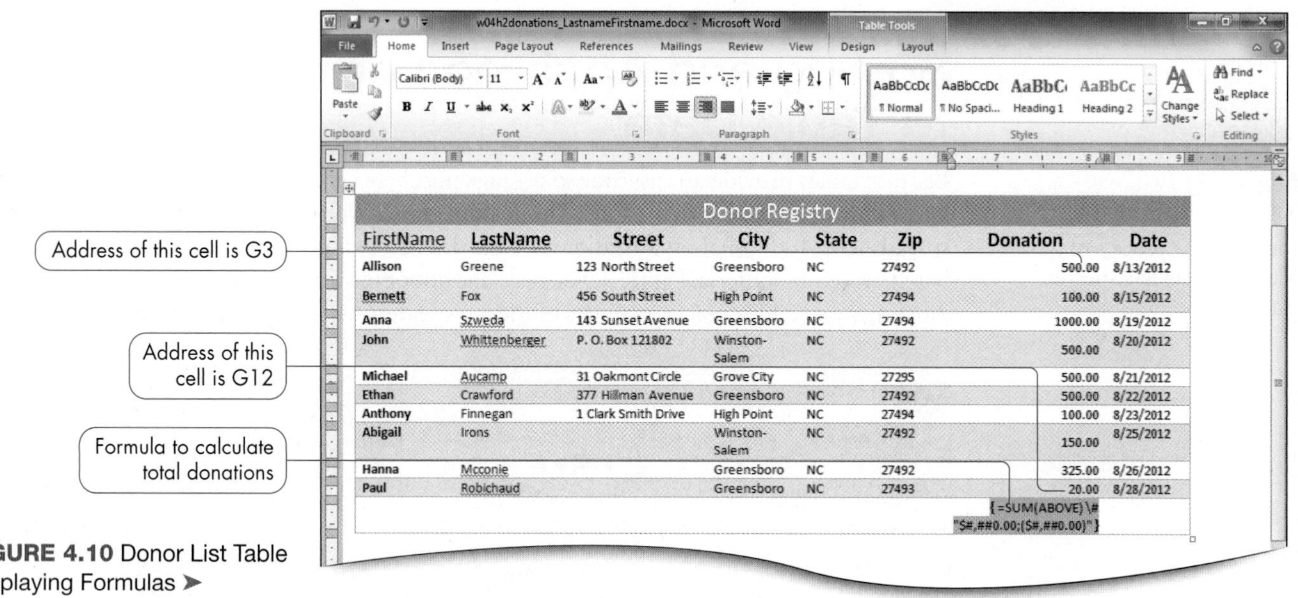

FIGURE 4.10 Donor List Table Displaying Formulas ➤

Sort Data in a Table

Ascending order arranges data from lowest to highest.

Descending order arranges data from highest to lowest.

At times, you might need to sort data in a table to enhance the order or understand the data. For example, when a list of employees is reviewed, a manager might prefer to view the names in alphabetical order by last name, or perhaps by department. You can sort data according to the entries in a specific column or row of the table. Sort orders include ***ascending order***, which arranges text in alphabetical or sequential order starting with the lowest letter or number and continuing to the highest (A–Z or 0–9). Or you can sort in ***descending order***, where data is arranged from highest to lowest (Z–A or 9–0).

You can sort the rows in a table to display data in different sequences, as shown in Figure 4.11, where the donor list items are sorted by date. You also could sort the data in descending (high to low) sequence according to the donation amount or alphabetically by last name. In descending order the largest amount displays at the top of the list, and the smallest amount appears last. The first row of the table contains the title and the second row contains the field names for each column, so they are not included in the sort. The next 11 rows contain the sorted data; the last row is not included in the sort because it displays the total amount donated.

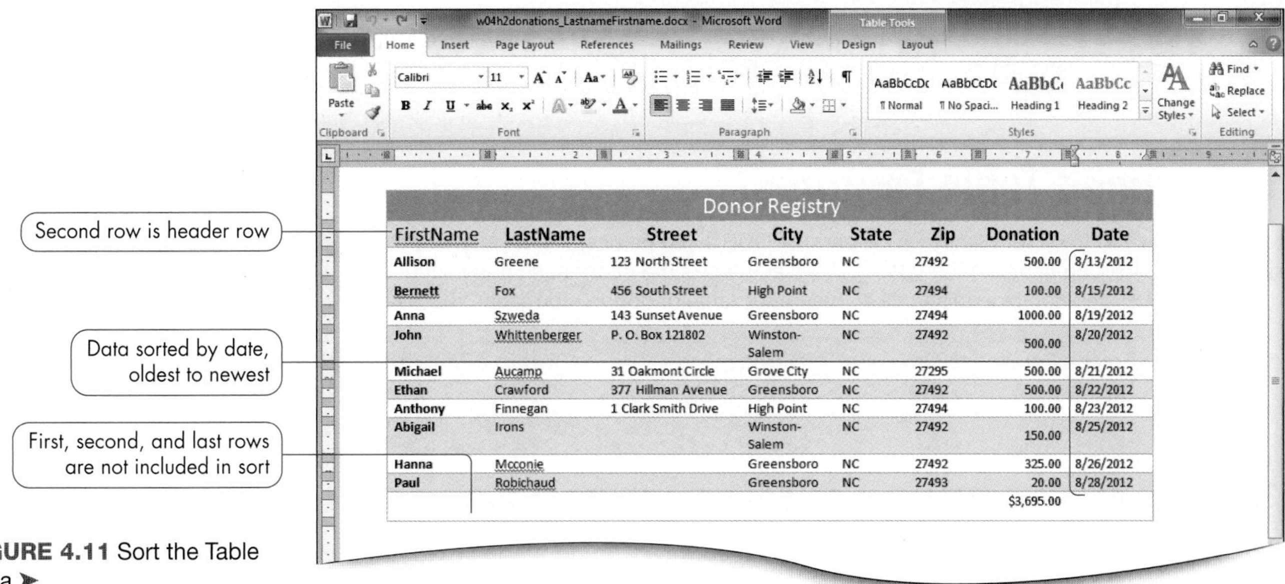

FirstName	LastName	Street	City	State	Zip	Donation	Date
Allison	Greene	123 North Street	Greensboro	NC	27492	500.00	8/13/2012
Bernett	Fox	456 South Street	High Point	NC	27494	100.00	8/15/2012
Anna	Szweda	143 Sunset Avenue	Greensboro	NC	27494	1000.00	8/19/2012
John	Whittenberger	P. O. Box 121802	Winston-Salem	NC	27492	500.00	8/20/2012
Michael	Aucamp	31 Oakmont Circle	Grove City	NC	27295	500.00	8/21/2012
Ethan	Crawford	377 Hillman Avenue	Greensboro	NC	27492	500.00	8/22/2012
Anthony	Finnegan	1 Clark Smith Drive	High Point	NC	27494	100.00	8/23/2012
Abigail	Irons		Winston-Salem	NC	27492	150.00	8/25/2012
Hanna	Mcconie		Greensboro	NC	27492	325.00	8/26/2012
Paul	Robichaud		Greensboro	NC	27493	20.00	8/28/2012
						$3,695.00	

FIGURE 4.11 Sort the Table Data ➤

To perform a sort of data in a table you select the rows that are to be sorted, rows 2 through 12 in this example, and then you click Sort in the Data group on the Layout tab. The Sort dialog box displays, as shown in Figure 4.12, which enables you to select the direction and sort criteria. In this case, you include the second row, which contains field names, and then select the option on the Sort dialog box that indicates your data includes a Header row. When you include the header row and then identify it to the sort program, it displays the header row names in the Sort by list so you can identify your sort criteria easily. Identifying the header row also removes it from the sort.

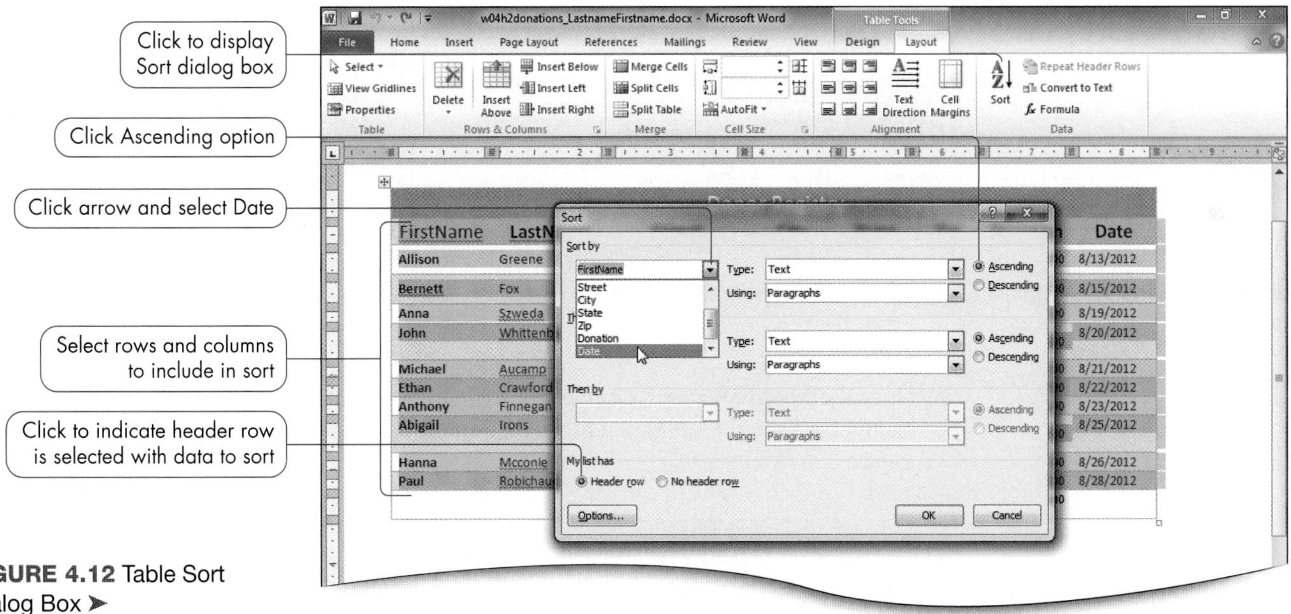

FIGURE 4.12 Table Sort Dialog Box ➤

Converting Text to a Table

The table feature is outstanding, but what if you are given a lengthy list of items that should have been formatted as a table but is currently just text? For example, you have a document containing a list of two items per line separated by a tab, and the list needs to be sorted. The Table command on the Insert tab includes the Convert Text to Table command, and it can aid you in this transformation. After you select the text and choose this command, the Convert Text to Table dialog box displays and offers several options to assist in a quick conversion of text into a table. The command also works in reverse; you can convert a table to text. You will perform a table conversion in the next Hands-On Exercise.

HANDS-ON EXERCISES

2 Advanced Table Features

The information you track for Wacey Rivale and the CDRC can be useful in a variety of ways. To prepare the information for reports and letters, you enhance the table in Word so it sorts the information and includes a row to display the total amount of donations. You also combine this table with another table of donor information that Wacey found on her flash drive.

Skills covered: Enter a Formula to Calculate Total Donations • Convert Text to a Table • Combine Two Tables into One • Sort Data in a Table

STEP 1 ENTER A FORMULA TO CALCULATE TOTAL DONATIONS

It is good to have an estimate of the amount of donations made to the CDRC over a period of time. Wacey would like you to include a row in the table that adds the donations together, and you agree that it can be done quickly and easily using the formula tool for tables. Refer to Figure 4.13 as you complete Step 1.

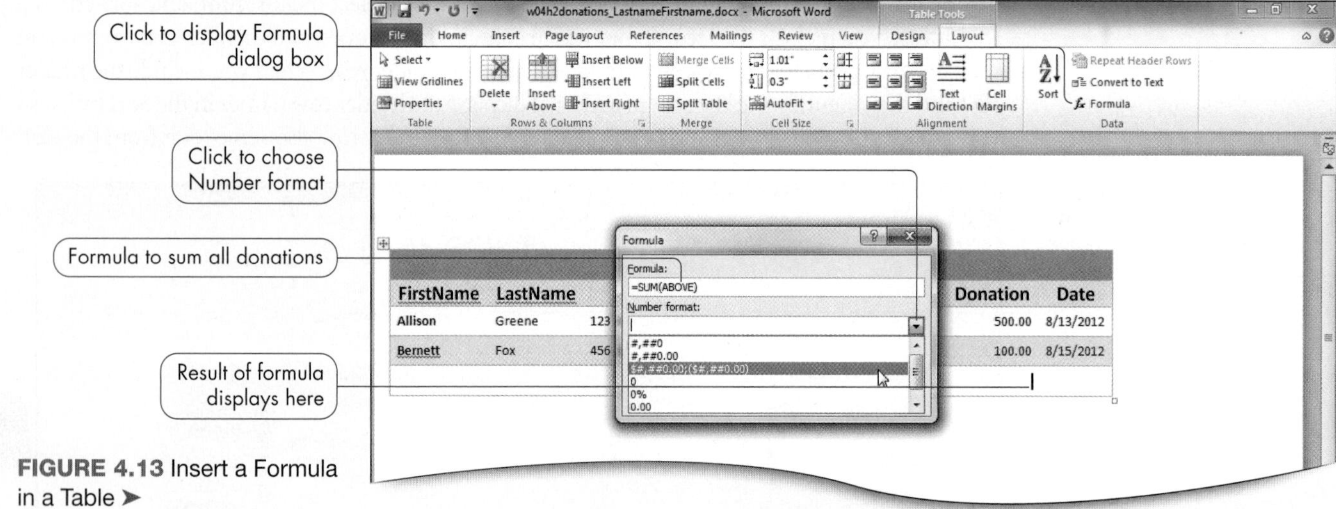

FIGURE 4.13 Insert a Formula in a Table ➤

a. Open the *w04h1donations_LastnameFirstname* document if you closed it after the last Hands-On Exercise, and save it as **w04h2donations_Lastname Firstname**, changing *h1* to *h2*.

> **TROUBLESHOOTING:** If you make any major mistakes in this exercise, you can close the file, open *w04h1donations_LastnameFirstname* again, and then start this exercise over.

b. Click in the last row of the table. Click the **Layout tab**, if necessary, and then click **Insert Below** in the Rows & Columns group.

   You add a new row where you can sum the total amount of donations.

c. Click in **cell G5**, the cell in the seventh column and fifth row. Click **Formula** in the Data group to display the formula box.

   Notice the formula *=SUM(ABOVE)* is entered by default. We can use the default formula because it will add the contents of cells directly above this one. The formula is not case sensitive; you can type formula references in lowercase or capital letters.

d. Click the **Number format arrow**, select **$#,##0.00;($#,##0.00)**, as shown in Figure 4.13, and then click **OK**.

The result of *$600.00* displays in a number format with a dollar sign and two decimal places because these numbers represent a monetary value.

e. Save the document and leave it open.

> **TIP Updating Formula Results**
>
> If you add or remove cells that affect the results of a formula in a table, the formula result will not change automatically. Right-click the formula, and then select Update Field to display the new results.

STEP 2 CONVERT TEXT TO A TABLE

Wacey remembered that she previously saved some raw data about donations received and asks you to put it in a table like the other information. You agree, knowing Word includes a feature for conversions of text to a table. Refer to Figure 4.14 as you complete Step 2.

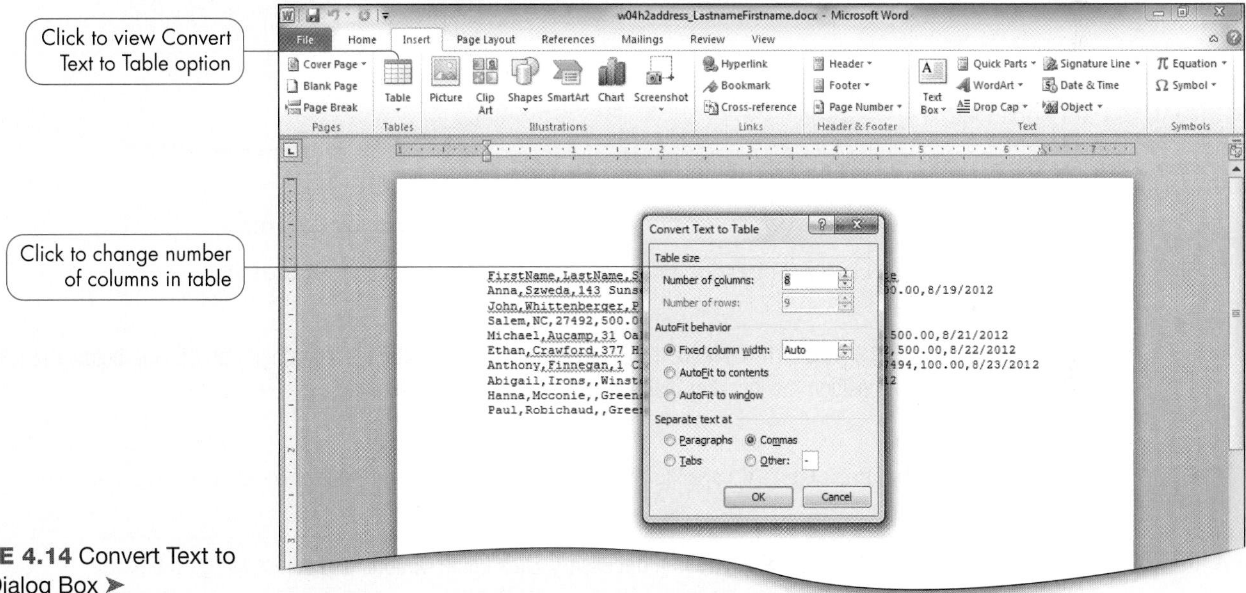

FIGURE 4.14 Convert Text to Table Dialog Box ➤

a. Open *w04h2address* and save it as **w04h2address_LastnameFirstname**.

b. Press **Ctrl+A** to select all text in this document, and then click the **Insert tab**.

c. Click **Table** in the Tables group, and then click **Convert Text to Table**. View the options in the Convert Text to Table dialog box, as shown in Figure 4.14, but do not make any changes at this time. Click **OK**.

The listing of donors and their related information now displays in a table and the commas that separated the data are removed.

d. Press **Ctrl+C** to copy the table to the clipboard.

> **TROUBLESHOOTING:** If you deselect the table after step C, click the Table Move handle to select the entire table, and then perform step D.

e. Save the document.

STEP 3 COMBINE TWO TABLES INTO ONE

Now that you have converted the additional data into a table, you want to combine it with the first table so you can manipulate all the data together. It is not always possible to combine two tables easily, but in this case, you can use Copy and Paste to merge the two tables that contain similar information into one. Refer to Figure 4.15 as you complete Step 3.

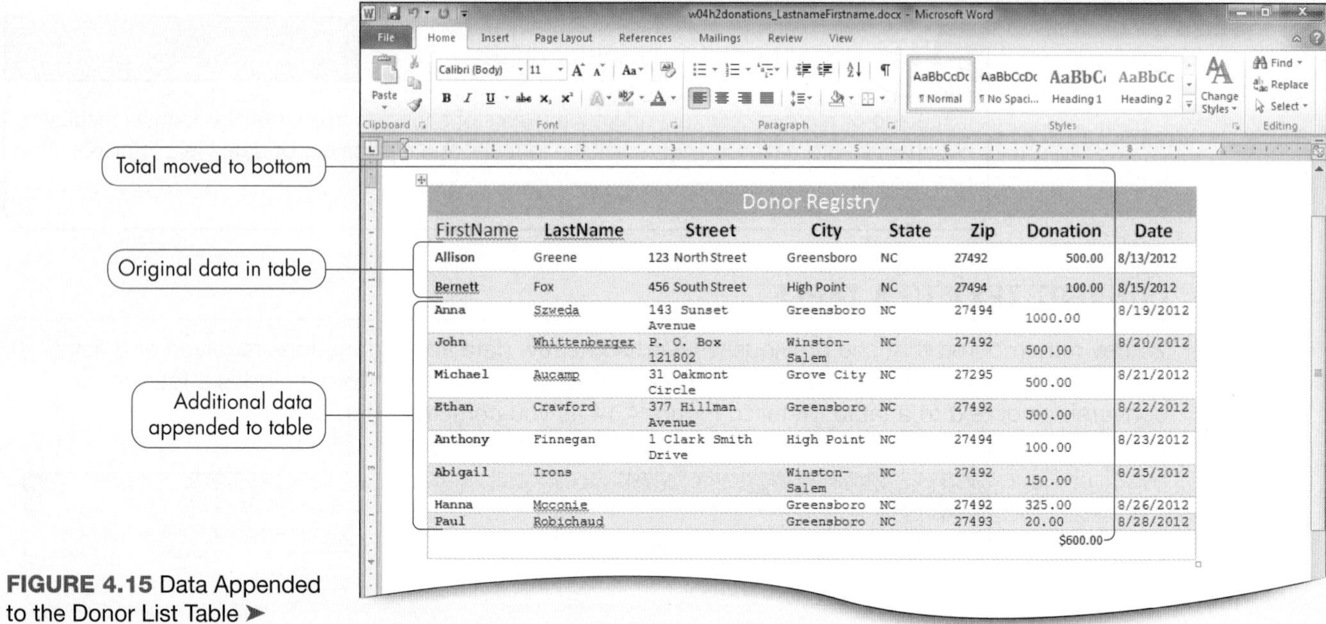

Donor Registry							
FirstName	LastName	Street	City	State	Zip	Donation	Date
Allison	Greene	123 North Street	Greensboro	NC	27492	500.00	8/13/2012
Bernett	Fox	456 South Street	High Point	NC	27494	100.00	8/15/2012
Anna	Szweda	143 Sunset Avenue	Greensboro	NC	27494	1000.00	8/19/2012
John	Whittenberger	P. O. Box 121802	Winston-Salem	NC	27492	500.00	8/20/2012
Michael	Aucamp	31 Oakmont Circle	Grove City	NC	27295	500.00	8/21/2012
Ethan	Crawford	377 Hillman Avenue	Greensboro	NC	27492	500.00	8/22/2012
Anthony	Finnegan	1 Clark Smith Drive	High Point	NC	27494	100.00	8/23/2012
Abigail	Irons		Winston-Salem	NC	27492	150.00	8/25/2012
Hanna	Mcconie		Greensboro	NC	27492	325.00	8/26/2012
Paul	Robichaud		Greensboro	NC	27493	20.00	8/28/2012
						$600.00	

FIGURE 4.15 Data Appended to the Donor List Table ➤

a. Make *w04h2donations_LastnameFirstname* the active document.

b. Place the insertion point on the line immediately below the table.

TROUBLESHOOTING: If you have trouble placing the insertion point on the line below the table, position the insertion point in the last cell of the table and click → two times.

c. Press **Ctrl+V** to paste the rows from the table in the clipboard into this document.

TROUBLESHOOTING: If necessary, click Paste Options and select Merge Table.

Because both tables contained the same number of columns, the copied table appends directly to the existing table, displaying a table with many more rows of donor information. Unfortunately, there is an extra header row which needs to be removed, and the row containing the total line is no longer at the bottom, so you must move it.

d. Select the entire sixth row, which is a repeat of the column headings. Right-click and select **Delete Rows**.

e. Select the entire fifth row, which displays the formula to total the donations. Press **Ctrl+X** to cut the row. Place the insertion point on the line directly below the last row of the table, and then press **Ctrl+V**.

The row now displays at the bottom of the table, but the formula results are the same (as seen in Figure 4.15). Next, you update the formula to reflect the additional donations that now display in the table.

f. Right-click the formula that displays on the last row of the table, and then select **Update Field**.

The new total of *$3,695.00* now displays.

g. Save the document but leave it open for the next step. Close *w04h2address_LastnameFirstname.*

STEP 4 SORT DATA IN A TABLE

The data are combined and you are almost ready to turn the document over to Wacey for review. You know that it will be helpful to display the information sorted by date so she can try to remember the people she visited with on certain occasions. You complete the sort and then make a few last adjustments so the information displays nicely on paper. Refer to Figure 4.16 as you complete Step 4.

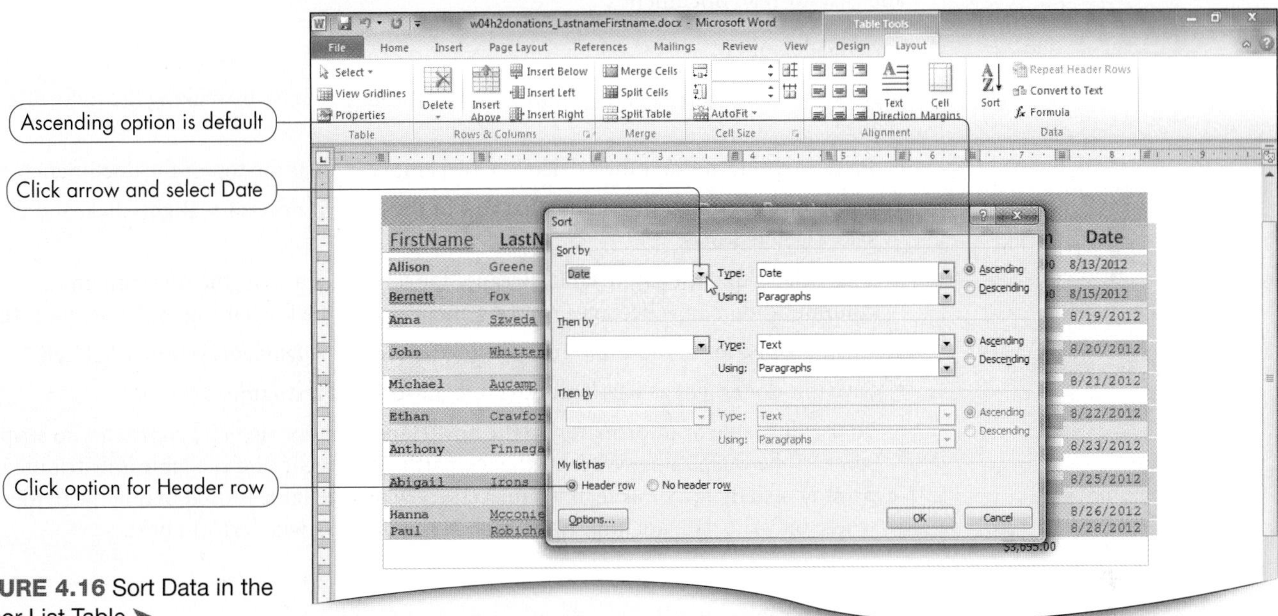

FIGURE 4.16 Sort Data in the Donor List Table ➤

a. Drag to select rows 2 through 12 in the table. That is, select all table rows *except* the first and last row. Click the **Layout tab**, and then click **Sort** in the Data group.

b. Click **Header row** in the *My list has* section, at the bottom of the dialog box.

c. Click the **Sort by arrow**, and then select **Date** (the column heading for the last column). Click **Ascending**, if necessary, and compare your settings to Figure 4.16. Click **OK**.

The entries in the table are rearranged chronologically from the oldest to most recent date of donation.

TROUBLESHOOTING: If you do not first click Header row, the headings for each column will not display in the Sort by list; instead you will see the column numbers listed. You can sort by column number (1, 2, 3, or 4), but it is important to click the Header row option before you leave this dialog box so the header row is not included in the sort.

d. Select **cells G5 through G12** (the donation data from the added table), and then click **Align Center Right** in the Alignment group.

Now the donation amounts for the data appended to this table are aligned with the other amounts that you typed in earlier.

e. Change the font of the newly inserted donors to match the first two donors by completing the following steps:

- Select the rows that contain the data appended to the table, and then right-click to display the Mini toolbar.
- Click the **Font arrow** on the Mini toolbar, and then click **Calibri.**
- Right-click the selected rows again to display the Mini toolbar, if necessary, click the **Font Size arrow**, and then click **11.**

f. Click **Properties** in the Table group.

g. Click the **Table tab**, if necessary, and then click **Center** in the *Alignment* section. Click **OK.** Click anywhere to deselect the table.

Your table is now centered between the left and right margins. This alignment alters the location of the table, but not the data inside the table. It also creates an attractively styled and easy-to-read document.

h. Save the document.

i. Modify the document in preparation for an upcoming exercise by making the following changes:

- Press **Ctrl+Home**, and then delete the two empty lines at the top of the document.
- Place the insertion point on the first row of the table, if necessary. Right-click, and then select **Delete Rows.**

  This deletes the title of the table. Because the table uses a style, the row containing column headers now becomes row one and assumes the formatting of the previous title.
- Click **Properties** in the Table group. Click **Left** in the *Alignment* section. Click **OK.**
- Save this document as **w04h2donortable_LastnameFirstname.**

  To use this table of information in the next Hands-On Exericse, it is necessary to strip out some of the formatting. Whereas the formatting is beneficial if the table is distributed in print or strictly for viewing, it is unnecessary when the table is used in other activities where only the data are important, such as the one you will perform next.

j. Close the document.

Mail Merge

At some point in your personal or professional life, you will need to send the same message to a number of different people. For example, you will send a graduation announcement to all your family and friends, you might send a cover letter with a résumé to several organizations, or you might need to send a letter to a group of customers informing them of an upcoming sale. In each case, you will need to personalize either the letter or the recipient's address on the letter or an envelope. You can use Word's Mail Merge feature to generate these types of documents easily and efficiently. ***Mail merge*** is a process that combines content from a main document and a data source, with the option of creating a new document.

Mail merge is a process that combines content from a main document and a data source.

A **form letter** is a letter you will print or e-mail many times, personalizing each one for the recipient.

Mail merge is used most frequently to create a set of ***form letters***, which are letters you might print or e-mail many times, personalizing or modifying each one for the recipient. When you apply for a job after graduation, you might send the same cover letter to many different companies. You could spend hours personalizing and resaving individual letters, but when you use mail merge, you can update several letters simultaneously and quickly. An example of a mail merge is illustrated in Figures 4.17, 4.18, and 4.19, in which Wacey Rivale has written a letter of appreciation to each person who donated to the CDRC, then merges that letter with her log that contains addresses, donation amount, and dates. When complete, she produces letters addressed to each donor individually.

... you might send the same cover letter to many different companies. You could spend hours personalizing and resaving individual letters, but when you use mail merge, you can update several letters simultaneously and quickly.

In this section, you will learn about the mail merge process by creating a main document and selecting a recipient list. You then will create form letters by combining the information from both sources.

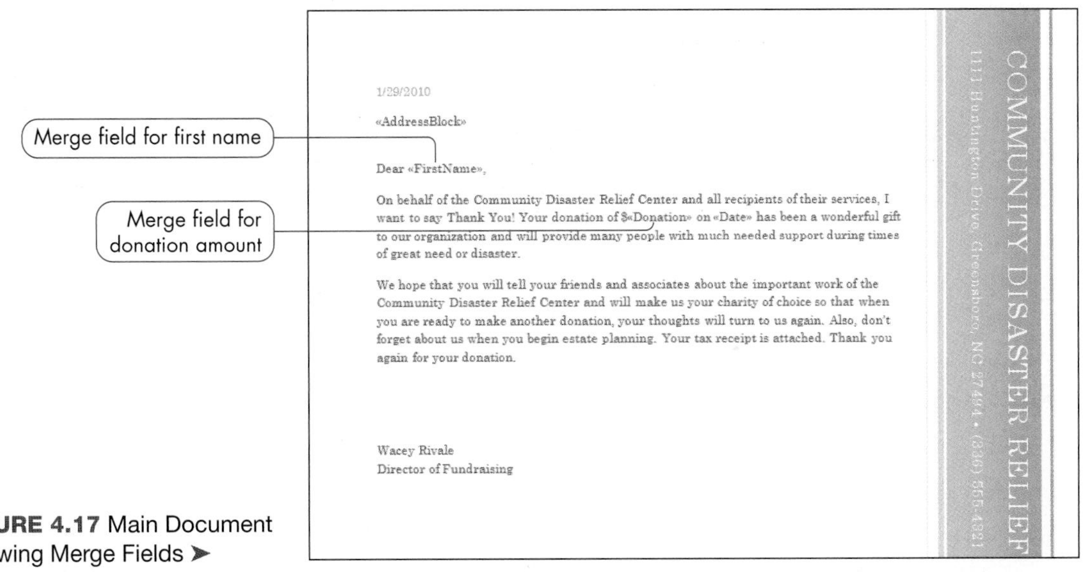

1/29/2010

«AddressBlock»

Dear «FirstName»,

On behalf of the Community Disaster Relief Center and all recipients of their services, I want to say Thank You! Your donation of $«Donation» on «Date» has been a wonderful gift to our organization and will provide many people with much needed support during times of great need or disaster.

We hope that you will tell your friends and associates about the important work of the Community Disaster Relief Center and will make us your charity of choice so that when you are ready to make another donation, your thoughts will turn to us again. Also, don't forget about us when you begin estate planning. Your tax receipt is attached. Thank you again for your donation.

Wacey Rivale
Director of Fundraising

FIGURE 4.17 Main Document Showing Merge Fields ➤

FirstName	LastName	Street	City	State	Zip	Donation	Date
John	Whittenberger	P. O. Box 121802	Winston-Salem	NC	27492	500.00	8/20/2012
Anna	Szweda	143 Sunset Avenue	Greensboro	NC	27494	1000.00	8/19/2012
Paul	Robichaud		Greensboro	NC	27493	20.00	8/28/2012
Hanna	Mcconie		Greensboro	NC	27492	325.00	8/26/2012
Abigail	Irons		Winston-Salem	NC	27492	150.00	8/25/2012
Allison	Greene	123 North Street	Greensboro	NC	27492	500.00	8/13/2012
Bernett	Fox	456 South Street	High Point	NC	27494	100.00	8/15/2012
Anthony	Finnegan	1 Clark Smith Drive	High Point	NC	27494	100.00	8/23/2012
Ethan	Crawford	377 Hillman Avenue	Greensboro	NC	27492	500.00	8/22/2012
Michael	Aucamp	31 Oakmont Circle	Grove City	NC	27295	500.00	8/21/2012

FIGURE 4.18 List of Names, Addresses, and Donations ➤

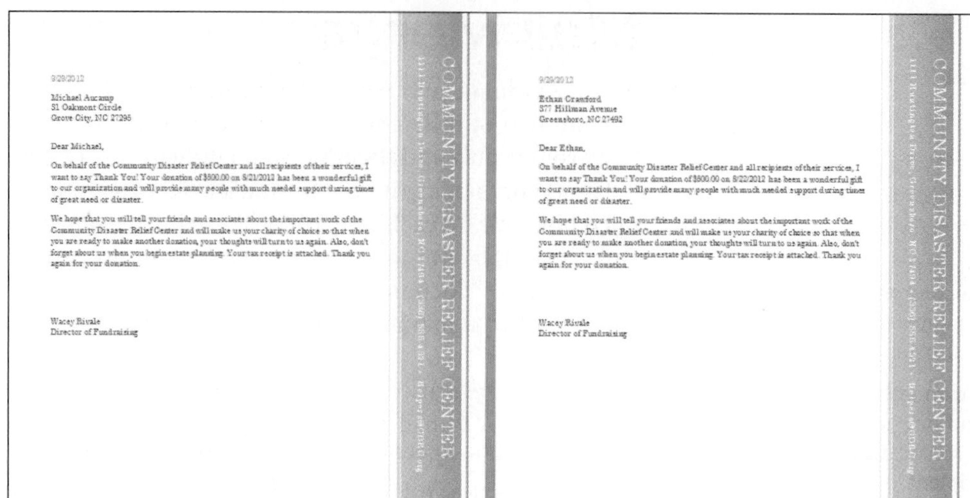

9/29/2012

Michael Aucamp
51 Oakmont Circle
Grove City, NC 27295

Dear Michael,

On behalf of the Community Disaster Relief Center and all recipients of their services, I want to say Thank You! Your donation of $500.00 on 8/21/2012 has been a wonderful gift to our organization and will provide many people with much needed support during times of great need or disaster.

We hope that you will tell your friends and associates about the important work of the Community Disaster Relief Center and will make us your charity of choice so that when you are ready to make another donation, your thoughts will turn to us again. Also, don't forget about us when you begin estate planning. Your tax receipt is attached. Thank you again for your donation.

Wacey Rivale
Director of Fundraising

COMMUNITY DISASTER RELIEF CENTER

9/29/2012

Ethan Cranford
377 Hillman Avenue
Greensboro, NC 27492

Dear Ethan,

On behalf of the Community Disaster Relief Center and all recipients of their services, I want to say Thank You! Your donation of $500.00 on 8/22/2012 has been a wonderful gift to our organization and will provide many people with much needed support during times of great need or disaster.

We hope that you will tell your friends and associates about the important work of the Community Disaster Relief Center and will make us your charity of choice so that when you are ready to make another donation, your thoughts will turn to us again. Also, don't forget about us when you begin estate planning. Your tax receipt is attached. Thank you again for your donation.

Wacey Rivale
Director of Fundraising

COMMUNITY DISASTER RELIEF CENTER

FIGURE 4.19 Merged Form Letters ➤

Selecting a Main Document

The **main document** contains the information that stays the same for all recipients.

A **merge field** serves as a placeholder for data that will be inserted into the main document during the mail merge.

The mail merge process uses two files as input, a main document and a data source; by merging these two files you can create a set of individualized letters, envelopes, e-mails, or other documents. The ***main document***, also known as a source or starting document, contains the information that stays the same for all recipients. The main document also includes one or more ***merge fields*** that serve as placeholders for the variable data that will be inserted into the individual letters, as shown in Figure 4.17.

You can use an existing document as a main document, or you can create one from a blank document. When you click *Start Mail Merge* in the Start Mail Merge group of the Mailings tab, you can choose from several categories to use as your main document. Table 4.3 describes the document types and how they are typically used in a mail merge.

TABLE 4.3 Main Document Types

Document Type	How It Is Typically Used in a Mail Merge
Letters	To send letters to a group after personalizing each letter.
E-Mail Messages	To send e-mail messages to a group of people after personalizing each message.
Envelopes	To print an address on an envelope for each person in the group.
Labels	To print address labels for each person in the group, which can then be attached to an envelope for mailing.
Directory	To create a single document that contains a list of addresses.

A **wizard** makes a process easier by asking a series of questions, then creating a document structure based on your answers.

The last option displayed when you click *Start Mail Merge* is the Step by Step Mail Merge Wizard. A ***wizard*** makes a process easier by asking a series of questions, then creating a customized document structure based on your answers. In this case, the wizard simplifies the process of creating form letters and other types of merge documents through step-by-step directions that appear automatically on the Mail Merge pane. The options for the current step appear in the top portion of the pane and are self-explanatory. Click the link to the next step at the bottom of the pane to move forward in the process, or click the link to the previous step to correct any mistakes you might have made. This is a very easy-to-follow process and helps you work through the mail merge procedure without knowing exactly what you need to click in the Mailings tab.

> **TIP** Printing Mailing Labels or Envelopes
>
> If you want to create mailing labels or envelopes, the Create group on the Mailings tab includes commands that help you select the correct settings. You can use these options to print items that would not necessarily be included in a mail merge, such as a single envelope or a sheet of return address labels.

Selecting or Creating Recipients

After you choose the type of document you will use in a merge, the next step is to create or select a list of recipients. Typically, this is the information you need to insert in an address block, or specific information, such as a company name. A recipient list, sometimes called a ***data source***, contains individual pieces of data and each is known as a ***field***. Common fields in a data source include first name, last name, address, city, state, ZIP code, phone number, and e-mail address. A group of fields for a particular person or thing is called a ***record***. Figure 4.18 demonstrates a sample data source. Your data source might come from:

A **data source** is a listing of information.

A **field** is a single piece of data used in a source document, such as last name.

A **record** is a group of related fields.

- A Word document that contains information stored in a table
- An Access database
- An Excel worksheet
- Your Outlook Contacts

The **header row** is the first row in a data source.

The first row in the data source is called the ***header row*** and identifies the fields in the remaining rows. Each additional row contains a record, and every record contains the same fields in the same order—for example, Title, FirstName, LastName, and so on.

> **TIP** Using a Word Table as a Data Source
>
> When your source data are stored in a table in Word, you can ensure the mail merge will work correctly if you save the table by itself in a separate file with no blank lines above the table. The first row of the table must contain field names. To use your table as a recipient list, click Use Existing List after you click Select Recipients in the Start Mail Merge group on the Mailings tab. Navigate to the location where the document is saved, select the file, and click Open.

If you do not have a preexisting list to use as a data source, you can create one in Word. Click Select Recipients in the Start Mail Merge group of the Mailings tab, and then click Type New List. A New Address List dialog box displays with the most commonly used fields for a mail merge, as shown in Figure 4.20. You can enter data immediately or click Customize Columns to add, delete, or rename the fields to meet your particular needs. When you save, the list is saved as a database file with the .mdb extension.

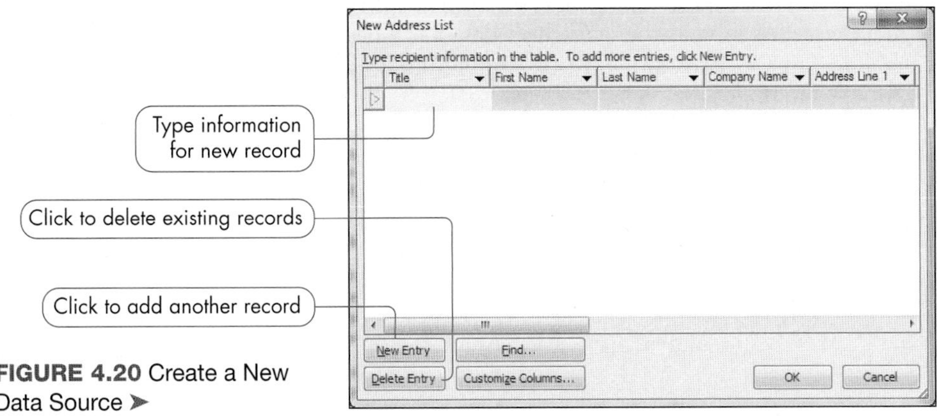

FIGURE 4.20 Create a New Data Source ➤

If you want to add new records to a source file you created in Word, you can click Edit Recipient List in the Start Mail Merge group of the Mailings tab. Note that you can only edit the list after it has been selected as a recipient list for the mail merge. When the Mail Merge Recipients dialog box displays, click the name of the data source, and then click Edit. The Edit Data Source dialog box displays. Click Add New and a blank form displays as the last record, and you can immediately populate the fields with your data (see Figure 4.21).

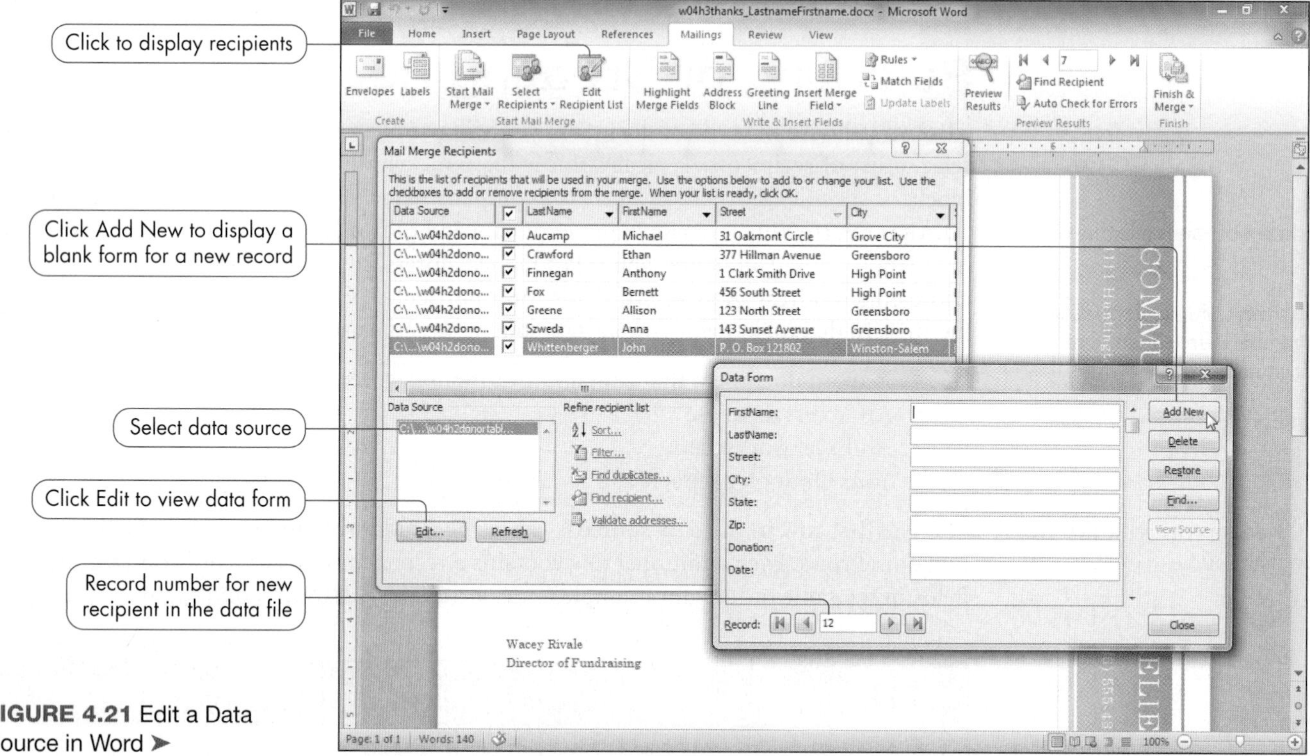

FIGURE 4.21 Edit a Data Source in Word ➤

Using Excel Worksheets as a Data Source

Even though you can create and use data sources in Word, there is a very good probability you will also need to perform a mail merge with a data source that was created and saved in a different Office application such as Access or Excel. The database and spreadsheet applications are designed to organize large amounts of information, so they are perfect candidates to hold the source data you want to use in a mail merge.

The database and spreadsheet applications are designed to organize large amounts of information, so they are perfect candidates to hold the source data you want to use in a mail merge.

An Excel worksheet is comparable to a giant table in Word; it can contain hundreds of rows and columns of data. A manager who must keep track of large amounts of information probably stores it in a spreadsheet, which makes a good candidate for a data source in a mail merge and prevents you from having to retype any data you might want to use in a merge. As long as the worksheet data has a header row, you can use it as a data source in a mail merge. Look at Figure 4.22 and notice how the worksheet displays data suitable for use in a mail merge.

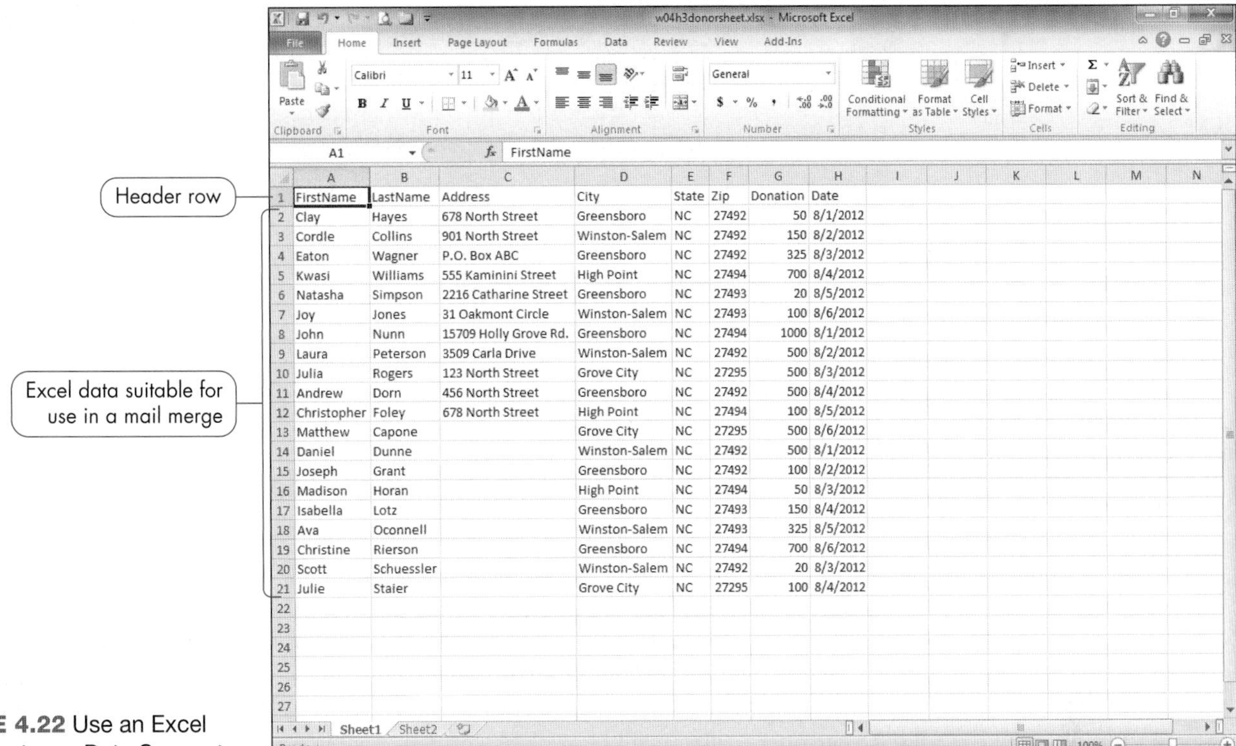

FirstName	LastName	Address	City	State	Zip	Donation	Date
Clay	Hayes	678 North Street	Greensboro	NC	27492	50	8/1/2012
Cordle	Collins	901 North Street	Winston-Salem	NC	27492	150	8/2/2012
Eaton	Wagner	P.O. Box ABC	Greensboro	NC	27492	325	8/3/2012
Kwasi	Williams	555 Kaminini Street	High Point	NC	27494	700	8/4/2012
Natasha	Simpson	2216 Catharine Street	Greensboro	NC	27493	20	8/5/2012
Joy	Jones	31 Oakmont Circle	Winston-Salem	NC	27493	100	8/6/2012
John	Nunn	15709 Holly Grove Rd.	Greensboro	NC	27494	1000	8/1/2012
Laura	Peterson	3509 Carla Drive	Winston-Salem	NC	27492	500	8/2/2012
Julia	Rogers	123 North Street	Grove City	NC	27295	500	8/3/2012
Andrew	Dorn	456 North Street	Greensboro	NC	27492	500	8/4/2012
Christopher	Foley	678 North Street	High Point	NC	27494	100	8/5/2012
Matthew	Capone		Grove City	NC	27295	500	8/6/2012
Daniel	Dunne		Winston-Salem	NC	27492	500	8/1/2012
Joseph	Grant		Greensboro	NC	27492	100	8/2/2012
Madison	Horan		High Point	NC	27494	50	8/3/2012
Isabella	Lotz		Greensboro	NC	27493	150	8/4/2012
Ava	Oconnell		Winston-Salem	NC	27493	325	8/5/2012
Christine	Rierson		Greensboro	NC	27494	700	8/6/2012
Scott	Schuessler		Winston-Salem	NC	27492	20	8/3/2012
Julie	Staier		Grove City	NC	27295	100	8/4/2012

FIGURE 4.22 Use an Excel Worksheet as a Data Source ➤

To merge a Word document with data stored in Excel, click Select Recipients in the Start Mail Merge group on the Mailings tab, and then click Use Existing List. When the Select Data Source dialog box opens, browse to the location where the Excel worksheet is stored, click the file name, and then click Open. Excel worksheets have the extension .xlsx (or .xls if an older version), so you might need to change the type of file in the *Files of type* box at the bottom of the window.

Using Access Databases as a Data Source

A **database table** is a collection of related records that contain fields to organize data.

Access is a database program, and databases are designed to store large amounts of data. Information in a database is stored in tables. A ***database table*** is a collection of related records that contain fields to organize data. Access also includes features that enable you to query the database tables so you can extract and view only data that meet your search criteria. Figure 4.23 provides a look at a database file. Because database files can contain so much data, it is advisable to use the query feature to narrow down the data to only that which will be needed in the mail merge. Filtering the data from the database is much more efficient and easier than sorting and deleting unwanted pages in a Word document after a mail merge.

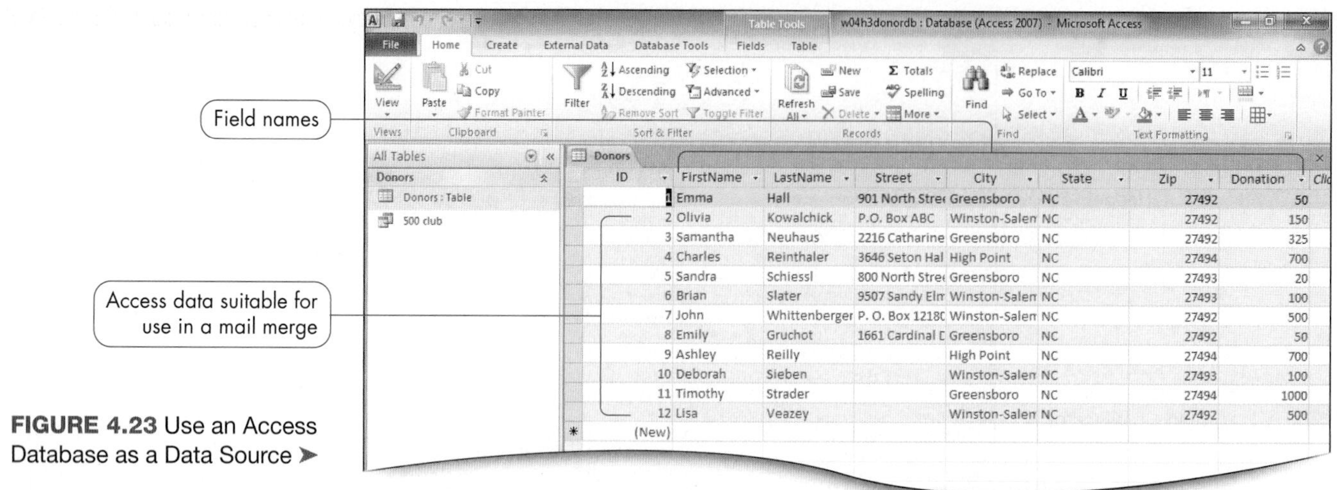

FIGURE 4.23 Use an Access Database as a Data Source ➤

The process of selecting recipients from a database for use in a mail merge is the same as in Excel. However, when you merge a Word document with an Access database, you can select to use a table or a query as the source of your data. If a database includes queries, the query names will display in the Select Table dialog box along with any tables it contains, as shown in Figure 4.24. When you select to use the query as a data source, only records that meet the query criteria will be available for your mail merge. This can be beneficial if you are certain all the data you need is extracted by that query, but it can limit your data and omit necessary records if the query is too restrictive.

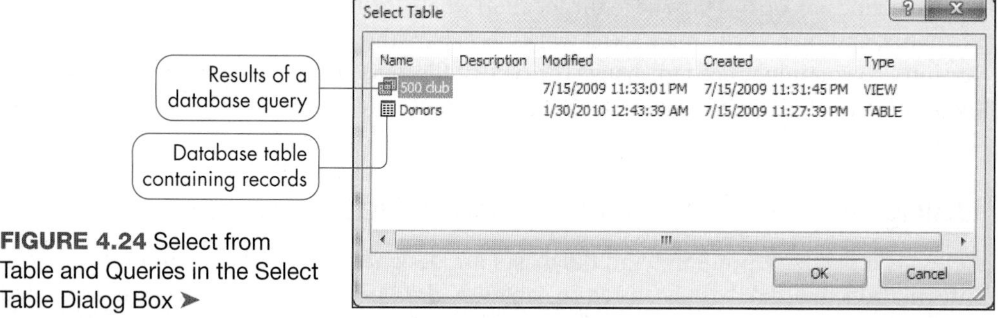

FIGURE 4.24 Select from Table and Queries in the Select Table Dialog Box ➤

Access database files have the extension .accdb (or .mdb if an older version). A database uses field names to classify the data it contains, which makes it very compatible for a mail merge. However, the Access file you use as a data source might not use the same field names as Word expects; for example, a database may use LNAME as a field name instead of LastName. In this situation, you can use the Match Fields command to create a link between the Word document fields and the Access database fields. After you select the recipient list for your mail merge, click Match Fields to display a list of fields that Word often uses and a list of the fields found in the data source. You can then select a database field that matches the required fields in Word.

Sorting and Filtering Records in a Data Source

Before merging the data source with the main document, you might want to rearrange the records in the data source. For example, you might want to sort the data source in alphabetical order by last name, or in descending order by sales, if included. If you have a large number of form letters to send, you can receive a discount at the post office if you follow certain procedures. One procedure is to sort the letters by ZIP code. You can save a lot of work hours if you sort the data source before merging instead of after merging and printing. When you click Edit Recipient List in the Start Mail Merge group on the Mailings tab to display the Mail

Merge Recipients dialog box, several options offer a variety of methods to sort the source data, as shown in Figure 4.25.

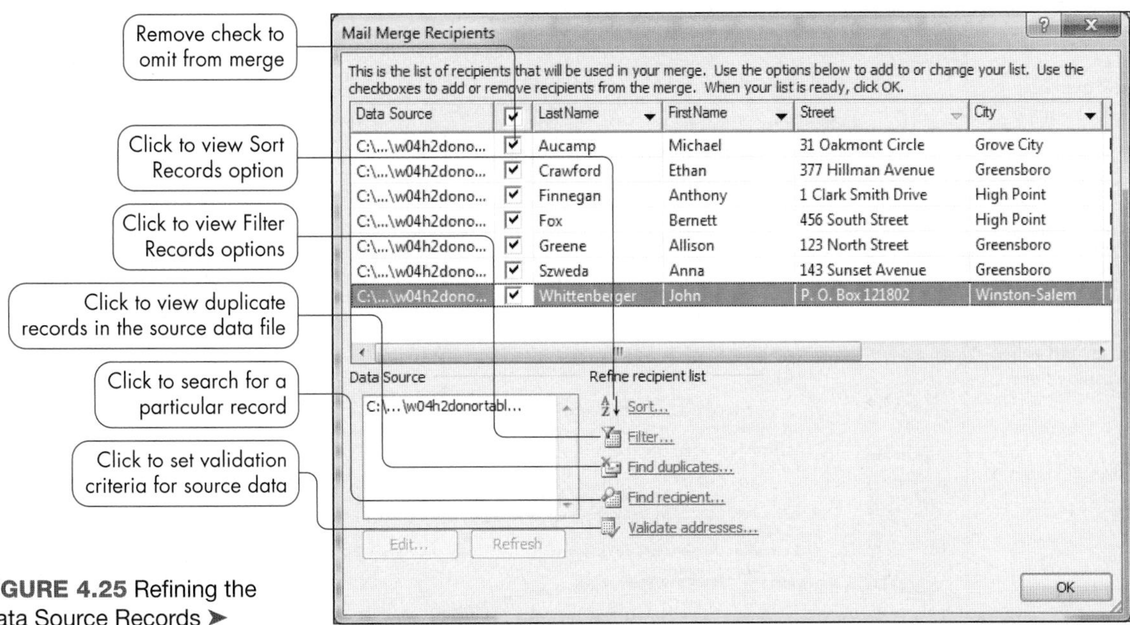

FIGURE 4.25 Refining the Data Source Records ➤

A **filter** specifies criteria for including records that meet certain conditions.

When you click Sort or Filter, the Filter and Sort dialog box displays and enables you to perform more complex sorts. The Filter Records tab enables you to ***filter***, or specify criteria for including records that meet certain conditions during the merge process. For example, you may want to filter the source data by state so only companies in the state of California are included in the mail merge.

The Sort Records tab enables you to specify up to three levels for sorting records. For example, you can first sort by state, further sort by city within state, and finally sort by last name within city (see Figure 4.26).

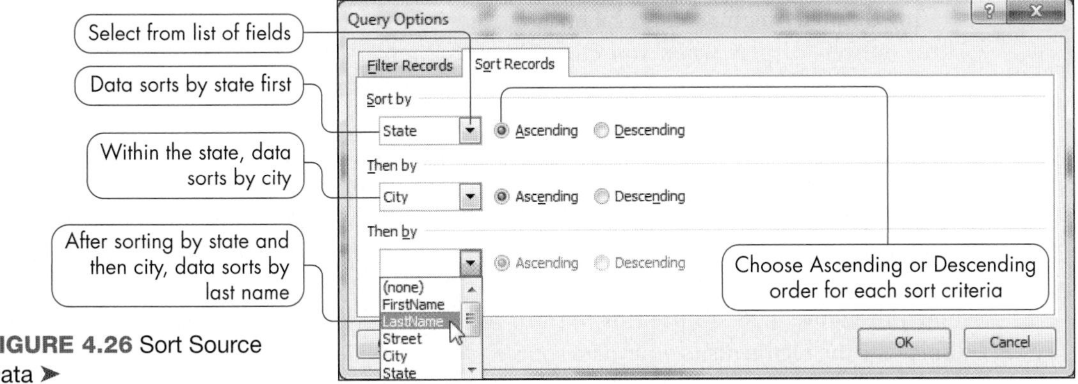

FIGURE 4.26 Sort Source Data ➤

Inserting Merge Fields

When you write a letter or set up your e-mail in preparation for a mail merge, you insert a merge field in the main document. The merge field is a placeholder that specifies where information from the data source will display in the main document. Because it corresponds with a field in the data source, matching the two fields guarantees that the right data will be inserted into the main document when you complete the merge. View Figure 4.17 again to view the merge fields that correspond to the fields in the source document in Figure 4.18.

The merge fields display in the main document within angle brackets, for example <<AddressBlock>>, <<FirstName>>, or <<Donation>>. These entries are not typed explicitly but are entered automatically when you select one of the source data fields that display when you click Insert Merge Field from the Write & Insert Fields group of the Mailings tab. (See Figure 4.27.)

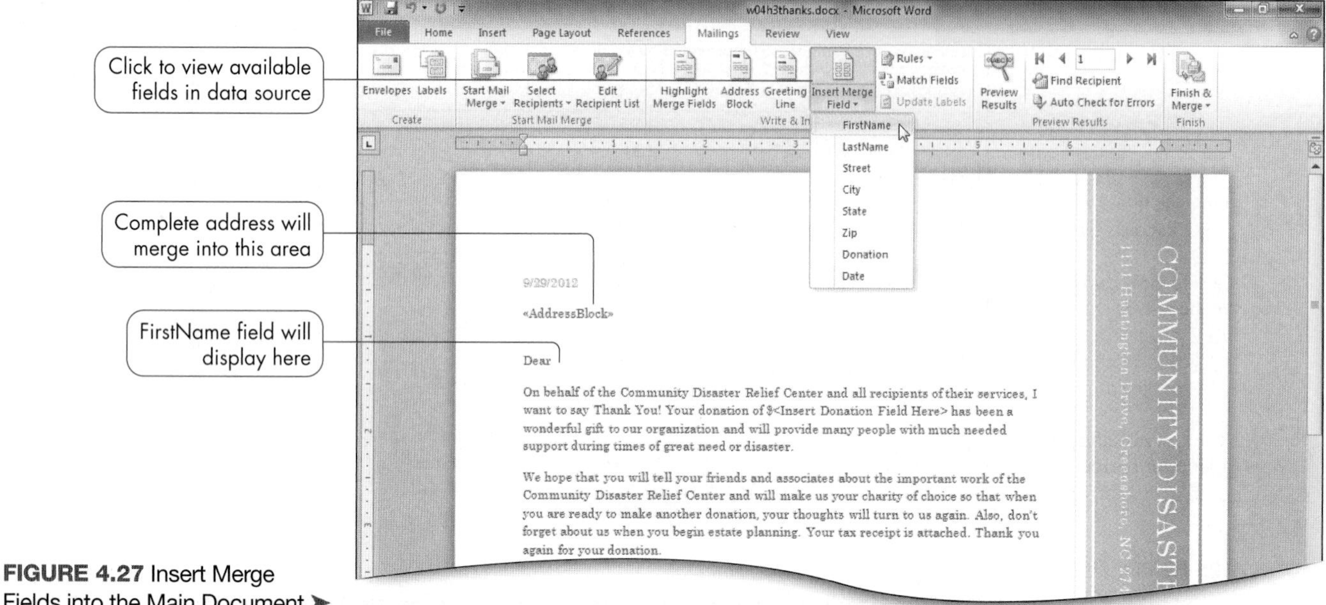

FIGURE 4.27 Insert Merge Fields into the Main Document ➤

Merging a Main Document and a Data Source

After you create the main document and identify the source data, you are ready to begin the merge process. The merge process examines each record in the data source, and when a match is found, it replaces the merge field in the main document with the information from the data source. A copy of the main document is created for each record in the data source, thus creating individual form letters, for example. Figure 4.19 displays two of the personalized letters after a mail merge.

To complete the merge, click Finish & Merge in the Finish group on the Mailings tab. Three options display when you click Finish & Merge: *Edit Individual Documents*, *Print Documents*, and *Send E-mail Messages*. To create a new document that contains the results of the merge, you should select Edit Individual Documents. This enables you to preview each page of the merged documents prior to saving or printing. If you select Print Documents, you will have the opportunity to specify which pages to print; however, you cannot preview the document prior to printing. To conserve paper, you should choose *Edit Individual Documents* and use Print Preview before you print. The last option, *Send E-mail Messages*, enables you to make selections and complete the e-mail information prior to sending, as shown in Figure 4.28. To use this option, you must have an e-mail field where addresses display for the recipients in your data source.

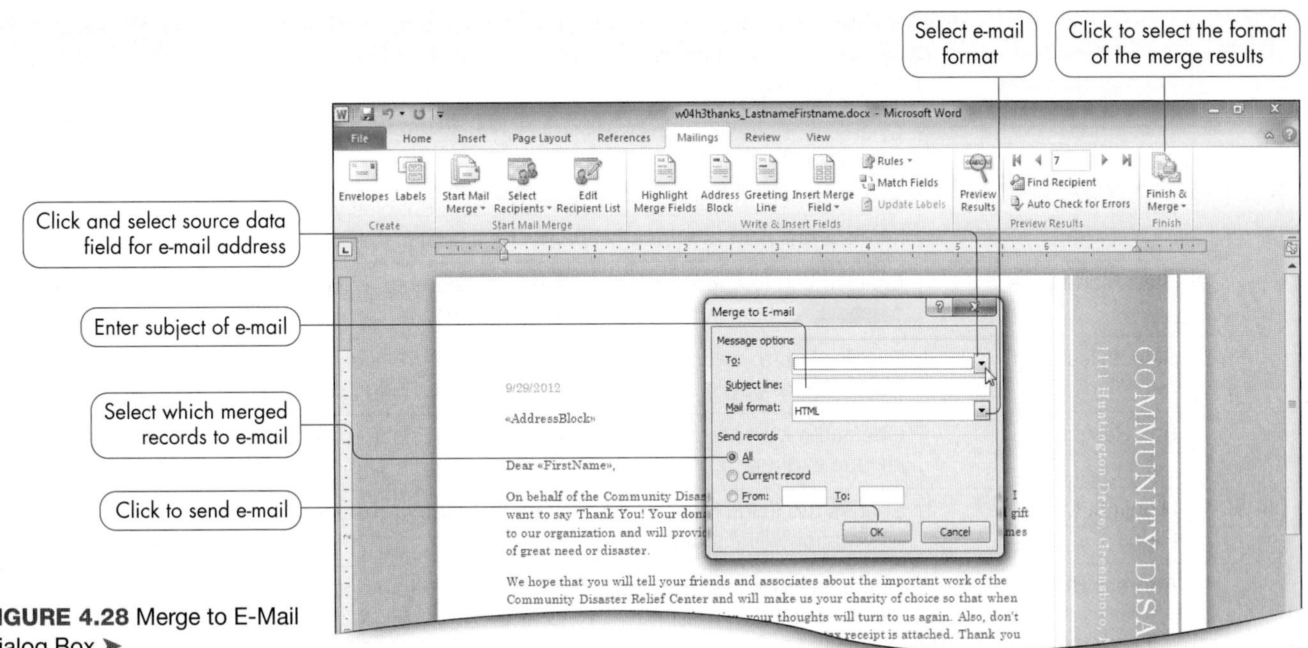

FIGURE 4.28 Merge to E-Mail Dialog Box ➤

The same data source can be used to create multiple sets of form documents. You could, for example, create a marketing campaign in which you send an initial letter to the entire list, and then send follow-up letters at periodic intervals to the same mailing list. Alternatively, you could filter the original mailing list to include only a subset of names, such as the individuals who responded to the initial letter. You could also create a different set of documents, such as envelopes or e-mail messages.

If you want to generate a list from the source data, you can use a Directory mail merge. Select Directory as your source document type and Word will merge all the source data onto the same page instead of merging each record onto a separate page.

The Mail Merge feature is exciting, yet a bit complex. Use Table 4.4 to acquaint yourself with the commands on the Mailings tab. Once you successfully complete a mail merge, you will enjoy finding ways to use it over and over!

TABLE 4.4 Mail Merge Commands

Icon	Command Name	Description
	Envelopes	Opens the Envelopes and Labels dialog box. Enables you to insert recipient and return address information.
	Labels	Opens the Envelopes and Labels dialog box. Enables you to insert an address for labels and select to print a full page of the same label or a single label.
	Start Mail Merge	Enables you to choose the type of main document, such as letters or envelopes, to create. Enables you to use Mail Merge Wizard.
	Select Recipients	Enables you to select the data source file that you want to open and use with the main document or opens a New Address List dialog box to create a data source.
	Edit Recipient List	Opens the Mail Merge Recipients dialog box. Enables you to sort or select records to include in a merge. Also enables you to add, edit, and delete the data source records.
	Highlight Merge Fields	Shades the fields in the main document so you can quickly see where the merged information will display.
	Address Block	Opens the Insert Address Block dialog box. Enables you to choose the formats for the inside address.
	Greeting Line	Opens the Greeting Line dialog box. Enables you to choose the level of formality for the salutation.
	Insert Merge Field	Opens the Insert Merge Field dialog box. Enables you to select and insert fields in the main document.
	Rules	Displays decision-making criteria to increase your options for filtering records.
	Match Fields	Opens the Match Fields dialog box. Enables you to select fields from another data source, such as an Access database table, to match with required fields in Word.
	Update Labels	Copies the merge fields from the first label to the other labels.
	Preview Results	Displays the data from the data source in the respective fields in the main document so that you can verify correct placement.
	First Record	Displays the first merged record. Works with Preview Results.
	Previous Record	Displays the previous merged record. Works with Preview Results.
1	Go to Record	Enables you to enter the number of a specific record to go to.
	Next Record	Displays the next merged record. Works with Preview Results.
	Last Record	Displays the last merged record. Works with Preview Results.
	Find Recipient	Opens the Find Entry dialog box. Enables you to find data in a specific field or in all fields.
	Auto Check for Errors	Enables you to check for errors and report those errors during the merge process.
	Finish & Merge	Enables you to choose how to display or process the results of the mail merge.

HANDS-ON EXERCISES

3 Mail Merge

Wacey Rivale always sends a letter of gratitude to the people who have donated to the CDRC. You will use an existing letter as the main document and use the table you recently created as a recipient list in a mail merge process, which makes sending letters quick and easy. Wacey later finds more donor information, created in Excel and Access, which you also use to generate letters. Lastly, you create mailing labels for the letters.

Skills covered: Start the Mail Merge Process and Select a Recipient List • Complete the Main Document • Complete the Mail Merge and View Results • Use an Excel Spreadsheet Recipient List • Use an Access Database Recipient List • Use Mail Merge Wizard to Create Mailing Labels

STEP 1 START THE MAIL MERGE PROCESS AND SELECT A RECIPIENT LIST

You open the letter of gratitude to use as a source document in the mail merge process. Then you must select recipient information, which includes address and amount received from each donor. The document that contains the table of donor information you created recently will work perfectly in this process. Refer to Figure 4.29 as you complete Step 1.

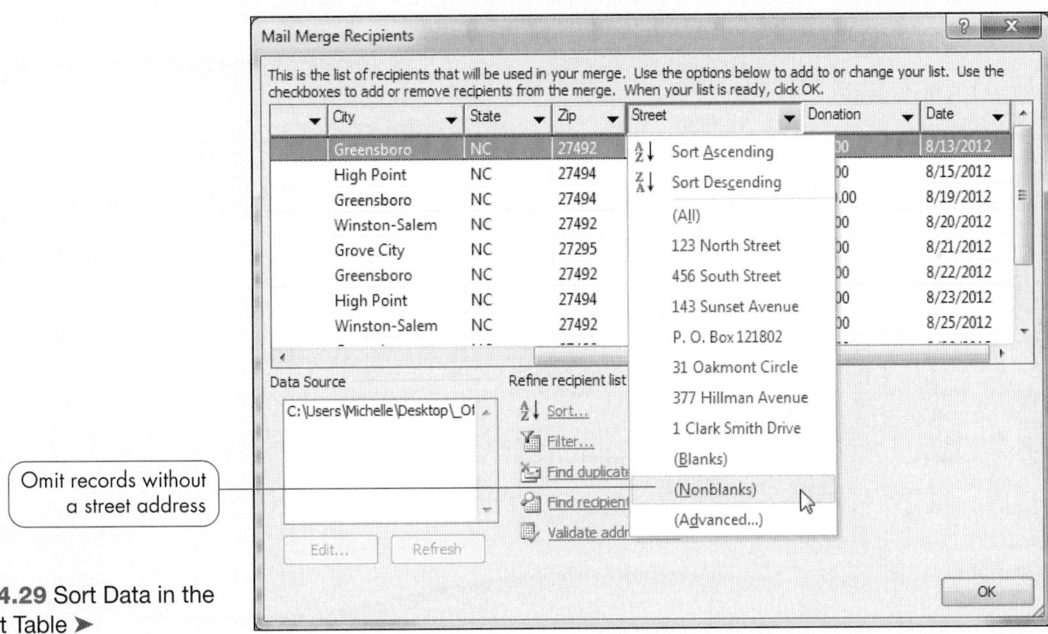

FIGURE 4.29 Sort Data in the Donor List Table ➤

a. Open *w04h3thanks*, and then save it as **w04h3thanks_LastnameFirstname**.

   The document contains a letter that you will mail to the people who have donated to the CDRC.

b. Click the **Mailings tab**, click **Start Mail Merge** in the Start Mail Merge group, and then click **Letters**.

   You are telling Word that this document onscreen is the main document you are using for the mail merge operation.

c. Click **Select Recipients** in the Start Mail Merge group, and then click **Use Existing List**. Navigate to the location where you store your documents, and then select *w04h2donortable_LastnameFirstname.*

   This is the last document you created in Hands-On Exercise 2, which contains the donor information in a table with no title row.

d. Click **Edit Recipient List** in the Start Mail Merge group.

   The Mail Merge Recipients dialog box opens and displays information about donors. It also provides features you use later, such as sort and filter.

e. Filter and sort the data used in the mail merge by completing the following steps:
   - Scroll to the right to view more columns.
   - Click the **Street arrow**, and then click (**Nonblanks**), as shown in Figure 4.29.
   - Click **Sort**.
   - Click the **Sort by arrow**, and then select **LastName**. Click **OK** to close the Query Options dialog box.
   - Click **OK** to close the Mail Merge Recipients dialog box.

   When the process is complete, letters will only be generated to people for whom Wacey has an address. When printed, the letters will be sorted by the donor's last name. This simplifies the process of matching letters with tax receipts before mailing.

f. Save the document.

STEP 2 COMPLETE THE MAIN DOCUMENT

Now you need to update the source of your mail merge, the letter of gratitude, to include placeholders for the information that it pulls in from the recipient list. You want to include the donor address, name, amount of donation, and date of donation. Refer to Figure 4.30 as you complete Step 2.

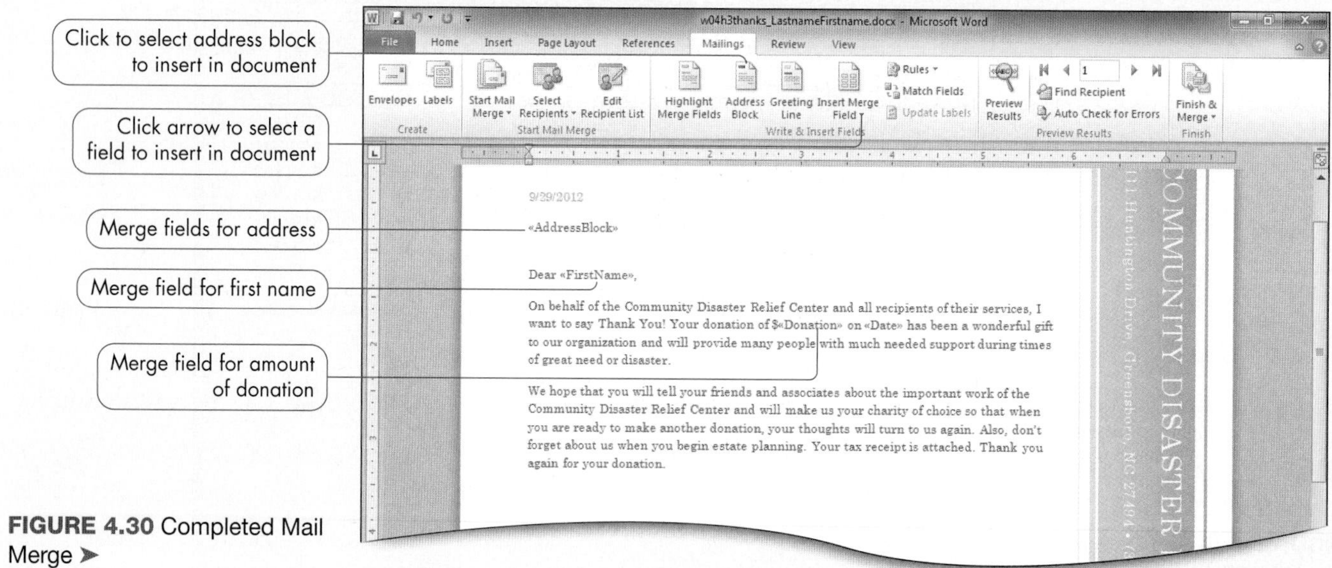

FIGURE 4.30 Completed Mail Merge ➤

a. Click **Pick the Date**, click the arrow, and then click **Today**.

b. Insert the address by completing the following steps:
   - Place the insertion point on the left side of the text *Insert Name and.*
   - Click **Address Block** in the Write & Insert Fields group. Look at the address in the Preview panel.

     Notice the first and last name display on the first line and the city, state, and ZIP display on the second line. The street address does not display, which is not correct. This is a problem with matching the names of the fields in the main letter and the source document which holds the recipient information.
   - Click **Match Fields** in the bottom-right corner of the Insert Address Block dialog box.
   - Locate *Address 1* in the column that displays fields in the Required for Address Block column.
   - Click the **Address 1 arrow**, and then click **Street**.

- Click **OK** to close the Match Fields dialog box.

  In the Preview window, the address displays for the first recipient, *Michael Aucamp.*
- Click **Next** (an arrow pointing right) in the *Preview* section of the Insert Address Block dialog box.

  The entry for *Ethan Crawford* displays in the *Preview* section of the dialog box.
- Click **OK** to close the Address Block dialog box.

  The AddressBlock field displays in the document.

c. Select and delete the three lines that display *Insert Name and, Street and, City, ST, ZIP fields Here.*

d. Insert a salutation by completing the following steps:

- Click one time to position the cursor on the left side of *Insert Greeting Line here.* Type **Dear** and press the **spacebar**.
- Click the **Insert Merge Field arrow** in the Write & Insert group.
- Click **FirstName**. Press **,** to display a comma after the name.
- Delete the text *Insert Greeting Line here* from that line.

  The merge fields show the recipient's first name in the salutation line.

e. Insert the donation date and amount in the letter for each person by completing the following steps:

- Select the text *<Insert Donation Field Here>* in the second line of the first paragraph.

TROUBLESHOOTING: If you find it difficult to drag to select the exact text and symbols to remove from this paragraph, position the insertion point at the left edge of the text, hold down Shift, and then press and hold → until all text is selected.

- Click **Insert Merge Field.**
- Click **Donation**, click **Insert**, and then click **Close**.
- Press **Spacebar**, type **on**, and then press **Spacebar**.
- Click the **Insert Merge Field arrow**.
- Click **Date.**

  The placeholder for donation and date displays in the paragraph, as shown in Figure 4.30. You now know two different ways to insert the individual fields into the main document.

f. Save the document.

STEP 3 COMPLETE THE MAIL MERGE AND VIEW RESULTS

You preview the final product before completing the mail merge, just to be sure you inserted the information correctly and included spaces where needed so words do not run together. Then you complete the merge and display the letters in a new document in which you can make individual edits if needed. Refer to Figure 4.31 as you complete Step 3.

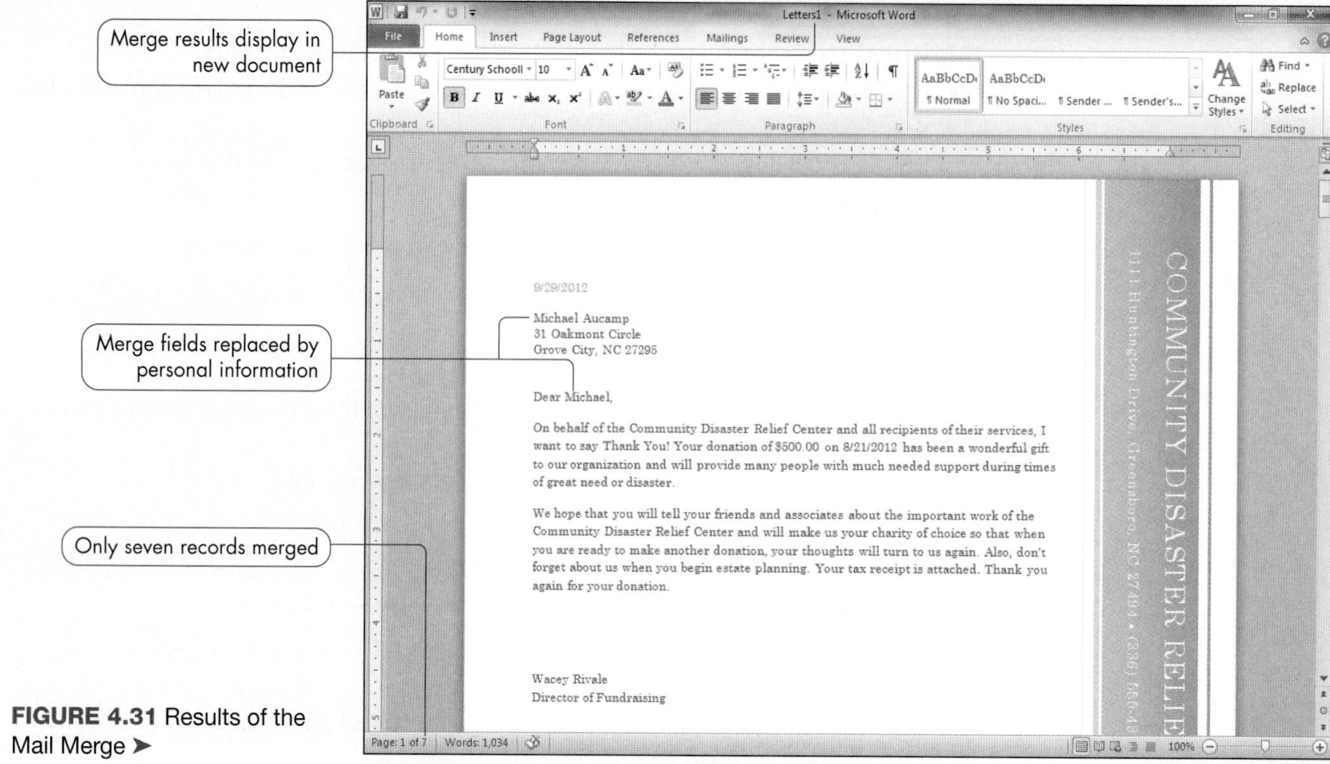

FIGURE 4.31 Results of the Mail Merge ➤

a. Click **Preview Results** in the Preview Results group. Click **Last Record** to preview the letter addressed to *John Whittenberger.*

You can navigate from record to record or specify a record to preview using the First Record, Previous Record, Go To Record, Next Record, and Last Record navigational commands in the Preview Results group on the Mailings tab.

b. Click **Preview Results** to return to the letter and view the mail merge fields.

The Preview Results command is a toggle that alternates between the original source document and a preview of the final documents.

c. Click **Finish & Merge** in the Finish group, and then click **Edit Individual Documents.** Click **OK** to merge all records with the letter.

The letter merges with the recipients and displays in a completely new document, as shown in Figure 4.31. Scroll through the new document and view the seven pages, one for each letter.

d. Press **Ctrl+S** to display the Save As dialog box, and then save the merged letters as **w04h3letters_LastnameFirstname.**

e. Save and close all documents.

STEP 4 USE AN EXCEL SPREADSHEET RECIPIENT LIST

Wacey has found another list of donor information which was stored in an Excel spreadsheet. You tell her you can print another set of letters with this information because the letter you use in the mail merge can be modified to use information from a different source or recipient list, such as a spreadsheet, just as easily as a Word table. Refer to Figure 4.32 as you complete Step 4.

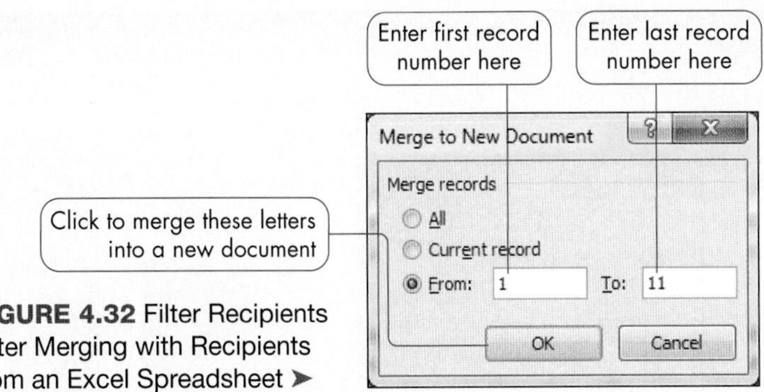

FIGURE 4.32 Filter Recipients After Merging with Recipients from an Excel Spreadsheet ➤

a. Open *w04h3thanks_LastnameFirstname*, and then click **Yes** if a screen displays the message *Opening this document will run the following SQL command.*

b. Click the **Mailings tab**, click **Select Recipients**, and then click **Use Existing List**.

   The Select Data Source dialog box displays.

c. Navigate to the location of your data files, select *w04h3donorsheet.xlsx*, and then click **Open**. When the Select Table dialog box displays, click **OK**.

d. Click **Preview Results** to view the first merged letter. Click **Last Record** to view the last letter.

   The last letter is number 20. Notice that there is no street address for that record. You do not want to print letters to people for whom addresses are unknown. You can do a manual filter when you complete the final merge step.

e. Click **Previous Record** again until you determine which letter has the last complete address.

   You find that the 11th letter has a complete address displaying.

f. Click **Finish & Merge**, and then click **Edit Individual Documents**. Click **From**, type **1** in the first box, and then type **11** in the second box, as shown in Figure 4.32. Click **OK**.

   You create a new document that contains letters for only the first 11 individuals in the recipient list.

g. Save the new file as **w04h3exletters_LastnameFirstname** and close the document. Leave *w04h3thanks_LastnameFirstname* open for the next step.

STEP 5 ➤ USE AN ACCESS DATABASE RECIPIENT LIST

Just as you finish the second mail merge, Wacey runs in to tell you she found another file that contains donor information. However, this list is in an Access database. You assure her that Word accepts Access tables and queries as source data too, so with one more round of mail merge, more letters will be ready today. Refer to Figure 4.33 as you complete Step 5.

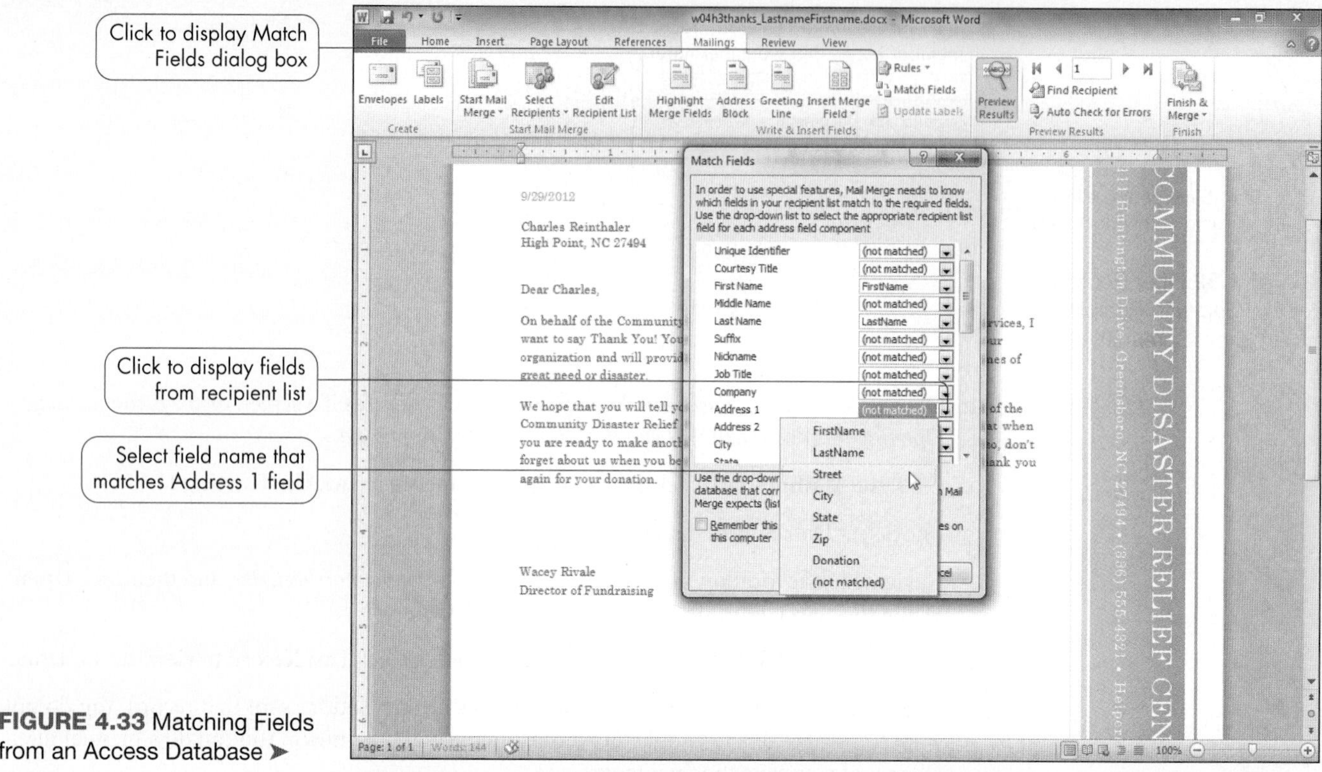

FIGURE 4.33 Matching Fields from an Access Database ➤

a. Click **Select Recipients** in the Start Mail Merge group, and then click **Use Existing List**.

b. Navigate to the location of your data files, select *w04h3donordb.accdb*, and then click **Open**. When the Select Table dialog box displays, click **OK** to select the data in a query named *500 club*.

   The Access database file contains a table of data, but it also includes a query created to extract specific information from the table. In this case, the query displays only patrons who donated more than $500.

> **TROUBLESHOOTING:** If you click the Donors table in the Select Table dialog box by mistake, you can repeat steps a and b to select the 500 Club query. You can use the Donors table for the merge, but you will have more fields to select from than you have in the 500 Club query.

c. Click **Remove Field** in the Invalid Merge Field dialog box.

   An Invalid Merge Field dialog box displays because your letter includes a merge field for date (of donation) and the data in the query does not have a match for the field. Since that information is not available, you will remove the merge field in the source document (the letter).

d. Click **Preview Results**, if necessary, to view the first merged letter.

   Notice you are viewing the letter to Charles Reinthaler but the address block does not include a street address. Next, you check for unmatched fields between the query and the letter.

e. Click **Match Fields** in the Write & Insert Fields group. Click the **Address 1 arrow**, select **Street** (shown in Figure 4.33), and then click **OK**.

f. Click **Next Record**, and then click **Previous Record** in the Preview Results group.

   Now the complete address for Charles Reinthaler displays.

g. Delete the word *on* and the space that follows it from the second sentence in the first paragraph.

   Since you are no longer displaying the date of the donation, the sentence must be corrected.

h. Ensure the letter is only mailed to people for whom we have a complete mailing address by completing the following steps:
   - Click **Edit Recipient List** in the Start Mail Merge group.
   - Click **Filter** to display the Filter and Sort dialog box.
   - Click the **Filter Records tab**, if necessary.
   - Click the **Field arrow**, and then select **Street**.
   - Click the **Comparison arrow**, and then select **Not equal to**.
   - Click **OK** to close the dialog box. Click **OK** to close the Mail Merge Recipients dialog box.

     You have set a filter so any record containing blanks in the address field will not be used in the mail merge. Only two records meet all criteria.

i. Click **Finish & Merge** in the Finish group, click **Edit Individual Documents**, click **All**, and then click **OK**.

   In a new document, two letters display.

j. Save the new document as **w04h3acletter_LastnameFirstname**, and then close it. Close *w04h3thanks_LastnameFirstname* without saving, but do not exit Word.

TIP Saving Merged Letters

Typically, you only save the original documents and recipient lists used in a mail merge. The document that contains the individual letters as a result of the mail merge is usually printed and mailed. You save the merged documents in this exercise so you can submit them to your instructor, if necessary.

STEP 6 USE MAIL MERGE WIZARD TO CREATE MAILING LABELS

Wacey is hoping you can help with one last request—she needs to send out the first set of letters today. If you can create mailing labels to put on the envelopes, it will prevent another assistant from having to address envelopes manually. You agree to do it because creating labels is as easy as generating a letter. Refer to Figure 4.34 as you complete Step 6.

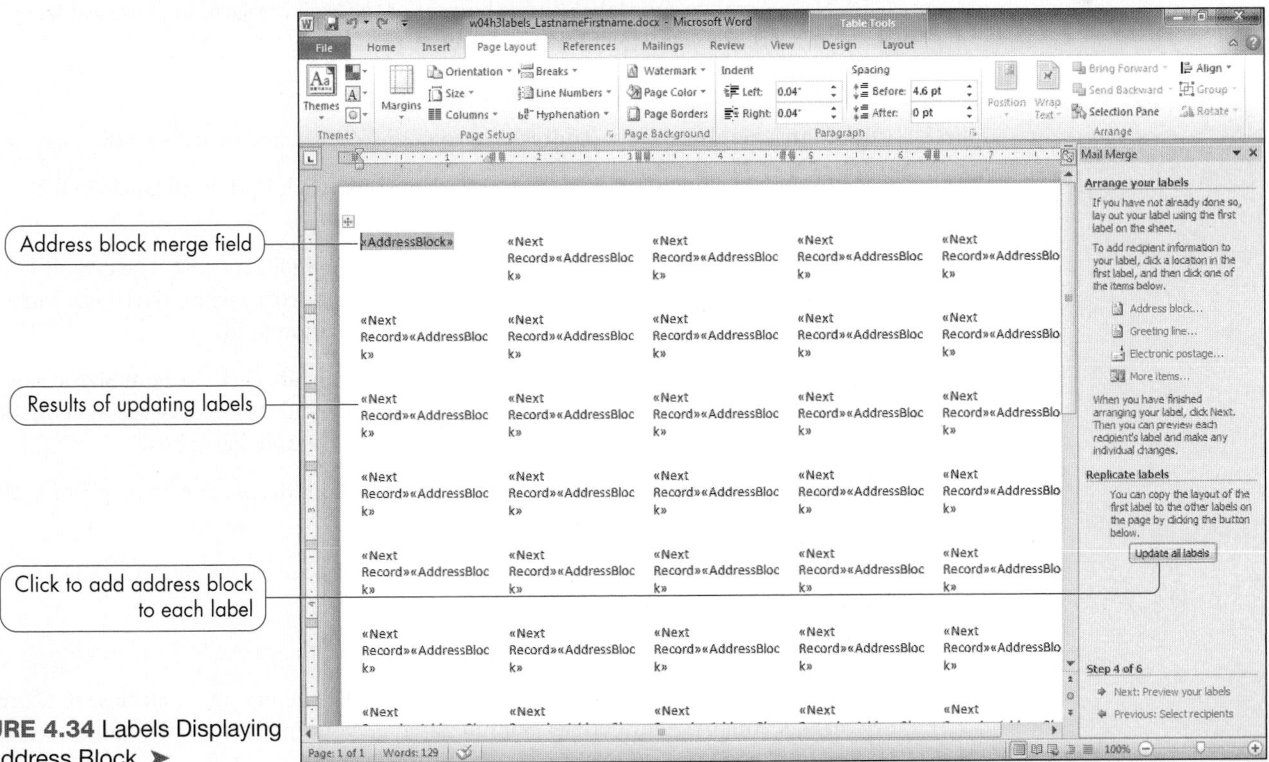

FIGURE 4.34 Labels Displaying the Address Block ➤

a. Press **Ctrl+N** to display a new document. Save the document as **w04h3labels_LastnameFirstname**.

b. Click the **Mailings tab**, click **Start Mail Merge**, and then click **Step by Step Mail Merge Wizard**.

The Mail Merge pane displays.

c. Click **Labels** in the *Select document type* section of the Mail Merge pane, and then click **Next: Starting document** at the bottom of the pane.

d. Click **Label options** in the *Change document layout* section of the pane.

The Label Options dialog box displays.

e. Click the **Label vendors arrow**, and then click **Avery A4/A5**. Click **C2651** from the Product number list. Click **OK**. Click **Next: Select recipients** at the bottom of the pane.

TROUBLESHOOTING: If you do not have the Avery A4/A5 label, consult with your instructor for an alternative product.

Most packages of labels will display a product number on the package that will also display in this list. This product number helps Word to set up a template that matches the layout of the labels, which then ensures the labels print correctly.

f. Click **Browse** in the *Use an existing list* section of the pane, and then navigate to the location where you saved the recipient list, *w04h2donortable_LastnameFirstname*. Select the file, and then click **Open**.

The Mail Merge Recipients dialog box displays.

g. Click the **Last Name arrow**. Click **Sort Ascending**.

h. Click the **Street arrow**, and then click **(Nonblanks)**.

i. Click **OK** to select the remaining recipients, and then close the dialog box.

The document displays the Next Record code throughout the document to indicate the labels are ready.

j. Click **Next: Arrange your labels** in the bottom of the Mail Merge pane. Click **Address block** in the *Arrange your labels* section of the pane.

The Insert Address Block dialog box displays.

k. Click **Match Fields**, click the **Address 1 arrow**, click **Street**, and then click **OK**.

l. Click **OK** to close the Insert Address Block dialog box. Click **Update all labels** in the *Replicate labels* section of the pane.

The Address Block field displays on each label, as shown in Figure 4.34. The default font size for the document is so large the addresses will not display correctly on the labels. You will reduce the size of the font to enable the address information to fit.

m. Press **Ctrl+A** to select all the label fields. Click the **Home tab**, click the **Font Size arrow**, and then select **9**. Click the **Paragraph dialog box launcher**, and then reduce the **Spacing Before** in the *Spacing* section to **0 pt**. Click **OK** to close the Paragraph dialog box.

n. Click **Next: Preview your labels** in Step 4 of 6 of the Mail Merge pane. In Step 5 of 6, click **Next: Complete the merge**.

o. Click **Edit individual labels** in the *Merge* section of the Mail Merge pane. Click **OK** in the Merge to New Document dialog box.

A new document displays with seven labels at the top of the page.

p. Save the document as **w04h3mergelabels_LastnameFirstname**, and then close it. Close the original document without saving. Submit based on your instructor's directions.

CHAPTER OBJECTIVES REVIEW

After reading this chapter, you have accomplished the following objectives:

1. **Insert a table.** Tables represent a very powerful capability within Word and are used to organize a variety of data in documents. Tables are made up of rows and columns; the intersection of a row and column is called a *cell.* You can insert additional rows and columns if you need to add more data to a table, or you can delete a row or column if you no longer need data in the respective row or column. Individual cells can be merged to create a larger cell. Conversely, you can split a single cell into multiple cells. The rows in a table can be different heights and/or each column can be a different width.
2. **Format a table.** Each cell in a table is formatted independently and may contain text, numbers, and/or graphics. To enhance readability of table data, you can apply a predefined style, which Word provides, or use Borders and Shading tools to add color and enhance it. Furthermore, you can align table data—at the left margin, at the right margin, or centered between the margins. You also can change the text direction within a cell.
3. **Sort and apply formulas to table data.** You can sort the rows in a table to display the data in ascending or descending sequence, according to the values in one or more columns in the table. Sorting is accomplished by selecting the rows within the table that are to be sorted, and then executing the Sort command on the Layout tab. Calculations can be performed within a table using the Formula command in the same tab.
4. **Convert text to a table.** If you have a list of tabulated items that would be easier to manipulate in a table, you can use the Convert Text to Table command. The command also works in reverse, enabling you to remove data from a table and format it as tabulated text.
5. **Select a main document.** The mail merge process uses two files as input, a main document and a data source; by merging these two files, you can create a set of individualized letters, envelopes, e-mails, or other documents. The main document, also known as a *source* or *starting document,* contains the information that stays the same for all recipients. A wizard makes a process easier by asking a series of questions, and then creating a template based on your answers. If you want to create individual envelopes or a sheet of mailing labels, which are not part of a mail merge process, the Create group on the Mailings tab includes commands that you use to select the correct settings.
6. **Select or create recipients.** A recipient list, sometimes called a *data source,* contains individual pieces of data known as *fields.* Common fields in a data source include first name, last name, street, city, state, ZIP code, phone number, and e-mail address. You can sort or filter the recipient list to specify criteria for including records that meet certain conditions during the merge process. The Sort Records tab enables you to specify up to three levels for sorting records. You can also use Excel spreadsheets or Access databases or queries as source data for a mail merge.
7. **Insert merge fields.** When you write your letter or set up your e-mail in preparation for a mail merge, you insert a merge field in the main document. The merge field is a placeholder that specifies where information from the data source will display in the main document. The merge fields display in the main document within angle brackets. Because it corresponds with a field in the data source, matching the two fields guarantees that the right data will be inserted into the main document when you complete the merge.
8. **Merge a main document and a data source.** The merge process examines each record in the data source, and when a match is found, it replaces the merge field in the main document with the information from the data source. A copy of the main document is created for each record in the data source, thus creating individual form letters.

KEY TERMS

Ascending order ***p.224***
Border ***p.214***
Cell ***p.212***
Cell margin ***p.216***
Column width ***p.213***
Data source ***p.233***
Database table ***p.235***
Descending order ***p.224***
Field ***p.233***
Filter ***p.237***
Form letter ***p.231***
Header row ***p.233***
Mail merge ***p.231***
Main document ***p.232***
Merge field ***p.232***
Record ***p.233***
Row height ***p.213***
Shading ***p.214***
Sorting ***p.223***
Syntax ***p.223***
Table ***p.212***
Table alignment ***p.216***
Table Move handle ***p.213***
Table style ***p.215***
Text direction ***p.216***
Wizard ***p.232***

MULTIPLE CHOICE

1. You have created a table containing numerical values and have entered the SUM(ABOVE) function at the bottom of a column. You then delete one of the rows included in the sum. Which of the following is true?
   (a) The row cannot be deleted because it contains a cell that is included in the sum function.
   (b) The sum is updated automatically.
   (c) The sum cannot be updated.
   (d) The sum will be updated after you right-click the cell and click the Update Field command.

2. What happens when you press Tab from within the last cell of a table?
   (a) A Tab character is inserted just as it would be for ordinary text.
   (b) Word inserts a new row below the current row.
   (c) Word inserts a new column to the right of the current column.
   (d) The insertion point appears in the paragraph below the table.

3. What happens when you type more than one line of text into a cell?
   (a) The cell gets wider to accommodate the extra text.
   (b) The row gets taller as word wrapping occurs to display the additional text.
   (c) The first line is hidden by default.
   (d) A new column is inserted automatically.

4. Assume you created a table with the names of the months in the first column. Each row lists data for that particular month. The insertion point is in the first cell on the third row, which lists goals for April. You realize that you left out the goals for March. What should you do?
   (a) Display the Insert tab, and then click the Table command.
   (b) Display the Table Tools Design tab, and then click the Insert Cell command.
   (c) Display the Table Tools Layout tab, and then click the Insert Left command.
   (d) Display the Table Tools Layout tab, and then click the Insert Above command.

5. You have a Word document that contains a list of people who were sent an invitation to a wedding. You are responsible for monitoring their responses to the invitation, whether they will attend or not, and to determine the grand total of those attending. Using skills learned in the chapter, what would be a good way to track this information?
   (a) Copy the names into an Excel spreadsheet, and then use mail merge to populate a table in Word.
   (b) Convert the list of names to a table; add columns that enable you to mark their response, including the number who will attend, and use a formula to add up the numbers when all responses are received.
   (c) Type the list of names into a Word table; add columns to mark a response, and a formula to add up responses.
   (d) Insert a two-column table beside the names and mark the responses as declined or attending.

6. When you generate a new data source during the mail merge process, what type of file do you create when it saves?
   (a) Document (.docx)
   (b) Worksheet (.xlsx)
   (c) Database (.mdb))
   (d) Rich text (.rtf)

7. During a mail merge process, what operation can you perform on a data source so only data that meet specific criteria, such as a particular city, are included in the merge?
   (a) Sort
   (b) Propagate
   (c) Delete
   (d) Filter

8. When you click Edit Individual Documents on the Mail Merge pane, and then click OK, the merged document _____.
   (a) appears in a new document window
   (b) is automatically printed
   (c) is saved to a new document file
   (d) overwrites the main document

9. When you use mail merge to create address labels, what option do you click to copy the address field from the first label to the rest of the labels before performing the merge?
   (a) Copy and paste
   (b) Update all labels
   (c) Edit recipient list
   (d) Sort and filter

10. Which of the following is not a good use for mail merge?
   (a) To print mailing labels for Christmas cards from a list of addresses in an Excel spreadsheet
   (b) To send the same personalized letter to all your business clients
   (c) To create return address labels that display your home address
   (d) To e-mail a meeting announcement to every member of your professional organization

1 Jacksonville City Theatre

You are the manager of the Jacksonville City Theatre and each month you mail tickets to patrons who have placed orders over the phone or online. You know that it is time-consuming to copy and paste the patrons' names and addresses from your Excel worksheet into the cover letter you send with the tickets, so you decide to create a mail merge document that you can quickly update and send each month. Later, you decide to use a filter so you print only letters to patrons attending the January performance. This exercise follows the same set of skills as used in Hands-On Exercise 3 in the chapter. Refer to Figure 4.35 as you complete this exercise.

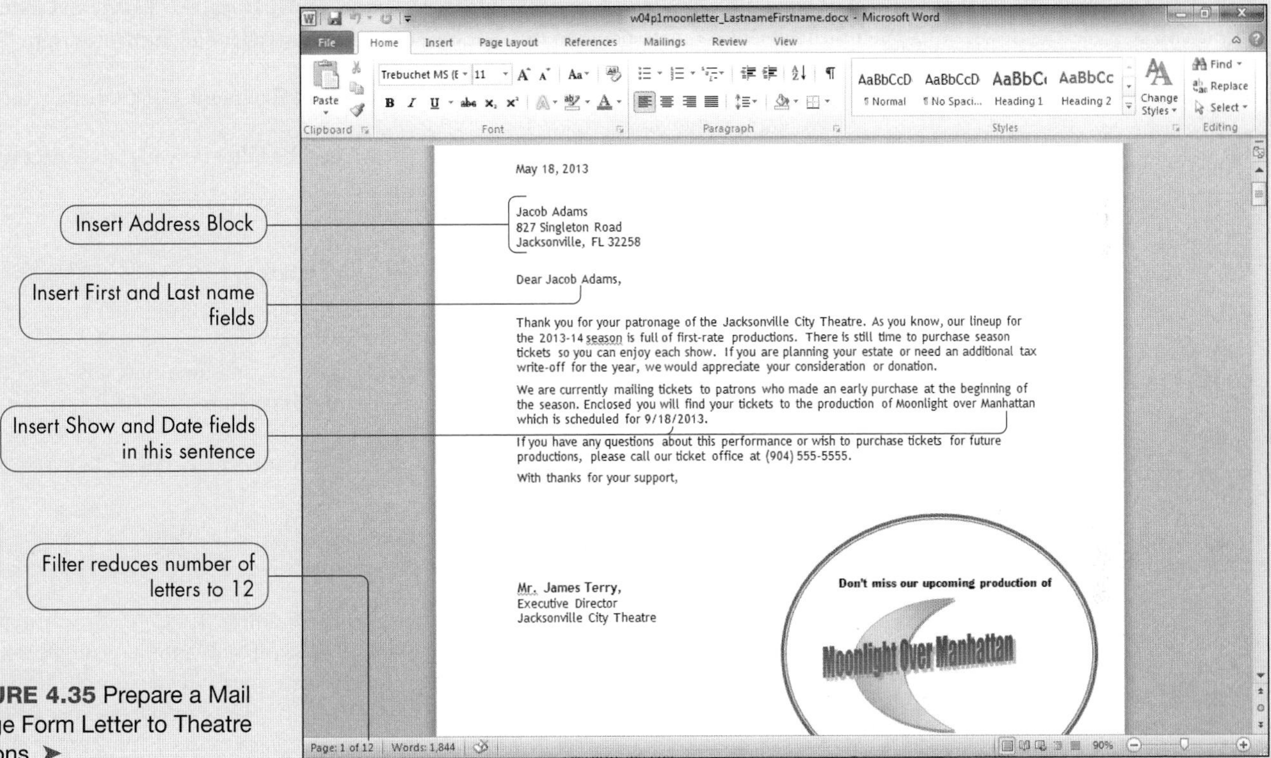

FIGURE 4.35 Prepare a Mail Merge Form Letter to Theatre Patrons ➤

a. Open *w04p1theatre* and save it as **w04p1theatre_LastnameFirstname**.

b. Click the **Mailings tab**, click **Start Mail Merge** in the Start Mail Merge group, and then click **Letters**.

c. Select a recipient by completing the following steps:
   - Click **Select Recipients**, and then click **Use Existing List**.
   - Navigate to the location where data files are stored, click **w04p1patrons.xlsx**, and then click **Open**.
   - Make sure *Sheet1* is selected, and then click **OK** when the Select Table dialog box displays.

d. Insert merge fields by completing the following steps:
   - Move the insertion point two lines below the date. Click **Address Block**, and then click **OK** to insert the patron's address at the top of the letter.
   - Move the insertion point to the left side of the comma in the salutation line *Dear*, and then click the **Insert Merge Field arrow**. Click **Fname**, press **Spacebar**, click **Insert Merge Field**, and then click **Lname**.
   - Place the insertion point between the two spaces on the right side of the word *of* in the last sentence of the second paragraph. Click **Insert Merge Field arrow**, and then click **Show**.

> **TROUBLESHOOTING:** If you find it difficult to determine where to place the cursor, click Show/Hide (¶) on the Home tab to display formatting marks such as spaces.

- Move the insertion point to the end of the last sentence of the second paragraph, just before the ending period. Click **Insert Merge Field arrow**, and then click **Date**.

e. Click **Preview Results**. To correct the extra spacing around the address block, complete these steps:
   - Select the three lines that make up the address block.
   - Click the **Page Layout tab**.
   - Click the **Spacing After arrow** in the Paragraph group until **0 pt** displays.

f. Finish the merge by completing these steps:
   - Click the **Mailings tab**, click **Finish & Merge**, and then click **Edit Individual Documents**.
   - Click **From**, type **1** in the first box, type **34** in the second box, and then click **OK**. There were four records at the end of the list that did not contain addresses. You do not want to print those letters.
   - Save the new document as **w04p1ticketletter_LastnameFirstname**. Close the file.

g. Select *w04p1theatre_LastnameFirstname*, and then save it as **w04p1theatre2_LastnameFirstname**.

h. Filter the recipient list in preparation for creating letters to patrons attending the January production by completing the following steps:
   - Click the **Mailings tab**, if necessary, and then click **Edit Recipient List** to display the Mail Merge Recipients dialog box.
   - Click **Filter** to display the Filter and Sort dialog box. Click the **Filter Records tab**, if necessary.
   - Click the **Field arrow**, and then click **Show**.
   - Click the **Comparison arrow**, and then click **Contains**.
   - Type **Moon** in the **Compare to box**, and then click **OK**.
   - Click **OK** again to close the Mail Merge Recipients dialog box.

i. Click **Last Record** to determine how many pages your merge will create. If the filter is set correctly, your merge will create 12 letters.

j. Click **Finish & Merge**, click **Edit Individual Documents**, click **All**, and then click **OK**.

k. Save the new document as **w04p1moonletter_LastnameFirstname**. Compare your letter to Figure 4.35, and then close the document.

l. Save and close all documents, and submit based on your instructor's directions.

2 Marti Appraisal Company

You work as a real estate assessor and must bill for services each month. Traditionally, you type the total amount of your services in the document, but after a discussion with another assessor you discover how to use table formulas and begin to use them to calculate your total fees on the invoice. In this exercise, you develop a professional-looking invoice and use formulas to calculate totals within the table. This exercise follows the same set of skills as used in Hands-On Exercises 1 and 2 in the chapter. Refer to Figure 4.36 as you complete this exercise.

Marti Appraisal Company, LLC	
Invoice Number: 300	Invoice Date: 8/20/2012
Bill to: Heartcountry Bank 33252 S. Campbell Ave. Springfield, MO 65807	Submit Payment to: Marti Appraisal Company, LLC 2048 S. Glenn Ave. Springfield, MO 65807

File #	Appraisal Date	Property Address	Appraisal Fee Due
75	8/1/2012	335 Valley Vista Dr., Springfield	800.00
70	8/2/2012	105 Amanda Ln., Nixa	300.00
65	8/4/2012	2402 E. Lee St., Republic	300.00
77	8/4/2012	3324 N. Hickory Hills Ct., Nixa	100.00
		Total	$1,500.00
Thank You for your business!			

FIGURE 4.36 Completed Invoice ➤

a. Open a blank document and save it as **w04p2invoice_LastnameFirstname.**
b. Click the **Insert tab**, and then click **Table**. Drag to select one column and three rows (1 × 3 table).
c. Add information in the first row by completing the following steps:
   - Type **Marti Appraisal Company, LLC.**
   - Right-click to display the Mini toolbar, and then click **Center**.
   - Select the text, click the **Font size arrow** on the Mini toolbar, and then select **28**.
   - Click the **Page Layout tab**, and then click the **Spacing After arrow** until **12 pt** displays.
   - Press [→] to move the insertion point to the right side of the text.
   - Click the **Insert tab**. Click **Clip Art**.
   - Search for **House** and insert a graphic in the first row next to the Company name. Close the Clip Art pane.
   - Click the **Format tab**, if necessary, click **Position** in the Arrange group, and then click **Position in Middle Right with Square Text Wrapping**.
   - Reduce the height of the Clip Art so it is no more than 1″ high; the width can adjust proportionally to the height.

d. Select the second and third rows. Click the **Layout tab**, click **Split Cells** in the Merge group, and then click **OK** to accept the new size of 2 columns by 2 rows.
e. Fill in the last two rows of the table with the following information:

Invoice Number: 300	**Invoice Date: 8/20/2012**
Bill to: Heartcountry Bank 33252 S. Campbell Ave. Springfield, MO 65807	Submit Payment to: Marti Appraisal Company, LLC 2048 S. Glenn Ave. Springfield, MO 65807

f. Select the text you just typed and use the Mini toolbar to increase the font size to **14**. Press **Ctrl+L** to left justify, if necessary.
g. Select the second row of the table, click the **Page Layout tab**, and increase both **Spacing before** and **Spacing after** to **6 pt**.
h. Format the table borders by completing the following steps:
   - Click the **Table Move handle** to select the whole table.
   - Click the **Design tab,** click the **Borders arrow** in the Table Styles group, and then click **Borders and Shading**.
   - Click the **Borders tab** in the Borders and Shading dialog box, if necessary.
   - Click **Box** in the Setting area on the left side. Click **OK**.
   - Select the second row of the table.
   - Click the **Borders arrow** in the Table Styles group, and then click **Bottom Border**.
   - Select the first row of the table.
   - Click the **Borders arrow**, click **Borders and Shading**, and then click the **Shading tab**.
   - Click the **Fill arrow**, select **Red, Accent 2, Darker 25%**, and then click **OK**.

i. Add a second table for invoice details by completing the following steps:
   - Press **Ctrl+End** to move your cursor to the end of the document.
   - Press **Enter** two times.
   - Click the **Insert tab.**
   - Click **Table.**
   - Drag to select a four column by five row table (4 × 5).

j. Type the following column headings in the first row:

File #	**Appraisal Date**	**Property Address**	**Appraisal Fee Due**

k. Modify the size of the columns in this table by completing the following steps:
   - Click the **Table Move handle** to select the whole table.
   - Click the **Layout tab**, if necessary.
   - Click the **Width arrow** until **1″** displays.
   - Place the insertion point in the third column.
   - Click the **Width arrow** until **2.5″** displays.

l. Type the following appraisal information in rows 2 through 4.

65	8/4/2012	2402 E. Lee St., Republic	300.00
70	8/2/2012	105 Amanda Ln., Nixa	300.00
75	8/1/2012	335 Valley Vista Dr., Springfield	800.00

m. Add the total amount due in row five by completing the following steps:
- Drag to select the first three cells in row five. Click **Merge Cells** in the Merge group on the Layout tab.
- Type **Total** in this new larger cell, and then press **Ctrl+R.**
- Place the insertion point in the last column of this row (**cell D5**), and then click **Formula** in the Data group.
- Make sure *=SUM(ABOVE)* displays in the Formula box. Click the **Number format arrow**, select **$#,##0.00;($#,##0.00)**, and then click **OK.**

n. Press **Tab** to add one more row to the table. In that row, complete the following steps:
- Drag your mouse across each cell in the last row to select the whole row.
- Click **Merge Cells** in the Merge group.
- Type **Thank you for your business!**
- Press **Ctrl +E** to center the sentence in the row.

o. Place the insertion point in the first cell of the fourth row, and then click **Insert Below** in the Rows & Columns group. In the new blank row, type the following:

77	8/4/2012	3324 N. Hickory Hills Ct., Nixa	100.00

p. Sort the information in the table by date by completing the following steps:
- Select rows one through five.
- Click **Sort** in the Data group.
- Click **Header row** under *My list has.*
- Click the **Sort by arrow**, and then select **Appraisal Date.**
- Click **OK.**

q. Click in **cell D6**, which holds the formula. Right-click, and then select **Update Field.**

r. Format the table for readability by completing the following steps:
- Click the **Design tab.**
- Click anywhere in the second table, and then click the **More button** in the Table Styles group.
- Select **Medium Shading 1 - Accent 2** (third column, fourth row) from the gallery.
- Select **cells D1 through D6** (the first six rows of the last column), and then press **Ctrl+R** to right align.
- Click the **Layout tab**, click **AutoFit**, and then click **AutoFit Window** to expand the size of the table to the right margin.
- Select the total amount due in **cell D6**, and then click **Bold** on the Mini toolbar.
- Click the **Table Move handle** to select the whole table, and then increase the font size to **12 pt** using the Mini toolbar.
- Select the *Thank you* sentence in the last row, and then select **Bold** from the Mini toolbar, if necessary. Compare your results to Figure 4.36.

s. Save and close the document, and then submit based on your instructor's directions.

MID-LEVEL EXERCISES

1 Regional Science Fair

The Regional Science Fair will occur on the campus of Missouri State University in the spring, and students from schools across the southwest portion of the state compete in areas such as physics, chemistry, environment, meteorology, and astronomy. As the volunteer coordinator, you must maintain a list of people who will donate their time to the event. You decide to send a reminder to each volunteer so they will be sure to arrive at their designated time.

a. Open *w04m1reminder* and save it as **w04m1reminder_LastnameFirstname**.
b. Use the reminder as the main document in a mail merge.
c. Use *w04m1times.xlsx* as your data source. Insert fields for first and last name, time in (start time), and time out (end time) in the appropriate locations in the reminder document. Center the start and end time fields in the table.
d. Preview the merge results, and then edit the recipient list. Sort the source data so that it sorts the Time In field in ascending order.
e. Filter the source data so that any record containing a Time Out of *9:00:00 PM* will not be included in the merge.
f. Merge the documents, and then display the results in a new file. Save the merged reminders as **w04m1mergedreminder_LastnameFirstname**.
g. Save and close all documents, and then submit based on your instructor's directions.

2 Building Materials

You are the executive assistant to a general contractor, and your duties include listing the materials that will be used on a home remodeling project. Due to the large number of people who work on the project, from plumbers to electricians to carpenters, it is necessary to keep detailed records of the materials and supplies to use during the remodel. After the first job, you decide to provide the crew with a table of materials that includes pictures. This also might be helpful for any crew member who does not speak English. Refer to Figure 4.37 as you complete this exercise.

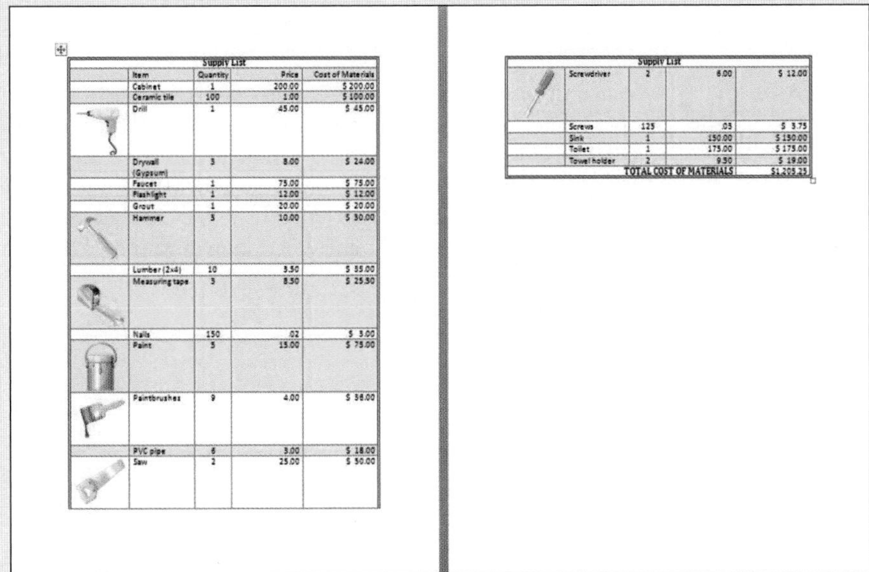

Supply List

	Item	Quantity	Price	Cost of Materials
	Cabinet	1	200.00	$ 200.00
	Ceramic tile	100	1.00	$ 100.00
	Drill	1	45.00	$ 45.00
	Drywall (Gypsum)	3	8.00	$ 24.00
	Faucet	1	75.00	$ 75.00
	Flashlight	1	12.00	$ 12.00
	Grout	1	20.00	$ 20.00
	Hammer	3	10.00	$ 30.00
	Lumber (2x4)	10	3.50	$ 35.00
	Measuring tape	3	8.50	$ 25.50
	Nails	150	.02	$ 3.00
	Paint	5	15.00	$ 75.00
	Paintbrushes	9	4.00	$ 36.00
	PVC pipe	6	3.00	$ 18.00
	Saw	2	25.00	$ 50.00

Supply List

	Screwdriver	2	6.00	$ 12.00
	Screws	125	.03	$ 3.75
	Sink	1	150.00	$ 150.00
	Toilet	1	175.00	$ 175.00
	Towel holder	2	9.50	$ 19.00
			TOTAL COST OF MATERIALS	$1,205.25

FIGURE 4.37 Supply List ➤

a. Open *w04m2construction* and save it as **w04m2construction_LastnameFirstname**.
b. Convert this list to a three-column table so you can organize the list of materials and add more data.
c. Insert two rows at the top to use for a heading and item descriptions.
   - Create a title row on the table by merging cells in the first row.
   - Insert the text **Supply List** as the title.
   - Use the second row as a header for the columns.
   - Enter the following labels for each column: **Item**, **Quantity**, **Price**.
d. Align the prices of each item in the third column. The prices should appear to align on the decimal point.
e. Center the data in the second column, which displays the quantity of each item you will use in the project.
f. Sort the data in ascending order by Item.
g. Use the **Split cell option** to split the third column in two. The label for the fourth column is **Total Cost**.
h. Insert a column to the left of the first column. Insert a picture of the supplies in the first column.
   - Use symbols, clip art, or pictures to visually describe the following materials in your table: drill, hammer, paint, paintbrushes, saw, and screwdriver. You might not be able to locate a graphic for each item, but you should be able to find at least five to use in the table.
   - Include Office.com content in your search, if needed.
   - Resize the graphics as necessary so they do not exceed 1″ in height or width.
   - Align each graphic in the center of the cell.

i. Use a formula to calculate the total cost of each item and display it in the fifth column. To calculate the cost of materials, multiply the cell that contains the quantity by the cell that contains the price. For example, the formula for the cabinet is =C3*D3. You might also explore the Product function to calculate the cost of items. If you use a function, you can copy the formula from cell to cell, but must update each one to reflect the different data they calculate.
j. Add a row at the bottom of the table. Merge the first four columns of this row into one cell, and then type **TOTAL COST OF MATERIALS**. Insert a formula in the last column to calculate the total cost of materials used in this project.
k. Apply the **Light Grid - Accent 1** (sixth column, nineth row) style to the table. Use the Borders (and Shading) feature on the Design tab to add a double-line outside border to the table. (Hint: Use the Custom setting.) Center the table horizontally on the page.

l. Use Help if needed to indicate the first row will repeat as a header row at the top of each page if your table spans more than one page. Merge cells in the first row to enlarge the cell containing the title.
m. Save and close the document, and then submit based on your instructor's directions.

3 Finding Dakota

CREATIVE CASE

In an unfortunate mishap, your five-year-old dog, Dakota, escaped from your yard and is now missing. After calling local shelters and pet stores, you decide to create a flyer to post around the neighborhood and shops so that people will know whom to contact if they see her. Figure 4.38 displays a flyer that is intended to give information about your dog and also provide a tag with contact information that someone can pull from the flyer and take home. Use a table as the basis of this document. If allowed by your instructor, use a picture and description of your own pet or other animals. Refer to Figure 4.38 as you complete this exercise.

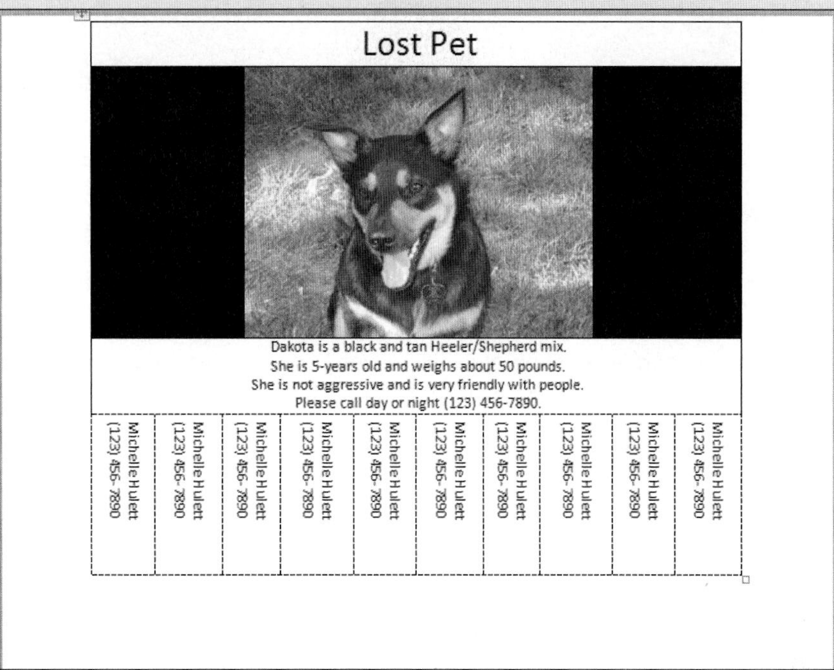

FIGURE 4.38 Lost Pet Flyer ➤

a. Open a new document and save it as **w04m3lostpet_LastnameFirstname**.

b. Create a table with five columns and four rows (5 × 4 table).

c. Merge all the cells in the first row, and then enter the text **Lost Pet**. Select the text, and then change the font size to **26 pt**. The row height will increase automatically to accommodate the larger text. Center the text in the cell.

d. Merge the cells in row 2. Use shading to place a black background in the cell. Locate pictures of your pet or pets; we have provided a picture of Dakota, *dakota.jpg*, in the Exploring Word folder. When you locate the file, insert the picture. The row height will expand automatically to accommodate the picture. Center the picture in the cell. You should use the Size features in Word to reduce the size of the photo if it displays too large for the page.

e. Merge cells in the third row, and then enter text to describe your pet or pets. Feel free to duplicate the information provided in Figure 4.38. Change the font size to **14 pt**, and then center the text in the cell.

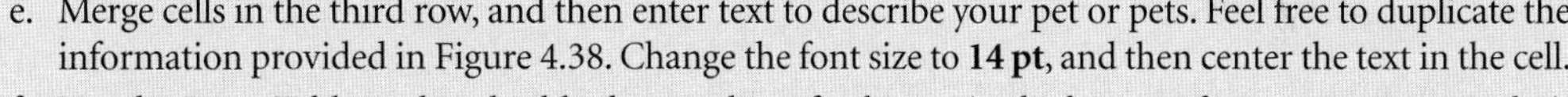

f. Use the Draw Table tool to double the number of columns in the last row from 5 to 10. Use Help if needed to learn about this tool.

g. Type your name and phone number in the first cell of the fourth row. Use the Text Direction feature to rotate the text, as shown in Figure 4.38. Center and align the text at the top of the cell and increase the height of the cell, if necessary, to display the contents on two lines.

h. Use Copy and Paste to populate the remaining cells with the owner information.

i. Change the formatting of the fourth row to display a dashed line around each of the cells.

j. Save and close the document, and then submit based on your instructor's directions.

CAPSTONE EXERCISE

You work as the business manager for the local Sports Medicine Clinic and are responsible for many forms of correspondence. This week, you want to send a letter of welcome to three physical therapists recently hired at the clinic. Additionally, you need to send your weekly reminders to patients who are scheduled for upcoming treatment or consultations. In the past, the letters were generated manually and names were typed in each letter separately. However, because you now use Word 2010, you decide to create and use source data documents and implement a mail merge so you can produce the letters quickly and accurately.

Create a Table Containing Therapist Information

You will create a new document that includes a table of information about the new physical therapists. Then you personalize the welcome letter created for the therapists and use information from the table to create a personal letter for each person.

a. Open a new, blank document and save it as **w04c1therapists_LastnameFirstname.**

b. Create a table with the following information:

Name	Credentials	Street	Days working	Salary
Mike Salat	M.S., ATC	2342 W. Cardinal Street	Monday–Thursday	$60,000
Justin Ebert	M.S., ATC	34234 S. Callie Place	Monday–Friday	$65,000
Karen Rakowski	ATC, PT	98234 E. Shepherd Lane	Monday–Friday	$65,000

c. Separate the name into two columns because it will be easier to use in form letters using mail merge features. Make necessary changes to the table to display the therapists' first and last names in two separate columns. (Hint: Uncheck the option *Merge cells before split* in the Split Cells dialog box.)

d. Create three new columns for the City, State, and ZIP Code information, and then populate each one with **Conway, AR 72032.**

e. Create a new row, and then use a formula to total the Salary column. This amount is referenced in the letter, although you do not use it in the mail merge. Use Currency formatting, which will cause total salary amount to display with two decimal places, unlike the salary entries in the cells above.

f. Sort the data in the table by Last Name.

g. Save the document.

Merge Therapist Information into a Welcome Letter

Now that you have documented information about the new Physical Therapists, you can use it as a source for the welcome letter.

a. Open *w04c1welcome* and save it as **w04c1welcome_LastnameFirstname.**

b. Start a mail merge using the welcome letter as the source document. The recipient information will come from *w04c1therapists_LastnameFirstname.*

c. Replace the starred placeholders in the letter with the fields from the recipient table. Insert today's date in the appropriate place.

d. Preview the results before merging. Filter the recipients so the fourth record does not generate a letter.

e. Complete the mail merge, displaying the results in a new document. Save the merged letters as **w04c1ptwelcome_LastnameFirstname.** Close all files.

Produce a Reminder Letter for Patients

Your second project for the day is the generation of a letter to remind patients of their appointment with the therapists. For this project, you use an Access database as the source because that is how your office stores patient information.

a. Open a new document and save it as **w04c1reminder_LastnameFirstname.** Start a mail merge letter and pull your recipients from *w04c1patients.accdb.* When you select the database file, use the Patients table.

b. Insert today's date in the top-right corner of the letter. Insert an address block in the return address area of the letter. Add an appropriate salutation of greeting to the patient.

c. Type the following for the body of the reminder letter: **Please remember that you have an appointment at the Sports Medicine Clinic of Conway on **date**, at **time**. If you have paperwork to fill out, please arrive at our office 15 minutes prior to your appointment time stated above. Thank you!**

d. Insert the fields for date and time in the first sentence and remove the markers.

e. Finish the letter by typing the closing salutation:

Sincerely,
The Sports Medicine Clinic of Conway
(501) 555-5555

f. Edit the recipient list and add your name, address, and a date for an appointment. If file or network security does not enable you to modify the source data file, copy the file to your own disk and redirect the mail merge to use the file from the new location. If you cannot copy the file, omit this step.

g. Sort the recipient list by appointment date, and then appointment time. Do not print letters for people who do not have a scheduled appointment.

h. Change the formatting of the document so the letter is single spaced with no spacing before or after any paragraph.

i. Merge the documents into a new document, and then save it as **w04c1appointments_LastnameFirstname**. If a Mail Merge dialog box displays indicating Word found locked fields during the update, click **OK** to clear the dialog box.

j. Save and close all documents, and submit based on your instructor's directions.

BEYOND THE CLASSROOM

Employee Directory

GENERAL CASE 

The management of your company requires you to keep a current list of employee contact information in case you need to contact someone for an emergency situation. You have a worksheet that contains the contact information, but you do not yet know how to use Excel and you need to create and format a list very quickly. You are mastering the Mail Merge feature of Word and remember you have the option of creating a directory, which lists the source data on one page instead of printing each one on a separate page. This would be a good tool to use in generating the master list. Open a new document and prepare the contact information list using a mail merge operation. Use the file *w04b1personnel.xlsx* as your data source. Save the main document as **w04b1directory_LastnameFirstname**, and save the result of your mail merge as **w04b1directorylist_LastnameFirstname**. Use the Microsoft Help feature, if necessary. It might be helpful to format your data in a table so it is easier to read. Close all documents and submit based on your instructor's directions.

Great Plains Travel Agency

RESEARCH CASE 

You are a travel agent at the Great Plains Travel Agency and your boss wants you to develop a travel itinerary to a popular destination. Choose a location, and then use the Internet to help you determine the expenses that a customer will incur if he or she chooses that location. Create a table in Word that details costs associated with transportation, lodging, activities, and food. Create multiple columns that enable you to break down costs by category and by day (such as seven nights in a hotel that costs $200 per night) and add formulas to show subtotals and the total cost of the trip. Save your work as **w04b2travel_LastnameFirstname**. Close the document and submit based on your instructor's directions.

Wedding Invitations

DISASTER RECOVERY 

Your friend is experiencing high levels of anxiety because she cannot complete a mail merge operation to create labels for her wedding invitations. She has used the Mail Merge feature previously; however, when you open the labels, a dialog box appears and indicates there is no link from that main document to the data source (address list). You decide to troubleshoot the operation by first opening the file *w04b3labels*, to see how it was set up to use the addresses in *w04b3labeladdresses.accdb*, and then determine if you can find the reason why it does not work. If you can solve the problem, create mailing labels for the wedding and save the new file as **w04b3weddinglabels_LastnameFirstname**. Rename and save the original file you fix as **w04b3labels_LastnameFirstname**. Close all documents and submit based on your instructor's directions.

WORD

5 DESKTOP PUBLISHING AND GRAPHIC DESIGN

Creating a Newsletter, Working with Graphics, and Linking Objects

CASE STUDY | Along The Greenways

Watch the
Set-up
Video
for this
Case Study!

Kody Allen is director of The Greenways, a nonprofit organization. The organization was formed to generate interest in outdoor activities, as well as to provide support and funding for additional walking and biking trails in the city and surrounding counties. Maintaining positive public relations is a key to generating support for this organization, and providing a quarterly newsletter is one way to do this. Kody hired you as the assistant director because you enjoy cycling, you have been an outstanding volunteer for this organization, and you have good computer skills.

Director Allen has asked you to create the newsletter in a format that is easy to read but also informative. Kody wants you to limit the information to only what can be printed on a single page, even though there is much to convey. In addition to mailing the newsletter, it will also be posted on The Greenways' Web site.

OBJECTIVES

AFTER YOU READ THIS CHAPTER, YOU WILL BE ABLE TO:

1. Construct a newsletter ***p.262***
2. Develop a document design ***p.265***
3. Insert graphical objects ***p.273***
4. Manipulate graphical objects ***p.278***
5. Use OLE to insert an object ***p.290***
6. Update a linked object ***p.293***

Desktop Publishing

Desktop publishing is the merger of text with graphics to produce a professional-looking document.

Desktop publishing evolved through a combination of technologies, including faster computers, laser printers, and sophisticated page composition software that enables users to manipulate text and graphics to produce a professional-looking document. Desktop publishing was initially considered a separate application, but today's generation of word processors has matured to such a degree that it is difficult to tell where word processing ends and desktop publishing begins. Word is, for all practical purposes, a desktop publishing program that can be used to create all types of documents.

You can enjoy the challenge of creating a document that contains many graphical design techniques, but it can be time consuming and require an eye for detail, which is why documents such as brochures, newsletters, and flyers are often prepared by skilled professionals. Nevertheless, with a little practice and a basic knowledge of graphic design, you will be able to create effective and attractive documents like the newsletter you see in Figure 5.1.

In this section, you will learn how to develop a simple newsletter that includes a multi-column layout, clip art, and other objects, and position those objects within a document.

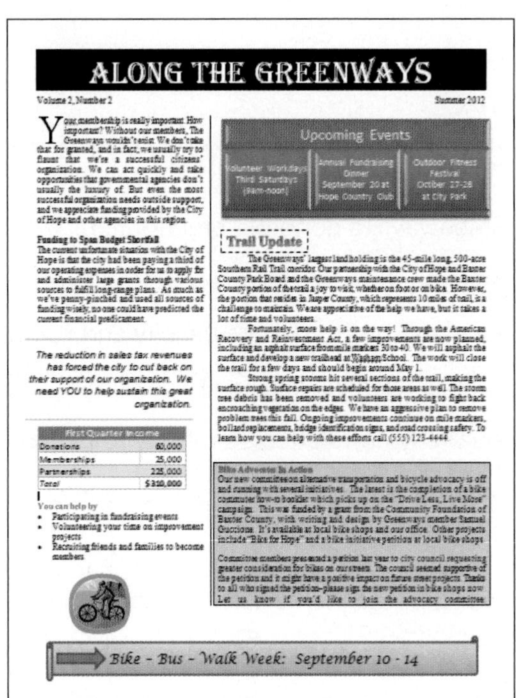

ALONG THE GREENWAYS

Volume 2, Number 2 Summer 2012

Your membership is really important. How important? Without our members, The Greenways wouldn't exist. We don't take that for granted, and in fact, we usually try to flaunt that we're a successful citizens' organization. We can act quickly and take opportunities that governmental agencies don't usually the luxury of. But even the most successful organization needs outside support, and we appreciate funding provided by the City of Hope and other agencies in this region.

Funding to Span Budget Shortfall
The current unfortunate situation with the City of Hope is that the city had been paying a third of our operating expenses in order for us to apply for and administer large grants through various sources to fulfill long-range plans. As much as we've penny-pinched and used all sources of funding wisely, no one could have predicted the current financial predicament.

The reduction in sales tax revenues has forced the city to cut back on their support of our organization. We need YOU to help sustain this great organization.

First Quarter Income	
Donations	60,000
Memberships	25,000
Partnerships	225,000
Total	$310,000

You can help by

- Participating in fundraising events
- Volunteering your time on improvement projects
- Recruiting friends and families to become members

Upcoming Events

Volunteer Workdays Third Saturdays (9am-noon)

Annual Fundraising Dinner September 20 at Hope Country Club

Outdoor Fitness Festival October 27-28 at City Park

Trail Update

The Greenways' largest land holding is the 45-mile long, 500-acre Southern Rail Trail corridor. Our partnership with the City of Hope and Baxter County Park Board and the Greenways maintenance crew made the Baxter County portion of the trail a joy to visit, whether on foot or on bike. However, the portion that resides in Jasper County, which represents 10 miles of trail, is a challenge to maintain. We are appreciative of the help we have, but it takes a lot of time and volunteers.

Fortunately, more help is on the way! Through the American Recovery and Reinvestment Act, a few improvements are now planned, including an asphalt surface from mile markers 30 to 40. We will asphalt the surface and develop a new trailhead at Wickham School. The work will close the trail for a few days and should begin around May 1.

Strong spring storms hit several sections of the trail, making the surface rough. Surface repairs are scheduled for those areas as well. The storm tree debris has been removed and volunteers are working to fight back encroaching vegetation on the edges. We have an aggressive plan to remove problem trees this fall. Ongoing improvements continue on mile markers, bollard replacements, bridge identification signs, and road crossing safety. To learn how you can help with these efforts call (555) 123-4444.

Bike Advocates In Action
Our new committee on alternative transportation and bicycle advocacy is off and running with several initiatives. The latest is the completion of a bike commuter how-to booklet which picks up on the "Drive Less, Live More" campaign. This was funded by a grant from the Community Foundation of Baxter County, with writing and design by Greenways member Samuel Guccione. It's available at local bike shops and our office. Other projects include "Bike for Hope" and a bike initiative petition at local bike shops.

Committee members presented a petition last year to city council requesting greater consideration for bikes on our streets. The council seemed supportive of the petition and it might have a positive impact on future street projects. Thanks to all who signed the petition—please sign the new petition in bike shops now. Let us know if you'd like to join the advocacy committee.

Bike - Bus - Walk Week: September 10 - 14

FIGURE 5.1 Newsletter ➤

Constructing a Newsletter

Reverse is the technique that uses light text on a dark background.

A **masthead** is the identifying information at the top of a newsletter or other periodical.

A **drop cap** is a large capital letter at the beginning of a paragraph.

When you use desktop publishing to create a document such as a newsletter, you should use several techniques to enhance readability and attractiveness. One technique desktop publishers use to emphasize text is called a ***reverse***, and it consists of using light-colored text on a dark-colored background. It is often used in the ***masthead***, which is the identifying information at the top of the newsletter or other periodical. It provides a distinctive look to the publication and often has the characteristics of a banner. The number of the newsletter and the date of publication also appear in the masthead in smaller letters.

When you use desktop publishing to create a document such as a newsletter, you should use several techniques to enhance readability and attractiveness.... Your objective should be to create a document that is easy to read and visually appealing.

Another way to catch the reader's eye and call attention to the associated text is a drop cap. A ***drop cap***, or dropped-capital letter, is a large capital letter at the beginning of a paragraph. The Drop Cap command in Word enables you to determine if the dropped cap will align with the text or display off to the side. The choice you make will largely depend on the style of the newsletter and how you design it. You can determine the size of a drop cap initial from the Drop Cap dialog box. Options for a drop cap include how many lines to drop, or how far from the text the drop cap displays. You can display a drop cap in the margin and turn it off from this dialog box. Click Drop Cap on the Insert tab, and then click Drop Cap Options to display the dialog box, as shown in Figure 5.2.

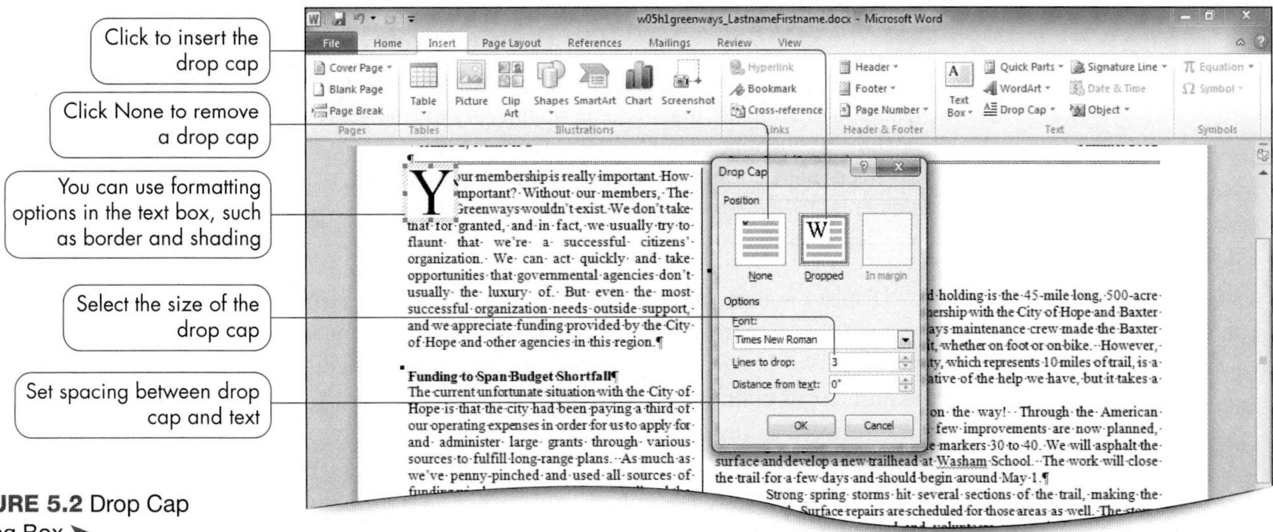

FIGURE 5.2 Drop Cap Dialog Box ➤

Many features you use frequently in word processing are also very effective individually or in combination with one another, to emphasize important information within the newsletter. These features include:

- **Clip art.** When used in moderation, clip art will catch the reader's eye and enhance almost any newsletter. It is also used to prevent using so much text on a page that the document bores the reader.
- **Images.** An image or photograph can showcase people, events, or topics discussed in a newsletter. They are often reduced in size to take up only a small amount of space.
- **Borders.** A line border might surround a paragraph, or a page border might consist of a series of small graphics.
- **Shading.** When used as the background color of an element, such as a text box or as simple vertical and/or horizontal lines, it is effective in drawing attention. These techniques are especially useful in the absence of clip art or other graphics and are a favorite of desktop publishers to draw the reader's eye to a location on the document.
- **Lists.** Whether bulleted or numbered, lists help to organize information by emphasizing important topics.
- **Typography.** The arrangement and appearance of information is essential in adding personality to your newsletter. The selection of fonts, font styles, and font sizes that enhance the appearance of a document is a critical, often subtle, element in the success of a document. You should not, for example, use the same design to announce a year-end bonus and a plant closing. Indeed, good typography goes almost unnoticed, whereas poor typography draws attention to and detracts from a document.
- **Styles.** You can also use predefined styles in desktop publishing to add personality to your newsletter. Remember that a style is a set of formatting options you apply to characters or paragraphs. It can store formats such as alignment, line spacing, indents, tabs, borders, and shading. You can use the same styles from one edition of your newsletter to the next to ensure consistency. Additionally, the use of styles in any document promotes uniformity and increases flexibility.

No hard and fast rules exist to dictate how many or which features you should include when designing a newsletter. Your objective should be to create a document that is easy to read and visually appealing. You will find that the design that worked so well in one document may not work at all in a different document. An effective presentation is often the result of trial and error, and you should experiment freely to find it.

TIP Limit Use of Typography

More is not better, especially in the case of too many typefaces and styles, which produce cluttered documents that impress no one. Try to limit yourself to a maximum of two fonts per document, but choose multiple sizes or a variety of formatting treatments on those fonts. Use boldface or italic for emphasis, but do so in moderation, because if you emphasize too many elements, the effect is lost. A simple design is often the best design.

Displaying information vertically in a newsletter is implemented through the Columns command, as shown in Figure 5.3. Start by selecting one of the column preset designs, and Microsoft Word takes care of everything else. It calculates the width of each column based on the number of columns, the left and right margins on the page, and the specified (default) space between columns. The newsletter in Figure 5.1, for example, uses a two-column layout with wide and narrow columns. This design is preferred over columns of uniform width, as it adds interest to the document. Note, too, that once columns have been defined, text will flow continuously from the bottom of one column to the top of the next.

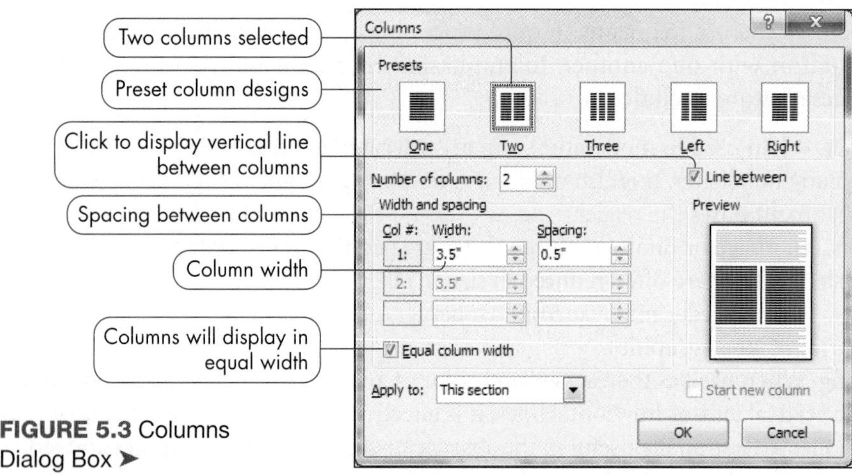

FIGURE 5.3 Columns Dialog Box ➤

Notice also that in Figure 5.1, the number of columns varies from one part of the newsletter to another. The masthead is displayed over a single column at the top of the page, whereas the remainder of the newsletter is formatted in two columns of different widths. The number of columns is specified at the section level, and thus, a section break is required whenever the column specification changes. A section break is also required at the end of the last column to balance the text within the columns. Insertion of the continuous section break, as shown in Figure 5.4, enables you to determine where columns start and end on a single page. To insert a continuous section break, click the Page Layout tab, click Breaks, and then select Continuous.

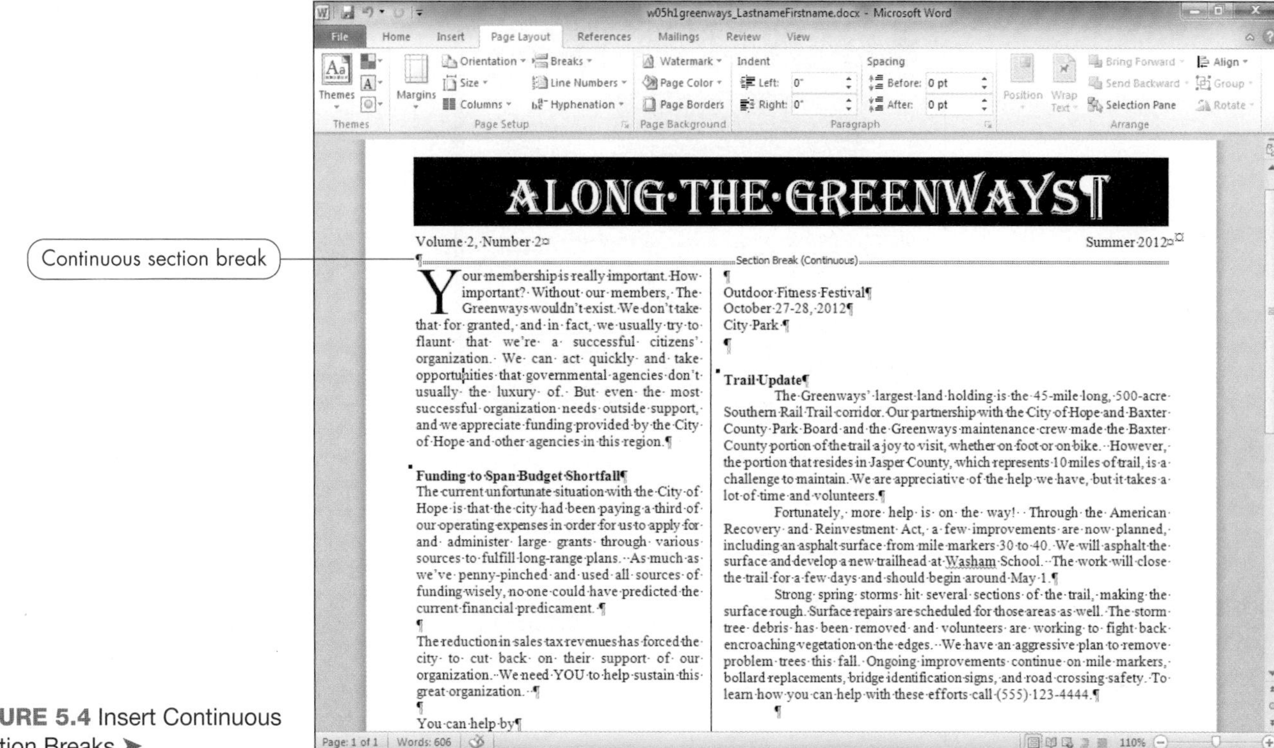

FIGURE 5.4 Insert Continuous Section Breaks ➤

A column break also plays an important role in the development of a newsletter. You use a column break to force a paragraph to start at the top of the next column. This prevents you from having to display text or other materials all the way to the bottom of one column before it wraps to the top of the next. To insert a column break, click the Page Layout tab, click Breaks, and select Column.

Developing a Document Design

The most difficult aspect of creating a newsletter is to develop the design in the first place; the mere availability of a desktop publishing program does not guarantee an effective document any more than a word processor will turn its author into another Shakespeare. Other skills are necessary, and so it is helpful to read a brief introduction to graphic design.

Much of what you write is subjective, and what works in one situation will not necessarily work in another. Your eye is the best judge of all, and you should follow your own instincts. Seek inspiration from others by collecting samples of real documents that capture your attention, and then use those documents as the basis for your own designs.

A **grid** is an underlying, but invisible, set of horizontal and vertical lines that determine the placement of major elements.

The design of a document is developed on a ***grid***, an underlying, but invisible, set of horizontal and vertical lines that determine the placement of major elements. A grid establishes the overall structure of a document by indicating the number of columns; the space between columns; the size of the margins; and the placement of headlines, art, and so on. The grid does not appear in the printed document—you draw or sketch it on a piece of paper to solidify the layout prior to creating the newsletter in Word. Figures 5.5 through 5.7 show a document which was developed using different grid designs; the grid design displays on the right side of each completed newsletter document.

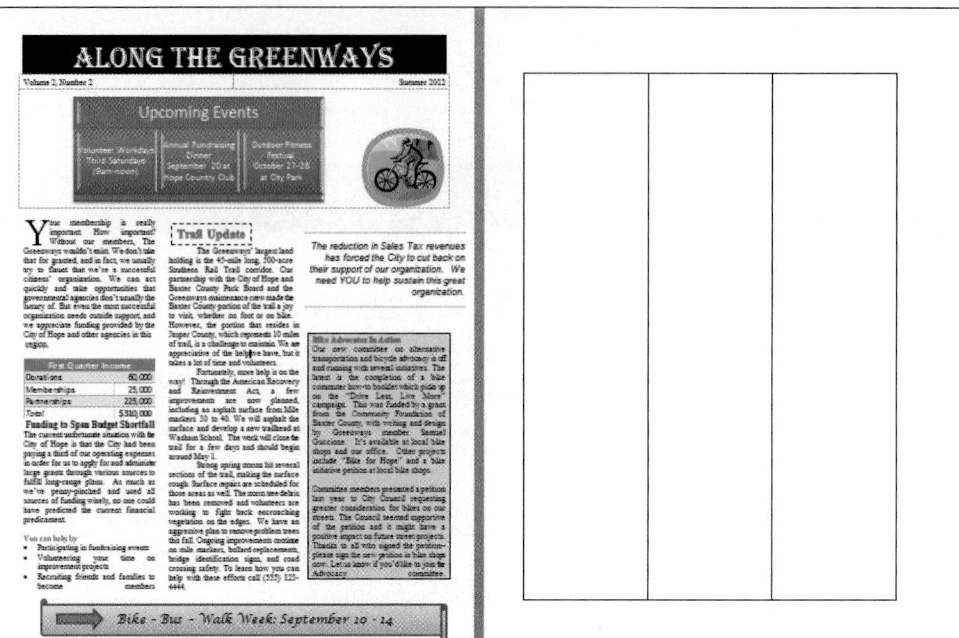

FIGURE 5.5 Three-Column Grid ➤

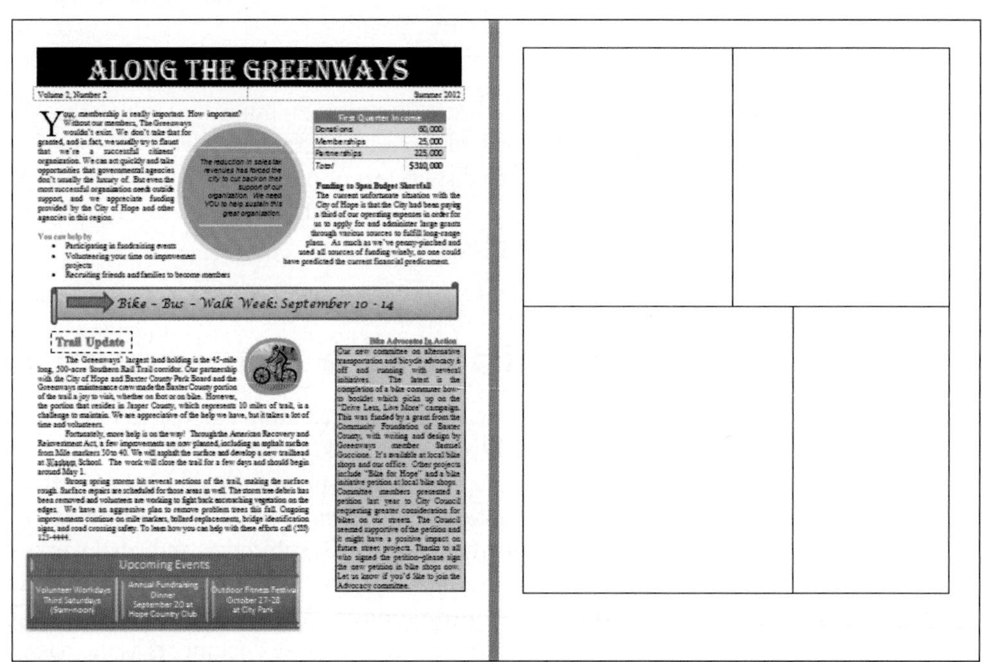

FIGURE 5.6 Two-Column Grid with Unequal Column Widths ➤

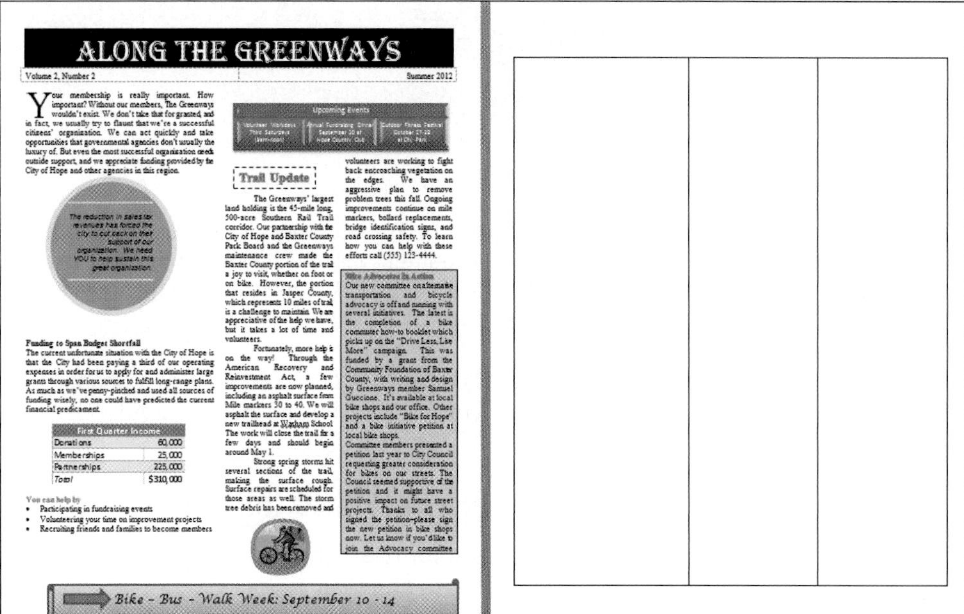

FIGURE 5.7 Three-Column Grid with Unequal Column Widths ➤

A grid may be simple or complex, but it is always distinguished by the number of columns it contains. The three-column grid of Figure 5.5 is one of the most common and utilitarian designs. Figure 5.6 shows an unequal two-column design for the same document. Figure 5.7 illustrates a three-column grid with unequal column widths to provide interest. Many other designs are possible as well. A one-column grid is used for term papers and letters. A two-column, wide-and-narrow format is appropriate for some textbooks and manuals. Two- and three-column formats are often used for newsletters and magazines.

The simple concept of a grid makes the underlying design of any document obvious, and it also helps you determine the page composition. Moreover, the conscious use of a grid will help you organize your material and will result in a more polished and professional-looking publication. It will also help you to achieve consistency from page to page within a document (or from issue to issue of a newsletter).

Good design makes it easy for the reader to determine what is important. As indicated earlier, emphasis can be achieved in several ways, the easiest being variations in type size and/or type style. Headings should be set in type sizes at least two points larger than body copy. The use of bold and italic formatting is effective, but both should be done in moderation. UPPERCASE LETTERS and underlining are alternative techniques but are less effective. Uppercase letters are often associated with screaming, because that is how you portray a raised voice in e-mail. They can also be harder to read because of the close spacing. Underlining is often associated with hyperlinks on a Web page, so it should be used on a limited basis, unless you are actually displaying a Web link.

Boxes and/or shading call attention to selected articles. Horizontal lines are effective to separate one topic from another or to call attention to a pull quote. A reverse can be striking for a small amount of text. Clip art, used in moderation, will catch the reader's eye and enhance almost any newsletter. Color is also effective, but it is more costly if you print a document.

All of the techniques and definitions discussed can be implemented with commands you already know, as you will see in Hands-On Exercise 1.

Saving in PDF Format

If your newsletter, or other document, will display on a Web page you should consider saving it as a PDF file. ***PDF*** stands for ***Portable Document Format*** and was developed by Adobe Systems as a way to share information across platforms, or computer systems, such as Microsoft Windows or Macintosh operating systems. By presenting your information as a PDF file, the reader does not have to have Word to open or view it; however, they do have to install the free Adobe Reader program. Saving in this form can also preserve a document that you do not want altered in its native Word format.

Portable Document Format (PDF) is a format that allows users to view a document regardless of the platform they use.

HANDS-ON EXERCISES

1 Desktop Publishing

Kody Allen, the director of The Greenways, forwarded you a document with short articles that he would like to include in the newsletter you are preparing. You must design a layout that will display the information in an easy-to-read and visually appealing manner. You will also consider how to display the masthead and other visual elements, and then you will take steps to set up the document and add each feature.

Skills covered: Change Page Setup Options and Implement Column Formatting • Change Column Layout • Create a Masthead and a Reverse • Create a Drop Cap • Apply Borders and Shading and Insert Clip Art

STEP 1 CHANGE PAGE SETUP OPTIONS AND IMPLEMENT COLUMN FORMATTING

After you open the file that Director Allen provides, you consider the margins needed to display all the information and make appropriate changes in your document. You decide the newsletter will display in two columns, so you quickly set them. Refer to Figure 5.8 as you complete Step 1.

FIGURE 5.8 Document Displaying Text in Two Columns ➤

a. Start Word. Open *w05h1greenways* and save it as **w05h1greenways_LastnameFirstname**.

> **TROUBLESHOOTING:** If you make any major mistakes in this exercise, you can close the file, open *w05h1greenways* again, and then start this exercise over.

b. Click the **Page Layout tab**, click **Margins** in the Page Setup group, and then select **Narrow**.

   Because the newsletter contains many items, you need smaller margins that allow more usable space on the document.

c. Click **Columns** in the Page Setup group, and then select **Two**.

   The text of the newsletter displays in two columns. The column width for each column and the spacing between columns is determined automatically from the existing margins.

d. Click the **Zoom slider**, and then decrease the zoom to **50%** and view the whole page.

   You can see both columns, as shown in Figure 5.8.

e. Save the document.

STEP 2 CHANGE COLUMN LAYOUT

In consideration of the best way to display the articles and information in the newsletter, you decide it would look better if you use unequal column widths for the two columns. You display the Columns dialog box so you can change the preset, set the width to your specifications, and add a line to separate the columns. Refer to Figure 5.9 as you complete Step 2.

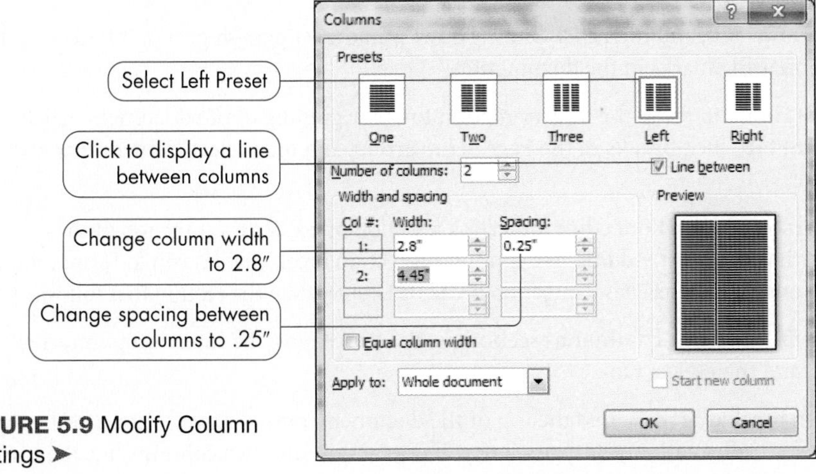

FIGURE 5.9 Modify Column Settings ➤

a. Click the **Zoom slider**, and then increase the zoom to **80%**. Click **Columns** in the Page Setup group, and then select **More Columns** to display the Columns dialog box.

b. Click **Left** in the *Presets* section, and then click **Line between** to display a line between the columns.

c. Press **Tab** to select the Width list for the first column, and then type **2.8**. Press **Tab**, and then type **.25** in the **Spacing list** for the first column. Press **Tab**, and then notice that the width of the second column automatically changes to *4.45″*, as shown in Figure 5.9. Click **OK**.

   The columns are no longer the same width, and the vertical line displays as a separator.

d. Press **Ctrl+End** to move the insertion point to the end of the document. Click **Breaks** in the Page Setup group. Select **Continuous** under Section Breaks.

   The columns are now balanced.

e. Save the document.

STEP 3 CREATE A MASTHEAD AND A REVERSE

The main title of your newsletter is important to design because it is most likely the first element the reader will view. You decide to insert a masthead and use a reverse technique so that it is very distinctive. To make it display properly as one column, you will first need to add a continuous section break at the top of the page. Refer to Figure 5.10 as you complete Step 3.

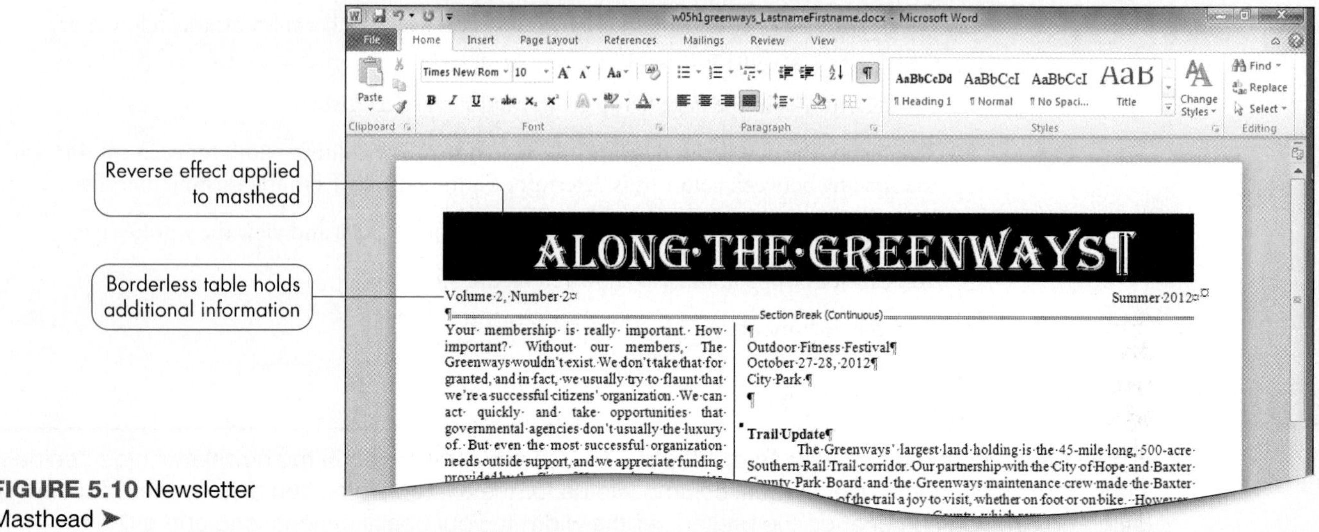

FIGURE 5.10 Newsletter Masthead ➤

a. Click the **Zoom slider**, and then increase the zoom to **110%**.

b. Click the **Home tab**, and then click **Show/Hide** (¶) in the Paragraph group, if necessary, to display formatting marks in the document.

c. Press **Ctrl+Home** to move the insertion point to the beginning of the document. Click the **Page Layout tab**, click **Breaks** in the Page Setup group, and then select **Continuous** under Section Breaks.

   You should see a double dotted line indicating a section break occurs at the top of the left column in the document. Adding this continuous section break enables you to format the area of the document that precedes the section break differently than the section that follows it.

d. Click the left side of the continuous section break line to move the insertion point, click **Columns**, and then select **One**.

   The section break extends across the top of the document, creating one column at the top of the page. Now information you type there will not be split into two columns like the text in the next section.

e. Type **Along the Greenways** and press **Enter** twice. Select the text you just typed, and then click **Center** on the Mini toolbar. Click the **Font arrow** on the Mini toolbar, click **Algerian**, click the **Font Size arrow**, and then select **36**.

   This large heading is the masthead for the newsletter.

f. Click the left side of the section break, just below the masthead, to move the insertion point. Click the **Insert tab**, click **Table**, and drag your mouse over the cells until you select two columns and one row (2 × 1 table). Click to insert the table.

   A table displays below the masthead and above the section break.

g. Make the following changes in the table:
   - Click in the left cell of the table, if necessary, and then type **Volume 2, Number 2**.
   - Click in the right cell (or press **Tab**), and then type **Summer 2012**.
   - Press **Ctrl+R** to right align text in the cell on the right.
   - Select the entire row, click the **Page Layout tab**, and then click the **Spacing Before arrow** until **6 pt** displays.

h. Press **Ctrl+Home** to move the insertion point to the beginning of the masthead. Click the **Home tab**, click the **Border arrow** in the Paragraph group, and then select **Borders and Shading.**

   The Borders and Shading dialog box displays. The Borders tab is active.

i. Click the **Shading tab**, click the **Style arrow**, select **Solid (100%)**, and then click **OK**. Click in the table to deselect the masthead.

   The masthead displays white text on a black background.

j. Click the **Table Move handle** to select the entire table. Click the **Borders and Shading arrow** in the Paragraph group, and then select **No Border**. Compare your work to Figure 5.10.

k. Click outside the table, and then view the masthead.

l. Save the document.

STEP 4 CREATE A DROP CAP

You decide to pull the reader into the articles in your newsletter by adding features such as a drop cap, which is often applied to the very first paragraph of a document. Refer to Figure 5.11 as you complete Step 4.

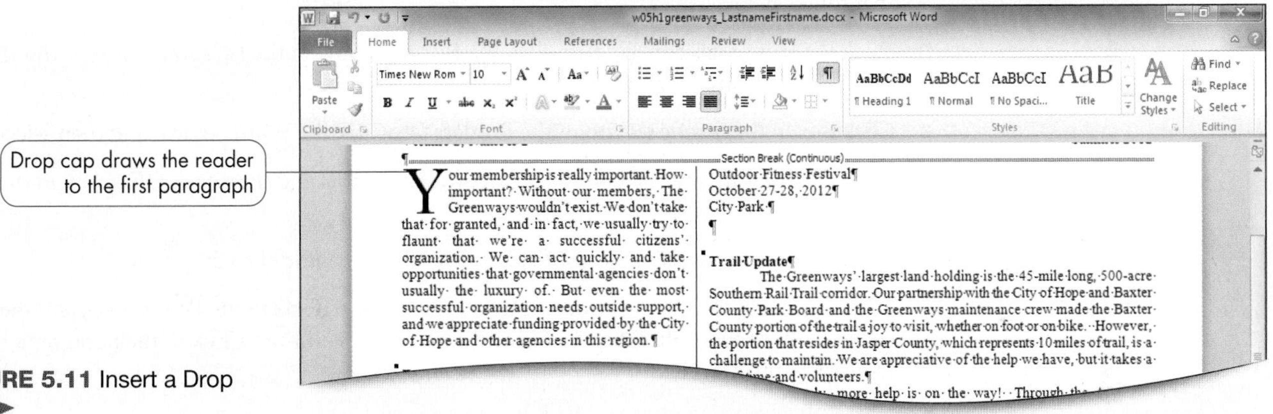

FIGURE 5.11 Insert a Drop Cap ➤

a. Click to move the insertion point to the left of the first letter in the first paragraph on the top left of the page, which displays *Your membership is really important.* Click the **Insert tab**, click **Drop Cap** in the Text group, and then select **Dropped**.

b. Click anywhere outside the Drop Cap frame, and then compare your document to Figure 5.11.

c. Select the first sentence of the fourth paragraph in the left column, *You can help by.* Click the **Home tab**, click **Text Effects** in the Font group, and then click **Gradient Fill - Orange, Accent 6, Inner Shadow** (fourth row, second column).

d. Select the three items below the *You can help by* heading, and then click **Bullets** in the Paragraph group. Click **Decrease Indent** in the Paragraph group to align the bullets with the left edge of the heading.

e. Save the document.

STEP 5 APPLY BORDERS AND SHADING AND INSERT CLIP ART

Because some of the paragraphs look very similar, you decide to add distinction by using shading and placing a border around one of them. You also add clip art to add variety and a little fun to the page. Refer to Figure 5.12 as you complete Step 5.

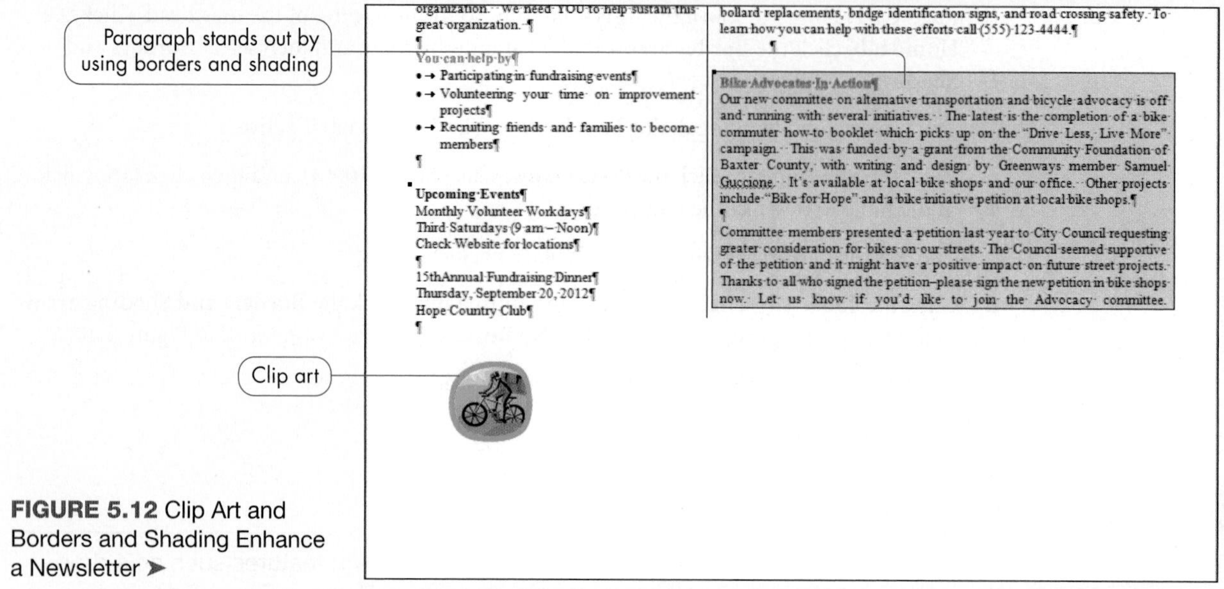

organization. We need YOU to help sustain this great organization.

You can help by

- Participating in fundraising events
- Volunteering your time on improvement projects
- Recruiting friends and families to become members

Upcoming Events
Monthly Volunteer Workdays
Third Saturdays (9 am – Noon)
Check Website for locations

15thAnnual Fundraising Dinner
Thursday, September 20, 2012
Hope Country Club

bollard replacements, bridge identification signs, and road crossing safety. To learn how you can help with these efforts call (555) 123-4444.

Bike Advocates In Action
Our new committee on alternative transportation and bicycle advocacy is off and running with several initiatives. The latest is the completion of a bike commuter how-to booklet which picks up on the "Drive Less, Live More" campaign. This was funded by a grant from the Community Foundation of Baxter County, with writing and design by Greenways member Samuel Guccione. It's available at local bike shops and our office. Other projects include "Bike for Hope" and a bike initiative petition at local bike shops.

Committee members presented a petition last year to City Council requesting greater consideration for bikes on our streets. The Council seemed supportive of the petition and it might have a positive impact on future street projects. Thanks to all who signed the petition–please sign the new petition in bike shops now. Let us know if you'd like to join the Advocacy committee.

FIGURE 5.12 Clip Art and Borders and Shading Enhance a Newsletter ➤

a. Select the heading in the right column, *Bike Advocates in Action*, and the two paragraphs that follow it.

b. Click the **Home tab**, if necessary, click the **Border arrow** in the Paragraph group, and then select **Borders and Shading**.

c. Click **Box** in the *Setting* section of the Borders tab. Click the **Width arrow**, and then select **1 pt**.

d. Click the **Shading tab**, click the **Style arrow**, select **15%**, and then click **OK**. Click in the article above to deselect the paragraph.

   A black border and gray shading display around and behind the paragraph.

e. Select the heading *Bike Advocates in Action*, click **Text Effects** in the Font group, and then click **Gradient Fill - Blue, Accent 1** (third row, fourth column). Click in the paragraph below to deselect the heading.

f. Insert Clip Art by completing the following steps:
   - Click the **Insert tab**, click **Clip Art** in the Illustrations group, and then type **bicycle** in the **Search for box**. Click **Include Office.com content**, and then click **Go**.
   - Click the clip art object of the bicycle rider, as seen in Figure 5.12, to insert it into the document. If you do not find the same clip art that displays in Figure 5.12, you can substitute something different. Close the Clip Art pane.
   - Click the **Format tab**, click **Wrap Text** in the Arrange group, and then click **Top and Bottom**.
   - Click the **Shape Height arrow** in the Size group until **.8″** displays.
   - Drag the clip art to the bottom of the left column and center it in that column.

TROUBLESHOOTING: Use Ctrl+arrow to nudge the clip art, if needed, for more exact positioning.

g. Click the **Home tab**, and then click **Show/Hide** (¶) in the Paragraph group to turn off the formatting marks. Drag the **Zoom Slider** to **50%**.

   As you view the whole document, notice how your changes already improve the look of the newsletter. You will add more enhancements in Hands-On Exercise 2.

h. Save the document and keep it onscreen if you plan to continue with Hands-On Exercise 2. If not, close the document and exit Word.

Decorative Text and Drawing Tools

Desktop publishing documents, and newsletters in particular, are more appealing to the reader when they display a variety of text and graphical objects. Word provides many graphical and drawing tools that enable you to enhance these documents. You can create boxes containing text and format them to grab the readers' attention, you can create professional looking diagrams, and you can use predefined shapes or create your own. For each graphical object, you can choose from dozens of options, which you can customize and manipulate to create the effect you want. One thing you should keep in mind when adding graphics to your document—some objects may display better onscreen than in print, so view them with a critical eye before you finalize your document.

In this section, you will learn how to insert a variety of graphical objects found on the Insert tab. You will then learn how to use tools to make adjustments such as changing colors, layering, and rotation.

Inserting Graphical Objects

A **shape** is a geometric or nongeometric object, such as a circle or an arrow.

Graphical elements—such as lines, arrows, diagrams, and text boxes—help enhance your documents by adding visual interest.

Graphical elements—such as lines, arrows, diagrams, and text boxes—help enhance your documents by adding visual interest. Microsoft Word provides a variety of graphical objects you can use individually or combine to produce one-of-a-kind drawings. For example, you can insert a ***shape***, a geometric or nongeometric object, which represents balloons on strings and formats the shapes by applying different fill colors. You can position, size, and overlap shapes to achieve the visual effect you desire.

Inserting SmartArt

SmartArt is a diagram-generating tool that presents information visually to effectively communicate a message.

Using shapes and text allows you to draw attention to your document; however, it is very time consuming to use these tools to create a complex and designer-quality illustration. Word includes ***SmartArt***, which enables you to create a diagram and enter the text of your message in one of many existing layouts to visually and effectively communicate your message. For example, you might insert a SmartArt diagram of an organizational chart, a list, or a process into your document to illustrate an important concept that is difficult to explain with simple text but easy to understand when viewed in an illustration. When you insert a SmartArt diagram in your document, you can select from several existing layouts, and it will conform to any theme you select for your document (see Figure 5.13).

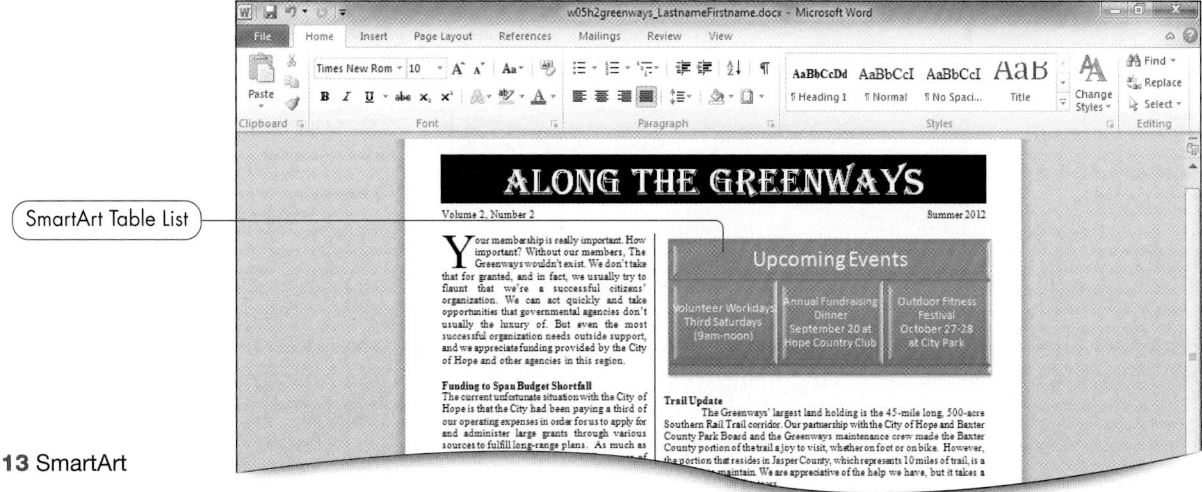

FIGURE 5.13 SmartArt Diagram ➤

To insert SmartArt into your document, click the Insert tab, click SmartArt, and then click one of the diagrams that displays in the gallery. A short description displays at the side of the gallery pane when you click any diagram, as shown in Figure 5.14. After you select the type and subtype of diagram you want to create, click OK.

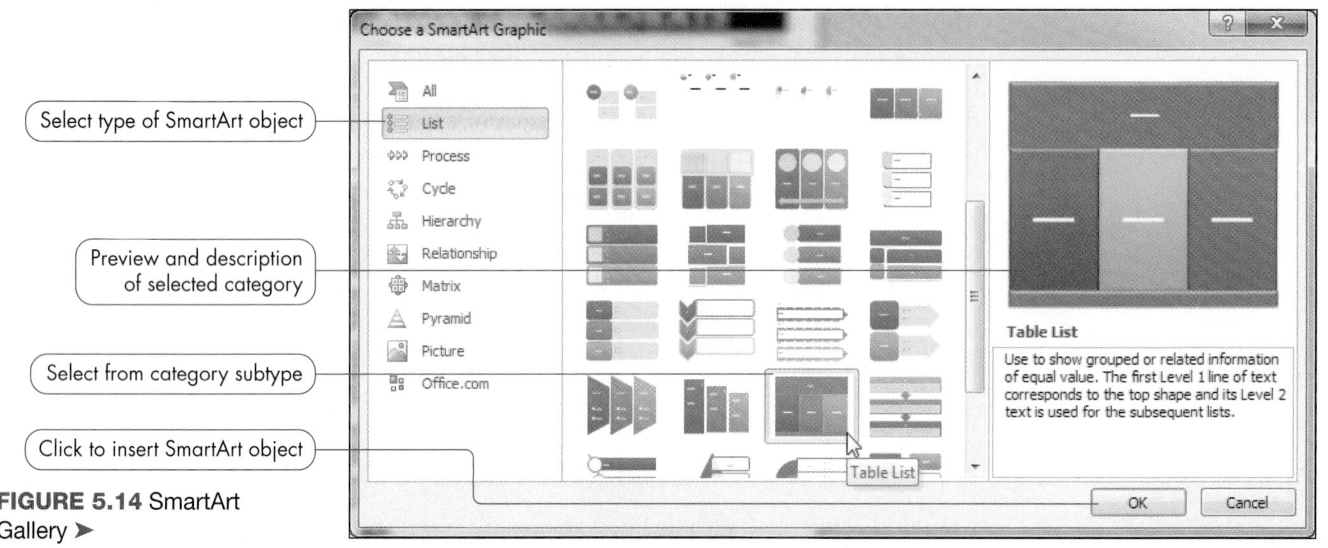

FIGURE 5.14 SmartArt Gallery ➤

The **Text pane** is a special pane that opens up for entering text when a SmartArt diagram is selected.

When the SmartArt diagram is inserted in your document, text placeholders display. You can click a placeholder and type the text that should appear in that location in the diagram. Alternatively, you can click the arrows on the left side of the diagram frame to view the Text pane. The ***Text pane*** displays an outline view of the text items and enables you to type or insert additional text into the SmartArt. The Design and Format tabs also display when you select a SmartArt object. The Design tab provides tools to change the appearance of the diagram, such as adding shapes and changing the style, as shown in Figure 5.15. The Format tab provides tools to modify the appearance of the diagram text.

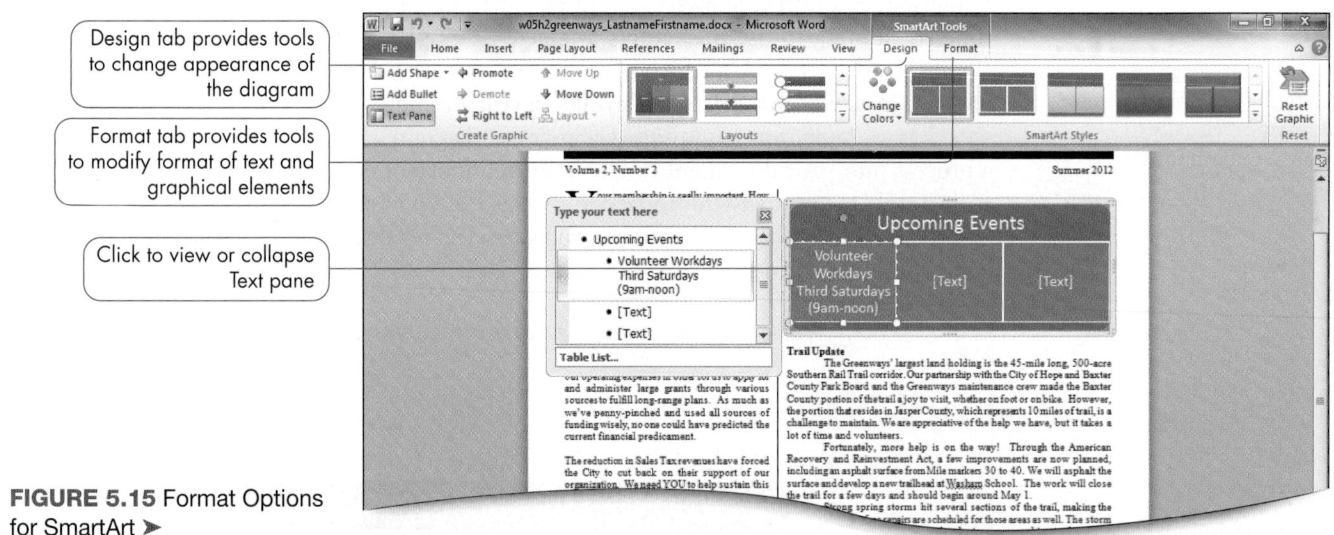

FIGURE 5.15 Format Options for SmartArt ➤

Inserting WordArt

WordArt is a feature that creates decorative text for a document.

WordArt is a Microsoft Office feature that creates decorative text that can be used to add interest to the text you use in a document. The advantage of using WordArt is that you can rotate text in any direction, add three-dimensional effects, display the text vertically, slant it, arch it, or even display it upside down.

WordArt is intuitively easy to use. You choose a style from the gallery (see Figure 5.16), then you enter the specific text in the text box, after which the results display (see Figure 5.17). The WordArt object can be moved and sized, just like any graphical object. A WordArt Tools tab provides many formatting features that enable you to change alignment, add special effects, and change styles quickly. It is fun and easy, and you can create some truly unique documents.

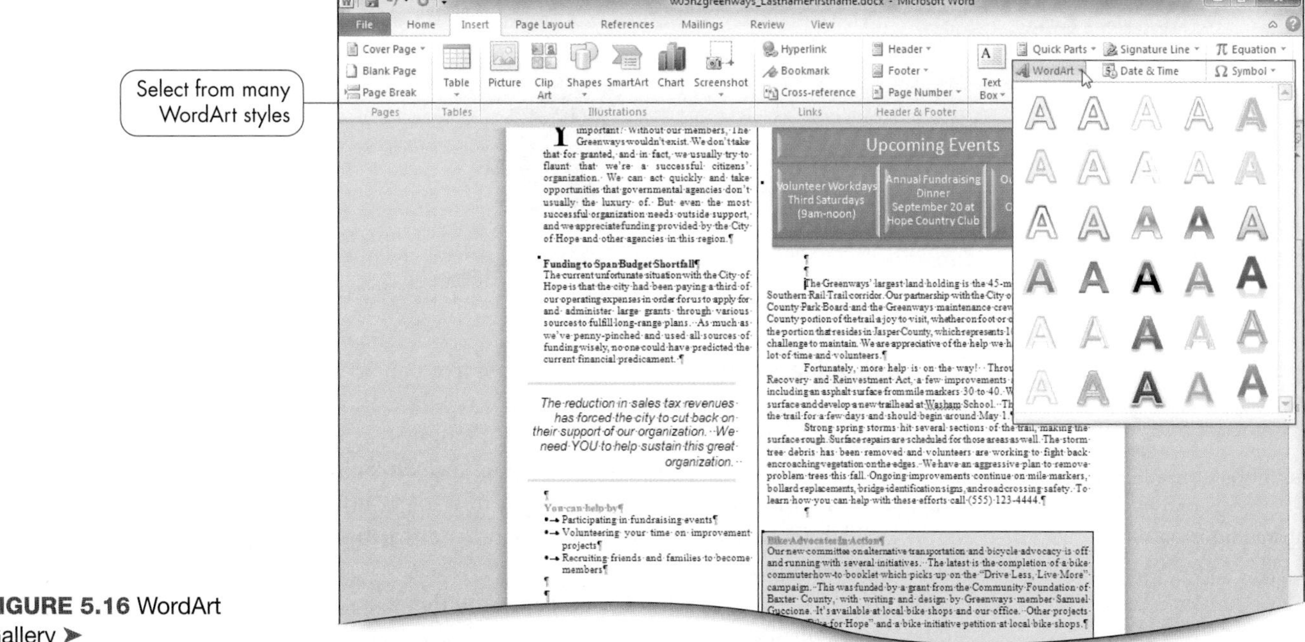

FIGURE 5.16 WordArt Gallery ➤

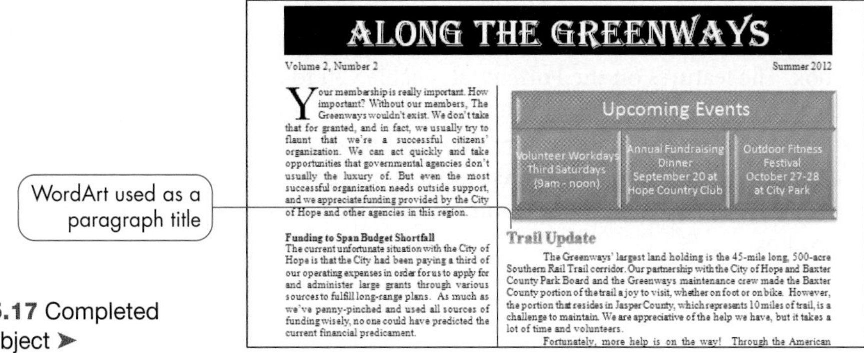

ALONG THE GREENWAYS

Volume 2, Number 2 Summer 2012

Your membership is really important. How important? Without our members, The Greenways wouldn't exist. We don't take that for granted, and in fact, we usually try to flaunt that we're a successful citizens' organization. We can act quickly and take opportunities that governmental agencies don't usually the luxury of. But even the most successful organization needs outside support, and we appreciate funding provided by the City of Hope and other agencies in this region.

Funding to Span Budget Shortfall
The current unfortunate situation with the City of Hope is that the City had been paying a third of our operating expenses in order for us to apply for and administer large grants through various sources to fulfill long-range plans. As much as we've penny-pinched and used all sources of funding wisely, no one could have predicted the current financial predicament.

Upcoming Events

Volunteer Workdays Third Saturdays (9am - noon)

Annual Fundraising Dinner September 20 at Hope Country Club

Outdoor Fitness Festival October 27-28 at City Park

Trail Update

The Greenways' largest land holding is the 45-mile long, 500-acre Southern Rail Trail corridor. Our partnership with the City of Hope and Baxter County Park Board and the Greenways maintenance crew made the Baxter County portion of the trail a joy to visit, whether on foot or on bike. However, the portion that resides in Jasper County, which represents 10 miles of trail, is a challenge to maintain. We are appreciative of the help we have, but it takes a lot of time and volunteers.

Fortunately, more help is on the way! Through the American

FIGURE 5.17 Completed WordArt Object ➤

Inserting a Text Box

A **text box** is simply a graphical object that contains text.

One way to combine the flexibility of a shape object with simple text is to create a text box. A ***text box*** is simply a graphical object that contains text. Magazine and newspaper articles often use text boxes as a visual tool to entice readers to focus on the contents of the text box, which then encourages them to read the accompanying article. Besides the obvious benefit of displaying text, you can layer it with other shapes. For example, you can position a text box on a callout shape object, and use it as a dialog bubble for a comic strip or clip art, as shown in Figure 5.18.

FIGURE 5.18 Insert a Text Box ➤

A **pull quote** is a phrase or sentence taken from an article to emphasize a key point.

A **sidebar** is supplementary text that appears on the side of the featured information.

A ***pull quote*** is a phrase or sentence taken from an article to emphasize a key point. It is typically set in larger type, often in a different typeface and/or italics, and may be offset with borders at the top, bottom, or on the sides. Pull quotes display throughout this book to draw attention to important topics in each chapter. ***Sidebars*** also enable you to call attention to information in a document by displaying it in a space along the side of the featured information. Sidebars might display supplementary information, or they can simply display information of interest to the reader.

To insert a text box, click the Insert Tab, and then click Text Box. A gallery of preformatted text boxes displays and you can click one of those or click Draw Text Box to create a custom text box. Several designs in the gallery are suitable for a sidebar or pull quote in your document, as shown in Figure 5.19, but you can also create your own. Because it is a graphical object, you can apply graphical formatting options such as wrapping style, horizontal alignment, outside borders, and font treatments. The Format tab displays when you click a text box. The features on the Format tab enable you to customize the border of the text box (you can give it a colored border, or no border at all), apply shadow and 3-D effects, and use positional attributes such as where the text box displays on the page and how text wraps around the text box. You can format the text using font properties you are already familiar with, such as size, type, and color, and you also can change the direction text displays within the text box.

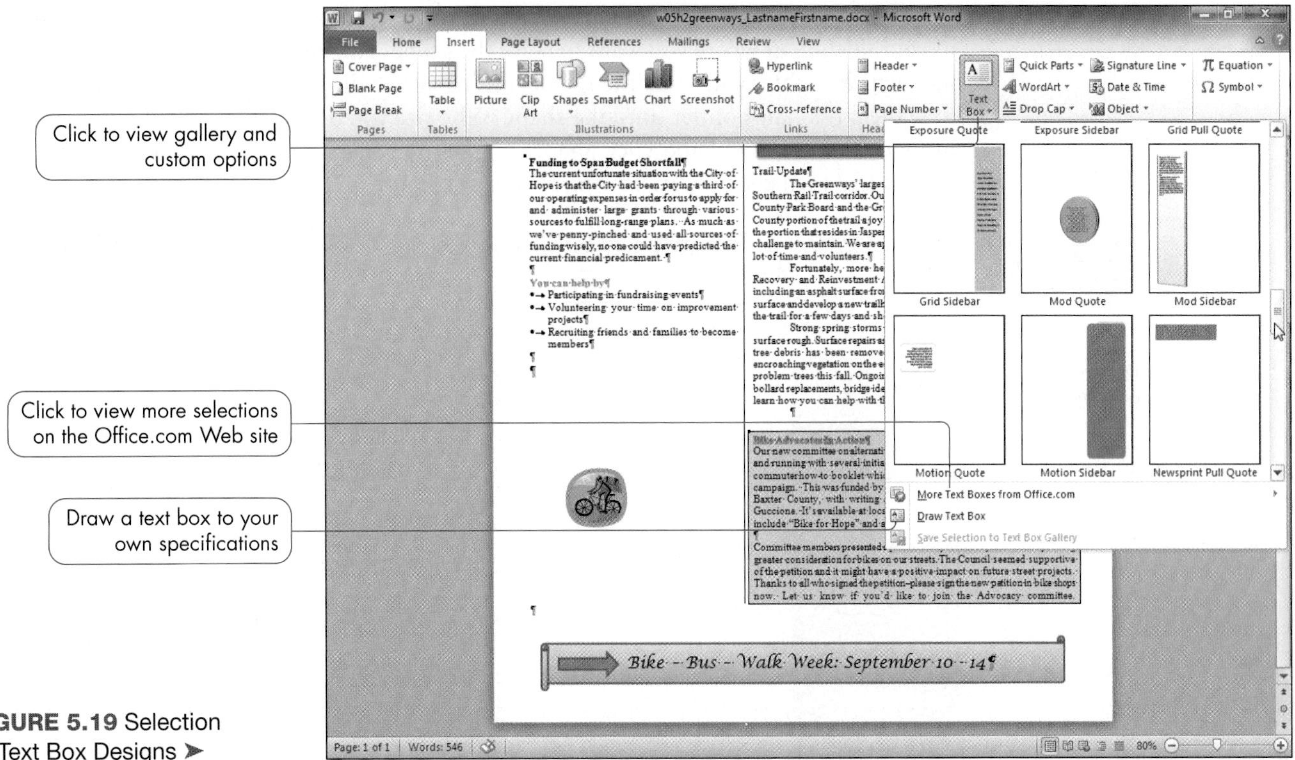

FIGURE 5.19 Selection of Text Box Designs ➤

You can link one text box to another so that when text runs out of space in one box it automatically continues into another, as shown in Figure 5.20. The best use for linking text boxes is creating a booklet. Each page contains two text boxes that include the booklet text. Because booklets print on both sides of the paper, the text boxes link in such a way so that the text flows from the back of one page to the front of another. When you view the pages in Word, they appear out of order, but when assembled for the booklet, they display correctly.

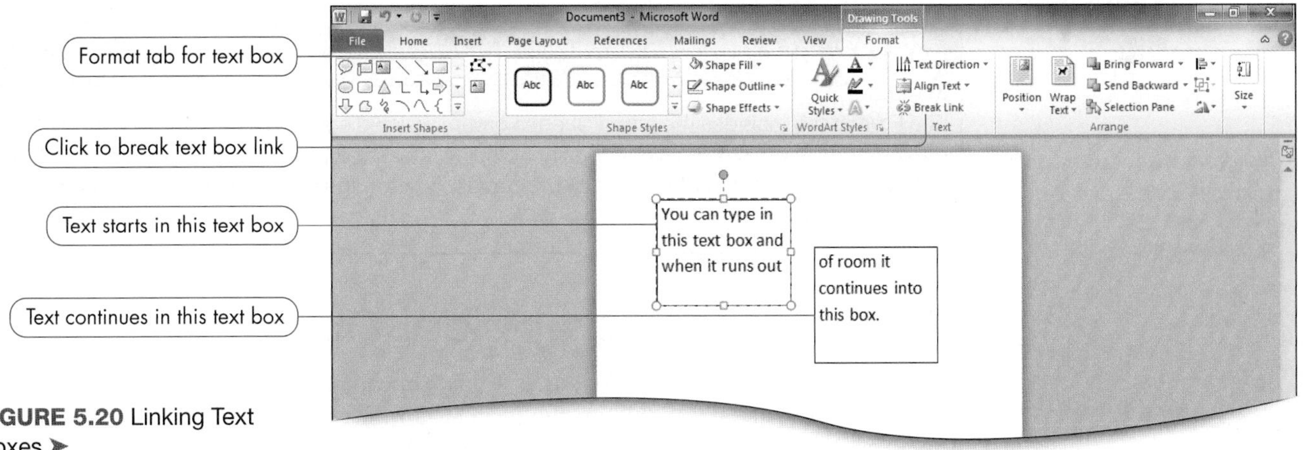

FIGURE 5.20 Linking Text Boxes ➤

Inserting Drawing Shapes

One tool that is especially useful is the Shapes command. A shape is an object, such as a circle or an arrow, which you can use as a visual enhancement. You can use one shape or combine multiple shapes to create a more complex image. When you click Shapes in the Illustrations group on the Insert tab, the Shapes gallery displays the following categories of shapes:

- Lines
- Basic Shapes
- Block Arrows
- Flowchart
- Callouts
- Stars and Banners

To insert a shape, select the shape from the gallery, and then position the mouse pointer in your document where you want to place the shape. The mouse pointer changes to a cross-hair, which enables you to define the beginning and ending points of your shape. Click and drag the cross-hair pointer until the shape is the size you desire. If you need to insert several instances of the same shape, click Shapes on the Insert tab, right-click the shape object in the gallery, and then click Lock Drawing Mode (see Figure 5.21).

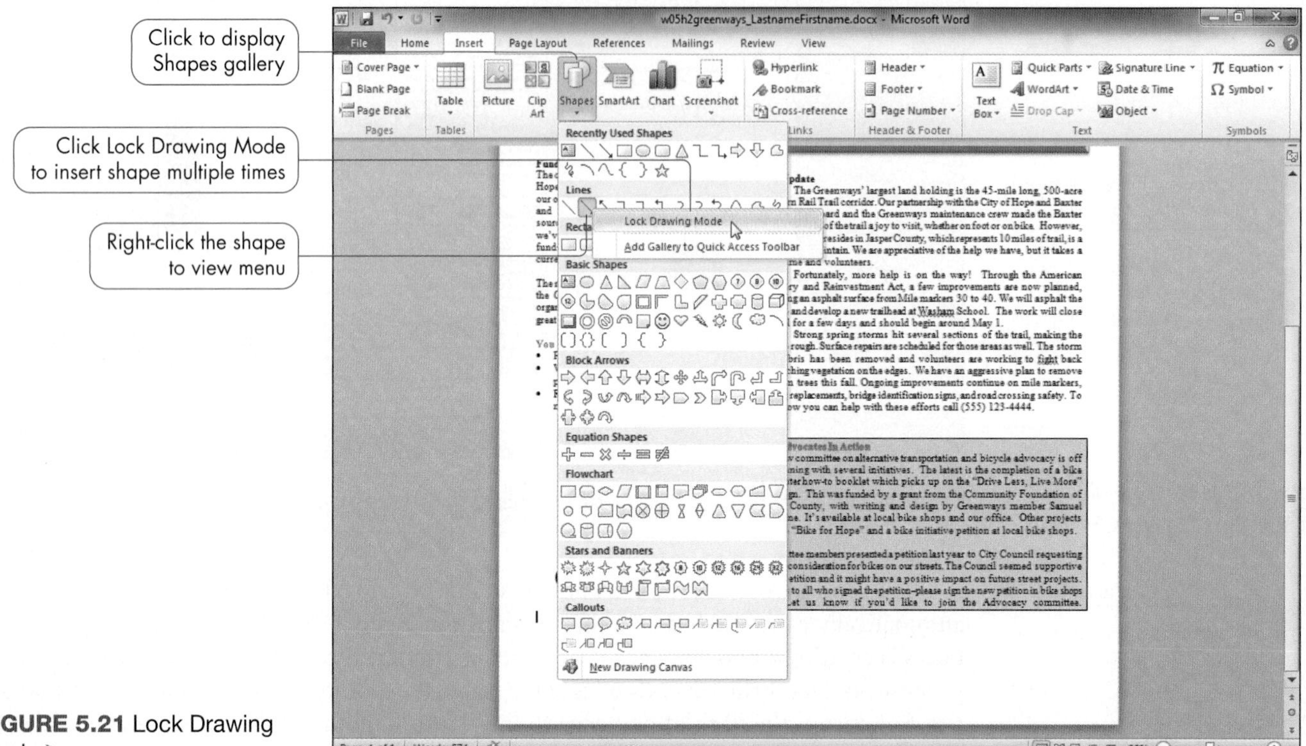

FIGURE 5.21 Lock Drawing Mode ➤

TIP Inserting Additional Shapes

The Format tab includes the Insert Shapes group, which displays a small gallery of commonly used shapes. If the small gallery does not display the shape you want, you can click the More button to view the complete gallery of shapes. This enables you to insert shapes without returning to the Insert tab.

Manipulating Graphical Objects

After you insert a shape, SmartArt, or text box, you can enhance its appearance by using one of the commands available on the Format tab for the object. Shapes and text boxes display initially with a simple black border and white fill. But to capture the attention of the reader, you will likely want to change the border style; and to shapes you can add color or fill effects as well.

Change Shape Fills and Borders

The **fill** is the interior space of an object.

Drawing shapes and text boxes have two main components that can contain color: the line or border and the ***fill***, or interior space of the object. Word provides a gallery of styles you can choose from, or you might prefer to pick the line and fill colors for the objects yourself.

You have so many options to use for line and fill that it can be overwhelming. Figure 5.22 shows the Shape Fill options you access from the Drawing Tools Format tab and Table 5.1 gives examples of several fill and border options. Shapes such as a straight line obviously do not contain an interior area for applying a fill color, but you can change the color, width, and style of the line itself.

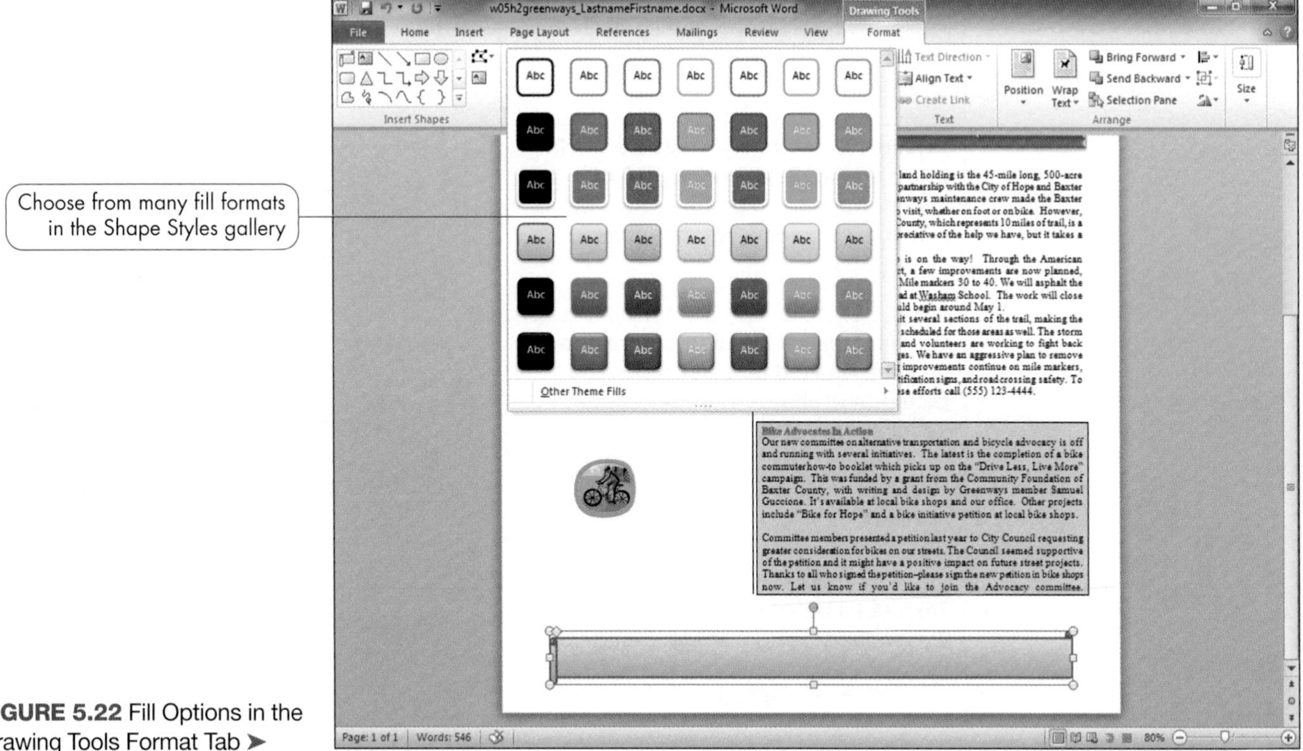

FIGURE 5.22 Fill Options in the Drawing Tools Format Tab ➤

TABLE 5.1 Results of Using Shape Fill, Outline, and Effects

Description	Example	Ribbon Command
Solid color fill is applied to the shape. No outline is selected. Outer Shadow effect is applied.		Shape Fill: Theme Colors; Standard Colors; No Fill; More Fill Colors...; Picture...; Gradient; Texture
Picture fill inserts an image from a file into a shape. Solid outline in 3 pt weight frames the picture and shape. Angle bevel special effect applied.		Shape Outline: Theme Colors; Standard Colors; No Outline; More Outline Colors...; Weight; Dashes; Arrows
Gradient fill is a blend of colors and shades. Dashed outline frames the picture and shape. Tight reflection special effect applied.		Shape Effects: Preset; Shadow; Reflection; Glow
Texture fill inserts textures, such as woven fabric, into a shape. Solid color in 4½ pt weight outlines shape. Glow special effect applied.		Soft Edges; Bevel; 3-D Rotation

TIP The Drawing Canvas

If you plan on combining multiple shapes in one area, you should consider using the Drawing Canvas. The ***Drawing Canvas*** is a frame-like area that helps you keep parts of your drawing together while you arrange them. The Drawing Canvas frame does not display in your document, but you can format it to display as a border if you choose. To use the Drawing Canvas, click the Insert tab, click Shapes, and then click New Drawing Canvas. You can then insert shapes onto the canvas. To delete the Drawing Canvas, select the frame sizing handles, which resemble crop handles rather than graphic sizing handles, and then click Delete. The canvas and any shapes it contains are removed.

The **Drawing Canvas** is a framelike area that helps you keep parts of your drawing together.

Grouping and Layering Objects

It is fun to work with shapes because you can manipulate them in so many different ways. You have already seen how to manipulate the appearance of a shape. Not only can you format and manipulate a single shape or object, but you can manipulate several objects together.

When you work with several graphical objects, you might find that you need to arrange them so that a part of one overlaps another. This process is appropriately called ***layering*** because objects are stacked on each other. However, the reason for layering is to enable you to separate a complex grouping of objects so you can format and revise each object (or layer) individually. It is similar to working on a project on a desk: You pick up a piece of paper and place it on top of another piece. At any time, you can rearrange the order of the papers, write on one, or add to the stack of papers on your desk. Figure 5.23 shows two objects that are layered.

Layering is the process of placing one shape on top of another.

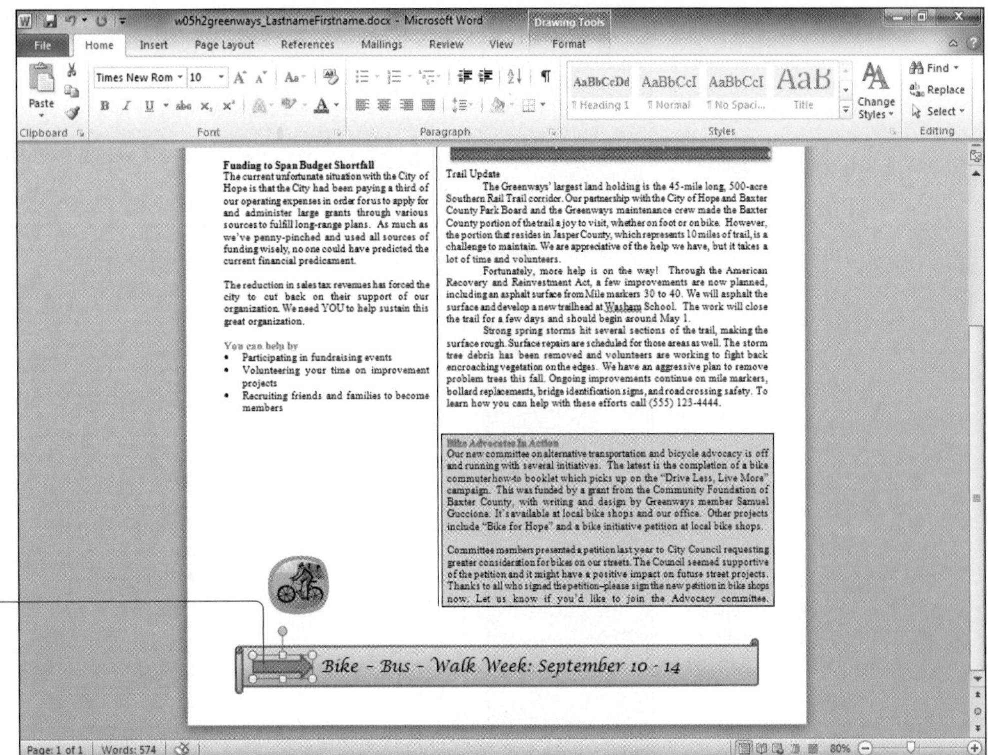

Arrow object is layered on top of banner object

FIGURE 5.23 Layering Objects ➤

As you work with shapes in Word, you can bring a shape to the front by one layer, push a shape back by one layer, move a shape to the front of all layers, or push a shape to the back of all layers. The commands in Table 5.2 are found in the Arrange group on the Format tab and are very valuable when you layer objects.

TABLE 5.2 Layering Options

Bring to Front	Moves an object to the top of all other objects
Bring Forward	Places an object on top of the object directly in front of it
Bring in Front of Text	Enables an object to display in front of text
Send to Back	Moves an object to the back of all other objects
Send Backward	Places an object behind the object directly in back of it
Send Behind Text	Enables an object to display behind text

Grouping is the process of combining objects so they appear as a single object.

After you layer objects, you might need to group them so you can manipulate them together. ***Grouping*** is the process of combining selected objects so that they appear as a single object. When objects are grouped, you can move them together or apply a quick style to all the objects at one time. To select multiple objects for grouping, click one object, hold down Shift, and then click the remaining objects. After you select all the objects, click Group on the Format tab, as shown in Figure 5.24.

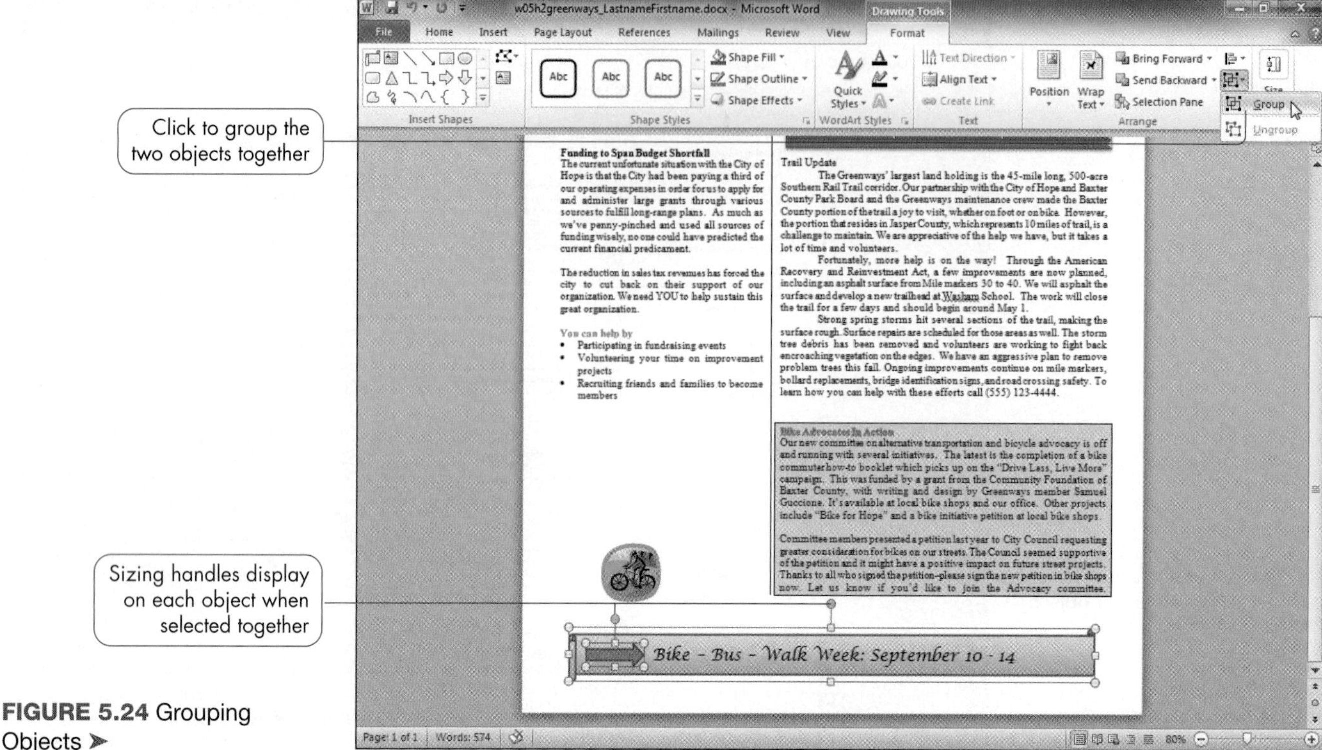

FIGURE 5.24 Grouping Objects ➤

Ungrouping breaks a combined single object into individual objects.

Regrouping is the process of grouping objects together again.

You can separate grouped objects by ungrouping them. ***Ungrouping*** breaks a combined single object into individual objects. You might ungroup objects because you need to make modifications, such as size or position, to an individual object. Or you might want to delete or add another object to the group. After you ungroup, Word remembers how you grouped the objects originally and enables you to regroup them. ***Regrouping*** is the process of grouping objects together without having to select them again individually. Regrouping only works with the objects you group initially. If you want to add another object to the group, use the Group command instead of Regroup.

You can quickly access grouping or layering options by right-clicking the object. When the menu displays, click Grouping to view the Group commands, or click Order to view the layering commands.

Text Wrapping

If you encounter difficulties when working with graphical objects, you might need to change the text wrapping format of the object. The Advanced Layout properties dialog box, which you access from the Format tab, includes the Square text wrapping setting. This setting is often necessary to layer and group objects. Additionally, you can find the Lock anchor setting in this dialog box, which is useful when you want to assign an absolute position to a graphic.

Flipping and Rotating Objects

If you decide that a shape should be turned in a different direction, you can quickly flip or rotate an object using tools on the Format tab. When you click Rotate in the Arrange group, you can select from several commands that enable you to rotate the object in a particular direction, or to flip it in such a way that you get a mirror image. If you click the More Rotate options, a dialog box displays and you can use precise measurements to modify the object. Figure 5.25 demonstrates the different Rotate commands.

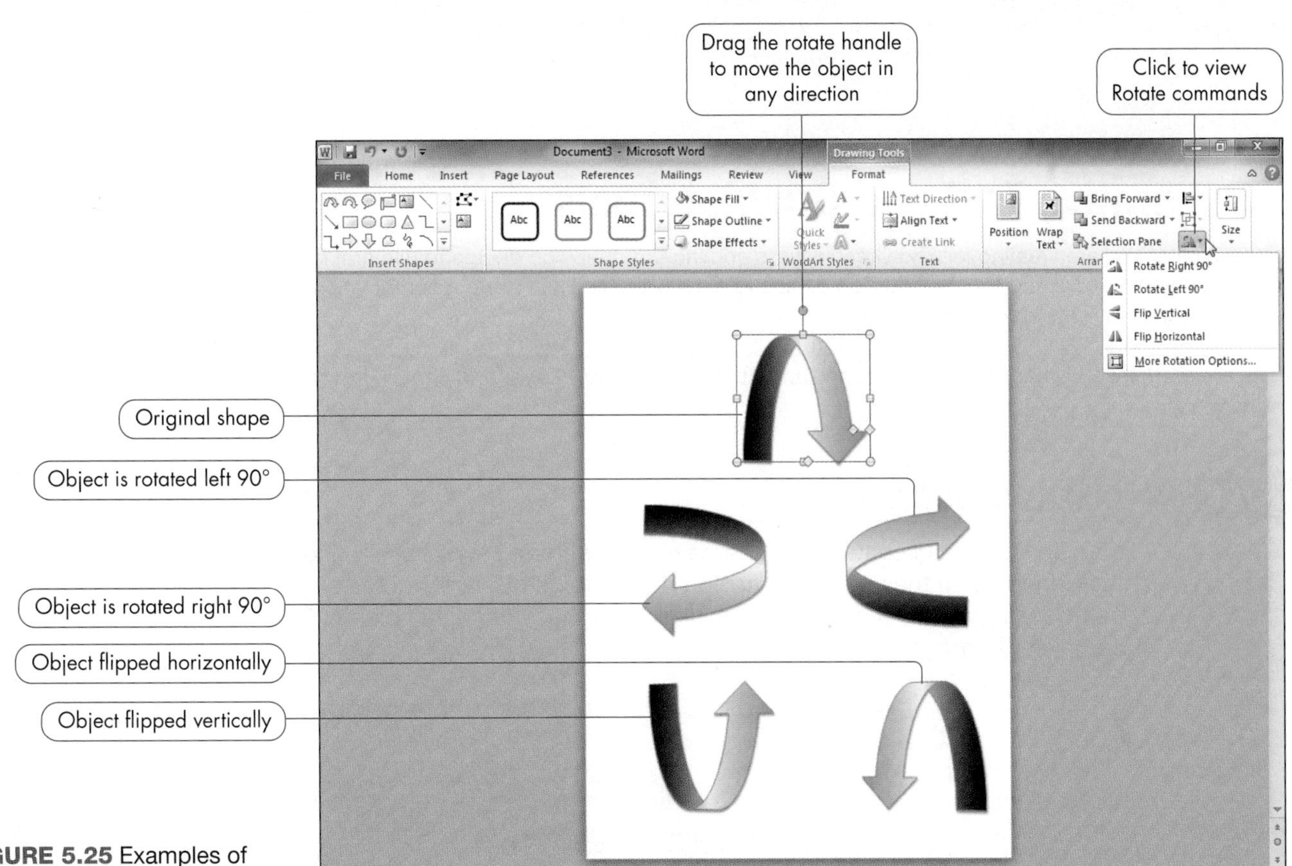

FIGURE 5.25 Examples of Rotating an Object ➤

HANDS-ON EXERCISES

2 Decorative Text and Drawing Tools

The newsletter you are creating for The Greenways is coming together. You decide to use graphical features in Word to display information about upcoming events. You also decide to display article titles using a combination of graphics and text rather than simply changing the size and color of fonts.

Skills covered: Insert SmartArt • Insert Shapes and Apply Formatting • Layer and Group Drawing Objects • Create a Pull Quote • Insert WordArt

STEP 1 INSERT SMARTART

Members of The Greenways should be made aware of several upcoming events. You want to be sure they stand out in the newsletter, so you decide to use SmartArt to display them. This will give this particular news item a unique look and will fit in the wider right column. Refer to Figure 5.26 as you complete Step 1.

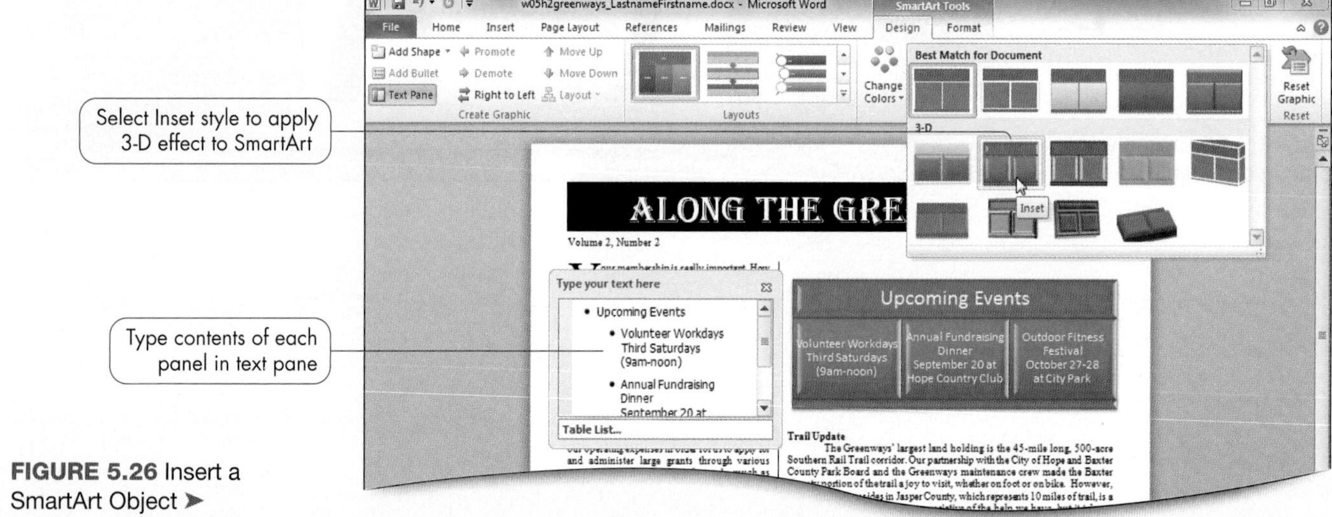

FIGURE 5.26 Insert a SmartArt Object ➤

a. Open *w05h1greenways_LastnameFirstname*, if you closed it after Hands-On Exercise 1, and save it as **w05h2greenways_LastnameFirstname**, changing *h1* to *h2*.

b. Click the **Zoom slider**, and then increase the zoom to **80%**. Delete the heading *Upcoming Events* and the event information that follows. Click to position the insertion point on the blank line above the *Trail Update* heading.

TROUBLESHOOTING: If there is not a blank line above the *Trail Update* heading, position the insertion point on the left side of *Trail Update*, and then press Enter.

c. Click the **Insert tab**, and then click **SmartArt** in the Illustrations group.

The Choose a SmartArt Graphic dialog box displays with a list of categories on the left side of the box.

d. Click **List** on the left side, scroll down to view the additional designs at the bottom of the right pane, and then click **Table List** (eighth row, third column). Click **OK** to close the dialog box.

A representation of the table list displays in your document.

e. Hold your mouse over the bottom-right corner of the SmartArt shape until the two-headed arrow displays, and then drag to the right margin and release the mouse.

   This increases the size of the SmartArt object to create additional space for the information you type next.

f. Click the **Text pane arrows** to expand the text pane, if necessary. Type **Upcoming Events**.

   This places text in the panel that displays at the top of the SmartArt object.

g. Populate the remaining panels by completing the following steps:

   - Click one time in the first sub-bullet, type **Volunteer Workdays**, press **Shift+Enter** to move the insertion point to the next line without a bullet, type **Third Saturdays**, press **Shift+Enter**, and then type (**9am-noon**).
   - Type the following text in the two remaining panels.

Annual Fundraising Dinner September 20 at Hope Country Club	Outdoor Fitness Festival October 27–28 at City Park

TROUBLESHOOTING: If you have trouble displaying the information above on multiple lines in each text box, type directly in the text boxes that display in the object instead of typing in the Text pane.

h. Click the **Close button** in the top-right corner of the text pane.

i. Confirm the entire SmartArt object is selected, click the **Design tab**, if necessary, and then click the **More button** in the SmartArt Styles group to display a variety of styles for this object. Click **Inset** (second row, second column) under the *3D* heading, as shown in Figure 5.26.

j. Save the document.

STEP 2 INSERT SHAPES AND APPLY FORMATTING

You notice there is a significant amount of white space at the bottom of the newsletter and decide to use this space to add a shape object that will span the width of the newsletter and display text to remind readers of an upcoming event. Refer to Figure 5.27 as you complete Step 2.

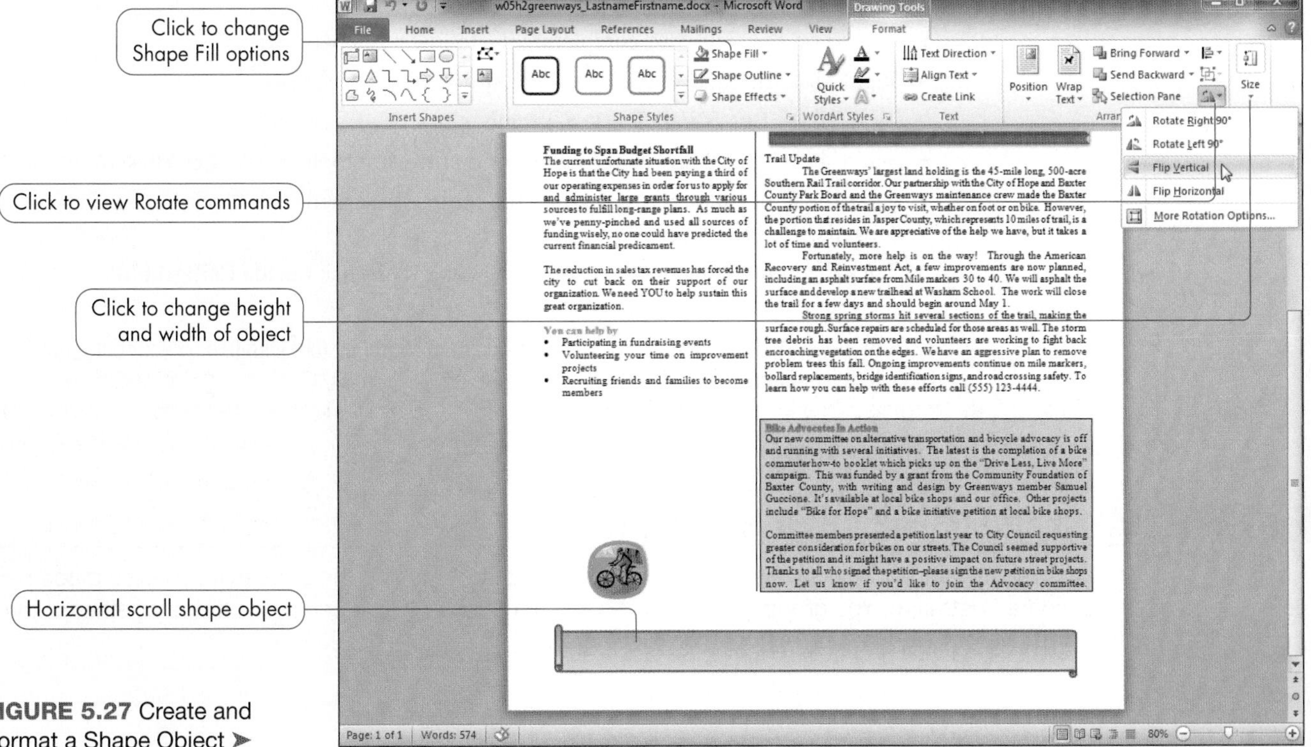

FIGURE 5.27 Create and Format a Shape Object ➤

a. Press **Ctrl+End** to move the insertion point to the bottom of the page.

b. Click the **Insert tab**, click **Shapes** in the Illustrations group, and click **Horizontal Scroll** (second row, sixth column) in the *Stars and Banners* set.

   After you click the shape, the mouse cursor takes the form of a cross-hair.

c. Drag the mouse at the bottom of the newsletter to create a scroll that extends across the width of the page.

   The scroll remains selected after you release the mouse, as indicated by the sizing handles. You can click and drag the yellow diamond to change the appearance of the scroll.

d. Click the **Height arrow** in the Size group until **.7** displays. Click the **Width arrow** until **7.2** displays.

   The Format tab displays a variety of formatting commands, in addition to Height and Width.

> **TROUBLESHOOTING:** If you release the mouse before the scroll is the desired size, click the sizing handles to stretch it to the desired size or just type in the height and width.

e. Click **Wrap Text**, and then click **More Layout Options**. Click the **Position tab**, and then click **Alignment** in the *Horizontal* section. Click the **Alignment arrow**, select **Centered**, click the **relative to arrow**, and then select **Margin**. Click **OK**.

f. Click the **Shape Fill arrow** in the Shape Styles group. Click the color **Blue, Accent 1, Darker 25%** (fifth row, fifth column).

g. Click the **Shape Fill arrow** again, point to **Gradient**, and then click **Linear Up** (third row, second column) under the *Light Variations* section.

   The scroll color changes to display a lighter blue color that gradually lightens as it nears the top of the object.

h. Click the **Shape Outline arrow** in the Shape Styles group, select **Weight**, and then select **2¼ pt**.

i. Click **Rotate** in the Arrange group, and then select **Flip Vertical**, as shown in Figure 5.27.

   The two previous steps enhance the outline of the object and flip it so that the edges of the scroll display differently.

j. Insert text on the banner by completing the following steps:
   - Right-click the banner, and then click **Add Text**.
   - Type **Bike—Bus—Walk Week: September 10 - 14**.
   - Select the text, click the **Font Size arrow** on the Mini toolbar, and then click **16**.
   - Click the **Font Color arrow** on the Mini toolbar, and then click **Black, Text 1** (first row, second column).
   - Click the **Font arrow** on the Mini toolbar, and then click **Lucida Calligraphy**.

> **TROUBLESHOOTING:** If you do not have the Lucida Calligraphy font installed on your computer, substitute a different font.

k. Save the document.

STEP 3 LAYER AND GROUP DRAWING OBJECTS

You can display shape objects together as layered objects, but moving the objects for precise placement can become frustrating. You group the shapes so, when necessary, you can move them together at the same time. Refer to Figure 5.28 as you complete Step 3.

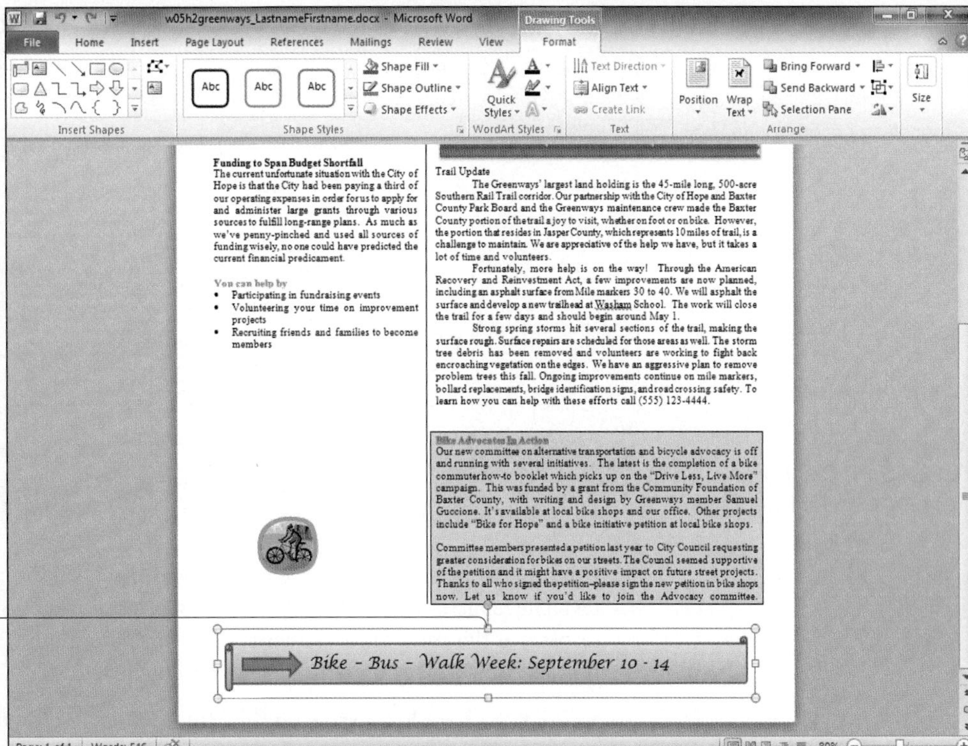

Only one set of sizing handles display after grouping items together

FIGURE 5.28 Grouping Objects ➤

a. Click the **Insert tab**, click **Shapes** in the Illustrations group, and then select the **Right Arrow** from the *Block Arrows* section. Drag your mouse to create the arrow on the left side of the word *Bike* that displays in the scroll object at the bottom of the page.

b. Click the **Height arrow** in the Size group until **.3** displays. Click the **Width arrow** until **.8** displays.

c. Click the arrow one time, and then hold down **Ctrl** and press ↑ or ↓ to nudge the arrow shape into the middle of the scroll shape.

   Using the Ctrl+arrow combination enables you to position an object very precisely.

d. Press **Shift**, and then click the banner.

   Both objects, the banner and the arrow, are selected and sizing handles for both objects display.

e. Click **Group** in the Arrange group, and then select **Group**.

   Only one set of sizing handles displays because the two objects are grouped and function as one, as shown in Figure 5.28.

f. Save the document.

STEP 4 CREATE A PULL QUOTE

You decide to move one paragraph into a text box, which has the effect of a pull quote. This is an effective way to display a statement that is so important you want to make sure the members notice it. Refer to Figure 5.29 as you complete Step 4.

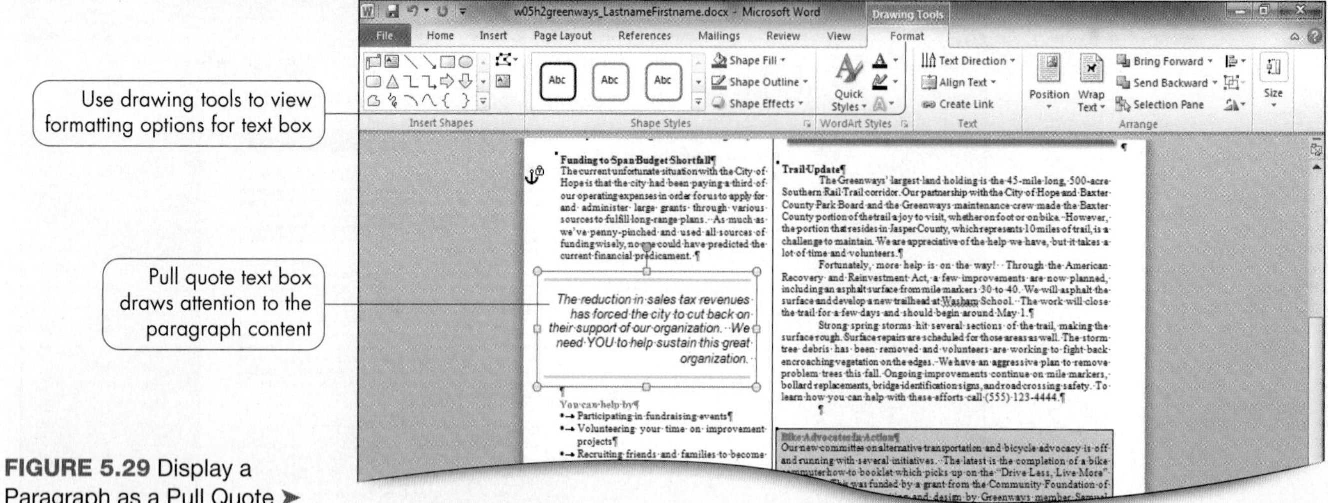

FIGURE 5.29 Display a Paragraph as a Pull Quote ➤

a. Click the **Home tab**, and then click **Show/Hide** (¶). Select the paragraph that begins with the text *The reduction in sales tax revenue has forced*, but do not select the paragraph symbol that displays at the end of the last sentence of this paragraph. To modify the format and prepare this text for a pull quote, complete the following steps:

- Click the **Font Size arrow** on the Mini toolbar, and then select **12**.
- Click the **Font arrow**, and then select **Arial**.
- Click **Italic**.
- Press **Ctrl+X** to cut the text from the document.
- Press **Backspace** two times to remove the paragraph marks that display between the two paragraphs.

Now you do not have any empty lines between the paragraphs that will cause large gaps of white space between the elements in this newsletter. This will enable you to position the pull quote more precisely.

b. Click the **Insert tab**, click **Text Box** in the Text group, scroll down, and then click **Stacks Quote** from the gallery.

The Text Box gallery includes building blocks that are preformatted for a variety of pull quote styles.

c. Press **Ctrl+V**.

The text you copied earlier displays in the text box.

d. Click the border of the text box to select it. To position it more precisely on the page, complete the following steps:

- Click the **Format tab**, click **Position** in the Arrange group, and then click **More Layout Options**.
- Click **Absolute position** in the *Horizontal* section, and then click the arrow until **–0.3″** displays. Click the **to the right of arrow**, and then select **Margin**.
- Click **Absolute position** in the *Vertical* section, and then click the arrow until **1.4″** displays. Click the **below arrow**, and then select **Paragraph**.
- Click **Lock anchor**.
- Click **OK** to save the settings.

e. Save the document.

STEP 5 INSERT WORDART

The large article in the middle of the right column looks pretty plain, but contains some very important information about the trails. You decide that it deserves a more attractive title and will replace the current title text with WordArt. You also use fun formatting features on the WordArt to coordinate better with the SmartArt you added earlier. Refer to Figure 5.30 as you complete Step 5.

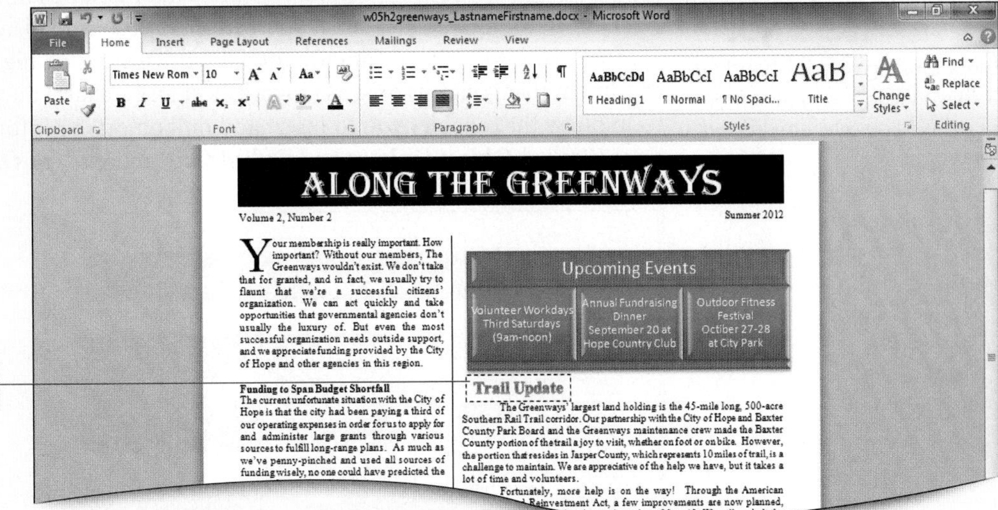

WordArt replaces paragraph title

FIGURE 5.30 Using WordArt for a Paragraph Heading ➤

a. Select the heading *Trail Update*, and then press **Enter** two times.

   This removes the current title and makes room for the WordArt you will insert.

b. Click the **Insert tab**, and then click **WordArt** in the Text group. Select **Gradient Fill - Blue, Accent 1** (third row, fourth column).

   The text box where you type the phrase displays on top of the paragraph. You will relocate the text box later.

c. Press **Backspace** three times, and then type **Trail Update** to insert the paragraph heading into the **WordArt box**. Select **Trail Update**, click the **Font size arrow** on the Mini toolbar, and then select **16**.

   The paragraph heading *Trail Update* displays in the text box in the WordArt style you select. You will move it into the proper position in the next step.

d. Drag the text box to the right column; position it under the SmartArt object and just above the paragraphs it describes.

TROUBLESHOOTING: Use the arrow keys to nudge the object into exact positioning, if necessary.

e. Click **Shape Outline** in the Shape Styles group, select **Dashes**, and then select **Dash** (fourth item in the list). Click anywhere to remove the sizing handles.

f. Click the **Home tab**, and then click **Show/Hide** (¶). Compare your work to Figure 5.30.

g. Save the document and keep it onscreen if you plan to continue with Hands-On Exercise 3. If not, close the document and exit Word.

Object Linking and Embedding

Microsoft Office enables you to create documents that contain objects from other applications.... The technology that enables you to insert and link objects ... is called Object Linking and Embedding.

Object Linking and Embedding (OLE) is a technology that enables you to insert objects into different applications.

Microsoft Office enables you to create documents that contain objects from other applications. For example, you might create a report in Word that explains the results of a survey. The survey data are saved in an Excel spreadsheet that also includes a chart to summarize the data. Rather than re-creating the data in a Word table, you can insert the spreadsheet and chart into your Word document. The document in Figure 5.31 is a Microsoft Word document that contains objects (a worksheet and a chart) developed in Microsoft Excel. The technology that enables you to insert and link objects or information into different applications is called ***Object Linking and Embedding*** (abbreviated ***OLE***; it is pronounced "oh-lay").

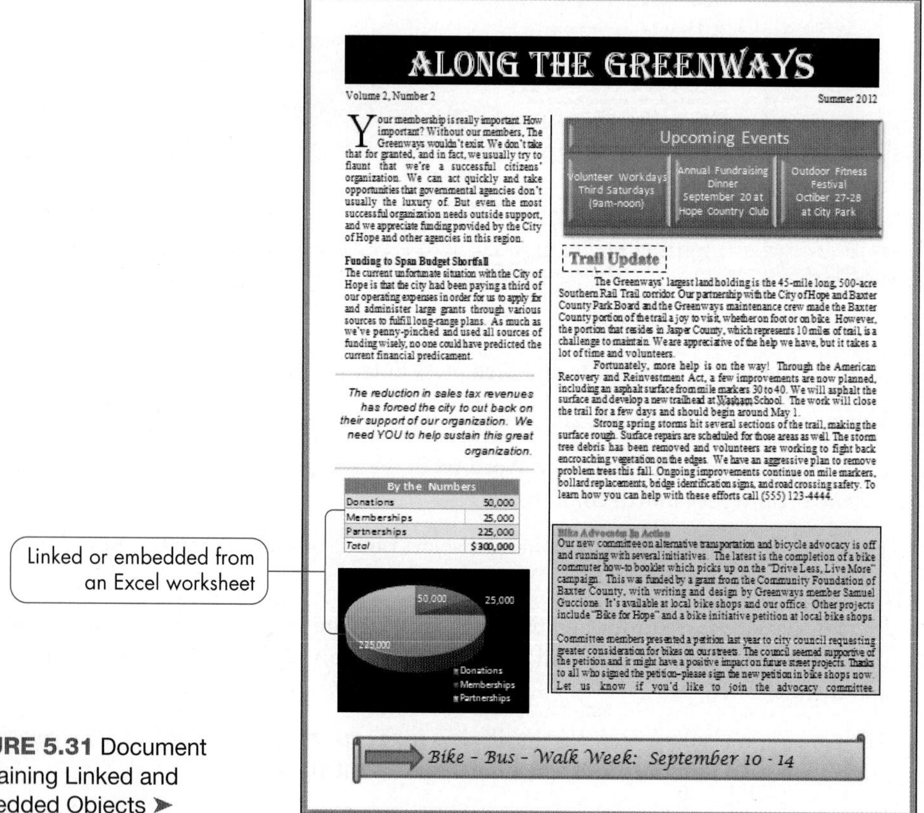

ALONG THE GREENWAYS

Volume 2, Number 2 — Summer 2012

Your membership is really important. How important? Without our members, The Greenways wouldn't exist. We don't take that for granted, and in fact, we usually try to flaunt that we're a successful citizens' organization. We can act quickly and take opportunities that governmental agencies don't usually the luxury of. But even the most successful organization needs outside support, and we appreciate funding provided by the City of Hope and other agencies in this region.

Funding to Span Budget Shortfall
The current unfortunate situation with the City of Hope is that the city had been paying a third of our operating expenses in order for us to apply for and administer large grants through various sources to fulfill long-range plans. As much as we've penny-pinched and used all sources of funding wisely, no one could have predicted the current financial predicament.

The reduction in sales tax revenues has forced the city to cut back on their support of our organization. We need YOU to help sustain this great organization.

By the Numbers	
Donations	50,000
Memberships	25,000
Partnerships	225,000
Total	$300,000

Upcoming Events

Volunteer Workdays Third Saturdays (9am-noon)	Annual Fundraising Dinner September 20 at Hope Country Club	Outdoor Fitness Festival October 27-28 at City Park

Trail Update

The Greenways' largest land holding is the 45-mile long, 500-acre Southern Rail Trail corridor. Our partnership with the City of Hope and Baxter County Park Board and the Greenways maintenance crew made the Baxter County portion of the trail a joy to visit, whether on foot or on bike. However, the portion that resides in Jasper County, which represents 10 miles of trail, is a challenge to maintain. We are appreciative of the help we have, but it takes a lot of time and volunteers.

Fortunately, more help is on the way! Through the American Recovery and Reinvestment Act, a few improvements are now planned, including an asphalt surface from mile markers 30 to 40. We will asphalt the surface and develop a new trailhead at Washam School. The work will close the trail for a few days and should begin around May 1.

Strong spring storms hit several sections of the trail, making the surface rough. Surface repairs are scheduled for those areas as well. The storm tree debris has been removed and volunteers are working to fight back encroaching vegetation on the edges. We have an aggressive plan to remove problem trees this fall. Ongoing improvements continue on mile markers, bollard replacements, bridge identification signs, and road crossing safety. To learn how you can help with these efforts call (555) 123-4444.

Bike Advocates In Action
Our new committee on alternative transportation and bicycle advocacy is off and running with several initiatives. The latest is the completion of a bike commuter how-to booklet which picks up on the "Drive Less, Live More" campaign. This was funded by a grant from the Community Foundation of Baxter County, with writing and design by Greenways member Samuel Guccione. It's available at local bike shops and our office. Other projects include "Bike for Hope" and a bike initiative petition at local bike shops.

Committee members presented a petition last year to city council requesting greater consideration for bikes on our streets. The council seemed supportive of the petition and it might have a positive impact on future street projects. Thanks to all who signed the petition–please sign the new petition in bike shops now. Let us know if you'd like to join the advocacy committee.

Bike - Bus - Walk Week: September 10 - 14

FIGURE 5.31 Document Containing Linked and Embedded Objects ➤

In this section, you will learn about the many ways to embed and link an object, and then you will learn to update a linked object.

Using OLE to Insert an Object

Embedding pulls an object into a document, where you can edit it without changing the source.

Linking inserts an object from another program, but retains a connection to the original data.

When you insert objects into your document, you really have two options for how the object will work within your document. The first option is ***embedding***. Embedding pulls an object into a document from its original source and enables you to edit it without changing the source. For example, if you embed a portion of an Excel worksheet, it becomes part of your document; you can make modifications to the copied data at any time, and those changes do not affect the original worksheet. Likewise, any changes to the original Excel file will not display in your document.

The second option for inserting an object into your document is linking. ***Linking*** is the process of inserting an object from another program, but the object retains a connection to the original file. If you change the data in the original source file, the data in the destination file will reflect the changes. A linked object is stored in its own file and may be tied to many documents. The same Excel chart, for example, can be linked to a Word document and a PowerPoint presentation. Any changes to the Excel chart are automatically reflected in the document and the presentation to which it is linked.

The advantage of linking over embedding is that a linked object will reflect the most current information. This might be important, for example, when you insert the stock prices for your company into your weekly newsletter—you would always want the most current prices to display. An embedded object is a snapshot of the information at the time you embedded it; if that is sufficient for your document, it is a good option to use because you don't have to worry about having access to the source file at a later date. If you want to display the previous year-ending sales figures in your January newsletter, you would embed the data because those numbers won't change.

You have several methods to link and embed data into a document, including:

- Copy and Paste
- Drag and Drop
- Display the Insert tab and click Object

If you use the Copy and Paste method, you first copy a selection from the source, such as an Excel spreadsheet or a PowerPoint slide, and then use Paste to insert it into the destination document. If you use a simple paste command, the object will be embedded. When you paste Excel data into Word, the data are pasted into table cells and do not retain Excel spreadsheet capabilities and formatting. For example, all formulas and functions convert to actual values, and if you change one value it will not change any results that use that value. Additionally, the numbers will not align on the decimal points. If you click Paste Special, you can invoke the Paste link option from the Paste Special dialog box, as shown in Figure 5.32, which creates the connection to the original file.

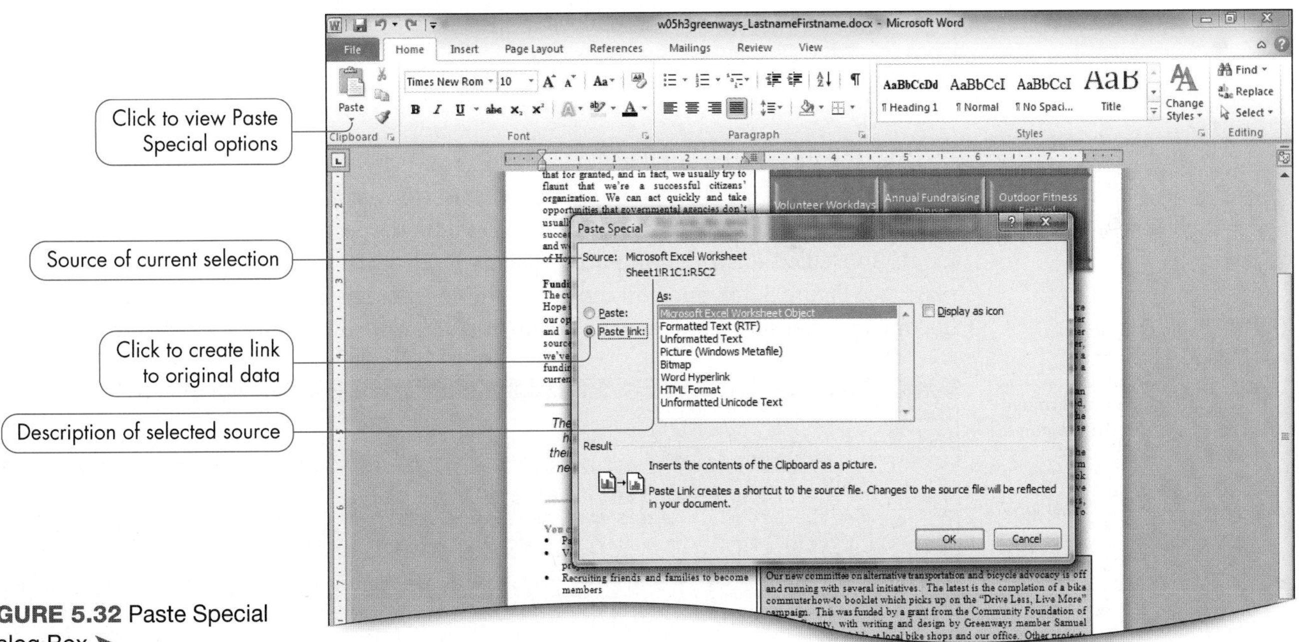

FIGURE 5.32 Paste Special Dialog Box ➤

If you use the drag-and-drop method, you display both source and destination documents simultaneously, click the object in the source, and then drag and drop it in the destination. It is important to note that when you want to copy the object from the source to the destination, then you must hold down Ctrl while dragging. If you do not hold down Ctrl during the entire drag-and-drop process, you will move the object instead of copying it.

You can insert an object, such as an Excel workbook, within a Word document without displaying the contents of the Excel workbook at all. The contents of the entire Excel workbook, which may contain several worksheets, appear as an icon in the document, and when you click it the Excel workbook opens in a separate window. This allows you to associate the data or information with your document without using space to display it. To use this method, click the Insert tab, and then click Object. The Object dialog box displays, as shown in Figure 5.33, with two tabs across the top. Click the Create from File tab to browse to the location of the file you want to insert.

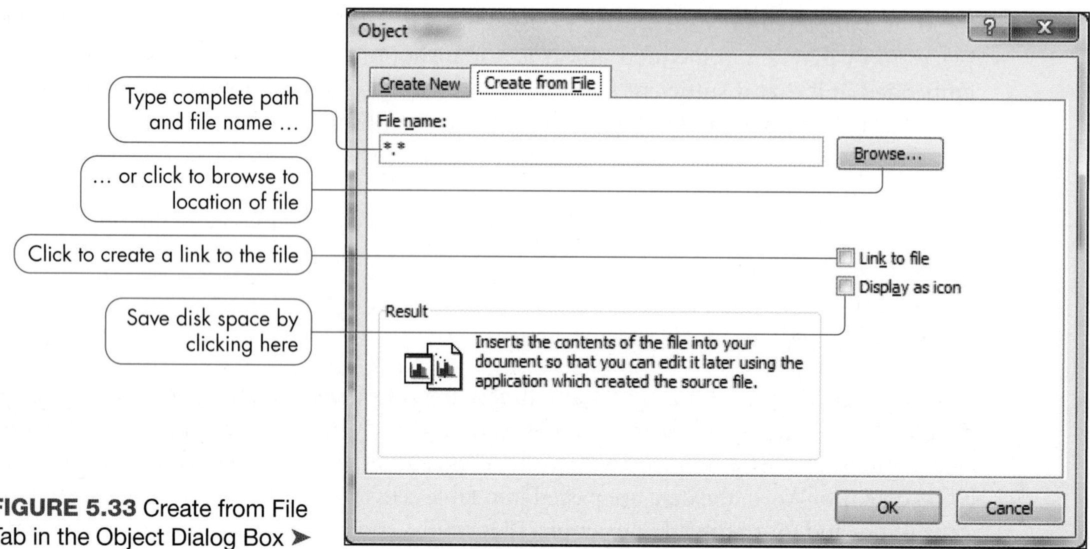

FIGURE 5.33 Create from File Tab in the Object Dialog Box ➤

TIP Displaying a Link as an Icon

You can save disk space by inserting the link as an icon instead of displaying the actual linked data. When you are selecting options in the Paste Special dialog box or the Object dialog box, click the Display as icon check box.

The Create New tab, in the Object dialog box, is helpful when you do not have an existing file to insert as an object. The Object type list box displays many types of objects you can create; however, you can only create the object if the respective application, such as Microsoft Excel, is installed on your computer. When you click the Object type, a small window displays (see Figure 5.34), and you can create the content for the object that will display in your document. After it displays in your document, you can edit it by double-clicking the object.

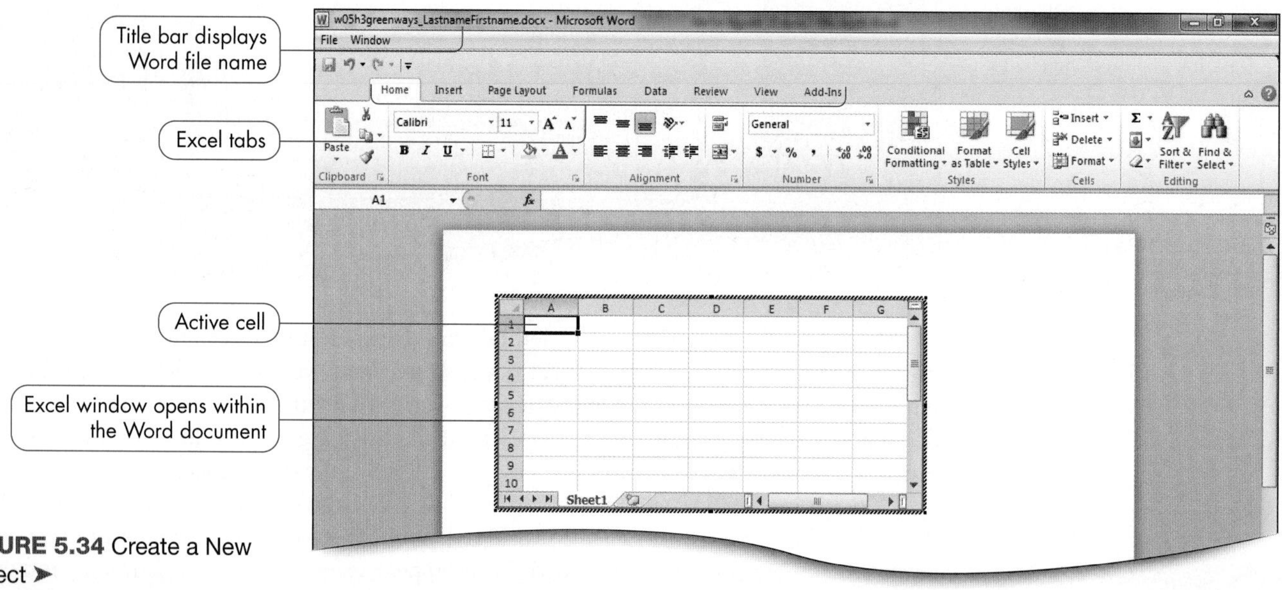

FIGURE 5.34 Create a New Object ➤

Updating a Linked Object

After you link an object to your document, you can still make modifications to the source file. At any time, you can open a source file in its native application—Excel, for example—to make modifications. You can also open the application by clicking the linked object in the Word document. To use this method, right-click the linked object in your document, point to Linked Object, and then select Edit Link or Open Link, as shown in Figure 5.35. When you click Edit Link, the editing tools display and you can make modifications to the object from within Word. If you click Open Link, the application starts and displays the complete interface and Ribbon.

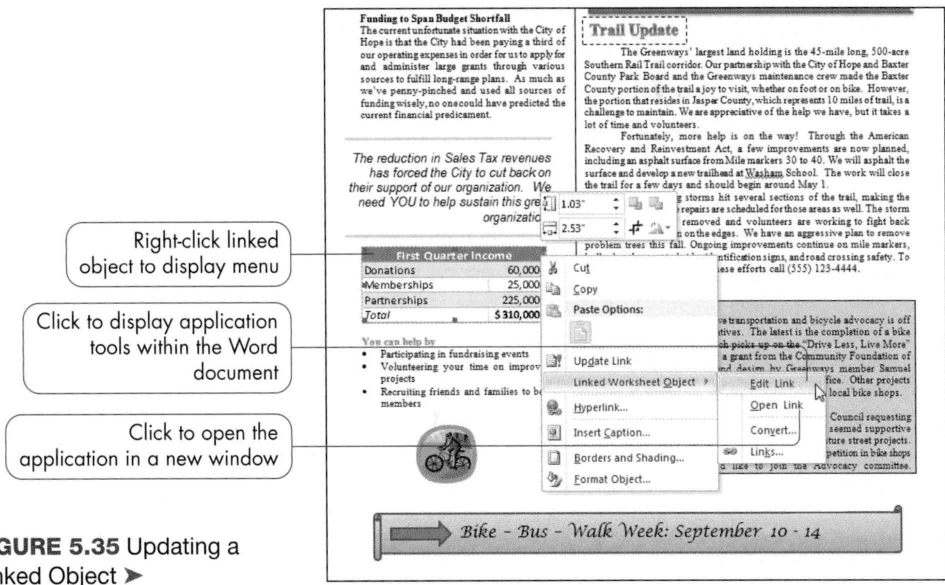

FIGURE 5.35 Updating a Linked Object ➤

If you linked an object to the document, there is also an Update Link command in the menu, as shown in Figure 5.35. When you click Update Link, Word retrieves the most updated form of the object from the source; any changes in the source file will display in the Word document. Some updates to the source do not display automatically, so this provides you the ability to check and update.

HANDS-ON EXERCISES

3 Object Linking and Embedding

The newsletter for The Greenways is nearly complete. Director Allen requests space to display first-quarter financial information, and provides the information in an Excel worksheet. You will add this information by inserting a chart into the newsletter, and then you will save the final copy before leaving for a bike ride!

Skills covered: Copy and Link a Worksheet • Change the Source Data and Update the Document • Save as a PDF File

STEP 1 COPY AND LINK A WORKSHEET

When Director Allen sends you the Excel worksheet that contains the first-quarter income sources, he tells you that it should be added to the newsletter, but some changes to the worksheet might be necessary in the near future. You decide the proper course of action is to insert the information with a link to the original file so you have the option to update it later. Refer to Figure 5.36 as you complete Step 1.

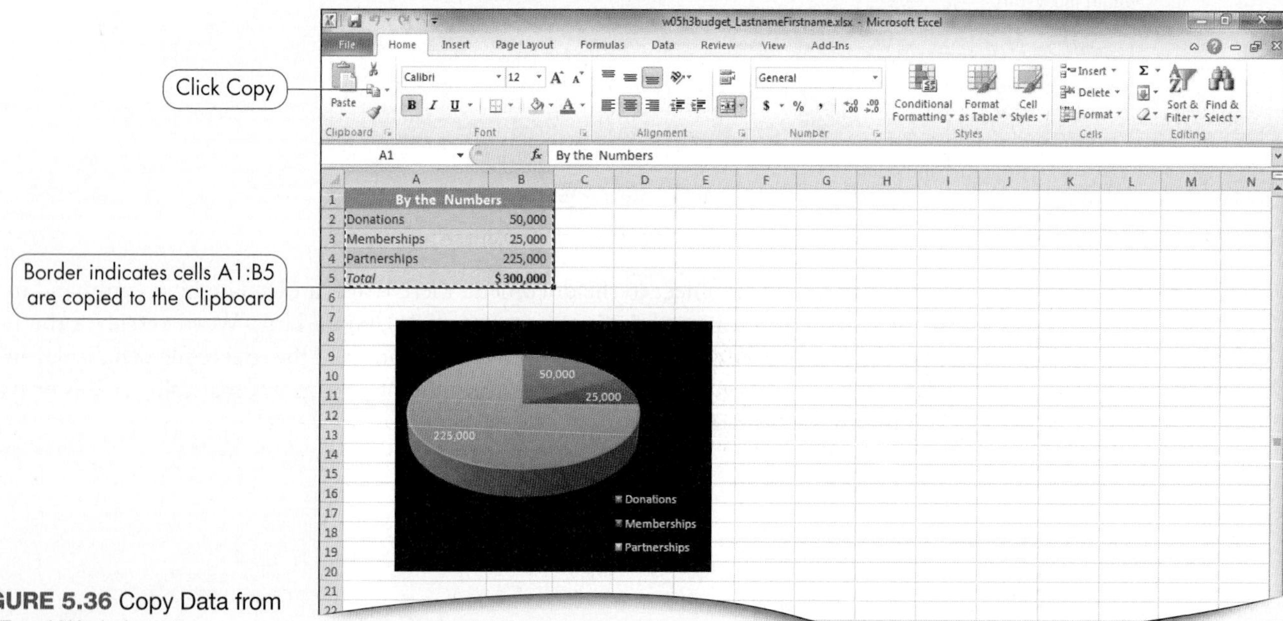

FIGURE 5.36 Copy Data from an Excel Worksheet ➤

a. Start Word, open *w05h2greenways_LastnameFirstname* if you closed it after Hands-On Exercise 2 and save it as **w05h3greenways_LastnameFirstname**, changing *h2* to *h3*.

   In the next step, you will open an Excel workbook. You might find it easier to work with the Excel spreadsheet if you minimize your Word document. Do not forget to save your document.

b. Start **Excel**. Open *w05h3budget.xlsx* and save it as **w05h3budget_LastnameFirstname**.

   The file displays in an Excel window. The Windows taskbar now contains icons for both Word and Excel; click either icon to move back and forth between the applications.

c. Drag to select **cells A1 through B5** in the Excel worksheet.

d. Click **Copy** in the Clipboard group (or click **Ctrl+C**).

   A moving border displays around the selection, indicating it has been copied to the Clipboard, as shown in Figure 5.36.

e. Click the **Word icon** on the Windows taskbar to return to the Word document. Place the insertion point on the first blank line above the *You can help by* paragraph. This is where you will insert the Excel worksheet.

> **TROUBLESHOOTING:** If necessary, press Enter to insert a blank line before the paragraph heading *You can help by.*

f. Click the **Paste arrow** in the Clipboard group on the Home tab. Click **Paste Special** to display the Paste Special dialog box. In the **As list**, click **Microsoft Excel Worksheet Object**.

g. Click **Paste link** on the left side of the dialog box, and then click **OK**.

h. Press **Enter** one time to add one blank line between the table and the next heading.

> **TROUBLESHOOTING:** If you do not see the Update Link option when you right-click an object, it is not linked to the source. Click Undo on the Quick Access Toolbar, and then repeat steps g and h, making sure you click Paste Special and Paste Link.

i. Save the document.

STEP 2 CHANGE THE SOURCE DATA AND UPDATE THE DOCUMENT

As expected, Director Allen sends the changes you need to make in the budget worksheet and thus on the newsletter. You make the changes in the Excel worksheet, and then update the table in your newsletter to reflect them. Refer to Figure 5.37 as you complete Step 2.

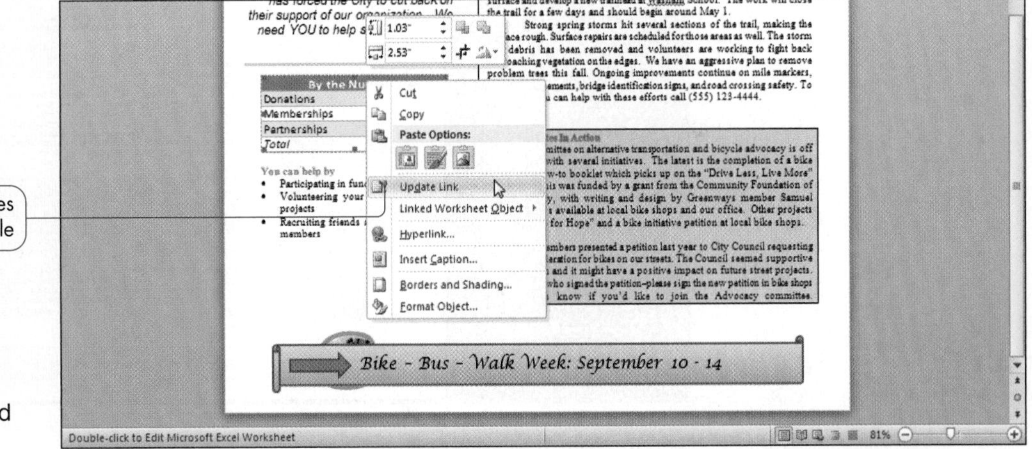

FIGURE 5.37 Update Linked Data ➤

a. Click the **Excel icon** on the Windows taskbar to return to the worksheet. Press **Esc** to deselect the cells.

b. Click **cell A1**, type **First Quarter Income**, and then press **Enter**.

   The text you type automatically replaces the original text.

c. Click **cell B2**, type **60000**, and then press **Enter**.

d. Save the workbook.

e. Click the **Word icon** on the Windows taskbar to return to the Word document. Right-click the Excel worksheet object, and then click **Update Link**, as shown in Figure 5.37.

   The linked object reflects the changes you made in the Excel workbook. Notice the bicycle clip art object has moved below and behind the grouped object. Next, you will take steps to reset it to the previous position.

f. Click the bicycle clip art object. Click the **Format tab**, click **Wrap Text**, and then click **More Layout Options**. Click **Square Wrapping style**, click the **Position tab**, and then click **Lock Anchor**. Click **OK**. Drag the object up so it displays between the bulleted list and the grouped shape object.

   The addition of more objects changes the way the clip art displays on the page. To maintain control of its position, you can change the text wrapping options and reposition the object.

g. Save the document.

STEP 3 SAVE AS A PDF FILE

Because you will post the newsletter on The Greenways' Web site, you decide to save the document as a PDF file. By doing so, anyone can view the newsletter regardless of the type of computer they are using. You can also e-mail the PDF version to members and know they can read it even if they do not have Microsoft Word installed on their PC. Refer to Figure 5.38 as you complete Step 3.

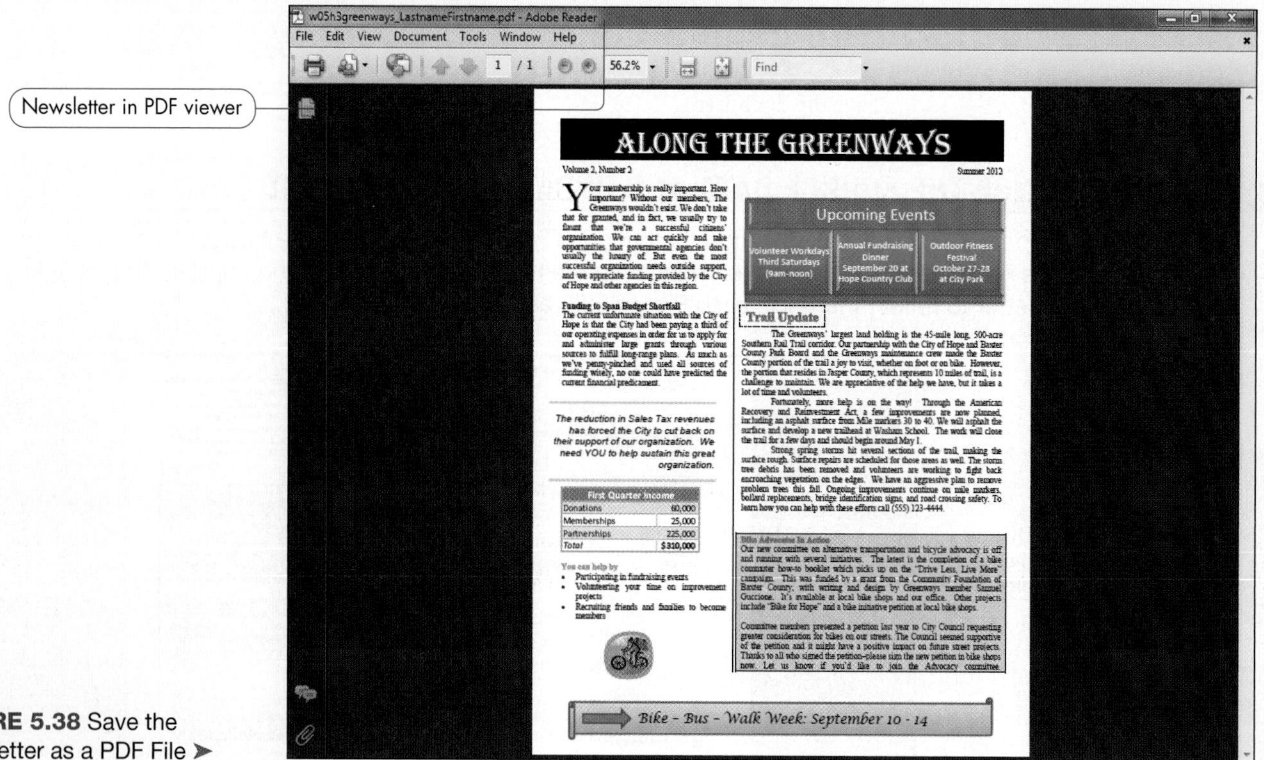

FIGURE 5.38 Save the Newsletter as a PDF File ➤

a. Click **File**, and then click **Save As**.

b. Click the **Save as type arrow**, and then select **PDF (*.pdf)**.

c. Click **Save**.

   An additional window displays the file in Adobe Reader. The file now exists in both Word and Adobe PDF formats. Note that in some situations, formatting, such as double line borders, may not display in the PDF file exactly as formatted in Word.

d. Close *w05h3greenways_LastnameFirstname* and submit based on your instructor's directions. Close the Adobe Reader (PDF) version of the file and submit based on your instructor's directions.

CHAPTER OBJECTIVES REVIEW

After reading this chapter, you have accomplished the following objectives:

1. **Construct a newsletter.** When you use desktop publishing to create a document such as a newsletter, you should use several techniques to enhance readability and attractiveness. You can create a masthead to display at the top of the page to introduce the document and use a reverse to enhance the appearance. When used in moderation, clip art, pull quotes, sidebars, and drop caps will catch the reader's eye and enhance almost any newsletter. Borders and shading are effective individually, or in combination with one another, to emphasize important stories within the newsletter. Lists, whether bulleted or numbered, help to organize information by emphasizing important topics. Typography is a critical, often subtle, element in the success of a document; good typography goes almost unnoticed, whereas poor typography draws attention and detracts from a document. No hard and fast rules exist for the selection of type and style—your objective should be to create a document that is easy to read and visually appealing. Try to limit yourself to a maximum of two fonts per document, but choose multiple sizes and styles.
2. **Develop a document design.** A grid establishes the overall structure of a document by indicating the number of columns, the space between columns, the size of the margins, the placement of headlines, art, and other objects. The grid does not appear in the printed document—you draw or sketch it on a piece of paper to solidify the layout prior to creating the newsletter in Word. Good design makes it easy for the reader to determine what is important.
3. **Insert graphical objects.** Word includes SmartArt to assist you in creating visually stimulating diagrams to represent your information and effectively communicate a message. When you insert a SmartArt diagram in your document, you can select from several existing layouts, and it will follow any theme you select for your document. One way to combine the flexibility of a shape object with simple text is to create a text box. Besides the obvious benefit of displaying text, you can layer it with other shapes. A shape is an object, such as a circle or an arrow, which you can use as a visual enhancement. You can use one shape or combine multiple shapes to create a more complex image.
4. **Manipulate graphical objects.** After you insert a graphical object, you can enhance the appearance by using one of the commands available on the Format tab for the object, such as fill, outline, and effects. Layering is the process of placing one shape on top of another. After you layer objects, you might need to group them so you can manipulate them more easily. Grouping is the process of combining selected objects so that they appear as a single object. When grouped, you can move objects simultaneously or apply a Style to all at one time. Also, Word makes it easy to flip or rotate an object. When you click the Rotate command, you can select from several commands that enable you to rotate the object in a particular direction or to flip it in such a way that you get a mirror image.
5. **Use OLE to insert an object.** When you insert objects into your document, you have two options for how the object will work within your document. The first option, embedding, pulls information from its original source into your document, but does not change or maintain a link to that source file. The second option for inserting an object into your document is linking. Linking is the process of inserting an object from another program, but the object retains a connection to the original data and file. If you change the data in the original source program, you can quickly update the data in the destination program to reflect the changes. The advantage of linking over embedding is that a linked object will reflect the most current information.
6. **Update a linked object.** After you link an object into your document, you can still make modifications to the source file. At any time, you can open a source file in its native application, Microsoft Excel, for example, to make modifications. But you can also open the application by double-clicking the linked object in a Word document. When you click Update Link, Word retrieves the most updated form of the object from the source; any changes in the source file will display in the Word document.

KEY TERMS

Desktop publishing ***p.262***
Drawing Canvas ***p.280***
Drop cap ***p.262***
Embedding ***p.290***
Fill ***p.278***
Grid ***p.265***
Grouping ***p.281***
Layering ***p.280***
Linking ***p.290***
Masthead ***p.262***
Object Linking and Embedding (OLE) ***p.290***
Portable Document Format (PDF) ***p.267***
Pull quote ***p.276***
Regrouping ***p.282***
Reverse ***p.262***
Shape ***p.273***
Sidebar ***p.276***
SmartArt ***p.273***
Text box ***p.275***
Text pane ***p.274***
Ungrouping ***p.282***
WordArt ***p.274***

MULTIPLE CHOICE

1. What format do you see when you use a reverse effect on a masthead?
   (a) Light text on a clear background
   (b) Dark text on a clear background
   (c) Dark text on a light background
   (d) Light text on a dark background

2. How do you balance the columns in a newsletter so that each column contains the same amount of text?
   (a) Insert a section break at the end of the last column and use the Balance Columns feature.
   (b) Insert a page break at the end of the last column.
   (c) Manually set the column widths in the Columns dialog box.
   (d) Press Enter until the text lines up at the bottom of each column.

3. Which feature would not be used to add emphasis to a document?
   (a) Pull Quote
   (b) Borders and Shading
   (c) Paste Link
   (d) Bulleted and Numbered List

4. Which feature enables you to quickly insert an organizational chart, which you can modify and enhance as needed?
   (a) WordArt
   (b) SmartArt
   (c) Shapes
   (d) Clip Art

5. You insert an arrow shape in your document that points left, but you need it to point right. Which command will you use?
   (a) Flip Horizontal
   (b) Rotate Right 90°
   (c) Flip Vertical
   (d) Rotate Left 90°

6. To move several shapes as one object, you should:
   (a) Layer the shapes.
   (b) Anchor the shapes.
   (c) Position the shapes.
   (d) Group the shapes.

7. Which of the following inserts Excel data in a way that enables you to edit the values in Word, but does not change the source?
   (a) Embedding
   (b) Copying and Pasting
   (c) Linking
   (d) Find and Replace

8. Which process should you use to insert Excel data into Word so that any changes you make to the original Excel worksheet can be automatically updated in Word?
   (a) Copying and Pasting
   (b) Linking
   (c) Embedding
   (d) Find and Replace

9. To quickly determine if a spreadsheet that displays in a Word document is linked to the source file, what can you do?
   (a) Click the Insert tab, and then click Object.
   (b) Single-click the object.
   (c) Click Paste Special.
   (d) Right-click the object, and then look for the Update Link option.

10. You just inserted two shape objects, a triangle and circle, into your document; the circle is larger and was inserted on top of the triangle, so now you cannot see the triangle. What can you do to display the triangle on top of the circle?
    (a) Click the circle, and then click Bring to Front.
    (b) Click the triangle, and then click Bring to Front.
    (c) Click the circle, and then click Send to Back.
    (d) Click the circle, and then click Bring in Front of Text.

PRACTICE EXERCISES

1 Personal Computer Consulting

You are a local computer expert who operates a business named Personal Computer Consulting. You are often asked to give advice on purchasing a personal computer. Because the basic considerations are the same for everyone, you decide to create a simple shopping guide to explain those steps. You want it to look professional, so you use several features in Word to develop an attractive document that is easy to read and that will make a good handout for anyone who asks how to buy a PC. This exercise follows the same set of skills as used in Hands-On Exercises 1 and 2 in the chapter. Refer to Figure 5.39 as you complete this exercise.

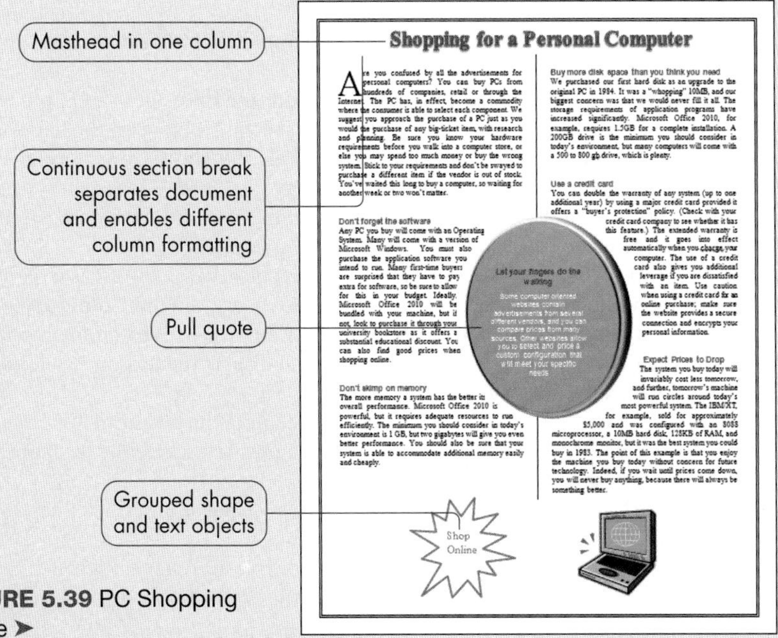

FIGURE 5.39 PC Shopping Guide ➤

a. Open *w05p1pchandout* and save it as **w05p1pchandout_LastnameFirstname.**

b. Click the **Page Layout tab**, click **Columns** in the Page Setup group, and then select **More Columns.** Click **Two** in the *Presets* section, click the **Line between box**, and then click **OK.** Click **Breaks** in the Page Setup group, and then select **Continuous.**

c. Click the **Home tab**, and then click **Show/Hide** (¶) in the Paragraph group to display formatting marks. Move the insertion point to the left side of the section break. Click the **Page Layout tab**, click **Columns** in the Page Setup group, and then select **One.**

d. Create a masthead for this document by completing the following steps:
   - Click **Enter** two times, and then press **Ctrl+Home** to move the insertion point to the beginning of the document.
   - Click the **Insert tab**, and then click **WordArt** in the Text group. Select the red colored style named **Fill - Red, Accent 2, Warm Matte Bevel** (fifth row, third column).
   - Type **Shopping for a Personal Computer** and select the text. On the Mini toolbar, click **Font size**, and then select **26.**
   - Click the **Format tab**, and then click the **Size arrow**, if necessary. Click the **Height arrow** until **.6″** displays, and then click the **Width arrow** until **6″** displays.
   - Click the **Position arrow**, and then select **Position in Top Center with Square Text Wrapping.** Place the insertion point on the left side of the blank line between the WordArt object and the section break, and then press **Delete.**

e. Press **Ctrl+End** to move the insertion point to the end of the document. Click the **Page Layout tab**, click **Breaks** in the Page Setup group, and then select **Continuous** to display the content in two equally balanced columns.

f. Insert a text box to display a quote by completing the following steps:
   - Select the heading and text in the paragraph titled *Let your fingers do the walking.* Press **Ctrl+X** to cut the paragraph.

- Click the **Insert tab**, if necessary, click **Text Box** in the Text group, and then select **Mod Quote**. Click **Ctrl+V** to insert the paragraph you cut in this step.
- Click the **Bring Forward arrow** in the Arrange group, and then select **Bring in Front of Text**.
- Click the **Size arrow**, and then click the **Width arrow** until **3.4** displays. Click the paragraph heading and text in the pull quote, and then press **Ctrl+E** to center it. If necessary, delete any extra line returns in the pull quote.
- Omit the heading, but select the whole paragraph in the pull quote, click **Font** on the Mini toolbar, and then select **Arial**. Click the **Font Color arrow**, and then select **White, Background 1**. Click outside the pull quote to deselect it.

g. Insert clip art, a shape, and a text box by completing the following steps:
- Click the **Insert tab**, click **Clip Art** in the Illustrations group, and then type **laptop** in the **Search for box** in the Clip Art pane. Click **Go**. Select the clip of a laptop computer with a green screen, or substitute as needed. Close the Clip Art pane.
- Click the graphic one time. Click the **Format tab**, if necessary, click **Wrap Text**, and then click **Square**. Drag the object to the bottom of the right column, which displays on a second page.
- Click the **Height arrow** in the Size group until **1.5″** displays. Click the **Width arrow** until **1.4″** displays.
- Click the **Insert tab**, click **Shapes** in the Illustrations group, and then click the **Explosion 1 shape** in the *Stars and Banners* section (first shape in that section). Drag on the left side of the computer graphic to create a shape that is approximately the same size as the clip art. Click the **More button** in the Shape Styles group to display the Quick Styles gallery. Click **Colored Outline - Blue, Accent 1** (first row, second column). Click **Rotate** in the Arrange group, and then select **Rotate Left 90°**.
- Click **DrawText Box** in the Insert Shapes group. Drag a text box that is almost as large as the explosion. Type **Shop Online** in the text box. Select the text, click the **Font Color arrow** on the Mini toolbar, and then click **Dark Blue, Text 2, Lighter 40%** (fourth row, fourth column). Click the **Font Size arrow**, and then click **14**. Press **Enter** to display the text on two lines, so it will be easier to display in the shape.
- Click the blue line that surrounds the text. Click the border, drag the box until it is large enough to display all the text, and then drag the box into a position where the text appears centered in the explosion shape.
- Click the **Format tab**, if necessary, click **Shape Fill**, and then click **No Fill**. Click **Shape Outline**, and then click **No Outline**.
- Click the text box, press and hold **Shift**, and then click the explosion shape. Right-click, point to **Group**, and then click **Group**. Click anywhere outside the explosion shape to deselect it.

h. Click the **Page Layout tab**, click **Page Borders**, drag the **Style scroll bar** down until a double line style displays, and then select the double line. Click the **Width arrow**, and then select **2¼ pt**. Click **Box** in the *Setting* section, and then click **OK**. Click the **Home tab**, and then click **Show/Hide** (¶) to remove formatting marks.

i. Click the **Page Layout tab**, click **Margins**, and then click **Custom Margins**. Type **.7** in each box for **Top**, **Bottom**, **Left**, and **Right**. In the Apply to: box, select **Whole document**, and then click **OK**.

j. Drag the **Zoom slider** to **60%**. Adjust all objects as necessary so they match Figure 5.39. Click the **WordArt masthead**, and then use the arrow keys to nudge it higher on the page, if necessary. Delete or add line returns, if necessary, so a paragraph starts at the very top of the right column. Delete the extra blank line that displays before the *Use a credit card* paragraph. Compare your work to Figure 5.39.

k. Position the insertion point on the left side of the first paragraph. Click the **Insert tab**, click **Drop Cap**, and then select **Dropped**.

l. Save and close the file, and submit based on your instructor's directions.

2 IBC Enterprises

You are the lead financial analyst for IBC Enterprises, a technology manufacturing organization. Each year you are responsible for preparing a summary of the annual report. After you summarize the main points, you decide the report should include a chart and graph to emphasize certain points as well as give a visual summary of the information. You begin this exercise by opening the general summary, and then you add data from an Excel spreadsheet that contains the information you want to summarize. You also utilize SmartArt graphics to display an organization chart of the new administration. This exercise follows the same set of skills as used in Hands-On Exercises 1, 2, and 3 in the chapter. Refer to Figure 5.40 as you complete this exercise.

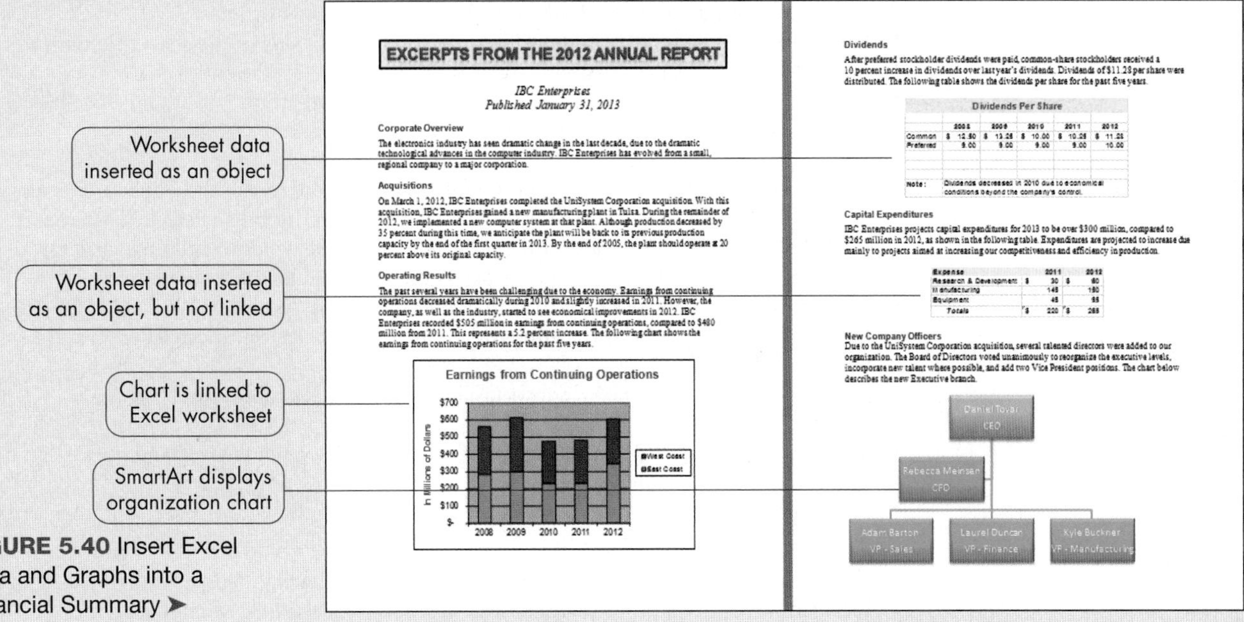

FIGURE 5.40 Insert Excel Data and Graphs into a Financial Summary ➤

a. Open *w05p2report* and save it as **w05p2report_LastnameFirstname**.

b. Insert an Excel object by completing the following steps:
   - Place the insertion point on the blank line just above the heading *Capital Expenditures.* Press **Enter** one time.
   - Click the **Insert tab**, click the **Object arrow** in the Text group, click **Object**, and then click the **Create from File tab.**
   - Click **Browse**, and then browse and select *w05p2dividends.xlsx.*
   - Click **Insert** in the Browse dialog box. Click **OK** in the Object dialog box, and then scroll down to view the object, if necessary.
   - Double-click the worksheet object, and then click **cell F5**.
   - Type **10.00** and press **Enter**.
   - Click anywhere outside the object to save the change.
   - Click the object one time to display sizing handles, and then click **Center** on the Home tab (or press **Ctrl+E**).
   - Press → one time to deselect the chart, and then press **Enter** to insert a blank line between the object and the next paragraph.

c. Click one time on the worksheet object to select it. Right-click the object, select **Worksheet Object**, and then select **Open**. Save the workbook as *w05p2dividends_LastnameFirstname.* To insert and link a worksheet object into the document, complete the following steps:
   - Click the **Expenses worksheet tab** at the bottom of the Excel window.
   - Position the mouse pointer over **cell A4**. When the mouse pointer resembles a big plus sign, drag down and over to **cell C8**, which contains the total $265.
   - Click **Copy** in the Clipboard group on the Home tab (or press **Ctrl+C**).
   - Click the **Word icon** on the Windows taskbar to toggle back, and then view *w05p2report_LastnameFirstname.* Click once on the blank line following the *Capital Expenditures* paragraph.
   - Click the **Home tab**, if necessary, and then click the **Paste arrow** in the Clipboard group.
   - Click **Paste Special** to display the Paste Special dialog box. In the **As list**, click **Microsoft Excel Worksheet Object.** Click **Paste link** on the left side of the window, and then click **OK.**
   - Right-click the object, and then click **Format Object.**
   - Click the **Layout tab**, and then click **Square** under Wrapping style. Under Horizontal alignment, click **Center**, and then click **OK.**
   - Click to position the insertion point on the left side of the *New Company Officers* heading, which has been separated by the table, and then press **Enter** five times to separate the object and the next paragraph.

d. Insert an Excel chart into the document by completing the following steps:
   - Click once on the blank line above the *Dividends* heading, and then press **Enter** one time.
   - Click the **Excel icon** on the Windows taskbar to toggle to the *w05p2dividends_LastnameFirstname* workbook.
   - If the moving border remains on the range you copied earlier, press **Esc**.

- Click the **Earnings worksheet tab** at the bottom of the Excel window.
- Position the mouse pointer in the white space on the right side of the chart title *Earnings from Continuing Operations*, and then click one time to select the entire chart.
- Click the **Home tab**, and then click **Copy** in the Clipboard group.
- Click the **Word icon** on the Windows taskbar to toggle back to *w05p2report_LastnameFirstname*.
- Click the **Home tab**, if necessary, and then click the **Paste arrow** in the Clipboard group.
- Click **Paste Special** to display the Paste Special dialog box. In the **As list**, click **Microsoft Excel Chart Object**. Click **Paste link** on the left side of the window, and then click **OK**.
- Press **Enter** one time to insert space between the chart and the next paragraph.
- Right-click the white space near the top of the chart, point to **Linked Worksheet Object**, and then click **Open Link**. In the Earnings tab of the Excel worksheet, click **cell F5**, type **345**, and then press **Enter**.
- Click the **Word icon** on the Windows taskbar to toggle back to *w05p2report_LastnameFirstname*.
- Right-click the white space near the top of the chart, click **Update Link**, and notice that the column for 2012 increases in height.
- Press **Ctrl+E** to center the chart. Click the bottom-left handle of the object, and then drag to reduce the size of the object so that it will display at the bottom of the first page.

e. Create a document title using WordArt by completing the following steps:
- Press **Ctrl+Home**, and then select the title *Excerpts from the 2012 Annual Report*.
- Click the **Insert tab**, and then click **WordArt** in the Text group. Click the style **Gradient Fill - Purple, Accent 4, Reflection** (fourth row, fifth column).
- Select the WordArt text, click the **Font Size arrow** on the Mini toolbar, and then select **20**.
- Click the **Format tab**, if necessary, click **Position** in the Arrange group, and click **Position in Top Center with Square Text Wrapping**.
- Click **Shape Fill** in the Shape Styles group, and then click **Yellow**. Click **Shape Outline** in the Shape Styles group, select **Weight**, and then select **2¼**.
- Click **Shape Effects** in the Shape Styles group, select **Bevel**, and then click **Cool Slant** (first row, fourth column).
- Delete additional line returns between the heading and the first line of the subheading so that only one displays.

f. Create an organization chart with SmartArt by completing the following steps:
- Press **Ctrl+End** to move the insertion point to the end of the document. Press **Enter** one time.
- Click the **Insert tab**, and then click **SmartArt** in the Illustrations group.
- Click **Hierarchy** in the left panel, and then click **Organization Chart**. Click **OK**.
- Type the following names and positions in the chart, starting from the top and then from left to right on the third level.

Daniel Tovar **CEO**
Rebecca Meinsen **CFO**
Adam Barton **VP — Sales**
Laurel Duncan **VP — Finance**
Kyle Buckner **VP — Manufacturing**

- Click **Change Colors** in the SmartArt Styles group, and then select **Colorful Range - Accent Colors 4 to 5** (second row, fourth column).
- Click the **More button** in the SmartArt Styles, and then select **Intense Effect** (first row, fifth column).
- Click the **Format tab**, click the **Size arrow**, and then click the **Height arrow** until **3″** displays. Click the **Width arrow** until **5.5″** displays.

g. Drag the **Zoom slider** in the status bar to **50%**. Compare your document to Figure 5.40.

h. Save and close all files, and submit based on your instructor's directions.

MID-LEVEL EXERCISES

1 Computer Training Association, Inc.

You are preparing a report that announces the implementation of new technology for your computer training company. You need to include a chart that was created in Excel. Because you want the chart in Word to reflect changes in the original Excel workbook, you decide to link the chart.

a. Open *w05m1CTA*, and then save it as **w05m1CTA_LastnameFirstname**.
b. Open the Excel workbook *w05m1chart*, and then save it as **w05m1chart_LastnameFirstname**.
c. Select the **Projected Costs chart** in Excel, and then copy it to the Clipboard.
d. Link the Projected costs chart as a chart object to the bottom of the *w05m1CTA_LastnameFirstname* document.
e. Make the following changes in the *w05m1chart_LastnameFirstname* worksheet:
    - Phase 1 Hardware value: **1.40**
    - Phase 2 Software value: **.75**
    - Phase 3 Software value: **.80**
    - Phase 4 Software value: **1.20**
    - Phase 3 Training value: **.50**
    - Phase 4 Training value: **1.00**

f. Update the linked chart object in the Word document. Center the chart horizontally on the page.

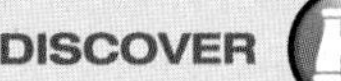

g. Select the heading *Computer Training Association, Inc.* and display the text as WordArt using **Gradient Fill - Blue, Accent 1**. Modify the format of the WordArt by completing the following steps:
    - Change the font size to **24**.
    - Use Help to learn how to create a custom Fill color. Use the RGB values **196, 200, 234** as the custom color.
    - Apply a **10 pt Soft Edges Shape Effect**.
    - Increase width to **6″**.
    - Set the position to display the object in the Top Center with Square Text wrapping.

h. Save and close all files, and submit based on your instructor's directions.

2 Marlborough Woods Homeowners Association

You are a member of the Marlborough Woods Homeowners' Association and have been asked to assemble the next quarterly newsletter. You have many events to advertise, so the layout of the newsletter is important. The text you use for the newsletter is included in a file. Refer to Figure 5.41 as you complete this exercise.

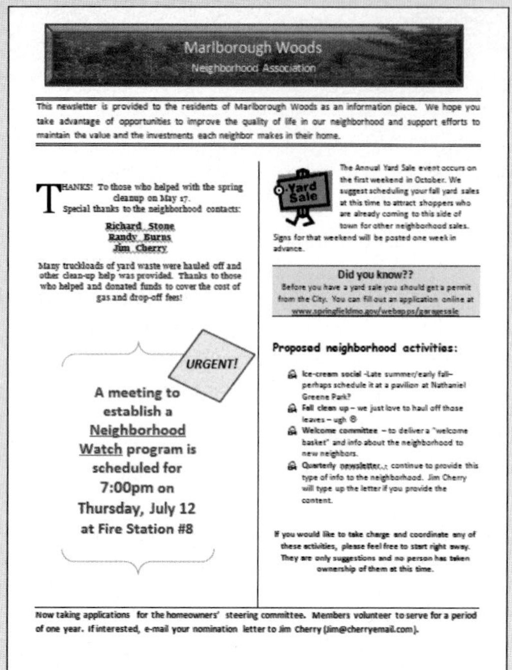
Marlborough Woods
Neighborhood Association

This newsletter is provided to the residents of Marlborough Woods as an information piece. We hope you take advantage of opportunities to improve the quality of life in our neighborhood and support efforts to maintain the value and the investments each neighbor makes in their home.

THANKS! To those who helped with the spring cleanup on May 17.
Special thanks to the neighborhood contacts:

Richard Stone
Randy Burns
Jim Cherry

Many truckloads of yard waste were hauled off and other clean-up help was provided. Thanks to those who helped and donated funds to cover the cost of gas and drop-off fees!

URGENT!

A meeting to establish a Neighborhood Watch program is scheduled for 7:00pm on Thursday, July 12 at Fire Station #8

Yard Sale

The Annual Yard Sale event occurs on the first weekend in October. We suggest scheduling your fall yard sales at this time to attract shoppers who are already coming to this side of town for other neighborhood sales. Signs for that weekend will be posted one week in advance.

Did you know??
Before you have a yard sale you should get a permit from the City. You can fill out an application online at www.springfieldmo.gov/webapps/garagesale

Proposed neighborhood activities:

- Ice-cream social -Late summer/early fall– perhaps schedule it at a pavilion at Nathaniel Greene Park?
- Fall clean up – we just love to haul off those leaves – ugh ☹
- Welcome committee – to deliver a "welcome basket" and info about the neighborhood to new neighbors.
- Quarterly newsletter – continue to provide this type of info to the neighborhood. Jim Cherry will type up the letter if you provide the content.

If you would like to take charge and coordinate any of these activities, please feel free to start right away. They are only suggestions and no person has taken ownership of them at this time.

Now taking applications for the homeowners' steering committee. Members volunteer to serve for a period of one year. If interested, e-mail your nomination letter to Jim Cherry (Jim@cherryemail.com).

FIGURE 5.41 Neighborhood Association Newsletter ➤

a. Open *w05m2neighborhood*, and then save it as **w05m2neighborhood_LastnameFirstname**.
b. Set a **1.5″ top margin** and a **.18″ bottom margin** for the whole document. Change **left and right margins** to **.5″**. Increase the bottom margin as needed to comply with your printer's capability.
c. Create a two-column newsletter that displays a line between columns. Use a section break to enable a one-column masthead.

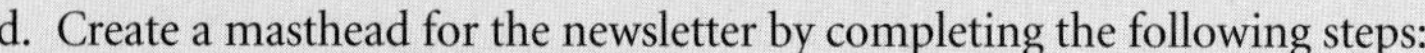

DISCOVER

d. Create a masthead for the newsletter by completing the following steps:
   - Insert a bevel shape (third row, first column in the Basic Shapes category) that spans the top of the page. Fill the bevel shape with the picture *woods.jpg*.
   - Add the text **Marlborough Woods Neighborhood Association** to display on the shape. Change **Spacing after** to **0 pt**.
   - The font size for *Marlborough Woods* should be 20 pt, and this should display on the first line. The font size for *Neighborhood Association* should be 14 pt, and it should display on the line below.
e. Move the first paragraph, which starts *This newsletter is provided*, to the one-column section, and then display it just below the masthead. Justify the text and apply a top and bottom double line border to the paragraph. The border should be 3/4 pt wide and colored dark blue.
f. Apply a drop cap to the first letter of the word *Thanks!*, which displays on the top of the left column.
g. Create a text box using the **Braces Quote style** to emphasize *A meeting to establish a neighborhood Watch Program.* Resize the box as necessary to extend across and display on the left column.
h. Insert a diamond shape that is 1.2″ high and 1.5″ wide. Use the rotate handle to display it, as shown in Figure 5.41. Fill the shape using a yellow color, and then group the diamond shape with a text box containing the text *URGENT!* Display the grouped item over the text in the Braces Quote in the left column.
i. Insert a column break that forces the article about the yard sale to display in the right column. Search for clip art with a Yard Sale theme and display it on the left side of the paragraph. Insert at least one line return at the end of the paragraph to add space before the *Did you know??* heading that follows.
j. Select the heading *Did you know??* and the sentence and hyperlink that follow it. Apply a black single-line top and bottom border, and also apply the shading pattern style 10%.
k. Create a bulleted list out of the proposed neighborhood activities. Change the bullet to a house symbol.
l. Select the paragraph that begins *Now taking applications.* Apply a one-column format to the paragraph and then apply a single-line top border. Increase the font size to **12 pt** and bold the text in this paragraph.
m. Save and close the file, and submit based on your instructor's directions.

3 Create a Family Tree

CREATIVE CASE 

You have decided to begin charting your genealogy. You have a number of different methods for displaying the family tree, but you decide to use SmartArt graphics to show your immediate family. If allowed by your instructor, substitute your own personal information and styles for those in the instructions below.

a. Open a new document, and then save it as **w05m3family_LastnameFirstname**.

b. Change document orientation to **Landscape** so you can more easily view the complete family tree.

c. Insert the **Horizontal Hierarchy SmartArt graphic** from the Hierarchy gallery. Populate the family tree by completing the following steps:
   - Click in the first element on the left, and then type **Michelle** in the first box.
   - Type **Gary** and **Sandra** in the second-level boxes to represent Michelle's parents.
   - Type **Lester** and **Verdene** in the boxes that represent Gary's parents.
   - Type **Sidney** in the box to represent Sandra's father.
   - Open the Text pane, add a box for Sandra's mother, and then type **Effie**.
   - With the text box open, create sub-bullets so you can add Lester's parents, Ralph and Emma. Then add sub-bullets to represent Verdene's parents, George and Mary. Add sub-bullets for Sidney's parents, Miles and Minnie, and finally, add bullets for Effie's parents, Jasper and Lou.

d. Modify the chart by completing the following steps:
   - Change the height of the chart to **6″** and the width to **9″**.
   - Change the color set to **Colorful Range - Accent Colors 3 to 4**.
   - Change the Shape Fill to use **Red, Accent 2, Lighter 80%.**
   - Modify Shape Effects to use **Glow variation Red, 8 pt glow, Accent color 2**.
   - Change the position to Middle Center with Square Text wrapping.

e. At the top of the document, insert a text box to display the heading **My Family Tree**. Make the following enhancements to the text box:
   - Change the size of the text to **28 pt**, and then center the text in the box.
   - Change the font to use **WordArt Quick Style Gradient Fill - Purple, Accent 4, Reflection**.
   - Modify the Shape Style to use **Subtle Effect - Red, Accent 2**.
   - Set the height of the text box to **.7″** and the width to **3″**.
   - Modify Shape Effects to use **Glow variation Red, 5 pt glow, Accent color 2**.
   - Change the position so that the text box displays in the top-left corner of the SmartArt diagram.

f. Save and close the file, and submit based on your instructor's directions.

You are hired as a marketing manager for a small airline service that provides transportation from Denver to frequently requested locations and vacation cities such as Las Vegas, Orlando, and New York. Your first big assignment is to develop a marketing flyer that can be printed and mailed to potential customers in the Denver area and also in the cities serviced by the airline. From your previous marketing experience, you know that it is important to emphasize the most positive attributes of the airline as well as provide information that will generate interest in, and eventually revenue for, the company. In this exercise, you will recreate the newsletter as you see it in Figure 5.42.

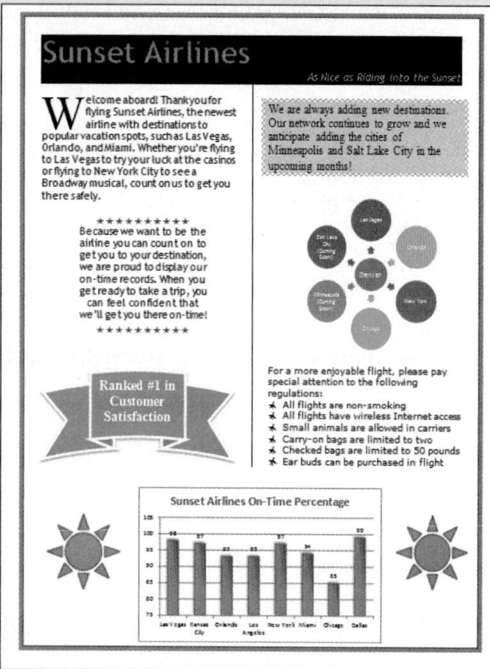

FIGURE 5.42 Sunset Airlines Flyer

Create the Masthead

You have a document with several important pieces of information that should be used in the marketing flyer. You must format the page so it can accommodate the amount of information you display, as well as any graphics you might add later.

a. Open the file named *w05c1airline*, and then save it as **w05c1airline_LastnameFirstname**.

b. Change the margins to **.7″** on all sides.

c. Set a **Continuous Section Break** at the beginning of the document. Use a single-column format for the masthead.

d. Create a masthead with the main heading **SUNSET AIRLINES**. Use a Reverse on the heading by changing the background to **100% solid black**, and then use the Text Effect **Gradient Fill - Orange, Accent 6, Inner Shadow** on *Sunset Airlines*. Increase font size to **36 pt**.

e. Create a second line of the masthead, type the subheading **As Enjoyable as Watching a Sunset**. Change the font size to **13 pt**, and then apply **Italics**. Change the color of the subheading to **Orange, Accent 6, Lighter 40%**. Right align the subheading.

Create Columns and Format Text

You now need to adjust the text to display in two columns below the masthead. You will also make several modifications to that text so that it is visually appealing and also conveys all the important information the airline wants to promote to potential customers.

a. Set a two-column format to arrange the text below the masthead. Display a line between the columns, and then set equal column width. Insert another **Continuous Section Break** at the end of the text, and then set the area below to display in one column.

b. Set a dropped cap letter on the first letter of the word *Welcome* in the first paragraph.

c. Cut the paragraph that starts with the phrase *Because we want to be the airline*, and then display it in a text box in the same place using the Stars Quote design from the Text Box gallery. Set it to wrap on top and bottom, and then center the text. Adjust the position of the text box so it is centered horizontally in the column.

d. Insert a column break to force the paragraph that starts with the phrase *We are always adding* to display at the top of the second column. Apply a box border around the paragraph using the wavy line style, colored **Orange, Accent 6**, and with a **1 1/2 pt** width. Set shading for the paragraph using the color **Orange, Accent 6, Lighter 60%**.

e. Insert a page border that uses the style found fourth from the bottom of the style list. Use the **Orange, Accent 6 color** and a **4 1/2 pt** width.

f. Use a bulleted list to organize the regulations listed in the paragraph that starts *For a more enjoyable flight*. Customize the bullets to use the airplane symbol, Webdings: 241. Decrease the indent of the bulleted list to display each item on one line.

g. Change the font of the paragraph and bulleted list to **Verdana**, and then set the size to **11 pt**.

Add Graphics for Visual Effects

You have several ways to make the flyer visually stimulating, but you know that it is easy to add too much and thus defeat the purpose of attracting customers. You decide to use SmartArt, WordArt, and a few shapes to complete the look.

a. Position the insertion point at the bottom of the document. Insert a SmartArt object; use the Diverging Radial from the *Cycle* section. Display the Text pane, and then type **Denver** on the first line to represent the circle in the middle. Press ↓ to move to the next bullet, and then type the next city, **Las Vegas**. Continue to click ↓ after each city to complete the graphic with the cities **Orlando**, **New York**, **Chicago**. Press **Enter** after you type **Chicago**, and then type **Minneapolis (Coming Soon!)**. Click **Enter** once again, and then type **Salt Lake City (Coming Soon!)**.

b. Change the Color scheme of the SmartArt to use **Colorful - Accent Colors**.

c. Format the SmartArt object with Square Text wrapping, and then change the size so the object is 2.5″ high and 3.5″ wide. Display the SmartArt below the shaded paragraph in the second column. Change the Layout properties to center the object horizontally in the column, and then use a Lock Anchor setting so it will remain in position.

d. Place the insertion point at the end of the document. Open the Excel workbook *w05c1flights.xlsx*, and then save it as **w05c1flights_LastnameFirstname.xlsx**. Copy the chart from the spreadsheet, and then link it into the Word document.

e. Reduce the chart size as needed so it fits centered on the bottom of the page, in the one-column section. If necessary, change the wrapping style and use the Lock Anchor setting for precise placement. Edit the data in the Excel worksheet so the Los Angeles on-time percentage increases to 93% in cell D5, and then update the chart in the flyer to reflect this change.

f. Insert a **Curved Down Ribbon shape** at the bottom of the first column. Flip the ribbon vertically, and then change the shape style to **Light 1 Outline, Colored Fill - Orange, Accent 6**. Display the text **Ranked #1 in Customer Satisfaction** on the Ribbon. Increase the size of the text to **16 pt**, and then bold the text. Use the yellow sizing handles on the top of the ribbon object to increase the size of the face of the ribbon so the text fits on it, if necessary.

g. Insert a **Sun shape** in the bottom-left corner of the flyer. The height and width of the object should be 1.2″. Change the shape style to **Colored Fill - Orange, Accent 6**. Copy the object, and then paste it to create a second identical object. Drag the second object to the bottom-right corner of the flyer so the two suns appear as bookends to the chart.

h. Make adjustments to spacing and line returns as necessary to display all text and objects without overlapping. Save and close all files, and then submit based on your instructor's directions.

Evaluating Political Issues

GENERAL CASE 

At any given time, there is often a political race or issue that will eventually be voted on by your state or community. As an informed citizen, you should be aware of any amendments, issues, or candidates running for office; you should also be able to give reasons why you would vote for or against them. Create a flyer that uses SmartArt and other graphical objects to describe candidates or amendments and list the issues they support or oppose. Remember that a few SmartArt objects enable you to include pictures or graphics in the diagram as well as insert bullet points to support the main subject. Save your work as **w05b1politics_LastnameFirstname**, and then submit based on your instructor's directions.

Astronomy Is Fun!

RESEARCH CASE 

You are a member of the local astronomy club and have been asked to create a monthly newsletter for elementary schools and home-schooled children. Some information and a few short articles have already been provided to you, but it is not enough material for a whole newsletter. You can perform an Internet search to gather information so you can provide a chart of times when they might see shuttles or the ISS pass overhead. You will probably want to use an Excel file to keep track of times so it is easy to update for the next newsletter. Use the techniques from this chapter to organize your facts and present a professional-looking newsletter that children will enjoy reading. Open the Word document *w05b2stars*, save your changes to **w05b2stars_LastnameFirstname**, and then submit based on your instructor's directions.

Car Financing Information

DISASTER RECOVERY 

You work for a local automotive dealer and your supervisor requests your help to fix a document he was unable to complete. He attempted to create a document that describes a vehicle, including a spreadsheet calculation for pricing that can be updated automatically. He thinks this will be a great resource for all sales associates, but his first attempt to create the document was not successful. He did not properly link the document with the source file, nor did his graphical enhancements provide the effect he desires. You have been assigned the task of repairing the document so the pricing information from the *w05b3cooper.xlsx* spreadsheet can be updated easily and automatically. You must also modify the document to display the graphical elements correctly and make any other enhancements that create a professional-looking document. Open the Word document your supervisor created, *w05b3car*, save your changes to **w05b3car_LastnameFirstname**, and then submit based on your instructor's directions.

WORD

6 TIME SAVING TOOLS

Using Templates, Themes, and Multiple Documents

CASE STUDY | Computer Training Concepts, Inc.

Watch the
Set-up
Video
for this
Case Study!

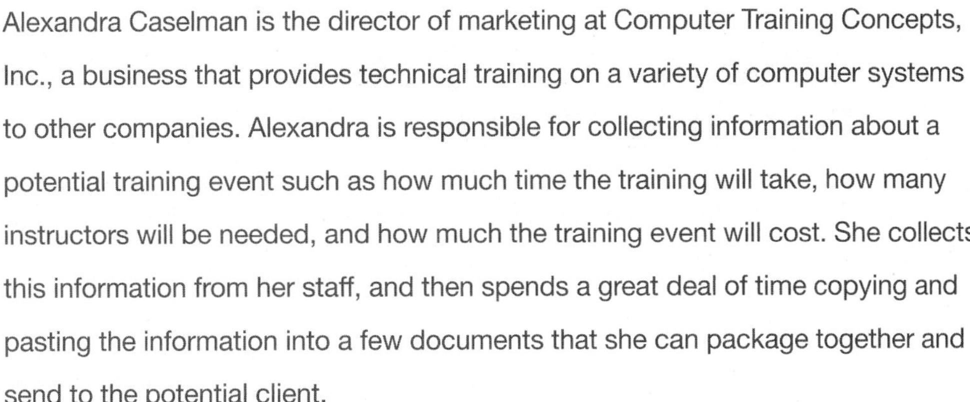

Alexandra Caselman is the director of marketing at Computer Training Concepts, Inc., a business that provides technical training on a variety of computer systems to other companies. Alexandra is responsible for collecting information about a potential training event such as how much time the training will take, how many instructors will be needed, and how much the training event will cost. She collects this information from her staff, and then spends a great deal of time copying and pasting the information into a few documents that she can package together and send to the potential client.

During a recent meeting she mentions this cumbersome task to you, her assistant director, and you mention that Word 2010 has features that will make the process of assembling the information more efficient. Alexandra decides to split the job with you since her method of compiling the information is outdated and slow. She decides to set up some of the documents, and then transfer all the files to you. At that point, you will take the information provided from a variety of sources and assemble one very nice looking document.

OBJECTIVES

AFTER YOU READ THIS CHAPTER, YOU WILL BE ABLE TO:

1. Select a template from the Backstage view ***p.310***
2. Create a Word template ***p.312***
3. Use Building Blocks ***p.313***
4. View documents side by side ***p.320***
5. Merge documents ***p.321***
6. Use navigational tools ***p.324***
7. Customize theme colors ***p.336***
8. Customize theme fonts and effects ***p.336***

Document Templates

A **template** is a partially completed document containing preformatted text or graphics.

Word 2010 is useful for creating very interesting and complex documents because it provides a variety of formatting features that you can apply on your own. You can jump-start the formatting process by using professional designs provided in the form of templates. A ***template*** is a partially completed document that contains formatting, text, and/or graphics. Word provides a variety of templates for common documents, and additional templates can be downloaded from Office.com. You can use Word templates to create letters, memos, reports, résumés, agendas, calendars, and brochures, as well as other documents. Each template contains the framework of formats and text to decrease the time it takes you to create a document. You can even develop your own templates to use when you create certain types of documents, such as specialized reports.

Word provides a variety of templates for common documents, and additional templates can be downloaded from Office.com. You can use Word templates to create letters, memos, reports, résumés, agendas, calendars, and brochures, as well as other documents.

In this section, you will use a template to start a document. You save time doing so because you do not have to set fonts, bullets, or create a style for the résumé. You also will download and use a template from Office.com.

Selecting a Template from the Backstage View

Normal template is the framework that defines the default page settings.

Each time you create a new blank document, you use the ***Normal template***, the framework that defines the 1″ left, right, top, and bottom margins, left horizontal alignment, 11 pt Calibri font, and other settings. However, when you click File, and then click New, a menu of template options displays in the Backstage view from which you can select, as shown in Figure 6.1.

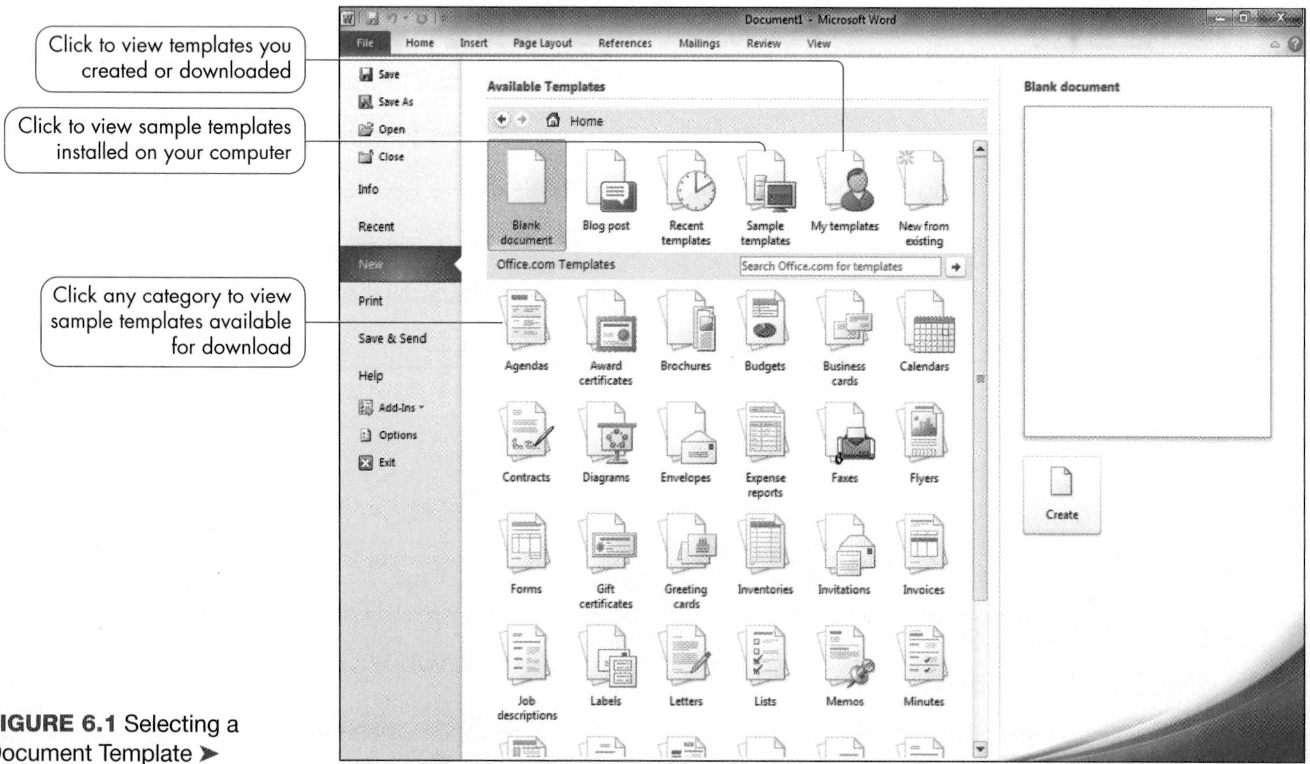

FIGURE 6.1 Selecting a Document Template ➤

After you use a template, it will display in the *Recent templates* category in the Backstage view for a New File. But you can also view other templates installed on your PC, or templates you have created. If you cannot find a template that meets your immediate needs, you can view templates available for download from Office.com.

TIP Document Template File Extensions

Document templates use the file extensions .dotx or .dotm (if it contains a macro) in Word 2010. Previous versions of Word use .dot as the extension for templates. When you search for a template on your computer, you must click the Files of type arrow and display All Word Templates (*.dotx; *.dotm; *.dot).

A **placeholder** is a field or block of text used to determine the position of objects in a document.

Word provides several different templates for different types of documents, such as résumés, letters, and faxes. Many of these templates are preformatted using styles or themes such as Adjacency, Equity, Median, Oriel, Origin, and Urban. By using templates with a similar style you can coordinate documents. To preview the templates, click Sample Templates in the Backstage view, as shown in Figure 6.2. Each template portrays a different style and when opened contains placeholders for information you provide to complete the résumé. A ***placeholder*** is a field or block of text used to determine the position of objects in a document. If you insert text beside a placeholder instead of replacing it, you should be sure to delete the placeholder before you save the document.

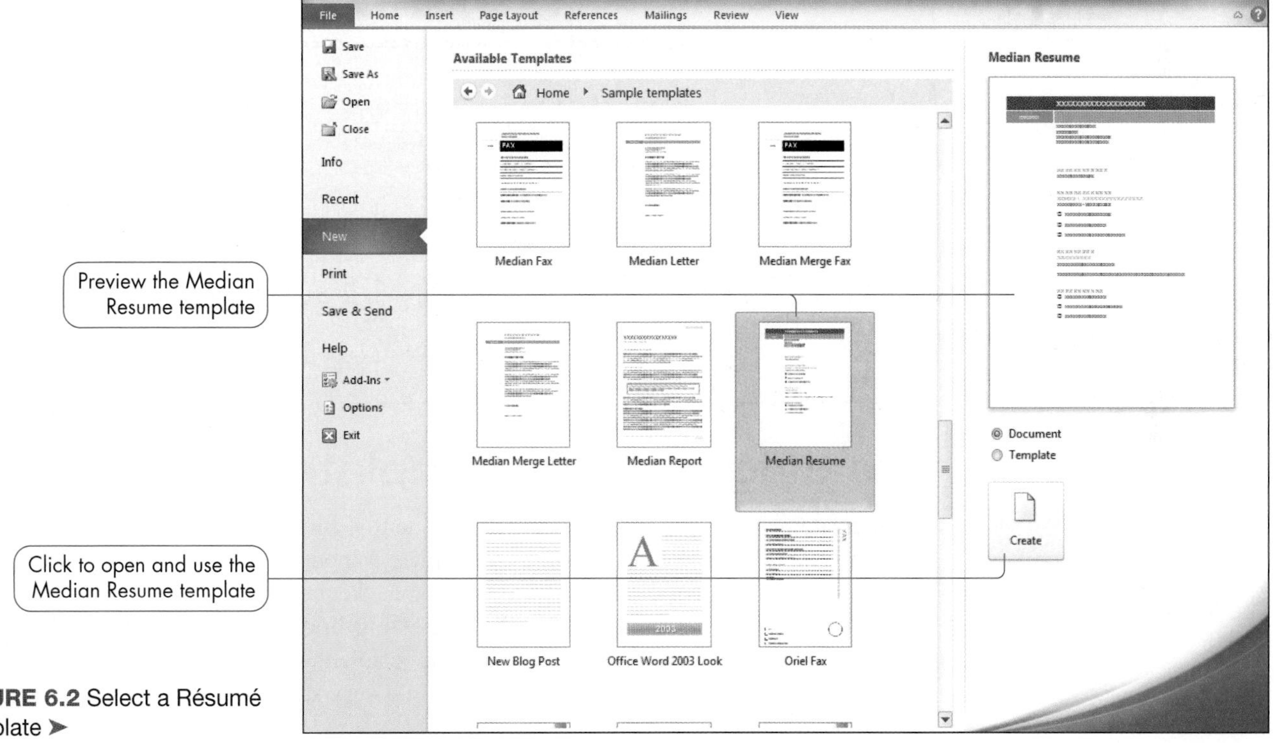

FIGURE 6.2 Select a Résumé Template ➤

Templates often help provide assistance with layout for some documents, such as résumés. A variety of different ways exist to lay out a résumé, and using a template can be an easy way to determine which style best matches your needs. If the default résumé templates do not meet your needs, you can look at others on Office.com. When you click *Resumes and CVs* in the Backstage view, there are three categories of résumé templates on Office.com: Basic, Job specific, and Situation specific.

A **curriculum vitae (CV)**, like a résumé, displays your skills, accomplishments, and job history.

After you select a template category, you then choose a style from the long list of choices, and then download the template to your computer. Existing templates include résumé and vitae templates. A ***curriculum vitae*** (***CV***) is similar to a résumé; it displays your skills, accomplishments, job history, or other employment information, and is often used by academics.

To transfer the template to your computer, click Download after you select a template from the gallery. After the template downloads, it opens in a new document window to display placeholders and sample text as shown in Figure 6.3. You can then begin the process of replacing placeholders with your personal information. When you save the résumé, it will save as a Word document, not a document template, unless you change the file type to template.

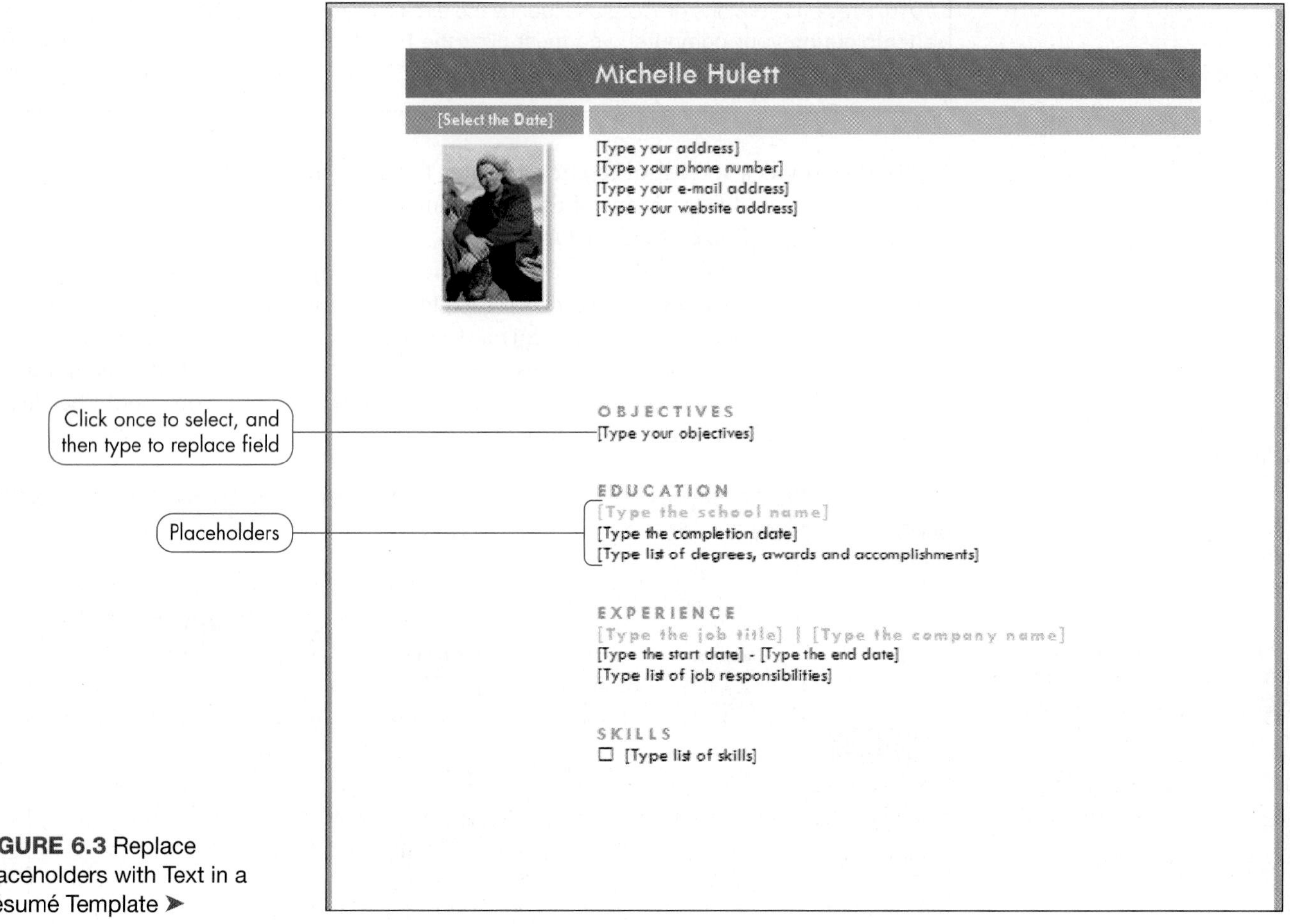

FIGURE 6.3 Replace Placeholders with Text in a Résumé Template ➤

Creating a Word Template

If you create or use a particular document frequently, with only minor modifications each time, you should save the document as a template. When you create the template, you can insert placeholders for the information you change frequently. You can create a document template that contains a company letterhead, greeting, body, and salutation, thereby requiring you to replace only the information for the recipient. Or if you have a report that you update on a regular basis, which is contained in a very structured and detailed table, you might consider making it a template as well.

To save a document as a template, simply click the File tab, click Save As, and then change the *Save as type* to a Word template (*.dotx), as shown in Figure 6.4. The file extension is added for you, and you only need to click Save. You should, however, note the location where the template saves. You can specify a location on your own hard drive or portable storage device, or you can enable it to save in the Documents Library, which saves to your hard drive. When you create and save a Word template in the Documents Library, it displays in the New Document dialog box when you click *My templates.*

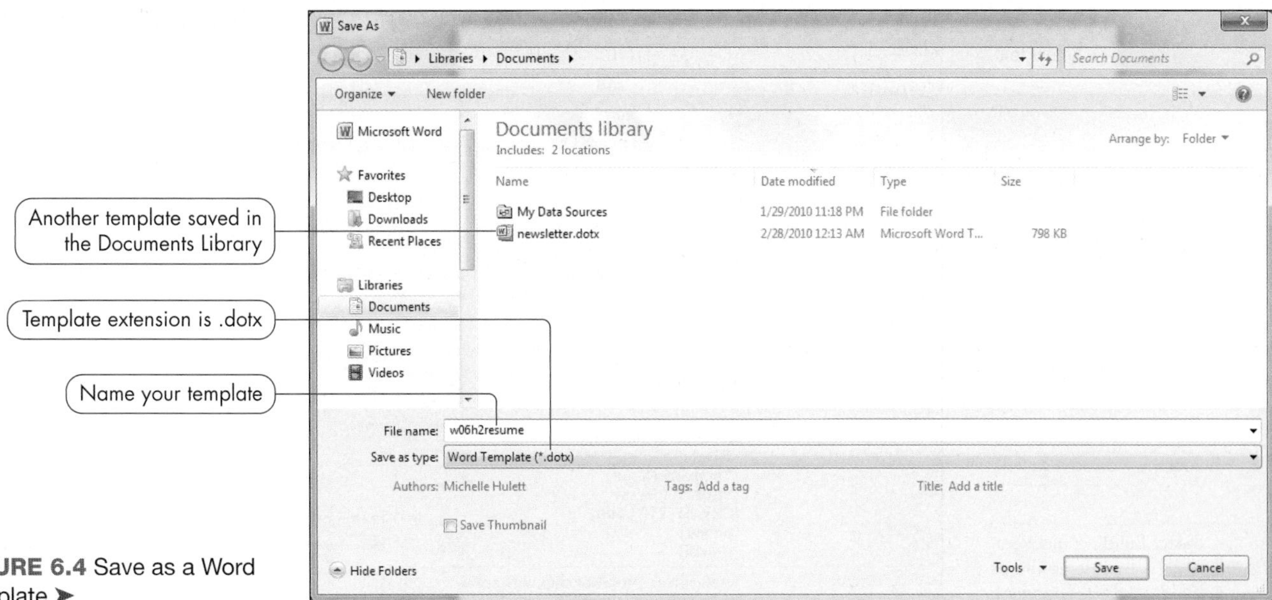

FIGURE 6.4 Save as a Word Template ➤

Using Building Blocks

A **Building Block** is a document component used frequently, such as a disclaimer, company address, or cover page.

When you create templates that frequently contain particular content or objects, you might want to save the content or objects so that you can use them again without re-creating or retyping. Word enables you to create or save objects, called ***Building Blocks***, which are used frequently. Building Blocks might include disclaimers that display at the bottom of a document, a company address or logo, or a cover page to a letter. By saving information into a Building Block, it is quick and easy to insert in a document. Other objects that you can save as a Building Block include watermarks, headers or footers, tables, or logos; and they can also include larger objects such as a whole page with specific tables and formatting.

You can also save information as AutoText, which is a type of Building Block, to store text or graphics that you want to use again, such as a standard contract clause or a long distribution list. To save an item as AutoText or a Building Block, you

- Select the item.
- Click the Insert tab.
- Click Quick Parts.
- Select Save Selection to Quick Part Gallery.
- In the Create New Building Block dialog box, assign a name that reflects the object, select AutoText from the Gallery, and click OK.

Each selection of text or graphics that you add to the Quick Part Gallery is stored in the Building Blocks Organizer and is assigned a unique name that makes it easy for you to find the content when you want to use it. You can also assign a name you prefer. After you add text to the Quick Part Gallery, you can type a portion of the entry, and then press F3 to insert the remainder into your document. Figure 6.5 demonstrates the creation of the AutoText. Word 2010 contains many Building Blocks already, which you can view and insert into your document by clicking the Insert tab, clicking Quick Parts, and then clicking Building Blocks Organizer, as shown in Figure 6.6.

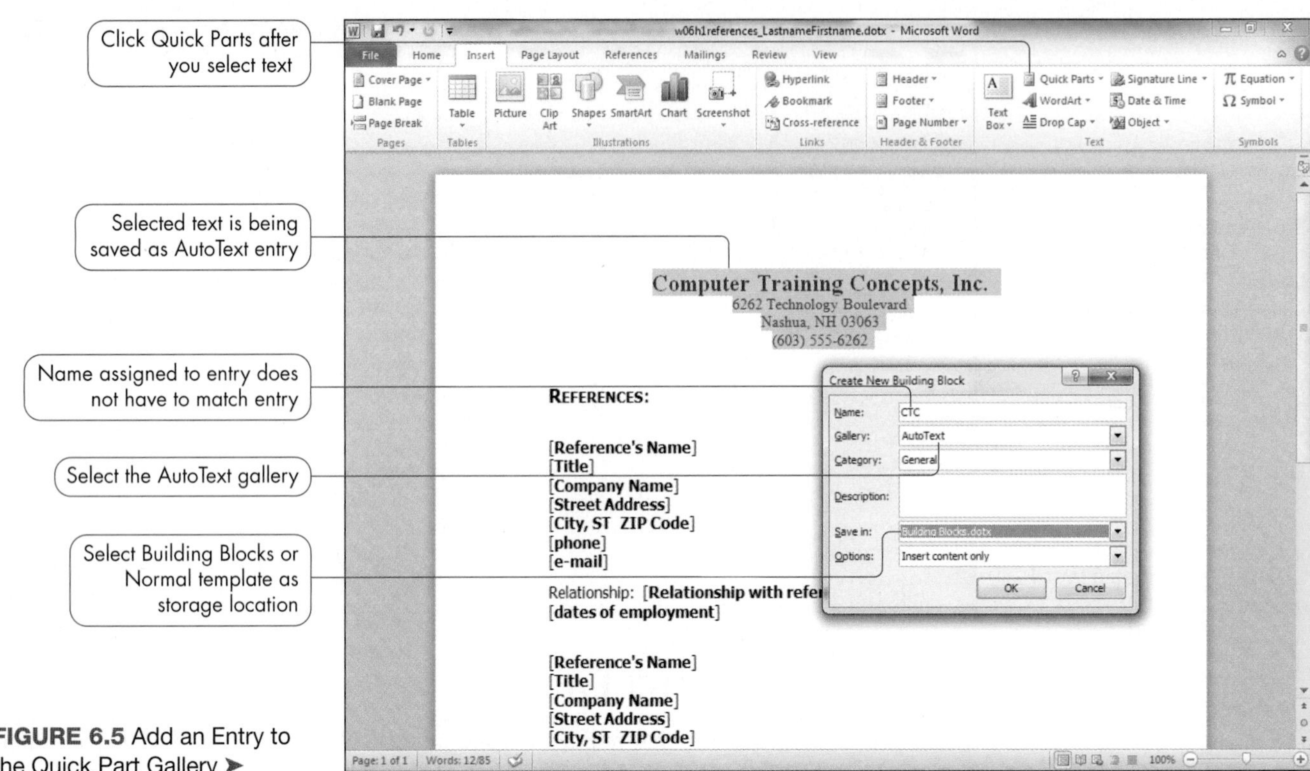

FIGURE 6.5 Add an Entry to the Quick Part Gallery ➤

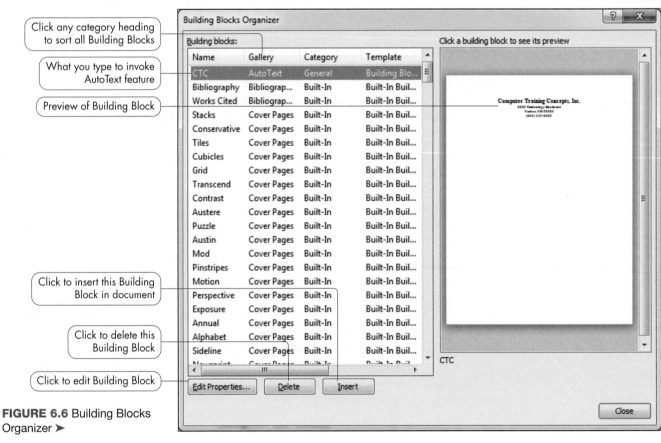

Click any category heading to sort all Building Blocks

What you type to invoke AutoText feature

Preview of Building Block

Click to insert this Building Block in document

Click to delete this Building Block

Click to edit Building Block

Building Blocks Organizer

Building blocks:

Name	Gallery	Category	Template
CTC	AutoText	General	Building Blo...
Bibliography	Bibliograp...	Built-In	Built-In Buil...
Works Cited	Bibliograp...	Built-In	Built-In Buil...
Stacks	Cover Pages	Built-In	Built-In Buil...
Conservative	Cover Pages	Built-In	Built-In Buil...
Tiles	Cover Pages	Built-In	Built-In Buil...
Cubicles	Cover Pages	Built-In	Built-In Buil...
Grid	Cover Pages	Built-In	Built-In Buil...
Transcend	Cover Pages	Built-In	Built-In Buil...
Contrast	Cover Pages	Built-In	Built-In Buil...
Austere	Cover Pages	Built-In	Built-In Buil...
Puzzle	Cover Pages	Built-In	Built-In Buil...
Austin	Cover Pages	Built-In	Built-In Buil...
Mod	Cover Pages	Built-In	Built-In Buil...
Pinstripes	Cover Pages	Built-In	Built-In Buil...
Motion	Cover Pages	Built-In	Built-In Buil...
Perspective	Cover Pages	Built-In	Built-In Buil...
Exposure	Cover Pages	Built-In	Built-In Buil...
Annual	Cover Pages	Built-In	Built-In Buil...
Alphabet	Cover Pages	Built-In	Built-In Buil...
Sideline	Cover Pages	Built-In	Built-In Buil...

Click a building block to see its preview

Computer Training Concepts, Inc.

CTC

Edit Properties... | Delete | Insert

Close

FIGURE 6.6 Building Blocks Organizer ➤

HANDS-ON EXERCISES

1 Document Templates

When Alexandra Caselman assembles a quote for the cost of training, she always includes a résumé of the instructors. She also creates a sheet of references—people who have used the services of Computer Training Concepts, Inc. She would like each résumé and reference sheet to have a similar look, so she decides to use document templates instead of starting with blank documents each time.

Skills covered: Select an Installed Résumé Template • Download a Template and Insert Building Blocks • Modify a Template and Save as a Document

STEP 1 SELECT AN INSTALLED RÉSUMÉ TEMPLATE

Alexandra recently found the selection of résumé templates that comes with Word, and learned there are even more online. She decides to select one style and fill in the information for the trainer she will send to the next job. Refer to Figure 6.7 as you complete Step 1.

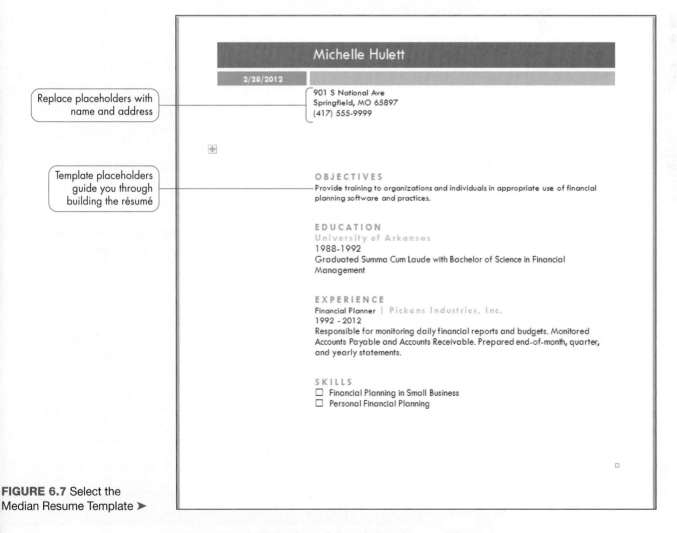

Replace placeholders with name and address

Template placeholders guide you through building the résumé

Michelle Hulett

2/28/2012

901 S National Ave
Springfield, MO 65897
(417) 555-9999

OBJECTIVES
Provide training to organizations and individuals in appropriate use of financial planning software and practices.

EDUCATION
University of Arkansas
1988-1992
Graduated Summa Cum Laude with Bachelor of Science in Financial Management

EXPERIENCE
Financial Planner | Pickens Industries, Inc.
1992 - 2012
Responsible for monitoring daily financial reports and budgets. Monitored Accounts Payable and Accounts Receivable. Prepared end-of-month, quarter, and yearly statements.

SKILLS
☐ Financial Planning in Small Business
☐ Personal Financial Planning

FIGURE 6.7 Select the Median Resume Template ➤

a. Start Word. Click **File**, and then click **New**.

The Backstage view displays and the Available Templates cover the middle section of the window.

b. Click **Sample Templates** in the Available Templates pane. In the Sample Templates pane, scroll down, and then click the **Median Resume template**. Click **Create** to open the template.

The Median Resume template opens as a new document and the User Name specified in Word Options displays at the top.

c. Click one time in the brown bar that displays your name at the top of the résumé, and then click the **Resume Name tab**. Click the **Quick Parts arrow** that displays on the right side of the tab, and then click **Name**.

This template has two formats—*Name* and *Name with Photo*. You choose the template without a photograph.

TROUBLESHOOTING: If your name does not display at the top of the résumé, you can click the name placeholder, and then type to replace it with your name. If it still does not display, place your cursor on the left side of the placeholder, type your name, and then delete the placeholder.

d. Click **Select the Date** in the template to view an arrow control. Click the arrow, and then click **Today**.

e. Replace the next three placeholders, address, phone, and e-mail, with the following information, and then delete the Web site address placeholder:

901 S National Ave
Springfield, MO 65897
(417) 555-9999

f. Type the following information in the résumé for each category:

Objectives	**Provide training to organizations and individuals in appropriate use of financial planning software and practices.**
Education	**University of Arkansas** **1988–1992** **Graduated Summa Cum Laude with Bachelor of Science in Financial Management**
Experience	**Financial Planner Pickens Industries, Inc.** **1992–2012** **Responsible for monitoring daily financial reports and budgets. Monitored Accounts Payable and Accounts Receivable. Prepared end-of-month, quarter, and yearly statements.**
Skills	**Financial Planning in Small Business** **Personal Financial Planning**

g. Click the **File tab**, and then click **Save As**. In the **File name box**, type **w06h1resume_LastnameFirstname**. Confirm the *Save as type* box displays *Word Document (*.docx)*, and then click **Save**.

TROUBLESHOOTING: If the Save as type box displays Word Template (*.dotx), click the Save as type arrow, and then click Word Document (*.docx) before you save.

h. Close the document, but do not exit Word.

TIP Change User Names

To replace the current User Name with your own, click File, click Options, click General, if necessary, and then type your name in the *User name* box in the *Personalize Your Copy of Microsoft Office* section.

STEP 2 DOWNLOAD A TEMPLATE AND INSERT BUILDING BLOCKS

The next step in compiling the proposal for a potential client is to generate a list of references. This information changes often, so Alexandra wants to use a template that she can update quickly. She also inserts the company letterhead frequently, so she decides to save that information as a Building Block, which can be inserted with only a few key strokes, instead of retyping the information each time. Refer to Figure 6.8 as you complete Step 2.

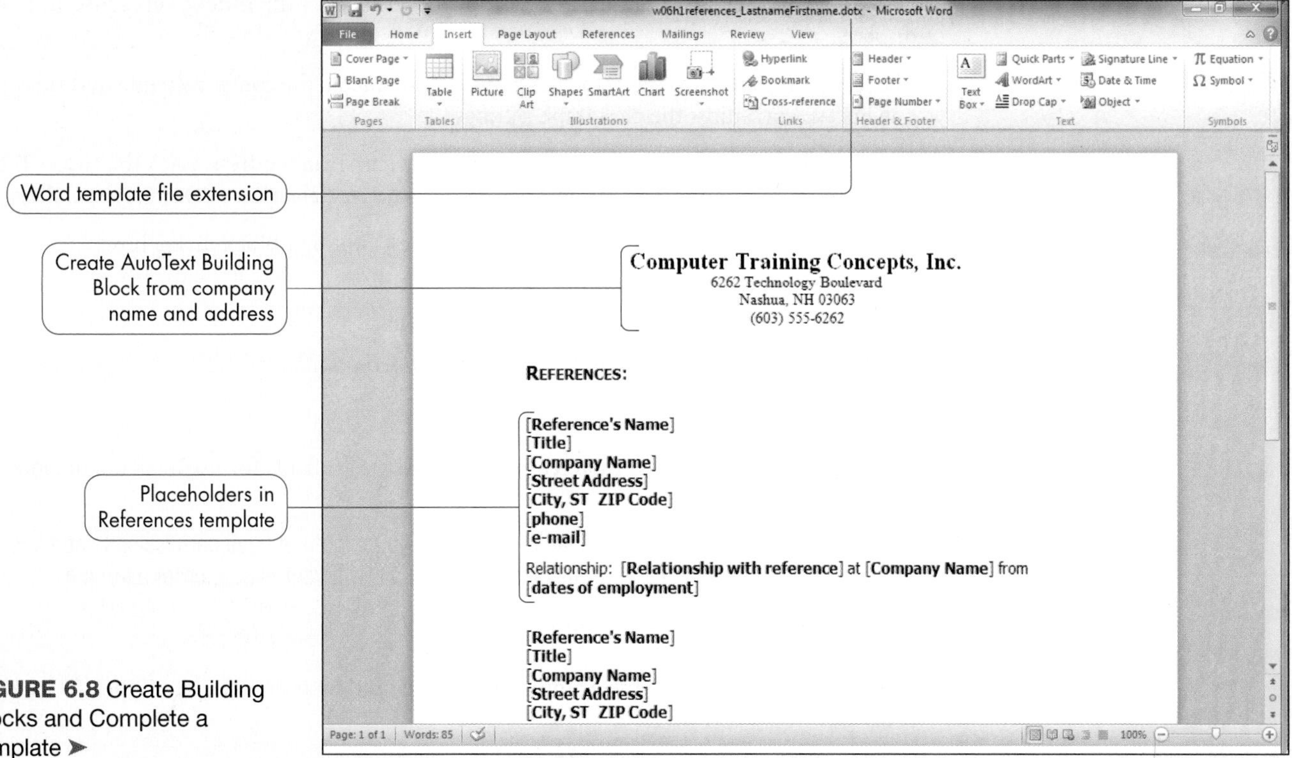

FIGURE 6.8 Create Building Blocks and Complete a Template ➤

a. Click the **File tab**, and then click **New**. In the Templates pane, click **Lists** in the Office.com *Templates* section. Click **Business**, select **Resume References**, and then click **Download**.

> **TROUBLESHOOTING:** If a Microsoft Office Genuine Advantage dialog box displays, click Do not show this message again, and then click Continue. If you work in a lab environment, you may not have permission to download document templates from Office.com. If that is the case, read Steps 2 and 3, and then continue to the next section.

A download window appears briefly, then the résumé reference template displays with placeholders and sample text.

b. Click the **File tab**, and then click **Save As**. When the Save As dialog box displays, click the **Save as type arrow**. Click **Word Template (*.dotx)**. Click in the **File name box**, type **w06h1references_LastnameFirstname**, and then click **Save**.

If a Microsoft dialog box displays with a message about saving in a new file format, click OK. When you save this document as a template, you can open it later and make modifications without changing the original. Be sure to save the file as a template (.dotx) and not a document (.docx).

c. Replace the placeholders at the top of the page by completing the following steps:
- Click the **[Your Name] placeholder**, and then type **Computer Training Concepts, Inc.**
- Click one time in the **[Street Address] placeholder**, and then type **6262 Technology Boulevard.**

- Click one time in the [City, ST ZIP Code] **placeholder**, and then type **Nashua, NH 03063**.
- Select the [phone] **placeholder**, and then type **(603) 555-6262**.
- Click the [E-mail] **placeholder**, right-click, and then click **Cut**.

d. Select all five lines that contain the company name and address, click **Font** on the Mini toolbar, and then select **Times New Roman**. Click **Center** on the Mini toolbar to center all lines horizontally.

e. Click the **Page Layout Tab** in the Text group, and then select the **Indent Left arrow** until **0″** displays.

The formatting that was set in the template did not enable the company name to display on one line, so you adjust the paragraph settings.

f. Select the four lines that now display the company name and address. Click the **Insert Tab**, click **Quick Parts** in the Text group, and then select **Save Selection to Quick Part Gallery**.

g. Complete the following steps within the Create New Building Block dialog box:

- Type **CTC** in the **Name box**.
- Click the **Gallery arrow**, and then select **AutoText**.
- Click the **Save In arrow**, and then select *Building Blocks.dotx.*
- Click **OK**.

The entry is added to the Normal template and will be available for use in all documents.

> **TROUBLESHOOTING:** If you are in a lab environment, you might not have permission to add this item or save the changes to the Normal template. Consult with your instructor for alternate instructions, if necessary.

h. Test your Building Block by selecting the four lines, and then press **Delete**. Type **CTC** and press **F3**.

The entry displays just as it was before. Now you can use this Building Block in other documents you design for the company.

i. Compare your results to Figure 6.8, and then save the template.

STEP 3 MODIFY A TEMPLATE AND SAVE AS A DOCUMENT

Now that the template is set up, Alexandra forwards it so you can add the information about companies that will be used as references in this proposal. After adding the references, you save it as a document instead of a template. Refer to Figure 6.9 as you complete Step 3.

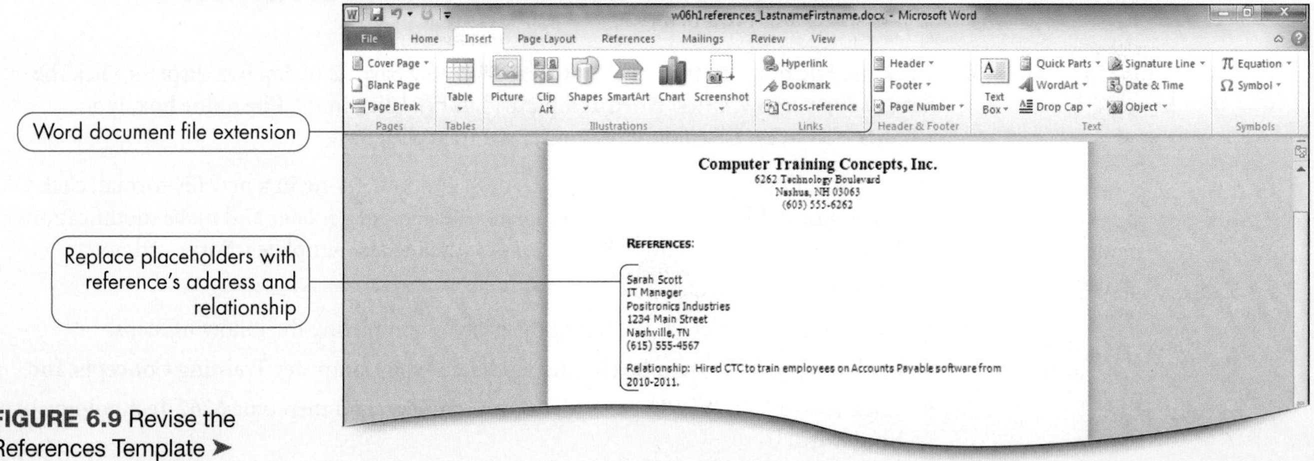

FIGURE 6.9 Revise the References Template ➤

a. Type the information from the list below into the respective reference placeholders. Remove the e-mail placeholders for each reference because they are not used.

Reference #1	Sarah Scott IT Manager Positronics Industries 1234 Main Street Nashville, TN (615) 555-4567
Reference #2	Noah Ward Director of Accounting State of Alaska 678 Pitka Place Juneau, AK (907) 555-1234
Reference #3	Kyler Funk Chief Financial Officer Orchestral Solutions 211 Shawna Street Fairfax, VA (703) 555-9876

b. Select the two lines that display placeholders for the *Relationship*, *Company Name*, and *dates of employment*. Type the following information to replace the placeholders:

Reference #1	Relationship: Hired CTC to train employees on Accounts Payable software from 2010-2011.
Reference #2	Relationship: Hired CTC to train employees on Accounts Payable and Accounts Receivable software from 2009-2011.
Reference #3	Relationship: Hired CTC to train employees on financial and budgeting software from 2010-2012.

c. Click **File**, and then click **Save As**. Click the **Save as Type arrow**, and then select **Word Document (.docx)**. If necessary, type in the file name **w06h1references_LastnameFirstname**.

Be sure to save the file as a document (.docx) and not a template (.dotx).

d. Close all files, and then submit based on your instructor's directions.

Multiple Documents

... features in Word enable you to work with multiple documents simultaneously—you can view multiple documents at one time, as well as combine them into one.

The collaboration features in Word facilitate an easy exchange of ideas and revisions to a document. But some users do not use the collaboration features, which causes the process of combining information into one document to be less efficient. Fortunately, other features in Word enable you to work with multiple documents simultaneously—you can view multiple documents at one time, as well as combine them into one.

In this section, you will view multiple documents side by side as well as compare and combine them. You will create a document that contains subdocuments, and then use tools to navigate within lengthy documents. Finally, you will create an electronic marker for a location in a document and use the Go To feature to find that marker.

Viewing Documents Side by Side

View Side by Side enables you to display two documents on the same screen.

The ***View Side by Side*** feature enables you to display two documents on the same screen. This is a useful tool when you want to compare an original to a revised document or when you want to cut or copy a portion from one document to another. To view two documents side by side, you must open both documents. The View Side by Side command is grayed out if only one document is open. When the documents are open, click View Side by Side in the Window group on the View tab, and the Word window will split to display each document as shown in Figure 6.10. If you have more than two documents open, when you click View Side by Side the Compare Side by Side dialog box displays, and you select which document you want to display beside the active document.

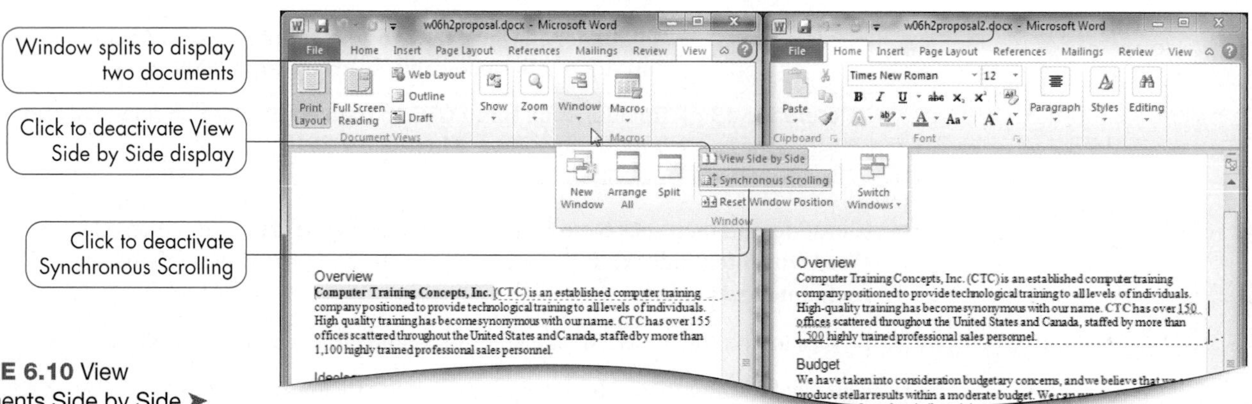

FIGURE 6.10 View Documents Side by Side ➤

Synchronous scrolling enables you to simultaneously scroll through documents in Side by Side view.

When the documents display side by side, synchronous scrolling is active by default. ***Synchronous scrolling*** enables you to scroll through both documents at the same time. If you want to scroll through each document independently, click Synchronous Scrolling on the View tab to toggle it off. If you are viewing two versions of the same document, synchronous scrolling enables you to view both documents using only one scroll bar. If you scroll through each document asynchronously, you must use the respective scroll bars to navigate through each document.

While in Side by Side view, you can resize and reposition the two document windows. If you want to reset them to the original side-by-side viewing size, click Reset Window Position on the View tab. To close Side by Side view, click View Side by Side to toggle it off. The document that contains the insertion point when you close Side by Side view will display as the active document.

Merging Documents

Besides viewing two documents simultaneously, Word also provides different ways to combine multiple documents into one. The particular method you use depends on the purpose of the document. You might simply want to combine two documents, deciding which portions of each to keep and omit. You might need to add the entire contents of one document into another, or you might want to include the entire contents of several documents in one.

Compare and Combine Documents

The **Compare** feature evaluates the contents of two or more documents and displays markup balloons showing the differences.

Ideally, when you have a document to submit to others for feedback, you want everyone to use the Track Changes feature in Word. However, sometimes it is necessary to have several people edit their own copy of the document simultaneously before they return it to you. When this occurs, you have several similar documents but with individual changes. Instead of compiling results from printed copies or viewing each one in Side by Side view to determine the differences, you can use a Compare feature. ***Compare*** automatically evaluates the contents of two or more documents and displays markup balloons that show the differences between the documents. You can display the differences in the original document, the revised document, or in a new document. You also can display the original and revised documents with the new document as shown in Figure 6.11. The Compare command is in the Compare group on the Review tab.

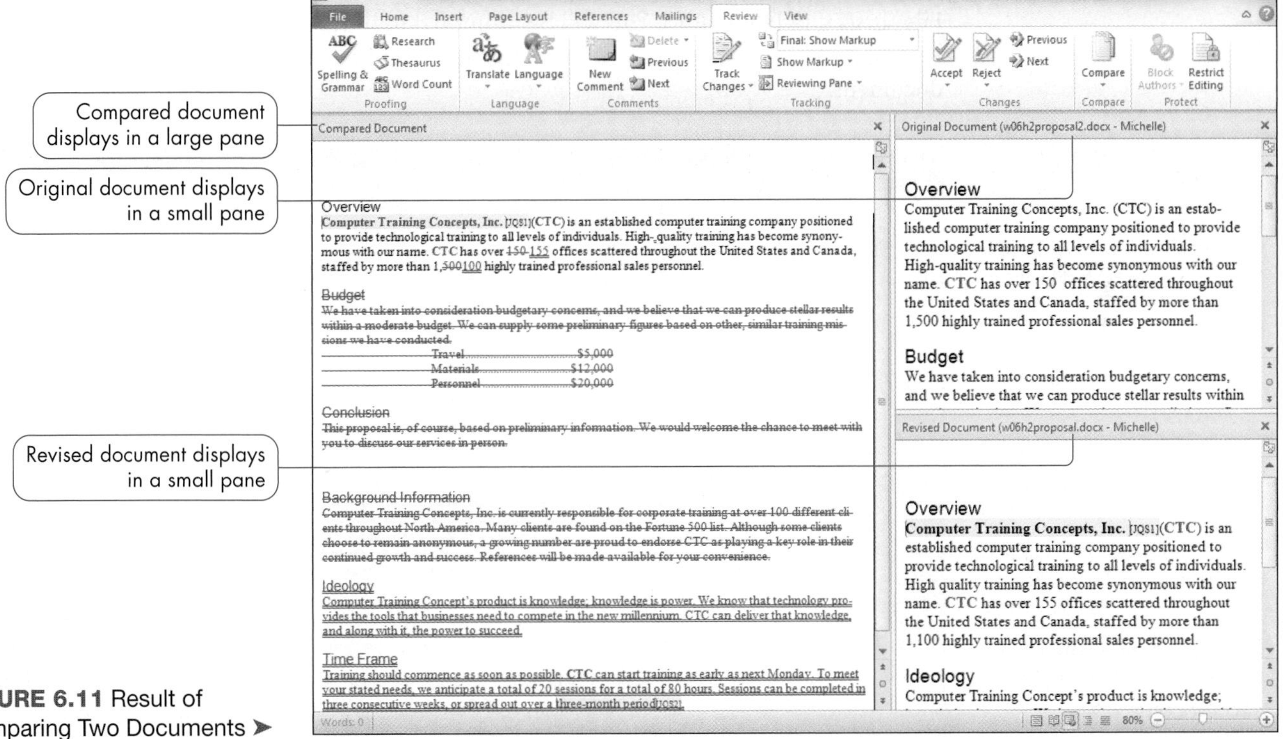

FIGURE 6.11 Result of Comparing Two Documents ➤

The **Combine** feature incorporates all changes from multiple documents into a new document.

If you want to go a step further than just viewing the differences, you can use the ***Combine*** feature to integrate all changes from multiple documents into one document. To use the Combine feature, click Compare in the Review tab, and then select Combine. The Combine Documents dialog box contains a variety of options you can invoke, as shown in Figure 6.12; however, options only display after clicking the More button. The option you are most likely to change is in the *Show changes* section where you determine in which document the Combined documents will display—in the original document, the revised document, or in a new document. If you want to be certain not to modify the original documents, you should combine the changes into a new document.

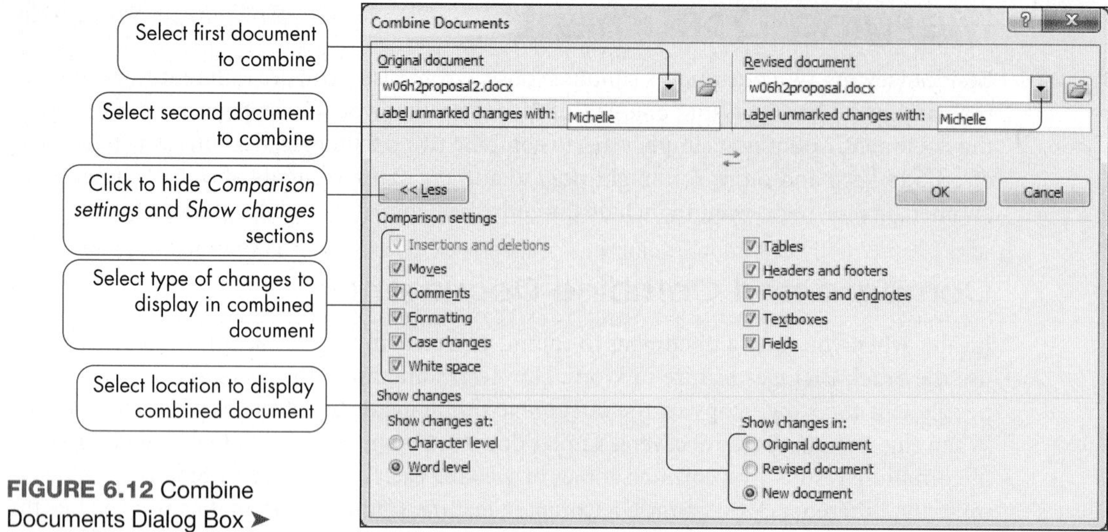

FIGURE 6.12 Combine Documents Dialog Box ➤

Insert a File Object

You can quickly add the contents of one document to another without opening both documents by using the Object command. When you use this method, you open one document and place the cursor where you want to insert the contents of the second (unopened) document. Click the Insert tab, click the Object arrow in the Text group, and then click Text from File, as seen in Figure 6.13. You will be prompted to browse to the file that contains the text you want to insert, and after you select the file the entire contents will be placed in the open document.

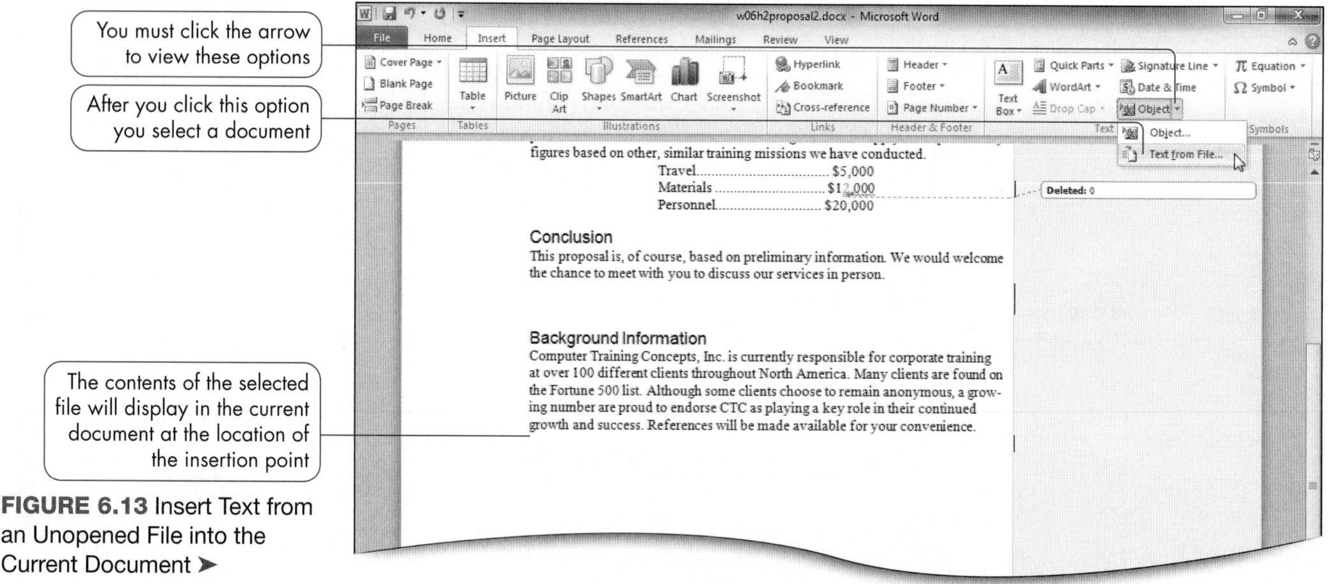

FIGURE 6.13 Insert Text from an Unopened File into the Current Document ➤

Create Master Documents and Subdocuments

A **master document** is a document that acts like a binder for managing smaller documents.

A **subdocument** is a smaller document that is a part of a master document.

Working with long documents can be cumbersome. You may notice your computer slows down when you are working in a lengthy document—scrolling, finding and replacing, editing, and formatting typically take longer to process. To improve this situation, you can create a ***master document***, a document that acts like a binder for managing smaller documents. A smaller document that is a part of a master document is called a ***subdocument***. The advantage of the master document is that you can work with several smaller documents, as opposed to a single large document. Thus, you edit the subdocuments individually and more efficiently than if they were all part of the same document. You can create a master document to hold the chapters of a book, where each chapter is stored as a subdocument. You also can use a master document to hold multiple documents created by others, such as a group project, where each member of the group is responsible for a section of the document.

To work with master and subdocuments, you need to click the View tab, and then click Outline to display the Outlining tab. You can also click Outline on the status bar. The Outlining tab contains the Collapse and Expand Subdocuments buttons, as well as other tools associated with master documents. Figure 6.14 displays a master document with three subdocuments. The subdocuments are collapsed in Figure 6.14 and expanded in Figure 6.15. The collapsed structure enables you to see at a glance the subdocuments that comprise the master document. You can insert additional subdocuments or remove existing subdocuments from the master document. Deleting a subdocument from within a master document does not delete the actual subdocument file. Look carefully at the subdocuments in Figure 6.14. A padlock appears to the left of the first line in subdocuments. All subdocuments are locked when collapsed.

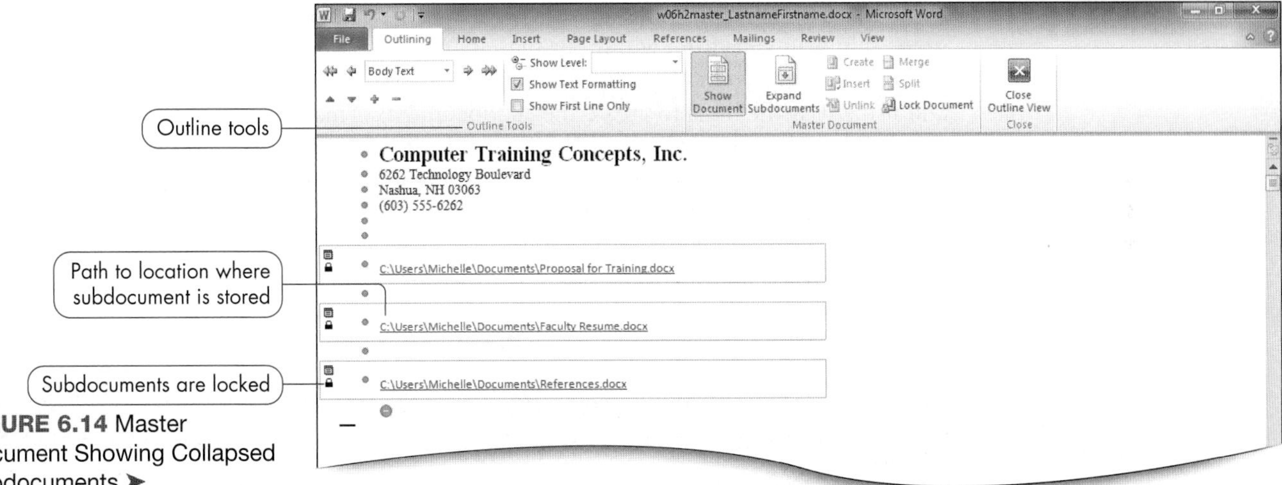

FIGURE 6.14 Master Document Showing Collapsed Subdocuments ➤

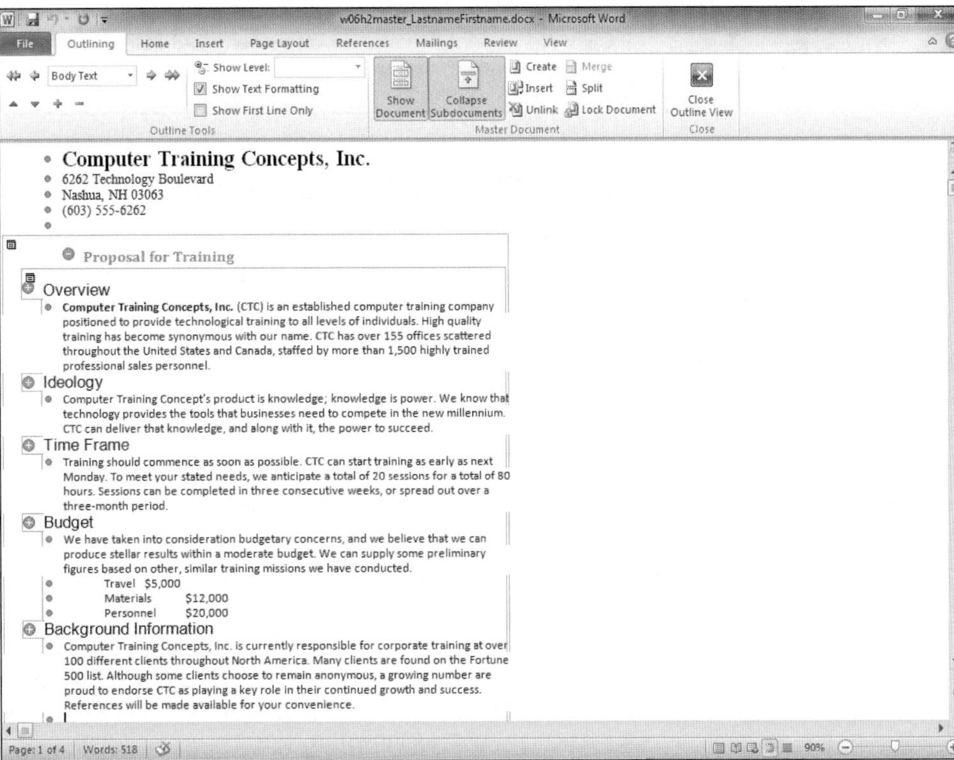

FIGURE 6.15 Master Document Showing Expanded Subdocuments ➤

The expanded structure enables you to view and edit the contents of the subdocuments. You can make changes to the master document at any time. However, you can make changes to the subdocuments only when the subdocument is unlocked. Note, too, that you can make changes to a subdocument in one of two ways, either when the subdocument is expanded (and unlocked) within a master document as in Figure 6.15 or by opening the subdocument as an independent document within Microsoft Word. You lock the subdocuments to prevent making changes to their content but also to prevent the subdocument from being deleted from the master document.

Regardless of how you edit the subdocuments, the attraction of a master document is the ability to work with multiple subdocuments simultaneously. The subdocuments are created independently of one another, with each subdocument stored in its own file. Then, when all of the subdocuments are finished, the master document is created, and the subdocuments are inserted into the master document, from where they are easily accessed. Inserting page numbers into the master document, for example, causes the numbers to run consecutively from one subdocument to the next. You also can create a table of contents or index for the master document that will reflect the entries in all of the subdocuments. And finally, you can print all of the subdocuments from within the master document with a single command.

Alternatively, you can reverse the process by starting with an empty master document and using it as the basis to create the subdocuments. This process is ideal for organizing a group project in school or at work, the chapters in a book, or the sections in a report. Start with a new document, and then enter the topics assigned to each group member. Format each topic in a heading style within the master document, and then use the Create Subdocument command to create subdocuments based on those headings. Saving the master document will automatically save each subdocument in its own file. This is the approach that you will follow in Hands-On Exercise 2.

TIP Printing a Master Document

If you click Print when a master document is displayed and the subdocuments are collapsed, the message *Do you want to open the subdocuments before continuing with this command?* appears. Click Yes to open the subdocuments so that they will print as one long document. Click No to print the master document that lists the subdocument file names as they display onscreen.

Using Navigational Tools

Without a reference source, such as a table of contents, it can be difficult to locate information in a long document. Even scrolling through a long document can be inefficient if you are uncertain of the exact location that you want to view. Fortunately, Word provides navigation tools that assist the author and reader in locating content quickly and easily.

Display the Navigation Pane

The **Navigation Pane** enables you to quickly move through documents using text, headings, or pages.

You can use the Find and Go To features in Word to move through a document. Another helpful feature is the ***Navigation Pane***, which enables you to navigate through the document by viewing headings, viewing pages, and browsing the results of your last search. To display the pane, click Navigation Pane in the Show group on the View tab. This setting is a toggle, enabling you to turn it on and off. When displayed, the Navigation Pane contains three tabs—one for each type of search. The first tab displays headings in a document. You can click a heading in the pane to move the insertion point to the location of that heading in the document. When working in long documents this view provides a way to navigate quickly to a particular topic, as shown in Figure 6.16.

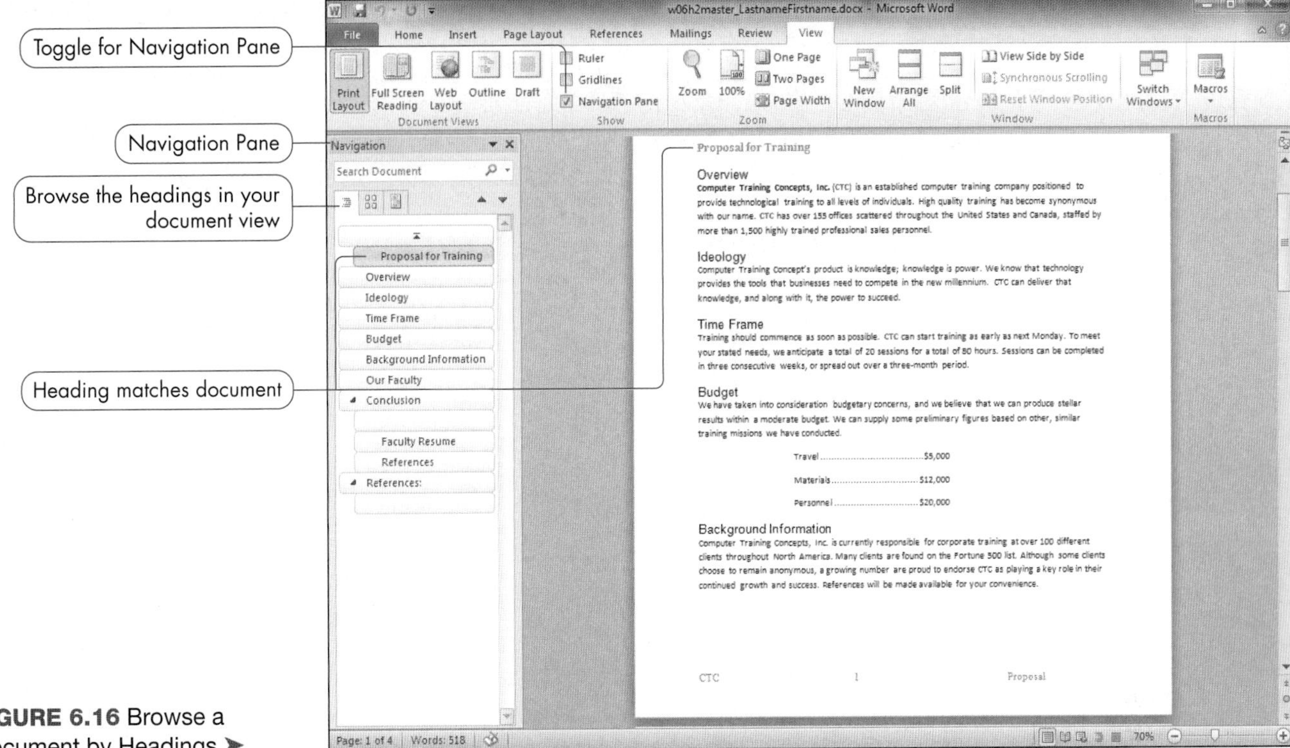

FIGURE 6.16 Browse a Document by Headings ➤

If you want to display the headings in a master document, be sure the master document is expanded to display the text of the subdocuments. The Navigation Pane will only display headings for a document that uses the styles feature to format headings. The best way to format headings is to apply the built-in title or heading styles from the Styles group on the Home tab.

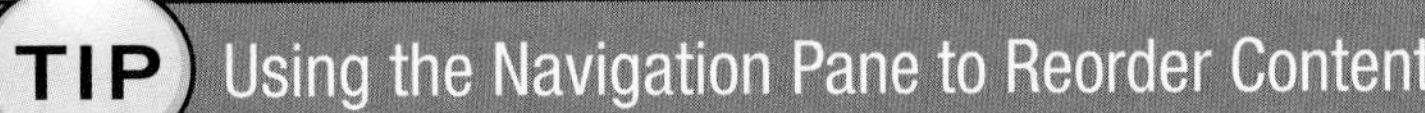

TIP Using the Navigation Pane to Reorder Content

You can use the Navigation Pane in a similar manner to the way you use the Outline view to reorganize content in a document when you display the browse by headings view. Select a paragraph heading, and then drag it to a different location in the Navigation Pane to move that heading and corresponding paragraph.

A **thumbnail** is a small picture of each page in your document that displays in the Navigation Pane.

In lieu of the document headings, you can display ***thumbnails***—small pictures of each page in your document—in the Navigation Pane. Thumbnails display when you click the *Browse the pages in your document* tab in the Navigation Pane. As with the headings, you can click a thumbnail to move the insertion point to the top of that page. This is another method of navigating quickly through a document.

Even though you cannot read the text on a thumbnail, you can see the layout of a page well enough to determine if that is a location you want to display (see Figure 6.17). And if you display revision marks and comments, the marks and comment balloons also display in the thumbnails.

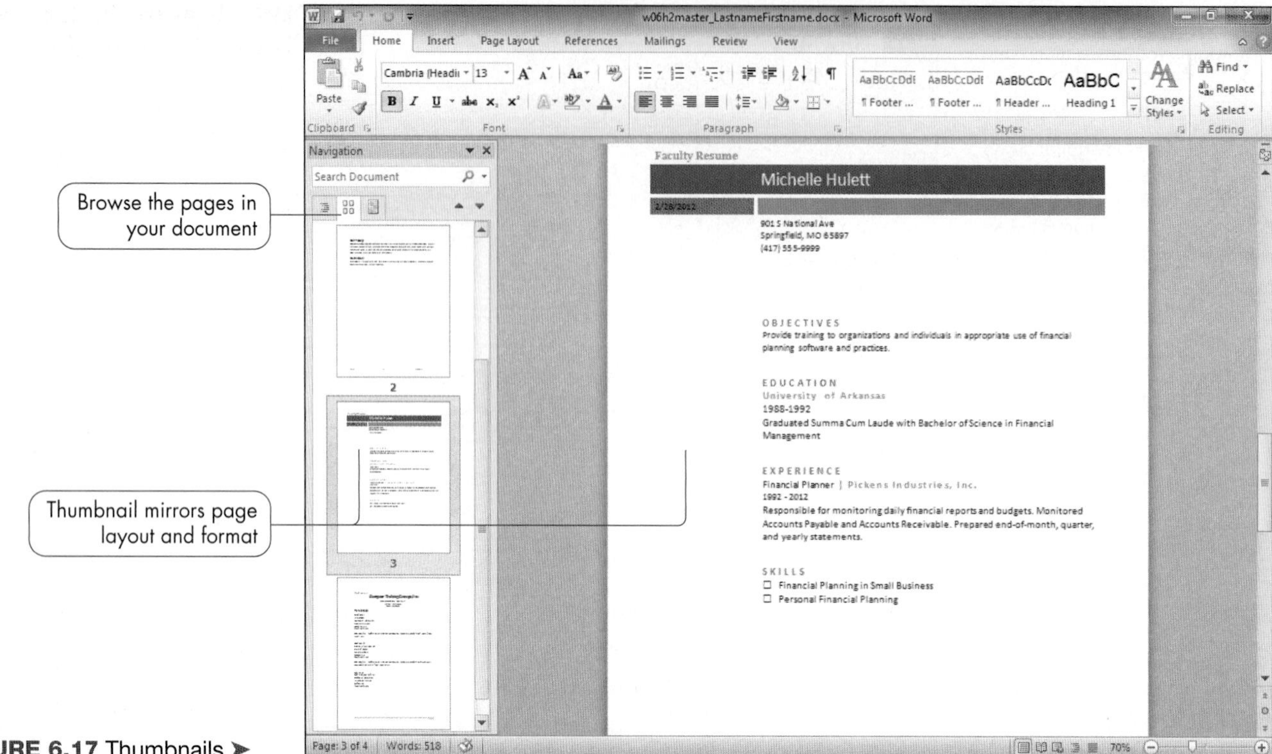

FIGURE 6.17 Thumbnails ➤

The third panel in the Navigation Pane displays the results of a text search. When you type in a word or a string of text, each occurrence displays, as shown in Figure 6.18. You can click the occurrence and the text is highlighted in the document. This pane also enables you to search for other objects in the document, such as graphics and tables.

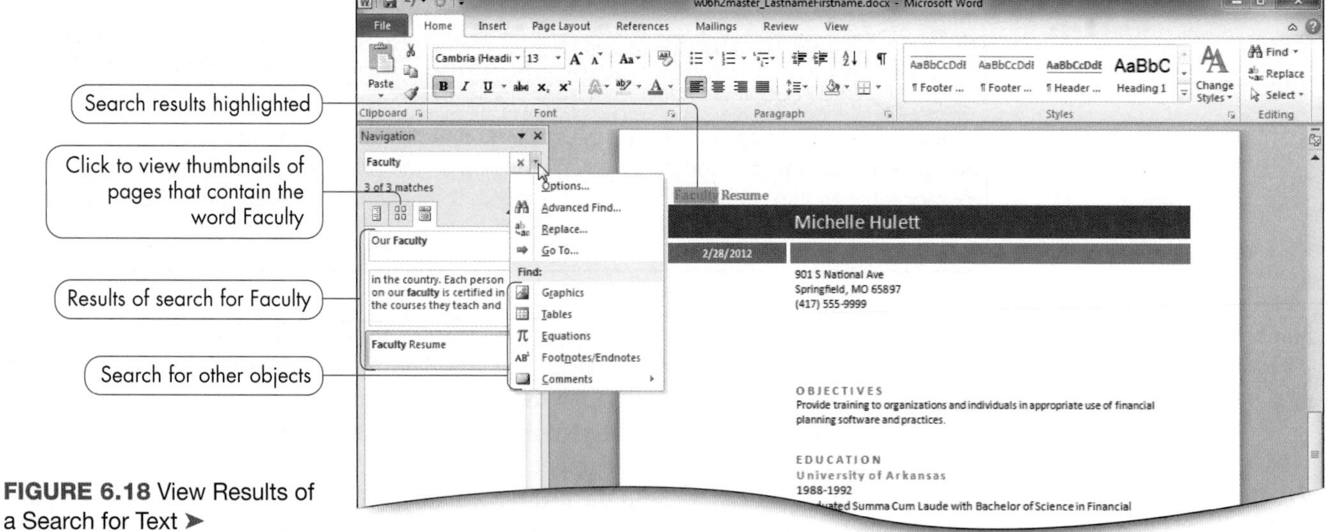

FIGURE 6.18 View Results of a Search for Text ➤

Insert Bookmarks

The **bookmark** feature is an electronic marker for a specific location in a document.

When you read a book you use a bookmark to help you return to that location quickly. Word provides the ***bookmark*** feature as an electronic marker for a specific location in a document, enabling the user to go to that location quickly. Bookmarks are helpful to mark a location where you are working. You can scroll to other parts of a document, and then quickly go back to the bookmarked location. The Bookmark command is in the Links group on the Insert tab. After you click the command, the Bookmark dialog box displays, and you can designate the name of the bookmark, as shown in Figure 6.19. Bookmarks are inserted at the loca of the insertion point. Bookmark names cannot contain spaces or hyphens; however, th may contain the underscore character to improve readability.

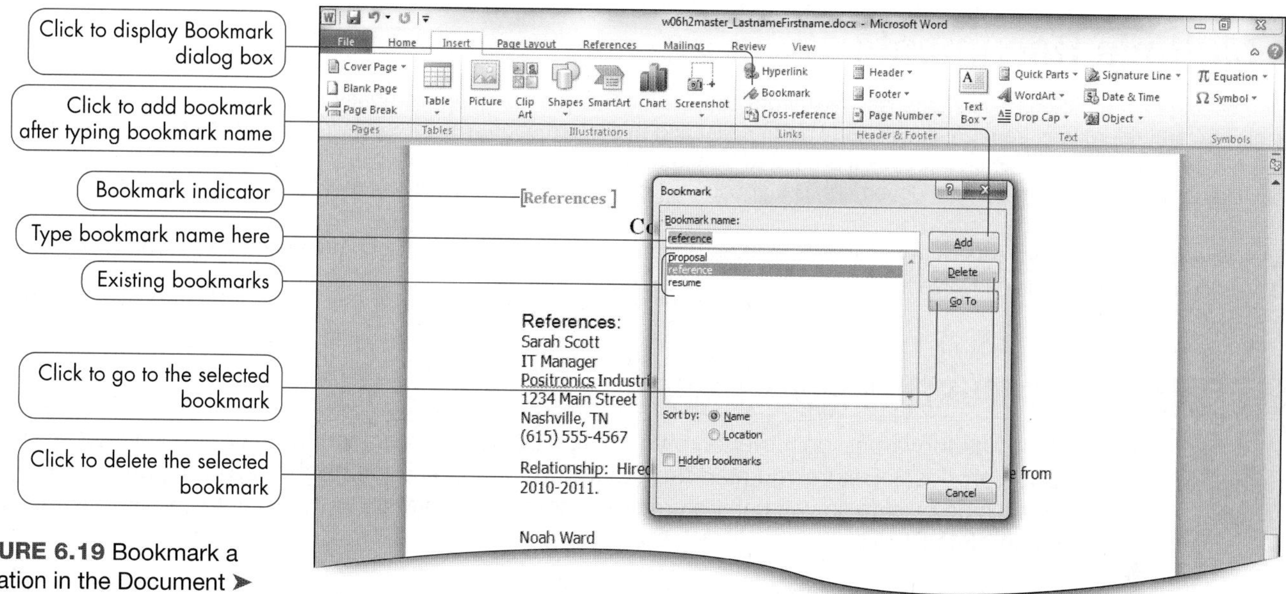

FIGURE 6.19 Bookmark a Location in the Document ➤

After you insert a bookmark, you can click Bookmark on the Insert tab to see a list of bookmarks in the current document. Click a bookmark in the Bookmark name list, and then click Go To to move the insertion point to that bookmarked location. You can also press Ctrl+G to open the Go To tab of the Find and Replace dialog box. When you click Bookmark in the *Go to what* section, a list of bookmarks is available to choose from.

TIP Using Numbers in Bookmark Names

You can use numbers within bookmark names, such as Quarter1. However, you cannot start a bookmark name with a number.

HANDS-ON EXERCISES

2 Multiple Documents

When setting up a prospective job proposal, Alexandra collects information about the company, the trainers who might work with the clients, and references from previous clients. After collecting this information, she forwards it to you to combine into one or more different documents. The final proposal is created from several files, and it is time-consuming to try to number each one so it looks like they all came from a single document. But you know how to use the master document feature to make that task easier.

Skills covered: View Documents Side by Side • Combine Documents • Create Master Documents and Subdocuments • Modify the Master and Subdocuments • Use the Navigation Pane and Create Bookmarks

STEP 1 VIEW DOCUMENTS SIDE BY SIDE

Alexandra has forwarded documents to you which contain information that should be included in the multi-page proposal. Before you start the process of combining information, you decide to view the documents side by side so you can determine if there is any overlap in the content. Refer to Figure 6.20 as you complete Step 1.

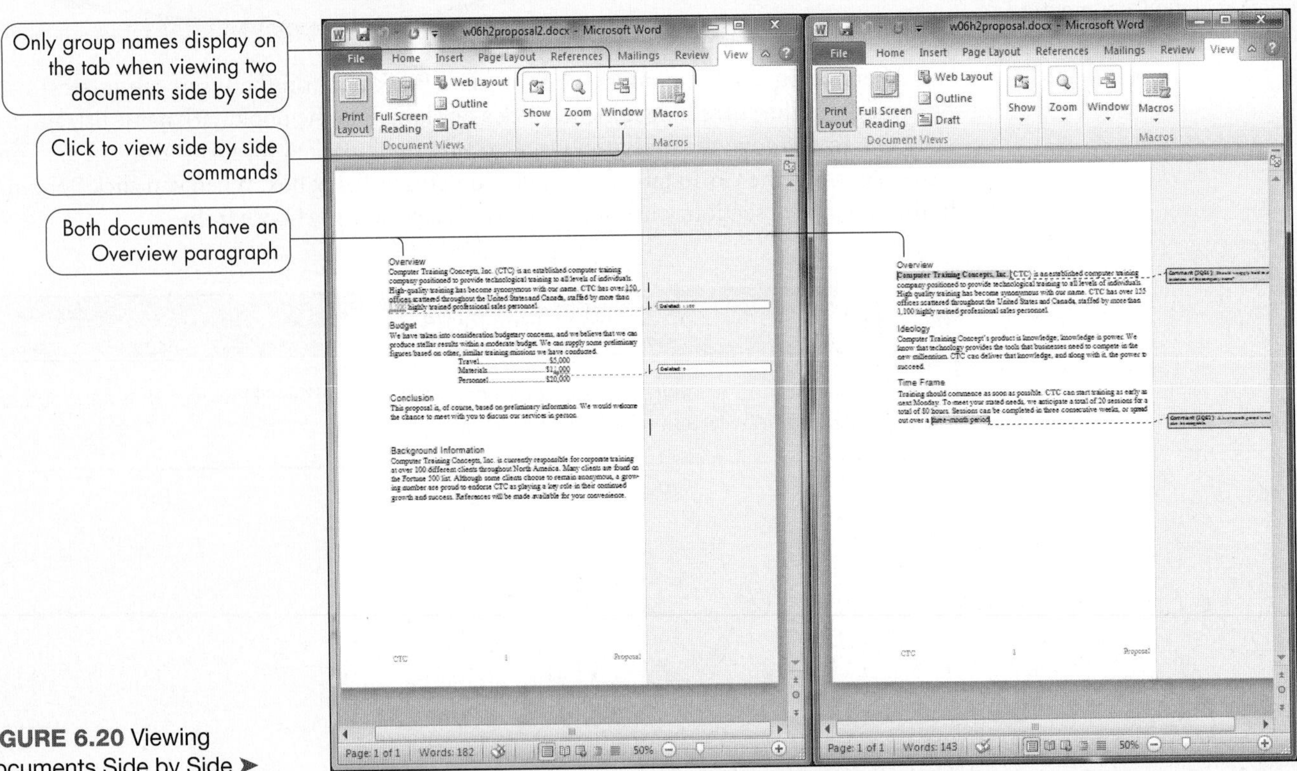

FIGURE 6.20 Viewing Documents Side by Side ➤

a. Open the files *w06h2proposal* and *w06h2proposal2*.

   w06h2proposal2 should be the active document since it was opened last.

b. Click the **View tab**, click **View Side by Side** in the Window group, click *w06h2proposal.docx*, and then click **OK**.

   Two windows display, containing the contents of each file. If you click the Window group arrow, you see Synchronous Scrolling is highlighted in an orange color to indicate the setting is on. As you scroll in one document, the other will scroll also.

TROUBLESHOOTING: If your view of one or both of the documents is insufficient, you can use the mouse to resize the window. Drag the border of the window until you reach an acceptable size to view the document information.

c. Click the arrow at the bottom of the scroll bar in the window on the left to scroll to the bottom of the page.

   Both documents scroll down evenly and you can view the footer of each document, as shown in Figure 6.20.

d. Click **Synchronous Scrolling** in the Window group to turn the toggle off.

   Now you can scroll through only one document at a time.

e. Close both documents without saving. Do not exit Word.

STEP 2 COMBINE DOCUMENTS

Now that you know the two files you just viewed are not identical, you decide to use the Combine feature in Word to pull all content into one location. You then make some minor formatting changes, insert the entire contents of another document, and then save the file so that it is ready to accompany the other files in the proposal. Refer to Figure 6.21 as you complete Step 2.

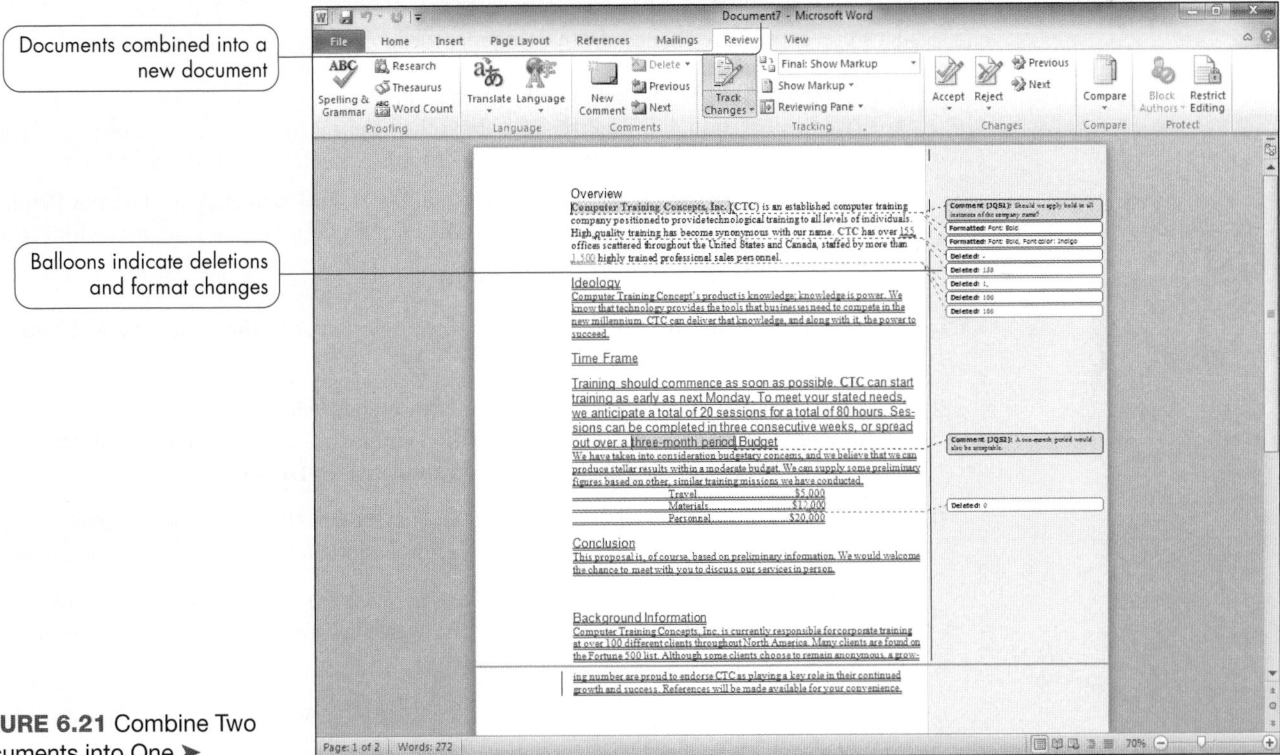

FIGURE 6.21 Combine Two Documents into One ➤

a. Press **Ctrl+N** to open a new document. Change the Zoom level to **70%**.

b. Combine the two documents you viewed in the last step by completing the following steps:
   - Click the **Review tab**, click **Compare** in the Compare group, and then select **Combine** to display the Combine Documents dialog box.
   - Click the **Original document arrow**, and then select *w06h2proposal2*. If necessary, click **Browse**, navigate to *w06h2proposal2*, and then click **Open**.
   - Click the **Revised Document arrow**, and then select *w06h2proposal*. If necessary, click **Browse**, navigate to *w06h2proposal*, and then click **Open**.

- Click the **More button**, if necessary, and then click **New document** below *Show changes in*, if necessary. Click **OK**. Click **Continue with Merge** if a Microsoft Word dialog box displays with a message about keeping formatting changes from only one document.

TROUBLESHOOTING: If the two documents you just merged display in small windows on the screen, select Show Source Documents in the Compare group on the Review tab, and then click Hide Source Documents to close them.

The document opens in a new window and contains markup balloons to indicate each difference in the two documents, as shown in Figure 6.21. Depending on your Track Changes settings, the balloons might display on either the left or right side of your document.

TROUBLESHOOTING: If the paragraphs in your document do not display in the same order as those in Figure 6.22, close the document and begin the process again. Make sure you select *w06h2proposal2* as the Original document.

c. Click the **Display for Review arrow** in the Tracking group, and then select **Final.**

The document in this view appears to include information from both files and is what you need to present to the customers. After some minor edits, it will be ready for use.

d. Click **Track Changes** in the Tracking group to turn off Track Changes.

This prevents future changes from being recorded.

e. Make the following format changes to the document:
   - Place the insertion point on the left side of the heading *Budget*, which displays at the end of the *Time Frame* paragraph. Press **Enter** to move the heading to the next line.
   - Right-click anywhere in the *Ideology* paragraph text, and then click the **Format Painter** in the Mini toolbar. Click anywhere in the *Time Frame* paragraph to change the font from Arial to Times New Roman.

f. Click the **Display for Review arrow** in the Tracking group, and then select **Final: Show Markup.**

g. Click the **Accept arrow** in the Changes group, and then click **Accept All Changes in Document.** Place the insertion point in the first comment, click the **Delete arrow** in the Comments group, and then click **Delete All Comments in Document.**

h. Press **Ctrl+End**, and then click **Enter**. Click the **Insert tab**, click the **Object arrow** in the Text group, and then click **Text from File.** Navigate to *w06h2faculty*, and then click **Insert.**

You insert the entire contents of the *w06h2faculty* document at the bottom of the page because it contains information that you want to display with the rest of the proposal. You will revise the order of the paragraphs later.

i. Save the document as **w06h2finalproposal_LastnameFirstname.** Close the document but leave Word open for the next step.

STEP 3 CREATE MASTER DOCUMENTS AND SUBDOCUMENTS

You now have the three main pieces of information that you will send to the potential client. You decide to create a master document so that you can insert each piece and make formatting modifications that will not affect the originals. Refer to Figure 6.22 as you complete Step 3.

Backing Up Your Files

Before you create a master document, you should back up all data files you will insert into the master document. Any changes made to the content in the master will alter the originals.

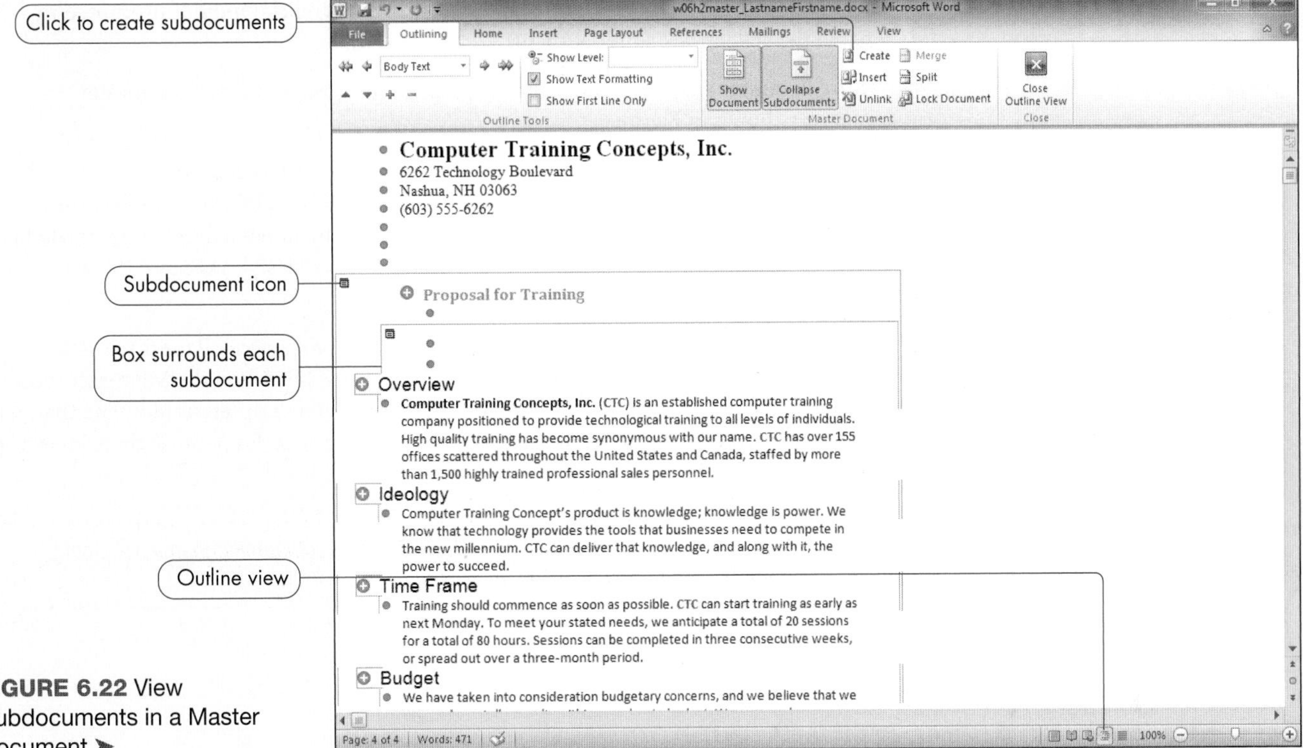

FIGURE 6.22 View Subdocuments in a Master Document ➤

a. Press **Ctrl+N** to open a new document, and then save it as **w06h2master_LastnameFirstname**.

b. Type **ctc** and press **F3** to insert the Building Block that contains the company name and address.

c. Press **Enter** one time. Type the following headings, each on a separate line, for the subdocuments: **Proposal for Training**, **Faculty Resume**, and **References**.

d. Select the three headings you just typed, and then click **Heading 2** from the Quick Styles gallery on the Home tab. Click **Outline** on the status bar.

> **TROUBLESHOOTING:** If the Heading 2 style does not display in the Quick Styles gallery, click the Styles dialog box launcher to display the Styles pane, select the Heading 2 style, and then close the Styles pane.

The Outlining tab displays, and the document text displays in Outline view. Be sure all three headings are still selected before you perform the next step.

e. Click **Show Document** in the Master Document group to display more master document commands. Click **Create** in the Master Document group.

   Individual subdocuments are created for the selected headings. A box surrounds each subdocument, and you see a subdocument icon in the top-left corner of each subdocument box. You also will see section breaks and other formatting marks if the Show/Hide (¶) feature is turned on.

f. Click **Collapse Subdocuments** in the Master Document group to collapse the subdocuments in the document, and then display the name and path where each subdocument is saved. Click **OK** if prompted to save changes to the master document.

g. Click **Expand Subdocuments** in the Master Document group to reopen and display the subdocuments.

h. Place the insertion point on the line below the first subdocument heading, *Proposal for Training*. To insert the appropriate subdocument complete the following steps:

   - Click **Insert** in the Master Document group to display the Insert Subdocument dialog box.

- Select *w06h2finalproposal_LastnameFirstname*, and then click **Open**. If prompted to rename the style in the subdocument, click **Yes to All**.

The entire document displays under the *Proposal for Training* section of the master document, as shown in Figure 6.22.

i. Move the insertion point to the line below the subheading *Faculty Resume*. Repeat the steps above to insert the file *w06h1resume_LastnameFirstname*. Click **OK** when the Microsoft Word information window displays indicating the subdocument has a different template than its master document. Click **Yes to All** when prompted to rename styles because there are several used in this document.

j. Move the insertion point to the line below the subheading *References*. Repeat the steps above to insert the file *w06h1references_LastnameFirstname*. Click **OK** when the Microsoft Word information window displays indicating the subdocument has a different template than its master document. Click **Yes to All** when prompted to rename styles because there are several used in this document.

> **TROUBLESHOOTING:** Be sure to insert the *w06h1references_LastnameFirstname* document, ending in *.docx*, and not the template which ends in *.dotx*.

k. Save the document.

STEP 4 MODIFY THE MASTER AND SUBDOCUMENTS

Now that you have all three documents inserted into the master document, you begin to make adjustments to the order of content from the subdocuments, and you add information from another document that you decide should be included. You also remove extra page breaks that are inserted automatically when inserting subdocuments into a master document. Refer to Figure 6.23 as you complete Step 4.

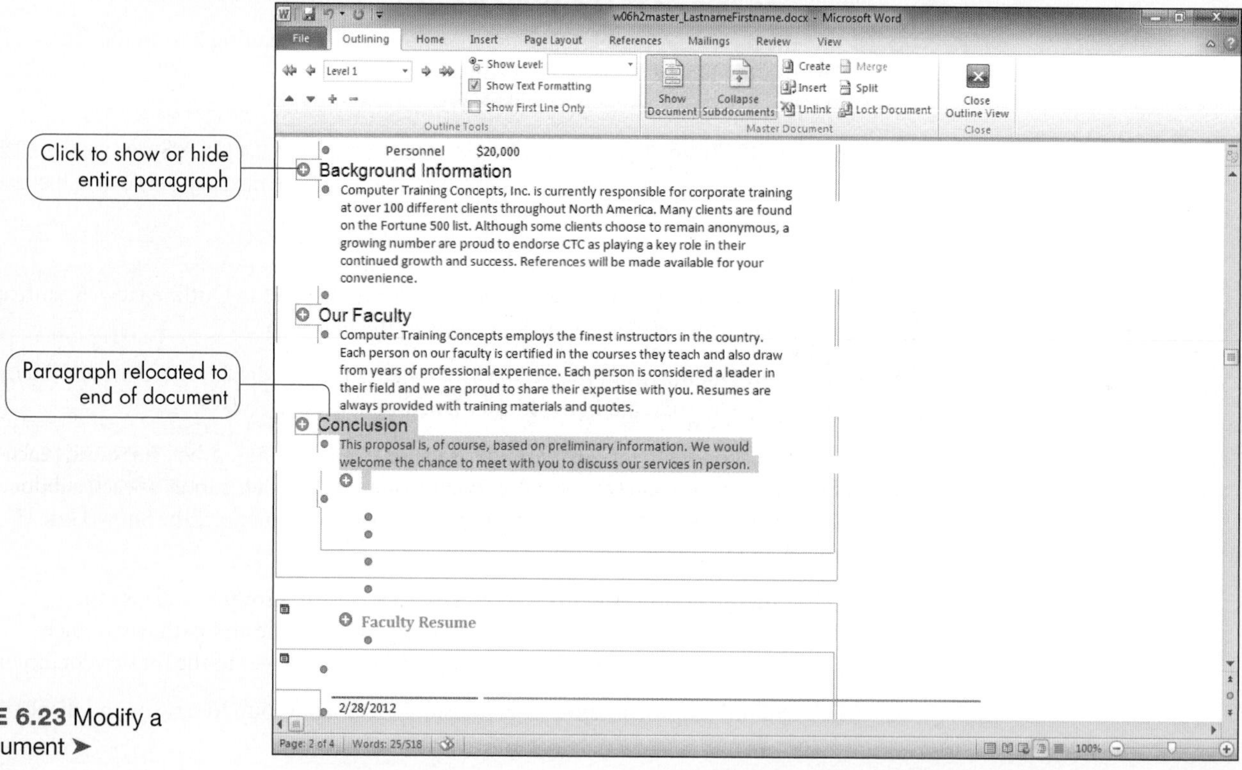

FIGURE 6.23 Modify a Subdocument ➤

a. Press **Ctrl+Home** to view the first subdocument. Scroll down until the *Conclusion* paragraph displays. Click the **Expand icon** on the left side of the *Conclusion* paragraph heading and paragraph, and then click **Move Down** in the Outline Tools group five times until the *Conclusion* paragraph displays below the *Our Faculty* paragraph, as shown in Figure 6.23.

b. Click **Show Document** in the Master Document group to view section and page breaks along with the paragraph headings and text.

   Notice there are several page breaks that will make the document split and display awkwardly. You want to remove those breaks so it displays professionally when printed.

c. Press **Ctrl+Home** to view the top of the document, click the following blank lines and breaks, and then press **Delete** to remove them.

   - Delete the *Section Break (Continuous)* that displays immediately before the *Proposal for Training* heading.
   - Delete the *Section Break (Continuous)* that displays immediately after the *Proposal for Training* heading.
   - Delete the two blank lines that display immediately after the *Proposal for Training* heading, if necessary.
   - Delete two of the *Section Break (Continuous)* that display immediately before the *Faculty Resume* paragraph.
   - Delete the *Section Break (Next Page)* that displays immediately after the *Faculty Resume* heading.
   - Delete the *Section Break (Next Page)* that displays immediately after the *References* heading.

d. Click **Show Document** in the Master Document group. Click **Lock Document** in the Master Document group. Press the letter **a** on the keyboard but notice the letter does not display at the insertion point.

   The padlock icon displays below the subdocument icon, and the Lock Document command is highlighted in an orange color. Attempts to type or edit text are not successful because the subdocument is locked.

e. Click **Lock Document** a second time to unlock the subdocument.

f. Click **Close Outline View** in the Close group to return to Print Layout view.

   The document now displays on four pages: The proposal displays on pages one and two, the faculty résumé displays on page three, and the references display on page four. If necessary, delete additional lines or breaks as necessary so your document displays on four pages also.

g. Save the document.

STEP 5 USE THE NAVIGATION PANE AND CREATE BOOKMARKS

You remember that inserting bookmarks is a quick way to get to different pages in a document, so you decide to insert one at the top of each section of the document. You decide to display the Navigation Pane so you can move quickly from one page to another to add those bookmarks. Refer to Figure 6.24 as you complete Step 5.

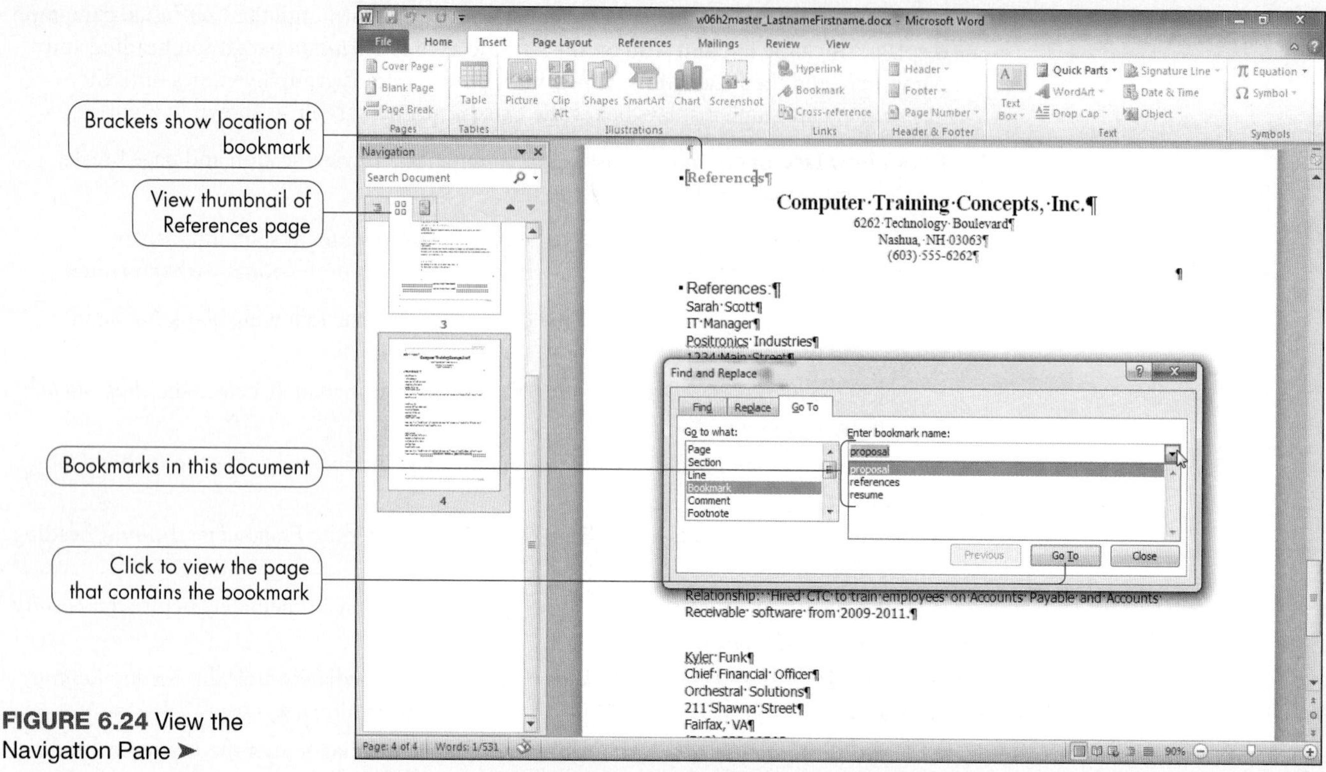

FIGURE 6.24 View the Navigation Pane ➤

a. Click the **View tab**, and then click **Navigation Pane** in the Show group to display the Navigation Pane on the left side of the window.

   The headings from the master document appear in the pane. An orange border appears around the heading of the paragraph where the insertion point displays.

b. Click the **Proposal for Training heading** in the Navigation Pane, if necessary.

   Word positions the insertion point at the beginning of that heading on the first page.

c. Click the **Insert tab**, and then click **Bookmark** in the Links group. Type **proposal** in the **Bookmark name box**, and then click **Add**.

   Word inserts a bookmark with the name you entered. A large, gray-colored I-beam indicates the location of the bookmark.

TROUBLESHOOTING: If you do not see the bookmark indicator, you can change a setting that enables it. Click File, and then click Options. Click Advanced, and then scroll down and click the *Show bookmarks* check box in the *Show document content* section. Click OK to save the settings and return to the document.

d. Click **Browse the pages in your document** in the Navigation Pane to display thumbnails of each page in the Navigation Pane. Click the thumbnail of page three, the résumé, to display the page and move the insertion point to the top of that page.

e. Click **Bookmark** in the Links group. Type **resume** in the **Bookmark name box**, and then click **Add**.

f. Type **reference** in the **Search Document box**. Click the **Browse the results from your current search tab**. Click the second item listed, which is the label *References* that displays at the top of page four.

g. Click **Bookmark** in the Links group. Type **reference** in the **Bookmark name box**, and then click **Add**.

   Notice the brackets that display to show the location of the bookmark. When a block of text is selected at the time you insert a bookmark, brackets display around the text to locate the bookmark instead of a single I-beam, which displays at the location of the cursor.

h. Press **Ctrl+G** to display the Go To tab of the Find and Replace dialog box. Click **Bookmark**, if necessary, in the **Go to what list**.

Word displays the first bookmark, *proposal*, in the *Enter bookmark name* box. If you click the *Enter bookmark name* arrow, the résumé and reference bookmarks also display in the list, as shown in Figure 6.24.

i. Click **Go To**.

The insertion point moves to the bookmark's location, and the Find and Replace dialog box remains onscreen in case you want to go to another bookmark.

j. Click **Close** to remove the Find and Replace dialog box. Click the **Close button** in the top-right corner of the Navigation Pane.

k. Save the document. Close the document, and then exit Word if you will not continue with the next exercise at this time.

TIP Displaying Subdocuments in a Master Document

After you create subdocuments, the link or path to the location where the subdocument is stored displays in the master document. If you move or rename the subdocument from that original location, the content will no longer display in the master document.

Document Themes

... creating and managing document design is very time-consuming. Word 2010 contains several document themes that enable you to focus on the content of your document instead of spending time creating a design for it.

To create a professional-looking document, you want to select features and styles that coordinate, but creating and managing document design is very time-consuming. Word 2010 contains several document themes that enable you to focus on the content of your document instead of spending time creating a design for it. A ***document theme*** is a set of coordinating fonts, colors, and special effects, such as shadowing or glows, that work together to provide a stylish appearance. Document themes are available in other Office applications also. This means you can use the same theme on different types of files that are used in a project, such as a report created in Word and a worksheet and chart created in Excel.

A **document theme** is a set of coordinating fonts, colors, and special effects that give a stylish and professional look.

In this section, you will apply themes to a document. You also will customize the theme elements and create a new theme.

Customizing Theme Colors

You can select a document theme from the Themes group on the Page Layout tab. When you select a document theme, formatting occurs immediately. If you wish to make changes to the design, you can modify the theme elements individually.

A **theme color** represents the current text and background, accent, and hyperlinks.

Theme colors include four text and background colors, six accent colors, and two hyperlink colors. When you click Theme Colors in the Themes group on the Page Layout tab, the accent and hyperlink colors display, as shown in Figure 6.25. To create a custom color theme you can modify the colors in the current theme, and then save the set with a new name. The new color theme will then display at the top of the theme color gallery.

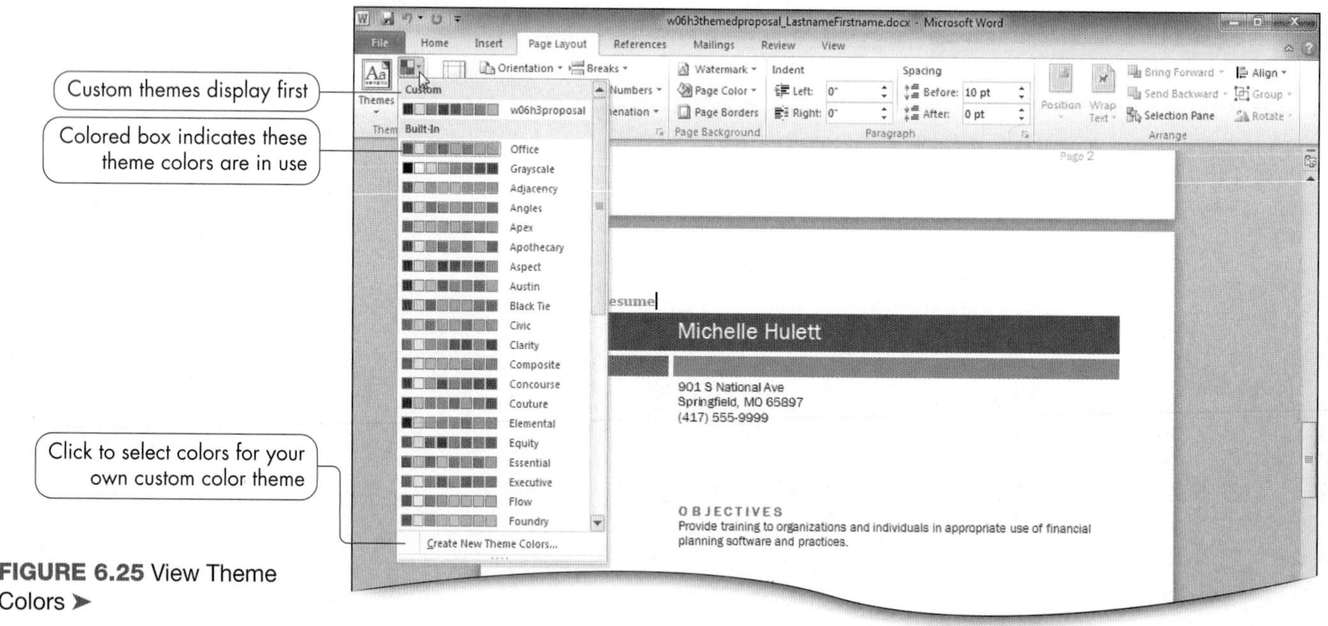

FIGURE 6.25 View Theme Colors ➤

Customizing Theme Fonts and Effects

A **theme font** contains a heading and body text font.

The ***theme fonts*** contain a coordinating heading and body text font for each different theme. You can view the fonts used in the theme when you click Theme Fonts in the Themes group on the Page Layout tab, as shown in Figure 6.26. Theme fonts display at the top of the font list when you click the Font down arrow on the Home tab or on the Mini toolbar. As with theme colors, you can change the fonts used in a theme, and you can create a new theme font set.

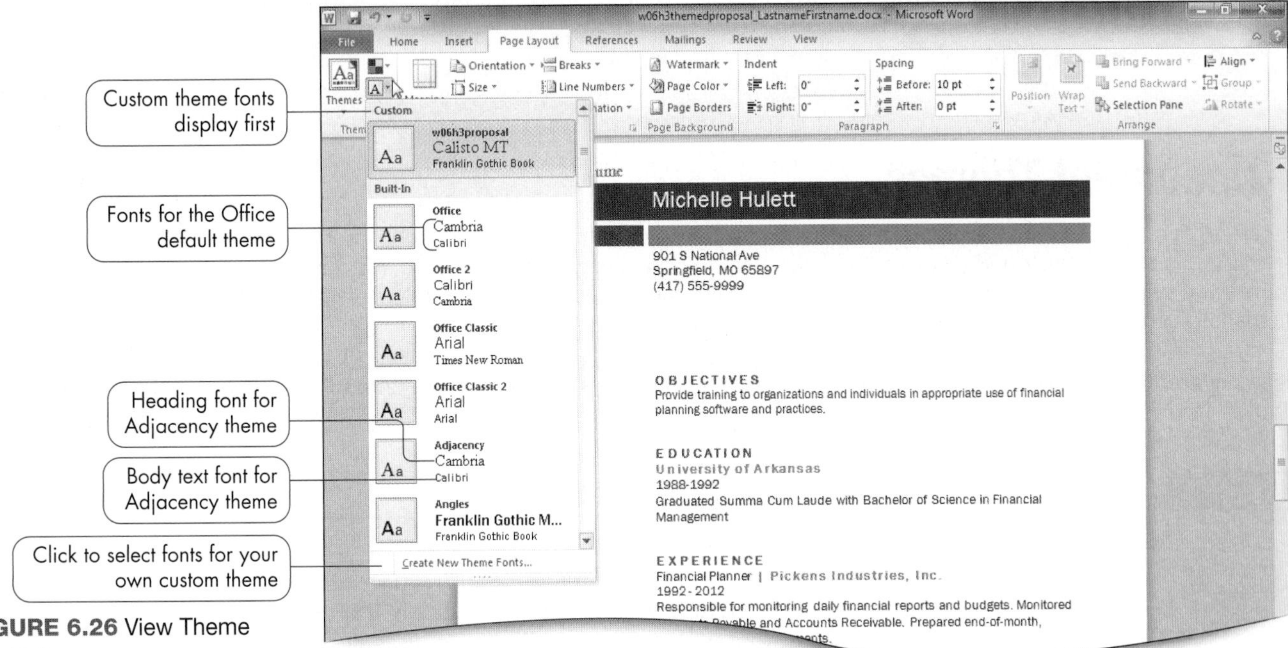

FIGURE 6.26 View Theme Fonts ➤

A **theme effect** includes lines or fill effects.

The ***theme effects*** include lines and fill effects, such as shadowing, glows, and borders. When you apply a theme, the theme effects will affect objects such as shapes, SmartArt, and borders around graphics, as shown in Figure 6.27. You cannot create your own set of theme effects, but you can choose from the built-in sets when compiling your own document theme.

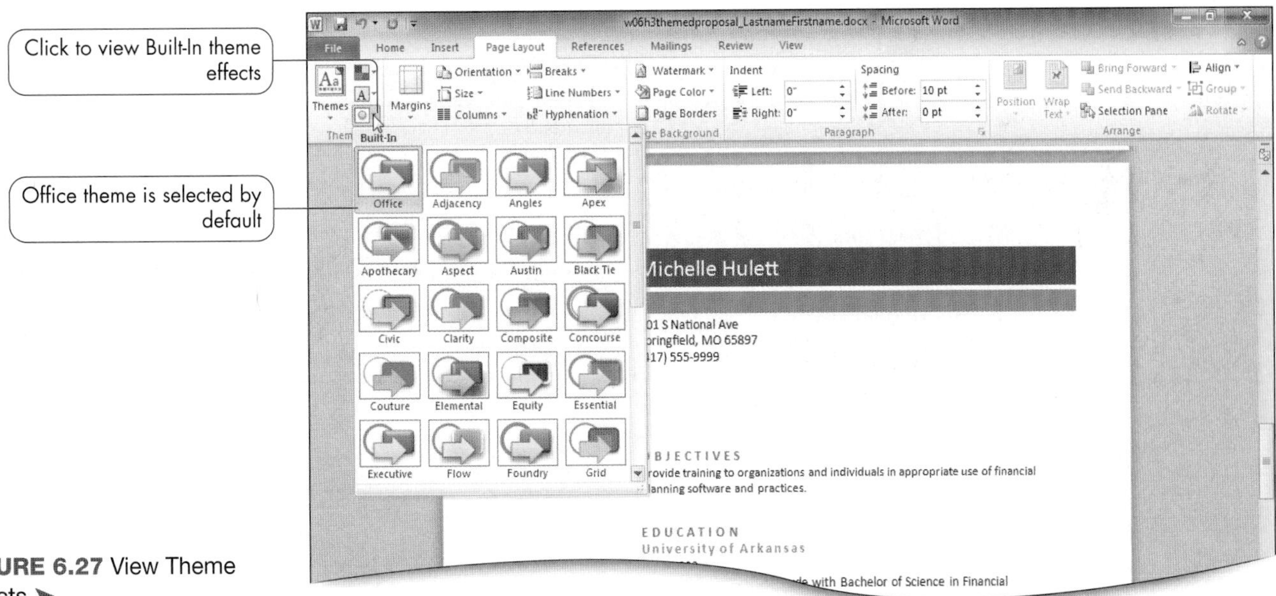

FIGURE 6.27 View Theme Effects ➤

TIP Delete Custom Theme Colors and Fonts

You can easily delete a custom theme, a custom theme color set, or custom theme fonts. To remove these custom sets, click Themes (or Theme Colors or Theme Fonts) on the Page Layout tab, right-click the custom set that displays in the top of the gallery, and then click Delete. You will see a confirmation dialog box before the set is removed permanently. You cannot delete the themes, color themes, or font themes that are included in Word.

HANDS-ON EXERCISES

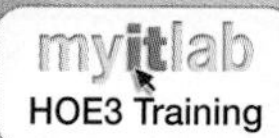

3 Document Themes

You are almost ready to print the proposal and send it to the potential client. But each document that you inserted into the master is formatted a bit differently, and you want this document to have a very consistent look. You remember that Microsoft Word enables you to apply a theme to documents so they use the same style of fonts and colors—which is exactly what you need to put the finishing touches on this proposal!

Skills covered: Apply a Theme to a Document • Revise Theme Color • Revise Theme Fonts • Save a Custom Theme

STEP 1 APPLY A THEME TO A DOCUMENT

Your proposal should have a very professional look to it, so you decide to apply one of the built-in themes in Word. By using the theme, all colors in the résumé template and colors used for headings in the other documents will coordinate. The colors in the Pushpin theme closely match the colors of your business, so you select that theme. Refer to Figure 6.28 as you complete Step 1.

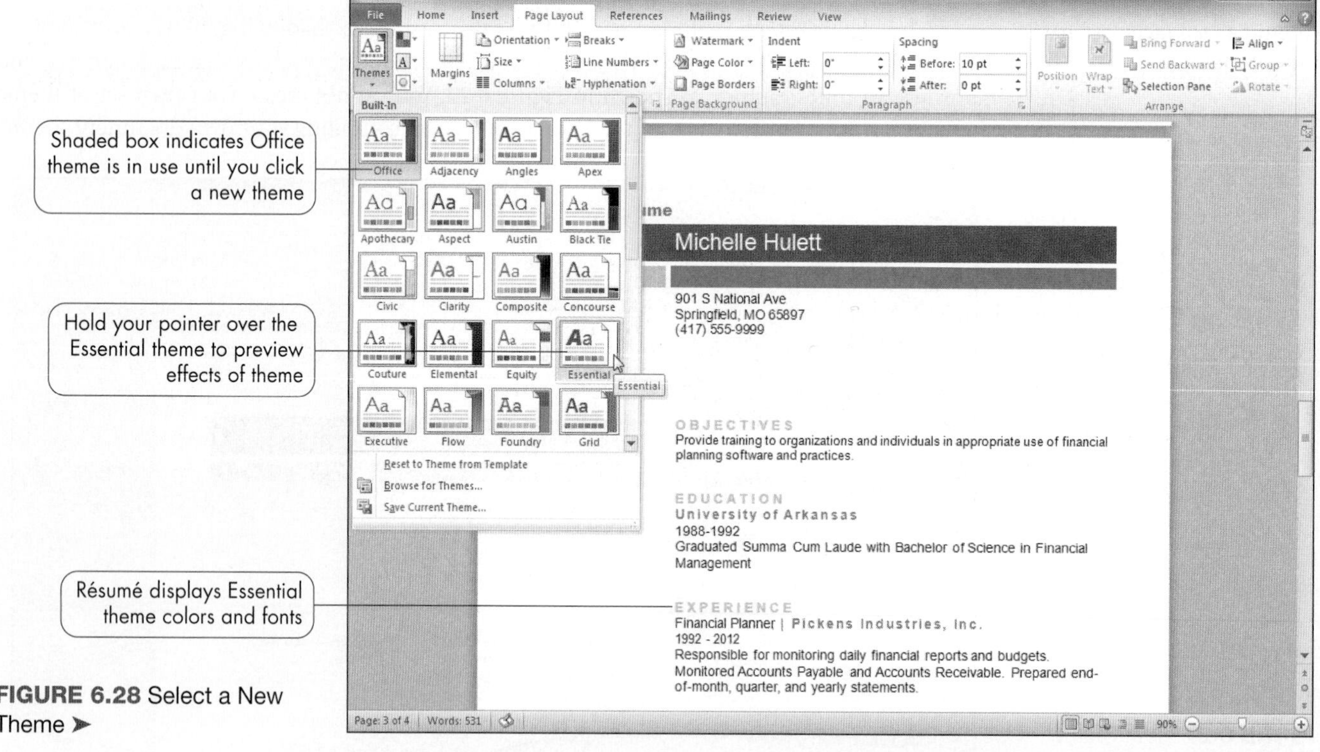

FIGURE 6.28 Select a New Theme ➤

a. Open the *w06h2master_LastnameFirstname* document if you closed it after the last Hands-On Exercise, and then save it as **w06h3themedproposal_LastnameFirstname.**

b. Click the **Home tab**, and then click **Show/Hide** (¶) in the Paragraph group to turn off formatting marks. If necessary, click **Outline** in the status bar to view the Outlining tab and commands. Click **Show Document** in the Master Document group on the Outlining tab, and then click **Expand Subdocuments**, if necessary, to view all of the content in the subdocuments. Click **Close Outline View** to return to Print Layout view.

c. Press **Ctrl+G**, and then click **Bookmark** in the **Go to what: box**. Click the **Enter bookmark name arrow**, and then select **resume.** Click **Go To**, and then when the résumé displays, close the Find and Replace dialog box.

d. Click the **Page Layout tab**, and then click **Themes** in the Themes group.

The gallery of themes displays and a shaded box surrounds the Office theme. It is active because that is the theme applied to the master document when it was created.

e. Hold your mouse over the Verve theme, but do not click it, and notice how the résumé features change to reflect that theme, as shown in Figure 6.28. Click **Pushpin** to apply the Pushpin theme to all pages in the master document.

f. Save the document.

> **TIP Using Themes in Compatibility Mode**
>
> If you click the Page Layout Tab and notice Theme is grayed out, and thus unavailable, your current document is probably open in Compatibility Mode. To use Themes, you must save your document in Word 2010 format (.docx). If you save a Word 2010 document in a compatible format, such as Word 97–2003, any theme previously applied to the document will be removed.

STEP 2 REVISE THEME COLOR

The Pushpin theme looks great on the master document; however, you would like to change a color that you do not particularly like. You take steps to make a color change in the theme, and you save the changes as a custom theme so you can use it again in other documents. Refer to Figure 6.29 as you complete Step 2.

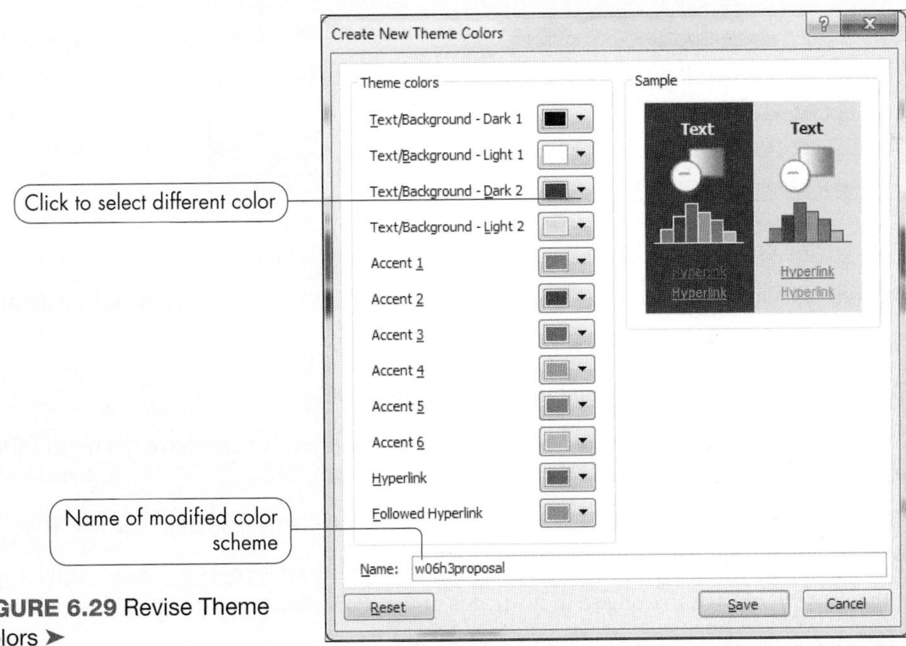

FIGURE 6.29 Revise Theme Colors ➤

a. Click **Theme Colors** in the Theme group, and then scroll down to view the themes near the bottom of the list.

A colored box displays around the color swatch for Pushpin to indicate it is in use. You can select the colors for other built-in themes from this gallery.

b. Click **Create New Theme Colors** at the bottom of the gallery.

The Create New Theme Color dialog box displays. Now you can customize the colors used in the theme that is currently applied to your document.

c. Click the **Text/Background - Dark 2 arrow**, and then click **Ice Blue, Text 2, Darker 75%** (fifth row, fourth column).

d. Type **w06h3proposal** in the **Name box**, as shown in Figure 6.29. Click **Save** to save this color scheme.

The *w06h3proposal* color theme is automatically applied to your document. When you click Theme Colors, *w06h3proposal* displays at the top of the gallery with a box around it.

e. Press **Ctrl+Home** to view the first page of the document. Select the title *Computer Training Concepts, Inc.*, and then click the **Font Color arrow** on the Mini toolbar.

Notice the top of the box displays *Theme Colors*, so you know any color you select will coordinate with the document theme.

f. Click **Orange, Accent 1** from the first row.

g. Save the document.

STEP 3 REVISE THEME FONTS

You notice the same font is used for headings and body text in the theme applied to this document. You would like to make a change so a different, yet coordinating font is used for the headings. And then the proposal is ready for the printer! Refer to Figure 6.30 as you complete Step 3.

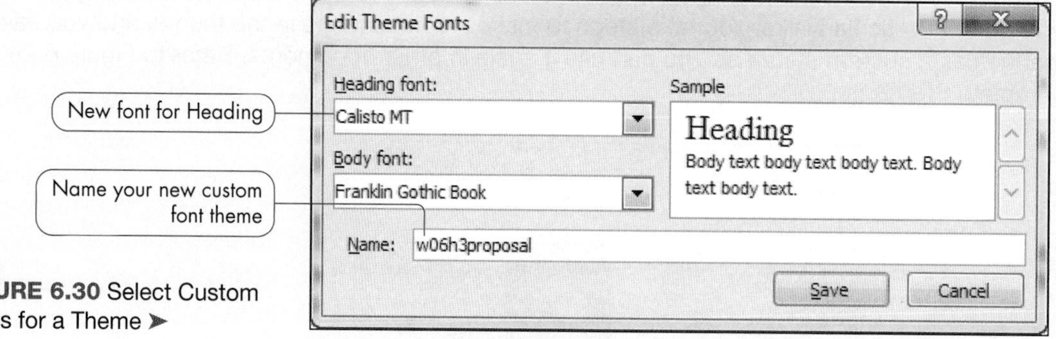

FIGURE 6.30 Select Custom Fonts for a Theme ➤

a. Click **Theme Fonts** in the Themes group of the Page Layout tab.

The fonts for each theme display. The font style in use for the Pushpin theme is Constantia.

b. Click **Create New Theme Fonts** at the bottom of the gallery.

c. Click the **Heading font arrow**, and then select **Calisto MT**.

d. Type **w06h3proposal** in the **Name box**, as shown in Figure 6.30. Click **Save** to save this font scheme.

The headings *Proposal for Training, Resume*, and *Resources* change to reflect the new font.

e. Click **Theme Fonts** in the Theme group, and then notice *w06h3proposal* displays at the top of the list with orange shading to indicate it is in use. Press **Esc** to return to the document.

f. Save the document.

STEP 4 SAVE A CUSTOM THEME

Since you made changes to both colors and fonts for this theme, you decide to take one more step and save the whole theme with a new name so you can use it again without modifying the individual features. Refer to Figure 6.31 as you complete Step 4.

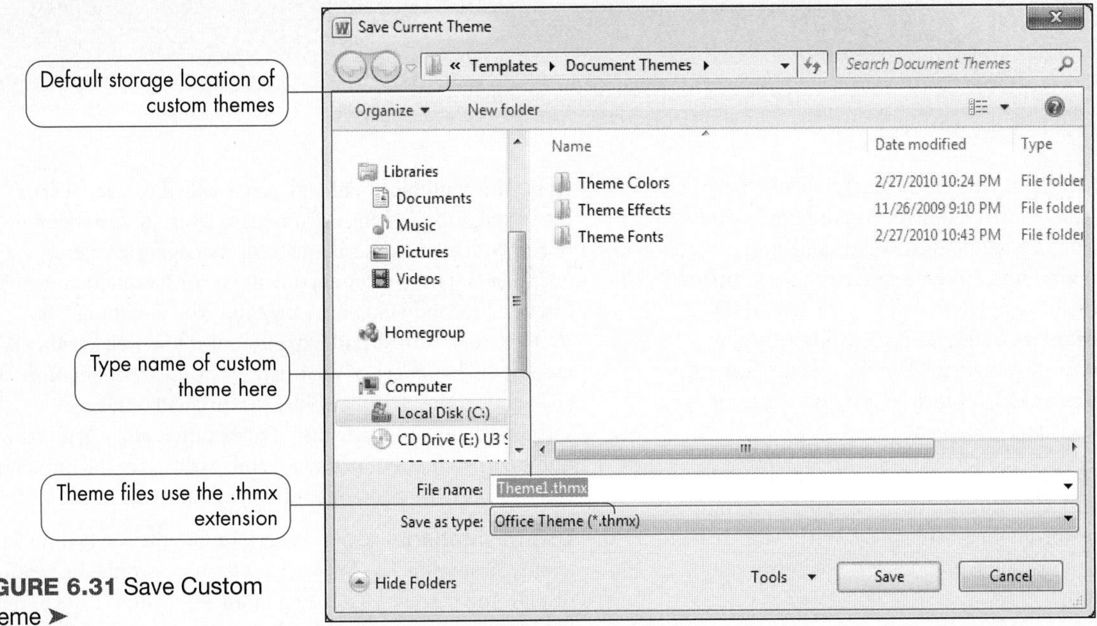

FIGURE 6.31 Save Custom Theme ➤

a. Click the **Page Layout tab**, if necessary, and then click the **Themes arrow** in the Themes group.

b. Click **Save Current Theme** at the bottom of the gallery.

   The Save Current Theme dialog box displays, as shown in Figure 6.31. By default, the new themes are saved in the Document Themes folder for the current user. They are not stored in a folder with the themes that install with Word 2010.

c. Type **w06h3proposaltheme** in the **File name box**.

d. Click **Save**.

TROUBLESHOOTING: If your lab environment does not enable you to save the template to the default folder, or if instructed by your teacher, save the theme file to your own storage media.

e. Save and close the document, and then submit based on your instructor's directions.

CHAPTER OBJECTIVES REVIEW

After reading this chapter, you have accomplished the following objectives:

1. **Select a template from the Backstage view.** Each time you create a new blank document, you use the Normal template. When you use a template, it will display under Blank and Recent documents, but you can also view other templates installed on your PC or templates you have created. Many people will take advantage of the résumé templates. By default, résumé templates are installed in Word and they contain placeholders, a field or block of text, to determine the position of objects in a document.
2. **Create a Word template.** If you create or use a particular document frequently, with only minor modifications each time, you should save the document as a template. When you create the template, you can insert placeholders for the information you change frequently.
3. **Use Building Blocks.** Building Blocks are document components you use frequently such as disclaimers, company addresses or logos, or your name and address. Word enables you to create Building Blocks in such a way that they are easy to insert as document parts. Each selection of text or graphics that you add to the Quick Part Gallery is stored in the Building Blocks Organizer and is assigned a unique name that makes it easy for you to find the content when you want to use it.
4. **View documents side by side.** This feature enables you to view two documents on the same screen. It is useful when you want to compare the contents of two documents or if you want to cut or copy and paste text from one document to another. To view two documents side by side, they must both be open in Word. While you display the two documents, you can use synchronous scrolling to move through both using only one scroll bar.
5. **Merge documents.** When you have several copies of the same document submitted from different people, you can use the compare and combine features. The compare feature evaluates the contents of two or more documents and displays markup balloons that show the differences between the documents. You can determine if the differences display in the original document, a revised document, or a new document. The combine feature goes a step further and integrates all changes from multiple documents into one. Another way to work with multiple documents, especially those that will be combined into one long document, is to create a master document that acts like a binder for managing smaller documents. The smaller document is called a subdocument and can be edited individually at any time. The Outlining tab contains the Collapse and Expand buttons, as well as other tools used to work on master documents. The great benefit of master and subdocuments is the ability to work with multiple subdocuments simultaneously. For example, you can create page numbers in a master document, and it will cause the numbers to run consecutively from one subdocument to the next.
6. **Use navigational tools.** When you use the Navigation Pane feature *Browse the headings in your document*, only the headings display. You can click a heading in the Navigation Pane to move the insertion point to that heading in the document. The feature is only available when headings are formatted using the Styles feature. You also can use thumbnails to navigate quickly through a document. Thumbnails are small pictures of each page that display in the Navigation Pane when the feature is toggled on. When you click a thumbnail, the insertion point moves to the top of that page. The Bookmark feature is an electronic marker for a specific location in a document. You can designate a bookmark in a particular location in a document, and then use the Go To feature to return to that bookmark.
7. **Customize theme colors.** You can select a document theme from the Themes group on the Page Layout tab. When you select a document theme, formatting occurs immediately. Theme colors represent the current text and background, accent, and hyperlinks. To create a custom color theme, you can modify the colors in the current theme, and then save the set with a new name.
8. **Customize theme fonts and effects.** The theme fonts contain a coordinating heading and body text font for each different theme. Theme fonts display at the top of the font list when you click the Font down arrow on the Home tab or on the Mini toolbar. The theme effects include lines and fill effects, such as shadowing, glows, and borders. You cannot create your own set of theme effects, but you can choose from the built-in sets.

KEY TERMS

Bookmark ***p.326***
Building Block ***p.313***
Combine ***p.321***
Compare ***p.321***
Curriculum vitae (CV) ***p.311***
Document theme ***p.336***
Master document ***p.322***
Navigation Pane ***p.324***
Normal template ***p.310***
Placeholder ***p.311***
Subdocument ***p.322***
Synchronous scrolling ***p.320***
Template ***p.310***
Theme color ***p.336***
Theme effect ***p.337***
Theme font ***p.336***
Thumbnail ***p.325***
View Side by Side ***p.320***

MULTIPLE CHOICE

1. If you create new documents every day that contain your company letterhead, which productivity tool would best fit your need?
   (a) Mail merge
   (b) Building Blocks
   (c) Document themes
   (d) Document templates

2. Which of the following is not a way you can obtain a document template?
   (a) Select it from the Styles gallery.
   (b) Download from Office.com.
   (c) Select an installed template on your computer.
   (d) Create a document yourself and save it as a template.

3. What file extension is given to a template?
   (a) .dotx
   (b) .docx
   (c) .xlsx
   (d) .accdb

4. What is another name for the text or fields that display in a document template so you will know where to insert your own information?
   (a) Flag
   (b) Extension
   (c) CV
   (d) Placeholder

5. Why would you use a document theme?
   (a) So you can restrict the use of color in the document
   (b) To merge information from a data source into a document
   (c) To color coordinate elements used in the document and give a professional appearance
   (d) To easily locate bookmarks

6. Which theme element are you unable to customize and save?
   (a) Theme effect
   (b) Theme font
   (c) Theme color
   (d) Document theme

7. Which of the document elements listed below can you find using the Go To command?
   (a) Hyperlink
   (b) Bookmark
   (c) Table of Contents
   (d) Cross-reference notation

8. After you use the styles feature to format headings, you can use this feature to view an outline of your document and click a heading to relocate the insertion point in your document.
   (a) Bookmarks
   (b) Navigation Pane—headings
   (c) Navigation Pane—thumbnails
   (d) Navigation Pane—search

9. What comprises a master document?
   (a) Subdocuments
   (b) Templates
   (c) Outline documents
   (d) Combined documents

10. Which feature enables you to display the differences in two documents in a separate document?
    (a) Side by side view
    (b) Compare documents
    (c) Master documents
    (d) Subdocuments

PRACTICE EXERCISES

1 Your Town Electric Company

You work in the Employee Benefits Department of the local utility company, Your Town Electric. You want to set up a form that all new and existing employees can use to document personal information and emergency contact numbers. Before you create a new form, you decide to look for an existing form in the Word templates gallery. You find just the right form and need to make only minor modifications, adding the company name and logo. You also insert the contents of another document to add insurance information, and the form is ready to be distributed to all employees. This exercise follows the same set of skills as used in Hands-On Exercises 1 and 2 in the chapter. Refer to Figure 6.32 as you complete this exercise.

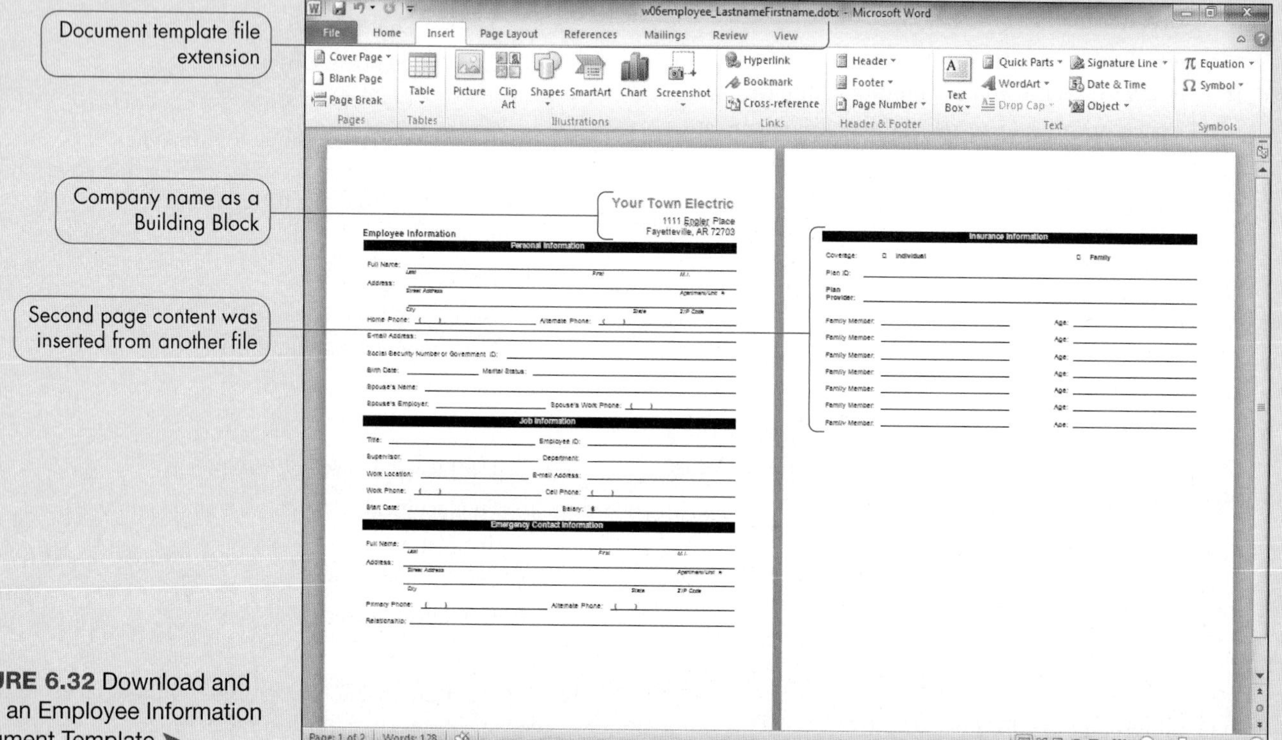

FIGURE 6.32 Download and Save an Employee Information Document Template ➤

a. Click **File**, click **New**, click **Forms** in the *Office.com Templates* section, click **Employment**, click **Employee information form** (second row, first column), and then click **Download.**

b. Click **File**, and then click **Convert.** Click **OK** if a dialog box confirms that you want to convert the document.

c. Select the border of the text box that displays *Your Logo Here*, and then press **Delete.**

d. Click one time on the text *Company Name* to display the text box. Select the text *Company Name*, and then type the following:

Your Town Electric

1111 Engler Place

Fayetteville, AR 72703

e. Select the two lines that contain the address, and then press **Ctrl+R** to align them on the right side of the text box.

f. Click one time on the border of the text box to select it, and then click the **Insert tab.** Click the **Quick Parts arrow** in the Text group, and then select **Save Selection to Quick Part gallery.**

g. Click the **Gallery arrow** in the Text group, and then select **Text Boxes** when the Create New Building Block dialog box displays. Click the **Save In arrow**, and then select *Building Blocks.dotx*, if necessary. Click **OK.**

h. Press **Delete** to remove the text box. Click **Quick Parts** in the Text group, select **Building Blocks Organizer**, click **Name** to sort the entries by name, scroll down to the bottom of the entries, click **Your Town**, and then click **Insert**.

i. Press **Ctrl+End** to move to the end of the document, and then press **Ctrl+Enter** to insert a page break. Click the **Object arrow** in the Text group, and then select **Text from File**. Browse to the location where data files are stored, select *w06p1insurance.docx*, and then click **Insert**.

j. Click **File**, click **Save As**, click the **Save as type arrow**, and then select **Word Template (*.dotx)**. Type **w06p1employee_LastnameFirstname** in the **File name box**, and then click **Save**. Notice the file name in the Title Bar reflects the template extension (see Figure 6.32).

k. Position the insertion point on the *Full Name:* line under *Personal Information*, type your last name, press **Tab**, and then type your first name.

l. Click **File**, click **Save As**, click the **Save as type arrow**, and then select **Word Document (*.docx)**. If necessary, type **w06p1employee_LastnameFirstname** in the **File name box**.

m. Save and close the file, and submit based on your instructor's directions.

2 Carver Middle School

You volunteer at the Carver Middle School library and have the opportunity to observe the computer skill level of many students. You decide to create a document that contains tips for using Windows 7 that the students can use as a reference. You found three sources of information and want to combine them into one document. Fortunately, you are familiar with the Master and Subdocument features in Word, so you can easily combine the documents into one and make modifications so that it is easy to read after printing. This exercise follows the same set of skills as used in Hands-On Exercises 2 and 3 in the chapter. Refer to Figure 6.33 as you complete this exercise.

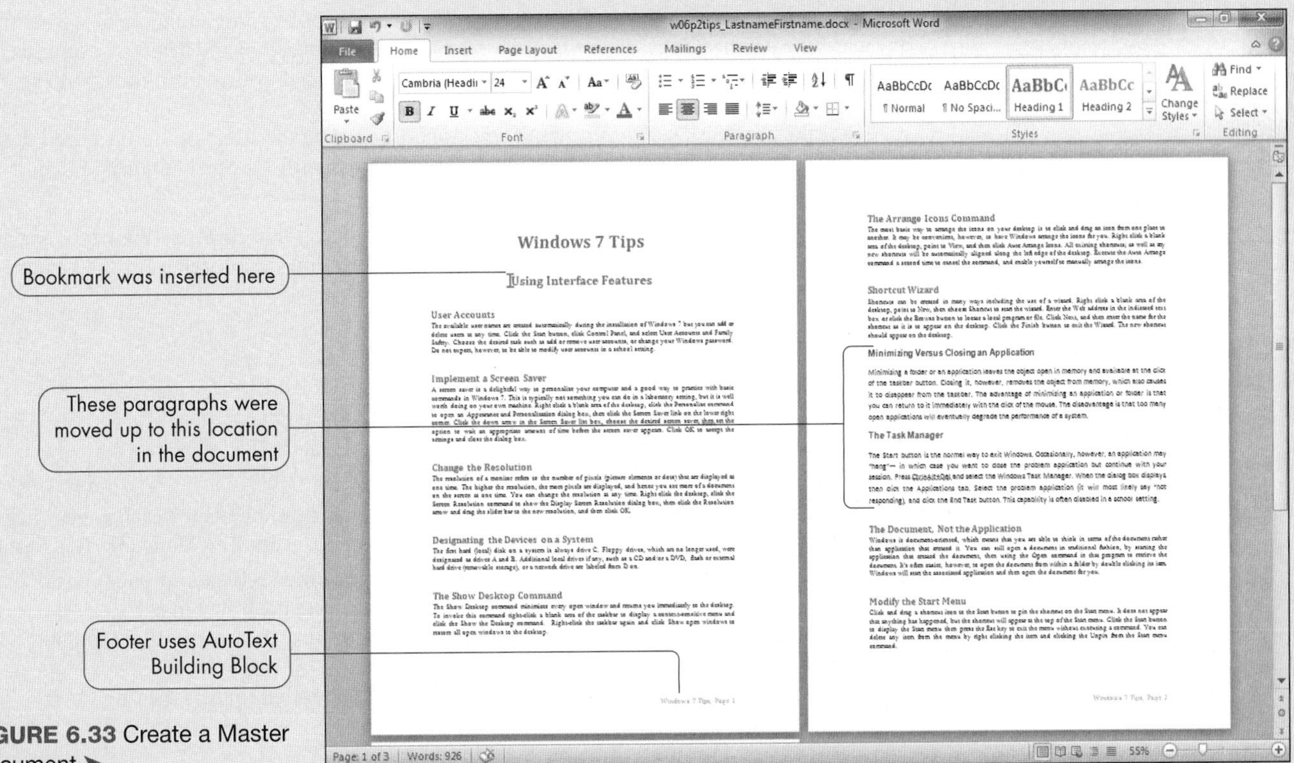

FIGURE 6.33 Create a Master Document ➤

a. Start Word, and then click **Ctrl+N** to create a new blank document. Click **Outline** on the status bar. The Outlining tab displays automatically. Save the document as **w06p2tips_LastnameFirstname**.

b. Type **Windows 7 Tips** as the title of the document. Save this title as a Building Block by completing the following steps:

- Select the text, click the **Insert tab**, click **Quick Parts** in the Text group, and then select **Save Selection to Quick Part Gallery**.

- Type **tips** in the **Name box** when the Create New Building Block dialog box displays.
- Click the **Gallery arrow**, and then select **AutoText**.
- Click the **Save in arrow**, and then select *Building Blocks.dotx*.
- Click **OK**.

c. Right-click the selected text, and then use the Mini toolbar to center the text and increase the size to **24 pt**. Move the insertion point to the right side of the heading, and then press **Enter**.

d. Create subdocuments by completing the following steps:
   - Type the following headings on separate lines:
     Using Interface Features
     Using Windows Explorer
   - Select the two lines, and then select the **Heading 1 style** from the Quick Styles gallery on the Home tab.
   - Click the **Outlining tab**, and then click **Show Document** in the Master Document group.
   - Click **Create** in the Master Document group to create two subdocuments, and then click **Save** on the Quick Access Toolbar.

e. Populate the subdocuments with content from existing documents by completing the following steps:
   - Place the insertion point on the line directly below the heading *Using Interface Features*.
   - Click **Insert** in the Master Document group, and then navigate to and open the file *w06p2tips1*. Click **Yes to All** when the dialog box displays a warning about styles used in the two documents.
   - Place the insertion point on the line directly below the heading *Using Windows Explorer*.
   - Click **Insert** in the Master Document group, and then open the file *w06p2tips2*. Click **Yes to All** when the dialog box displays a warning about styles used in the two documents.
   - Click **Insert** in the Master Document group, and then open the file *w06p2tips3*.
   - Click **Yes to All** when the dialog box displays a warning about styles used in the two documents.

f. Scroll to select all headings and paragraphs except the document heading, *Windows 7 Tips*, and then click **Collapse** in the Outline Tools group. Reorder the tips by completing the following steps:
   - Select the two headings, *Minimizing Versus Closing an Application* and *The Task Manager*, and then click **Move Up** in the Outline Tools group six times so they display in the *Using Interface Features* section.
   - Select the heading *The Document, Not the Application*, drag the selection upward until the insertion point displays on the left side of the heading *Modify the Start Menu*, and then release the mouse to drop the selection.

g. Click **Close Outline View** in the Close group on the Outlining tab, click the **View tab**, and then click **Navigation Pane** in the Show group. Click **Using Windows Explorer** from the heading list that displays in the Navigation Pane.

h. Insert a bookmark by completing the following steps:
   - Click the **Insert tab**, and then click **Bookmark** in the Links group.
   - Type **explorer** in the **Bookmark name box**, and then click **Add**.
   - Click the heading *Using Interface Features* in the Navigation Pane.
   - Click **Bookmark** in the Links group.
   - Type **interface** in the **Bookmark name box**, and then click **Add**.

i. Click the **Browse the pages in your document tab** to display thumbnails for each page. Click the **page 1 thumbnail**, and then notice the large gap of space after the heading *Using Interface Features*.

j. Click the **Home tab**, and then click **Show/Hide** (¶) to view the section and page breaks in the master document. To remove unnecessary page breaks, complete the following:
   - Place the insertion point on the **Section Break (Continuous)** that follows the *Windows 7 Tips* heading, and then press **Delete**.
   - Place the insertion point on the **Section Break (Next Page)** that follows the title *Using Interface Features*, and then press **Delete**.
   - Click the **page 3 thumbnail** in the Navigation Pane.
   - Place the insertion point on the **Section Break (Next Page)** that follows the title *Using Windows Explorer*, and then press **Delete**.
   - Scroll up to the previous page, and then place the insertion point on the **Section Break (Next Page)** that follows *The Document, Not the Application*. Press **Delete** to remove the break.
   - Place the insertion point on the right side of the paragraph symbol (¶) at the end of the paragraph that displays below *The Document, Not the Application*, and then press **Delete**, enabling the paragraph from the next page to display at the bottom of the current page.

- Press **Ctrl+End**, place the insertion point on the **Section Break (Continuous)** at the bottom of the last page in the document, and then press **Delete** to remove the extra blank page at the end of the document, if necessary. Place the insertion point on the remaining **Section Break (Continuous)**, and then press **Delete**.

k. Insert a footer that includes the title of the document by completing the following steps:
   - Double-click the white space at the bottom of the current page to display the Header and Footer Design tab.
   - Click **Quick Parts** in the Insert group, and then point to **AutoText**. Scroll down the AutoText entries, and then click **Windows 7 Tips**.
   - Press **Backspace** to remove the extra line return. Press **comma** (,), and then press **Spacebar**. Type **Page** and press **Spacebar**.
   - Click **Quick Parts** in the Text group, and then click **Field**. In the Field dialog box, scroll down the Field Names on the left, and then click **Page**. Click the **1, 2, 3, ... format**, and then click **OK**.
   - Select the entire line, and then select font size **10** on the Mini toolbar. Click one time on the text to remove the selection, and then click **Ctrl+R** to right align the footer. Click **Close Header and Footer**.

l. Click the **Home tab**, click **Show/Hide ¶** in the Paragraph group to remove the formatting marks, and then click the **Close button** on the Navigation Pane. Press **Ctrl+G**, select **Bookmark** in the **Go to what list**, and then select **explorer** in the **Enter bookmark name list**, if necessary. Click **Go To**, and then view the topics on page 3. Click **Close** to remove the Find and Replace dialog box.

m. Scroll up, and then place your cursor in the *Shortcut Wizard* paragraph title. Double-click the **Paintbrush** in the Clipboard group. Click one time on the **Minimizing Versus Closing an Application paragraph title**, and then click one time on **The Task Manager title**. Press **Esc**.

n. Place your cursor in the paragraph that follows the *Shortcut Wizard* paragraph title, and then double-click the **Paintbrush** in the clipboard group. Click one time on the paragraph that follows the *Minimizing Versus Closing an Application* paragraph title, and then click one time on the paragraph that follows *The Task Manager.*

o. Save and close the file, and submit based on your instructor's directions.

3 Cancer Information

You receive two documents from coworkers who searched for information about cancer on the Internet. The information is interesting and could be valuable to other people you know, so you decide to create a well-formatted document that you can distribute to anyone who expresses an interest in basic information about cancer. And you also apply a document theme so it will look more professional. This exercise follows the same set of skills as used in Hands-On Exercises 1, 2, and 3 in the chapter. Refer to Figure 6.34 as you complete this exercise.

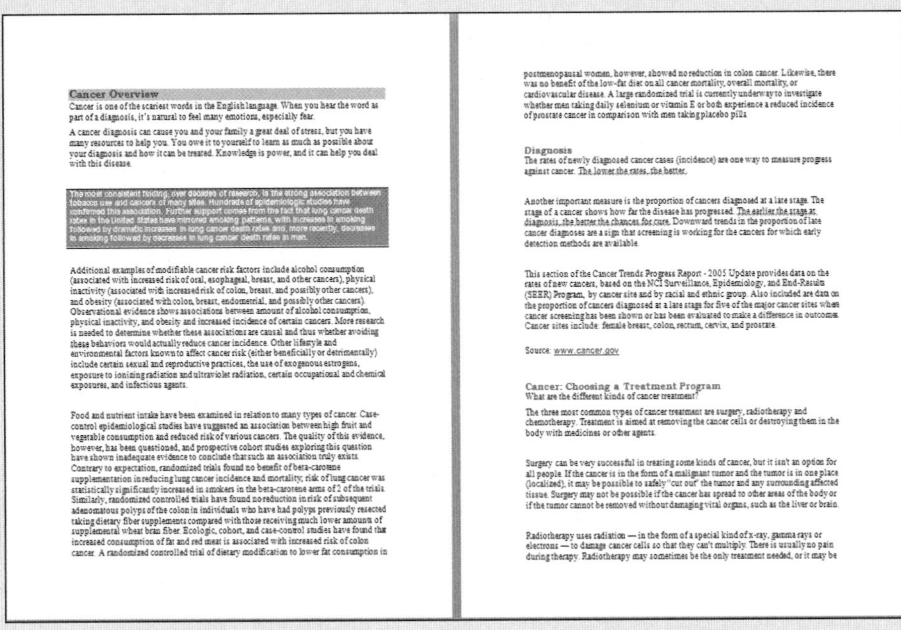

Cancer Overview

Cancer is one of the scariest words in the English language. When you hear the word as part of a diagnosis, it's natural to feel many emotions, especially fear.

A cancer diagnosis can cause you and your family a great deal of stress, but you have many resources to help you. You owe it to yourself to learn as much as possible about your diagnosis and how it can be treated. Knowledge is power, and it can help you deal with this disease.

The most consistent finding, over decades of research, is the strong association between tobacco use and cancers of many sites. Hundreds of epidemiologic studies have confirmed this association. Further support comes from the fact that lung cancer death rates in the United States have mirrored smoking patterns, with increases in smoking followed by dramatic increases in lung cancer death rates and, more recently, decreases in smoking followed by decreases in lung cancer death rates in men.

Additional examples of modifiable cancer risk factors include alcohol consumption (associated with increased risk of oral, esophageal, breast, and other cancers), physical inactivity (associated with increased risk of colon, breast, and possibly other cancers), and obesity (associated with colon, breast, endometrial, and possibly other cancers). Observational evidence shows associations between amount of alcohol consumption, physical inactivity, and obesity and increased incidence of certain cancers. More research is needed to determine whether these associations are causal and thus whether avoiding these behaviors would actually reduce cancer incidence. Other lifestyle and environmental factors known to affect cancer risk (either beneficially or detrimentally) include certain sexual and reproductive practices, the use of exogenous estrogens, exposure to ionizing radiation and ultraviolet radiation, certain occupational and chemical exposures, and infectious agents.

Food and nutrient intake have been examined in relation to many types of cancer. Case-control epidemiological studies have suggested an association between high fruit and vegetable consumption and reduced risk of various cancers. The quality of this evidence, however, has been questioned, and prospective cohort studies exploring this question have shown inadequate evidence to conclude that such an association truly exists. Contrary to expectation, randomized trials found no benefit of beta-carotene supplementation in reducing lung cancer incidence and mortality; risk of lung cancer was statistically significantly increased in smokers in the beta-carotene arms of 2 of the trials. Similarly, randomized controlled trials have found no reduction in risk of subsequent adenomatous polyps of the colon in individuals who have had polyps previously resected taking dietary fiber supplements compared with those receiving much lower amounts of supplemental wheat bran fiber. Ecologic, cohort, and case-control studies have found that increased consumption of fat and red meat is associated with increased risk of colon cancer. A randomized controlled trial of dietary modification to lower fat consumption in postmenopausal women, however, showed no reduction in colon cancer. Likewise, there was no benefit of the low-fat diet on all cancer mortality, overall mortality, or cardiovascular disease. A large randomized trial is currently underway to investigate whether men taking daily selenium or vitamin E or both experience a reduced incidence of prostate cancer in comparison with men taking placebo pills.

Diagnosis

The rates of newly diagnosed cancer cases (incidence) are one way to measure progress against cancer. The lower the rates, the better.

Another important measure is the proportion of cancers diagnosed at a late stage. The stage of a cancer shows how far the disease has progressed. The earlier the stage at diagnosis, the better the chances for cure. Downward trends in the proportion of late cancer diagnoses are a sign that screening is working for the cancers for which early detection methods are available.

This section of the Cancer Trends Progress Report - 2005 Update provides data on the rates of new cancers, based on the NCI Surveillance, Epidemiology, and End-Results (SEER) Program, by cancer site and by racial and ethnic group. Also included are data on the proportion of cancers diagnosed at a late stage for five of the major cancer sites when cancer screening has been shown or has been evaluated to make a difference in outcomes. Cancer sites include: female breast, colon, rectum, cervix, and prostate.

Source: www.cancer.gov

Cancer: Choosing a Treatment Program

What are the different kinds of cancer treatment?

The three most common types of cancer treatment are surgery, radiotherapy and chemotherapy. Treatment is aimed at removing the cancer cells or destroying them in the body with medicines or other agents.

Surgery can be very successful in treating some kinds of cancer, but it isn't an option for all people. If the cancer is in the form of a malignant tumor and the tumor is in one place (localized), it may be possible to safely "cut out" the tumor and any surrounding affected tissue. Surgery may not be possible if the cancer has spread to other areas of the body or if the tumor cannot be removed without damaging vital organs, such as the liver or brain.

Radiotherapy uses radiation — in the form of a special kind of x-ray, gamma rays or electrons — to damage cancer cells so that they can't multiply. There is usually no pain during therapy. Radiotherapy may sometimes be the only treatment needed, or it may be

FIGURE 6.34 Theme Applied to Combined Document ➤

a. Open *w06p3cancer1*, and then open *w06p3cancer2*. Click the **View tab**, and then click **View Side by Side** in the Window group. Use **Synchronous Scrolling** to scroll down to view the contents of each, and then click **View Side by Side** again to turn off the feature.

b. Click the **Review tab**, click the **Compare arrow** in the Compare group, and then select **Combine**.
   - Click the **Original document arrow**, and then select *w06p3cancer1.docx*. If necessary, click **Browse**, and then navigate to the document. Click **Open**.
   - Click the **Revised document arrow**, and then select *w06p3cancer2.docx*. If necessary, click **Browse**, and then navigate to the document. Click **Open**.
   - Click the **More button**, and then click **New document** below *Show changes in*, if necessary. Click **OK**.

c. Save the document as **w06p3cancer_LastnameFirstname**. To accept and reject the tracked changes, complete the following steps:
   - Click the balloon which describes the change in Style Definition, and then click **Accept** in the Changes group.
   - Click **Accept** to keep the blue shading on the heading.
   - Click **Reject** to remove the extra space between paragraphs.
   - Click **Accept** to keep the paragraphs with shading.
   - Scroll down until you see the balloon with a large amount of deleted text. Right-click the balloon, and then click **Reject Deletion**.

d. Press **Ctrl+Home** to view the first page. Close the Reviewing Pane, if necessary.

e. Click the **Page Layout tab**, and then click **Themes** in the Theme group. Click **Opulent** to apply colors from that theme on the text. Modify theme features by completing the following steps:
   - Click **Colors** in the Themes group, and then click **Create New Theme Colors**.
   - Click the **Accent 1 arrow**, and then click **Purple, Accent 2, Darker 25%** (fifth row, sixth column).
   - Click in the **Name box**, type **Cancer colors**, and then click **Save**.
   - Click **Fonts** in the Themes group, and then click **Create New Theme Fonts**.
   - Click the **Heading font arrow**, and then select **Bookman Old Style**.
   - Click in the **Name box**, type **Cancer fonts**, and then click **Save**.
   - Click **Themes**, and then click **Save Current Theme**. Navigate to the location where you save your solution files, type **w06p3cancertheme** in the **File name box**, and then click **Save**.

f. Save and close the file, and submit based on your instructor's directions.

1 Humane Society Recipe Book

You work as a volunteer at the local humane society. The board of directors asked you to coordinate a fund-raising effort in which books that contain animal treat recipes will be sold. You have been receiving recipes from several supporters via e-mail, and you place each one in a Word document for the particular type of animal. To create the recipe book, you decide to create a master document that contains all of the individual documents that contain recipes. After you add the documents, you can format and print the master document in preparation for the big sale.

a. Create a new master document. Save the file as **w06m1recipemaster_LastnameFirstname**.
b. Display the document in Outline view. At the top of the page, add the title **Recipes for the Animals in Your Life**, and then center the line horizontally.
c. Type the following categories on different lines below the heading: **Dogs**, **Cats**, **Birds**, and **Horses**. These category headings classify the type of recipes that follow. Center each heading, and then use the outline tools to reorder the categories of animal alphabetically.
d. Create subdocuments for each animal heading, and then save the document.
e. Insert the following subdocuments into the master document below the appropriate category heading: *w06m1dogs*, *w06m1cats*, *w06m1birds*, and *w06m1horses*.
f. Take appropriate actions so the recipes for each category of animal start on the top of a page. Remove any section breaks that create large gaps of white space within the group of recipes for a particular animal. If removal of breaks changes formatting of category headings, reapply the center formatting.
g. Create a Building Block with the following information and format it with single line spacing and center horizontal alignment. Display the Building Block in the header of the first page and in the footer of each page in the remainder of the document. Reduce the font size in the footer to **9 pt**.

   Humane Society Animal Recipe Book

   Compiled by and for Friends of the Humane Society

   Distributed Fall 2012
h. Display the Navigation Pane, and then use the headings to locate each animal category. Create a bookmark for each type of animal. Use the Navigation Pane and the GoTo feature as needed while you work through the remaining steps of this exercise.
i. Display the Theme gallery, and then select the **Apex theme**. Create a new color theme. Change the Text/Background - Dark 2 color to **Aqua, Accent 3**, which is located on the top of the seventh column. Change the Accent 1 color to **Lavender, Accent 5** (top of ninth column), and change Accent 2 to **Blue, Accent 4** (top of eighth column). Save the new color theme as **w06m1recipetheme**.
j. Save the master document. Open the subdocument *horses.docx*, and then apply bold formatting to the recipe headings *Birthday Cake for a Horse* and *Cold Weather Treat for Horses and Ponies*. Save and close the subdocument.
k. Confirm the change displays in the master document. Save and close the master document. Submit based on your instructor's directions.

2 Sidewalk Café

Your friend, Mary Guccione, just purchased the Sidewalk Café restaurant. She prepared an information sheet to distribute to several office buildings within the neighborhood and she asked you to look at it and offer suggestions. Before you start reviewing the information sheet she sends another version with new changes. With two different documents, you use the Compare and Combine features to view them, and then consolidate the documents into one final copy, add your suggested changes, and return it to Mary.

a. Use the **Compare feature** to open the two documents Mary sends, *w06m2cafe* and *w06m2caferevision*, and then display the results in a new document. View the differences, save the new document as **w06m2cafecompare_LastnameFirstname**, and then close the document.

b. Use the **Combine feature** to combine *w06m2caferevision* (hint: open this as an original document) and *w06m2cafe*. Save the newly combined file as **w06m2cafecombined_LastnameFirstname**.

c. Accept and reject the following changes that display in the document:
   - Accept the tracked change *Formatted: Space Before: 0 pt.*
   - Reject the tracked change *Formatted: Font: 10 pt.*
   - Reject the addition of text *on a daily basis* that displays above the SmartArt.
   - Reject the insertion of the SmartArt object that includes *Fresh Seafood, Homemade Soup, etc.*
   - Reject the tracked change that displays in the text *is homey and* in the third paragraph.
   - Accept the tracked change *Deleted: those in the know.*
   - Accept the inclusion of the text *trendy-conscience people.*
   - Accept all remaining changes in the document.

d. Apply the **Module theme** to the document.

e. Type **Mary Guccione's** on the title line, so that the title reads *Mary Guccione's Sidewalk Café.* Apply the **Intense Emphasis style** from the style gallery to this text. Change the font color to **Gold, Accent 1, Darker 25%**. Select the name, *Mary Guccione's*, and add it as an AutoText entry in the Building Block Organizer.

f. Display the Building Block in front of each occurrence of the *Sidewalk Café* title throughout the document, replacing *The*, where necessary. Bold the AutoText entry, if necessary.

g. Italicize all instances of Mary Guccione and Doug Guccione, or any variation of their names.

h. Save and close all documents, and submit based on your instructor's directions.

3 Creating Themes

Because you learned about the themes that Word 2010 provides, you decide that you need to use them more often and also create your very own custom theme. You download a letter that incorporates a theme already, add a custom Building Block, and then make modifications to create your own custom theme that you can use in other documents.

a. Open a new document, and then browse the Sample templates. Find and open the Median Letter template. Save the file as a document template named **w06m3custom_LastnameFirstname**. Make certain the Save as type box displays *Word Template (*.dotx)*.

b. Create a Building Block that contains your name and address. Use a style from the style gallery to format the name and/or address.

c. Remove the template placeholder for *Name* and *Address*, and insert your new Building Block entry. Select today's date.

d. Display the Theme gallery, and then select a theme that closely fits your personality.

e. Display the Theme Colors gallery, and then change the color of any two objects. Save the new color theme as **w06m3colortheme**.

f. Create a new font theme. Change the heading font to any Sans Serif font. Save the font theme as **w06m3fonttheme**.

g. Save the Current Document Theme as **w06m3mytheme_LastnameFirstname**, since you have personalized several pieces of the theme.

h. Save and close the document template. Submit based on your instructor's directions.

You have recently been elected secretary of the local professional chapter of Information Technologist Professionals (ITPs). You decide to send professional-looking documents to the other officers so they can prepare for meetings, as well as collect and distribute information. Your next meeting occurs in one week, so you begin the process of assembling your information.

Download a Word Template

You want to prepare a meeting agenda that is comprehensive, yet looks nice and is easy to read. Instead of creating one from scratch, you download a meeting agenda document template from Office.com. Once you personalize these templates with the organization name and logo, you save them as templates so you can use them for each monthly meeting.

a. Open a new document, and then download the **Agenda (Capsules design) template**, which is found in the Agendas template folder.

b. Save the file as a Word template named **w06c1agenda_LastnameFirstname.dotx**.

c. Delete the text box that displays *Your Logo Here*. In its place, insert the graphic *w06c1logo.png*, which is stored with other data files for this chapter.

d. Create a Building Block out of the logo, name it **Logo**, and then save it to the Quick Part Gallery.

e. Remove the bullet points under *Chairperson's Report* and *Treasurer's Report*.

f. Replace the following text in the document template:

Replace This Text	With This Text
Meeting Name	ITP Monthly Board Meeting
Place of Meeting	The Library Center
Status of landscaping bids	Membership update
Status of water quality control	Status of
Possible pending litigation	Assign student chapter liaison

g. Save and close the template.

Combine Documents to Create an Agenda with Minutes

After you create the agenda template, you send it to the president and vice president and ask them to revise it and add their topics for the meeting. When they each return their version to you, you combine them into one final agenda for the upcoming meeting. You also attach the minutes from the last meeting to the end of the agenda.

a. Use the **Combine feature** to view the returned agendas named *w06c1Fordagenda* and *w06c1Factoragenda*. Save the combined file as a document named **w06c1combinedagenda_LastnameFirstname**.

b. Accept all changes to the agenda after the files are combined.

c. Change the date to **October 16**. Change the time to **6:30 pm**.

d. Insert a blank page after the agenda. Use the **Insert Text from File object feature** to add the minutes of the meeting, stored in *w06c1minutes*, to the end of the agenda.

e. Type your name as Note taker/Secretary for the September 18 Minutes.

f. Insert the logo Building Block at the bottom of the page where you just inserted the minutes.

Apply a Document Theme to the Meeting Agenda and Minutes

After you combine the agendas and insert the minutes, you decide to customize the document to reflect the national organization's colors. You begin by selecting a theme, but decide to modify it so your colors match and fonts are easier to read. You save your custom settings so you can use them again on other documents.

a. Change the document theme to **Urban**.

b. Modify the colors used in this theme by changing the Accent 1 color to **Blue-Gray, Background 2** (first row, third column), and then changing the Text/Background - Light 1 color to **Black, Background 1** (first row, first column). Save the font colors as **w06c1agendacolors**.

c. Create new Theme Fonts replacing the heading font with **Arial Black** and the body font with **Arial Narrow**. Save the font theme as **w06c1agendafonts**.

d. Save the current theme, which includes the revisions you just made, as **w06c1agenda**.

e. Click the green-colored graphic on the page where the agenda displays. Change the fill color of that object to the theme color **Blue-Gray, Accent 1, Lighter 60%** (third row, fifth column), and apply the Shape Style **Diagonal Gradient - Dark** (sixth row, first column).

f. Save and close the document.

Add Bookmarks to a Document

After the minutes for each meeting are approved, you are responsible for adding them to a document which holds the minutes for a whole year. The document becomes so lengthy that it is easier to navigate when bookmarks are applied to each month. You will add the minutes from the last meeting and add missing bookmarks.

a. Open *w06c1yearlyminutes*. Save the document as **w06c1yearlyminutes_LastnameFirstname**.

b. Add a page break at the beginning of the document, and then use the **Insert Text from File object** to add the minutes of the September meeting, *w06c1minutes*.

c. Insert a bookmark named **September** at the left edge of the date *September 18*, which displays in the second line of the table holding the minutes.

d. Insert a bookmark named **August** at the left edge of the date *August 21*, which displays on the next page.

e. Press **Ctrl+G**, and then go to the bookmark named *June*. Close the Find and Replace dialog box.

f. Type your name as the Timekeeper. Apply the **w06c1agenda theme**.

g. Save and close the document. Submit based on your instructor's directions.

BEYOND THE CLASSROOM

Employee Handbooks

GENERAL CASE 

Meghan Bisi has recently started her own company and wants to establish an employee policy manual immediately. She has recruited graduate assistants at the local university to help her compile information and write sections of policy which she will include in the manual. Each student has forwarded her a copy of their work and now she asks you, her new executive assistant, to assemble the policy manual. You will create one single document using the following files: *w06b1handbook*, *w06b1eligibility*, *w06b1employment*, *w06b1leave*, and *w06b1conduct*. Accept or reject changes as you see fit so the manual is an orderly document. Use or modify document themes to add consistency to the newly combined sections. Save your final document as **w06b1policymanual_LastnameFirstname**, and submit based on your instructor's directions.

Use the Calendar Wizard

RESEARCH CASE 

You want to create a monthly calendar for the current year. However, you do not want to manually create and populate 12 tables, one for each month, typing in dates within cells. You know there are many calendar templates on Office.com and decide to find one there. Find and download the Calendar Wizard, and after you complete the steps you can apply Document Themes and modify colors and fonts for a very personalized and custom calendar. Save the calendar as a template, which you can share with others, naming it **w06b2calendar_LastnameFirstname.dotx**. For your personal calendar, insert information for important dates such as birthdays and anniversaries; create Building Blocks for frequently used names. Save the calendar as **w06b2calendar_LastnameFirstname.docx**, and submit based on your instructor's directions.

Repairing Bookmarks

DISASTER RECOVERY 

You work in the city's Planning and Zoning department as an analyst. You begin to prepare the Guide to Planned Developments document for posting on the city's intranet. The administrative clerk who typed the document attempted to use bookmarks for navigation purposes, but he did not test the bookmarks after inserting them. You must review the document and repair the bookmarks. Additionally, several cross-reference statements are embedded in the document, but appear to be erroneous. The cross-references are highlighted in the document so you can locate them; the highlights should be removed when you have corrected the references. Open *w06b3bookmarks* and save your revised document as **w06b3bookmarks_LastnameFirstname**. Close the document and submit based on your instructor's directions.

WORD

7 DOCUMENT AUTOMATION

Forms, Macros, and Security

Watch the
Set-up Video
for this Case Study!

CASE STUDY | Oak Grove Products, Inc.

Cassie Artman has purchased Oak Grove Products, Inc., a company that sells tulip, hyacinth, and crocus bulbs. Cassie wants to take the company to the next level by automating some of the resources they use. One of the first projects she assigns to you, her technology coordinator, is to create a sales invoice that can be filled out quickly by salespeople who take phone or online orders. The invoice will include check boxes, drop-down menus, and fields that calculate prices automatically. She also wants you to incorporate an informational document about the products sold. She has created a document that she considers complete, so she wants you to password-protect it to prevent any accidental editing. But she also wants you to get feedback from staff before you consider it final and stamp it with a digital certificate.

In the Hands-On Exercises, you will create the invoice form, work with macros, and practice protecting documents.

OBJECTIVES

AFTER YOU READ THIS CHAPTER, YOU WILL BE ABLE TO:

Forms

A **form** is a document designed for collecting data for a specific situation.

Forms are quite common in our society. A ***form*** is a document designed for collecting data for a specific situation. For example, you complete a medical history form when you visit a doctor's office, you complete forms when you open a bank account, other forms help you register software and hardware, and you fill out a form when you apply for a job. Forms are also used for class registrations, purchase orders, and invoices. The form may be electronic and completed online, or it may exist as a printed document. Figure 7.1 displays a completed form that is an invoice for goods or services.

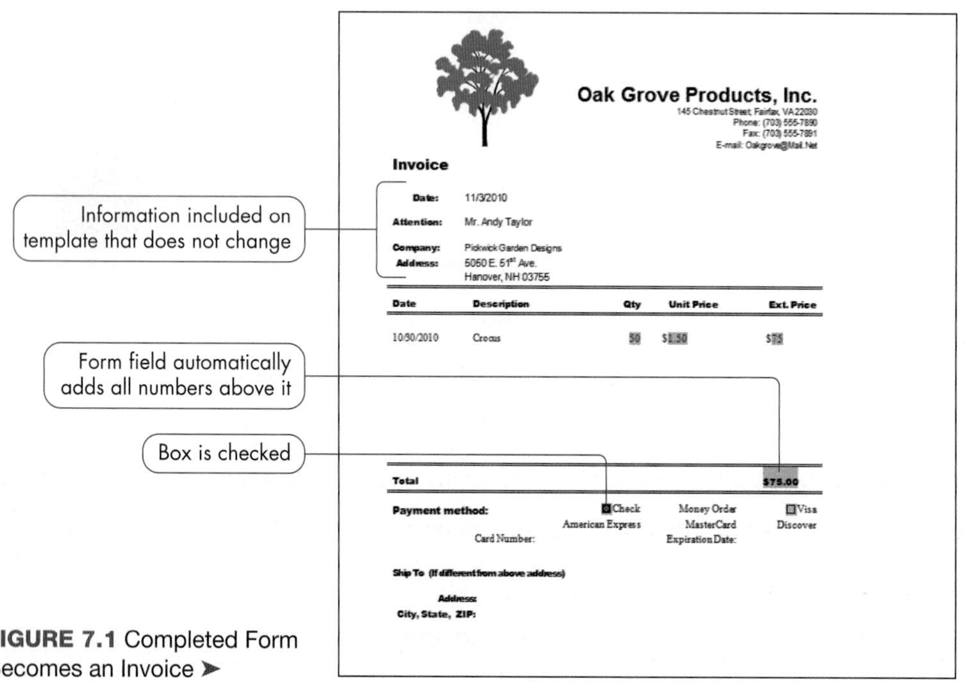

Information included on template that does not change
Form field automatically adds all numbers above it
Box is checked

Oak Grove Products, Inc.
145 Chestnut Street, Fairfax, VA 22030
Phone: (703) 555-7890
Fax: (703) 555-7891
E-mail: Oakgrove@Mail.Net

Invoice

Date: 11/3/2010
Attention: Mr. Andy Taylor
Company: Pickwick Garden Designs
Address: 5050 E. 51st Ave.
Hanover, NH 03755

Date	Description	Qty	Unit Price	Ext. Price
10/30/2010	Crocus	50	$1.50	$75
Total				**$75.00**

Payment method: ☒ Check Money Order ☐ Visa American Express MasterCard Discover
Card Number: Expiration Date:

Ship To (If different from above address)
Address:
City, State, ZIP:

FIGURE 7.1 Completed Form Becomes an Invoice ➤

In this section, you will create and use a simple form that can be printed and filled in or completed onscreen. You will learn how to create and customize form controls, you will perform calculations in a table form, and then you will protect the document so you can use the form.

Creating an Electronic Form

A **form template** is a document that defines the standard layout, structure, and formatting of a form.

In Word, you can create a ***form template***, a document that defines the standard layout, structure, and formatting of a form. You save the document as a Word template, and then establish settings to enable the user to enter data in specific places, but prevent editing it in any other way. The process requires you to create the form and save it to disk, where it serves as an original template for future documents. Then, when you need to enter data for a specific situation, you open the template form, enter the data, and save the completed form as a document. This process is more efficient than removing old information from a standard document so you can replace it with current data for the new situation. It also minimizes errors that sometimes occur when you intend to replace old information with updated data but overlook some portion of the older data. Using a form enables you to maintain the integrity of an original document or template while also allowing you to customize it.

In Word, you can create a form template, a document that defines the standard layout, structure, and formatting of a form. You … then establish settings to enable the user to enter data in specific places, but prevent editing it in any other way.

Figure 7.2 displays a blank form. The shaded entries indicate where a user enters information into a form. To complete the form, the user presses Tab to move from one field to the next and enters data as appropriate. Then, when all fields have been filled, the form is printed to produce the finished document (an invoice). The data entered into the various fields appear as regular text when printed.

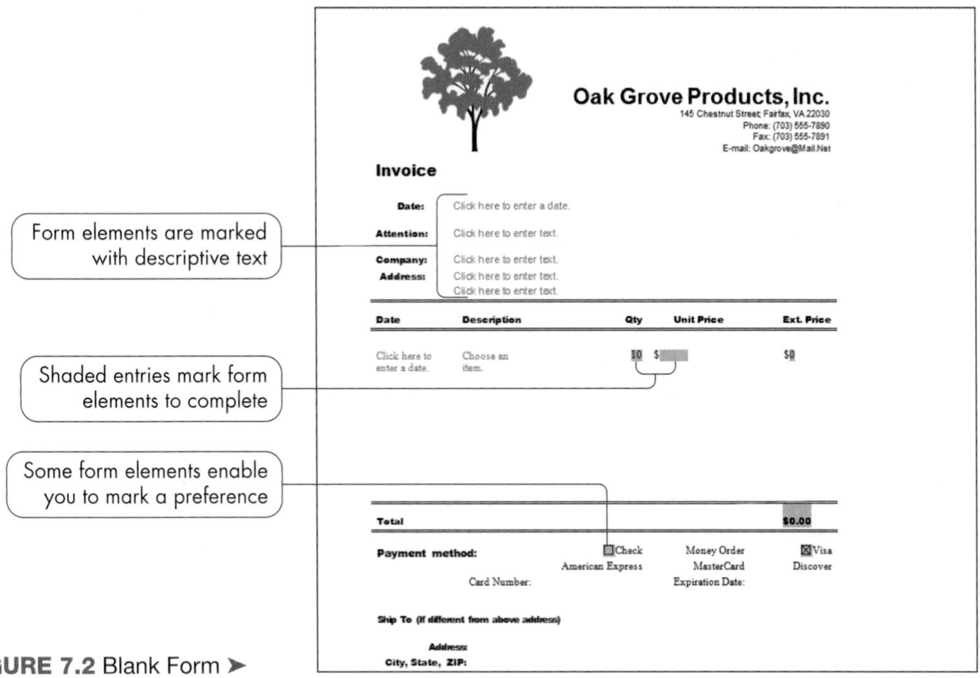

FIGURE 7.2 Blank Form ➤

Inserting Form Controls

You must display the Developer tab to use the form development tools in Word. This tab does not display automatically but is easy to activate. If you need to display the Developer tab, complete the following steps:

- Click File.
- Click Options.
- Click Customize Ribbon.
- Click Developer in the *Customize the Ribbon* column on the right.
- Click OK.

Design Mode enables you to view and modify control fields.

On the Developer tab, you see the form controls as well as other commands you use while creating the form. Before you insert the controls in your document, you must enter Design Mode. ***Design Mode*** enables you to view and select the control fields so you can make any necessary modifications to their layout or options. Design Mode is a toggle; click it once to activate Design Mode, and then click it again to deactivate it.

Using a table in a form template helps you align information and makes the form easier for users to fill out. In addition, you can use the Table feature to format and manipulate the fields and data to improve the form. For example, you can right-align labels, such as Name and Address, in one table cell, and then you can left-align the form field the user completes. This alignment clarifies the instructional information that accompanies the field.

A **form control** helps a user complete a form by displaying prompts such as text boxes and drop-down lists.

You can design forms that will be printed and also forms that will be completed electronically. If you want users to fill out a form electronically, you must insert ***form controls***, also called form fields, into the form template. Form controls help the user complete a form by displaying prompts such as drop-down lists and text boxes. Table 7.1 describes several of the most common types of controls.

TABLE 7.1 Form Controls

Control Type	Description
Rich Text	User can enter text or numbers, and can modify the format of the text they enter.
Text	User can enter text or numbers, but cannot modify the format of the text.
Picture Content Control	User can insert a drawing, shape, chart, table, clip art, or SmartArt object in a field.
Combo Box	User selects from a list of choices that displays in a drop-down box, but the user can modify the choices in the list.
Drop-Down List	User selects from a predefined list of choices that displays in a drop-down box.
Date Picker	User selects a date from the calendar that displays.
Building Block Gallery	User selects a building block item to insert in the document, such as cover pages, headers, footers, or predefined text such as a disclaimer.
Check Box	User selects or deselects an item by clicking the check box that displays beside the item.
Option Button	User selects from a predefined list by clicking the option button that displays beside the item.

A **text content control** is used to enter any type of text into a form.

The controls you use most often are text, check boxes, and drop-down lists. A ***text content control*** is the most common and is used to enter any type of text into a form. It usually displays in the form of a box, and it collects information such as name and address, and even numerical data such as a phone number. The length of a text box can be set exactly or can be left unspecified, in which case the field will expand to the exact number of positions that are required as the data are entered.

When you have a form that uses numerical information, you can use a text content control to perform calculations. You can use basic formulas, such as those that add or multiply the numbers that display in text form fields. The properties for the text form content control enable you to select the form fields you include in the calculation. You can adjust the format of the numbers; for example, you can change the format for a field that displays a price using currency format that displays dollar signs and decimal points.

A **check box form field** consists of a box that can be checked or unchecked.

A ***check box form field***, as the name implies, consists of a box that is checked or not. A check box might include the responses Yes or No, or Male or Female, for example. You can customize check box form fields so they display checked by default, or not checked. You can also specify the size of the check box.

A **drop-down list** enables the user to choose from one of several existing entries.

A ***drop-down list*** enables the user to choose from one of several existing entries. This type of control should only be used on electronic forms because the list of options will not display on a printed form. A drop-down list enables users to click a down arrow and then click one option from the list; the option they click will then display on the form. A list of cities or states is appropriate to display in a drop-down list.

The **Date Picker** displays a calendar that the user can click rather than typing in a date.

Many forms require a date. The ***Date Picker*** displays a calendar that the user can navigate and click rather than typing in a date. If the user wants to select the current date, the Date Picker calendar has a Today button. The Properties dialog box for the Date Picker enables you to select from several date formats, such as 3/2/2012 or 2-Mar-12.

TIP Planning the Order of Fields

When a user completes an onscreen form, Word moves through fields in the order in which you inserted them. You should plan how you want users to fill out the form before inserting form fields. If you want users to move from left to right across the page, insert form fields from left to right. If you want users to move down the page, insert form fields down the page. You should also keep labels close to the form controls because programs that are used by the visually impaired cannot distinguish which label matches a particular field when they are not positioned closely.

A **Legacy form field** is a form element that can be used in Word 2010 and also in previous versions of Word.

An **ActiveX control** is a form element that works in a Word 2007 or 2010 document or template.

Some controls are designated as ***Legacy form fields*** because they were used in previous versions of Word. These controls can be used in Word 2010 and also in documents or templates you open in Compatibility Mode, meaning they were created with a previous version of Word. ***ActiveX controls*** are form elements designed for use in Office 2007 and 2010. These controls are easy to insert in a Word 2010 document or template. You can insert them in a document saved in Compatibility Mode; however, the Properties dialog box is confusing to those not familiar with programming. If you create forms that might be used by people who are not yet using Word 2010, you should remember to use only legacy controls and save the document or template in Compatibility Mode. Figure 7.3 shows the Developer tab and available controls.

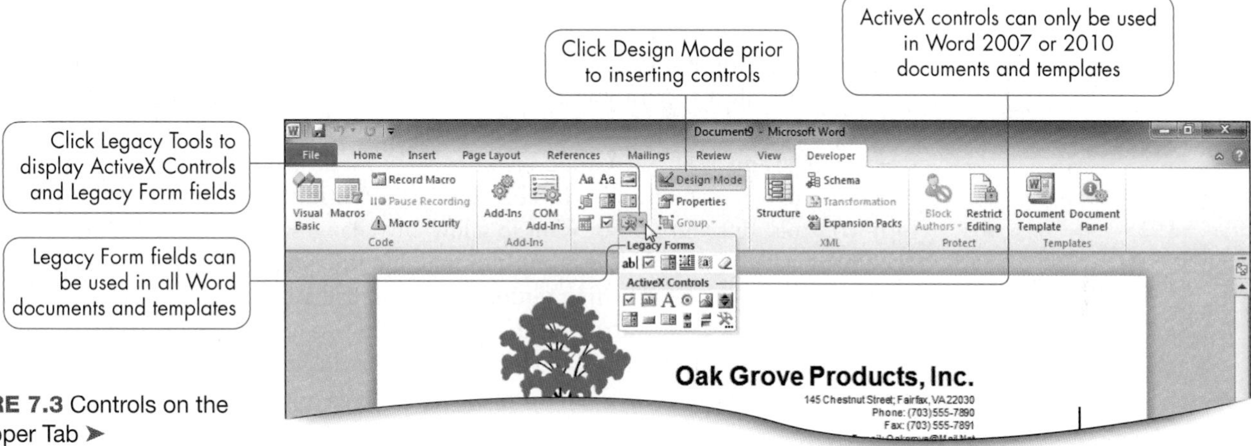

FIGURE 7.3 Controls on the Developer Tab ➤

Protecting a Form

After the form is created, it should be protected to prevent modification other than data entry. To protect the form, deactivate Design Mode, if necessary, and then click Restrict Editing in the Protect group of the Developer tab. The Restrict Formatting and Editing pane displays, as shown in Figure 7.4. Click *Allow only this type of editing in the document* in the *Editing restrictions* section, then click the arrow and select *Filling in forms* to enable the user to type in, click, or select only the form fields in the form.

FIGURE 7.4 Restrict Formatting and Editing of a Form ➤

A **password** is a security feature required to gain access to a restricted document.

After you enforce the protection of a form, you are prompted for a password. A ***password*** is a security mechanism consisting of case-sensitive characters entered to gain access to a restricted document. You can create a password for the form that serves as another layer of protection and prevents other users from deactivating the protection unless they know the password. Without a password, anyone can deactivate the protection. However, if you forget the password, it cannot be recovered. You can skip the password protection by omitting a password in the Enter new password box and clicking OK. If you want to revise the form, click Stop Protection in the Restrict Formatting and Editing pane.

You can protect specific controls on a form without restricting access to the entire document by using the Group command, in the Controls group on the Developer tab. When you select a range and apply the Group command, the range is protected from editing. This feature is useful when you want to be able to make modifications to a document that contains form controls, but you do not want to allow any changes to the form controls within that document. After you apply the Group command to the range, click Properties and set one of the two locking options. The first option—Content control cannot be deleted—enables you to edit the content of a control but does not enable you to remove the control. The second option—Contents cannot be edited—enables you to delete the control, but you cannot edit the content in the control.

1 Forms

As the new owner of Oak Grove Products, Inc., Cassie Artman wants to improve the resources used by employees in the sales and accounting departments. She asks you to update and automate the invoice form so that it is easier to use. You begin by inserting form controls and using automated calculations from those controls. You then save the document so that employees can open and enter data without affecting the content or structure of the invoice document.

Skills covered: Create a Document Template • Insert Form Controls in a Document • Insert Form Controls in a Table • Perform Calculations with Form Control Data • Add Check Box Controls and Protect the Form • Use an Electronic Form

STEP 1 CREATE A DOCUMENT TEMPLATE

Cassie has passed along an invoice form which you can use as a starting point for your automated invoice. You decide to save it as a Word template so it will be easy and efficient to update it for each new customer transaction. Refer to Figure 7.5 as you complete Step 1.

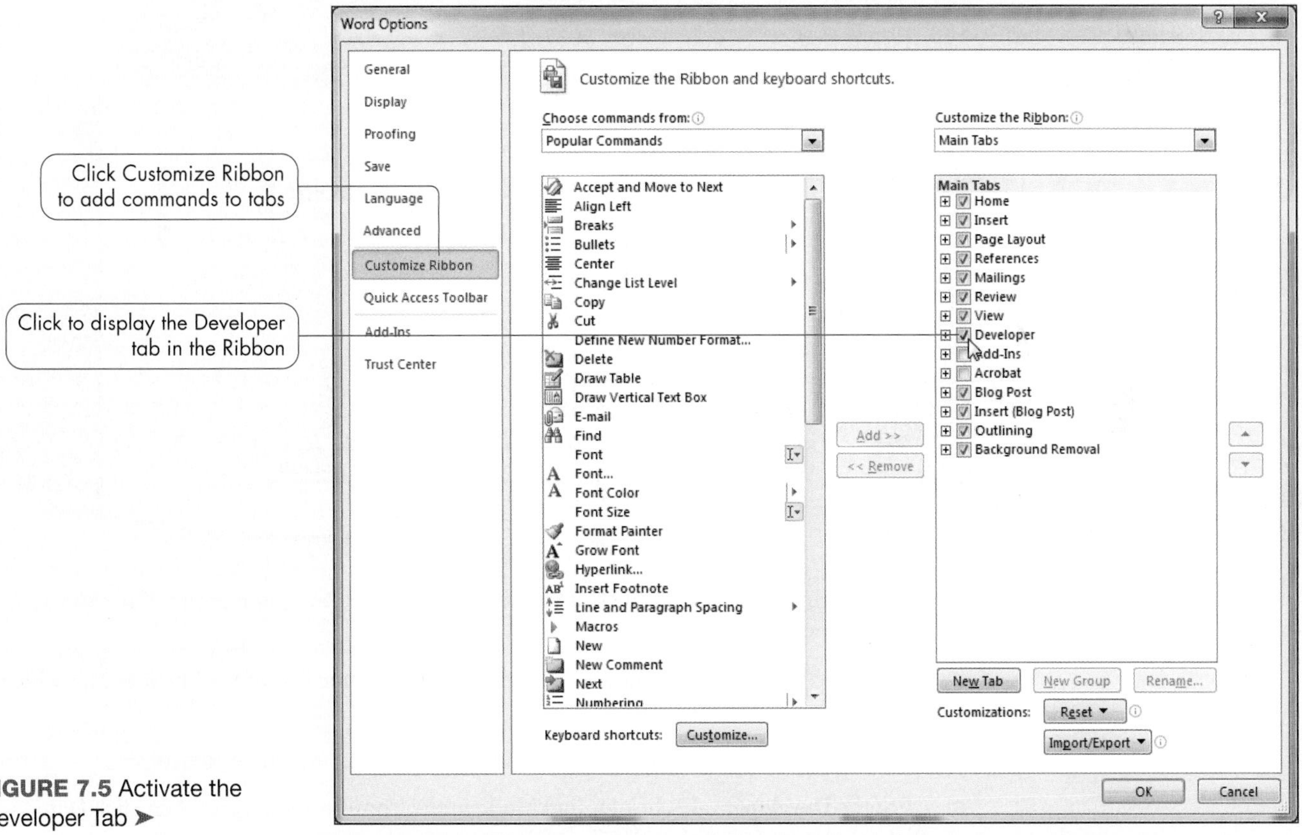

Click Customize Ribbon to add commands to tabs

Click to display the Developer tab in the Ribbon

FIGURE 7.5 Activate the Developer Tab ➤

a. Open *w07h1invoice.doc.*

   This file is saved as a Word 97–2003 document and will open in Compatibility Mode.

> **TROUBLESHOOTING:** If you make any major mistakes in this exercise, you can close the file, open *w07h1invoice* again, and then start this exercise over.

b. Click **File**, click **Options**, click **Customize Ribbon**, and then click the **Developer check box**, which displays in the Customize the Ribbon column on the right, as shown in Figure 7.5. Click **OK**.

   This step is necessary to display the Developer tab, which contains all form controls.

c. Click the **Developer tab**, and then locate the Controls group.

Notice that most of the Controls in the Controls group are grayed out. These ActiveX controls cannot be used in a document that opens in Compatibility Mode.

d. Click **File**, click **Save As**, click the **Save as type arrow**, and then select **Word Template (*.dotx)**. Type **w07h1invoice_LastnameFirstname** in the **File name box**, and then click **Save.**

If a Microsoft Office Word dialog box displays with a warning that you are about to save your document in one of the new formats, click OK. If a Microsoft Office Word dialog box asks if you want to continue to save as a macro-free document, click Yes.

STEP 2 INSERT FORM CONTROLS IN A DOCUMENT

Now that the document is saved as a template, you insert form controls for the customer's name, address, and date of the sale. You especially appreciate the Date Picker control, which enables you to click the date from a calendar; this process prevents mistyped dates and should reflect more accurate record keeping. Refer to Figure 7.6 as you complete Step 2.

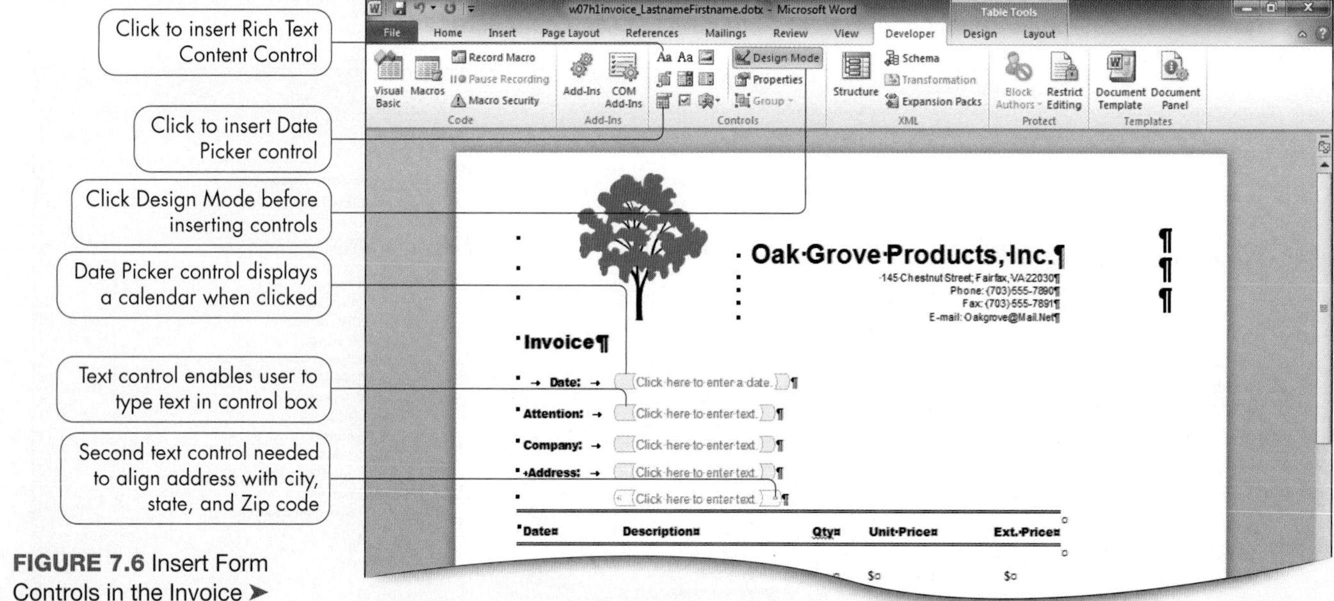

FIGURE 7.6 Insert Form Controls in the Invoice ➤

a. Click the **Home tab**, and then click **Show/Hide** (¶) in the Paragraph group, if necessary, to display formatting marks.

b. Click the left side of the paragraph mark that displays at the end of the line for *Date*, which is just below the text *Invoice.*

You are positioning the insertion point here prior to inserting a date control.

c. Click the **Developer tab**, click **Design Mode** in the Controls group, and then click **Date Picker Content Control** in the Controls group.

The control for choosing a date displays with a light blue border and the text *Click here to enter a date.*

d. Press ↓ one time to move the insertion point to the end of the line for *Attention:*, and then click **Rich Text Content Control** in the Controls group.

The control for entering text displays with a light blue border and the text *Click here to enter text.*

e. Repeat the process from step d to insert Rich Text Content Controls at the end of the *Company:* and *Address:* lines.

f. Click the left side of the paragraph mark that displays on the line just below the *Address:* line. Click **Rich Text Content Control** in the Controls group.

You must insert a second text control here for the city, state, and Zip code portions of the address. The text controls do not align text properly when you press Enter when typing within them, so a second box is necessary to align all the address information.

g. Compare your document to Figure 7.6, and then save the document.

STEP 3 INSERT FORM CONTROLS IN A TABLE

Customer purchases are recorded in an area of the invoice that is formatted in a Word table. By using a table, you have more control over the placement and alignment of the controls and text that display in the invoice. Because this invoice will be used in digital form, you insert form controls that enable the salesperson to pick the product purchased—another way to reduce the possibility of error that occurs when information is typed into a form. Refer to Figure 7.7 as you complete Step 3.

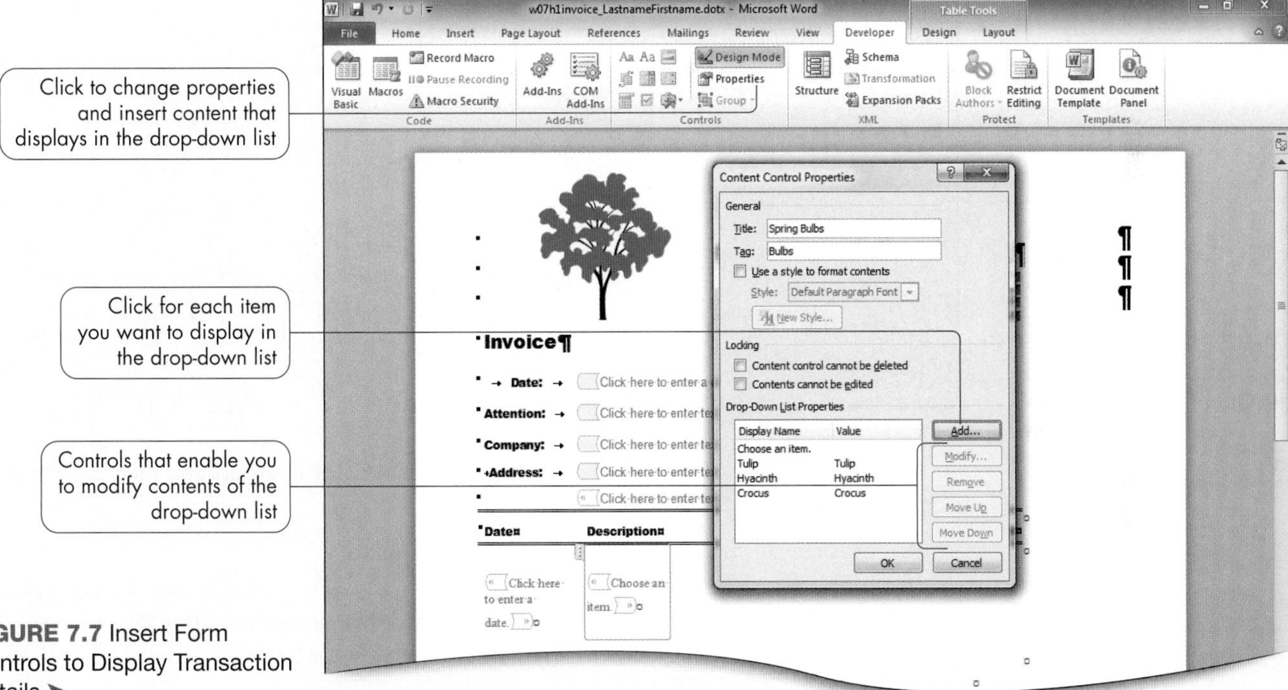

FIGURE 7.7 Insert Form Controls to Display Transaction Details ➤

a. Click the left side of the first blank row in the table, just below the text *Date*. Click **Date Picker Content Control** from the Controls group. Click the left side of the next cell, below the text *Description*.

> **TROUBLESHOOTING:** If you have difficulty positioning the cursor in the table, click the Layout tab, and then click View Gridlines so you can view each cell border. This border does not display when printed.

b. Click **Drop-Down List Content Control** in the Controls group. Click **Properties** in the Controls group to display the Content Control Properties dialog box.

Users will select from a predefined list of products when they click this control in the form.

c. Type **Spring Bulbs** in the **Title box**. Type **Bulbs** in the **Tag box**.

d. Click **Add** to display the Add Choice dialog box. Type **Tulip** in the **Display Name box**, and then click **OK**.

e. Repeat the process in step d to add two more types of bulbs: Hyacinth and Crocus. Compare your work to Figure 7.7.

f. Click **OK** to close the dialog box. Save the document.

STEP 4 PERFORM CALCULATIONS WITH FORM CONTROL DATA

The next few pieces of information entered into the invoice will reflect the quantity and amount paid for the products. Because these fields work with numbers, you use form controls that enable you to format the price entered using currency symbols. The controls also perform calculations using formulas resembling those used in table cell calculations. By using these form controls, you increase the frequency of very accurate sales figures that display on the invoices. Refer to Figure 7.8 as you complete Step 4.

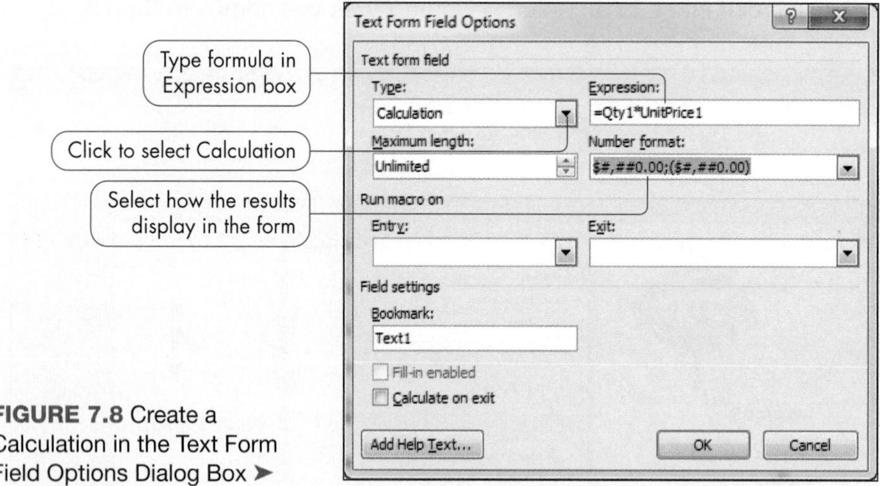

FIGURE 7.8 Create a Calculation in the Text Form Field Options Dialog Box ➤

a. Click in the cell below *Qty*. Click **Legacy Tools** in the Controls group, and then click **Text Form Field** below the heading *Legacy Forms*.

A series of small circles displays with a gray background.

TROUBLESHOOTING: If the gray background does not display behind the circles, click Legacy Tools, and then click Form Field Shading below the Legacy Forms heading.

b. Set up this form field by completing the following steps:

- Click **Properties** in the Controls group to display the Text Form Field Options dialog box.
- Click the **Type arrow**, and then select **Number**.
- Type **10** in the **Default number text box**.
- Press **Tab** four times, and then replace the contents of the **Bookmark box** with **Qty1**.
- Click the **Calculate on exit box**, confirm *Fill-in enabled* is checked, and then click **OK**.

By naming the bookmark *Qty1*, you will be able to add more product items to the invoice. The next row can contain a bookmark named Qty2, and eventually, you can use the bookmark names to create formulas to perform calculations within the form. Checking Calculate on exit ensures that calculations are updated after users enter numbers.

c. Click in the cell below *Unit Price*, placing your cursor on the right side of the dollar sign, and then complete the following steps:

- Click **Legacy Tools** in the Controls group, and then click **Text Form Field** below the heading *Legacy Forms*.
- Click **Properties** in the Control group.

- Replace the contents of the **Bookmark box** with **UnitPrice1**.
- Click the **Calculate on exit box**, and then confirm *Fill-in enabled* is checked.
- Click **OK** to close the Text Form Field Options dialog box.

d. Click in the cell below *Ext. Price*, placing your cursor on the right side of the dollar sign, and then complete the following steps:

- Click **Legacy Tools** in the Controls group, and then click **Text Form Field.**
- Click **Properties.**
- Click the **Type arrow**, and then select **Calculation.**
- Type **Qty1*UnitPrice1** after the equal sign in the **Expression box.**

The equal sign in the Expression box specifies that you are creating a mathematical formula. This formula multiplies the value in the Qty field by the value of the UnitPrice field. Because you assigned bookmark names to the fields, you can use the bookmark names in the formula.

e. Click **OK** to close the dialog box.

The Ext. Price field immediately displays *$0*, which is the result of multiplying the default value of 10 in the Qty field by the empty value in the Unit Price field.

f. Click in the cell at the right end of the Total row, below *Ext. Price*, and then complete the following steps:

- Click **Legacy Tools** in the Controls group, and then click **Text Form Field.**
- Right-click the shaded field that displays on the invoice, and then click **Properties.**
- Click the **Type arrow**, and then select **Calculation.**
- Click in the **Expression box**, and then type **SUM(ABOVE)** after the equal sign.
- Click **OK.**

You want to add all the values in as many fields as appear in the Ext. Price column. You use the SUM function to add values in all fields in this column. You will add more rows to the invoice later. The results display as a dollar value.

g. Save the document.

STEP 5 ADD CHECK BOX CONTROLS AND PROTECT THE FORM

Your changes to the invoice are almost complete. You decide to add only one more form control, a check box for the type of payment, which displays at the bottom of the invoice. You then use the document protection tools to prevent editing of the document, allowing only edits that serve to fill out the form. Refer to Figure 7.9 as you complete Step 5.

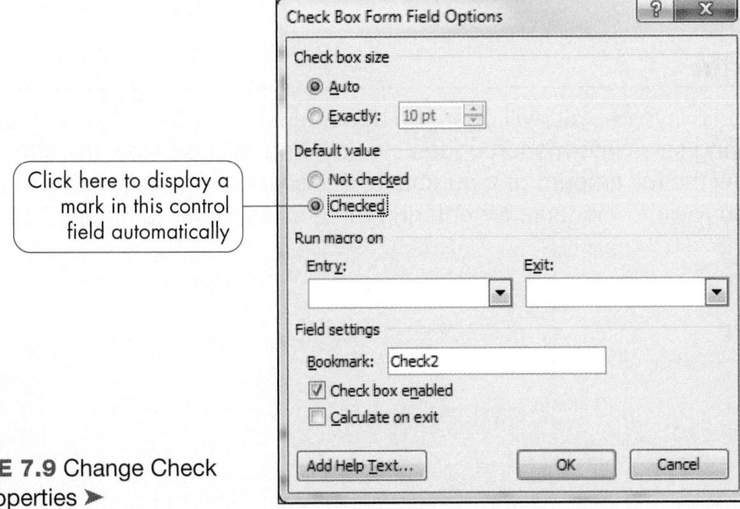

FIGURE 7.9 Change Check Box Properties ➤

a. Click the left side of the cell containing *Check*, click **Legacy Tools** in the Controls group, and then select **Check Box Form Field** below *Legacy Forms*.

   This action inserts a check box form field in the cell to the left of the Check payment method. Users can mark the check box next to the payment method they prefer. You use the Legacy form field instead of the ActiveX form field because it enables you to set custom properties for that field, which you complete in a future step.

b. Click the left side of the cell containing *Visa*, click **Legacy Tools** in the Controls group, and then select **Check Box Form Field.**

   You do not yet display check boxes next to all the payment methods, but you will add them in a future Hands-On Exercise. However, you do have enough controls to test your form in the next step.

c. Right-click the **Visa check box**, and then click **Properties.** Click **Checked** in the *Default value* section, as shown in Figure 7.9. Click **OK.**

   Because the majority of purchases are charged to the Visa credit card, you decide to check this option automatically. If customers use a different type of payment, they can click the option, but this saves time if they use a Visa card for payment.

d. Click **Design Mode** to turn off Design Mode, if necessary. Save the document. Click **Restrict Editing** in the Protect group to display the pane.

   The Restrict Formatting and Editing pane displays.

e. Click **Allow only this type of editing in the document**, which displays in the *2. Editing restrictions* section. Click the down arrow in the box below this option, and then select **Filling in forms**, if necessary. Click **Yes, Start Enforcing Protection** in the *3. Start enforcement* section.

> **TROUBLESHOOTING:** If *Yes, Start Enforcing Protection* is grayed out, make sure you are not in Design Mode.

f. Click **OK** when the Start Enforcing Protection dialog box displays.

   If you want to password-protect a document, you can insert and confirm the password in this dialog box. Remember that if you forget the password, you cannot recover it and your document cannot be opened.

g. Click the **Close button** in the top-right corner of the Restrict Formatting and Editing pane. Click the **Home tab**, and then click **Show/Hide** (¶) to turn off formatting marks.

h. Save and close the document.

STEP 6 USE AN ELECTRONIC FORM

It is now time to test the electronic invoice. You will open the document template and save it as a Word document prior to entering sales information on the invoice. You will also view the automatic calculations that display to show the full amount of a purchase. If this works as designed, you will update the invoice later and add rows to the table for entering more sales. Refer to Figure 7.10 as you complete Step 6.

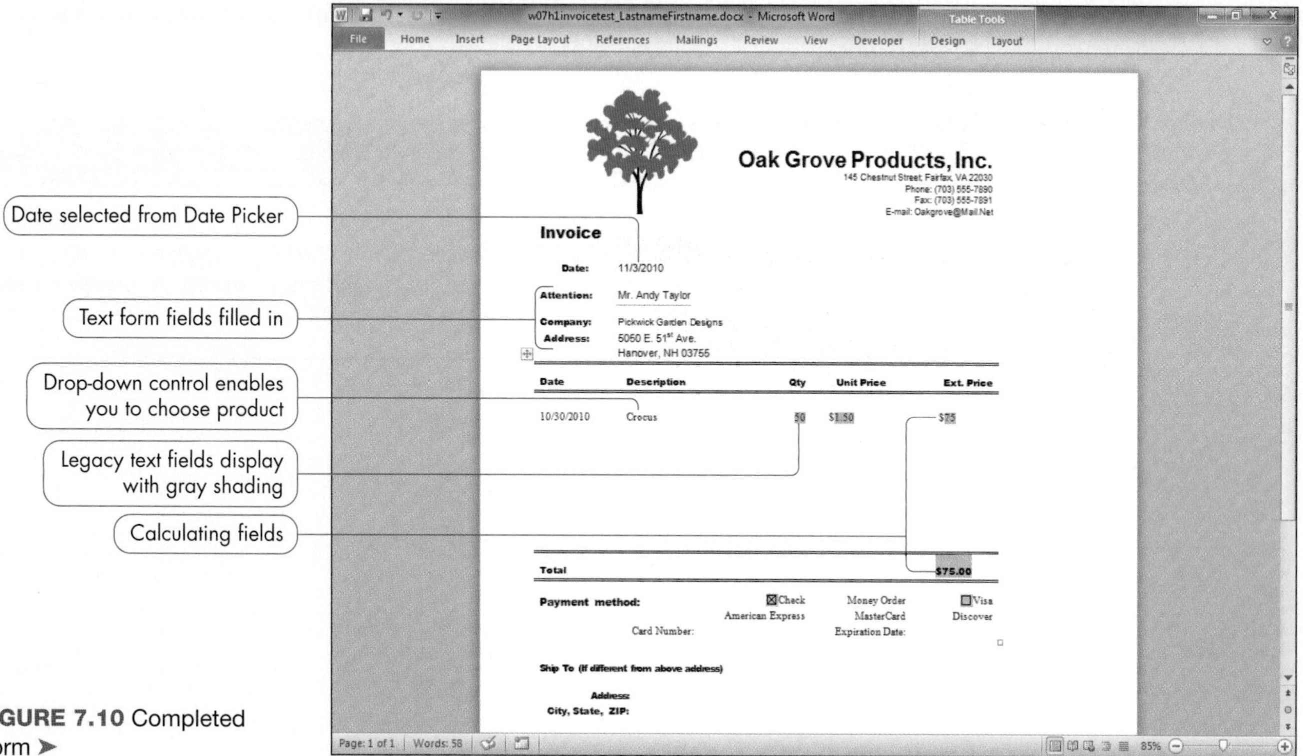

FIGURE 7.10 Completed Form ➤

a. Open the template *w07h1invoice_LastnameFirstname.dotx* and save it as a Word document named **w07h1invoicetest_LastnameFirstname**.

   Word creates the new file based on the template. By default, the first form control is selected. Notice the Ribbon is grayed out, preventing you from using the formatting commands, because the document is protected from editing. You will only be able to click and use the form controls.

b. Click the **Date Picker arrow** in the first control, which may already be selected. Click **Today**.

c. Click the words *Click here to enter text*, which display next to *Attention:*, and then type **Mr. Andy Taylor**. Press ↓.

   Word enters the name in the field and moves to the next field when you press the arrow keys.

d. Type **Pickwick Garden Designs**, press ↓, type **5050 E. 51st Ave.**, press ↓, type **Hanover, NH 03755**, and then press ↓.

e. Click the **Date Picker arrow** for the date of the first purchase, and then click **October 30** of the current year. Press **Tab**.

f. Click one time on the **Description field**, and then click the **Description arrow** to display the list of bulbs. Select **Crocus** from the list.

g. Double-click the **Qty control field**, type **50**, and then press **Tab**. Type **1.50** and press **Tab**.

   As soon as you click Tab to move out of the Unit Price control field, the insertion point moves forward in the form to the check box for the Check method of payment. As you continue completing the form, the calculations will take place.

h. Press the **Spacebar** to select *Check*. Press **Tab** one time, and then press **Spacebar** to deselect *Visa*. Press **Tab** two times to cycle through the text fields and update the calculations.

   You can also use your mouse to select or deselect a check box. You have completed the form, as shown in Figure 7.10.

i. Save and close the document. Exit Word if you will not continue with the next exercise at this time.

TIP Creating Hard Copy Forms

Many offices still use hard copy forms instead of electronic forms. For example, some job application forms are printed, and the job applicants must write or type on the hard copy form. These types of forms contain labels, text boxes, and check boxes. To create a hard copy form, open a document from the form template and print as many copies as you need.

Introduction to Macros

A **macro** is a set of instructions that executes a specific task.

Have you ever pulled down the same menus and clicked the same sequence of commands over and over? If you find yourself performing repetitive tasks, whether in one document or in a series of documents, you should consider using macros. A ***macro*** is a set of instructions (that is, a program) that executes a series of keystrokes, often to complete a task. Using a macro in Word is like recording your favorite television show: You turn on the DVR, record the show, and then play the show over and over again as often as you want.

A **Macro-Enabled Document** contains and enables execution of a macro.

Office 2010 enables you to save documents with macros automatically enabled or disabled. By default, Word documents with the .docx extension automatically disable any macros the file might contain. If you store a macro in a document, save it as a ***Macro-Enabled Document***, which adds the extension .docm to the file and stores VBA macro code in the document to enable execution of a macro.

In this lesson, you will record a macro that enables you to update and make repetitive modifications to the invoice you are updating for the Oak Grove Products company. Specifically, you will place additional form controls in the payment section you started in Hands-On Exercise 1. You will run the macro, and then you will modify the macro using the editor.

Recording a Macro

Record macro is the process of creating a macro.

The process of creating a macro is called ***record macro***. When you record a macro, Word records a series of keystrokes and command selections, and then converts the tasks into coded statements. Before recording a macro, you should decide what you want to accomplish (such as formatting a letter), and then plan exactly what commands and tasks to include (such as margins, alignment, tabs, and so on). Furthermore, you should practice completing the tasks and commands, and make notes of the sequence of steps to perform. Doing so helps you record the macro successfully the first time.

The macro commands are located on two tabs: the View tab and the Developer tab. You can start recording a macro by clicking the Macros arrow on the View tab, and then select Record Macro. On the Developer tab, you click Record Macro in the Code group. The Record Macro dialog box opens so that you can name the macro, as shown in Figure 7.11. You have the option of assigning the macro to a button, which can be assigned to the Quick Access Toolbar so that it is readily available, or you can assign a keystroke combination that runs the macro. If you do not choose either option, the macro is only available in the Macros dialog box. You also have the choice of storing a macro in a particular file, so that it can only be executed when that file is open, or you can store macros in the normal template so that they can run in all files.

When you close the Record Macro dialog box, Word records everything—every keystroke and click of the mouse. For this reason, you do not want to perform any unnecessary actions while recording a macro. For example, if you press Ctrl+Home to correct a mistake while recording the macro, Word records the command to move the insertion point to the beginning of the document. This is problematic if you run the macro in an existing document and the macro inserts or formats text in the wrong location. Keep in mind that it is easy to delete a macro that does not function as you intend, and record it again.

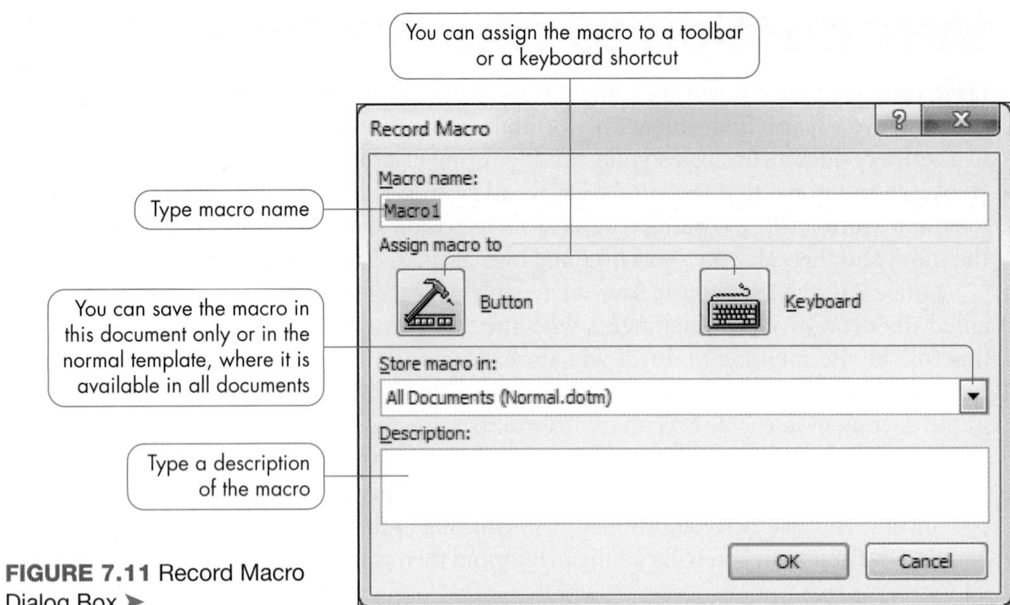
You can assign the macro to a toolbar or a keyboard shortcut
Type macro name
You can save the macro in this document only or in the normal template, where it is available in all documents
Type a description of the macro
Record Macro
Macro name:
Macro1
Assign macro to
Button
Keyboard
Store macro in:
All Documents (Normal.dotm)
Description:
OK
Cancel

FIGURE 7.11 Record Macro Dialog Box ➤

You can type text to include in a macro. If you want the macro text to contain character attributes, such as bold or font color, you should turn on the attribute before typing that particular text, type the text, and then turn off that attribute. While recording a macro, Word does not let you click and drag to select text to be able to apply formatting. If you already typed text and want to add an attribute while recording, you can select the text by pressing Shift and →. You can then apply the attribute you want to the selected text.

Edit a Macro

Visual Basic for Applications (VBA) is a programming language that is built into Microsoft Office.

Macro instructions are written in ***Visual Basic for Applications (VBA)***, a programming language that is built into Microsoft Office. Fortunately, however, you don't have to be a programmer to use VBA. Instead, the macro recorder within Word records your actions, which are then translated automatically into VBA. If you need to edit a macro, you can edit the statements after they have been recorded by opening the Visual Basic editor. The Developer tab includes the Visual Basic command, which opens the Visual Basic editor and displays the macro contents as programming statements, a set of code written in a specific syntax created by a particular programming language, such as Visual Basic. Each programming statement performs a specific task, such as setting a margin. Figure 7.12 displays the macro you will create in Hands-On Exercise 2.

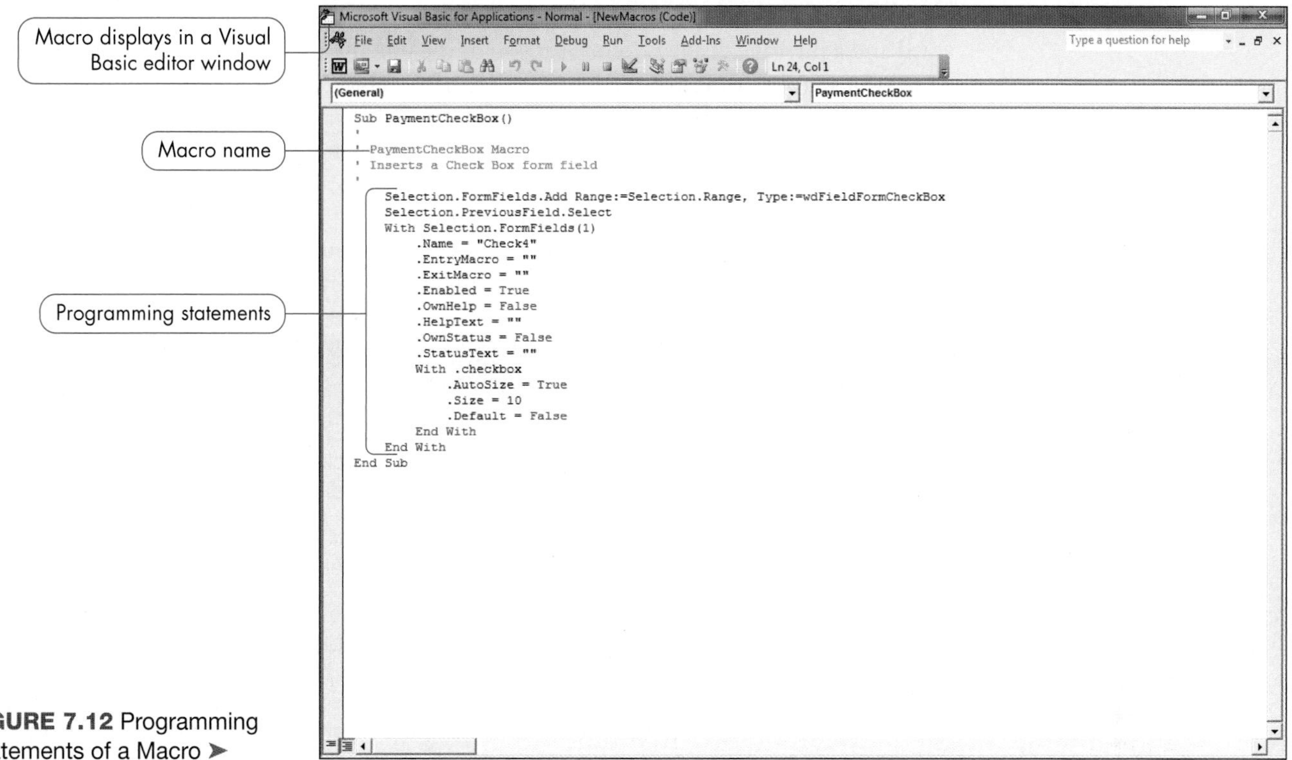

FIGURE 7.12 Programming Statements of a Macro ➤

It is helpful to have some knowledge of the Visual Basic programming language and how it works. When possible, you can make minor adjustments to improve the speed and efficiency of the macro. Every time you choose a dialog box option for a macro, the macro recorder records all dialog box settings, even those you do not change, such as the default font size.

When you record macros, Word saves them in the Normal template by default so that you can use them with other documents. Within the Normal template, macros are stored in a macro project called NewMacros, which is a collection of macros you create. You can copy a macro project to another template or document. To copy the NewMacros project to another template or document, click the Developer tab, and then click Macros. Click Organizer within the Macros dialog box. Specify the destination document or template in the list box on the left side of the dialog box, click NewMacros in the In Normal.dotm list box, and then click Copy. Use Help for more specific information on using the Organizer dialog box.

If you no longer need the macros, you can delete them from within the Macros dialog box. Select the name of the macro you want to delete, and then click Delete. Follow the onscreen prompts.

Security Risks of Macros

Because macros are coded in a Visual Basic application, they are essentially programs. As a program that executes commands, a macro has the potential to include code that imposes harmful viruses onto your computer. Microsoft Office includes a Trust Center to help protect users from unsafe macros. The Trust Center checks for the following scenarios before enabling a macro:

- The macro is signed by the developer using a digital signature.
- The digital signature is valid.
- The digital signature is not expired.
- The certificate associated with the digital signature was issued by a known certificate authority.
- The person who signed the macro is a trusted publisher.

If the Trust Center does not find any of these scenarios, the macro is automatically disabled and a message displays to inform you of the potential risk. You can edit the settings on your PC according to your preference for security. Table 7.2 describes the settings from the Trust Center in the Options dialog box.

To change the macro security settings, click File, click Options, click Trust Center, click Trust Center Settings, and then click Macro Settings, if necessary. Alternately, if the Developer tab is available, you can click Macro Security in the Code group to display the Trust Center dialog box and view the settings. When you change the settings in the Trust Center, they are only valid for the program you are currently using, such as Word 2010.

TABLE 7.2 Macro Security Settings

Macro Setting	Description
Disable all macros without notification.	If you do not trust macros, click this option. All macros and security alerts about macros are disabled.
Disable all macros with notification.	This is the default setting. All macros are disabled, but it alerts you when a document contains a macro.
Disable all macros except digitally signed macros.	This setting works similarly to Disable all macros with notification; however, it enables macros to run if they are digitally signed by a trusted publisher. If you have not included the publisher in your trusted list, you will be alerted about the macro. The alert enables you to allow a macro or to include a publisher in your trusted list. All unsigned macros are disabled and you will not see an alert.
Enable all macros (not recommended; potentially dangerous code can run).	This setting enables all macros to run regardless of their authenticity or signature. This option is not recommended because it exposes your computer to potential attacks by viruses.
Trust access to the VBA project object model.	This setting is for use by developers only.

If you open a document that contains macros and a security warning displays the message *Macros have been disabled*, you can click Options and display the Microsoft Office Security Options dialog box. From there, click Enable this content, and then click OK to return to the document and use any macros that were stored within the document.

Running a Macro

Run macro is the process of playing back or using a macro.

The process of playing back or using a macro is called ***run macro***. When you run a macro, Word processes the series of commands and keystrokes saved in the macro. Running a macro is faster than manually choosing each command when you need to use a series of commands frequently. To open the Macros dialog box, you have three options:

- Display the Developer tab, and then click Macros.
- Display the View tab, and then click Macros, View Macros.
- Press Alt+F8.

With the Macros dialog box open, as shown in Figure 7.13, you can run, edit, or delete a macro.

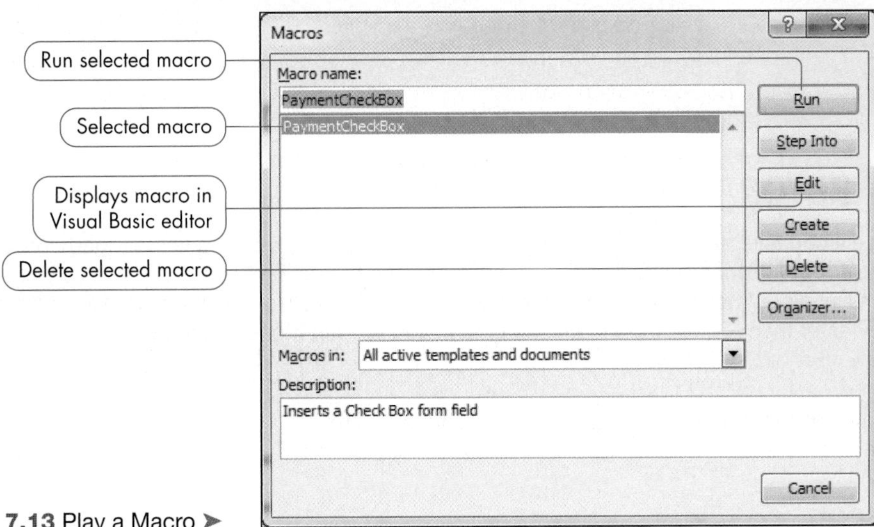

FIGURE 7.13 Play a Macro ➤

If your macro includes a command that types text, that text takes on the current document's formats when you run the macro. If you specially formatted the text while recording a macro, that special format is retained when you run the macro, regardless of the document's other formats.

2 Introduction to Macros

After modifying the invoice, you realize it can take several minutes to insert form fields one by one; if a field property needs changing, the time increases even more. But knowing that using a macro can shorten the time it takes for repetitive tasks, you decide to create a macro to update the invoice. After playing the macro to confirm how it works, you might make modifications using the Visual Basic editor, which is faster than re-creating the macro. Finally, you will run it one last time to finish revisions to the invoice.

Skills covered: Record a Macro • Play a Macro • Modify a Macro • Run an Edited Macro

STEP 1 RECORD A MACRO

After a successful test of the electronic invoice you created, you want to insert additional check boxes in the payment options section of the invoice. Instead of inserting each check box individually, you create a macro to insert them and change the property settings for that form control. Refer to Figure 7.14 as you complete Step 1.

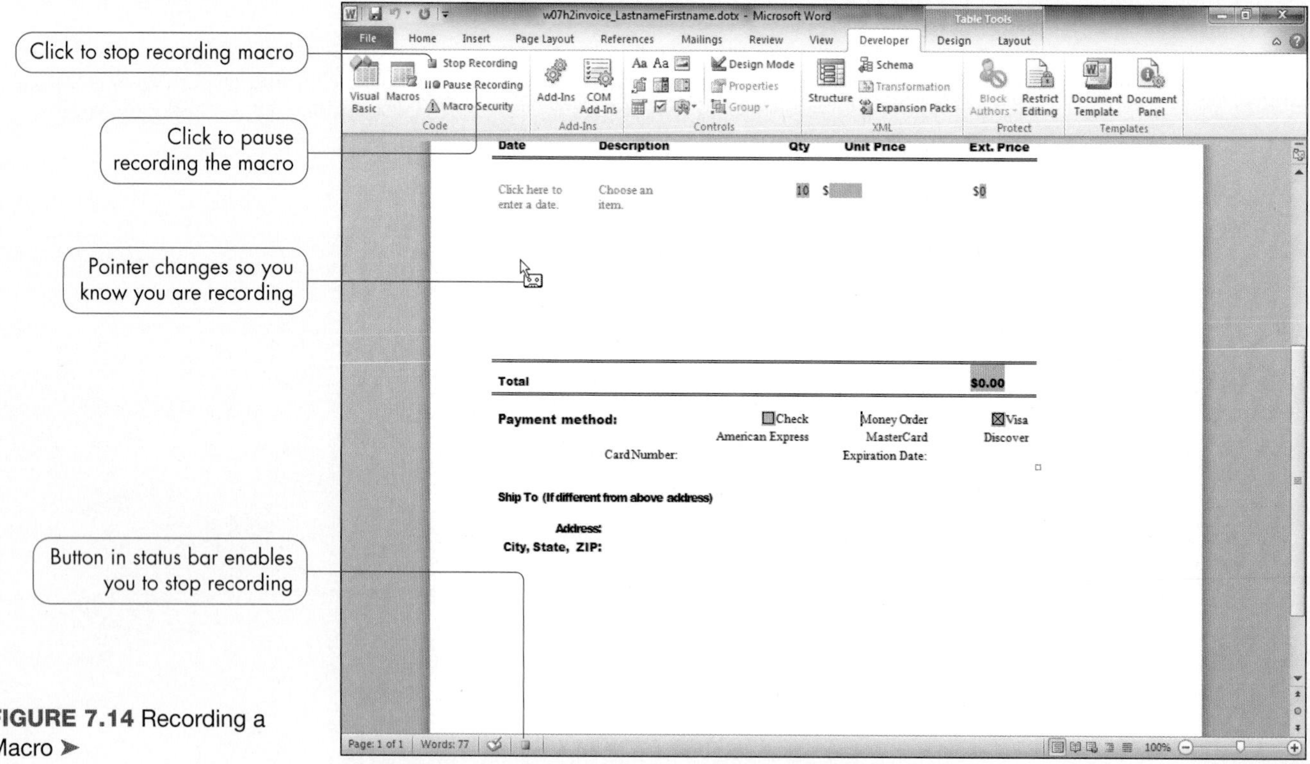

FIGURE 7.14 Recording a Macro ➤

a. Open *w07h1invoice_LastnameFirstname.dotx* and save it as a Word template named **w07h2invoice_LastnameFirstname**.

b. Click the **Developer tab**, and then click **Restrict Editing** to display the Restrict Formatting and Editing pane. Click **Stop Protection**. Close the Restrict Formatting and Editing pane.

   You must remove the form protection so you can edit the invoice.

c. Click to position the insertion point on the left side of the *Money Order* payment method.

d. Click **Record Macro** in the Code group.

The Record Macro dialog box displays so that you can name the macro before you record it. The macro name can consist of up to 80 characters, but no spaces.

> **TROUBLESHOOTING:** If the Developer tab does not display, click File, click Options, click Customize Ribbon, and then click Developer below the Customize the Ribbon pane on the right side of the window. Click OK to return to the document.

e. Type **PaymentCheckBox** in the **Macro name box.**

You want to provide a short description in addition to your name and the current date.

f. Click at the beginning of the **Description box**, and then type **Inserts a Check Box form field.**

g. Assign a keyboard shortcut to run the macro by completing the following steps:

- Click **Keyboard** to display the Customize Keyboard dialog box.
- Press **Alt+B**.
- Click **Assign**, and then click **Close.**

Later, after you complete the macro, you will click the keyboard combination Alt+B to execute it. The macro is saved in this document template only.

h. Click **OK** to start recording, if necessary.

Word assigns the macro name you entered. You see *Stop Recording* and *Pause Recording* display in the Code group of the Developer tab. The mouse pointer looks like an arrow with an attached recorder. A square button displays on the status bar, as shown in Figure 7.14; if you click it, the macro will stop recording.

i. Perform the following steps to create the macro:

- Click **Legacy tools** in the control group.
- Click **Check Box Form Field.**
- Click **Properties.**
- Click **Checked** in the *Default value* section.
- Click **OK.**

You insert a check box field that displays already checked next to the Money Order payment method.

> **TROUBLESHOOTING:** If you click something unintentionally or decide you are too far off track for the macro, click Stop Recording. Repeat the steps to begin recording again. You can use the same macro name and description; allow the new macro to overwrite the first attempt when prompted to replace it.

j. Click **Stop Recording.**

You can also click the gray square button in the Status bar to stop recording a macro.

k. Save the document.

STEP 2 PLAY A MACRO

Now that you have a macro that inserts the box to check when indicating the form of payment, you want to run the macro to display the box by other forms of payment. Refer to Figure 7.15 as you complete Step 2.

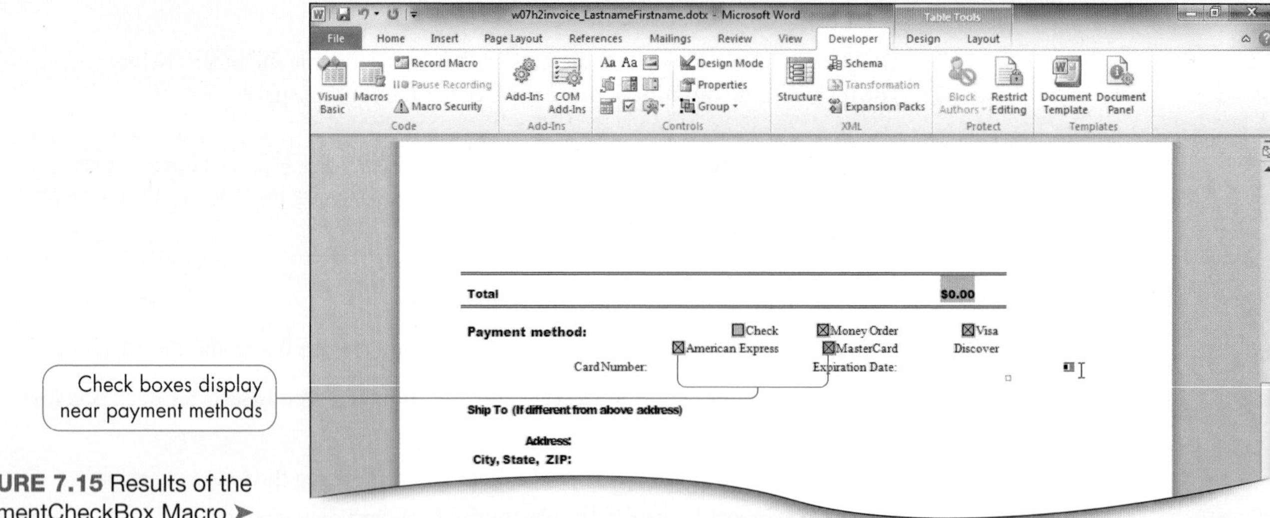
Check boxes display near payment methods

FIGURE 7.15 Results of the PaymentCheckBox Macro ➤

a. Click to position the insertion point on the left side of the payment method *American Express.*

> **TIP** Make a Backup
>
> To avoid destroying a document due to macro problems, you should save the document prior to running a macro. If the macro does not provide the desired results, you can close the document, and then open the original document again.

b. Click **Macros** in the Code group.

   The macros dialog box displays and the PaymentCheckBox macro is the only macro available to run.

c. Click **PaymentCheckBox**, if necessary, and then click **Run**.

   Word runs the macro and inserts a checked box next to the American Express payment method.

> **TROUBLESHOOTING:** The macro security level is too high if you receive a message stating that macros are disabled. A high security level protects you from running a macro that contains a virus. To disable this security so the macro can run, click Macro Security on the Developer tab, click *Enable all macros (not recommended; potentially dangerous code can run)*, and then click OK. Be sure to reset the security to *Disable all macros with notification* after completing this exercise.

d. Click to position the insertion point on the left side of the payment method *MasterCard*, and then click **Alt+B**.

   Word runs the macro again and inserts a checked box next to the MasterCard payment method. (See Figure 7.15.)

e. Save the document.

STEP 3 MODIFY A MACRO

The macro works well, but you realize that you only want one of the payment methods to be checked by default. Rather than delete each one and start all over, you modify the macro using the Visual Basic editor. Then you run the macro again to replace the incorrectly checked boxes. Refer to Figure 7.16 as you complete Step 3.

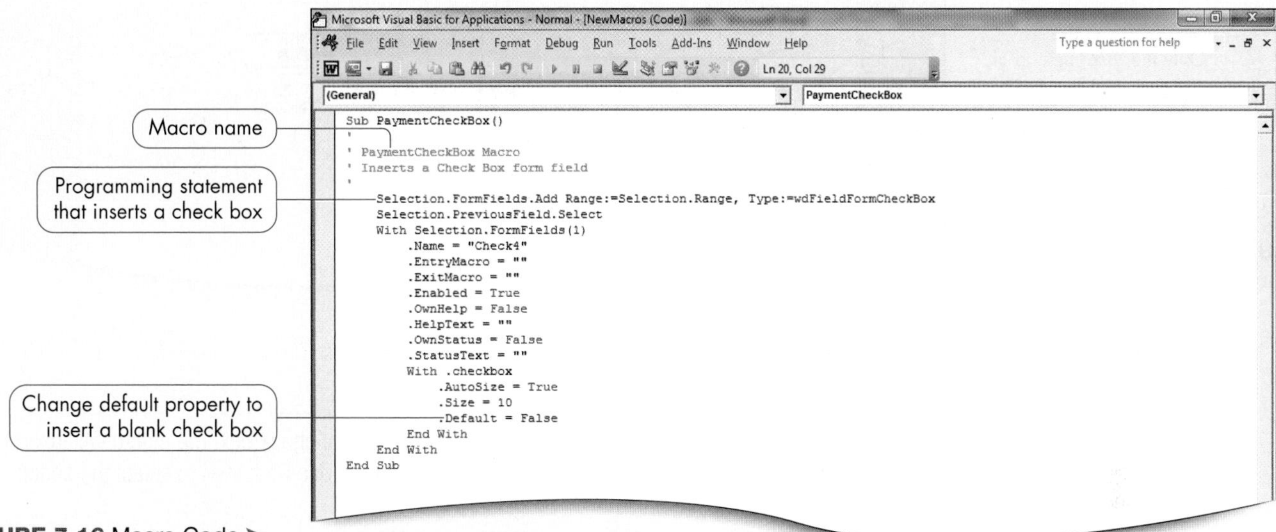

FIGURE 7.16 Macro Code ➤

a. Press **Alt+F8** to display the Macros dialog box. Select **PaymentCheckBox** in the **Macro name list**, and then click **Edit**.

   The Visual Basic Editor opens so that you can edit the programming statements. You will modify the .Default statement near the end of the code, which shows a *True* value; this causes the box to display as checked.

b. Delete the word *True* at the end of the statement *Default = True*, and then replace it with the word **False**, as shown in Figure 7.16.

> **TROUBLESHOOTING:** Do not delete any other part of the Default statement or any other statements. If you do, the macro may not run correctly. If you accidentally delete programming statements, refer to Figure 7.16 to retype them, and then edit the Default statement again.

c. Click **Save Normal** on the toolbar.

d. Click **File**, and then click **Close and Return to Microsoft Word**.

   You are ready to run the macro again to replace the checked boxes with boxes that are not checked.

e. Save the document.

STEP 4 RUN AN EDITED MACRO

Now that your macro is revised, you can replace the checked boxes for each payment method on the invoice. You want to leave only one box checked—the one that displays beside the Visa payment method. You select each one individually and run the macro to replace the form field check boxes. Refer to Figure 7.17 as you complete Step 4.

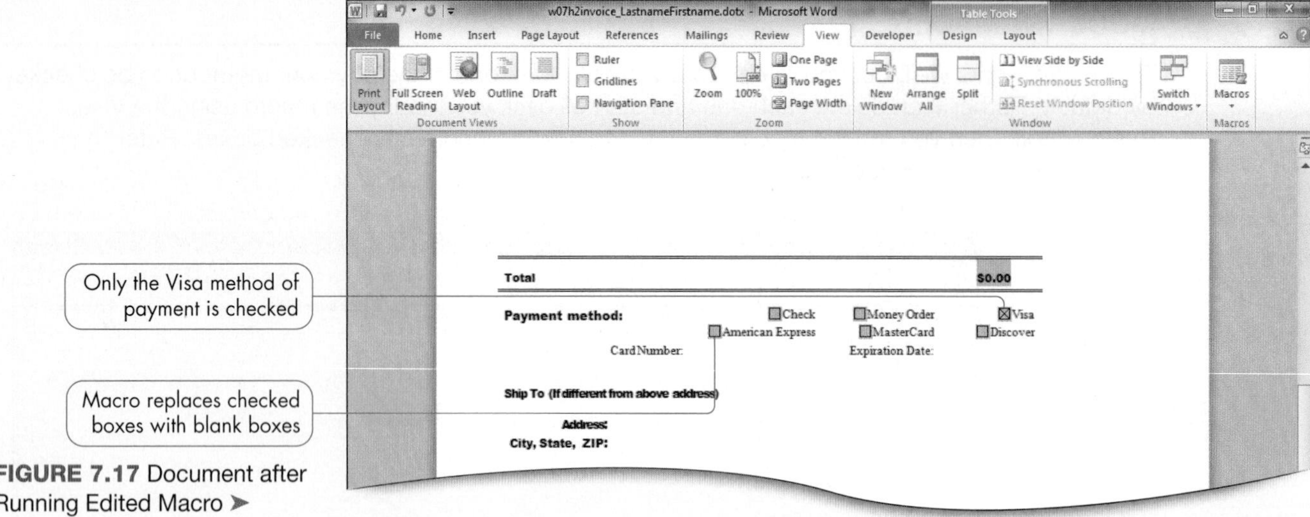

FIGURE 7.17 Document after Running Edited Macro ➤

a. Select the checked box that displays beside *Money Order.*

> **TROUBLESHOOTING:** If you do not properly select the original check box, the macro will insert a second check box beside the Money Order payment method. Use Shift+→ to select the check box, if necessary.

b. Click the **View tab**, click the **Macros arrow**, and then click **View Macros**.

   The Macros dialog box displays so that you can run a macro.

c. Click **PaymentCheckBox** in the Macro name box, and then click **Run**.

   The checked box is replaced by a box that does not display as checked.

d. Select the checked box that displays beside *American Express*, and then press **Alt+B**.

e. Press **Alt+B** to replace the checked box beside *MasterCard*, position the insertion point beside *Discover*, and then run the macro again.

   After you run the macro, all payment types display beside a box, and only the Visa payment displays beside a checked box, as shown in Figure 7.17.

f. Press **Ctrl+S** to save the document template. Click **File**, click **Save As**, click the **Save as type arrow**, and then select **Word Macro-Enabled Template (*.dotm)**. Click **Save** to save the template as **w07h2invoice_LastnameFirstname.dotm.**

g. Close the document. Exit Word if you will not continue with the next exercise at this time.

Document Protection and Authentication

As you work with documents containing confidential information, you might want to protect those documents from unauthorized access. In other situations, you might need to store reference documents, such as policies and procedures, on an organization's network for others to read but not change. You might also want to assure document recipients that particular documents have come from you and have not been tampered with during transit. To assist in situations such as these, Word provides tools that enable you to protect your documents on many levels.

In this section, you will learn to restrict permissions to documents against unauthorized access, formatting, or content changes. You also will learn how to mark a document as final, set passwords, and add digital signatures.

Applying Document Restrictions

Word provides a variety of ways to save a file to preserve the content or the formatting applied to the content. Some features enable you to protect the contents of a file so that anyone else who opens it cannot change the contents in any way. Other features allow the content to be altered, but restrict the use of formatting tools such as the bold feature or predefined styles. You can use these restrictive features independently or in combination with others.

Mark a Document as Final

Mark as Final creates a read-only file and also sets the property to Final on the status bar.

You may have occasion to share a file with other people, but before you send it you want to make it a read-only file, which prevents others from changing the document. The ***Mark as Final*** command enables you to create a read-only file and sets the property to Final on the status bar. To alert the reader to this status, it displays an icon in the status bar to indicate the file is in its final form, as shown in Figure 7.18. This is a helpful command for communicating with other people that the document is not a draft but a completed and final version. It also prevents unintentional changes to the document. When marked as final, typing, editing, and proofing marks do not display; all commands in the Ribbon are grayed out; and the document cannot be modified. To use this command, click File, click Protect Document, and then select Mark as Final.

Even though this feature provides a way to communicate the status of the document and enables you to set it as read-only, it does not completely secure the document. Mark as Final is a toggle setting and anyone can remove the status from the document as easily as it is set. Additionally, if you use the Mark as Final command on a Word 2010 document, it will not retain the read-only status if opened in an earlier version of Word.

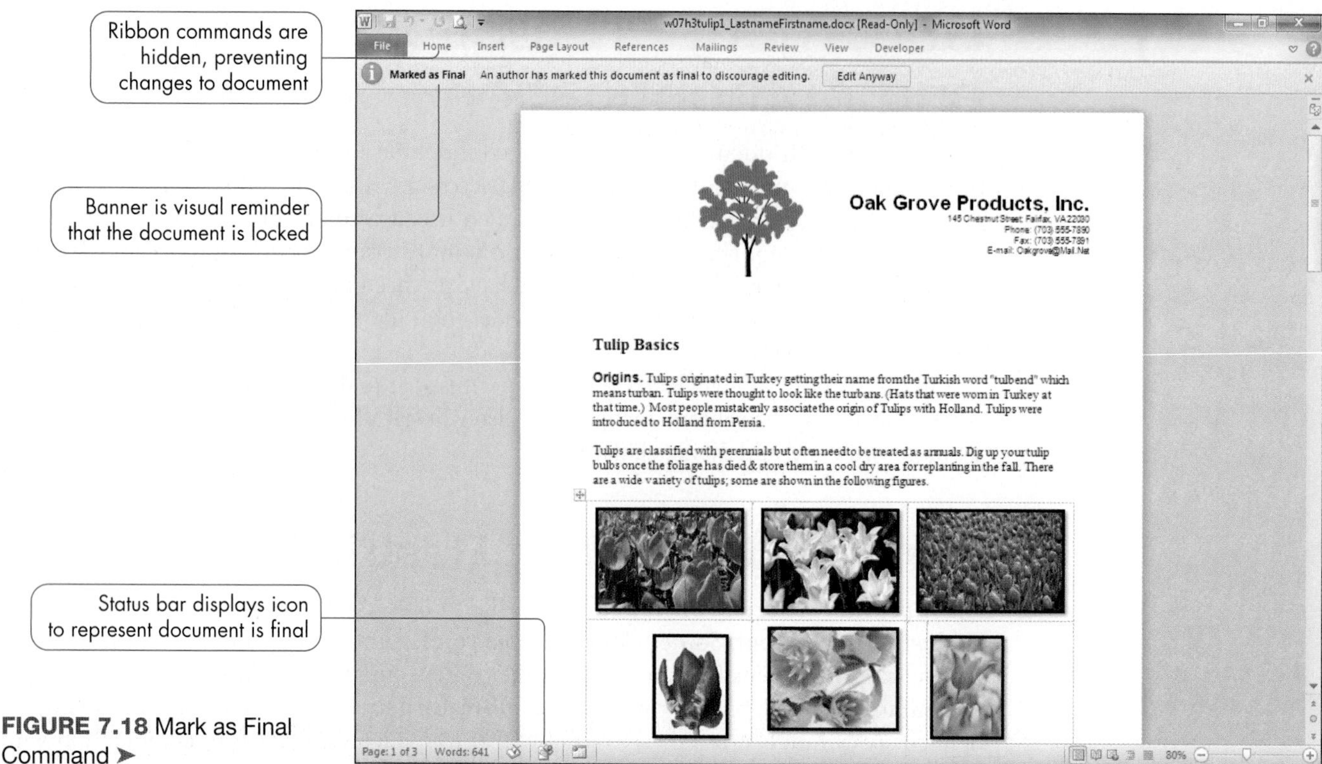

FIGURE 7.18 Mark as Final Command ➤

Set Formatting Restrictions

A **formatting restriction** guarantees that others do not modify formatting or styles in a document.

Organizations often use specific styles and formatting to ensure consistency among documents. The person who oversees document formatting might create or modify styles that should not be changed by other users. To ensure that others do not modify formatting or styles, you can set ***formatting restrictions*** on documents. When you set formatting restrictions, character formatting tools, such as bold and font size, are unavailable, as shown in Figure 7.19. Users cannot click Bold or press Ctrl+B to bold text.

To ensure that others do not modify formatting or styles, you can set formatting restrictions on documents. When you set formatting restrictions, character formatting tools, such as bold and font size, are unavailable....

FIGURE 7.19 Formatting Restrictions Disable Commands on the Home Tab ➤

In addition to restricting character format tools, Word also prevents users from changing the formats for font, paragraph, column, drop caps, bullets and numbering, and tabs. You may apply approved styles, such as Heading 1, to text. However, you cannot apply styles that you have restricted. For example, if you restrict the Heading 3 style, you cannot apply that style to text. Furthermore, you cannot modify the format settings for any styles, even those the user is authorized to apply.

To set formatting restrictions on a document, click Restrict Editing on the Review tab to display the Restrict Formatting and Editing pane. Then click Limit formatting to a selection of styles. Click Settings to display the Formatting Restrictions dialog box, where you specify exactly which formatting options to disable.

Set Editing Restrictions

An **editing restriction** specifies limits for users to modify a document.

When you set formatting restrictions, Word does not prevent you from changing content in a document. You might also want to set editing restrictions on particular documents. ***Editing restrictions*** specify limits for users to modify a document. For example, you might set the Tracked changes editing restriction to make sure the Track Changes feature is active when users make any changes to the document. Doing so lets you know what edits are made to collaborative documents, even if the users forget to activate Track Changes themselves. Other types of editing restrictions include limiting users to inserting comments without changing document content, restricting data entry to fields or unprotected areas within a form, and preventing users from making any changes to a letterhead template.

To set editing restrictions on a document, click Restrict Editing in the Protect group on the Review tab, and then click Allow only this type of editing in the document. After you click this setting, you can select from four editing restrictions, as outlined in Table 7.3. After the restriction is selected, click Yes, Start Enforcing Protection to activate it.

TABLE 7.3 Editing Restrictions

Restriction Type	Description
Tracked Changes	Enables the track changes feature automatically and marks document with any changes made.
Comments	Users can add comments to document, but cannot make any other changes.
Filling in Forms	Users can insert information into form controls or fields, but cannot modify other content.
No Changes (Read Only)	Users cannot make any changes to the document; they can only view it.

Allow User Exceptions from Restrictions

A **user exception** is an individual or group that is allowed to edit a restricted document.

If you apply the editing restriction *Comments* or *No changes (Read only)*, you can specify user exceptions. A ***user exception*** is an individual or group of individuals who are allowed to edit all or specific parts of a restricted document. For example, you might want all team members to edit only a particular section of a collaborative document. You can create an exception by enabling users to edit that section only. You can create various user exceptions throughout a document by enabling some individuals to edit particular text, while enforcing the editing restrictions for other individuals. Word color-codes text for which you create different user exceptions.

The default check box in the Exceptions list is Everyone. You can add individual users or groups to the list of exceptions. Click *More users* to open the Add Users dialog box, as shown in Figure 7.20. Type user names, domains, or e-mail addresses for individuals you want to add, separated by semicolons, and click OK. After you add users, you can continue selecting text and clicking the appropriate user name to create a user exception for editing text.

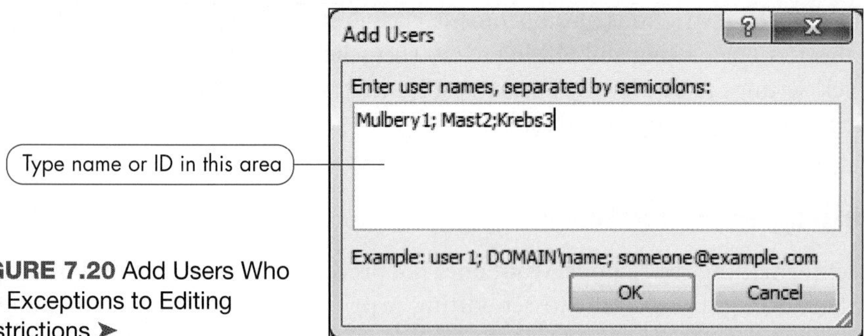

FIGURE 7.20 Add Users Who Are Exceptions to Editing Restrictions ➤

Information Rights Management (IRM) services are designed to help control who can access documents.

You must install a special service to add users in the Add Users dialog box. ***Information Rights Management (IRM)*** services are designed to help you control who can access documents containing sensitive or confidential information. By using an IRM, you can specify different users and the types of permissions you grant to them. If the IRM Services Client is not installed on your computer, a prompt to download it will display when you try to open files that have been rights-managed. Follow the prompts to download and install the software. If you work in a network lab, you might not be able to install it. Use Help to learn more about permissions, IRM, and adding users as exceptions.

Remove Editing Restrictions

To remove editing restrictions, click Stop Protection on the Restrict Formatting and Editing pane. If the formatting restrictions are password-protected, you must enter the correct password, and then click OK. If you did not assign a password, the restrictions are automatically removed. If you applied both formatting and editing restrictions, clicking Stop Protection removes both types of restrictions. If you want to remove only one type of restriction, you must reset the restriction you want to continue to enforce in the Restrict Formatting and Editing pane.

Setting Passwords to Open a Document

When creating the form in Hands-On Exercise 1, you had the opportunity to set a password for the document. Setting passwords is one way to secure a document. For example, you might want to password-protect highly confidential documents from being opened by unauthorized users. This is helpful when you need to store a document on a network drive but do not want everyone to be able to open the document. When you assign a password to the document, only those who know the password can open the document. Passwords are case-sensitive, meaning they must match upper- and lowercase letters perfectly. They may consist of letters, numbers, and symbols; a good password will use a combination of all three. You may even use a combination of upper- and lowercase characters, such as EW7_proj_2.

To set a password that must be entered before a document will open, click File, click Save As, click Tools, and then click General Options, as shown in Figure 7.21. Type your password in the *Password to open* box, and then click OK. The Confirm Password dialog box will prompt you to reenter the password. After you retype the password, click OK to close the dialog box, and then save the document.

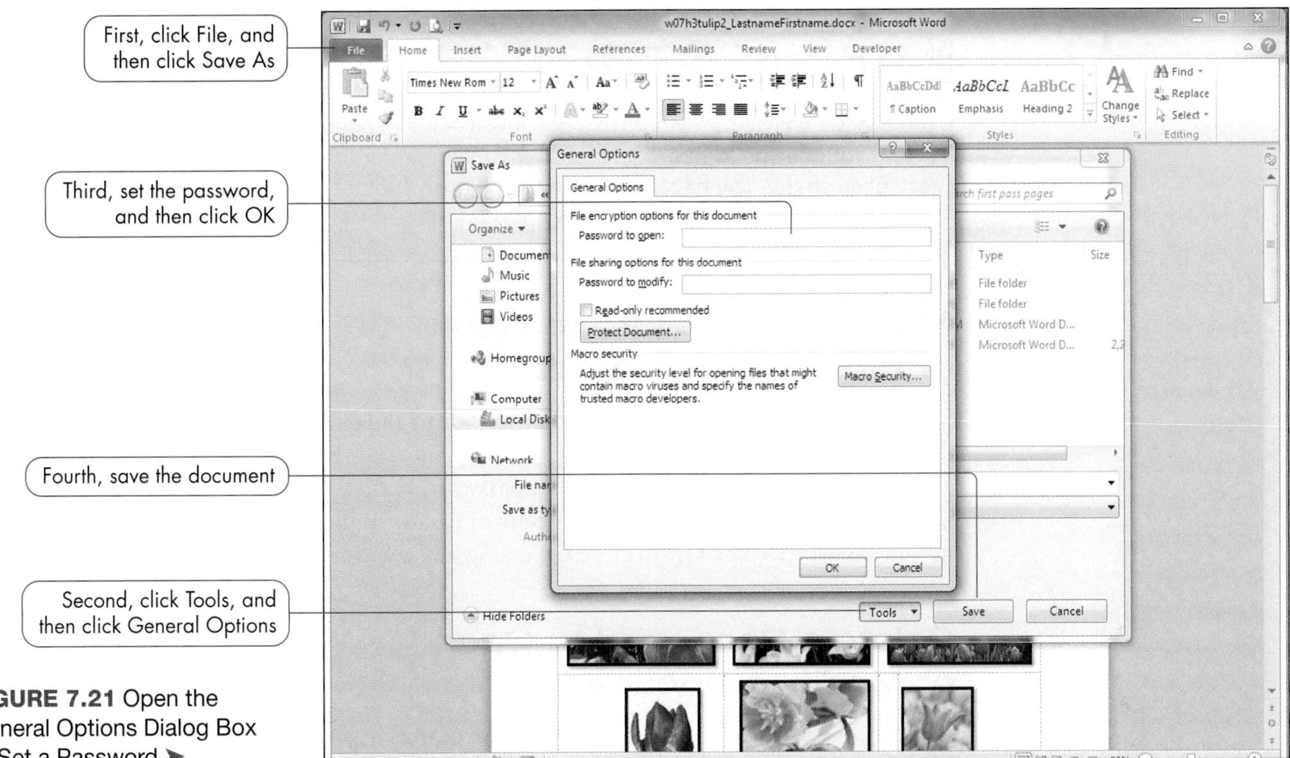

FIGURE 7.21 Open the General Options Dialog Box to Set a Password ➤

Set a Password to Modify a Document

You may want to allow others to open a document but not be able to modify the content. To restrict users from modifying a document, click File, click Save As, click Tools, and then click General Options. Type your password in the *Password to modify* box, and then click OK. You can set a password containing up to 15 characters. The Confirm Password dialog box will prompt you to reenter the password, and then you click OK. You return to the Save As dialog box, where you can proceed to save the document. People can now open the document, but they must know the password to modify the document. When users attempt to open a document protected against unauthorized modifications, the Password dialog box opens (see Figure 7.22).

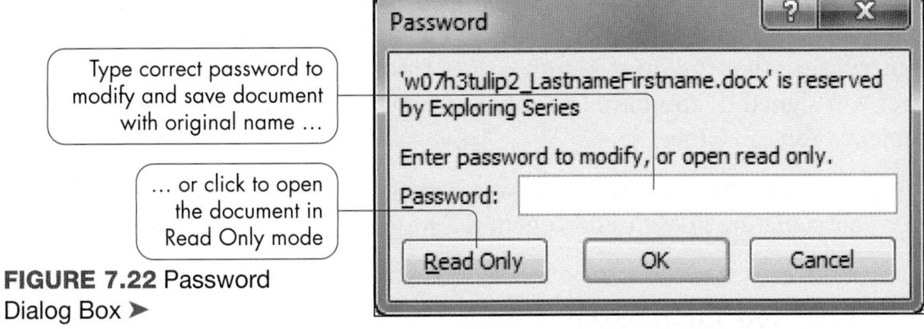

FIGURE 7.22 Password Dialog Box ➤

Authorized users can type the password in the Password box and click OK. They are able to make changes and save the document with those changes. Users who do not know the password can click Read Only to open the document in Read Only mode. In this mode, users can make changes; however, they cannot save those changes to the original file. They must choose a different folder or specify a different file name for saving the document through the Save As dialog box.

Set Passwords to Open and Modify a Document

You can assign two passwords to a document—one to open it and another to modify the content. If you choose to use both types, you might prefer to use different passwords for each restriction so that you have the option to authorize another person to open the document, by giving them the first password, but not to modify it.

Modify a Password to Open or Modify a Document

If you want to change a password, you must know the current password to open or modify the document. With the document open, click File, click Save As, click Tools, and then click General Options. Type the replacement password in the *Password to open* or the *Password to modify* box, and then click OK. The Confirm Password dialog box will prompt you to reenter the password. Click OK to close the dialog box, and then save the document again.

Delete a Password to Open or Modify a Document

You can remove a password for opening or modifying a document if you decide you no longer want to protect the document with a password. To remove the password, open the document by using the current password for opening or modifying the document. With the document open, click File, click Save As, click Tools, and then click General Options. Select the password in the *Password to open* or the *Password to modify* box, and then press Delete on the keyboard to remove it. Click OK to close the dialog box, and then save the document.

Using Digital Signatures to Authenticate Documents

A **digital certificate** is an attachment to a file that guarantees the authenticity of the file, provides a verifiable signature, or enables encryption.

Word uses Microsoft Authenticode technology to enable you to digitally sign a file by using a ***digital certificate***—an attachment to a file or e-mail that guarantees the authenticity of the file, provides a verifiable signature, or enables encryption. This authentication is important because as you share files with others, you increase your risk of having files tampered with or infected with a virus. By adding a digital signature to your documents, you confirm through electronic encryption that the information comes from you, is valid, and has not been changed after you signed it. You have two different ways to use digital signatures to sign Office documents. You can either:

- Add an invisible digital signature to a document or
- Add visible signature lines to a document to capture one or more digital signatures.

Attach a Digital Signature

A **digital signature** is an electronic stamp that displays information about a person or organization.

When you need to confirm the authenticity of a document you can attach a digital signature. ***Digital signatures*** are electronic stamps that display information about the person or organization that obtained the certification. You can obtain a digital certificate from a certification authority such as VeriSign by completing an application and paying a fee. Some companies have in-house security administrators who issue their own digital signatures by using tools such as Microsoft Certificate Server.

If you want to create your own digital certificate for personal use, you can do so by using the Selfcert.exe application included with Microsoft Office. This certification is unauthenticated but exposes you to how digital signatures work. When you sign your document, you are validating its contents and the document remains signed until it is modified. Therefore, signing a document and attaching the signature should be the last action you take before you distribute it. Adding a digital signature causes the document to be marked as final, so it also becomes a read-only document.

To use the built-in digital signature feature, you must first save the document, and then click File. Click Protect Document, and then select Add a Digital Signature. The first time you use this feature, you will see a Microsoft Word dialog box that explains the feature and asks you to click OK. After that, your signature stamp will attach automatically, as shown in Figure 7.23, but you can change the stamp if more than one certificate is available. You can also type in the purpose for signing the document, although it is not required.

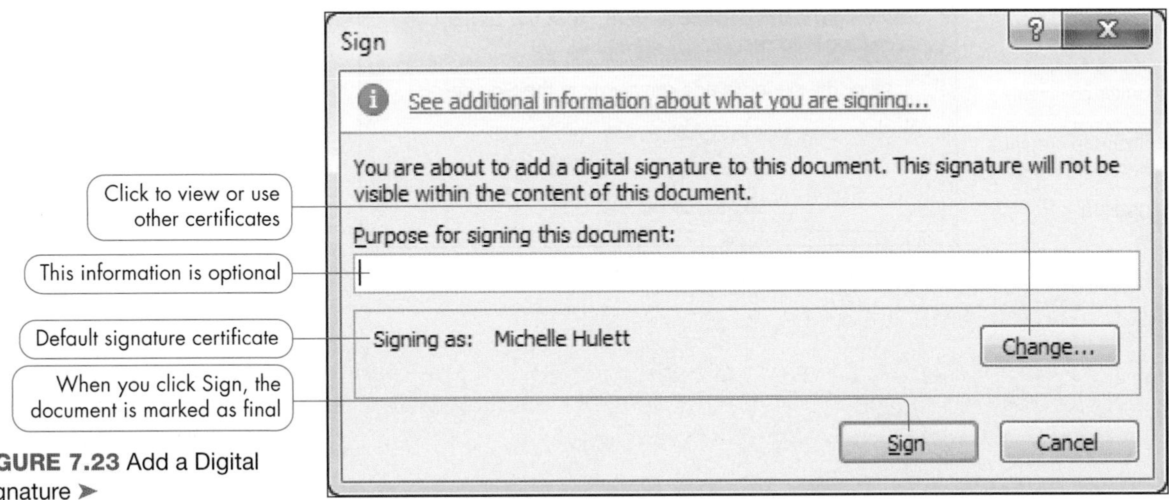

FIGURE 7.23 Add a Digital Signature ➤

You can also view and remove a digital signature from a signed document. Click File, and then click View Signatures to display the Signatures pane, which lists all signatures attached to the document. In the Signatures pane, you can click a particular signature to view a menu that includes Signature Details and Remove Signature. When all signatures are removed, the document is no longer marked as final and all formatting commands are available.

Add a Signature Line in a Document

The **signature line** enables the user of the document to digitally sign the document.

Word 2010 allows you to insert a signature line into a document. The ***signature line*** enables individuals and companies to distribute and collect signatures, and then process forms or documents electronically without the need to print and fax. The digital signatures, especially if verified by a certifying authority, provide an authentic record of the signer and enable the document to be verified in the future.

When the document opens and the signature line displays, users can type a signature, select a digital image of a signature, or write a signature if they use a tablet PC. After the user inserts his or her signature using one of the options listed above, a digital signature tag is attached to the document to authenticate the identity of the signer and the document becomes read-only to prevent modifications to the content.

To insert a signature line, click the Insert tab, click the Signature Line arrow in the Text group, and then click Microsoft Office Signature Line. Click OK to the Microsoft Word dialog box if it displays. The Signature Setup dialog box displays, as shown in Figure 7.24, and prompts you to enter information about the signer. You can enter the expected signer's name, title, e-mail address, and any additional instructions you want to display near the signature line. You can even enable signers to add comments to the document and attach the current date to the document when they sign.

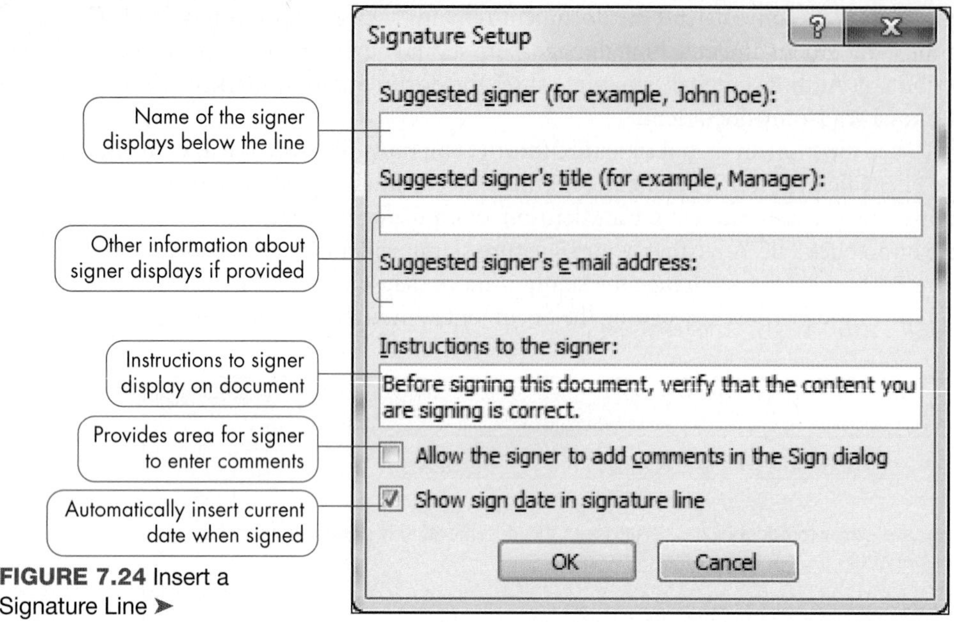

FIGURE 7.24 Insert a Signature Line ➤

3 Document Protection and Authentication

When someone purchases tulips, Cassie Artman wants to include information about bulbs in their package. You have put together a document about tulips, but you want staff members to review it for accuracy. After they return the document to you, edits will be incorporated, a final version will be saved, and you can then mark it with a digital signature. You also want to add a signature line to the invoice so that when it is delivered to a customer he or she will know it has come from the company and is a valid document.

Skills covered: Set a Password to Open a Document and Mark as Final • Set Formatting Restrictions and Modify a Document Password • Set Editing Restrictions • Set Exceptions for Restricted Documents • Attach a Digital Signature to a Document • Insert a Signature Line in a Document

STEP 1 SET A PASSWORD TO OPEN A DOCUMENT AND MARK AS FINAL

The tulip information document that will accompany all purchases has been created and you believe it to be in final form. To prevent anyone from opening it, you password-protect the file. Additionally, to prevent any accidental changes to the document when it is open, you mark it as final. Refer to Figure 7.25 as you complete Step 1.

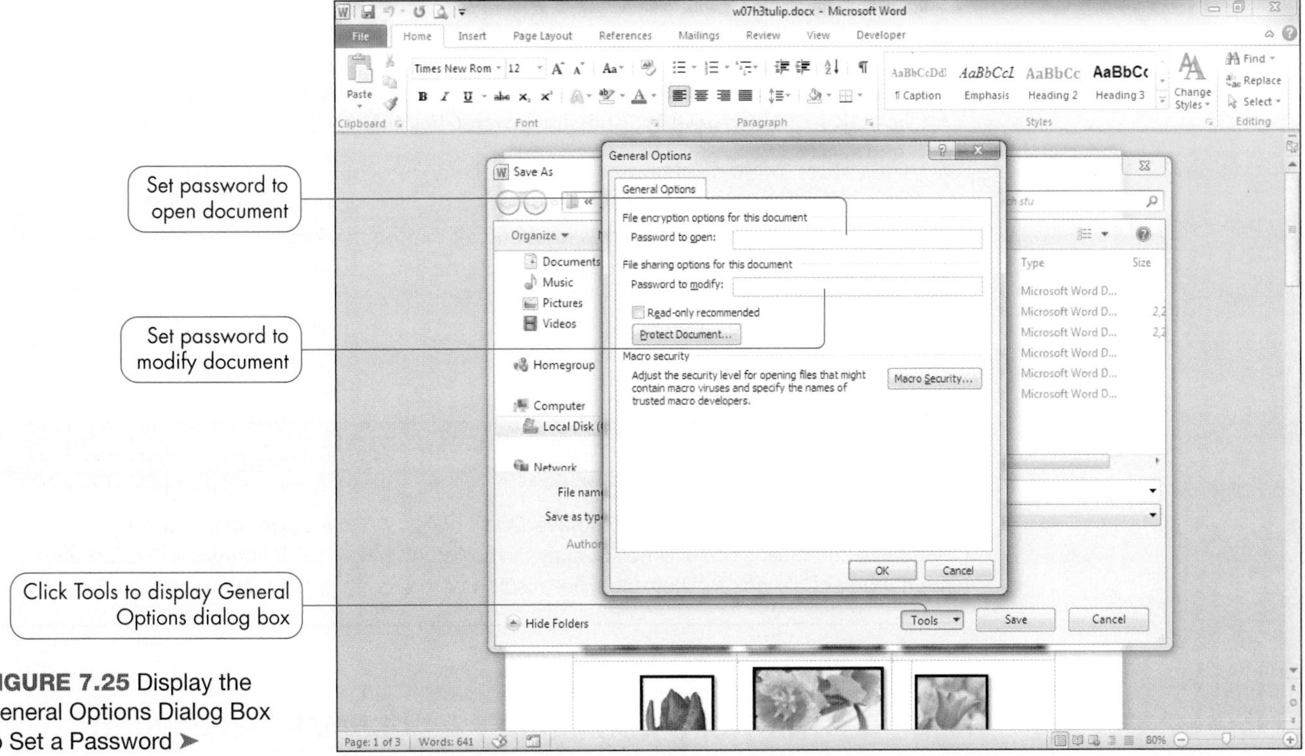

FIGURE 7.25 Display the General Options Dialog Box to Set a Password ➤

a. Open the document *w07h3tulip*.

   This is a draft of the document and you want to password-protect it until all modifications have been finalized.

b. Click **File**, and then click **Save As**. Replace the file name with **w07h3tulip1_LastnameFirstname** but do not close the Save As dialog box.

   You might prefer to click the end of the file name and add *1_FirstnameLastname* if you do not want to retype the whole file name.

c. Click **Tools**, and then click **General Options**, as shown in Figure 7.25.

The General Options dialog box displays; this is where you set passwords to open and modify a document.

TROUBLESHOOTING: The Tools menu is located in the Save As dialog box. If you closed that dialog box, click File, click Save As, and then repeat step c.

d. Type **W7h3a** in the **Password to open box**.

Security experts recommend you use a combination of upper- and lowercase letters, numbers, and special characters when you create passwords. Passwords are case-sensitive, meaning they must match upper- and lowercase letters perfectly. For that reason, you must pay special attention to capitalization when setting and using passwords to protect a document.

e. Click **OK**. In the Confirm Password dialog box, type **W7h3a** in the **Reenter password to open box**, click **OK**, and then click **Save** in the Save As dialog box.

TROUBLESHOOTING: Because passwords are case-sensitive, if you do not type the same password using the same capitalization, an error message appears stating you have not typed the same password. Click OK to close the message box, delete the passwords in the password dialog box, and then type the passwords again.

f. Click **File,** click **Protect Document**, and then click **Mark as Final** to avoid accidental editing. Click **OK** in all Microsoft Word dialog boxes. Click **File** to display the document.

Dialog boxes might display after you mark the document as final. The first informs you the document will be marked as final and then saved. The second dialog box informs you that the document has been marked as final and all editing marks are disabled. After these dialog boxes close and you return to the document, the banner displays at the top to indicate the document is Marked as Final.

g. Save and close the document.

TIP Don't Show This Message Again

If a Microsoft Word dialog box displays *Don't show this message again*, you can click the option so the dialog box will not display in the future. However, if you work in a lab environment, you should ask for instructor permission before changing a setting such as this.

STEP 2 SET FORMATTING RESTRICTIONS AND MODIFY A DOCUMENT PASSWORD

You are now ready to send the tulip information to a marketing manager so she can look over the document. She can make suggestions for changing the format because she will know how best to present the information. However, you do not want her to change any of the content of the document because that is not her area of expertise. You apply restrictions that only enable the marketing manager to change formatting, and she secures the restrictions with a password. Refer to Figure 7.26 as you complete Step 2.

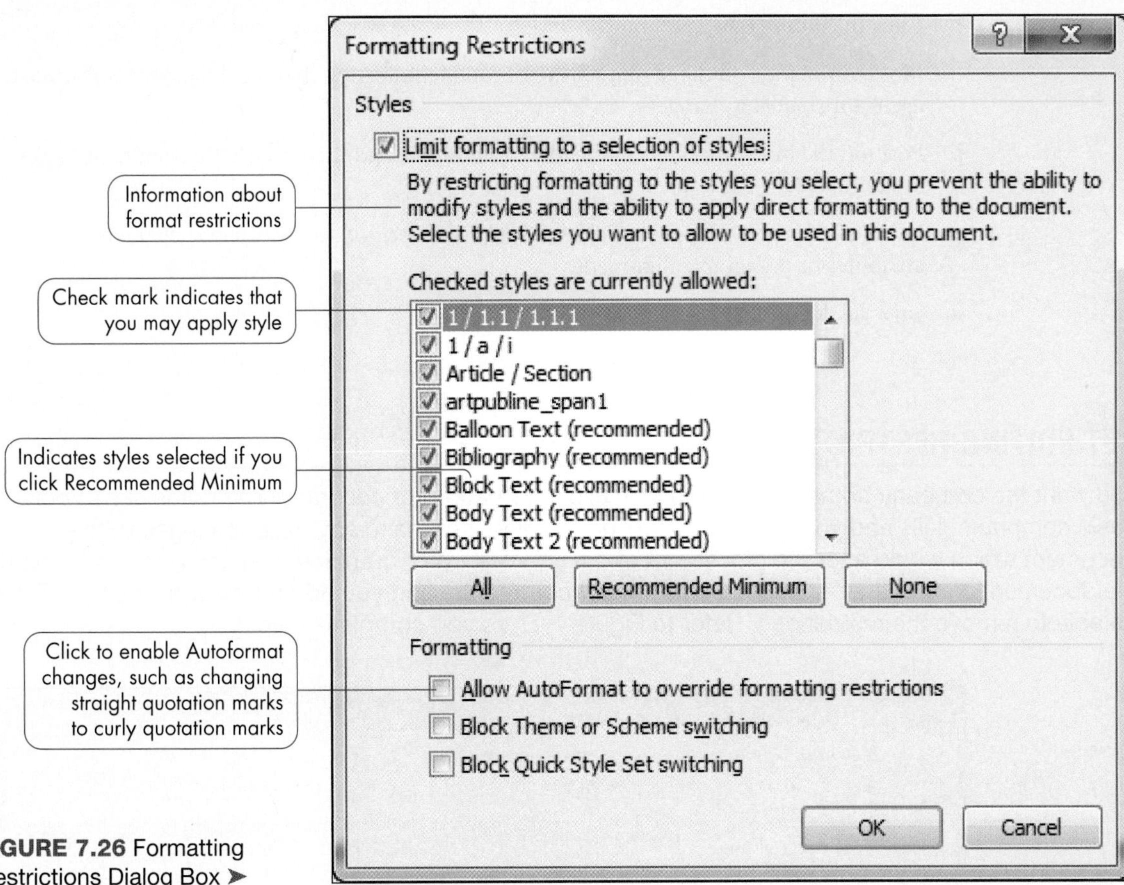

FIGURE 7.26 Formatting Restrictions Dialog Box ➤

a. Open *w07h3tulip1_LastnameFirstname*, enter the password **W7h3a** when prompted, and then click **OK**. Click **Edit Anyway** in the yellow bar across the top of the page to release the read-only status.

b. Click **File**, and then click **Save As**. Type **w07h3tulip2_LastnameFirstname** in the **File name box**, and then click **Tools**, **General Options**. Remove the existing password. Click **OK**, and then click **Save** to return to the document.

c. Click the **Review tab**, and then click **Restrict Editing** in the Protect group to display the Restrict Formatting and Editing pane.

d. Click **Limit formatting to a selection of styles** on the pane. Click **Settings** to display the Formatting Restrictions dialog box, as shown in Figure 7.26.

   In this dialog box, you can enable users to apply styles of your choice.

e. Click **None**.

   Notice that the check marks beside each style disappear. If you click OK, none of the styles can be used in this document. Next, you reselect the styles.

f. Click **All**, and then click **OK**. Click **No** to the Microsoft Office Word dialog box that asks if you want to remove styles that are not allowed.

   The user can now apply any style. However, they cannot modify the styles. This option is useful when you want to be sure anyone who edits the document uses a style that is included in Office 2010.

g. Click **Yes, Start Enforcing Protection** on the Restrict Formatting and Editing pane.

   The Start Enforcing Protection dialog box opens. You can use this dialog box to set a password required to remove formatting restrictions.

h. Type **W7h3b** in the **Enter new password (optional) box**. Retype the password in the **Reenter password to confirm box**, and then click **OK**.

i. Click the **Home tab.**

   Most commands on the Home tab are dimmed, indicating that the document is restricted against formatting changes.

j. Position the insertion point in the title *Tulip Basics*, and then click **Title** from the Quick Styles gallery.

   Word enables you to apply a different style; however, you cannot change character or font attributes or paragraph alignment.

k. Save the document.

STEP 3 SET EDITING RESTRICTIONS

You want the company botanist to review the tulip information for accuracy. The botanist has only basic computer skills and you want to make sure he does not make any major changes to the document which would alter the placement of the information or graphics. You use features to restrict the document so that the botanist can only insert comments, and you add a password so he will not be able to remove the restrictions. Refer to Figure 7.27 as you complete Step 3.

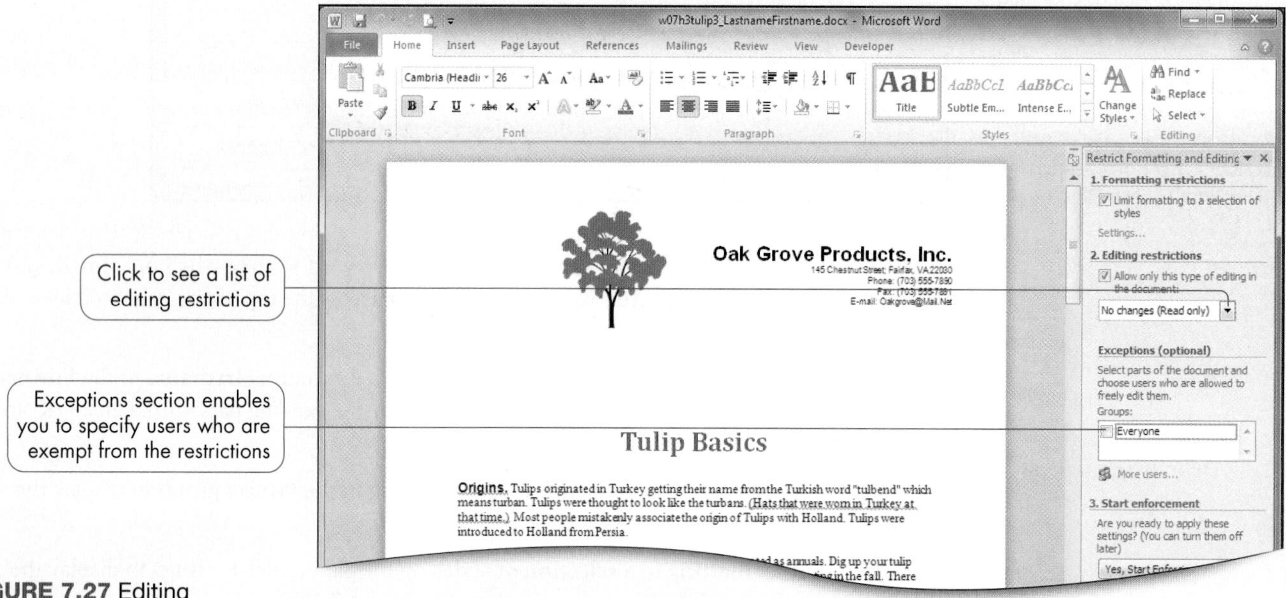

FIGURE 7.27 Editing Restrictions ➤

a. Save the document as **w07h3tulip3_LastnameFirstname.**

b. Click **Stop Protection**, which displays at the bottom of the Restrict Formatting and Editing pane, type **W7h3b** in the **Unprotect Document dialog box**, and then click **OK.**

   The formatting restriction is removed so that users may use any format features on the document.

> **TROUBLESHOOTING:** If the Restrict Formatting and Editing pane does not display, click the Review tab, and then click Restrict Editing.

c. Click **Allow only this type of editing in the document** in the *Editing restrictions* section.

   The Editing restrictions arrow is available so that you can specify the type of editing to restrict. Additionally, an *Exceptions (optional)* section appears on the pane so that you can apply exceptions to the editing restrictions, as shown in Figure 7.27.

d. Click the **Editing restrictions arrow**, and then click **Comments**.

e. Click **Yes, Start Enforcing Protection**. Type **W7h3c** in the **Enter new password (optional) box.** Retype the password in the **Reenter password to confirm box**. Click **OK**.

   Users are now restricted from editing the document content. They can only insert comments. The formatting restrictions are also still in place.

f. Press **Ctrl+Home** to move the insertion point to the beginning of the document. Select the title *Tulip Basics*, and then press **Delete**.

   You cannot delete the text. The status bar displays the message *This modification is not allowed because the selection is locked.* The Restrict Formatting and Editing pane now displays buttons to show document regions you can edit. However, because you restricted editing to comments only, no regions are available for editing.

g. Click the **Review tab**, click **New Comment**, and then type **Should we call this "Bulb Basics"?**.

   Because of the type of editing restrictions on the document you can insert a comment. The comment balloon appears on the side of the text.

h. Save the document.

STEP 4 SET EXCEPTIONS FOR RESTRICTED DOCUMENTS

After reflecting on the situation, you notice one section of the document where you should allow the botanist to modify content. You change the editing restrictions for the document to allow access to that one section, and then you reinforce the restrictions for the rest of the document again. Refer to Figure 7.28 as you complete Step 4.

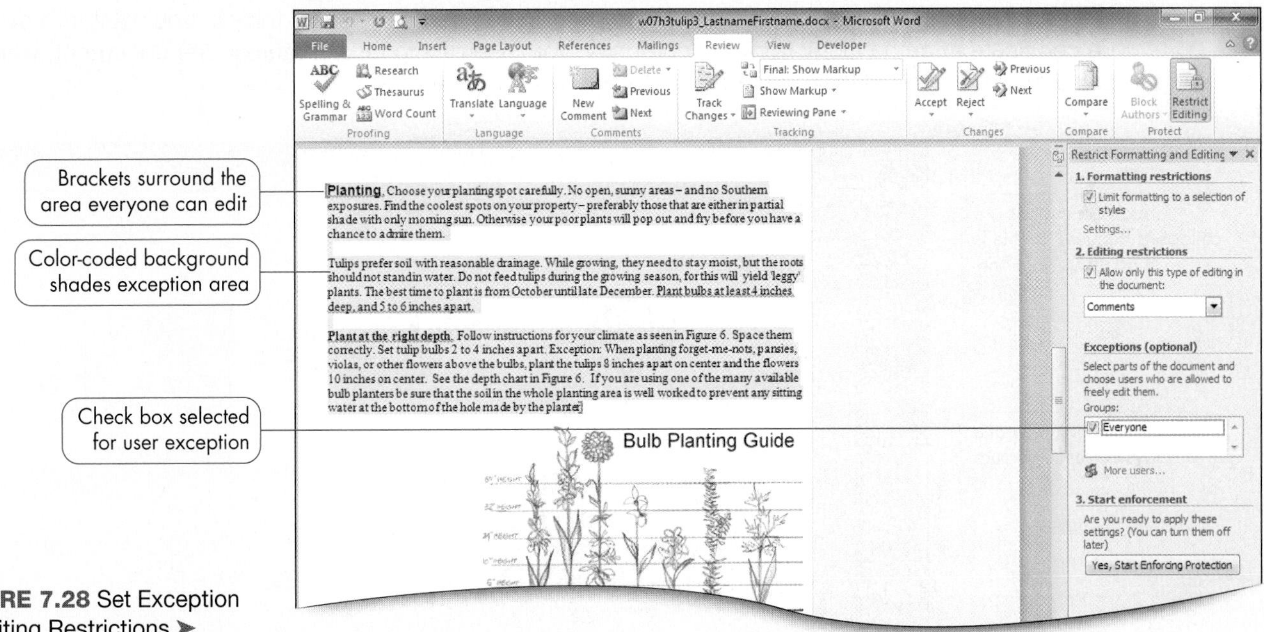

FIGURE 7.28 Set Exception to Editing Restrictions ➤

a. Display the Restrict Formatting and Editing pane, if necessary. Click **Stop Protection**. Type **W7h3c** in the **Password box**, and then click **OK**.

b. Confirm the first two boxes on the pane contain check marks. If they do not, click to mark those boxes.

c. Scroll to the top of page two, and then select the paragraph title *Planting*. Press **Shift+↓** to select the three paragraphs that follow it. Do not select the graphic titled *Bulb Planting Guide*.

   You want to set a user exception to allow all users to edit this section of the document. You do not want to include the graphic in your selection.

d. Click **Everyone** in the *Exceptions (optional)* section of the Restrict Formatting and Editing pane. Deselect the text.

The paragraphs you selected display with a light gray background, indicating that the user exception is applied to it, as shown in Figure 7.28.

> **TROUBLESHOOTING:** If you are unable to click the check box for *Everyone* in the *Exception* section of the Restrict Formatting and Editing pane, make sure you have first selected text in the document.

e. Click **Yes, Start Enforcing Protection**. Type **W7h3d** in the **Enter new password box**. Retype the password in the **Reenter password box**. Click **OK**.

f. Select the graphic titled *Bulb Planting Guide*, and then press **Delete**.

You cannot delete the graphic because it is protected against editing.

g. Click the paragraph heading *Planting*, click the **Home tab**, and then click **Book Title** from the Quick Styles gallery.

Word enables this editing because you are a part of *Everyone* included in the user exception for the heading.

h. Save the document.

STEP 5 ATTACH A DIGITAL SIGNATURE TO A DOCUMENT

After the document has been reviewed by the experts in the company, you take their changes into consideration, and then finalize it for distribution. When sent in a digital format, you want it to display a certificate of authenticity from the company; you insert a digital signature in the document, which also marks it as final. Refer to Figure 7.29 as you complete Step 5.

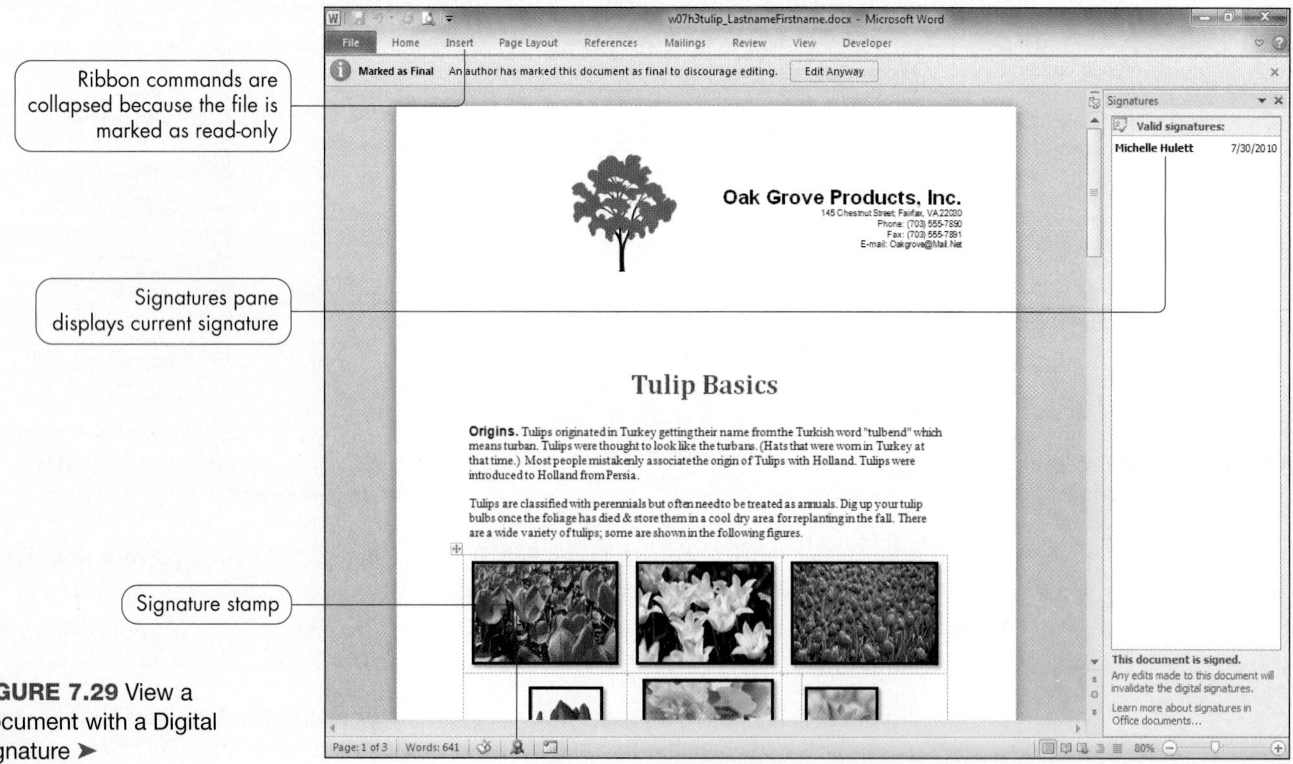

FIGURE 7.29 View a Document with a Digital Signature ➤

a. Click the **Start button**, and then type **SELFCERT.EXE** in the **Search Programs and Files box**. When Windows Explorer opens and displays the location of the file, double-click it.

The SELFCERT.EXE file should be located in the C:\Program Files\Microsoft Office\Office14 folder. The Create Digital Certificate dialog box opens and provides information about the self-certification program.

TROUBLESHOOTING: If you cannot find the *SELFCERT.EXE* file, or if your lab computer will not allow you to install the program, continue to read over the steps in this activity so that you can see how digital signatures work.

b. Type your name in the **Your Certificate's Name box**, and then click **OK**.

A message box appears, stating that you successfully created a certificate. Although your certificate is unauthorized, you can still use it to practice working with digital certificates.

c. Click **OK** to close the message box. Close Windows Explorer.

d. Remove all restrictions and prepare the final version of the document by completing the following steps:

- Click **Stop Protection** in the Restrict Formatting and Editing pane, enter the password **W7h3d** when prompted, and then click **OK**.
- Remove all check marks from the Restrict Formatting and Editing pane. When the Microsoft Word dialog box displays and asks if you want to remove the ignored exceptions, click **No**.
- Close the Restrict Formatting and Editing pane.
- Scroll to the top of page one. Right-click the **comment balloon**, and then click **Delete Comment**.

e. Save the document as **w07h3tulip_LastnameFirstname**.

f. Click **File**, click **Protect Document**, and then click **Add a Digital Signature**. Click **OK** in the Microsoft Office Word dialog box, if necessary.

The Sign dialog box displays. Your name displays at the bottom of the window because you recently created a digital signature.

TROUBLESHOOTING: If your name does not display in the Sign dialog box, click Change to display the Select Certificate dialog box. Click your name from the Issued to column, and then click OK.

g. Type **To validate contents** in the **Purpose for signing this document box**. Click **Sign** to close the Sign dialog box. Click **OK** to close the Signature Confirmation dialog box, and then click **File** to return to the document.

The signature stamp displays in the status bar and a yellow information bar displays *Marked as Final* below the ribbon. The Ribbon commands are hidden because the document has been marked as read-only.

h. Click one time on the signature stamp in the status bar.

The Signatures pane displays on the right side of the document, as shown in Figure 7.29. If you click a signature, a menu arrow displays enabling you to click an option to view details about the signature or to delete the signature.

i. Close the document.

STEP 6 INSERT A SIGNATURE LINE IN A DOCUMENT

You decide to add a signature line to the invoice, which will be signed by the person who completes the order. When printed, the customer service representative can sign his or her name on the signature line. When they send the invoice in digital format, the representative can type in his or her name or insert a graphic representation of his or her signature. Refer to Figure 7.30 as you complete Step 6.

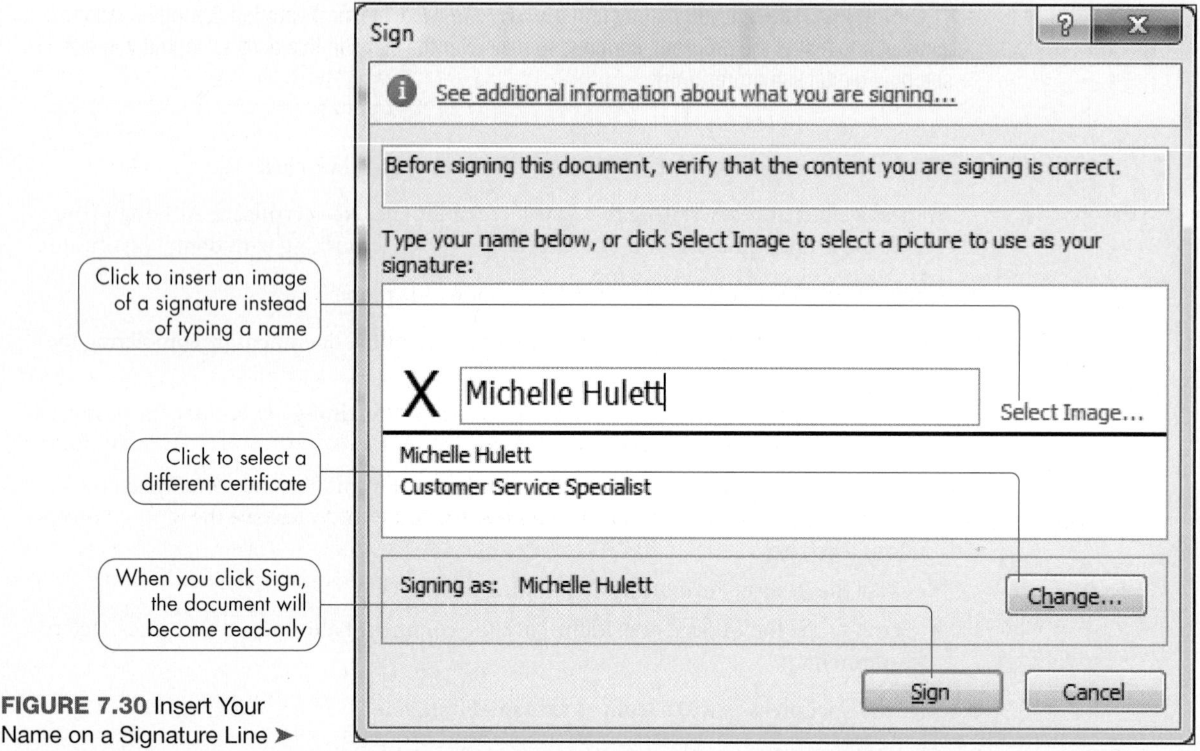

FIGURE 7.30 Insert Your Name on a Signature Line ➤

a. Open the document *w07h2invoice_LastnameFirstname.dotm*, and then save it as a Word Document, **w07h3invoice_LastnameFirstname**.

b. Press **Ctrl+End** to move the insertion point to the end of the document.

c. Click the **Insert tab**, and then click **Signature Line**. Click **OK** in the Microsoft Word dialog box, if necessary.

   The Signature Setup dialog box displays.

d. Type your name in the **Suggested signer box**. Type **Customer Service Specialist** in the **Suggested signer's title box**. Type **oakgrove@mail.net** in the **Suggested signer's e-mail address box**. Click **OK**.

   The signature line displays in the document, as well as the signer's information that you entered in the Signature Setup dialog box.

e. Click **OK** in the Microsoft Word dialog box, if necessary.

f. Insert a signature by completing the following steps:
   - Double-click the signature line to display the Sign dialog box. Click **OK** in the Microsoft Word dialog box.
   - Type your own name in the **Type your name below box** or click **Select Image** to select a picture to use as your signature box, as shown in Figure 7.30.
   - Click **Sign**.
   - Click **OK** in the Signature Confirmation dialog box, if necessary.

   The name displays above the signature line, and the date displays in the top-right corner of the signature line box. The document is marked as read-only and formatting features are grayed out.

g. Close the document, exit Word, and submit based on your instructor's directions.

CHAPTER OBJECTIVES REVIEW

After reading this chapter, you have accomplished the following objectives:

1. **Create an electronic form.** In Word 2010, you can create a form template—a document that defines the standard layout, structure, and formatting of a form. You can save the form as a Word document or a Word template. A form includes controls that enable the user to enter data in specific places.
2. **Insert form controls.** If you want users to fill out a form electronically, you must insert form controls, also called form fields, into the form template. Form controls help the user complete a form by displaying prompts such as drop-down lists and text boxes. A text content control is used most often and is used to enter any type of text or number into a form. A check box form field, as the name implies, consists of a box, which is checked or clear. A drop-down list enables the user to choose from one of several existing entries. The Date Picker displays a calendar that the user can navigate and click rather than typing in a date.
3. **Protect a form.** After you create a form, you can apply protection that prevents any modification except data entry. You must turn off the Design Mode before you protect a document. If you want to protect specific form controls without limiting access to the rest of the document, use the Group command on the Developer tab. After you group controls, click the Properties command and select a locking option.
4. **Record a macro.** When you create a macro, Word records a series of keystrokes and command selections and converts the tasks into specifically coded statements. Before recording a macro, you should decide what you want to accomplish with your macro, and then you should plan exactly which commands and tasks to include. When you start the macro, you can save it in the current document only or you can save it to the Normal template, where it will be available in all documents.
5. **Run a macro.** The process of playing back or using a macro is called run macro. When you run a macro, Word processes the series of commands and keystrokes saved in the macro. When you need to use a series of commands frequently, running a macro is faster than manually choosing each command. Furthermore, you can assign a keyboard shortcut to run a macro or edit the code to modify a macro.
6. **Apply document restrictions.** The Mark as Final command enables you to create a read-only file, and the status property is set to Final. This is a helpful command for communicating with other people that the document is not a draft but a completed and final version. You can set restrictions that prevent users from modifying the content of a document. Features are also available that prevent users from changing the formats for font, paragraph, column, drop caps, bullets, numbering, and tabs. When you set formatting restrictions, Word does not prevent users from changing content in a document. You might also want to set editing restrictions on particular documents. Editing restrictions specify conditions for users to modify a document. If you set the editing restriction to Comments or No changes (Read only), you can specify user exceptions. A user exception is an individual or group of individuals who are allowed to edit all or specific parts of a restricted document. Information Rights Management (IRM) services are designed to help you control who can access documents containing sensitive or confidential information and must be installed to restrict user access.
7. **Set passwords to open a document.** Setting passwords is one way to secure a document. When you assign a password to the document, only those who know the password can open the document. Passwords may consist of letters, numbers, and symbols; a good password will use a combination of all three. You may even use a combination of upper- and lowercase characters, such as W7h3a. Users who do not know the password can open the document in Read Only mode.
8. **Use digital signatures to authenticate documents.** Word uses Microsoft Authenticode technology to enable you to digitally sign a file by using a digital certificate—an attachment to a file or e-mail that guarantees the authenticity of the file, provides a verifiable signature, or enables encryption. You have two different ways to use digital signatures to sign Office documents. You can add an invisible digital signature to a document or add visible signature lines to a document to capture one or more digital signatures. When you need to confirm the authenticity of a document, you can attach a digital signature. Digital signatures are electronic stamps that display information about the person or organization that obtained the certification. The signature line enables individuals and companies to distribute and collect signatures, and then process forms or documents electronically without the need to print and fax.

KEY TERMS

ActiveX control ***p.359***
Check box form field ***p.358***
Date Picker ***p.358***
Design Mode ***p.357***
Digital certificate ***p.384***
Digital signature ***p.384***
Drop-down list ***p.358***
Editing restriction ***p.381***
Form ***p.356***
Form control ***p.357***
Form template ***p.356***
Formatting restriction ***p.380***
Information Rights Management (IRM) ***p.382***
Legacy form field ***p.359***
Macro ***p.369***
Macro-Enabled Document ***p.369***
Mark as Final ***p.379***
Password ***p.360***
Record macro ***p.369***
Run macro ***p.372***
Signature line ***p.385***
Text content control ***p.358***
User exception ***p.381***
Visual Basic for Applications (VBA) ***p.370***

MULTIPLE CHOICE

1. Which of the following is true about password protection?
   (a) All documents are automatically saved with a default password.
   (b) The password assigned to a document should use a combination of upper- and lowercase letters, numbers, and special characters.
   (c) A password must be set on a document that is restricted from editing.
   (d) A password cannot be changed after it has been established.

2. When you create a form template that will be broadly distributed outside your organization, you should do all of the following except:
   (a) Insert form controls where needed.
   (b) Protect the template using Restrict Formatting and Editing features.
   (c) Save the template with a .dotx extension.
   (d) Set a password to protect the template.

3. Which form control will enable a user to choose from a list of options?
   (a) Combo Box
   (b) Check Box
   (c) Date Picker
   (d) Text

4. Which of the following statements about protecting a form is false?
   (a) The Restrict Formatting and Editing pane enables you to prevent users from modifying the content of a form.
   (b) The Restrict Formatting and Editing pane enables you to prevent users from modifying the styles used in a form.
   (c) If you forget the password that protects a form, you can recover it by running a macro.
   (d) You can specify certain individuals who are exempt from the formatting and editing restrictions placed on a form.

5. Which of the following can you use to authenticate the contents of a document?
   (a) Password
   (b) Digital signature
   (c) Macro
   (d) Form control

6. How can you tell if a document has been digitally signed?
   (a) An icon that looks like a certificate displays on the status bar.
   (b) You must open the Add Digital Signature dialog box.
   (c) A message appears when you open the document.
   (d) A signature line displays at the bottom of the document.

7. What is the default location for a macro created in Microsoft Word?
   (a) In the Normal template, where it is available to every Word document
   (b) In the document in which it was created, where it is available only to that document
   (c) In the Macros folder on your hard drive
   (d) In the Office folder on your hard drive

8. Which of the following is the least appropriate advice to give to someone who wants to learn how to create and run macros?
   (a) Decide what you want the macro to accomplish.
   (b) Make a list of the sequence of tasks you want to perform prior to recording the macro.
   (c) Change your macro security settings to enable all macros all the time.
   (d) Practice completing the steps before actually recording the macro.

9. Before you can insert form controls into a form or display the Visual Basic editor to modify macros, what tab must you display in the Ribbon?
   (a) View
   (b) Review
   (c) Developer
   (d) Add-Ins

10. Which statement about a signature line is false?
    (a) If you specify a name and e-mail address of the signer, they do not display with the signature line.
    (b) You can insert a digital image of a signature on the line.
    (c) If you specify instructions for the signer, they display in the document along with the signature line.
    (d) You can have the date inserted automatically when a signature is inserted on the line.

1 White Glove Cleaners

You are the Marketing Manager for White Glove Cleaners, a small but growing company that offers a residential and commercial cleaning service. When potential customers are contacted they receive a printed document that highlights the cleaning services. You recently decided to update the document so it looks more professional and draws attention to the key services. You also want to include a signature line where clients can sign before they return it and set an appointment for a free estimate. After you make the changes, you mark the document as final to prevent further changes. This exercise follows the same set of skills as used in Hands-On Exercises 2 and 3 in the chapter. Refer to Figure 7.31 as you complete this exercise.

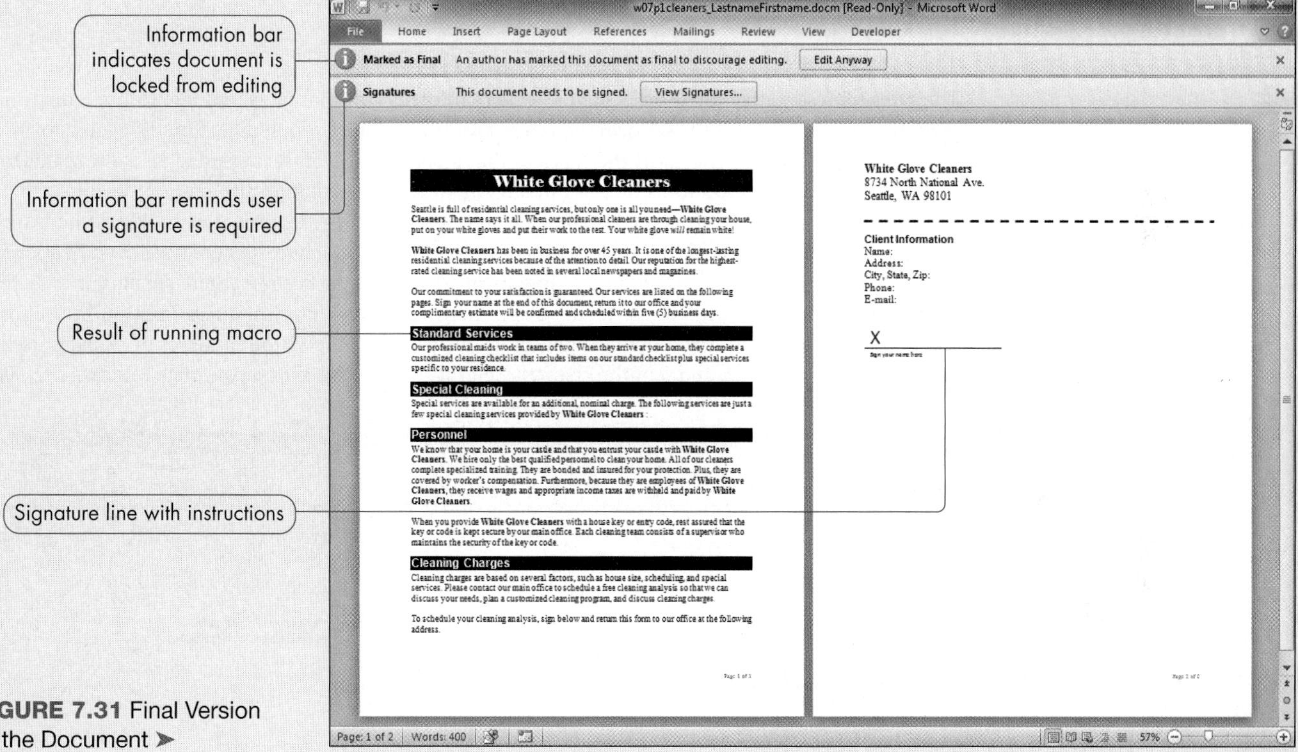

FIGURE 7.31 Final Version of the Document ➤

a. Open the document *w07p1cleaners*. Click **File**, and then click **Save As**. Click the **Save as type arrow**, and then click **Word Macro-Enabled Document** (*.docm). Type **w07p1cleaners_LastnameFirstname** in the **File name box**, and then click **Save**.

b. Display the Developer tab, if necessary. Click **File**, click **Options**, click **Customize Ribbon**, and then check **Developer**, which displays on the right side under the *Main Tabs* section. Click **OK**.

c. Record a macro by completing the following steps:
   - Click the left side of the heading *Standard Services* on the first page.
   - Click the **View tab**, click **Macros** in the Macros group, and then click **Record Macro**.
   - Type **reverse** in the **Macro name box**.
   - Click **Keyboard** to display the Customize Keyboard dialog box.
   - Press **Alt+R** to assign the keystroke combination to the macro.
   - Click the **Save changes in arrow**, click *w07p1cleaners_LastnameFirstname.docm*, and then click **Assign**.
   - Click **Close** to return to the document, where the macro recording symbol displays with the pointer. You are now recording the macro.
   - Click the **Home tab**, click the **Border arrow**, and then click **Borders and Shading**.
   - Click the **Shading tab**, click the **Style arrow**, click **Solid (100%)**, and then click **OK**.
   - Click **Stop recording** on the status bar.

d. Click the left side of the heading *Special Cleaning* on the second page. Press **Alt+R** to run the macro and apply the reverse effect to the heading. Run the macro on the headings *Personnel* and *Cleaning Charges.*

e. Press **Ctrl+End** to move the insertion point to the bottom of the document. Click the **Insert tab**, click **Signature Line** in the Text group, and then click **OK** to any Microsoft Office Word dialog boxes.

f. Type **Sign your name here** in the **Suggested signer box**, and then click **OK** to insert the signature line in the document.

g. Click **File**, click **Protect Document**, and then click **Mark as Final**. Click **OK** in all Microsoft Office Word dialog boxes that explain the document will be marked as final and saved. Click **File** to return to the document.

h. Select the address for White Glove cleaners, and then press **Delete.** Because the document is marked as final, it is also protected from any changes, and you cannot delete the address.

i. Close the document, and submit based on your instructor's directions.

2 White Glove Cleaners Service Plan

The sales representative for White Glove Cleaners informs you that he would like to use a document that offers more details of the services offered to customers, but he would like it modified as a form. He would like to be able to check off the services that a customer is most interested in contracting from your company. In addition to using a printed form, he indicates that he also communicates with several clients electronically, so he needs an electronic version of the document as well. And he wants it certified to assure the clients that the document is authentic. You make the necessary modifications by replacing bullets with check boxes and adding form controls at the bottom where clients can type their name and address. You protect the form so the clients can only enter their information in the form, and you finish up by adding a digital signature. This exercise follows the same set of skills as used in Hands-On Exercises 1, 2, and 3 in the chapter. Refer to Figure 7.32 as you complete this exercise.

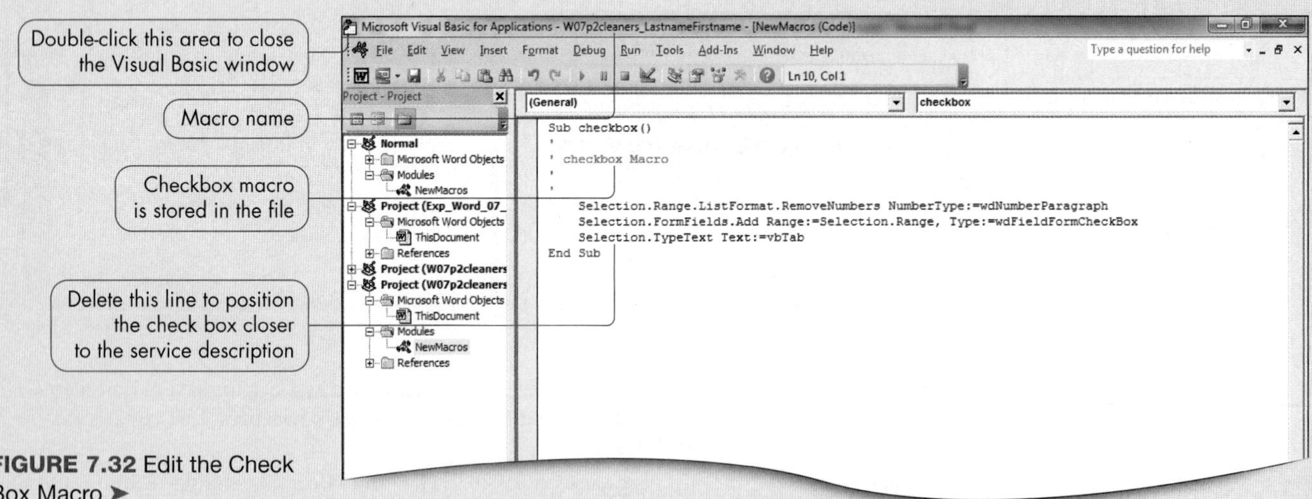

FIGURE 7.32 Edit the Check Box Macro ➤

a. Open *w07p2cleaners*, and then save it as a macro-enabled document, **w07p2cleaners_LastnameFirstname.docm**. Click **Edit Anyway**, which displays in the red bar at the top of the document, if necessary.

b. Position the insertion point on the left side of the word *Sweep* that displays in the first bulleted list under the *Entryway* paragraph. Record a macro by completing the following steps:
   - Click the **Developer tab**, and then click **Record Macro** in the Code group.
   - Type **checkbox** in the **Macro name box.**
   - Click the **Store macro in arrow.**
   - Click the *w07p2cleaners_LastnameFirstname.docm* document.
   - Click **Keyboard.**
   - Press **Alt+C.**
   - Click the **Save changes in arrow**, click *w07p2cleaners_LastnameFirstname.docm*, click **Assign**, and then click **Close.**

- Click the **Home tab**, click the **Bullets arrow**, and then click **None**.
- Click the **Developer tab**, click **Legacy Tools** in the Controls group, and then click **Check Box Form Field**.
- Press **Tab**, and then click **Stop Recording** in the Code group.

c. Press [↓] on the keyboard to move the insertion point to the next bulleted list item that starts *Shine both sides*. Press **Alt+C** to run the macro, and then replace the bullet with a check box. You adjust the alignment of the check box in the next step.

d. Edit the macro by completing the following steps:
   - Click **Macros** in the Code group.
   - Click **checkbox**, and then click **Edit**.
   - Press **Ctrl+End** to move to the bottom of the window and view the programming statements for the check box macro, as shown in Figure 7.32.
   - Select the third statement, *Selection.TypeText Text:=vbTab*, and then press **Delete**.
   - Press **Alt+Q** to close the window.

e. Select the check box and white space that precedes the first bulleted item (*Sweep*), and then press **Delete**. Press **Alt+C** to replay the macro, which removes the space between the check box and the service description. Run the macro on each bulleted list item on the page (those on the latter pages are completed for you).

f. Move the insertion point to the right side of *Name* in the *Client Information* section. Click the **Developer tab**, click **Legacy Tools** in the Controls group, and then click **Text Form Field**. Add a Text Form Field for each of the remaining client information items.

g. Add the signature line by completing the following steps:
   - Press **Ctrl+End** to move the insertion point to the bottom of the document.
   - Click the **Insert tab**, click **Signature Line** in the Text group, and then click **OK** in any Microsoft Office Word dialog box.
   - Type **Sign your name here** in the **Suggested signer box**, and then click **OK** to insert the signature line in the document.

h. Protect the document by completing the following steps:
   - Click the **Developer tab**, and then click **Design Mode**, if necessary, to toggle the setting off.
   - Click **Restrict Editing**.
   - Click **Limit formatting to a selection of styles**, and then click **Settings**.
   - Click **None**, and then click **OK**.
   - Click **No** in the Microsoft Office Word dialog box that asks if you want to remove styles that are not allowed.
   - Click **Allow only this type of editing in the document** in the *Editing restrictions* section, click the arrow below that line, and then select **Filling in forms**.
   - Click **Yes, Start Enforcing Protection** from the *Start enforcement* section.
   - Click **OK** to close the Start Enforcing Protection dialog box.

i. Close the Restrict Formatting and Editing pane.

j. Save and close the document, and submit based on your instructor's directions.

MID-LEVEL EXERCISES

1 Real Estate Appraisal Report

Angela Marti is a real estate appraiser who estimates the value of residential homes. At the end of each week, she must submit a report to her supervisor of the properties she appraised during the past seven days. She decides to create a form that she can fill out quickly, even while she is on location with her laptop. She has a document containing a table for the information, but she decides to automate it using form fields; then she will use features to protect the form and create a digital signature prior to submitting it to her boss.

a. Open *w07m1appraisal.dotx*, and then save it as **w07m1appraisal_LastnameFirstname.dotx** (a Word template).

b. Insert a **Rich Text Content Control** on the right side of *Completed by*. This is where Angela enters her name.

c. Insert the **Date Picker Content Control** on the right side of *Week ending* and in each cell in the Date column in the table.

d. Insert **Rich Text Content Controls** in each cell in the Address column.

e. Add **Combo Box Content Controls** in each cell for City and Zip Code. Since she only assesses homes in four cities, populate the City combo box with **Ava**, **Salem**, **Ozark**, and **Nixa**. Create a Combo Box Content Control for Zip codes using **65800**, **65801**, **65802**, and **65803**. Insert the state abbreviation **MO** in each cell in the state column. Hint: You can create one combo box for each category, and then copy it into other cells in the column.

f. Enter a **Text Form Field** in each cell of the Appraised Value column. Format the Text Form Field in the last row to calculate the total of the Appraised Value column. Hint: Select the **Calculate on exit property** for each Text Form Field.

g. Protect the document; allow users to fill in form controls only. Save and close the template.

h. Open the template you just created and save it as **w07m1appraisal_ LastnameFirstname.docx** (a Word document).

i. Fill out the form by entering the following information:
   - Type your name in the **Completed by text form control**.
   - Select **Today** in the date picker control.
   - Type the address and appraised value information below into the table. Select specified dates from the date picker controls.

Address	1387 E. Main Street	8977 N. Fremont Ave.
City	Ava	Ozark
State	MO	MO
Zip	65803	65801
Appraised Value	129,900	225,000
Date	Select **Today**	Select yesterday's date

j. Apply a digital signature to the document when complete. Enter your name in the signature. Type **This report is submitted as correct and valid** as the purpose for signing the document.

k. Save and close the document, and submit based on your instructor's directions.

2 Regional Science Fair Results

After the Regional Science Fair is held on the campus of Missouri State University, the director of the event must document the winners and distribute the awards in each category of the competition. The director's assistant has created an initial list of the winners in the Senior Division and has applied several layers of protection, including a password that you must enter to make modifications. You will open the document, make any necessary changes, and then protect the document again. All participants will receive the results via e-mail, and the document should be certifiable for accuracy. You do not want to assign a password to open the document, as that is not appropriate when distributing a public record, but you can use your knowledge of other forms of document protection so that it will be recognized as the official results, which cannot be altered.

a. Open the *w07m2results* document, and then type **Chap7_mid2** as the password to modify the document. Save it as **w07m2results_LastnameFirstname**.
b. Remove any formatting and editing protection that is applied to the document so you can make the following changes.
c. Change the name of the *Second Alternate*, which is incorrect, to display **Sydni Michelle Sanders**.
d. Change the main heading of the document to use the **Title style**. Decrease the font size to **20**, center the heading, and insert a line break so *Senior Division* appears on the first line and the remaining title displays below it.
e. Set editing restrictions so the document is read-only and no changes are allowed.
f. Remove the password necessary to open the document.
g. Mark the document as final.
h. Save and close the document, and submit based on your instructor's directions.

3 Computer Training Concepts

Your company, Computer Training Concepts, was recently purchased and the new owner is considering a new name for the organization. His first choice for a new name is *Computer Training Solutions*. The new CEO asked you to automate the process of changing the name of the company on all documentation and correspondence. As company documents are used, modifications to reflect the new name should take place. You decide to create a macro that will quickly search each document and replace the old name with the new name. You are also directed to change the appearance of the new name so it is more distinguishable in the documents.

a. Open *w07m3training* and save it as a Macro-Enabled document named **w07m3training_LastnameFirstname**.
b. Create a macro named **ReplaceName**. Save it in the *w07m3training_LastnameFirstname* file. Press **Alt+R** to run the macro and save changes to the macro in *w07m3training_LastnameFirstname.docm*.
c. Perform the following steps in the **ReplaceName macro**: Activate the **Find and Replace command**. Find occurrences of *Computer Training Concepts*, and then replace them with **Computer Training Solutions**. Change the font attributes of Computer Training Solutions to bold and italic from the Find and Replace dialog box.
d. Replace all occurrences, and then close the Find and Replace dialog box. Stop recording the macro.
e. Edit the header in each section by replacing *Student's Name* with your name.
f. Restrict formatting of the document to a selection of styles. When you enforce that protection, use a password to secure it. Set the password to modify as **Chap7_mid3**.
g. Edit the macro to reflect the CEO's latest decision to name the company **Digital Training Solutions**. Change the *.Text* statement in the macro to find **Computer Training Solutions**, and then change the *.Replacement.Text* statement to use **Digital Training Solutions**. Save and close the macro, and then run it to make the new corrections. Pay special attention to all the locations in the document where the company name displays, including headers and footers.
h. Insert a Signature Line at the end of the document. The name that displays beneath the line is *Tyler Batten* and his title is *CEO*. Insert Mr. Batten's name in the signature line so that it displays on the document.
i. Save and close the document, and submit based on your instructor's directions.

CAPSTONE EXERCISE

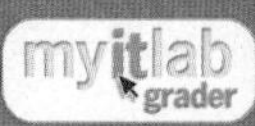

Many professionals have a job that requires travel. In most organizations, individuals must pay for all travel-related expenses and then submit a form in order to receive reimbursement. The form details every expense—from food to hotel to airfare—and at the end of the form the total of all expenses is calculated. The company you work for has a travel reimbursement form that all employees must print, fill in, and then submit via interoffice mail. You are responsible for converting that form so that it can be completed online and e-mailed to the accounting office.

Create a Macro That Inserts Text Controls

The travel expense form will require several text controls to enter information such as name, department, and phone number. To expedite the process of inserting text controls, you create a macro that inserts the field as soon as you press a keyboard combination.

a. Open the file *w07c1travel*. The password to open is **Chap7_cap** and the password to modify is **2Travel**.

b. Save the file as a Macro-Enabled Document named **w07c1travel_LastnameFirstname**.

c. Display the Developer tab, if necessary. Record a macro named **TextControl**. Store it in the *w07c1travel_LastnameFirstname* document. Assign the macro to the keyboard combination **Ctrl+L**, and then save changes to the macro in *w07c1travel_LastnameFirstname*.

d. Perform the following commands in the macro: Click the **Developer tab**, and then click the **Rich Text Content Control**. Click **Properties**, and then select the **Content control cannot be deleted option**. Close the Content Control Properties dialog box, and then stop the macro.

e. Deselect the control, and then press **Ctrl+L** to confirm that the macro runs correctly. Switch to Design Mode, and then delete all text controls that display in inappropriate locations in the document.

Insert Text and Date Controls on a Form

The Word document you opened in the last steps is the basis for the printed travel reimbursement form. You decide to keep the basic outline of the document and add form controls for users to enter their personal information. The document contains asterisks to mark the location where you want to enter the personal information, so you will delete the asterisks before you insert form controls.

a. Delete the asterisks, and then use the **TextControl macro** to insert text controls on the right side of *Name*, *Office Phone*, *Department*, and *Purpose of Trip*.

b. Insert **Date Picker controls** on the right side of *Request Date*, *Departure Date*, and *Return Date*.

c. Save the document.

Insert Controls That Compute Totals

The actual expenses are entered in a table in the document that sorts by category such as transportation, accommodations, and meals. Some expenses, such as Personal Car, might require a calculation of miles driven multiplied by the reimbursement amount per mile. After all information is entered in the table, a grand total is calculated by adding all the expenses. You decide to use legacy text fields in the table, which allow calculations.

a. Insert **legacy text form fields** within the table, and then apply **Number formats** for each expense in the second and third columns that requires a number to be entered.

b. Assign bookmark names to all fields you insert in the second and third columns. For example, you might use *ToAirport* (for the shuttle expense to the airport), *DriveMiles* (for number of miles driven), and *Brkdays* (for number of days you ate breakfast on the trip).

c. Insert the form field for Personal Car Mileage, using **.55** as the default entry, because this is the current mileage allowance.

d. Use Help to learn how to edit field properties so you can display Help text for form controls. The Help message you insert will display on the status bar to tell the user what to do (such as *Enter number of miles driven* or *Enter mileage allowance*) for fields in the second and third columns.

e. Insert a text form field that calculates the total amount in the fourth column. Create formulas that use the form field bookmark names from fields in columns two and three. For example, use *=Brkdays*Brkamt* to calculate the total amount spent for breakfasts during a trip. Notice that some fields will add the results from columns 2 and 3, and others will multiply them. Format calculating fields in the last column with **Currency format** and set them to calculate on exit.

f. Insert text form fields in the first column below the Other Expenses category.

g. Insert a calculation field in the last cell with this formula: **=SUM(D2:D17)**. Format the field to display the results as **Currency**.

h. Set right alignment on the text and fields in the second, third, and fourth columns.

i. Save the document.

Protect the Form

To make a true digital form, you wisely decide to add a line for a signature, and then protect the document so users can only enter information in the control field areas. You remove all passwords, and then you certify the form for authenticity by attaching a digital signature.

a. Insert a Signature Line at the bottom of the document. Below the line, display the text *Employee Signature.*

b. Remove the passwords that are required to open and modify the document.

c. Restrict formatting to a selection of styles (none) and restrict the type of editing to filling in forms. Enforce the protection without setting passwords.

d. Close all panes; save and close the document.

Fill Out a Travel Expense Form

Now, it is time to test the travel expense reimbursement form. You recently completed a trip to visit a client and will use that information to complete the form.

a. Open the travel reimbursement form and save it as a Word document named **w07c1reimburse_LastnameFirstname**. Click **Yes** to save it as a macro-free document.

b. Use information from the following table to complete the form. The total expenses should equal $830.00.

Form Control	Your information
Name	Enter your name
Office Phone	(555) 555-0001
Department	Sales—Western Division
Request Date	Today's date
Purpose of Trip	Client meeting
Departure Date	September 19, 2012
Return Date	September 21, 2012
Shuttle to Airport	25
Airfare	375
Hotel	2 nights @ 125
Breakfast	3 days @ 10
Lunch	3 days @ 15
Dinner	3 days @ 35

c. Sign your name on the digital signature line after you complete the form.

d. Save and close the document, and submit based on your instructor's directions.

Black Tie, Incorporated

GENERAL CASE 

You have just been hired as manager of a new tuxedo rental company named Black Tie, Incorporated. You need to hire employees, but you do not yet have an application form. Create an application form that potential employees can fill out onscreen. Provide a place for personal information, education and training, employment history, and references. Include any other information you think is necessary. Be sure to add default text for each field to indicate what the user should insert into the field. Protect the form, and then save the form template as **w07b1tuxedo_LastnameFirstname**. Enter data as if you were applying for a position, and then save the document as **w07b1tuxapp_LastnameFirstname.docx**. Save and close the document, and then submit based on your instructor's directions.

So Many Features to Choose From

RESEARCH CASE 

In this chapter, you learned the benefit of using macros to perform a repetitive task. Other features in Word also help you with a repetitive task. Which feature should you use for a particular task? Take this opportunity to create a chart that lists the features and tools in Word such as macros, Format Painter, and Building Blocks, and then compare each feature. Consider a scenario that would require the use of each feature and why you would use one instead of the other. Use Microsoft Office Word Help to learn more about each feature, if necessary. Save your work as **w07b2features_LastnameFirstname**, close the document, and then submit based on your instructor's directions.

Calculating Form Fields

DISASTER RECOVERY 

A colleague wants to use a form as a purchase order for his small company. He created the form, but it does not work as he expected. The calculating fields do not function properly, the customer information does not appear as a form field, and to top it off, he's no longer able to type anything into his form. His frustration has forced him to call you and ask for advice on solving his problems. Your task is to troubleshoot the form and make corrections or additions that will turn it into a functioning and professional-looking electronic form that is suitable for use. Open the file *w07b3problem.dotx* and save it as **w07b3problem_LastnameFirstname.dotx**. Determine the reason why the form fields are not calculating, make corrections to fix the problem, add any other form features that would make this a true digital form, and then save and test the form. When complete, save and close the document, and then submit based on your instructor's directions.

WORD

8 WORD AND THE INTERNET

Creating Web Pages, XML, and Blogs

Watch the
Set-up Video
for this Case Study!

CASE STUDY | Happy Haunting Online

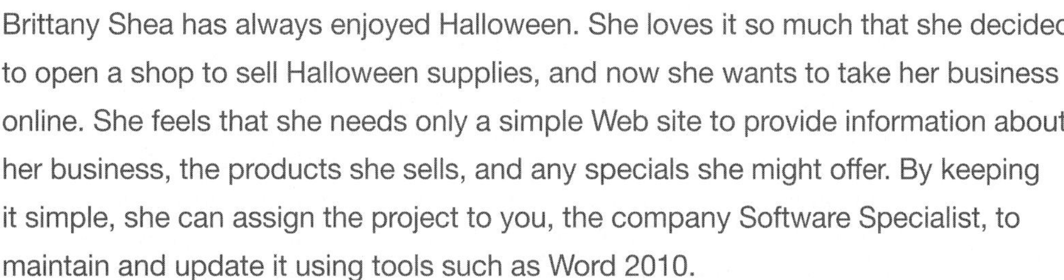

Brittany Shea has always enjoyed Halloween. She loves it so much that she decided to open a shop to sell Halloween supplies, and now she wants to take her business online. She feels that she needs only a simple Web site to provide information about her business, the products she sells, and any specials she might offer. By keeping it simple, she can assign the project to you, the company Software Specialist, to maintain and update it using tools such as Word 2010.

Your knowledge of the Office suite enables you to set up the Web pages to be multifunctional. You can format information about her products in a way that displays well on a Web site, and you can also format it using XML. By using XML, you can export and import into other programs such as Excel 2010. You will use these tools to get started, and then you can create a blog where you post more personal notes and links about Brittany's favorite Halloween happenings.

OBJECTIVES

AFTER YOU READ THIS CHAPTER, YOU WILL BE ABLE TO:

1. Customize the Ribbon ***p.406***
2. Build a Web page ***p.409***
3. Publish a Web page ***p.415***
4. Understand XML ***p.424***
5. Attach an XML schema ***p.424***
6. Create a blog post ***p.435***

Web Pages

The **Internet** is a network of networks that connects computers anywhere in the world.

The **World Wide Web (WWW)** is a very large subset of the Internet that stores Web page documents.

A **Web page** is any document that displays on the World Wide Web.

For most students, the Internet is as much a part of their education as books and teachers. The ***Internet*** is a network of networks that connects computers anywhere in the world. It is easy to connect your computer to the Internet, and that connection enables you to view an abundance of information about every imaginable topic.

The ***World Wide Web*** (***WWW*** or, simply, the Web) is a very large subset of the Internet, consisting of those computers that store a special type of document known as a ***Web page***. Any document that displays on the WWW is a Web page. Web pages may be self-contained and might provide all the information you need about a topic, or they may offer links to other Web pages. And therein lies the fascination of the Web—you simply click link after link to go effortlessly from one document or resource to the next.

In this section, you will learn to create a Web page. You will customize the Ribbon to display commands you will use for Web page development, then you will format the page, add hyperlinks and bookmarks, and finally save the document as a Web page.

Customizing the Ribbon

The features in Word enable you to create just about any kind of document you could want, and the Ribbon makes it easy to find the commands that you use when creating those documents. But did you know you can create a custom tab for the Ribbon that contains just the commands you want to use? Customization is new to Office 2010 and enables you to include features that you use most frequently or features that are not available on the standard Ribbon. By creating a custom tab, you have access to these features. In addition to creating a new tab, you can change the order of the tabs, change the order of the groups that appear within the tabs, and create new groups within a tab.

To customize the Ribbon, right-click the Ribbon, and then click Customize Ribbon, or do the following:

1. Click File to open the Backstage view.
2. Click Options.
3. Click Customize Ribbon.

Figure 8.1 shows the Customize Ribbon options displaying the current arrangement of the Ribbon in the right pane. To expand the view to display the groups within a tab, click +, and to collapse the view to hide the groups, click –. To change the order of the existing tabs or groups, drag and drop a selected tab and group to a new position.

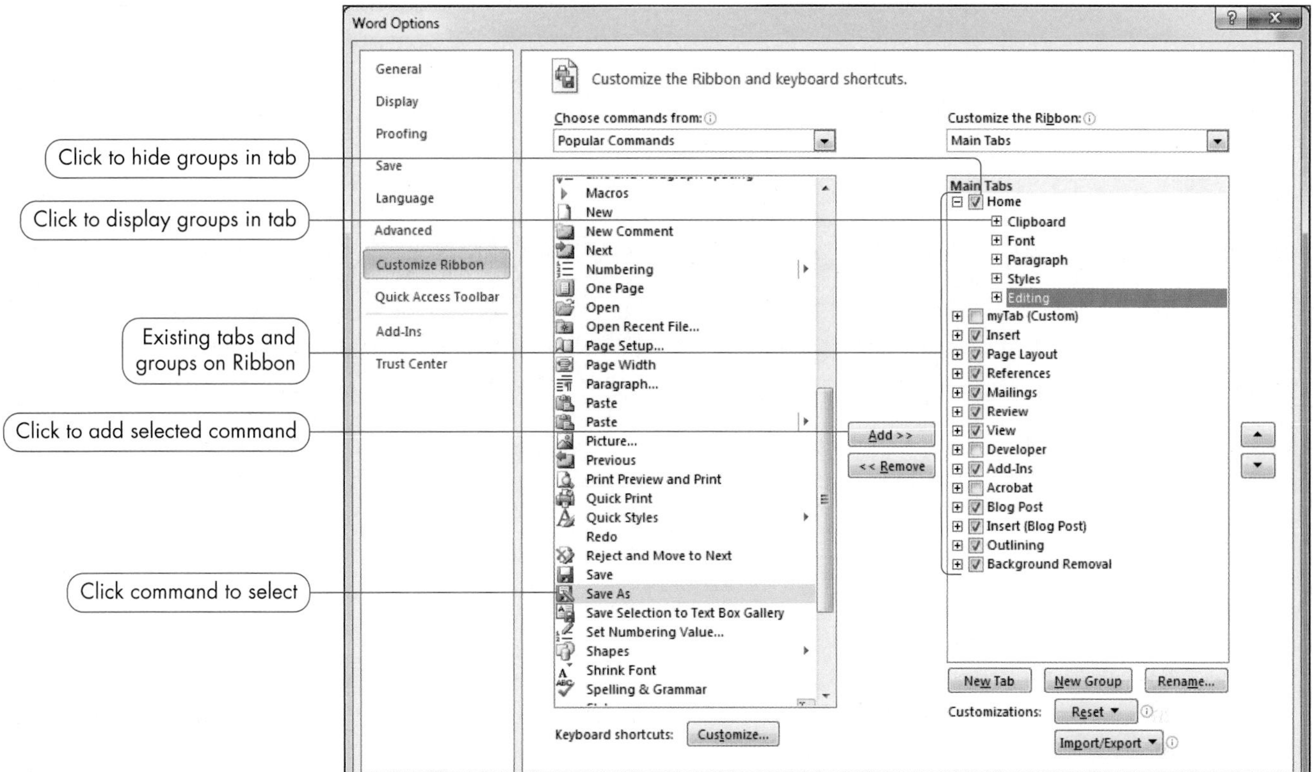

Click to hide groups in tab
Click to display groups in tab
Existing tabs and groups on Ribbon
Click to add selected command
Click command to select

FIGURE 8.1 Customize Ribbon Options ➤

> **TIP** Restore the Ribbon
>
> You can restore the Ribbon to its original arrangement by clicking *Reset* at the bottom of the Customize the Ribbon view, and then clicking *Reset all customizations*. Reset also enables you to reset individual tabs.

Add a New Tab

To have access to the commands you use most, add a new tab to the Ribbon, and then add the frequently used commands. Below the Customize the Ribbon pane, click New Tab. The new tab displays immediately below the tab in the pane that is also the active tab in your document and is named *New Tab (Custom)*. The new tab contains a new group named *New Group (Custom)*. To add additional groups, click New Group below the pane. You can rename tabs or groups by clicking Rename. When you rename a group, you can select a colorful symbol to represent the contents of the group. You can reorder the tab in the Ribbon by clicking the Move Up and Move Down arrows on the right side of the pane. Figure 8.2 displays a new tab containing a new group.

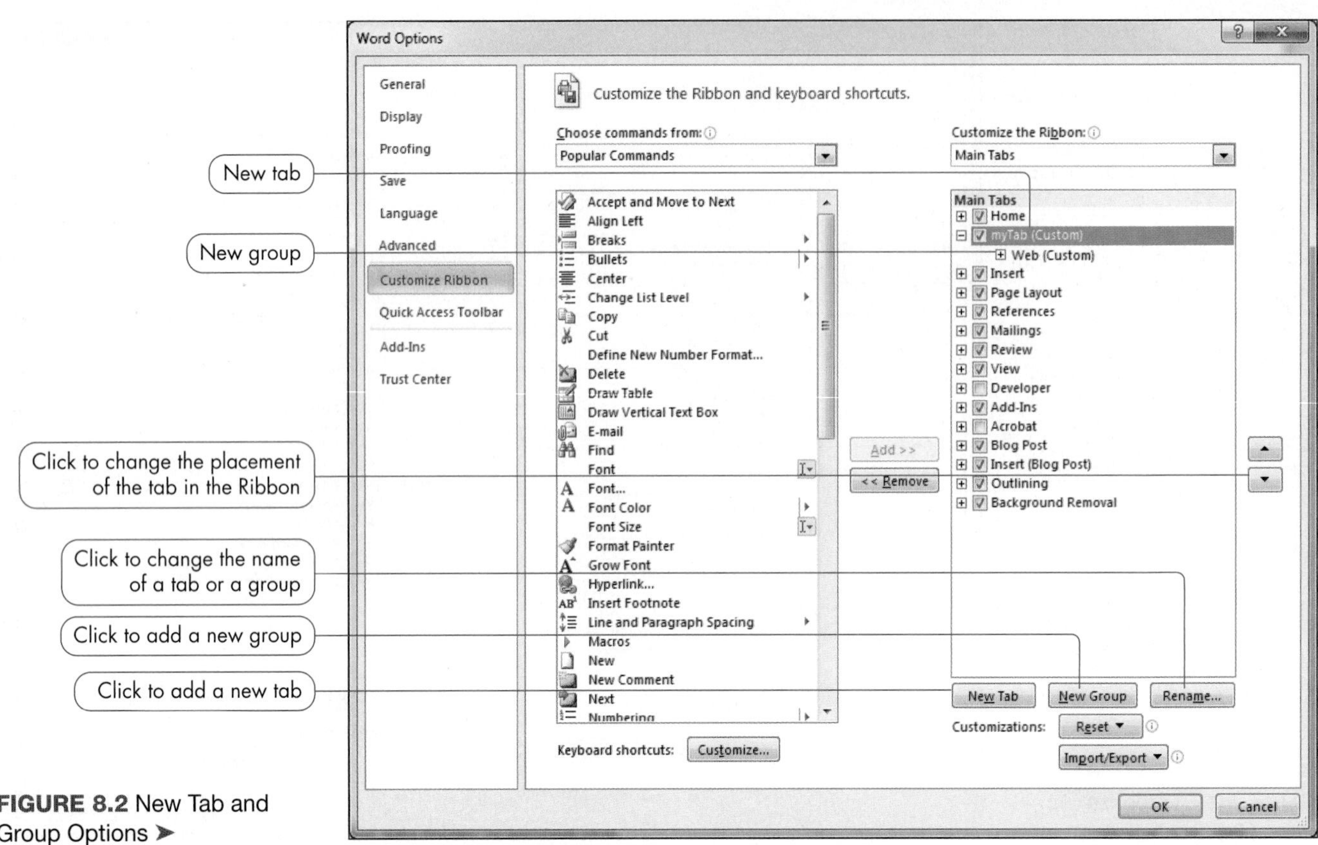

FIGURE 8.2 New Tab and Group Options ➤

Add Commands to a Group

To add commands to an existing tab or group or to a newly created tab, click a command from the *Choose commands from* pane, and then click Add. Popular commands that you can add are displayed in the default view, but you can click the *Choose commands from* arrow to choose from additional commands and macros. You will also find a category named Commands Not in the Ribbon. For example, you can add commands that are not on the default tabs, such as Web Page Preview, to a group in a personalized tab. Figure 8.3 displays a customized tab with commands you use while creating Web pages.

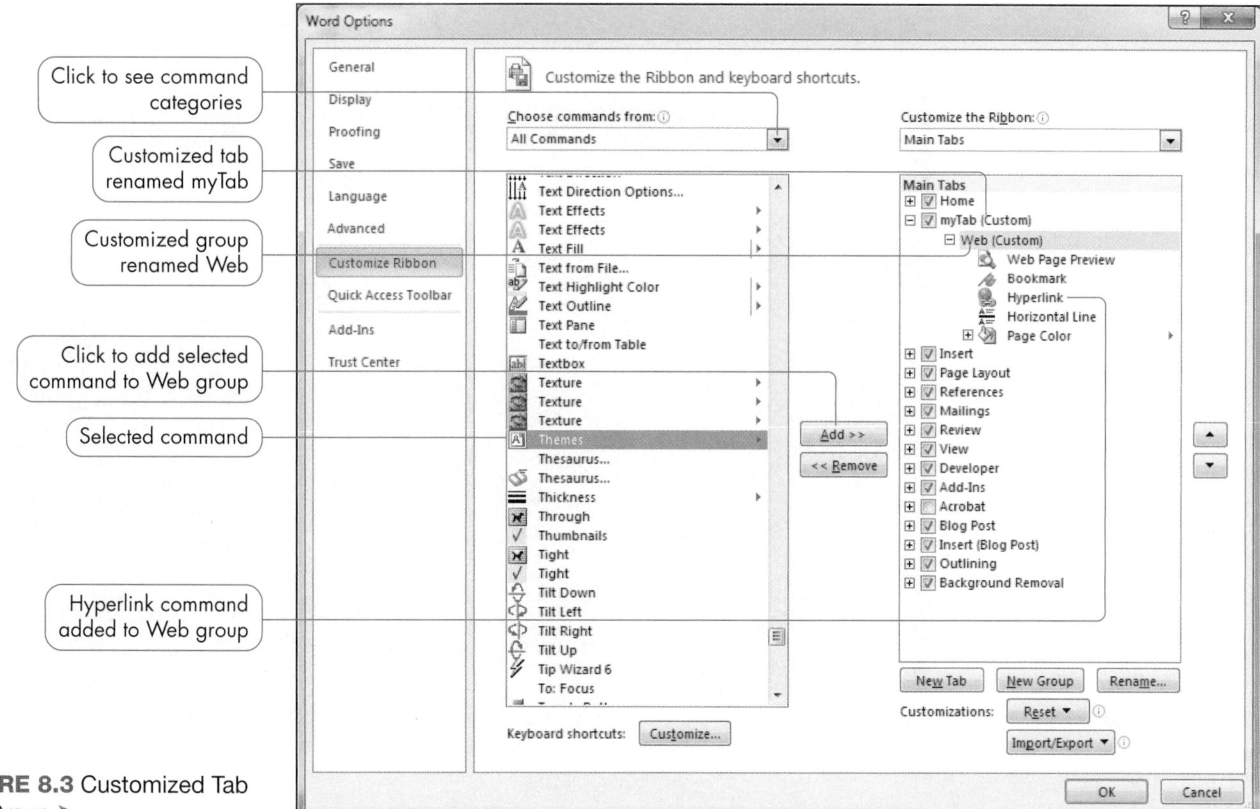

FIGURE 8.3 Customized Tab and Group ➤

TIP Export and Import a Custom Tab

If you customize a tab or the Quick Access Toolbar (QAT), you can export them to a file that can be imported on a different computer. Click Import/Export at the bottom of the Word Options dialog box to save your customizations. Copy the file you save on a different computer, and then click Import/Export again on the new computer to import your custom tab or QAT.

Building a Web Page

Sooner or later, anyone who cruises the World Wide Web wonders if he or she can create a home page or a Web site of his or her own. Word provides all the tools necessary to create a basic Web page.

Sooner or later, anyone who cruises the World Wide Web wonders if he or she can create a home page or a Web site of his or her own. Word provides all the tools necessary to create a basic Web page. You can use tables to organize and lay out the page elements, clip art and pictures to enhance the page with visual elements, bulleted and numbered lists to organize information on the page, WordArt for text, and so on. You can use Word to create a more advanced Web page; however, if your Web page design is complex, you will want to use a Web development and design program, such as Microsoft Expression.

HyperText Markup Language (HTML) uses codes to describe how a document appears when viewed in a Web browser.

Web pages are developed in a special language called ***HyperText Markup Language (HTML)***. Initially, the only way to create a Web page was to learn HTML, which consists of a set of codes (or tags) that are assigned to the content and describe how the document is to appear when viewed in a Web browser such as Internet Explorer.

Office 2010 simplifies the process because you can create the document in Word and then simply save it as a Web page. Word converts the document and generates the HTML code for you. You can continue to type text or change the formatting just as you can with an ordinary document. Figure 8.4 shows a Web page you will create in the next Hands-On Exercise, and Figure 8.5 displays the HTML code for that page.

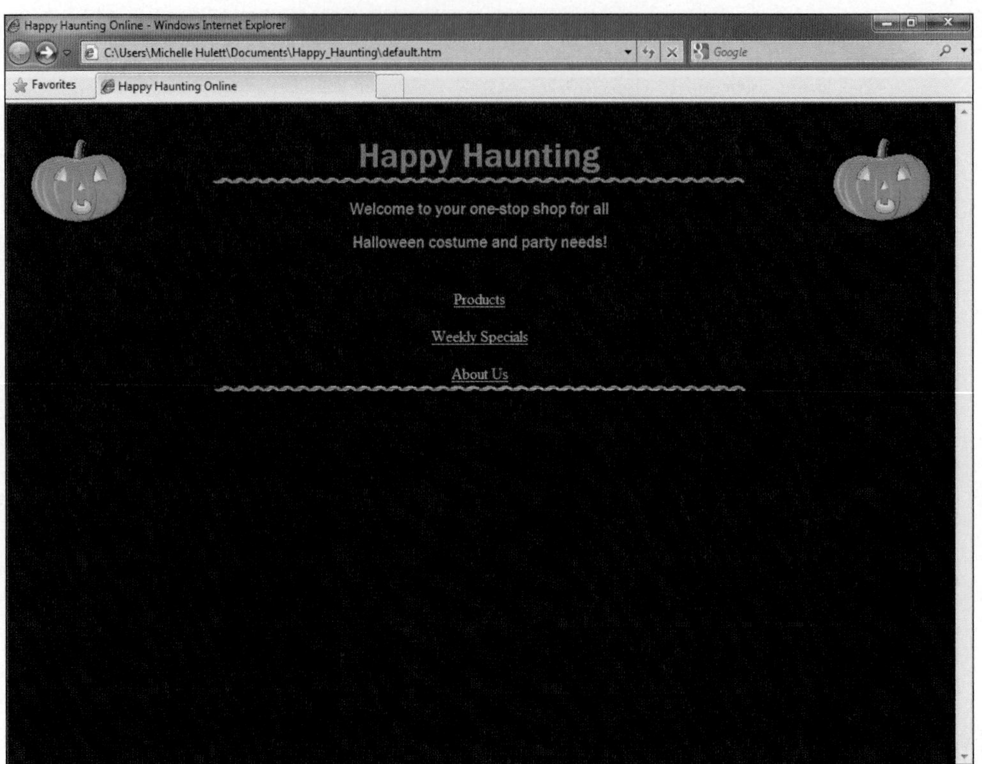

FIGURE 8.4 Halloween Shop Web Page ➤

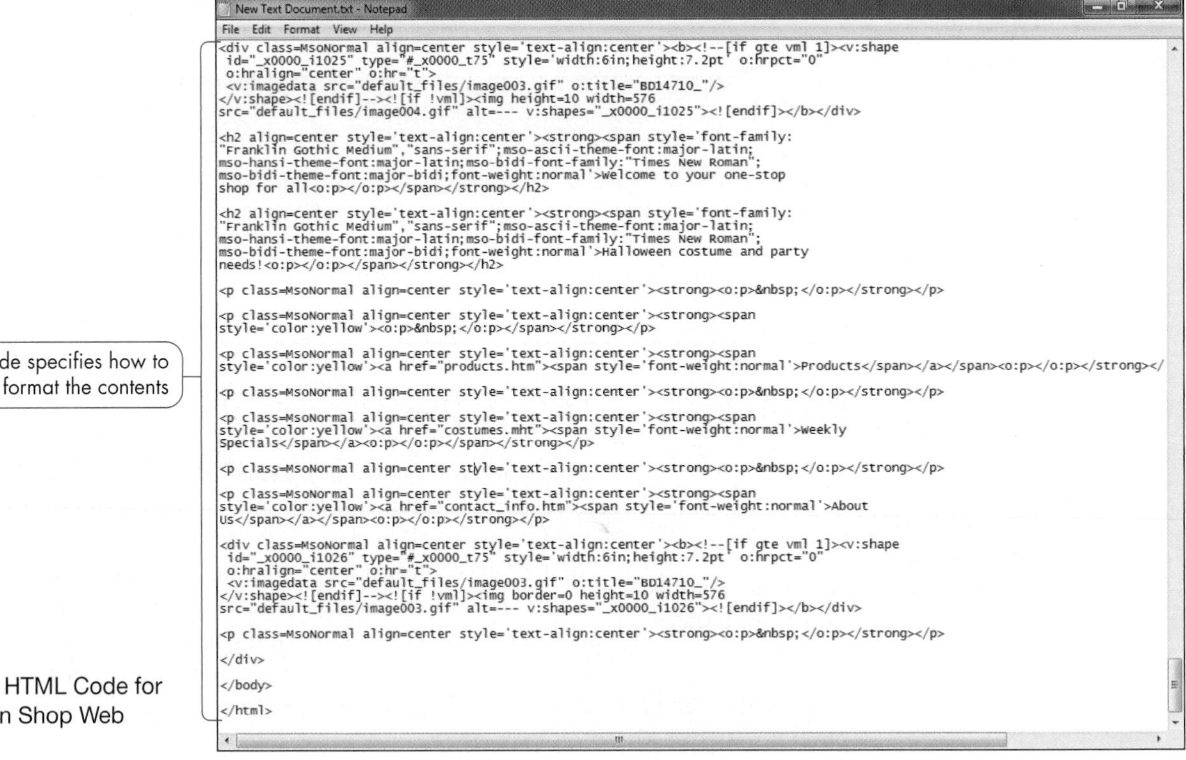


```
<div class=MsoNormal align=center style='text-align:center'><b><!--[if gte vml 1]><v:shape
 id="_x0000_i1025" type="#_x0000_t75" style='width:6in;height:7.2pt' o:hrpct="0"
 o:hralign="center" o:hr="t">
 <v:imagedata src="default_files/image003.gif" o:title="BD14710_"/>
</v:shape><![endif]--><![if !vml]><img height=10 width=576
src="default_files/image004.gif" alt=--- v:shapes="_x0000_i1025"><![endif]></b></div>

<h2 align=center style='text-align:center'><strong><span style='font-family:
"Franklin Gothic Medium","sans-serif";mso-ascii-theme-font:major-latin;
mso-hansi-theme-font:major-latin;mso-bidi-font-family:"Times New Roman";
mso-bidi-theme-font:major-bidi;font-weight:normal'>Welcome to your one-stop
shop for all<o:p></o:p></span></strong></h2>

<h2 align=center style='text-align:center'><strong><span style='font-family:
"Franklin Gothic Medium","sans-serif";mso-ascii-theme-font:major-latin;
mso-hansi-theme-font:major-latin;mso-bidi-font-family:"Times New Roman";
mso-bidi-theme-font:major-bidi;font-weight:normal'>Halloween costume and party
needs!<o:p></o:p></span></strong></h2>

<p class=MsoNormal align=center style='text-align:center'><strong><o:p> </o:p></strong></p>

<p class=MsoNormal align=center style='text-align:center'><strong><span
style='color:yellow'><o:p> </o:p></span></strong></p>

<p class=MsoNormal align=center style='text-align:center'><strong><span
style='color:yellow'><a href="products.htm"><span style='font-weight:normal'>Products</span></a></span><o:p></o:p></strong></

<p class=MsoNormal align=center style='text-align:center'><strong><o:p> </o:p></strong></p>

<p class=MsoNormal align=center style='text-align:center'><strong><span
style='color:yellow'><a href="costumes.mht"><span style='font-weight:normal'>Weekly
Specials</span></a><o:p></o:p></span></strong></p>

<p class=MsoNormal align=center style='text-align:center'><strong><o:p> </o:p></strong></p>

<p class=MsoNormal align=center style='text-align:center'><strong><span
style='color:yellow'><a href="contact_info.htm"><span style='font-weight:normal'>About
Us</span></a></span><o:p></o:p></strong></p>

<div class=MsoNormal align=center style='text-align:center'><b><!--[if gte vml 1]><v:shape
 id="_x0000_i1026" type="#_x0000_t75" style='width:6in;height:7.2pt' o:hrpct="0"
 o:hralign="center" o:hr="t">
 <v:imagedata src="default_files/image003.gif" o:title="BD14710_"/>
</v:shape><![endif]--><![if !vml]><img border=0 height=10 width=576
src="default_files/image003.gif" alt=--- v:shapes="_x0000_i1026"><![endif]></b></div>

<p class=MsoNormal align=center style='text-align:center'><strong><o:p> </o:p></strong></p>

</div>

</body>

</html>
```

FIGURE 8.5 HTML Code for the Halloween Shop Web Page ➤

When you create a document in Word, you can display it in Web Layout view. This particular view enables you to continue using regular Word formatting features while displaying the document as it will appear in a Web browser. After you create and format documents, you can save them as Web pages. From within the Save As dialog box, click the *Save as type* arrow and choose an appropriate Web format. Table 8.1 lists and describes the three Web file types.

TABLE 8.1 Options for Saving Web Pages	
File Type	**Description**
Single File Web Page (*.mht; *.mhtml)	Save all Web site files, including graphics, into one file so that you can send it to someone.
Web Page (*.htm; *.html)	Create and edit Web page documents and use regular Word editing tools. Keep saving in this format until you are done.
Web Page, Filtered (*.htm; *.html)	Save the final Web page in this format to reduce file size and reduce Word editing options. Upload this file to a Web server.

Applying Themes and Background Color to a Web Page

Web pages are more interesting when you add design elements such as background images, bullets, numbering, lines, and other graphical features. They also display better when colors and fonts are coordinated among the design elements. You can use the Word themes while developing a Web page, which enables you to coordinate colors and fonts. To make sure themes are as effective as possible, you should format your document by using Word heading styles, such as Heading 1.

A **background** is a color, design, image, or watermark that appears behind text in a document or on a Web page.

Themes assign colors to the elements on the page, such as fonts, numbers, and horizontal lines, which enable you to emphasize key information. However, the theme does not automatically add a background to the Web page. A ***background*** is a color, design, image, or watermark that appears behind text in a document or on a Web page. A colored background adds visual enhancement to the Web page. You can use the Page Color command on the Page Layout tab to quickly add color to the page. If a theme is selected, the Page Color palette automatically displays colors that coordinate with the theme, as shown in Figure 8.6.

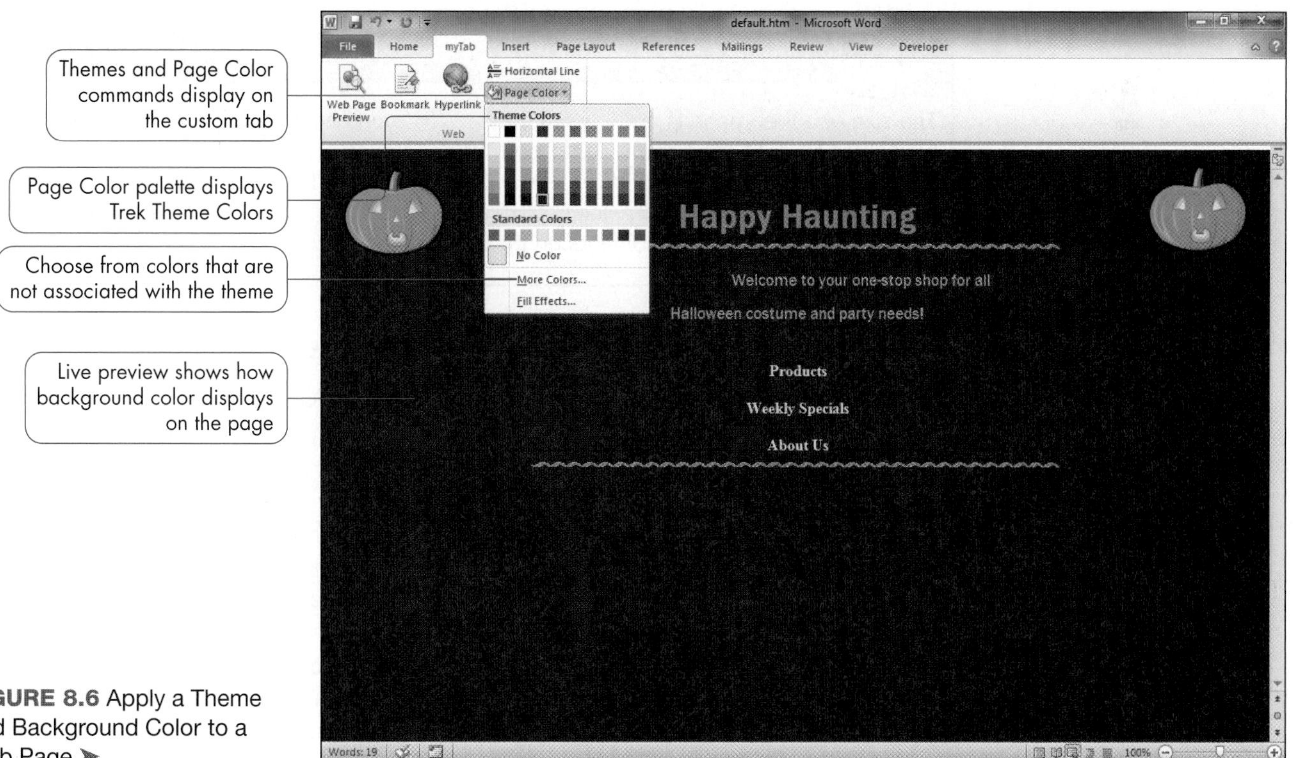

FIGURE 8.6 Apply a Theme and Background Color to a Web Page ➤

If you prefer to customize the background color, design, or image, you can click the Page Color command on the Page Layout tab, and then select from the commands that display below the theme color gallery. The More Colors command displays the Colors dialog box, which enables you to choose from the standard colors or to mix a custom color. The Fill Effects command that displays when you click Page Color enables you to apply a gradient, texture, pattern, or picture background. Figure 8.7 shows the Gradient tab of the Fill Effects dialog box, where you can select a gradient design to display on the background of your Web page.

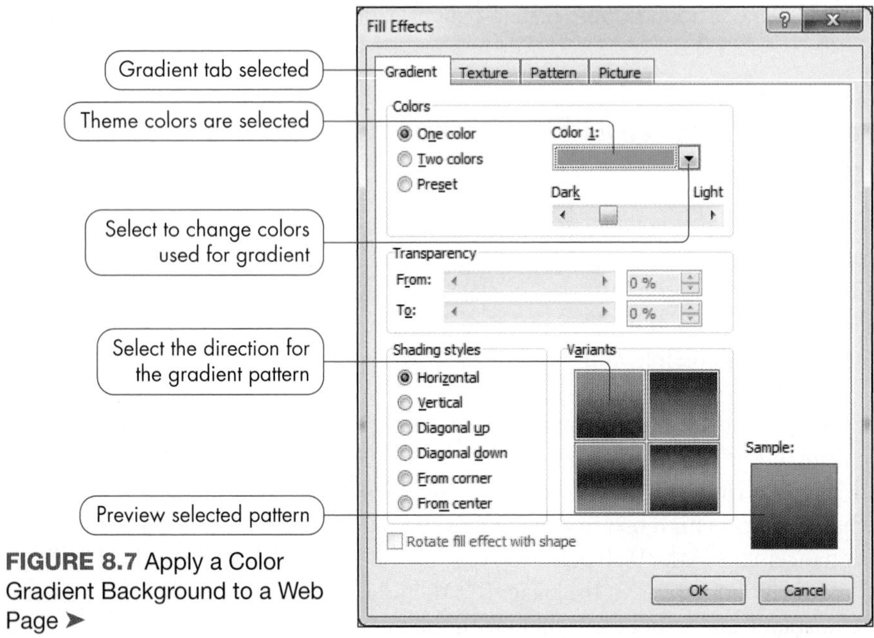

FIGURE 8.7 Apply a Color Gradient Background to a Web Page ➤

TIP Web Page Backgrounds

The size of a Web page is not the same as a Word document; Web pages are wider than a typical 8 1/2" x 11" document using portrait orientation. Therefore, any color, pattern, or image you use as a background will repeat so that it covers the entire Web page. You want to carefully select a background color, pattern, or image so that it is not distracting and does not affect the readability of the contents on the page.

Inserting Hyperlinks in a Web Page

A **hyperlink** is an electronic marker that points to a different location or displays a different Web page.

One benefit of a Web page is that it contains references, called hyperlinks, to other Web pages. ***Hyperlinks*** are electronic markers that, when clicked, move the insertion point to a different location within the same document, open another document, or display a different Web page in a Web browser. Hyperlinks can lead you to Web pages stored on different computers that may be located anywhere in the world.

Hyperlinks can be assigned to text or graphics. For example, consider a Web page you might create to document your visit to several national parks. You will display several pictures of the beautiful scenery and provide a summary of the trip. In your summary, you might mention a particular lodge where you spent a few nights, so you create a hyperlink from your Web page to the home page of the lodge. Anyone who reads your page can click the name of the lodge, and then be directed to the Web site, where they can inquire about reservations for themselves. Additionally, you might want to create a link to a particular park from a picture that was taken there. You can select the picture and assign a hyperlink that, when clicked, will direct the reader to the Web site for that national park.

To create a hyperlink in your document, select the text or picture, and then click Hyperlink in the Links group on the Insert tab. From the Insert Hyperlink dialog box, as shown in Figure 8.8, you can specify several types of hyperlinks:

- You can link to another Web page by inserting the address (or URL).
- You can link to another place within the same document.
- You can link to an e-mail address, which opens a new e-mail message when clicked.

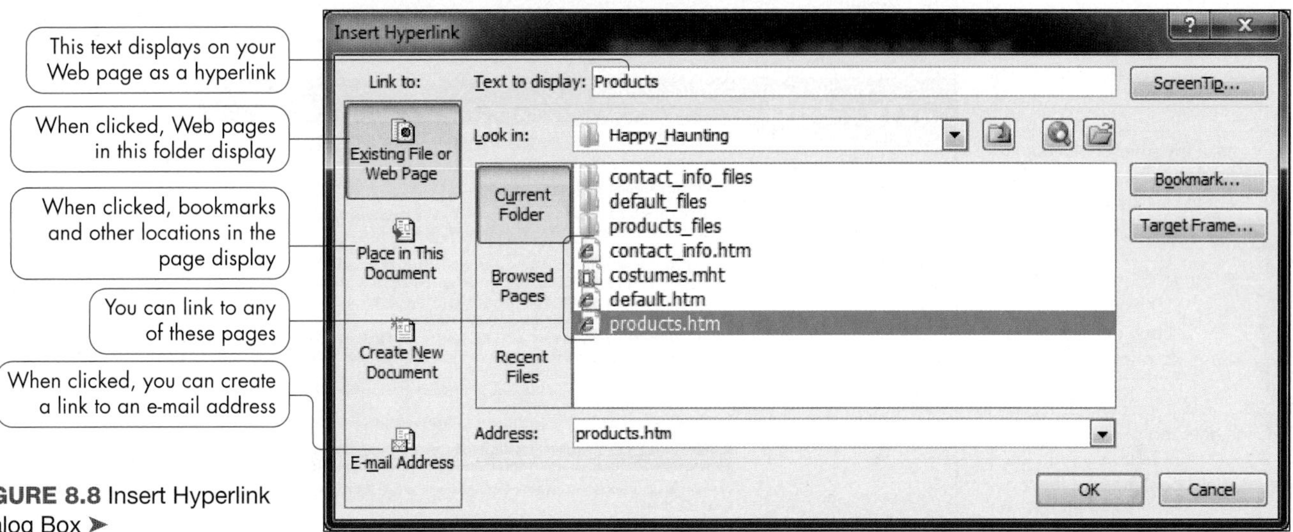

FIGURE 8.8 Insert Hyperlink Dialog Box ➤

When you point to a hyperlink in a Word document, you see a ScreenTip that directs you to press Ctrl+Click to follow the link, which is not the way you use hyperlinks in a Web Page. However, this gives you more control over the link from a development standpoint because you are able to select the link and make changes without it automatically opening in a new page. If you right-click a hyperlink in a Word document, you will see several options for working with the hyperlink, including Edit Hyperlink (which opens the Edit Hyperlink dialog box), Copy Hyperlink, and Remove Hyperlink (which removes the link but does not remove the text or graphic).

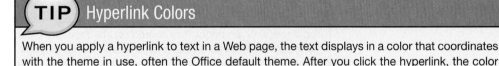

When you apply a hyperlink to text in a Web page, the text displays in a color that coordinates with the theme in use, often the Office default theme. After you click the hyperlink, the color of the text changes to the theme or default color for a followed link.

Inserting Bookmarks in a Web Page

Some Web pages are very lengthy and require the viewer to scroll a great deal to view all the contents on the page. You can help the viewer to return to the top, bottom, or other location in that page by inserting bookmarks. A bookmark is an electronic marker for a specific location in a document, enabling the user to go to that location quickly. A hyperlink takes you to a different page and can even take you to a specific location on a page, but the location must be identified somehow so the hyperlink knows exactly where to go; a bookmark provides that identification. Bookmarks are helpful in long documents because they enable you to move easily from one place to another within that document, without having to manually scroll. They are often used on FAQ (Frequently Asked Questions) Web pages, which list several questions and their answers. Consider the FAQ page in Figure 8.9. A bookmark was created for each question and answer set, so that when you click the question at the top of the page, you immediately move to that question and answer set further down the page.

Additionally, the placement of a bookmark at the top of the page enables the user to click a link at the conclusion of each question to return the user to the top of the page and the list of questions. Creating a bookmark and linking to it is a two-step process. You first create the bookmark(s) throughout the document, and then you insert a hyperlink that links to that bookmark. A bookmark for the top of the page is created automatically, so you do not have to create that one manually.

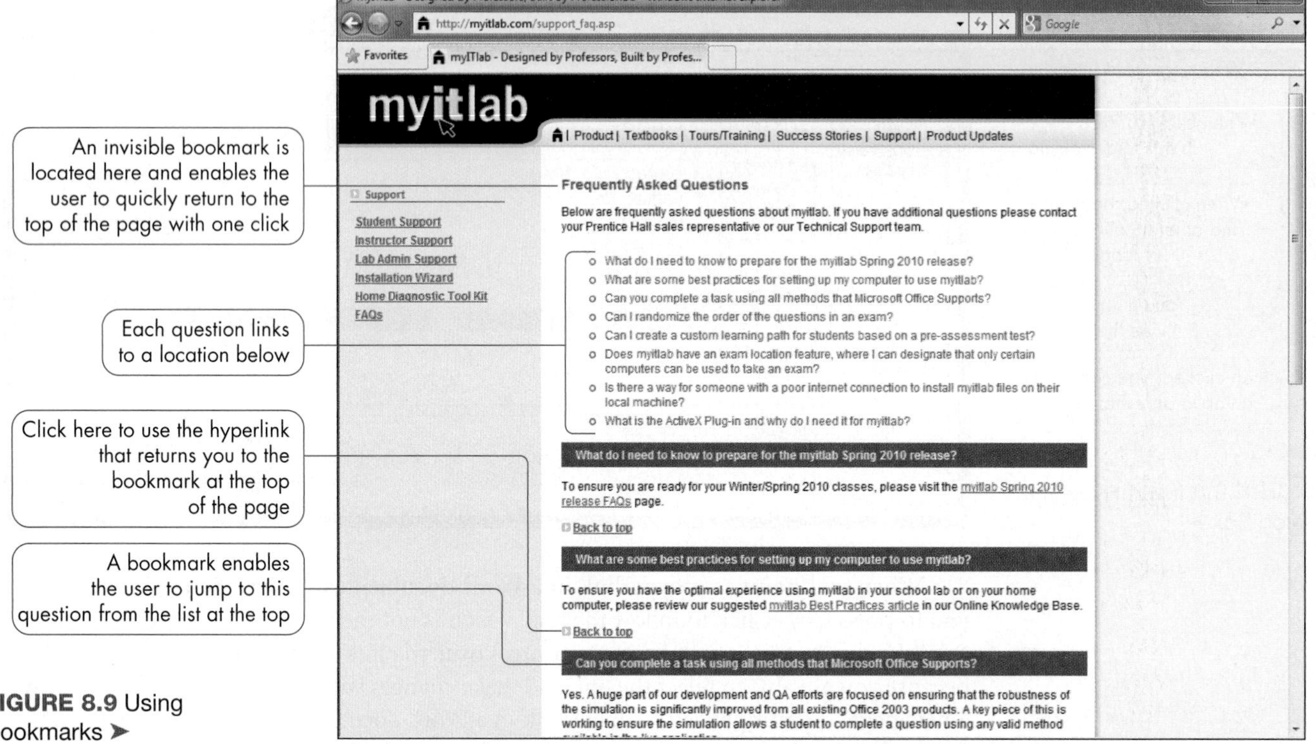

FIGURE 8.9 Using Bookmarks ➤

Bookmark Names

Spaces are not allowed in bookmark names. You can use a combination of capital and lowercase letters, numbers, and the underscore character, but you cannot begin the name of a bookmark with a number. You should create descriptive names so you can identify the bookmark easily when you create a hyperlink to it. For example, a bookmark to question #1 in a FAQ listing might be Q1.

Previewing a Web Page

After finalizing pages for a Web site, you save the document(s) as described earlier. The Web Layout view gives you a very accurate representation of how the page will look when published. You can also preview the page in an actual Web browser before you upload and publish it so that you can confirm it contains the content and is formatted to your specifications. Word contains a Web Page Preview command that you can add to a tab in the Ribbon or to the Quick Access Toolbar before you use it.

You can also open the page from within Internet Explorer, or the browser of your choice, when Word is not active. To view a Web page in Internet Explorer:

- Click File, and then click Open (or press Ctrl+O if the menu bar does not display).
- Click Browse.
- Select the folder where the page is stored.
- Select the file name of your Web page.

- Click Open.
- Click OK.

The document opens in an Internet Explorer window, as shown in Figure 8.10.

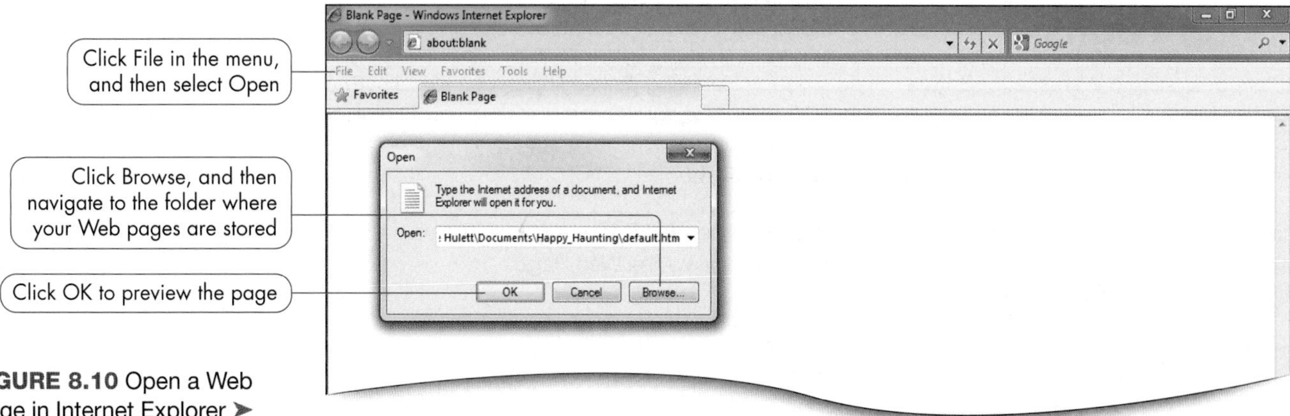

FIGURE 8.10 Open a Web Page in Internet Explorer ➤

Publishing a Web Page

A **Web server** is a computer system that hosts pages for viewing by anyone with an Internet connection.

File Transfer Protocol (FTP) is a process that uploads files from a PC to a server or from a server to a PC.

You can easily save the pages to your local computer. However, to view the pages on the Internet, you must save or publish to a ***Web server***, which is a computer system that hosts pages so that they are available for viewing by anyone who has an Internet connection. You will need additional information from your instructor about how to obtain an account on a Web server at your school, if available, as well as how to upload the pages from your PC to the server. The most common method of uploading Web pages to the server is by using ***File Transfer Protocol (FTP)***, a process that uploads files from a PC to a server or from a server to a PC.

HANDS-ON EXERCISES

1 Web Pages

You are designing a Web site for Brittany Shea's Happy Haunting Online Halloween supply store. She wants a simple design that provides basic information about her products and company. You have a few documents started but need to refine each one to use a common theme, add color, and add general Web components such as hyperlinks and bookmarks. When complete, you will preview the results to make sure it is ready to go live on the Web.

Skills covered: Create a Custom Tab • Save Documents as Web Pages • Add a Theme and Background • Insert and Link to Bookmarks • Insert Hyperlinks and a Horizontal Line • Preview the Web Page

STEP 1 CREATE A CUSTOM TAB

Before you begin designing a Web page, you want to organize the tools that will enable you to work quickly and efficiently. You decide to create a custom Tab to display the commands you will use most frequently while designing the Web site. Refer to Figure 8.11 as you complete Step 1.

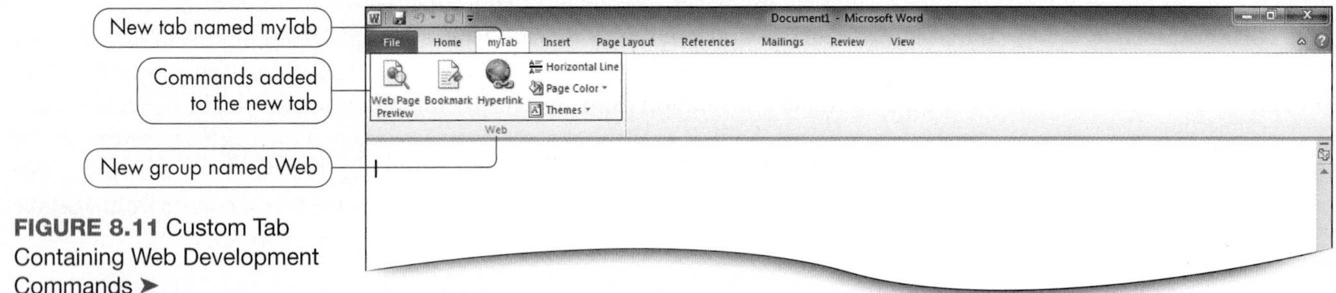

FIGURE 8.11 Custom Tab Containing Web Development Commands ➤

a. Start Word, and then open a new document.

   You can create a custom tab or group in any open document, and it can be used in all documents.

b. Click the **Home tab**, if necessary. Click **File**, click **Options**, and then click **Customize Ribbon**.

   The Word commands available display in the pane on the left side. On the right side, you customize the tabs and groups with the available commands.

> **TROUBLESHOOTING:** If you work in a lab environment where you are unable to customize the applications on your PC, read through the remainder of Step 1.

c. Click **New Tab**, which displays below the Customize the Ribbon pane on the right side of the window.

   A new tab is created in the Main Tabs list and positioned between the *Home* tab and the *Insert* tab. The tab is named *New Tab (Custom)* and contains a new group named *New Group (Custom)*.

d. Click **New Tab (Custom)**, and then click **Rename**, which displays below that pane. Type **myTab** in the **Display name box**, and then click **OK**.

   The new tab displays as *myTab (Custom)*.

e. Click **New Group (Custom)**, and then click **Rename**.

   The Rename dialog box opens.

f. Click the first symbol (first row, first column) in the *symbol* section. Type **Web** in the **Display name box**, and then click **OK**.

   The group displays as *Web (Custom).*

g. Click the **Choose commands from arrow**, and then click **Commands Not in the Ribbon**.

h. Scroll down the list of commands, click **Web Page Preview**, and then click **Add**.

   Web Page Preview is added to myTab (Custom) in the Web (Custom) group.

i. Click the **Choose commands from arrow**, and then click **All Commands**. Select each of the following commands, and then click **Add** to display them in the Web (Custom) group on the myTab (Custom) tab:
   - **Bookmark...**
   - **Horizontal Line...**
   - **Hyperlink...**
   - **Page Color**
   - **Themes**
   - **Web Layout**

j. Confirm that the myTab tab is checked so that it will display on the Ribbon, and then click **OK** to close the Options dialog box.

k. Click the **myTab tab**, and then notice the Web group contains seven commands. Right-click the **Ribbon**, and then click **Customize the Ribbon**.

   The Word Options dialog box opens.

l. Click the **plus sign** (+) to display all commands in the Web group on the myTab tab.

m. Click to select **Hyperlink**, and then drag and drop it above *Horizontal Line.* Click **Web Layout**, and then click **Remove**. Click **OK** to close the Options dialog box.

   This removes the Web Layout command, which you can access from the status bar. It also changes the order in which the commands display on the tab, as shown in Figure 8.11.

n. Leave the blank document open for the next step.

STEP 2 SAVE DOCUMENTS AS WEB PAGES

You have a few documents prepared as a foundation for the Web site, but before you get started, you first create a folder for storing Web page files. Then you open each one and save it as a Web page, which places it in the proper format for viewing in a Web browser. You recognize that the name of the page displays in the task bar in Windows and Internet Explorer, so you are careful to change the title for each page. Refer to Figure 8.12 as you complete Step 2.

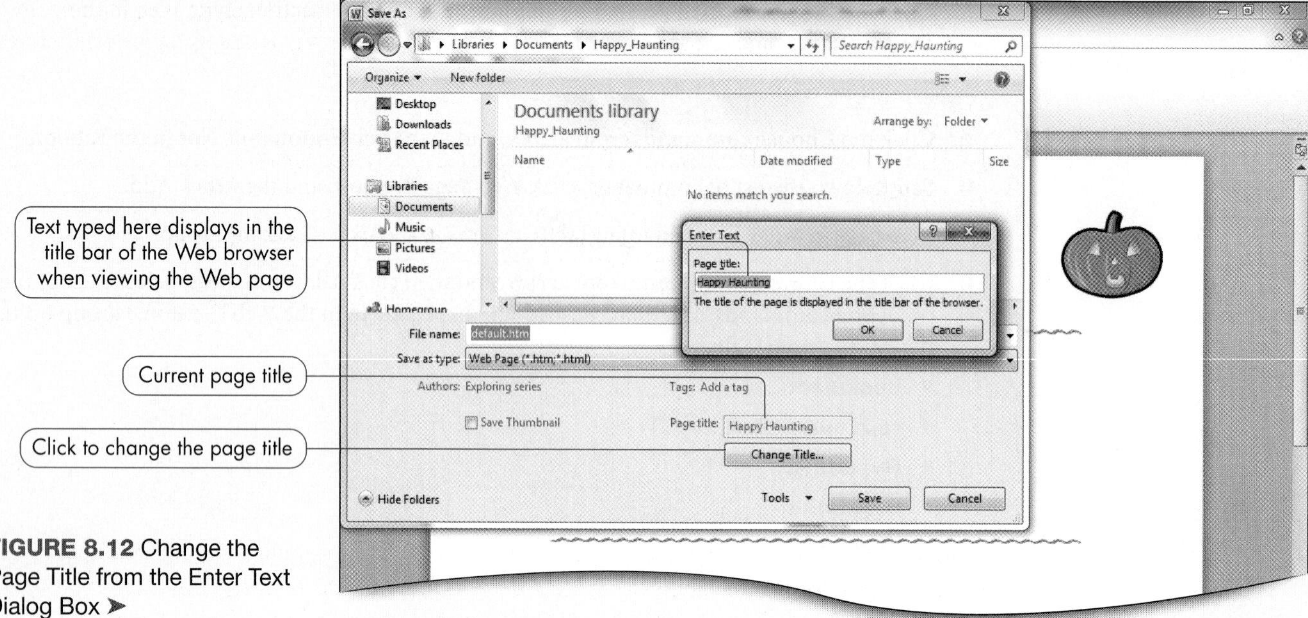

FIGURE 8.12 Change the Page Title from the Enter Text Dialog Box ➤

a. Open *w08h1default.*

This document is designed to be the home page for the Happy Haunting Web site. In the next step, you create a folder and save the document in that folder.

b. Click **File**, and then click **Save As**. In the Save in box, navigate to the drive and folder in which you want to create a folder.

Before you start creating Web documents, you need to create a folder to store all Web documents for a specific Web site.

c. Click **New Folder** on the Save As dialog box toolbar, type **Happy_Haunting**, and then press **Open**. Double-click the new folder to open it.

TIP Naming a Web Site Home Page

A Web site's home page is typically saved as default.html or index.html so that it loads automatically when you type the main URL in a Web browser address box.

d. Type **default** in the **File name box**.

e. Click the **Save as type arrow**, and then click **Web Page (*.htm; *.html)**.

When you save as a Web page, the Save As dialog box displays the Page title text area and the Change Title button.

f. Click **Change Title** to display the Enter Text dialog box, as shown in Figure 8.12.

In this dialog box, you can edit the Web page title—the text that appears on the Web browser's title bar when the Web page displays.

g. Press →, press the **Spacebar** to add a space, type **Online** in the **Page title text box** following the text *Happy Haunting*, and then click **OK**. Click **Save**.

The page displays in Web Layout view.

h. Drag the second pumpkin graphic from the left side of the page back to the top-right corner.

i. Open the Word documents listed in the table below. Save each document as a Web page in the Happy_Haunting folder. Assign new file names and Web page titles using the information in the following table.

Open This File	Save As	Web Page Title
w08h1products	products	*Happy Haunting Products*
w08h1contact	contact_info	*Happy Haunting Contact Information*

The Happy_Haunting folder now contains three Web pages that you use to complete your Web site.

j. Leave each document open for the next step.

TIP Naming Pages in Your Web Site

When you save a folder or page that you plan to use on a Web site, you should refrain from using spaces in the folder or file name. Even though it is possible to include spaces, it forces the Web browser to insert codes in place of the spaces when it displays the file name and path in the Address bar. For example, if you name a Web page *contact info*, it displays as *contact%20info* when viewed in a Web browser. If you need to use a long name, consider using dashes or underscores in place of spaces.

STEP 3 ADD A THEME AND BACKGROUND

Now that your Web pages are in the proper form, you select a common theme to use on each one. The theme affects the fonts but not the background. So you also select a background color that gives a dramatic look to your simple pages. Refer to Figure 8.13 as you complete Step 3.

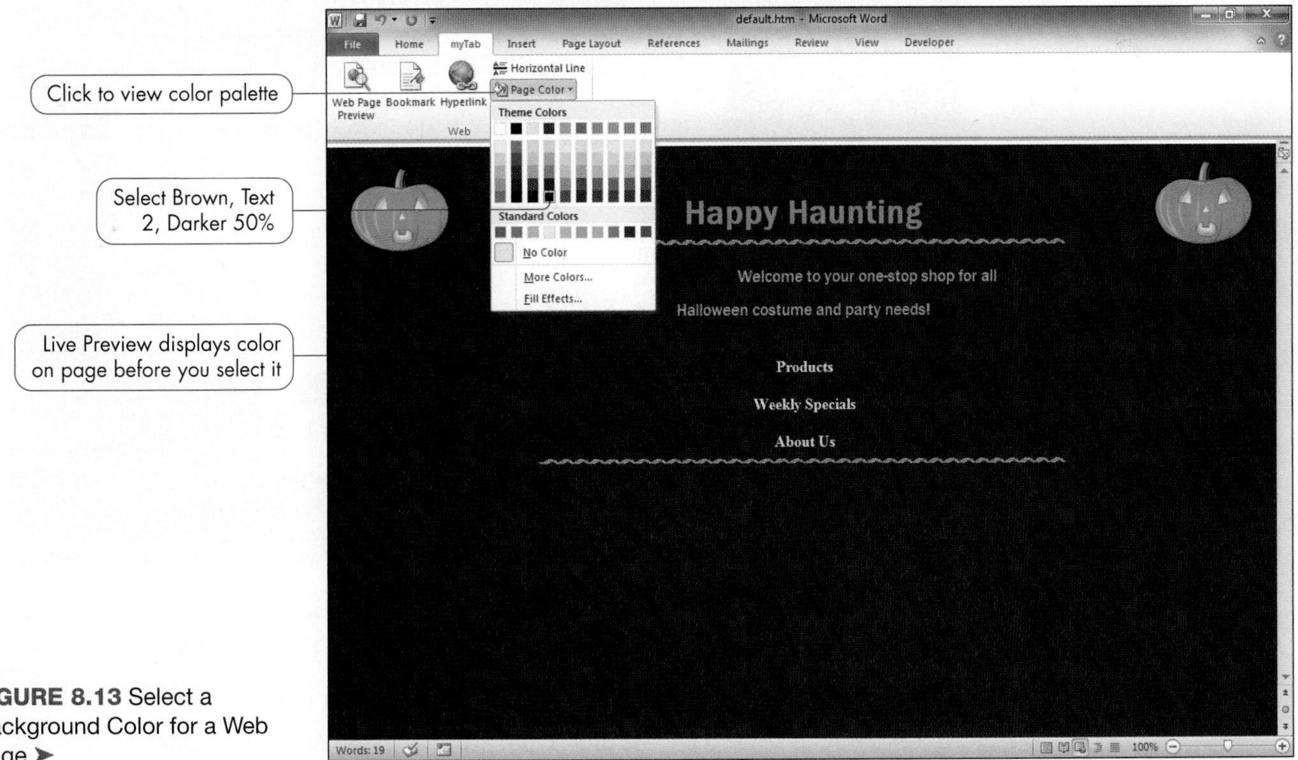

FIGURE 8.13 Select a Background Color for a Web Page ➤

a. Click the **View tab**, click **Switch Windows** in the Window group, and then click **default.htm** from the list of open files.

b. Click the **myTab tab**, click **Themes** in the Web group, and then click **Trek**.

The *Happy Haunting* title and text below it display in colors represented in the Trek theme.

c. Click **Page Color** in the Web group. Click **Brown, Text 2, Darker 50%** (sixth row, fourth column), as shown in Figure 8.13.

You applied a dark brown background color that covers the entire page.

d. Click **Save** in the Quick Access Toolbar to save the changes to the default.htm document.

e. Press **Alt+Tab** repeatedly until the *contact_info.htm* document displays. Repeat steps b and c to apply the same theme and background color to the page. Click **Save** on the Quick Access Toolbar to save the changes.

f. Press **Alt+Tab** repeatedly until the *products.htm* document displays. Repeat steps b and c to apply the theme and background color to the page. Click **Save** on the Quick Access Toolbar to save the changes.

STEP 4 INSERT AND LINK TO BOOKMARKS

The Web page that describes the products for sale is quite lengthy. You know that a good Web design will assist the viewer in navigating up and down the page without having to scroll. With that in mind, you incorporate bookmarks, which are a type of hyperlink, to help the reader move from section to section on the page. Refer to Figure 8.14 as you complete Step 4.

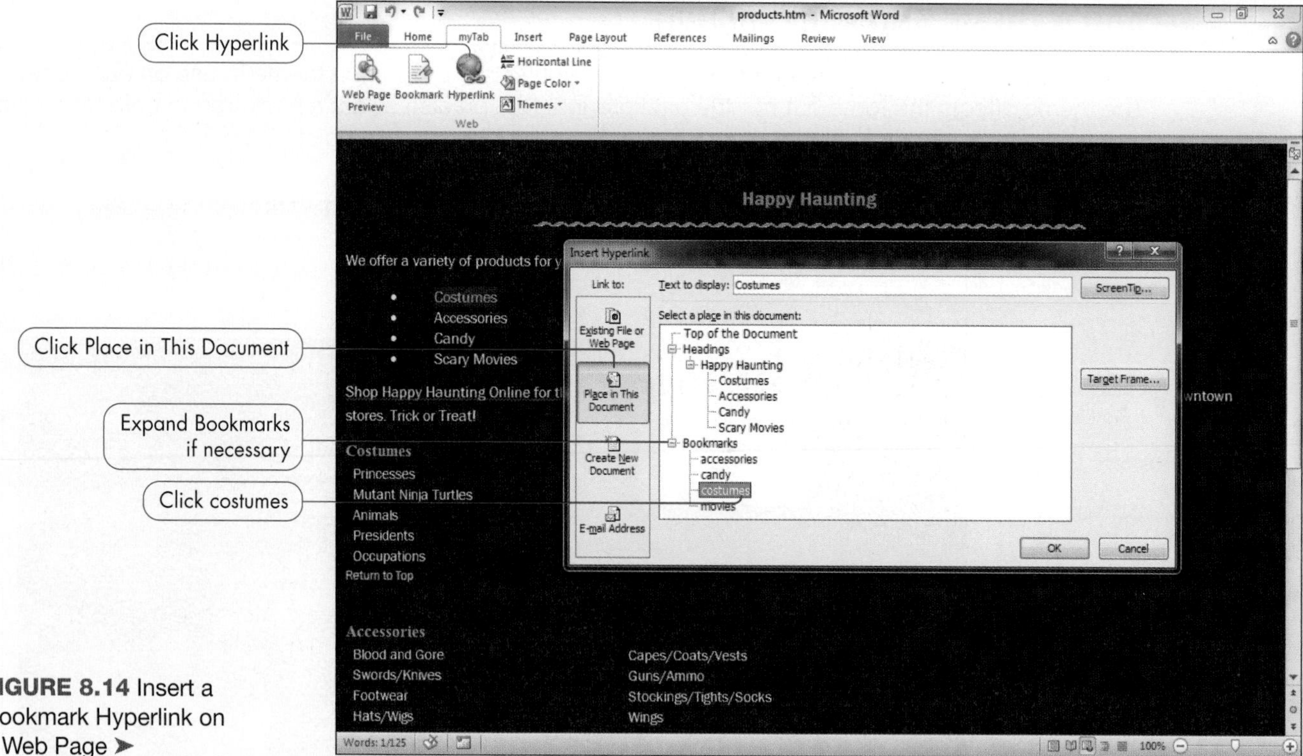

FIGURE 8.14 Insert a Bookmark Hyperlink on a Web Page ➤

a. Display the products page, if necessary. Place the insertion point on the left side of the word *Costumes*, which displays as a heading for the first table on the products page.

This table describes the variety of costumes that sell on the Happy Haunting Web site.

b. Click **Bookmark** in the Web group, type **costumes** in the **Bookmark name text box**, and then click **Add**.

c. Repeat step b to create bookmarks at the beginning of the headings *Accessories*, *Candy*, and *Scary Movies* that display down the page. The bookmarks should be named **accessories**, **candy**, and **movies**.

> **TROUBLESHOOTING:** If you insert a bookmark in the wrong location or name it incorrectly, click Bookmark on the myTab tab, select the incorrect bookmark from the list that displays in the Bookmark name list box, and then click Delete. You can recreate the bookmark to meet your specifications, if necessary.

d. Press **Ctrl+Home** to view the top of the page. Select **Costumes** in the **bullet list**, and then click **Hyperlink** from the Web group on the myTab tab.

   The Insert Hyperlink dialog box displays. You will select the bookmark to create a link from the word Costumes to the location in the document where the costume varieties display.

e. Click **Place in This Document** in the *Link to* panel of the Insert Hyperlink dialog box. If necessary, click the **plus sign** (+) next to *Bookmarks*. Click **costumes**, as shown in Figure 8.14, and then click **OK**.

   The Costumes bullet displays as a hyperlink, and the text color changes to red.

f. Hover your mouse over the Costumes hyperlink and view the ScreenTip that displays the name of the bookmark and *Ctrl+Click to follow link*. Press **Ctrl**, and then click the hyperlink to move the insertion point to the listing of costumes.

   The page scrolls so the heading *Costumes* displays near the top of the screen, and the insertion point moves as well. This simplifies navigation on the page. Additionally, the color of the hyperlink changes as a visual indication that it has been clicked.

g. Repeat steps d and e to create hyperlinks from each bullet list item to the corresponding bookmarks for *accessories*, *candy*, and *movies*.

h. Select the text *Return to Top* that displays below the costumes table. Click **Hyperlink** in the Web group, click **Top of the Document** that displays at the very top of the *Select a place in this document* list, and then click **OK**.

   This bookmark to the top of the page is created automatically when you save the document as a Web page. When you click this link, the page scrolls to the very top and displays the page heading. This enables you to return to the top of the page after you view content at the bottom of the page.

i. Repeat step h to create a hyperlink from each occurrence of *Return to Top* that displays below each product table.

j. Save the Web page.

STEP 5 INSERT HYPERLINKS AND A HORIZONTAL LINE

Your last modification is the addition of hyperlinks to other pages. You want the viewer to have the ability to click from one page to another in this site with ease, so you add hyperlinks on each page that link to the others. Refer to Figure 8.15 as you complete Step 5.

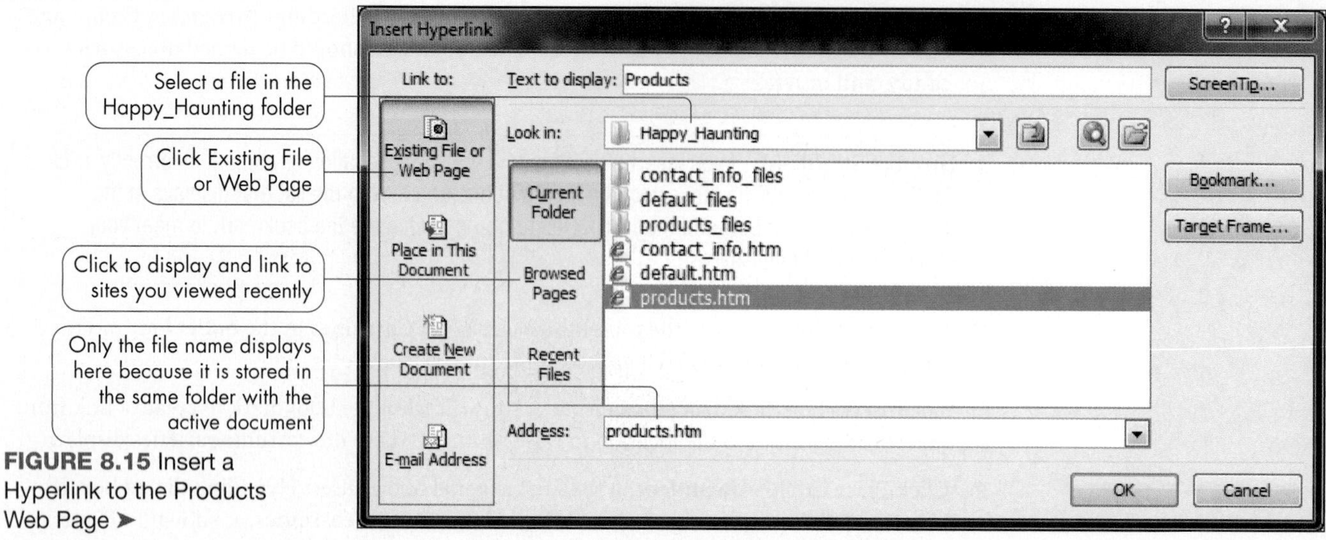

FIGURE 8.15 Insert a Hyperlink to the Products Web Page ➤

a. Click **default.htm - Microsoft Word** on the task bar to display the default Web page. Select **Products**, right-click to display the shortcut menu, and then click **Hyperlink** to display the Insert Hyperlink dialog box.

b. Click **Existing File or Web Page** in the *Link to* panel of the Insert Hyperlink dialog box. Scroll, if necessary, and click the *products.htm* file, as shown in Figure 8.15. Click **OK.**

   By creating this link, the Products page displays when you click *Products* on the home page.

c. Repeat step b to create a hyperlink from *About Us* on the default page to the contact_info .htm Web page. Click **Save** in the Quick Access Toolbar.

   You will create a link using the *Weekly Specials* text in a future exercise.

> **TROUBLESHOOTING:** If your link does not work properly, right-click the hyperlink, and then select Edit Hyperlink, which displays the Edit Hyperlink dialog box and enables you to revise the link. Remove Hyperlink also displays when you right-click a hyperlink, and this enables you to remove the hyperlink completely.

d. Click **contact_info.htm - Microsoft Word** on the task bar to display the contact_info Web page. Complete the following steps to create a link to the default page:
   - Press **Ctrl+End**, and then press **Enter**.
   - Type **Return to the Home Page** and press **Ctrl+E**.
   - Select the text *Return to the Home Page*, and then click **Hyperlink**.
   - Select **default.htm**, and then click **OK**.

e. Press **Enter** two times to move the insertion point below the hyperlink. Click **Horizontal Line** in the Web group. Scroll down, and then select the orange-colored wavy line that displays *Citrus Punch* as a description when you hold your mouse over the line in the dialog box. Click **OK**.

   Now you have a second wavy line in the document that matches the graphic that displays below the Happy Haunting heading.

f. Click **Save** on the Quick Access Toolbar.

g. Click **Products.htm - Microsoft Word** on the task bar to display the Products Web page. Press **Ctrl+End**, and then press **Enter** one time. Type **Return to the Home Page**, select the text you just typed, and then click **Hyperlink**. Select **default.htm**, and then click **OK.**

   The contact_info and products pages now include a link back to the home page of the Web site.

h. Save each document.

STEP 6 PREVIEW THE WEB PAGE

With your changes and edits complete, you decide to take a look at the final product. All files are saved in the Happy_Haunting folder, so you can open and preview them from within a Web browser. If everything looks acceptable, you will later send them to the company that will host the Web site. Refer to Figure 8.16 as you complete Step 6.

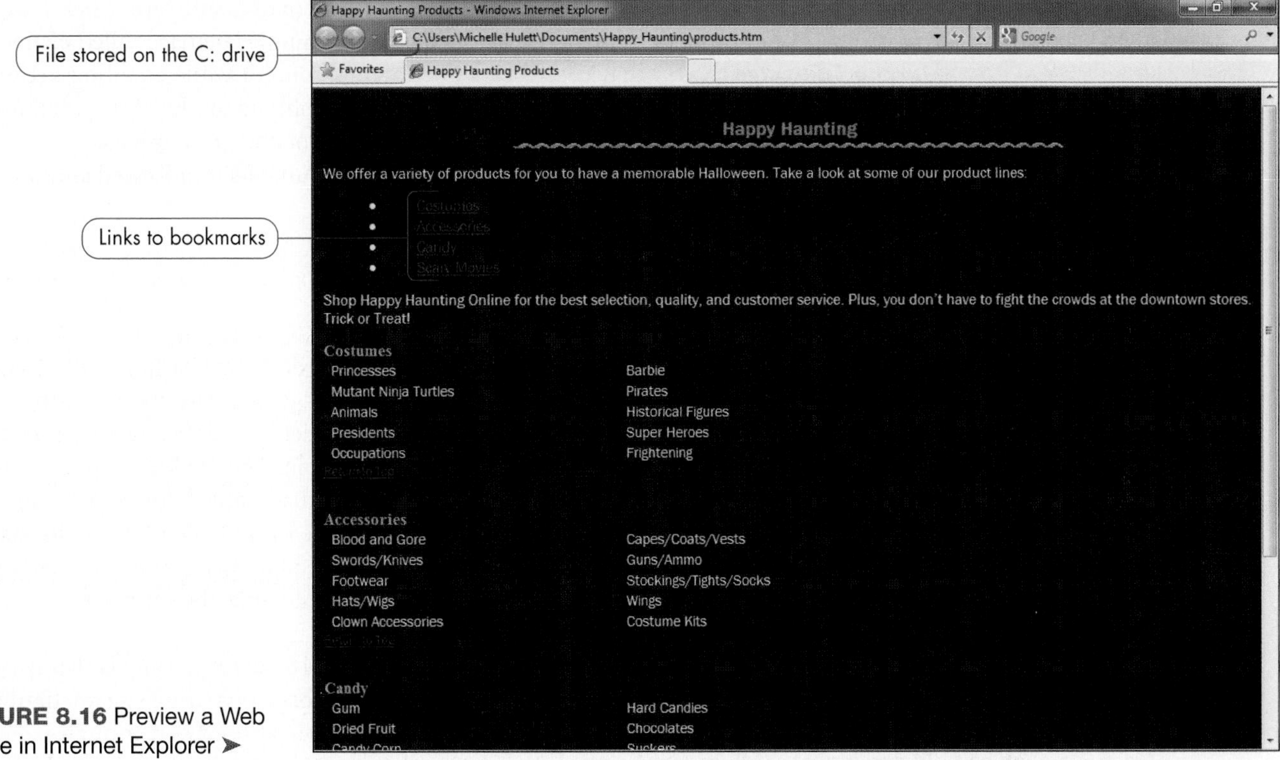

FIGURE 8.16 Preview a Web Page in Internet Explorer ➤

a. Display the default Web page. Click **Web Page Preview** in the Web group.

   The web browser window opens and the page displays. Look closely at the components of the URL in the Address bar, reading from right to left. You are viewing the *default.htm* document, which is stored in the Happy_Haunting folder, which is probably stored in one or more folders that are stored on the hard drive (C:). That means you are viewing the site locally, as opposed to seeing it on the Web. Next, you will open and view a page from within Internet Explorer. If your default web browser is not Internet Explorer, you can adjust the instructions as needed for your preferred browser.

b. Press **Ctrl+O** to display the Open dialog box in Internet Explorer. Click **Browse**, locate the Happy_Haunting folder, and then double-click **contact_info.htm**. Click **OK** in the Open dialog box to display the page.

> **TROUBLESHOOTING:** If the menu bar does not display in Internet Explorer, right-click anywhere in the toolbar area, and then click Menu Bar. You can also use this same procedure to remove the toolbar. If you do not want to display the menu bar, press Alt+F to display the menu on a temporary basis.

c. Click the **Return to Home Page** link to make sure it works properly.

d. From the home page, click the hyperlink to the **Products** page. Once the products page displays, click the hyperlinks to navigate from top to bottom and then back to top.

e. Click **Return to the Home Page** to verify the link to the default page works.

f. Exit Internet Explorer.

g. Close *default.htm*, *products.htm*, and *contact_info.htm*, and then exit Word.

eXtensible Markup Language (XML)

eXtensible Markup Language (XML) is a language that describes a document's content and enables easy exchange of data.

Electronic communication and data sharing are common, if not critical, today. People create electronic documents and distribute them all over the world using many types of devices such as cell phones, personal digital assistants (PDAs), and computers. Unfortunately, some documents may be incompatible with the receiver's system and software. Therefore, the World Wide Web Consortium (W3C) developed a programming language called ***eXtensible Markup Language (XML)*** that describes a document's content while enabling people to exchange information among various applications. The ability to apply XML functionality to your Word documents increases the usefulness of your documents to others.

In this section, you will learn how content in Word documents is processed and saved in XML format.

Understanding XML

XML goes a step beyond the code generated by HTML as described earlier in the chapter; HTML describes how a document should look by using tags that describe formatting features such as bold and indent. XML is data about data—it lets you define tags that describe the data or content in a document. Consider this example: The HTML code "<B>John Doe</B>" indicates that "John Doe" should appear in boldface, but it does not tell us anything more. You do not know that "John" is the first name or that "Doe" is the last name. XML lets you define your own tags; for example, "<name><first>John</first><last>Doe </last></name>." By tagging the content as first name or last name, the specific information can be extracted and entered into a database.

... HTML describes how a document should look by using tags that describe formatting features such as bold and indent. XML is data about data—it lets you define tags that describe the data or content in a document.

The major advantage of XML file formatting is that it is not constrained to a particular platform, operating system, hardware configuration, or software application. Even though it is not obvious, a Word 2010 document is actually saved in several XML files, which are compressed together to make a .docx file. This enables XML functionality, so that you can easily share information with others if needed. You can also specify that a file is saved strictly as an XML document, which is given an *xml* extension instead of *docx*. After you create XML documents in Word, database administrators can extract XML data and then import the data into a database, which in turn can be used to create brochures, catalogs, correspondence, and Web pages.

Attaching an XML Schema

An **XML schema** is a file that defines the structure and organization of content within an XML document.

Before saving a document in XML format, you must attach an XML schema to it. An ***XML schema*** is a file that defines the structure and organization of content within an XML document. For example, a schema can specify the number of characters allowed for a book title or dictate a range of acceptable values to be entered by a user. It is vaguely similar to a Word template in respect to being attached to a file and controlling the document. Whereas a template contains styles that dictate the formatting of a document, an XML schema dictates the structure of content in a document. Typically, the Information Technology (IT) department studies routine document creation and usage, analyzes how document content is stored and used, develops schemas for these types of documents, and makes the schemas available for end users. Figure 8.17 shows a schema that you attach to an existing document.

Subelements for Product element

Values allowed for product size

Root element

Main elements

Product element refers to ProductType subelements

```
<?xml version="1.0" encoding="utf-8" ?>
<xs:schema id="schema" targetNamespace="http://tempuri.org/schema.xsd" elementFormDefault="qualified"
       xmlns="http://tempuri.org/schema.xsd" xmlns:mstns="http://tempuri.org/schema.xsd"
 xmlns:xs="http://www.w3.org/2001/XMLSchema">
       <xs:complexType name="ProductType">
              <xs:complexContent>
                     <xs:restriction base="xs:anyType">
                            <xs:sequence>
                                   <xs:element name="Name" type="xs:string" />
                                   <xs:element name="Size" type="ProductSizes" />
                                   <xs:element name="RegPrice" type="xs:decimal" />
                                   <xs:element name="SalePrice" type="xs:decimal" />
                            </xs:sequence>
                     </xs:restriction>
              </xs:complexContent>
       </xs:complexType>
       <xs:simpleType name="ProductSizes">
              <xs:restriction base="xs:string">
                     <xs:enumeration value="S" />
                     <xs:enumeration value="M" />
                     <xs:enumeration value="L" />
                     <xs:enumeration value="XL" />
                     <xs:enumeration value="XXL" />
              </xs:restriction>
       </xs:simpleType>
       <xs:element name="Specials">
              <xs:complexType>
                     <xs:sequence>
                            <xs:element name="Caption" type="xs:string"></xs:element>
                            <xs:element name="NameHead" type="xs:string"></xs:element>
                            <xs:element name="SizeHead" type="xs:string"></xs:element>
                            <xs:element name="RegPriceHead" type="xs:string"></xs:element>
                            <xs:element name="SalePriceHead" type="xs:string"></xs:element>
                            <xs:element name="Product" type="ProductType" minOccurs="1"
maxOccurs="unbounded"></xs:element>
                     </xs:sequence>
              </xs:complexType>
       </xs:element>
</xs:schema>
```

FIGURE 8.17 XML Schema ➤

To add a schema, display the Developer tab, and then in the XML group, click Schema, which displays the Templates and Add-ins dialog box. Click the XML Schema tab to view options for adding a schema. When you add a schema, you make it available to new and existing documents. However, you must attach the schema to be able to tag a document. This process is similar to attaching templates: The Templates tab of the Templates and Add-ins dialog box contains available templates, but you must attach a template to a document to include its functionality. After attaching a schema to your document, you apply tags to the document text. A tag is a marker that indicates the beginning or end of particular content within a document. The ***tag*** enables the transferability of data in such a way that other applications can import the tagged data. Figure 8.18 shows tags applied to text within a table.

A **tag** is a marker that indicates the beginning or end of particular content within a document.

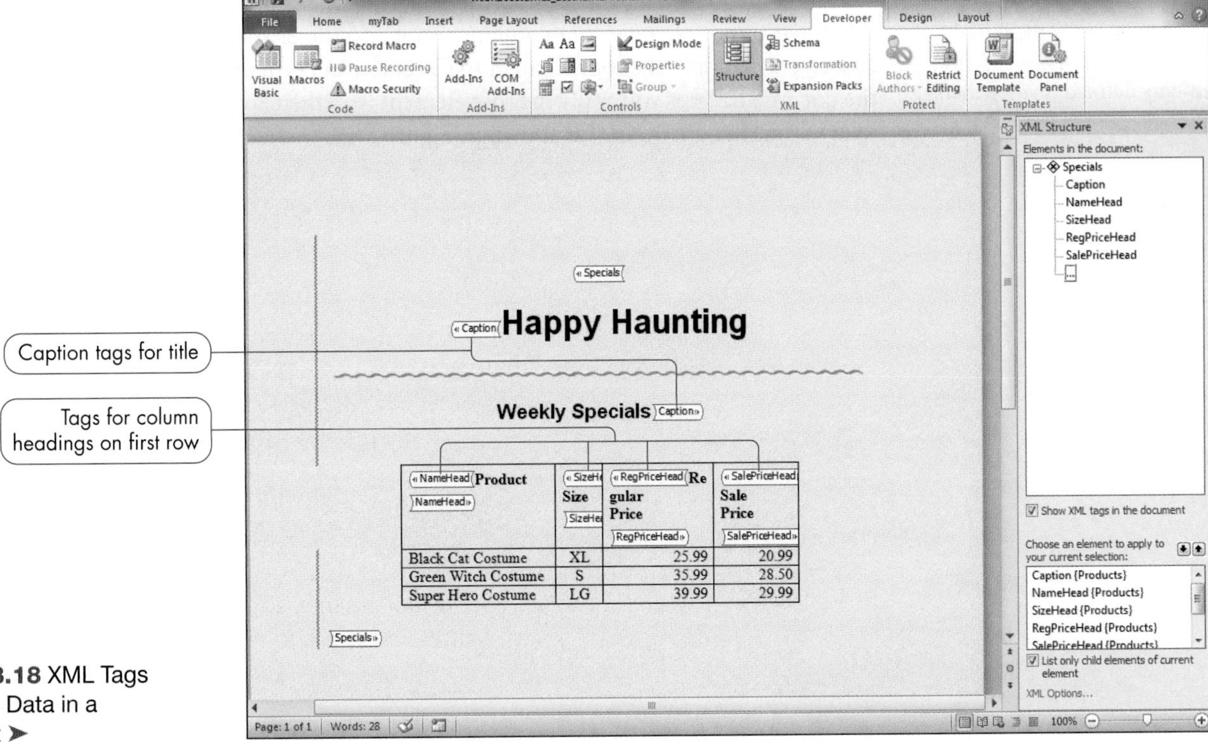

FIGURE 8.18 XML Tags Applied to Data in a Document ➤

You can add more than one schema to a particular document. To add more schemas, use the same process as you did for the first schema. Each schema you add is listed in the Available XML schemas list box in the Templates and Add-ins dialog box. When you add schemas, they are available for any document. You can click the check box next to the schema you want to attach to another document. Word alerts you to any conflicts that arise when you attach multiple schemas.

If you no longer want a schema attached to a document, you can deselect the schema's check box in the Available XML schemas list box in the Templates and Add-ins dialog box. This process does not delete the schema but removes it from the current document. If a conflict prevents you from using a particular schema because of the presence of another, you can delete the schema from the Schema Library and remove it completely.

TIP XML Files

Office 2010 uses XML format by default. The XML schemas and tags are compatible with those generated by Office 2003. However, Office 2007 and Office 2010 split the XML output into numerous files that are zipped together in a .docx file (for example, fonts are defined in a separate document, as are document styles).

Tag Text with XML Elements

An **element** is a descriptive name that identifies a piece of data.

A **root element** is the initial element that contains specific elements defined by the schema.

After you add a schema to a document, the XML Structure pane opens on the right side of the screen and displays elements defined by the attached schema. An ***element*** is a descriptive name that identifies a piece of data. It is similar to how a field name identifies data within an Access database table. For example, the field name FirstName identifies the data as a person's first name. One advantage of XML is its self-documenting characteristic. This means that developers can assign their own descriptive element names. These names should clearly indicate the specific types of data to be tagged in a document. You must use the schema's elements to tag the content within your document so that the association of tags and content will be available when you save the document in XML format. When you first attach a schema to a document, the XML Structure pane displays only one element. This initial element is the ***root element*** that contains more specific elements defined by the schema. Your first step is to apply the root element to the entire document or to a particular section within the document. After you apply the root element, you then apply individual elements to specific data within the document, as shown in Figure 8.19.

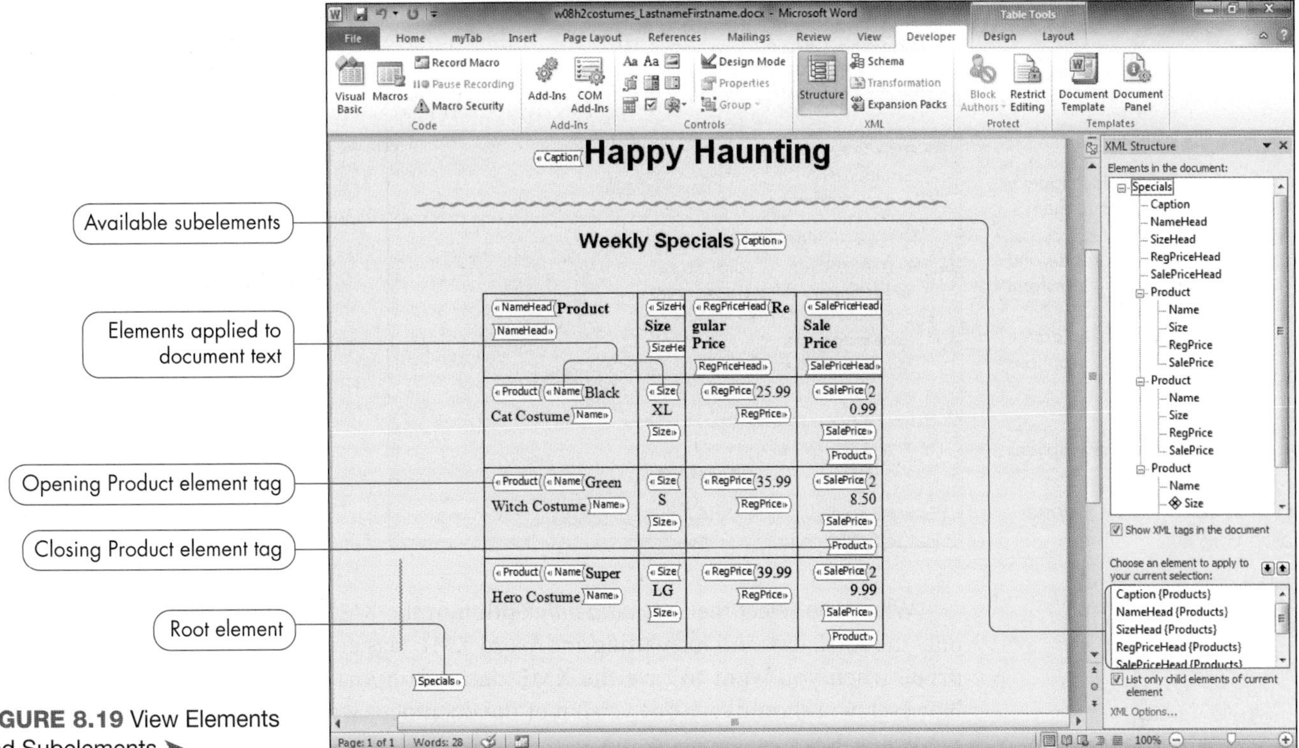

FIGURE 8.19 View Elements and Subelements ➤

Work with Elements

You can display or hide XML tags while working in the document. Click the Show XML tags in the document check box on the XML Structure pane or press Ctrl+Shift+X.

You can copy or move an element within an XML document. First, select the opening and closing element tags for a particular element. Then, use the Copy or Cut command to copy or cut, respectively, the selected element to the Clipboard. Finally, position the insertion point where you want the element and use the Paste command.

If you want to delete an element without deleting the text, right-click either the opening or closing tag in the document window or right-click the correct Element in the document list box in the XML Structure pane and choose Remove tag from the shortcut menu. The menu command displays the specific element name, such as Remove Size tag. If you apply the wrong element to text, you can change the element tag. You must first remove the existing tag. After removing that tag, select the text, and then apply the tag for the element that corresponds with the type of selected text.

Choose Default Save Options

You can further define XML settings through the XML Options dialog box. You can control how XML documents save, validate, and appear onscreen. Figure 8.20 shows the XML Options dialog box. The settings you apply in the XML Options dialog box are automatically applied when you save XML documents.

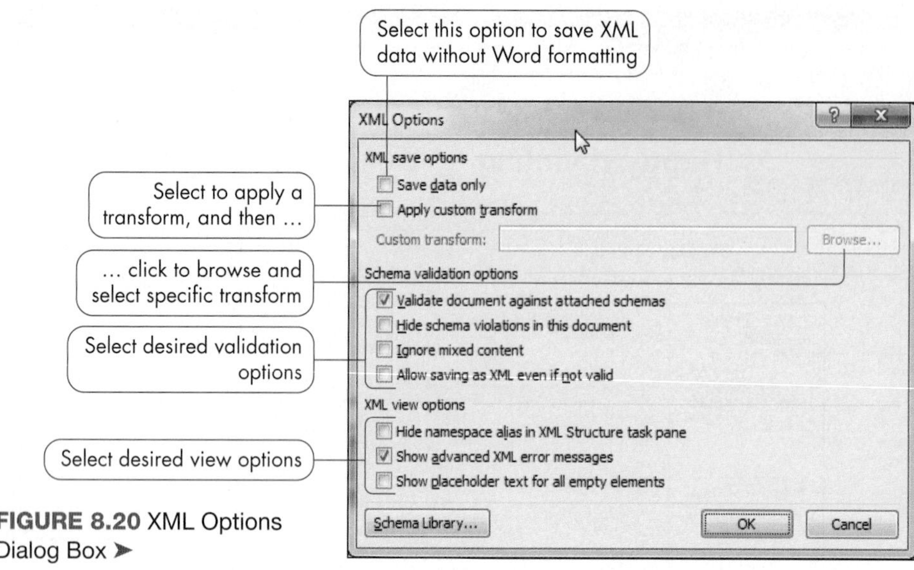

FIGURE 8.20 XML Options Dialog Box ➤

When you select the *Save data only* option in the XML Options dialog box, Word saves only the XML data. All formatting and Word XML tags are discarded. This option is appropriate when you want to save the XML data to import into another XML application. However, you should save one version of the document with formatting in case you want to modify or use the original document.

A **transform** is a file that converts XML documents into another type of formatted language, such as HTML.

Click the *Apply custom transform* check box in the XML Options dialog box if you want to apply a ***transform***—a file that converts XML documents into another type of formatted language, such as HTML. In other words, transforms specify how XML documents should be formatted and how they should display. After selecting the *Apply custom transform* check box, click Browse to select the transform file to apply. If you want to include the data in a Web page, you might use a transform to convert it to HTML format so it will insert easily into your page.

Schema validation is the process of examining the content and tags against the schema to ensure accuracy and conformity.

The *Schema validation options* section controls how Word checks the accuracy of the XML tags that you apply. ***Schema validation*** is the process of examining the content and tags against the schema to ensure that tags are correctly applied to the document content and that the content conforms to any schema requirements. For example, if you apply a numeric tag to a string of text, a validation error occurs. Additionally, the schema validation might allow only certain values for an element, such as the sizes S, M, L, and XL. Word flags validation errors in two ways: (1) a purple wavy line in the left margin area, and (2) an error symbol in the XML Structure pane next to the element that contains the validation problem. The *XML view options* section enables you to control the namespace alias listing in the XML Structure pane, advanced error messages, and the placeholder text view.

If you enforce validation, Word does not save an XML document that contains validation errors. Therefore, if you are working on a complicated XML document that will take some time to finish, you can select the *Allow saving as XML even if not valid* check box. This option enables you to save the XML document even though it might contain validation errors. However, you should deselect this check box after correcting validation errors before you publish the final XML document.

You can directly open an XML file that you saved in Word in other programs, such as Excel or Access. The program that you use to open the XML document recognizes the document's structure and displays it in a particular format.

2 eXtensible Markup Language (XML)

Brittany has a Word document that contains the costumes she wants to advertise as a weekly special. She would like you to export the data from that page and use it in an Access database where she tracks her products. One way you can guarantee the information will transfer from one to the other correctly is by applying XML formatting to define and identify the product information in the Word document. Of course, you will attach an XML schema to the document to define the data structure and to ensure products are tagged correctly. Once that process is complete, you will save the document as a Web page.

Skills covered: Add an XML Schema • Tag Text with XML Elements • Set XML Options and Validate Tagged Text • Save as a Web Page

STEP 1 ADD AN XML SCHEMA

You must display the Developer tab in Word before you can begin using the XML features. After you add it, you attach a predefined schema, which will define the costume information that displays on this page. Refer to Figure 8.21 as you complete Step 1.

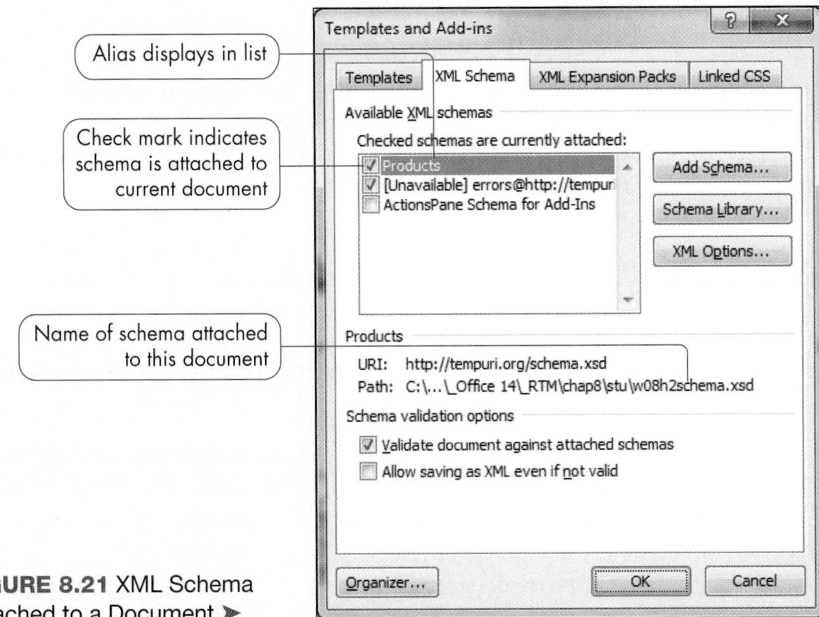

FIGURE 8.21 XML Schema Attached to a Document ➤

a. Start Word. Click **File**, click **Options**, click **Customize Ribbon**, and then click **Developer**, which displays below the Customize the Ribbon pane on the right side. Click **OK**.

   The Developer tab contains commands for working with XML documents, but the tab does not display automatically. Use this same procedure to remove the tab if you do not wish for it to display when you are not working with the commands it provides.

b. Click the **Developer tab**, click **Schema**, and then click **Schema Library** in the XML Schema tab. Confirm only one schema is listed in the *Select a schema* section—*ActionsPane Schema for Add-Ins*. Click **OK** to close the Schema Library dialog box, and then click **OK** to close the Templates and Add-ins dialog box.

> **TROUBLESHOOTING:** If any additional schemas display in the Schema Library, select the schema, and then click Delete Schema. Removing any and all schemas previously used will prevent error messages from displaying and will enable you to complete the remaining steps. Because the schemas you use in this chapter have similar design characteristics, you cannot add more than one at a time to the schema library. Deleting the schema from this library does not delete the schema file permanently.

c. Open the file *w08h2costumes*, and then save it as **w08h2costumes_LastnameFirstname** in the Happy_Haunting folder.

d. Click the **Developer tab**, and then click **Schema**. Click **Add Schema**, browse to the folder that contains files for this project, select *w08h2schema.xsd*, and then click **Open**.

The Schema Settings dialog box displays.

> **TROUBLESHOOTING:** If you do not see the file name extensions, you need to activate them through Windows. Click the Start button, and then select Computer. From that window, click Organize, and then select Folder and Search Options. Click the View tab, deselect the *Hide extensions for known file types* check box, and then click OK. Close the My Computer window.

e. Type **Products** in the **Alias box**, and then click **OK** to close the Schema Settings dialog box.

The *w08h2schema.xsd* schema, identified by the *Products* alias, is automatically attached to the current document (see Figure 8.21). It is also available to attach to other documents in the future. If you open another document, the schema is available but not attached. You can attach the schema to other documents by clicking its check box.

f. Click **OK** to close the Templates and Add-ins dialog box.

The XML Structure pane displays on the right side of the screen. This pane helps guide you through the process of preparing an XML document.

> **TROUBLESHOOTING:** If you do not see the XML Structure pane, click Structure in the XML group on the Developer tab.

g. Save the document.

STEP 2 TAG TEXT WITH XML ELEMENTS

Now that a schema is attached to the document, you must take the next step of tagging the text with XML elements. This process further defines each piece of information in the page so it will correctly transfer to a database later. Refer to Figure 8.22 as you complete Step 2.

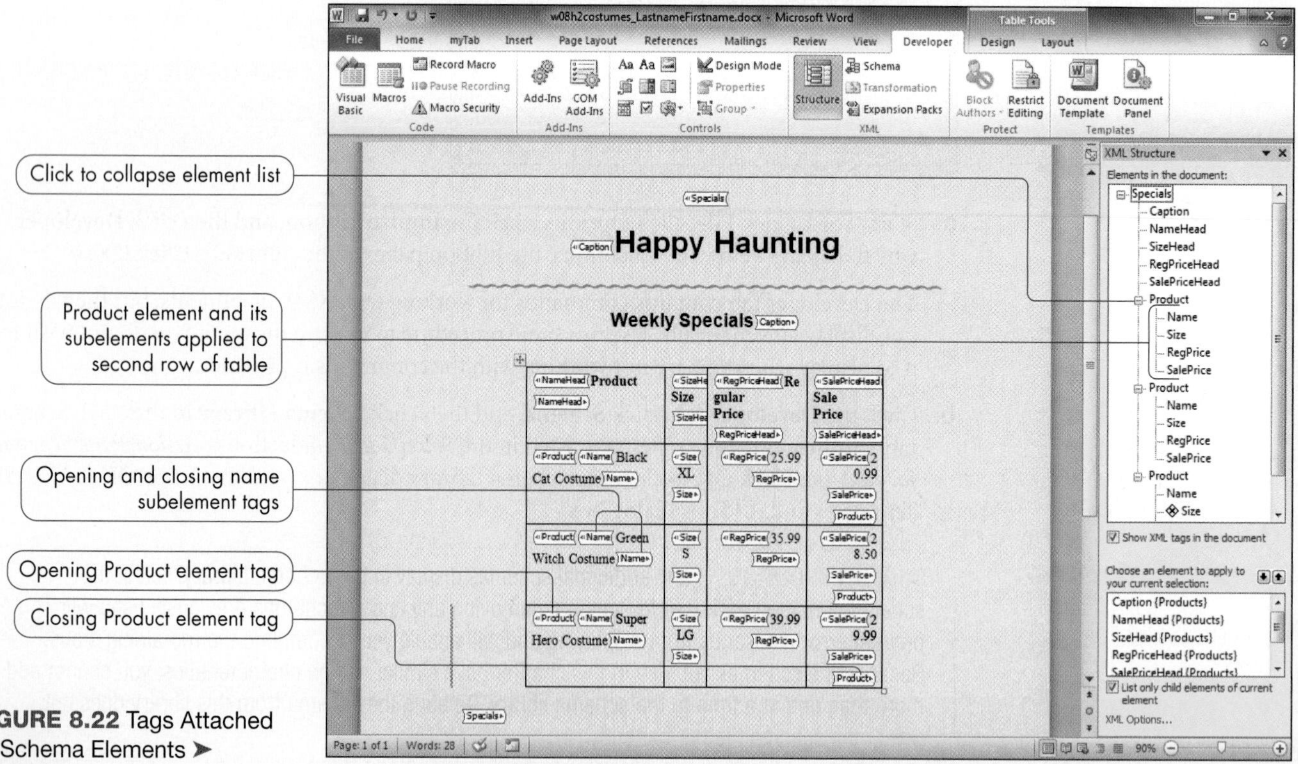

FIGURE 8.22 Tags Attached to Schema Elements ➤

a. Click **Specials** in the *Choose an element to apply to your current selection* list box, which displays at the bottom of the XML Structure pane. Click **Apply to Entire Document** in the dialog box.

   You applied the *Specials* root element to the entire document. Word inserts the root element opening tag at the beginning of the document and the closing tag at the end of the document. The XML Structure pane now displays a list of available elements to apply within the root element.

b. Select the **Happy Haunting** and **Weekly Specials titles**, and then click the **Caption {products} element** in the *Choose an element to apply to your current selection* list box at the bottom of the XML Structure pane.

   You tagged the *Happy Haunting* and *Weekly Specials* titles with the Caption XML element.

c. Select the **Product column heading text** in the first cell of the table, and then click the **NameHead {products} element** at the bottom of the XML Structure pane.

d. Repeat step c to apply the remaining three elements to the column headings, as described in this table:

Column Heading	Element
Size	SizeHead
Regular Price	RegPriceHead
Sale Price	SalePriceHead

e. Select all cells on the second row of the table—the row containing details about the Black Cat Costume—and then click **Product {Products}** in the *Choose an element to apply to your current selection* list box at the bottom of the XML Structure pane.

   The Product element contains subelements. When you apply an element that contains subelements, the *Choose an element to apply to your current selection* list box displays those subelements while the insertion point is located within the area to which you applied the element. You now see the following subelements: *Name, Size, RegPrice,* and *SalePrice.*

f. Select **Black Cat Costume** in the table, and then click **Name {Products}** in the *Choose an element to apply to your current selection* list box at the bottom of the XML Structure pane.

g. Select **XL** in the table, and then click **Size {Products}**. Select **25.99** in the table, and then click **RegPrice {Products}**. Select **20.99** in the table, and then click **SalePrice {Products}**.

h. Repeat steps e–g, adapting the steps to apply the Product element and the respective subelements to the remaining two rows of the table.

   Figure 8.22 shows the document after you tag it with the schema's elements.

i. Save the document.

STEP 3 SET XML OPTIONS AND VALIDATE TAGGED TEXT

The schema that you use on the page has been set up to perform error checking on some fields. Specifically, you are restricting the display of product sizes to only S, M, L, XL, and XXL. But before the errors display, you must activate the error checking, and then you can replace any information that the schema finds faulty. Refer to Figure 8.23 as you complete Step 3.

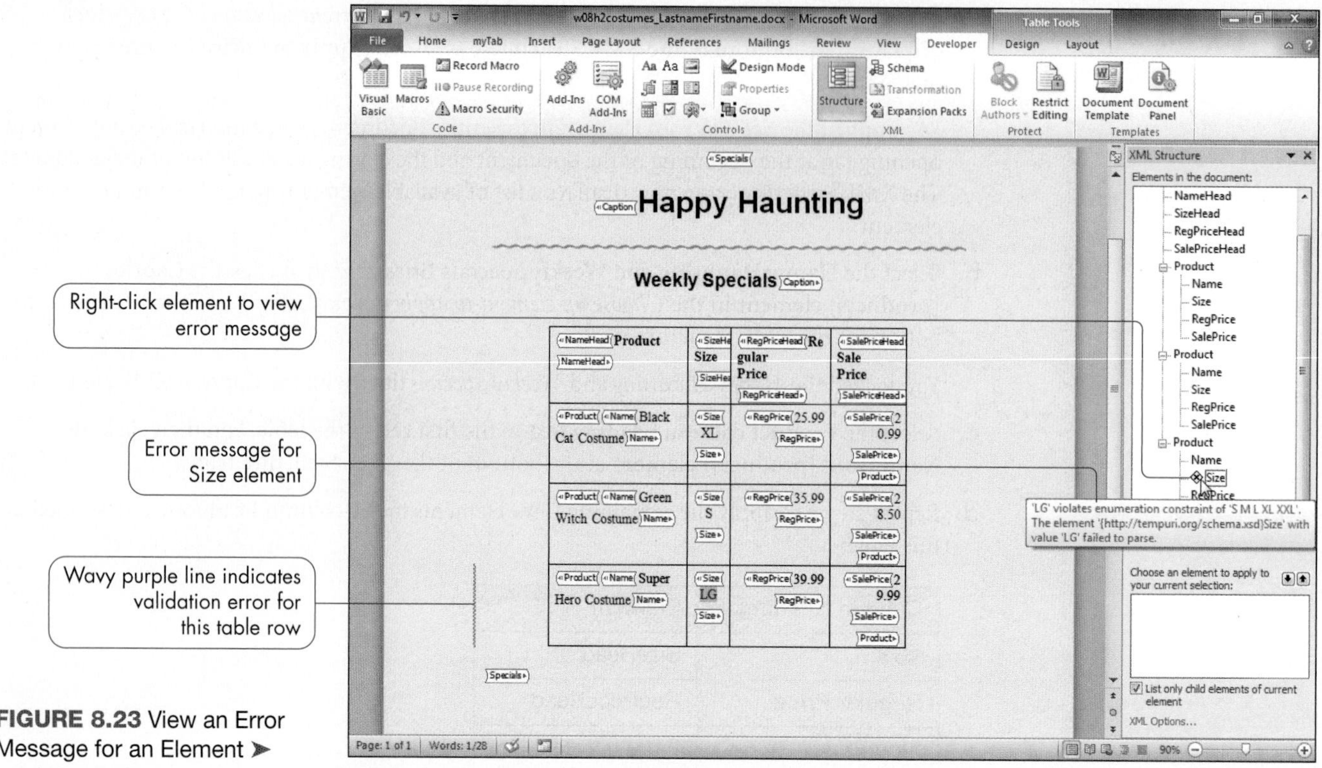

FIGURE 8.23 View an Error Message for an Element ➤

a. Click **XML Options** at the bottom of the XML Structure pane.

> **TROUBLESHOOTING:** If you closed the document at the end of Step 2, the XML Structure pane might not display when you open the document again. To display it, click the Developer tab, and then click Structure in the XML group.

b. Click **Show advanced XML error messages**, if it is not already selected.

When the *Show advanced XML error messages* check box is selected, Word displays more descriptive information about any validation errors when you position the mouse pointer over the error symbol in the XML Structure pane.

c. Click **Show placeholder text for all empty elements**, if it is not already selected.

When the *Show placeholder text for all empty elements* check box is selected, Word displays the placeholder text attribute if a tagged element does not contain any text.

d. Click **Validate document against attached schemas**, if it is not already selected, and then click **OK**.

The *Validate document against attached schemas* option ensures that you correctly applied XML tags to your document. Currently, a wavy vertical purple line appears in the left margin by the last table row. Furthermore, you might see a yellow diamond with an X next to the Size element name in the pane.

e. Right-click or hover your mouse over the yellow box beside the **Size subelement name** for the third product in the XML Structure pane.

Word displays an advanced error message, indicating specific values—S, M, L, XL, XXL—that are allowed for the Size subelement (see Figure 8.23).

f. Delete the letter *G* in *LG* that displays as the size of the Super Hero Costume in the Weekly Specials table.

After you correct the validation error, the yellow diamond no longer displays in the XML Structure pane.

g. Save the document.

After you save the document, the wavy purple line disappears.

h. Click **File**, and then click **Save As**. Click the **Save as type arrow**, click **Word XML Document (*.xml)**, and then click **Save**. Leave the document open for the next step.

STEP 4 SAVE AS A WEB PAGE

Now that the information has been refined and tagged for XML formatting, you are ready to save the document as a Web page. You will also create links to the Home page in the Web site. Refer to Figure 8.24 as you complete Step 4.

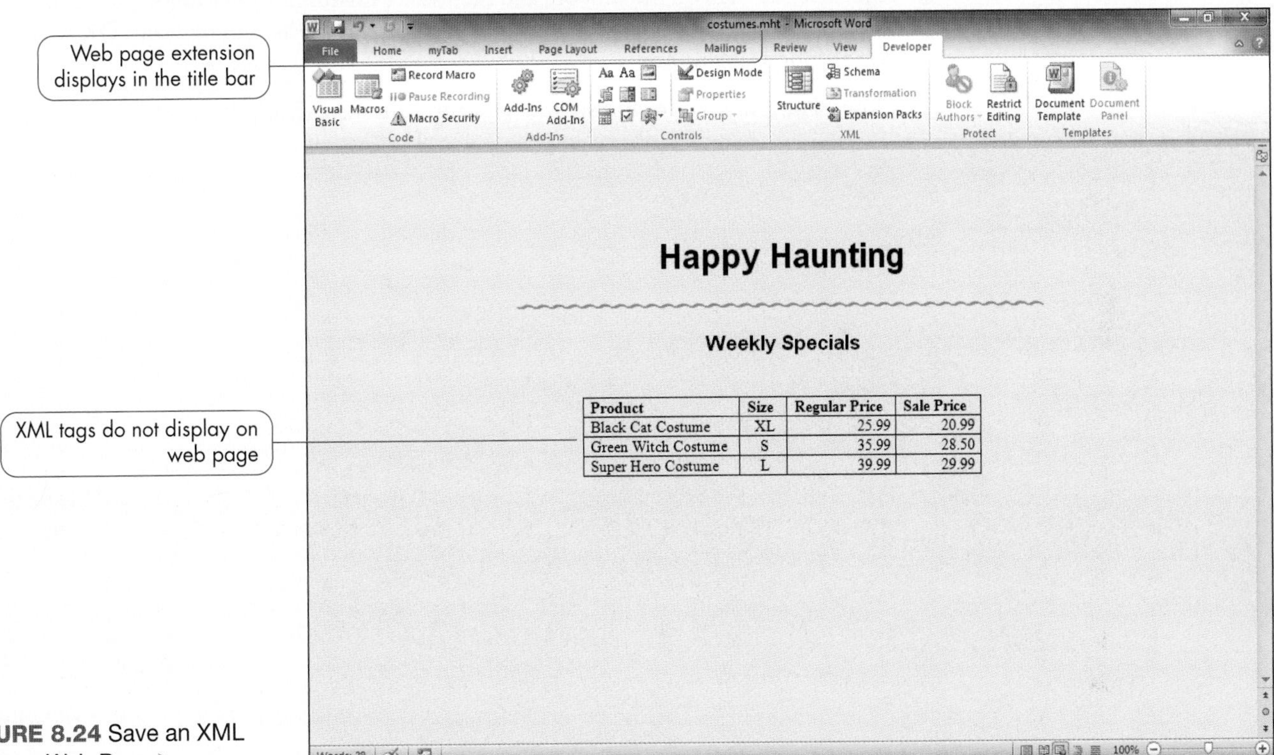

FIGURE 8.24 Save an XML File as a Web Page ➤

a. Click the **Developer tab**, and then click **Structure**, if necessary, to display the XML Structure pane.

b. Click **Show XML tags in the document** to hide the tags from the data in the table. Click **Structure** in the Developer tab to close the XML Structure pane.

c. Save the document as a Web page by completing the following steps:

- Click **File**, and then click **Save As**.
- Click the **Save as type arrow**, and then click **Single File Web Page (*.mht; *.mhtml)**.
- Type **costumes** in the **File Name box**.
- Click **Change Title**, and then type **Happy Haunting Specials** as the Page title. Click **OK**.
- Click **Save**.

The title bar displays the file with the Web page extension, as shown in Figure 8.24. You can now create a link to this page from the home page you created in Hands-On Exercise 1.

d. Create a link to the home page by completing the following steps:

- Press **Ctrl+End**, press **Enter**, and then type **Return to the Home Page**.
- Press **Ctrl+E** to center the text, select the text, and then click the **myTab tab**.
- Click **Hyperlink** in the Web group to open the Insert Hyperlink dialog box.

- Click **default.htm**, and then click **OK**.
- Click **Save** in the Quick Access Toolbar.

e. Create a link to this page from the home page by completing the following steps:
   - Click **File**, and then select **Open**.
   - Navigate to the Happy_Haunting folder, and then double-click **default.htm**.
   - Select **Weekly Specials**, right-click, and then click **Hyperlink**.
   - Click *costumes.mht*, and then press **OK**.
   - Save the document.

   Now the home page has a link to the page that contains the weekly specials.

f. Right-click any tab on the Ribbon, and then select **Customize the Ribbon**. Remove the check beside the myTab tab, so it will no longer display in the Ribbon. Click **OK** to close the Word Options dialog box.

g. Close all files, exit Word, and submit based on your instructor's directions.

Blogs

A **blog** is the chronological publication of personal thoughts.

Everyone has the ability to post information on the Internet about themselves, their thoughts, their interests, or simply whatever they want to make public. The chronological publication of personal thoughts and Web links is called a ***blog***. The term blog is derived from the words Web log, which refers to publishing personal information on the Web. Blogs can provide a vehicle to display the works of current or future journalists and authors, or they can simply reflect the emotions and ideas of an individual at a particular point in time.

In this section, you will learn how to create and publish a blog by using Word.

Creating a Blog Post

One exciting feature of Word 2010 is the Blog post template. This feature benefits people who are accustomed to working in Word but who also publish blogs on a frequent basis.

One exciting feature of Word 2010 is the Blog post template. This feature benefits people who are accustomed to working in Word but who also publish blogs on a frequent basis. When you open the New blog post template, the window looks different because the seven tabs in the Ribbon that you are accustomed to viewing are replaced with only two tabs that will provide commands you need to complete the blog post. The Blog Post tab contains commands you use to format text, but also commands that enable you to publish your blog directly to the host server for your blog, as shown in Figure 8.25. The Insert tab displays commands for items you might include in your blog, such as tables, illustrations, hyperlinks, WordArt, and symbols.

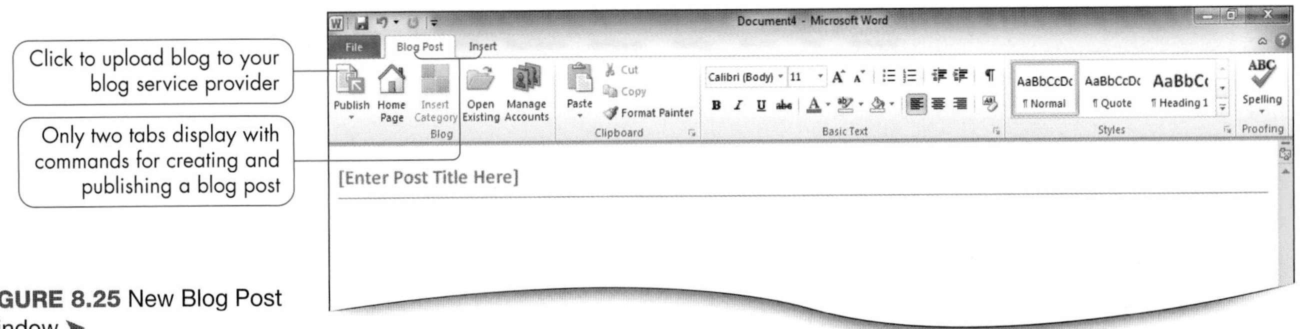

FIGURE 8.25 New Blog Post Window ➤

You can publish your blog posts by using one of several blog service providers. To learn about and find service providers, visit the Microsoft Office Marketplace, perform an Internet search, or ask your friends which service they use. Word supports several service providers, such as:

- Windows Live Spaces
- Microsoft Windows SharePoint blog
- Community Server
- WordPress
- Blogger
- TypePad

You must have an established blog account with a provider before you can register and publish blogs directly from Word. Click Manage Accounts in the Blog group on the Blog Post tab, and then click New in the Blog Accounts dialog box to view the New Blog Account dialog box. From this dialog box, the blog registration wizard prompts you for the service provider information and then configures Word to enable you to post your blog directly from Word. If you use a different service, you can click Manage Accounts, click New, click Other in the Blog list, click Next, and then type the account information, your user name, and your password. You can register several blog accounts in Word 2010. After they are registered, you can use the Manage Accounts command to change, delete, and set one account as your default blog location.

Some blogs include pictures. Even though they display with the blog post, pictures are stored in a file separate from the blog text. The file that stores the blog text includes a link to the path where the picture is stored. Your blog service provider might supply storage space for images, or you might have a completely different service provider for images. In the New Account dialog box, you can click Picture Options, and then specify the picture provider location where you store your images that display with the blog.

TIP Image Provider Considerations

If you sign up for an account with an image provider, pay special attention to the terms and conditions for using the service. Some free services might impose a limit on the maximum size of files, total amount of storage, or the types of files you are allowed to store.

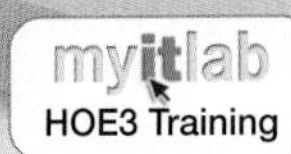

3 Blogs

The Web pages for the Happy Haunting online store are business-like, and their purpose is to display information about the products Brittany offers. However, she enjoys a personal relationship with customers and often chats with them about local events or party ideas. She asks you to start a blog to post some of the conversations and ideas she shares with customers, hoping that her online customers can enjoy them also.

Skills covered: Set Up a Blog Account • Write a Blog Entry • Publish a Blog Post

STEP 1 SET UP A BLOG ACCOUNT

In order to create a blog for the business, you must first set up an account with a service provider. You decide to use Blogger because it is one of the biggest blog providers on the Internet. Refer to Figure 8.26 as you complete Step 1.

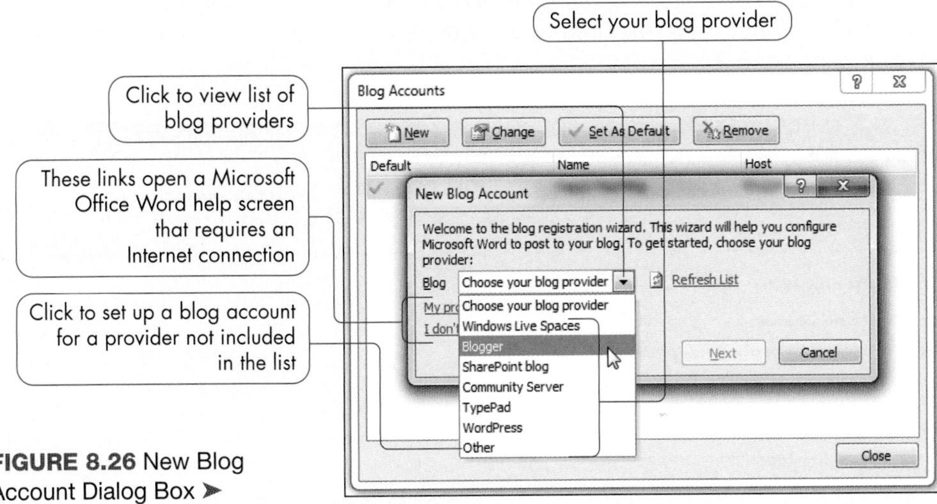

FIGURE 8.26 New Blog Account Dialog Box ➤

a. Start Word. Click **File**, click **New**, and then double-click **Blog post**. If the Register a Blog Account dialog box displays, click **Register Later**.

   A new document opens, and the Ribbon contains only two tabs: Blog Post and Insert. You might see more tabs if you install programs that create their own tabs. A placeholder prompts you to type the title of your post, and the insertion point is below the horizontal line, ready for you to create your post.

b. Click **Manage Accounts** in the Blog group on the Blog Post tab. Click **New**.

c. Click the **Blog arrow** in the New Blog Account dialog box. Click **Blogger**, as shown in Figure 8.26, and then click **Next**.

   If you have a different blog service provider, you should click the arrow, select that provider, and then type your personal identification and password in the next step. If you do not have an account with a blog service provider, you can create an account and return to this exercise or read through these steps and then continue with Step 2.

d. Type your blog service user name in the **User Name box**. Type your blog service password in the **Password box**. Click **OK**.

e. Click **OK** when the Picture Options dialog box displays.

   If you have a picture provider, you can click the Picture Provider arrow, and then select My own server. After you choose that option, boxes display where you type the Web address

(URL) for the location where you upload your pictures and where the pictures are stored. In this exercise, we will not specify a picture provider.

f. Click **Yes** to the Microsoft Office Word dialog box that tells you a possibility exists that the information you send to your blog service provider could be seen by other people.

   The information that passes from Word to your blog service provider is not encrypted, and this does provide the possibility of information being intercepted; however, this possibility is very small.

g. Select your blog in the Choose a Blog dialog box, and then click **OK**. Click **OK** to the Microsoft Office Word dialog box that indicates your account registration was successful.

   When you register a blog service successfully, the service will display in the Blog Accounts dialog box.

h. Click **Close** in the Blog Accounts dialog box.

STEP 2 WRITE A BLOG ENTRY

Now it is time for you to start posting information that customers will enjoy viewing. Brittany asks you to write about the hottest trends in costumes and theme parties for this year. You remember to use the spell check tool, which is an important resource to use before posting information publicly. Refer to Figure 8.27 as you complete Step 2.

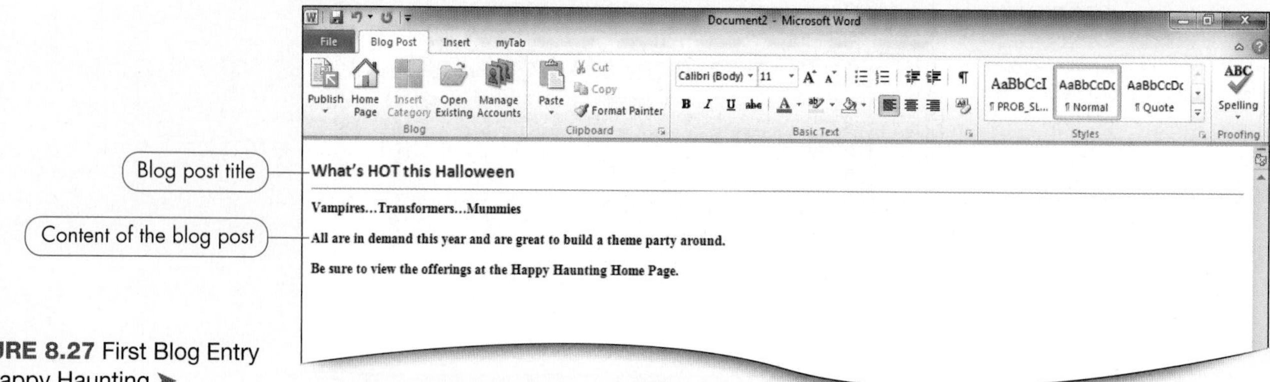

FIGURE 8.27 First Blog Entry for Happy Haunting ➤

a. Type the following text at the insertion point:

   Vampires...Transformers...Mummies

   All are in demand this year and are great to build a theme party around.

   Be sure to view the offerings at the Happy Haunting Home Page.

b. Click the placeholder *Enter Post Title Here*, and then insert the text **What's HOT this Halloween**. Click anywhere in the document to deselect the post title you just typed.

c. Click **Spelling** in the Proofing group on the Blog Post tab. When spell check is complete, click **OK**.

   Compare your post to Figure 8.27.

d. Click **File**, click **Save As**, navigate to the Happy_Haunting folder, and then type **w08h3blog_LastnameFirstname** in the **File name box**. Click **Save** to keep a copy of the post until you are ready to publish.

STEP 3 PUBLISH A BLOG POST

Now that you have completed the post, it is time to upload it to the Blogger site. You can publish the blog posts right from Word with only a few clicks! Once complete, you display your blog in an Internet Explorer window so you can see the final product. Refer to Figure 8.28 as you complete Step 3.

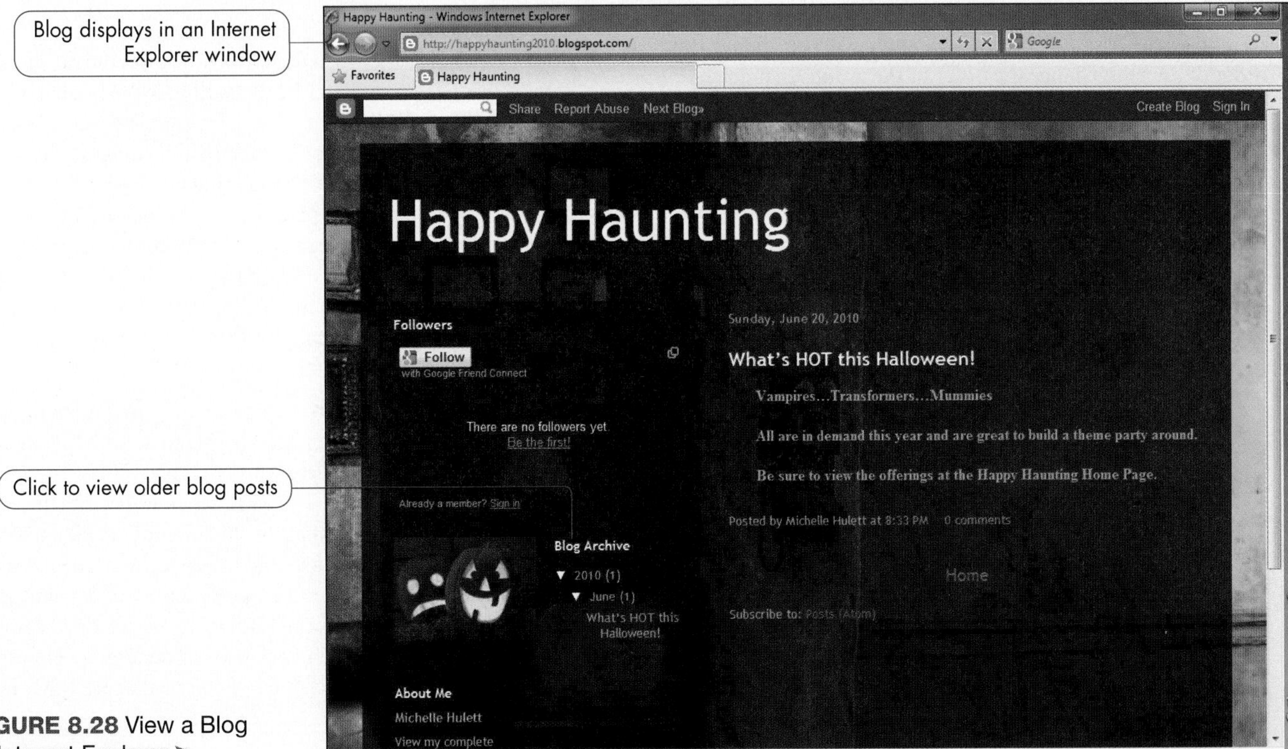

FIGURE 8.28 View a Blog in Internet Explorer ➤

a. Click **Publish** in the Blog group on the Blog Post tab.

b. Type your user name and password in the appropriate boxes in the **Connect to dialog box**.

   The dialog box displays the name of your blog. You can click Remember Password if you want to avoid typing the password each time you post to the blog server.

c. Click **OK** to save and post the blog. Click **Yes** in the Microsoft Office Word dialog box that tells you a possibility exists that the information you send to your blog service provider could be seen by other people. Click **Don't show this message again** if you want to avoid clicking *Yes* at this dialog box each time you post a blog.

d. Click **Home Page** on the Blog Post tab to display your blog in a separate Internet Explorer window, as seen in Figure 8.28.

e. Save and close the document. Exit Word. Submit based on your instructor's directions.

CHAPTER OBJECTIVES REVIEW

After reading this chapter, you have accomplished the following objectives:

1. **Customize the Ribbon.** You can create a custom tab for the Ribbon that contains just the features that you use most frequently or features that are not available on the standard Ribbon. In addition to creating a new tab, you can change the order of the tabs, change the order of the groups that appear within the tabs, and create new groups within a tab. You can also export and import custom tabs.
2. **Build a Web page.** Word provides all the tools necessary to create a basic Web page. You can use tables, clip art and pictures, bullet and numbered lists, and so on. Microsoft Word converts the document and generates the HTML codes for you. Web pages are developed in a special language called HyperText Markup Language (HTML).

   You can use the Word themes while developing a Web page, which enables you to coordinate colors and fonts. A colored background adds visual enhancement to the Web page. Hyperlinks are electronic markers that, when clicked, move the insertion point to a different location within the same document, open another document, or display a different Web page in a Web browser. A bookmark is an electronic marker for a specific location in a document, enabling the user to go to that location quickly. Bookmarks are helpful in long documents because they enable you to move easily from one place to another within that document, without having to manually scroll. As you prepare a Web page, the Web Layout view gives you a very accurate representation of how the page will look when published. You can also preview the page in an actual Web browser before you upload and publish it so that you can confirm it contains the correct content and is formatted to your specifications.
3. **Publish a Web page.** To view the pages on the Internet, you must save or publish them to a Web server, which is a computer system that hosts pages so that they are available for viewing by anyone who has an Internet connection.
4. **Understand XML.** XML goes a step beyond the code generated by HTML, which describes how a document should look by using tags that describe formatting features such as bold and indent. XML is data about data—it lets you define tags that describe the data or content in a document. The major advantage of XML file formatting is that it is not constrained to a particular platform, operating system, hardware configuration, or software application. After you create XML documents in Word, database administrators can extract XML data and then import the data into a database, which in turn can be used to create brochures, catalogs, correspondence, or Web pages.
5. **Attach an XML schema.** Before saving a document in XML format, you must attach an XML schema to it. An XML schema is a file that defines the structure and organization of content within an XML document. The XML schema specifies the type and location of content within the document. A tag is a marker that indicates the beginning or end of particular content within a document. The tag enables the transferability of data in such a way that other applications can import the tagged data. You can add more than one schema to a particular document. However, Word will alert you if the schemas conflict with each other in terms of tagging content.
6. **Create a blog post.** One of the most exciting features of Word 2010 is the new blog post template. This feature benefits people who are accustomed to working in Word but who also publish blogs on a frequent basis. You can publish your blog posts by using one of several blog service providers. You must have an established blog account with a provider before you can register and publish blogs directly from Word.

KEY TERMS

Background ***p.411***
Blog ***p.435***
Element ***p.426***
eXtensible Markup Language (XML) ***p.424***
File Transfer Protocol (FTP) ***p.415***
Hyperlink ***p.412***
HyperText Markup Language (HTML) ***p.409***
Internet ***p.406***
Root element ***p.426***
Schema validation ***p.428***
Tag ***p.425***
Transform ***p.428***
Web page ***p.406***
Web server ***p.415***
World Wide Web (WWW) ***p.406***
XML schema ***p.424***

MULTIPLE CHOICE

1. While you are creating and editing documents that will be part of a Web site, you should save them in which format?
   (a) XML
   (b) HTML
   (c) Compatibility Mode
   (d) Text

2. Which of the following is not a legitimate object to use in a hyperlink?
   (a) Schema
   (b) E-mail address
   (c) Web page
   (d) Bookmark

3. What is the advantage of applying a theme to a Web page?
   (a) It adds a background color automatically.
   (b) It cannot be removed after you apply it.
   (c) It applies a uniform design to the links and other objects in a document.
   (d) It is automatically applied to each additional Web page you create.

4. If you view a Web page and hyperlinks display in two different colors, what is the most likely explanation?
   (a) A different theme was applied to each hyperlink.
   (b) One of the hyperlinks is invalid.
   (c) One of the hyperlinks was previously visited.
   (d) One of the hyperlinks is a bookmark.

5. Which of the following is not a format used to save documents as Web pages?
   (a) Web Template
   (b) Single File Web Page
   (c) Web Page
   (d) Web Page, Filtered

6. What information is relayed to the Web browser by HTML tags?
   (a) How to categorize the data on the Web page
   (b) How to save the information on the Web page
   (c) How to transfer the data to a Web server
   (d) How to format the information on the Web page

7. What type of file should you attach to a document in order to apply XML tags?
   (a) XML
   (b) XML Library
   (c) XML transform
   (d) XML schema

8. Which feature enables users to manage schemas and solutions?
   (a) Alias
   (b) Schema Library
   (c) XML transform
   (d) Element

9. What type of Web site enables you to view the frequent, chronological publication of personal thoughts?
   (a) Search engine
   (b) FTP
   (c) Web server
   (d) Blog

10. What feature should you change in order to display information about your Web site at the top of the Internet Explorer window?
    (a) XML element
    (b) File name
    (c) Page title
    (d) Document theme

PRACTICE EXERCISES

1 Dave Meinert Realtors

Dave Meinert owns a large real estate company in New Orleans. The real estate company offers a comprehensive list of services beyond the standard commercial and residential real estate sales and listings, including management of retirement community and commercial properties. Although the company is profitable, Dave realizes it should post information about the organization and its services on a Web site. He prefers to establish a very simple Web site in the beginning, and then contract a Web site development professional to enhance the site if it generates a lot of business. Dave takes the following steps to turn a few basic Word documents into Web pages. This exercise follows the same set of skills as used in Hands-On Exercise 1 in the chapter. Refer to Figure 8.29 as you complete this exercise.

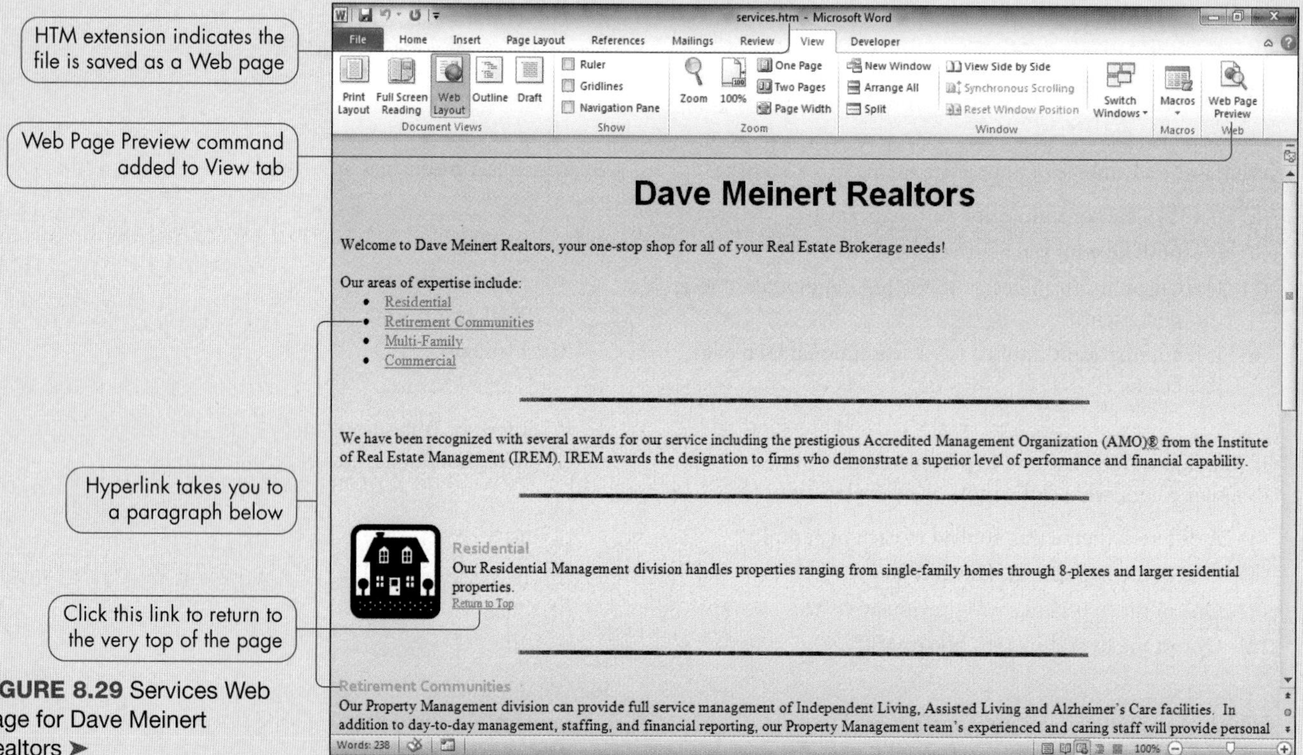

FIGURE 8.29 Services Web Page for Dave Meinert Realtors ➤

a. Start Word, and then open *w08p1default.*

b. Customize the Ribbon by completing the following steps:
   - Click **File**, click **Options**, and then click **Customize Ribbon.**
   - Click **View** to select the View tab. Click **New Group**, and then click **Rename.** Click the first icon, type **Web** in the **Name box**, and then click **OK.**
   - Click the **Choose commands from arrow**, and then select **Commands Not in the Ribbon.**
   - Scroll down and click **Web Page Preview.** Click **Add** to add the command to the Web group in the View tab.
   - Click **OK** to close the Word Options dialog box.

c. Click **File**, and then click **Save As.** In the Save As dialog box, navigate to the drive and folder in which you want to create a Web folder.

d. Create a folder and save the file as a web page by completing the following steps:
   - Click **New Folder** on the Save As dialog box toolbar, type **Realtor_LastnameFirstname**, and then click **Enter.** Click **Open.**
   - Type **default** in the **File name box.** Click the **Save as type arrow**, and then click **Web Page (*.htm; *.html).**
   - Click **Change Title** to display the Enter Text dialog box. Type **Dave Meinert Real Estate** in the **Page title box**, and then click **OK.** Click **Save.**

e. Open *w08p1services*, and then save it as a Web page named **services** in the Realtor_LastnameFirstname folder. Click **Change Title**, type **Dave Meinert Real Estate Services**, click **OK**, and then click **Save.**

f. Press **Alt+Tab** as needed to display the default file. Select **Real Estate Services**, and then click **Hyperlink** in the Links group on the Insert tab. Click **Existing File or Web Page** in the *Link to* panel of the Insert Hyperlink dialog box. Double-click the Realtor_LastnameFirstname folder, if necessary, click the file *services.htm*, and then click **OK**.

g. Apply themes and color to the pages by completing the following steps:
   - Click the **Page Layout tab**, click **Themes** in the Themes group, and then click **Module**.
   - Click **Page Color** in the Page Background group. Click **Fill Effects** to display the Fill Effects dialog box, and then click the **Gradient tab**, if necessary.
   - Click **Two colors** in the *Colors* section. Click the **Color 1 arrow**, and then select **Gold, Accent 1, Lighter 80%** (fifth column, second row). Click the **Color 2 arrow**, and then select **Gold, Accent 1, Lighter 60%** (fifth column, third row).
   - Click **Horizontal** in the *Shading styles* section, if necessary. In the *Variants* section, click the square in the top-right corner. Click **OK** to apply the background.

h. Press **Ctrl+S** to save the changes to *default.htm*.

i. Repeat step g to apply the theme and background color to the Services page.

j. Place the insertion point on the left side of the word *Residential*, which displays as a heading for the paragraph on the Services page. Click the **Insert tab**, click **Bookmark**, type **res** in the **Bookmark name box**, and then click **Add**.

k. Repeat step j to create bookmarks at the beginning of the headings *Retirement Communities*, *Multi-Family*, and *Commercial* that display down the page. The bookmarks should be named **retire**, **multi**, and **com**.

l. Select **Residential** in the bulleted list near the top of the page, and then click **Hyperlink** from the Links group. Click **Place in This Document** in the *Link to* panel of the Insert Hyperlink dialog box. Click **res**, and then click **OK**.

m. Repeat step l to create hyperlinks from each bulleted list item to the corresponding bookmarks for *Retirement Communities*, *Multi-Family*, and *Commercial*.

n. Select the text *Return to Top* that displays below the *Residential* paragraph. Click **Hyperlink** in the Links group, click **Top of the Document**, which displays at the very top of the *Select a place in this document* list, and then click **OK**.

o. Repeat step n to create a hyperlink from each occurrence of *Return to Top* that displays throughout the Services page.

p. Click the **View tab**, and then click **Web Page Preview** in the Web group to view the Services page in an Internet Explorer window. Click the hyperlinks in the Services page to navigate up and down the page. Close Internet Explorer.

q. Save and close all pages. Submit based on your instructor's directions.

2 Dave Meinert Realtors Property Listings

Rebecca Mitchell, a summer intern at Dave Meinert Realty, has been evaluating the progress of the Web pages Dave is creating to promote the agency. Her previous suggestions were well received and easy to implement, and now she has one last recommendation. Rebecca understands the importance of sharing information among staff and providing an efficient way to create, label, and use information. She conveys to Dave the benefit of using XML to label the real estate listings because the listings are often shared and communicated among the staff and clients of the company. Dave decides to let Rebecca develop a schema and apply the XML tags to the page that displays the current listings. Rebecca takes the following steps to create information that is easy to use between programs. This exercise follows the same set of skills as used in Hands-On Exercise 2 in the chapter. Refer to Figure 8.30 as you complete this exercise.

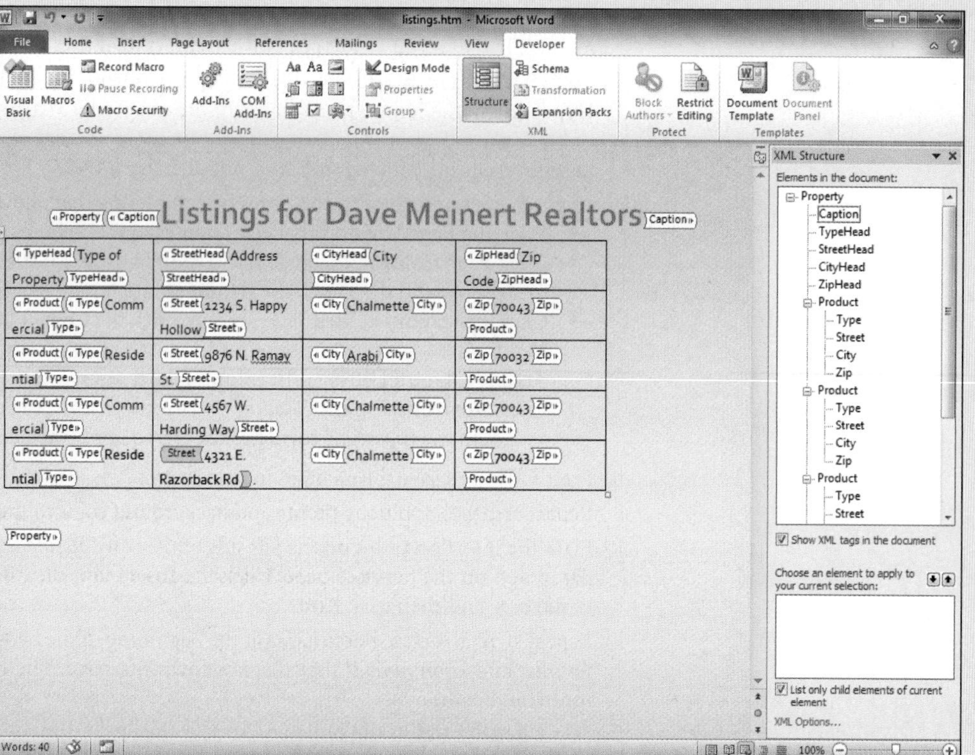

FIGURE 8.30 Schema Elements Applied to Directory Listing ➤

a. Open *w08p2listings*, and then save it in the Realtor_LastnameFirstname folder as **listings.htm**.
b. Click the **Developer tab**, and then click **Schema**. Click **Schema Library**, click **Products** from the **Select a schema list**, and then click **Delete Schema**. Click **Yes** in the Schema Library dialog box to continue.
c. Click **Add Schema**, browse to the folder that contains files for this project, select *w08p2propertyschema .xsd*, and then click **Open**. Type **Real Estate** in the **Alias box**, and then click **OK** to close the Schema Settings dialog box. Click **OK** to close the Schema Library dialog box. Select **Real Estate** in the *Checked schemas are currently attached* section of the Templates and Add-ins dialog box, and then click **OK**.
d. Click **Property** in the *Choose an element to apply to your current selection* list box. Click **Apply to Entire Document**. If necessary, click **Show XML tags** in the document in the XML Structure pane, if necessary.
e. Select the **Listings for Dave Meinert Realtors title**, and then click the **Caption element** in the *Choose an element to apply to your current selection* list box at the bottom of the XML Structure pane.
f. Select the **Type of Property column heading** in the first cell of the table, and then click the **TypeHead element** at the bottom of the XML Structure pane.
g. Repeat step f to apply an element to the three remaining column headings. Apply elements as described in the following table.

Column Heading	Element
Address	StreetHead
City	CityHead
Zip Code	ZipHead

h. Select all cells on the second row of the table—the row containing details about the commercial property on S. Happy Hollow—and then click **Product** in the *Choose an element to apply to your current selection* list box at the bottom of the XML Structure pane.
i. Apply the subelement tags to the property information by completing the following steps:
   - Select **Commercial** in the second row of the table, and then click **Type** in the *Choose an element to apply to your current selection* list box at the bottom of the XML Structure pane.
   - Select **1234 S. Happy Hollow** in the table, and then click the **Street subelement.**
   - Select **Chalmette**, and then choose the **City subelement.**
   - Select **70043** in the second row of the table, and then choose the **Zip subelement.**

j. Repeat steps h and i, adapting the steps to apply the Product element and the respective subelements to the remaining three rows of the table. When complete, compare your work to Figure 8.30.
k. Click **Show XML tags in the document** to hide the tags from the data in the table. Click **Structure** in the Developer tab to close the XML Structure pane. Save the document.
l. Click **File**, and then click **Save As**. Click the **Save as type arrow**, and then click **Word XML Document (.xml)**. Click **Save**.
m. Close all documents. Submit based on your instructor's directions.

3 Create a Blog Post

Simone Liburd is participating in a study abroad program at Missouri State University this fall and will spend the semester in Spain. She is excited about the opportunities to learn about a different country, the people, the language, and the culture. She is also very happy that they do not have classes on Friday, so she can travel and see as much of the country as possible. Her parents are nervous about her time away and want her to write home as much as possible. Her friends are also eager to hear about her experiences. Simone decides the most convenient and efficient way to communicate with everyone is to post blog entries as often as possible. She can use Word 2010 on her laptop, which she will have with her most of the time, to quickly write and post the blog entries to Blogger—the blog she set up using her Google account. Simone will follow these steps to connect to her blog account and prepare the first entry. This exercise follows the same set of skills as used in Hands-On Exercise 3 in the chapter. Refer to Figure 8.31 as you complete this exercise.

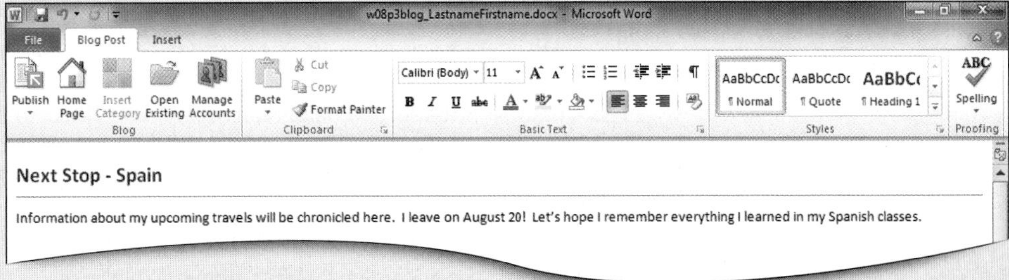

FIGURE 8.31 Blog Post ➤

a. Start Word. Click **File**, click **New**, and then double-click **Blog post**. If the Register a Blog Account dialog box displays, click **Register Later**. If you do not have an account with a blog service provider, you can create an account and return to this exercise. If you have a blog account, continue with step b.
b. Click **Manage Accounts** in the Blog group on the Blog Post tab. Click **New**. Click the **Blog arrow** in the New Blog Account dialog box. Click **Blogger**, and then click **Next**.
c. Type your blog service user name in the **User Name box**. Type your blog service password in the **Password box**. Click **OK**. Click **OK** when the Picture Options dialog box displays.
d. Click **Yes** in the Microsoft Office Word dialog box that tells you a possibility exists that the information you send to your blog service provider could be seen by other people.
e. Click **OK** in the Microsoft Office Word dialog box that indicates your account registration was successful. Click **Close** in the Blog Accounts dialog box.
f. Type the following text at the insertion point: **Information about my upcoming travels will be chronicled here. I leave on August 20! Let's hope I remember everything I learned in my Spanish classes.**
g. Click the placeholder *Enter Post Title Here*, and then insert the text **Next Stop–Spain**.
h. Click the **Spelling arrow** in the Proofing group on the Blog Post tab.
i. Click **File**, click **Save As**, and then navigate to the folder where you store solution files. Type **w08p3blog_LastnameFirstname** in the **File name box**. Click **Save** to keep a copy of the post until you are ready to publish. Compare to Figure 8.31.
j. Click **Publish** in the Blog group on the Blog Post tab to publish this blog to your account, if you previously created one. Type your user name and password in the appropriate boxes in the Connect to dialog box.
k. Click **OK** to save and post the blog. Click **Yes** in the Microsoft Office Word dialog box that tells you a possibility exists the information you send to your blog service provider could be seen by other people. Click **Don't show this message again** if you want to avoid clicking *Yes* at this dialog box each time you post a blog.
l. Click **Home Page** on the Blog Post tab to display the blog in a separate Internet Explorer window.
m. Close all documents. Submit based on your instructor's directions.

MID-LEVEL EXERCISES

1 FlyRight Airways

CREATIVE CASE 

The marketing manager at a fledgling airline company is hosting a competition that awards a prize to the employee who designs the best home page for their Web site. A document that provides a description of the company is given to each person, and the information in that page should display in the final version. You take the following steps to develop the page you will submit.

a. Open *w08m1airline*, and then save the document as a Single File Web page (*.mht; *.mhtml) using the name **w08m1airline_LastnameFirstname**.
b. Change the Page title to **Take off with FlyRight Airways**.
c. Customize the Ribbon to put the buttons you use most on one custom tab with groups. You can modify the myTab tab you created in Hands-On Exercise 1, or reset the Ribbon to its original state and create a new tab with groups.

DISCOVER 

d. Apply any theme to the page. Apply the **Intense Quote style** to the Company Name that displays at the top of the document and increase the font size to **20**. Use a different style if you do not find Intense Quote on your list of Styles.
e. Apply a background color to the page. Use a **Gradient fill effect** that uses two colors. Use a **Diagonal down shading style**, and then select **variant effect** in the top-left corner.
f. Select the text *Contact us* that displays near the top of the document. Insert a hyperlink that links to the e-mail address *help@flyrightairways.org* and that contains the subject *Request for information.*
g. Perform a Web search to find Web site addresses for the two companies mentioned—Boeing and FlyteComm—in the second paragraph. Create hyperlinks to those companies after you find their Web site addresses. The FlyteComm site enables you to track a flight from takeoff to landing.
h. Create bookmarks named **b737** and **b767** at the beginning of the paragraphs at the bottom of the page that describe the two types of aircraft. Create hyperlinks to these bookmarks from the text *Boeing 737* and *Boeing 767* that displays in the first paragraph.
i. Save and close the document. Start Windows Explorer, navigate to the folder containing your Web page, and then double-click the file you just created. Internet Explorer will start automatically because your document was saved as a Web page. Look carefully at the Address bar and note the local address, as opposed to a Web address.
j. Submit based on your instructor's directions.

2 FlyRight Airways Flight Schedules

The president of FlyRight Airways directs the Marketing Manager to create an XML document that will list the current flight schedule. This schedule can change frequently, so it should be formatted in such a way that information can be easily transferred between the company flight database and a Word or Web page. You are the resident XML expert, so you take the following steps to create an efficient solution for transferring flight schedules using XML technology.

a. Open *w08m2flights*, and then save it as **w08m2flights_LastnameFirstname**.
b. Delete any unused schemas, if necessary, and then attach *w08m2schema.xsd*. The schema alias should be **Fly**.
c. Select the whole document, and then apply the **Flights element**.
d. Apply the **Caption subelement** to the title of the page.
e. Attach the appropriate subelements to the heading and data in the table.
f. Check the cities listed in the destination column and make adjustments to comply with any schema restrictions for that field.
g. Save your changes, and then save as an XML document named **chap8_mid2_flights_LastnameFirstname .xml**. Do not show XML tags in the document, and then close the XML Structure pane.
h. Close all files and submit based on your instructor's directions.

CAPSTONE EXERCISE

Joyful Scents Candle Company is a family-owned business that manufactures and sells candles. So far, this company has relied on telephone and fax orders. Because of your extensive experience with Word 2010, the company president hired you to create a Web site.

Attach XML Schema to Product Information

You spoke with the database manager about exchanging product information between the database and your Web pages. He suggested you attach an XML schema and properly format any pages that contain product information. You also save the page as an XML document.

a. Open the file named *w08c1order.*
b. Display the Developer tab, if necessary, and then display the XML Structure pane.
c. Delete any schemas currently in the Schema Library, and then attach the schema in *w08c1schema.xsd.* Give the schema an alias of **Candles**.
d. Assign the **Candles element** to the table only. Assign the appropriate elements to the column headings in the table, and then assign the appropriate subelements to each product.
e. Verify that all product descriptions comply with schema restrictions, and make changes as necessary.
f. Hide the XML tags in the document, and then close the XML Structure pane.
g. Create a folder named **Candles_LastnameFirstname**. Save the file as a Word XML Document named **w08c1order_LastnameFirstname** in the Candles_ LastnameFirstname folder.

Design a Set of Web Pages

You need to convert existing documents to Web pages for Heavenly Scents, but before you save them as Web pages, you redesign the pages to incorporate visual enhancements, such as color and graphics.

a. Open the documents *w08c1default* and *w08c1 products.*
b. Customize the Ribbon to put the buttons you use most on one custom tab with groups. You can modify the myTab tab you created in Hands-On Exercise 1, or reset the Ribbon to its original state and create a new tab with groups.
c. Display the default document, which will become the home page of the Web site. Create a background color that uses the **Bouquet Texture fill effect** (fourth column, fifth row). Apply the **Verve theme**. Increase font sizes of headings to **22 pt** and use the text effect named **Gradient Fill - Pink, Accent 1** (fourth column, third row).
d. Insert clip art of a candle, and then display it on the right side of the home page. Use picture format tools to resize the picture to **2″** tall and apply the **Soft Edge Oval effect**. If you do not have access to the Internet, use your judgment on the image you use and use the picture format tools that would be most appropriate for that image.
e. Save this document in the Candles_LastnameFirstname folder as a Web Page (*.htm, *.html) named **w08c1default_ LastnameFirstname**.
f. Display the products document. Apply the **Verve theme** and **Bouquet Texture fill effect** to the document. Apply the same text effect used on the default page to the products page heading. Save this document in the Candles_LastnameFirstname folder as a Web Page (*.htm, *.html) named **w08c1products_ LastnameFirstname**.
g. Display *w08c1order_LastnameFirstname*, which is in XML format, and then change to Web Layout view. Apply the **Verve theme** and **Bouquet Texture fill effect** to the document. Apply the same text effect used on the default page to the order page heading. Center the text that is currently left justified. Save this document in the Candles_ LastnameFirstname folder as a Web Page (*.htm, *.html) named **w08c1order_LastnameFirstname**, and then change the Page title to **Joyful Scents Ordering Information**.
h. Leave all documents open for the next phase of development.

Add Navigation Elements to Web Pages

Your pages are looking good. Now you want to add the ability to navigate within a long page and also to navigate easily between the pages.

a. Display the default page. Type **View Our Products** and **Ordering Information** on the bottom of the default page. Create hyperlinks to the Products and Order Web pages from these lines of text.
b. Display the Products page. Create the following bookmarks in the appropriate places that correspond with the information on the page: **standard**, **exotic**, **sizes**, and **descriptions**.
c. Create a list near the top of the page for the categories that display down the page. Center the list, and then create a hyperlink from each item on the list to the appropriate bookmark.
d. At the end of each category, create a **Back to Top hyperlink** that will use a bookmark to navigate back to the top of the document.
e. At the bottom of the page, type **HOME**, and then create a hyperlink to the default page. Save the page.

f. Display the order page. Type **HOME** at the bottom of the page, and then create a hyperlink to the default page. Save the page.

Document Progress in a Blog Post

The president of Joyful Scents Candle Company is a strong proponent of documentation. She would like to know how much time you spent on this project and what resources you used. She advocates a casual workplace, so she recommended you just post a blog on the company server so she can read it later. You start the blog and then find the server is down for maintenance, so you save your work and post it at a later time.

a. Open a new blog post document.

b. The title of the blog post is *Preparing the Company Web Site.* Type the following sentence for the post: **I used Word 2010 to design the Web site. Features such as background color, themes, hyperlinks, and bookmarks made the process easy.**

c. Save the blog post in the Candles_LastnameFirstname folder as **w08c1blog_LastnameFirstname.**

d. Save and close all files. Submit based on your instructor's directions.

Create Your Own Design

GENERAL CASE 

After you complete the Capstone Exercise, you decide you have better ideas for the design of the Web site. You now have the opportunity to implement those ideas and modify the Joyful Scents Candle Web site. Open the three solution files from the Capstone Exercise, *w08c1default_LastnameFirstname.htm*, *w08c1order_LastnameFirstname.htm*, and *w08c1products_LastnameFirstname.htm*, and then save them in a folder named **Beyond1_LastnameFirstname**. Use formatting tools discussed in this chapter, but also use any of the formatting and layout tools you are familiar with in Word, such as tables (to lay out and position text and graphics), text boxes and shape tools (to create buttons), and WordArt. Be sure you change the hyperlinks to reflect the new files so that all the links work correctly. Rename the files **w08b1default_LastnameFirstname.htm**, **w08b1order_LastnameFirstname.htm**, and **w08b1products_LastnameFirstname.htm**, respectively, and then submit based on your instructor's directions.

Track Your Investments

RESEARCH CASE 

As soon as you graduate from school, you will begin saving for retirement. You can start tracking stock prices now to determine which companies you might invest in later. Create a table in Word that lists company names in the first row and that has a date listed in the first column. Use the Internet to look up stock prices for several weeks to see how the company stocks perform. Save the document in XML format, so you can later import the results into an Excel worksheet and graph the change over time. Name your file **w08b2stocks_LastnameFirstname**, and then submit based on your instructor's directions.

Modify a Schema

DISASTER RECOVERY 

A schema is necessary to tag elements of data so they can be used in other applications. Typically, an IT department develops the schemas used by its organization. However, with a basic schema in place, you can modify the code for use in a different scenario. The schemas used in this chapter are all very similar but include subtle changes that make them appropriate for the exercise. Open the file *w08b3schema.xsd* in Notepad (or WordPad), and then save it as **w08b3schema_LastnameFirstname.xsd**. Use your critical thinking skills to modify the code in the schema so that it will be appropriate to use with the data in *w08b3construction.docx*. Test your schema by attaching it to the data file, and then tag the data in that file with the appropriate elements and subelements. Save the results as an XML file with the name **w08b3construction_LastnameFirstname.xml**. Save and close all files and submit based on your instructor's directions.

GLOSSARY

Access A database program that is included in Microsoft Office.

ActiveX control A form element that works in a Word 2007 or 2010 document or template.

Ascending order A feature that arranges data in alphabetical order or sequential order from lowest to highest.

AutoRecover Enables Word to recover a previous version of a document.

Background A color, design, image, or watermark that appears behind text in a document, on a graphical image, or on a Web page.

Backstage view Display that includes commands related to common file activities and that provides information on an open file.

Backup A copy of a file, usually on another storage medium.

Bar tab Tab that inserts a vertical line at the location of a tab setting. Useful as a separator for text printed on the same line.

Bibliography A list of works cited or consulted by an author in his or her work and should be included with the published work.

Blog The chronological publication of personal thoughts.

Bookmark An electronic marker for a specific location in a document.

Border A line that surrounds a paragraph, a page, a table, or an image in a document, or that surrounds a cell or range of cells in a worksheet.

Brightness The ratio between lightness and darkness of an image.

Building Block A document component used frequently, such as a disclaimer, company address, or cover page.

Bulleted list Itemizes and separates paragraph text to increase readability.

Caption A descriptive title for an image, an equation, a figure, or a table.

Cell The intersection of a column or row in a worksheet or table.

Cell margin The amount of space between data and the cell border in a table.

Center tab Sets the middle point of the text you type; whatever you type will be centered on that tab setting.

Change Case Feature that enables you to change capitalization of text to all capital letters, all lowercase letters, sentence case, or toggle case.

Changed line A vertical bar in the margin to pinpoint the area where changes are made in a document when the Track Changes feature is active.

Character spacing The horizontal space between characters.

Character style Stores character formatting (font, size, and style) and affects only selected text.

Check box form field Consists of a box that can be checked or unchecked.

Citation A note recognizing a source of information or a quoted passage.

Clip art An electronic illustration that can be inserted into an Office project.

Clipboard An Office feature that temporarily holds selections that have been cut or copied.

Column A format that sections a document into side-by-side vertical blocks in which the text flows down the first vertical block and then continues at the top of the next vertical block.

Column width The horizontal measurement of a column in a table or a worksheet.

Combine A feature that incorporates all changes from multiple documents into a new document.

Command A button or area within a group that you click to perform tasks.

Comment A private note, annotation, or additional information to the author or another reader about the content of a document.

Compare A feature that evaluates the contents of two or more documents and displays markup balloons showing the differences.

Compatibility Checker Looks for features that are not supported by previous versions of Word.

Compress The process of reducing the file size of an object.

Contextual tab A Ribbon tab that displays when an object, such as a picture or clip art, is selected.

Contrast The difference between the lightest and darkest areas of an image.

Copy Duplicates a selection from the original location and places the copy in the Office Clipboard.

Cropping (or to **crop)** The process of reducing an image size by eliminating unwanted portions of an image or other graphical object.

Cross-reference A note that refers the reader to another location for more information about a topic.

Current List Includes all citation sources you use in the current document.

Curriculum vitae (CV) A document like a résumé that displays your skills, accomplishments, and job history.

Cut Removes a selection from the original location and places it in the Office Clipboard.

Data source A listing of information.

Database table A collection of related records that contain fields to organize data.

Date Picker Displays a calendar that the user can click rather than typing in a date.

Decimal tab Marks where numbers align on a decimal point as you type.

Default A setting that is in place unless you specify otherwise.

Descending order Arranges data in alphabetical or sequential order from highest to lowest.

Design Mode Enables you to view and modify control fields.

Desktop publishing The merger of text with graphics to produce a professional-looking document.

Dialog box A window that opens when you are accomplishing a task that enables you to make selections or indicate settings beyond those provided on the Ribbon.

Dialog Box Launcher An icon in Ribbon groups that you can click to open a related dialog box.

Digital certificate An attachment to a file that guarantees the authenticity of the file, provides a verifiable signature, or enables encryption.

Digital signature An electronic stamp that displays information about a person or organization.

Document Inspector Checks for and removes different kinds of hidden and personal information from a document.

Document Panel Provides descriptive information about a document, such as a title, subject, author, keywords, and comments.

Document theme A set of coordinating fonts, colors, and special effects that give a stylish and professional look.

Draft view Shows a simplified work area, removing white space and other elements from view.

Drawing Canvas A framelike area that helps you keep parts of your drawing together.

Drop cap A large capital letter at the beginning of a paragraph.

Drop-down list Enables the user to choose from one of several existing entries.

Editing restriction Specifies limits for users to modify a document.

Element A descriptive name that identifies a piece of data.

Embedding Pulls an object into a document, where you can edit it without changing the source.

Endnote A citation that appears at the end of a document.

Enhanced ScreenTip Provides a brief summary of a command when you place the mouse pointer on the command button.

Excel Software included in Microsoft Office that specializes in organizing data in worksheet form.

eXtensible Markup Language (XML) A language that describes a document's content and enables easy exchange of data.

Field The smallest data element contained in a table, such as first name, last name, address, and phone number.

File A document or item of information that you create with software and to which you give a name.

File Transfer Protocol (FTP) A process that uploads files from a PC to a server or from a server to a PC.

Fill The interior space of an object.

Filter Specifies criteria for including records that meet certain conditions, and displays a subset of records based on specified criteria.

Final: Show Markup A view that displays inserted text in the body of the document and shows deleted text in a markup balloon.

Find Locates a word or phrase that you indicate in a document.

First line indent Marks the location to indent only the first line in a paragraph.

Folder A named storage location where you can save files.

Font A complete set of characters—upper- and lowercase letters, numbers, punctuation marks, and special symbols with the same design that includes size, spacing, and shape.

Footer Information that displays at the bottom of each document page, presentation slide, handout, or notes page.

Footnote A citation that appears at the bottom of a page.

Foreground Appears in front of text or images in a document or on a graphical image.

Form A document designed for collecting data for a specific situation.

Form control Helps a user complete a form by displaying prompts such as text boxes and drop-down lists.

Form letter A letter with standard information that you personalize with recipient information. You might print or e-mail this to many people.

Form template A document that defines the standard layout, structure, and formatting of a form.

Format Painter A Clipboard group command that copies the formatting of text from one location to another.

Formatting restriction Guarantees that others do not modify formatting or styles in a document.

Full Screen Reading view A viewing format that eliminates tabs and makes it easier to read a document.

Gallery A set of selections that appears when you click a More button, or in some cases when you click a command, in a Ribbon group.

Grid An underlying, but invisible, set of horizontal and vertical lines that determine the placement of major elements.

Group A subset of a tab that organizes similar tasks together.

Grouping The process of combining objects so they appear as a single object.

Hanging indent Aligns the first line of a paragraph at the left margin and indents the remaining lines.

Hard page break Forces the next part of a document to begin on a new page.

Hard return Created when you press Enter to move the insertion point to a new line.

Header Information that displays at the top of each document page, presentation slide, handout, or notes page.

Header row The first row in a data source that contains labels describing the data.

Hidden text Document text that does not appear onscreen.

Highlighter Background color used to mark text that you want to stand out or locate easily.

Horizontal alignment The placement of data or text between the left and right margins in a document, or cell margins in a spreadsheet.

Hyperlink An electronic marker that points to a different location or displays a different Web page.

HyperText Markup Language (HTML) Uses codes to describe how a document appears when viewed in a Web browser.

Index An alphabetical listing of topics covered in a document, along with the page numbers where the topic is discussed.

Information Rights Management (IRM) Services that are designed to help control who can access documents.

Internet A network of networks that connects computers anywhere in the world.

Kerning Automatically adjusts spacing between characters to achieve a more evenly spaced appearance.

Key Tip The letter or number that displays over features on the Ribbon and Quick Access Toolbar.

Landscape Page or worksheet that is wider than it is tall.

Layering The process of placing one shape on top of another.

Leader character Typically dots or hyphens that connect two items, to draw the reader's eye across the page.

Left tab Sets the start position on the left so as you type, text moves to the right of the tab setting.

Legacy form field A form element that can be used in Word 2010 and also in previous versions of Word.

Library An organization method that collects files from different locations and displays them as one unit.

Line spacing The vertical space between the lines in a paragraph and between paragraphs.

Linking Inserts an object from another program, but retains a connection to the original data.

Live Preview An Office feature that provides a preview of the results of a selection when you point to an option in a list.

Macro A set of instructions that executes a specific task.

Macro-Enabled Document Contains and enables execution of a macro.

Mail merge A process that combines content from a main document and a data source.

Main document Contains the information that stays the same for all recipients.

Margin The blank space around the sides, top, and bottom of a document or worksheet.

Mark as Final Creates a read-only file and also sets the property to Final on the status bar.

Markup balloon A colored circle that contains comments, insertions, or deletions in the margin with a line drawn to where the insertion point was in the document prior to inserting the comment or editing the document.

Master document A document that acts like a binder for managing smaller documents.

Master List A database of all citation sources created in Word on a particular computer.

Masthead The identifying information at the top of a newsletter or other periodical.

Merge field Serves as a placeholder for the variable data that will be inserted into the main document during the mail merge.

Microsoft Office A productivity software suite that includes word processing, spreadsheet, presentation, and database software components.

Mini toolbar An Office feature that provides access to common formatting commands when text is selected.

Monospaced typeface Uses the same amount of horizontal space for every character.

Multilevel list Extends a numbered list to several levels, and is updated automatically when topics are added or deleted.

Navigation Pane (Office) Located on the left side of the Windows Explorer window, providing access to Favorites, Libraries, Homegroup, Computer, and Network areas. (Word) Enables you to quickly move through documents using text, headings, or pages.

Nonbreaking hyphen Keeps text of a hyphenated word on both sides of the hyphen together, thus preventing the hyphenated word from becoming separated at the end of a line.

Nonbreaking space A special character that keeps two or more words together.

Normal template The framework that defines the default page settings.

Numbered list Sequences and prioritizes the items in a list and is automatically updated to accommodate additions or deletions.

Object Linking and Embedding (OLE) A technology that enables you to insert objects into different applications.

OpenType A form of font designed for use on all platforms.

Original: Show Markup A view that shows deleted text within the body of the document (with a line through the deleted text) and displays inserted text in a markup balloon.

Orphan The first line of a paragraph appearing by itself at the bottom of a page.

Outline view Displays varying amount of detail; a structural view of the document or presentation that can be collapsed or expanded as necessary.

Paragraph spacing The amount of space before or after a paragraph.

Paragraph style Stores paragraph formatting such as alignment, line spacing, and indents, as well as the font, size, and style of the text in the paragraph.

Password A security feature required to gain access to a restricted document.

Paste Places a cut or copied item in another location.

Picture A graphic file that is retrieved from the Internet, a disk, or CD and placed in an Office project.

Picture Styles A gallery that contains preformatted options that can be applied to a graphical object.

Placeholder A field or block of text used to determine the position of objects in a document.

Plagiarism The act of using and documenting the works of another as one's own.

Portable Document Format (PDF) A format that allows users to view a document regardless of the platform they use.

Portrait Page or worksheet that is taller than it is wide.

Position Raises or lowers text from the baseline without creating superscript or subscript size.

PowerPoint A Microsoft Office software component that enables you to prepare slideshow presentations for audiences.

Print Layout view The default view that closely resembles the printed document.

Proportional typeface Allocates horizontal space to the character.

Pull quote A phrase or sentence taken from an article to emphasize a key point.

Quick Access Toolbar Provides one-click access to commonly used commands.

Record A group of related fields, representing one entity, such as data for one person, place, event, or concept.

Record macro The process of creating a macro.

Regrouping The process of grouping objects together again.

Replace Finds text and replaces it with a word or phrase that you indicate.

Reverse The technique that uses light text on a dark background.

Reviewing Pane A window that displays all comments and editorial changes made to the main document.

Revision mark Indicates where text is added, deleted, or formatted while the Track Changes feature is active.

Ribbon The long bar of tabs, groups, and commands located just beneath the Title bar.

Right tab Sets the start position on the right so as you type, text moves to the left of that tab setting and aligns on the right.

Root element The initial element that contains specific elements defined by the schema.

Row height The vertical measurement of a row in a table or a worksheet.

Run macro The process of playing back or using a macro.

Sans serif typeface A typeface that does not contain thin lines on characters.

Scaling (or to **scale**) Increases or decreases text or a graphic as a percentage of its original size.

Schema validation The process of examining the content and tags against the schema to ensure accuracy and conformity.

Section break A marker that divides a document into sections, thereby allowing different formatting in each section.

Serif typeface A typeface that contains a thin line or extension at the top and bottom of the primary strokes on characters.

Shading A background color that appears behind text in a paragraph, a page, a table, or within a cell.

Shape A geometric or nongeometric object, such as a circle or an arrow.

Shortcut menu Provides choices related to the selection or area at which you right-click.

Show Markup Enables you to view document revisions by reviewer; it also allows you to choose which type of revisions you want to view such as comments, insertions and deletions, or formatting changes.

Show/Hide feature Reveals where formatting marks, such as spaces, tabs, and returns, are used in the document.

Sidebar Supplementary text that appears on the side of the featured information.

Signature line Enables the user of the document to digitally sign the document.

Sizing handles The small circles and squares that appear around a selected object and enable you to adjust the height and width of an object.

SmartArt A diagram-generating tool that presents information visually to effectively communicate a message.

Soft page break Inserted when text fills an entire page and continues onto the next page.

Soft return Created by the word processor as it wraps text to a new line.

Sorting Listing records or text in a specific sequence, such as alphabetically by last name.

Status bar The horizontal bar located at the bottom of an Office application containing information relative to the open file.

Style A set of formatting options you apply to characters or paragraphs.

Subdocument A smaller document that is a part of a master document.

Subfolder A folder that is housed within another folder.

Synchronous scrolling Enables you to simultaneously scroll through documents in Side by Side view.

Syntax The rules that dictate the structure and components required to perform the necessary calculations in an equation or evaluate expressions.

Tab (Office Fundamentals) Ribbon area that contains groups of related tasks. (Word) A marker that specifies the position for aligning text in a document.

Table Organizes information in a series of records (rows), with each record made up of a number of fields (columns).

Table alignment The position of a table between the left and right document margins.

Table Move handle The graphical image that displays in the top-left corner of a table and enables you to select a whole table at one time.

Table of authorities Used in legal documents to reference cases and other documents referred to in a legal brief.

Table of contents Lists headings in the order they appear in a document and the page numbers where the entries begin.

Table of figures A list of the captions in a document.

Table style The rules that control the fill color of the header row, columns, and records in a table.

Tag A marker that indicates the beginning or end of particular content within a document.

Template A predesigned file that incorporates formatting elements, such as a theme and layouts, and may include content that can be modified.

Text box A graphical object that contains text.

Text content control Used to enter any type of text into a form.

Text direction The degree of rotation in which text displays.

Text pane A special pane that opens up for entering text when a SmartArt diagram is selected.

Text wrapping style The way text wraps around an image.

Theme color Represents the current text and background, accent, and hyperlinks.

Theme effect Includes lines or fill effects.

Theme font Contains a heading and body text font.

Thumbnail A small picture of each page in your document that displays in the Navigation Pane.

Title bar A horizontal bar that appears at the top of each open window. The title bar contains the current file name, Office application, and control buttons.

Toggle Commands such as bold and italic that enable you to switch from one setting to another.

Track Changes Monitors all additions, deletions, and formatting changes you make in a document.

Transform A file that converts XML documents into another type of formatted language, such as HTML.

Type style The characteristic applied to a font, such as bold.

Typeface A complete set of characters—upper- and lowercase letters, numbers, punctuation marks, and special symbols.

Typography The arrangement and appearance of printed matter.

Ungrouping Breaks a combined single object into individual objects.

User exception An individual or group that is allowed to edit a restricted document.

User interface A collection of onscreen components that facilitates communication between the software and the user.

View The way a file appears onscreen.

View Side by Side Enables you to display two documents on the same screen.

Visual Basic for Applications (VBA) A programming language that is built into Microsoft Office.

Watermark Text or graphic that displays behind text.

Web Layout view View to display how a document will look when posted on the Web.

Web page Any document that displays on the World Wide Web.

Web server A computer system that hosts pages for viewing by anyone with an Internet connection.

Widow The last line of a paragraph appearing by itself at the top of a page.

Windows Explorer A Windows component that can be used to create and manage folders.

Wizard A tool that makes a process easier by asking a series of questions, then creating a document structure based on your answers.

Word A word processing program that is included in Microsoft Office.

Word processing software A computer application, such as Microsoft Word, used primarily with text to create, edit, and format documents.

Word wrap The feature that automatically moves words to the next line if they do not fit on the current line.

WordArt A feature that creates decorative text for a document.

World Wide Web (WWW) A very large subset of the Internet that stores Web page documents.

XML schema A file that defines the structure and organization of content within an XML document.

Zoom slider Enables you to increase or decrease the size of file contents onscreen.

INDEX

D

E

F

G

H

N

O

P

Q

R

S

T

U

V

W

X

Z